MARRIAGE IN COMPARATIVE CONFLICT OF LAWS: SUBSTANTIVE CONDITIONS

LENNART PÅLSSON

Professor of International Law,
University of Lund

1981

Springer-Science+Business Media, B.V.

Library of Congress Catalog Card Number: 81-50362

ISBN 978-94-017-5585-6 ISBN 978-94-017-5583-2 (eBook)
DOI 10.1007/978-94-017-5583-2

The publication of this work has been made possible by Institutet för rättsvetenskaplig forskning (The Institute for Legal Research) in Stockholm, Sweden.

PREFACE

This book was originally intended as a second volume of "Marriage and Divorce in Comparative Conflict of Laws" (Leyden 1974) and is in fact a continuation of that work. Its scope is, however, limited to the substantive conditions of marriage (the form of marriage, as well as the general aspects of the subject, being treated in the 1974 volume). The original plan, as stated in the earlier work, was for the problems of divorce and legal separation also to be dealt with in the second book. On further consideration, however, this was found to be impractical. In the first place, to do so would have defeated any attempt to keep the size of the book within reasonable limits. Secondly, the ground has meanwhile been covered by my contribution to the International Encyclopedia of Comparative Law (Volume III, Chapter 16: "Marriage and Divorce", 1979), which I did not want to duplicate. In view of this change in the original project, it was thought appropriate to publish the present work as a separate monograph under its own title, rather than as a volume forming part of a larger work.

The research undertaken for this book was essentially completed by the end of 1978. It has generally not been possible to take account of material which was not available at that time. This applies, *inter alia,* to the new Austrian statute on the conflict of laws, which was enacted on 15 June 1978 and took effect on 1 January 1979, and to the Swiss draft statute on the matter, which was published in 1978.

During the time of gestation of the book I have continuously received financial support from Institutet för rättsvetenskaplig forskning (The Institute for Legal Research), Stockholm. Expenses incurred in the course of my work have been covered by grants from the Faculty of Law in Lund and from Emil Heijnes Stiftelse för rättsvetenskaplig forskning (Emil Heijne's Foundation for Legal Research), Stockholm. I am greatly indebted to these institutions for their support.

In collecting the material for the book I have drawn on the

resources of and received very useful help from several research institutes and libraries in and outside my home country. I wish to express my sincere gratitude particularly to the University Library in Lund, the Max-Planck-Institut für ausländisches und internationales Privatrecht in Hamburg, the Institute of Advanced Legal Studies in London and the Bodleian Law Library in Oxford.

Mrs. Lea Hatzidaki-Dahlström, Lund, has assisted me in drawing up the tables of statutes etc. preceding the text of the book. Mrs. Ylva Bolding and Mr. Mats Lidgard have helped me to produce a readable manuscript. Dr. Neville March Hunnings, London, has gone through the manuscript and given me much valuable advice on matters of style and linguistic accuracy. I wish to thank them all cordially for their cooperation.

Lund, November 1980 *Lennart Pålsson*

TABLE OF CONTENTS

TABLE OF STATUTES

Note. This table covers statutes, decrees, orders etc. cited in the book. For the United States it also includes the Restatements of the Conflict of Laws, which do not have the force of law.

The titles of the enactments are given in the original language, normally followed by an English translation within parentheses, wherever the original version has been used by the author. In other cases the title is given in English translation only.

References to official or semi-official law reports containing the text of the statutes etc. as originally adopted have only been made in some instances where the statute remains essentially unaltered by subsequent legislation and where it is not easily available in current national editions of codes etc. In most cases it has been thought preferable to refer to private collections (such as *Makarov's* Quellen des Internationalen Privatrechts), law reviews or books containing the current texts, whether in the original language or in English, French or German translation. In addition, a general reference should be made to the work of *Bergmann(-Ferid),* where most of the statutory texts cited in this book, including some texts for which no particular source is given in the table, are reproduced, usually in German translation.

References to place of citation in this book are to the footnotes, except where preceded by an "s.", which indicates the consecutively numbered sections of the text of the book.

CANON LAW (Law of Roman Catholic Church)

1917	Codex Iuris Canonici (CIC)	
	– canons 1060, 1070	1103
	– canons 1072-1073	1145

ALBANIA

1964 21 Nov. (No. 3920)	Act on the Enjoyment of Civil Rights by Foreigners and on the Application of Foreign Laws German transl.: *Makarov*, Quellen 22	
	– art. 5	285, 613
	– art. 7	613
1966 5 Dec.	Decree Concerning Marriages between Albanian Citizens and Aliens German transl.: WGO 9 (1967) 79	
	–	1176

BRAZIL

1916 1 Jan. Código Civil
— art. 183, 207 883

1942 4 Sept. (No. 4657) Lei de Introdução ao Código Civil (Introductory Act to the Civil Code)
Portuguese text and German transl. (extract): *Makarov*, Quellen 52
English transl.: *Garland* 111
— art. 7 293, 338, 631, 883

BULGARIA

1968 15 March Family Code (FC)
German transl.: WGO 10 (1968) 84
— art. 9 635, 953, 1003
— art. 10 635, 1088
— art. 91 285, 635, 953, 1003, 1088
— art. 92 1244
— art. 93 609

CANADA

Quebec

1866 1 Aug. Civil Code of Lower Canada
— art. 6 290
— art. 135 498

CHILE

1855 14 Dec. Código Civil
Spanish text and German transl. (extract): *Makarov*, Quellen 66
— art. 14 248
— art. 15 251

1884 10 Jan. Ley de Matrimonio Civil (Civil Marriage Act)
French and German transl. of art. 15: *Makarov*, Quellen I, Chile, no. 3
— art. 15 248, 251

COLOMBIA

1873 26 May Código Civil
French and German transl. (extract): *Makarov*, Quellen I, Kolumbien, no. 1
— art. 18 248
— art. 19 251

CZECHOSLOVAKIA

1963 4 Dec. (No. 97) Act on Private International Law and the Rules of Procedure Relating Thereto
Czech text and German transl. (extract): *Makarov*, Quellen 292

	English transl.: Bull. Czech. L. 1963, 249	
	– § 19	285
	– § 22	613
	– § 67-68	687

DENMARK

1969 18 Dec. (No. 559)	Bekendtgørelse om aegteskabs indgåelse (Marriage Order, issued by the Minister of Justice) *Karnovs Lovsamling* 2623	
	– § 22	270-274
	– § 25-27	1240
1969 18 Dec. (No. 261)	Cirkulaere om aegteskabs indgåelse (Circular Letter, issued by the Minister of Justice, Relating to Solemnisation of Marriage) *Karnovs Lovsamling* 2625	
	– § 5	273

ECUADOR

1860 14 Dec.	Código Civil French and German transl. (extract): *Makarov,* Quellen I, Ecuador, no. 1	
	– art. 13	248
	– art. 14	251
	– art. 91	248, 251

EGYPT

1948 16 July (No. 131)	Civil Code French text (official transl.) and German transl. (extract): *Makarov,* Quellen 16 English transl.: The Egyptian Civil Code, 1949. By Perrott, Fanner & Sims Marshall. Alexandria 1952.	
	– art. 12	287, 336, 653
	– art. 14	336, 1117

FINLAND

1929 5 Dec. (No. 379)	Lag angående vissa familjerättsliga förhållanden av internationell natur (International Family Relations Act) Swedish text: *Finlands Lag* 1978, 67 (Ci 24). Do. with German transl. (extract): *Makarov,* Quellen 88. French transl. of amendments made in 1967: Rev. crit. d.i.p. 1969, 851	
	– § 1	286, 622
	– § 2	286, 622, 635, 638, 1093
	– § 9-10	622
	– § 11-13	687
	– § 49	720

	GBl DDR 1975 I 748; *Makarov*, Quellen 76	
	English transl.: 25 Am. J. Comp. L. 354 (1977)	
	– § 3	462
	– § 18	285, 1176
	– § 20	609

[WEST] GERMANY

1896 18 Aug.	Einführungsgesetz zum Bürgerlichen Gesetzbuch (EGBGB) (Introductory Law to the Civil Code) *Makarov*, Quellen 82 (extract) English transl. of conflicts provisions: *Drobnig*, PIL 401	
	– art. 13	284
	– art. 17	725
1935 15 Sept.	Gesetz zum Schutze des deutschen Blutes und der deutschen Ehre (Act for the Protection of German Blood and Honour) (repealed) RGBl 1935 I 1146	
	– § 1	s. 110 (at n. 1156-1157, 1163-1167)
1938 6 July	Gesetz zur Vereinheitlichung des Rechts der Eheschliessung und der Ehescheidung im Lande Österreich und im übrigen Reichsgebiet (Marriage Act of 1938) (repealed) RGBl 1938 I 807	
	– § 23	972
1946 20 Feb. (Control Council Law No. 16)	Ehegesetz (EheG) (Marriage Act of 1946) KRABl 77, corr. 294	
	– § 6 (repealed)	1216
	– § 10	1244
	– § 19 (repealed)	962
	– § 20	846
	– § 23	739
	– § 24	846
	– § 41	875
1949 23 May	Grundgesetz für die Bundesrepublik Deutschland (Basic Law of the Federal Republic of Germany) English transl.: *Peaslee* III 361	
	– art. 6	776
1961 11 Aug.	Gesetz zur Vereinheitlichung und Änderung familienrechtlicher Vorschriften (Familienrechtsänderungsgesetz) (Family Law Alteration Act) BGBl 1961 I 1221	
	– art. 7	687
1968	Dienstanweisung für die Standesbeamten und ihre Aufsichtsbehörden – DA – Neufasung 1968 (Service Instruction for the Civil Registrars and Their Supervisory Bodies – New version 1968) Herausgegeben von R. Baumann und A. Koehler. Frankfurt a.M. & Berlin 1968.	
	– § 140	306
	– § 156-157	1212
	– § 161	384, 1212

	– § 163	1212
	– § 166-169 a	1244
	– § 170-171	1253
	– § 172	1261
	– § 178	647
	– § 383	384

GREECE

1940 15 March (No. 2250)	Civil Code French transl.: Code Civil Hellénique. Traduction de l'Institut hellénique de droit international et étranger. Effectuée par P. Mamopoulos. Athens 1956. German transl.: Das Zivilgesetzbuch von Griechenland (1940) mit dem Einführungsgesetz. Übersetzt und eingeleitet von D. Gogos. Berlin & Tübingen 1951.	
	– art. 13	284, 401
	– art. 32	401
	– art. 1350	347, 401
	– art. 1353	1105, 1116
	– art. 1355	927
	– art. 1356	1098
	– art. 1363	881
	– art. 1364	1146

GUATEMALA

1936 25 Jan. (No. 1781)	Ley de Extranjería (Act on Foreigners) Spanish text and German transl. (extract): *Makarov*, Quellen 136	
	– art. 35	248
	– art. 36	248, 251
1963 14 Sept. (No. 106)	Código Civil	
	– art. 86	248, 251

HUNGARY

1952 (No. IV)	Act on Marriage, Family and Guardianship French and German transl. (extract): *Makarov*, Quellen I, Ungarn, no. 1	
	– § 6 (as amended)	1244
	– § 7-8	635
1952 (No. 23)	Decree-Law on the Entry into Force and Implementation of Act no. IV/1952 French and German transl. (extract): *Makarov*, Quellen I, Ungarn, no. 2	
	– § 16	285, 635
1974 (No. I)	Act amending Act no. IV/1952 German transl.: WGO 16 (1974) 273	
	–	1244

IRAN

1935 16 Feb.	Civil Code French and German transl. (extract): *Makarov*, Quellen I, Iran, *sub* I	
	– art. 6-7	287
	– art. 1060	1176, 1194
	– art. 1061	1179

IRAQ

1951 4 June (No. 40)	Civil Code French transl. (extract): Rev. crit. d.i.p. 1959, 182	
	– art. 19	287, 336

ITALY

1929 27 May (No. 847)	Disposizioni per l'applicazione del concordato dell'11 febbraio 1929 tra la Santa Sede e l'Italia nella parte relativa al matrimonio (Provisions for the Application of the Concordat of 11 Feb. 1929 between the Holy See and Italy in the Part Relating to Marriage)	
	–	548
1929 24 June (No. 1159)	Disposizioni sull'esercizio dei culti ammessi nello Stato e sul matrimonio celebrato davanti ai ministri dei culti medesimi (Provisions on the Activity of Religious Orders Recognised by the State and on Marriages Celebrated before Ministers of Such Religious Orders)	
	–	554
1938 17 Nov. (No. 1728)	Provvedimenti per la difesa della razza italiana (Provisions for the Protection of the Italian Race) (repealed) G.U. 19 Nov. 1938 no. 264	
	–	1161
	– art. 1	1157, 1167
1940 28 Oct. (No. 1443)	Codice di Procedura Civile (CCP) French transl. (extract): Rev. crit. d.i.p. 1950, 262 German transl. (extract): RabelsZ 15 (1949/50) 124	
	– art. 796-799, 801, 804	687
1942 16 March (No. 262)	Codice Civile English transl.: *M. Beltramo, G.E. Longo and J.H. Merryman*, The Italian Civil Code. Dobbs Ferry, N.Y., 1969. Disposizioni sulla legge in generale (Disp. prel.) (Provisions on the Law in General)	
	– art. 17	284
	The Code	
	– art. 82	548
	– art. 83	554
	– art. 85	635, 953
	– art. 86	395, 635
	– art. 87	635, 1086
	– art. 88	635, 883
	– art. 89	635, 911

SENEGAL

1972 12 June (No. 72-61)	Code de la Famille (Family Code) (FC) French text and German transl. (extract): *Makarov*, Quellen 234	
	– art. 843	287

SOUTH AFRICA

1949 (No. 55)	Prohibition of Mixed Marriages Act	
	– s. 1 (as amended by the Act cited below)	281, 1158
1968 (No. 21)	Prohibition of Mixed Marriages Amendment Act	
	– s. 1	see the above-cited Act of 1949

SOVIET UNION

1968 27 June	Fundamental Principles of Legislation of the U.S.S.R. and the Union Republics on Marriage and the Family Russian text and German transl.: *Makarov*, Quellen 250 English transl.: (1) *J.N. Hazard, I. Shapiro and P.B. Maggs*, The Soviet Legal System (ed. 2; Dobbs Ferry, N.Y., 1969) 528. (2) 18 I.C.L.Q. 410 (1969)	
	–	312
	– art. 7-8	312
	– art. 31	257, 258
	– art. 32	257, 259, 260, 312

SPAIN

1889 24 July	Código Civil Spanish text and English transl. of conflicts provisions as amended in 1974: N.T.I.R. 21 (1974) 367	
	–	355
	– art. 9	284
	– art. 42, 75	548, 1105, 1146
	– art. 76-79	548
	– art. 80	548, 549
	– art. 81-82	548
	– art. 83	994, 1038, 1146
	– art. 101-102	1038

SWEDEN

1904 8 July (No. 26, p. 1)	Lag om vissa internationella rättsförhållanden rörande äktenskap och förmynderskap (Act on the Conflict of Laws in Regard to Marriage and Guardianship) *Sveriges Rikes Lag* 1979, 34	
	– ch. 1 § 1	286
	– ch. 1 § 2	295, 296, 472, 578
	– ch. 1 § 3	348, 635, 638, 684, 1062, 1086, 1093
	– ch. 2 (repealed)	617
	– ch. 3 § 7	721

SWITZERLAND

1953 1 June	Verordnung über das Zivilstandswesen (Zivilstandsverordnung) (Civil Status Order)	
	French and German texts (extract): *Makarov*, Quellen I, Schweiz, no. 4	
	– art. 168, 170	1245

SYRIA

1949 16 May	Civil Code	
	French text and German transl. (extract): *Makarov*, Quellen I, Syrien	
	– art. 13	287, 336
	– art. 15	336

THAILAND

1938 10 March	Act on Conflict of Laws	
	Official English transl.: *Makarov*, Quellen 278	
	– § 19	287

TUNISIA

1956 12 July	Decree on the Conflict of Laws in Matters of Personal Status	
	– art. 1, 2, 4	287

TURKEY

1926 17 Feb. (No. 743)	Civil Code	
	French transl.: Code civil turc. Ed. 3. Istanbul 1937.	
	– art. 96, 142	878

UNITED KINGDOM

1925 (15 & 16 Geo. 5, c. 49)	Supreme Court of Judicature (Consolidation) Act	
	– s. 31 (as amended)	868
1929 (19 & 20 Geo. 5, c. 36)	Age of Marriage Act (repealed)	
	– s. 1	365
1949 (12, 13 & 14 Geo. 6, c. 76)	Marriage Act	
	– s. 1	1084
	– s. 2	365
	– s. 32	542
	– Schedule I (as amended)	1084
1960 (8 & 9 Eliz. 2, c. 29)	Marriage (Enabling) Act	
	– s. 1	418, 602, 1101
1963 (c. 37)	Children and Young Persons Act	
	– s. 2 (repealed)	1066
1965 (c. 53)	Family Allowances Act (repealed)	
	– s. 12	643
1971 (c. 44)	Nullity of Marriage Act (repealed)	
	– s. 1	413, 650
	– s. 4	413

1971 (c. 53)	Recognition of Divorces and Legal Separations Act	
	– s. 7 (as amended)	809-811
1972 (c. 38)	Matrimonial Proceedings (Polygamous Marriages) Act	
	– s. 1-3 (s. 1 repealed)	643
	– s. 4 (repealed)	413
1973 (c. 18)	Matrimonial Causes Act	
	– s. 11	413, 418, 650, 846
	– s. 12	994, 997, 998
	– s. 13	846, 997, 1037
	– s. 14	413
	– s. 16	1021
	– s. 47	643
1973 (c. 45)	Domicile and Matrimonial Proceedings Act	
	– s. 2, 15	809
	– s. 16	682
1975 (c. 14)	Social Security Act	
	– s. 162	643
1975 (c. 18)	Social Security (Consequential Provisions) Act	
	– Schedule 2	643
1975 (S.I. No. 561)	Social Security and Family Allowances (Polygamous Marriages) Regulations	
	–	643

UNITED STATES

Federal Statutes

1787 17 Sept.	Constitution of the United States *Peaslee* IV 1195	
	– art. IV § 1 (full faith and credit clause)	102, 128, 178
	– amendment XIV § 1 (1868) (due process and equal protection clauses)	102, 128, 245

Uniform Acts, Approved by the National Conference of Commissioners on Uniform State Laws

1912	Uniform Marriage Evasion Act (withdrawn)*	
	–	s. 6, 8, 15
	– § 1	s. 15
	– § 2-3	s. 8

State Statutes

1872	California Civil Code	
	– § 133 (repealed) and 4515	174
1932	Massachusetts General Laws	
	– c. 207 § 6 (and predecessor)	s. 25 (at n. 166-172)

Restatements

1934	Conflict of Laws	
	– § 122	30
	– § 129	77
	– § 132	69, 93

*For state statutes based on or resembling this Act see Index, *s.v.* Evasion

TABLE OF CONVENTIONS
and other international instruments

Note. The references are to the footnotes, except where preceded by an "s.", which refers to the consecutively numbered sections of the text of the book. The footnotes referred to are those where the respective conventions are cited or in which (or in the text pertaining to which) they are considered.

Annexed to the Convention on Private International Law
86 LNTS 111

	– art. 7	292
	– art. 36	292, 630
	– art. 37	630, 1235, 1261
	– art. 38	630, 883
	– art. 40	640, 883, 1095
	– art. 48	949

1929

11 Feb. — Rome — HOLY SEE-ITALY
Concordat
Schöppe 172

	– art. 34	548, 549

1931

6 Feb. — Stockholm — DENMARK, FINLAND, ICELAND, NORWAY, SWEDEN

(amended 26 March 1953, 3 Nov. 1969 and 20 Nov. 1973)

Convention Containing Provisions in the Field of Private International Law Relating to Marriage, Adoption and Guardianship
SÖFM 1931 no. 19. Amendments: SÖFM 1954 no. 2, 1969 no. 11, 1973 no. 70
English transl.: *Norwegian Laws* XIX-A-3

	–	s. 3, 4
	art. 1	s. 35; n. 374, 1072, 1214, 1235
	Final Protocol	268

1940

19 March — Montevideo — Multipartite
Treaty on International Civil Law
Hudson VIII 513

	– art. 13	247, 249

1948

10 Dec. — Paris — General Assembly Resolution
Universal Declaration of Human Rights
GA Res. 217 (III)

	– art. 2	1109
	– art. 16	776, 1109

1950

4 Nov. — Rome — Multipartite
Convention for the Protection of Human Rights and Fundamental Freedoms
213 UNTS 221

	–	1137, 1172, 1180
	– art. 12	776, 1110, 1192
	– art. 14	1110, 1192

1963		
11 Dec.	Vienna AUSTRIA-POLAND Vertrag über die wechselseitigen Beziehungen in bürgerlichen Rechtssachen und über Urkundenwesen (Austrian) BGBl no. 79/1974	
	– art. 24	289
	– art. 27	612
1964		
20 Jan.	Belgrade CZECHOSLOVAKIA-YUGOSLAVIA Treaty Regulating Legal Relations in Civil, Family and Criminal Cases 538 UNTS 197	
	– art. 23	288, 635
	– art. 26	615
	– art. 27	614
10 Sept.	Paris Multipartite Convention tendant à faciliter la célébration des mariages à l'étranger C.I.E.C., Conventions no. 7	
	–	1226
	– art. 1-2	1227, 1228
	– art. 3	1227, 1229
	– art. 9	1227
1966		
7 March	New York Multipartite International Convention on the Elimination of All Forms of Racial Discrimination 660 UNTS 195	
	– art. 5	1173
16 May	Sofia BULGARIA-HUNGARY Treaty Concerning Legal Assistance in Civil, Family and Criminal Cases 724 UNTS 101	
	– art. 18	288
	– art. 21	610
20 May	Belgrade EAST GERMANY-YUGOSLAVIA Vertrag über den Rechtsverkehr in Zivil-, Familien- und Strafsachen GBl DDR 1966 1 96	
	– art. 31	288, 635
	– art. 34-35	615
	– art. 36	614
19 Dec.	New York Multipartite International Covenant on Civil and Political Rights GA Res. 2200 (XXI) of 16 Dec. 1966	
	–	1112
	– art. 2, 23	1113, 1114

1967

5 April	Warsaw	FRANCE-POLAND	
	Convention relative à la loi applicable, la compétence et l'exequatur dans le droit des personnes et de la famille 677 UNTS 235		
	– art. 4		289
	– art. 7		612
8 Sept.	Luxembourg	Multipartite	
	Convention sur la reconnaissance des décisions relatives au lien conjugal C.I.E.C., Conventions no. 11		
	– art. 9		804, 807, 815

1968

27 Nov.	Sofia	BULGARIA-MONGOLIA	
	Treaty Concerning the Provision of Legal Assistance in Civil, Family and Criminal Cases 677 UNTS 35		
	– art. 18		288
	– art. 21		610

1969

30 April	Ulan Bator	EAST GERMANY-MONGOLIA	
	Treaty Concerning Legal Assistance in Civil, Family and Criminal Cases 718 UNTS 153		
	– art. 28		288
	– art. 33		614

1970

1 June	The Hague	Multipartite	
	Convention on the Recognition of Divorces and Legal Separations Act. Doc. La Haye 11 (1968) II 201		
	–		806
	– art. 1		895
	– art. 11		805, 807, 808

1971

18 May	Paris	FRANCE-YUGOSLAVIA	
	Convention relative à la loi applicable et à la compétence en matière de droit des personnes et de la famille Clunet 1974, 198; Rev. crit. d.i.p. 1973, 570		
	– art. 3		289, 635

TABLE OF CASES

Note. This table shows the date or the name of cases cited in the present work. It refers to the footnotes in which the cases are cited, in some instances also to other footnotes which (or the text pertaining to which) have a bearing on a particular case. References to collections, periodicals, etc., containing the report of the cases are given in the footnotes.

CANADA

Common Law Provinces

Quebec

CHILE

DENMARK

EGYPT

FRANCE

[WEST] GERMANY

GREECE

ITALY

[1] Cases decided during the time of the French Protectorate (1912-1956) are listed under FRANCE.

[2] Including decisions of the House of Lords on appeals from Scotland and of the Privy Council on appeals from Commonwealth countries.

BIBLIOGRAPHY

Note. This bibliography is selective. As a rule, only works which are cited more than twice in the book have been included. References to other works are given in the footnotes.

Works listed in this bibliography are cited by the name of the author or authors alone or, where necessary, by the author's name and volume number or one or more descriptive words of the title. Titles consisting of or including the words "Droit international privé", "Internationales Privatrecht" ("International Privatret") or "Private International Law" are abbreviated DIP, IPR and PIL, respectively.

Aguilar Benítez de Lugo, M., "Estatuto personal y órden público en el derecho internacional privado español": Rev. Esp. Der. Int. 20 (1967) 217-246.

Aguilar Navarro. See Derecho Civil Internacional.

Albers, J., Die Befreiung von der Beibringung des Ehefähigkeitszeugnisses: StAZ 1954, 145-149, 170-173.

Albisetti, E., Die Eheschliessung, die Trennung und die Auflösung der Ehe der Italiener in der Schweiz und der Schweizer in Italien. Thesis, Bern 1937.

Alfonsín, Q., Régimen internacional del matrimonio. Montevideo 1958.

Ansay, T., American-Turkish Private International Law. Dobbs Ferry, N.Y., 1966.

Anton, A.E., Private International Law. A treatise from the standpoint of Scots law. Edinburgh 1967.

Anton, A.E., and Francescakis, Ph., Modern Scots "Runaway Marriages": 1958 Jur. Rev. 253-285.

Arndt, K., Erfahrungen eines Oberlandesgerichtspräsidenten bei der Erteilung der Befreiung vom Ehefähigkeitszeugnis: ZfRV 11 (1970) 241-252.

Audinet, E., Les conflits de lois en matière de mariage et de divorce: Rec. des Cours 11 (1926-I) 171-252.

Audit, B., La fraude à la loi. Paris 1974.

Baade, H.W., Marriage and Divorce in American Conflicts Law – Governmental-Interests Analysis and the Restatement (Second): 72 Colum. L. Rev. 329-381 (1972).

Balladore Pallieri, G., Diritto internazionale privato. Ed. 2. Milan 1950.

Ballarino, T., Costituzione e diritto internazionale privato. Padua 1974.

Balogh, E., Studien aus dem Gebiete der Rechtsvergleichung und des internationalen Privatrechts. Vol. II, Erste Lieferung: Vergleichender Überblick und international-privatrechtliche Untersuchungen über den Rechtszustand in Bezug auf die religiöse, zivile und "de facto" Ehe unter besonderer Berücksichtigung der letzten. Paris 1934.

Bartin, E., Principes de droit international privé. Vol. II. Paris 1932.

Batiffol, H., and Lagarde, P., Droit international privé. 2 vol. Ed. 5. Paris 1970-1971; ed. 6, 1974-1976. (References are to the fifth edition).

Baty, Th., Capacity and Form of Marriage in the Conflict of Laws: 26 Yale L.J. 444-463 (1916/17).
Bayitch, S.A., and Siqueiros, J.L., Conflict of Laws – Mexico and the United States. Coral Gables, Fla., 1968.
Beale, J.H., A Treatise on the Conflict of Laws. Vol. II. New York 1935.
Beck. See Kommentar zum Schweizerischen Zivilgesetzbuch.
Begeja, K., Das Eherecht der Volksrepublik Albanien: Leske and Loewenfeld 833-853.
Beitzke, G., Die deutsche internationale Zuständigkeit in Familienrechtssachen: FamRZ 1967, 592-605.
Beitzke, G., Internationalrechtliches zu Ehevoraussetzungen und Eheverboten: StAZ 1967, 285-290.
Beitzke, G., Kommentar. See Staudinger.
Benattar, R., Problèmes relatifs au droit international privé de la famille dans les pays de droit personnel: Rec. des Cours 121 (1967-II) 1-111.
Bendermacher-Geroussis, E., Die gültige Eheschliessung im griechischen internationalen Privatrecht: Rev. Hell. 22 (1969) nos. 3-4, p. 1-16.
Bergmann, Internationales Ehe- und Kindschaftsrecht. Begründet von A. Bergmann, fortgeführt von M. Ferid. Ed. 5. Frankfurt a.M. 1976- (looseleaf service). (Cited *Bergmann (-Ferid)*).
Bernecker, D., Internationales Privat- und Prozessrecht im Grossherzogtum Luxemburg: RabelsZ 27 (1962/63) 263-346.
Berner Kommentar. Kommentar zum Schweizerischen Privatrecht begründet von M. Gmür. Ed. 3. Vol. II/1/1/1: Die Eheschliessung. Artikel 90-136 ZGB erläutert von E. Götz. Bern 1964. (Cited *Götz*).
Betti, E., Problematica del diritto internazionale. Milan 1956.
Beyer, Betrachtungen über die Befreiung von der Beibringung des ausländischen Ehefähigkeitszeugnisses: StAZ 1957, 29-36.
Bischoff, J.-M., Mariage: Rép. dr. int. II 285-307.
Blagojević, B.T., Das Eherecht der Föderativen Volksrepublik Jugoslawien: Leske and Loewenfeld 57-120.
Böhmer, Ch., Die Gültigkeit der "Tondern-Ehen" in Deutschland: StAZ 1969, 85-91.
Bottini, R. de, La Convention franco-polonaise relative à la loi applicable, la compétence et l'exequatur dans le droit des personnes et de la famille: Rev. crit. d.i.p. 1970, 1-43.
A British Digest of International Law. Phase I – 1860-1914. Vol. VIII. London 1965.
Bucher, A., Grundfragen der Anknüpfungsgerechtigkeit im internationalen Privatrecht (aus kontinentaleuropäischer Sicht). Basle & Stuttgart 1975.
Buzzati, G.C., Le droit international privé d'après les conventions de la Haye. I. Le mariage d'après la convention du 12 juin 1902. Paris 1911.
Bystrický, R., The New Czechoslovak Act Concerning Private International Law and the Rules of Procedure Relating Thereto: Bull. Czech. L. 21 (1963) 209-232.

Caicedo Castilla, J.J., Derecho internacional privado. Ed. 6. Bogotá 1967.
Cappelletti, M., and Perillo, J.M., Civil Procedure in Italy. The Hague 1965.
Carter, P.B., Decisions of British Courts During 1962-1963 Involving Questions of ... B. Private International Law: 39 Brit. YB. Int. L. 474-492 (1963).

Carter, P.B., Decisions of British Courts During 1968 Involving Questions of ... B. Private International Law: 43 Brit. YB. Int. L. 239-252 (1968/69).
Carter, P.B., Decisions of British Courts During 1970-1971 Involving Questions of ... B. Private International Law: 45 Brit. YB. Int. L. 402-418 (1971).
Carter, P.B., Decisions of British Courts During 1972-1973 Involving Questions of ... B. Private International Law: 46 Brit. YB. Int. L. 428-437 (1972/73).
Castel, J.-G., Canadian Conflict of Laws. Vol. I. Toronto 1975.
Castel, J.-G., La fraude à la loi en droit international privé québecois: R. du B. 1964, 1-35.
Castel, J.-G., Private International Law. Toronto 1960.
Cavers, D.F., Contemporary Conflicts Law in American Perspective: Rec. des Cours 131 (1970-III) 75-308.
Cheshire, G.C., The English Private International Law of Husband and Wife: Rec. des Cours 108 (1963-I) 115-188.
Cheshire, G.C., Private International Law. Ed. 7. London 1965.
Cheshire's Private International Law. Ed. 9 by P.M. North. London 1974. (Cited *Cheshire and North*).
Clark, H.H., The Law of Domestic Relations in the United States. St. Paul, Minn., 1968.
Commission Internationale de l'Etat Civil, Statuts et Conventions (loose-leaf service). (References to this work are to the part entitled "Conventions et recommandations").
Cook, W.W., The Logical and Legal Bases of the Conflict of Laws. Cambridge, Mass., 1942.
Delaume, G.R., American-French Private International Law. Ed. 2. New York 1961.
Derecho Civil Internacional. Vol. II of Derecho Internacional Privado. Obra dirigida por M. Aguilar Navarro. Ed. 4. Madrid 1975. (Cited *Aguilar Navarro*).
Dicey and Morris on the Conflict of Laws. Ed. 9. London 1973 (with updating supplements).
Dieckmann, A., Eheschliessung eines katholischen Spaniers mit einer geschiedenen Deutschen – BGHZ 41, 136: JuS 1966, 99-108.
Dieckmann, A., Zur internationalen Zuständigkeit eines deutschen Vormundschaftsgerichts aus "unaufschiebbarem Fürsorgebedürfnis": StAZ 1970, 8-12.
Dietz. See Staudinger.
Dölle, H., Familienrecht. Vol. I. Karlsruhe 1964.
Dölle, H., Internationales Privatrecht. Ed. 2. Karlsruhe 1972.
Dorenberg, K., Hinkende Rechtsverhältnisse im internationalen Familienrecht. Berlin 1968.
Drobnig, U., American-German Private International Law. Ed. 2. Dobbs Ferry, N.Y., 1972.
Drobnig, U., Die Kollisionsnormen in den Rechtshilfeverträgen der Staaten des Ostblocks: OER 1960, 154-184.
Dutoit, B., L'avenir possible du rattachement à la loi nationale en droit international privé suisse: Schw. Jb. Int. R. 26 (1969/70) 41-64.
Dyer, A., Report on the Conflict of Laws in Respect of Marriage and Recognition Abroad of Decisions in Respect of the Existence or Validity of Marriages: Act. Doc. La Haye 13 (1976) III 14-66 (Cited *Dyer Report*).

Eder, Ph.J., American-Colombian Private International Law. New York 1956.

Eek, H., The Swedish Conflict of Laws. The Hague 1965.

Ehrenzweig, A.A., Miscegenation in the Conflict of Laws: 45 Cornell L.Q. 659-678 (1960).

Ehrenzweig, A.A., A Treatise on the Conflict of Laws. St. Paul, Minn., 1962.

Ehrenzweig, A.A., Fragistas, Ch., and Yiannopoulos, A., American-Greek Private International Law. New York 1957.

Ehrenzweig, A.A., and Jayme, E., Private International Law. Vol. II. Leyden & Dobbs Ferry, N.Y., 1973.

Ekteskapslovgivningen (The Norwegian Legislation on Marriage). Lütken og Platous kommentarutgave. Ed. 3 by V. Holmøy. Oslo 1971. (Cited *Holmøy*).

Elgeddawy, A.K., Relations entre systèmes confessionnel et laïque en droit international privé. Paris 1971.

El-Mikayis, 'Abdel-Wahhāb, Internationales und interreligiöses Personen-, Familien- und Erbrecht in der Vereinigten Arabischen Republik: RabelsZ 33 (1969) 517-543.

Encyclopedia. See International Encyclopedia of Comparative Law.

Etcheberry, A., American-Chilean Private International Law. New York 1960.

Falconbridge, J.D., Essays on the Conflict of Laws. Toronto 1947; ed. 2, 1954. (Unless otherwise indicated, references are to the second edition).

Das Familienrecht der DDR. Kommentar zum Familiengesetzbuch der Deutschen Demokratischen Republik vom 20. Dezember 1965 und zum Einführungsgesetz zum Familiengesetzbuch der Deutschen Demokratischen Republik vom 20. Dezember 1965. Herausgegeben vom Ministerium der Justiz. Ed. 3. Berlin 1970. (Cited *FGB-Kommentar*).

Fernández Flores, J.L., Principios que rigen la validez del matrimonio, con elemento extranjero, en derecho español: Rev. Esp. Der. Int. 21 (1968) 781-797.

Ferrer-Correia, A., Les problèmes de codification en droit international privé: Rec. des Cours 145 (1975-II) 57-203.

Festschrift Dölle. See Vom Deutschen zum Europäischen Recht.

Festschrift für Hans Carl Nipperdey zum 70. Geburtstag am 21. Januar 1965. Vol. I. Munich & Berlin 1965.

Festschrift für Hans Schima zum 75. Geburtstag. Vienna 1969.

Festschrift Hans Lewald. Basle 1953.

Festschrift Rheinstein. See Ius Privatum Gentium.

FGB-Kommentar. See Das Familienrecht der DDR.

Ficker, H.G., Verknüpfung von Anknüpfungen?: Festschrift Nipperdey I 297-322.

Finlands Lag (The Statutes of Finland, Swedish edition). Redigerad av Lars Karlsson under medverkan av Sören Karlsson. Helsinki 1978.

Florio, F., La codificazione del diritto internazionale privato e processuale in Cecoslovacchia. Milan 1967.

Frankenstein, E., Internationales Privatrecht. Vol. III. Berlin-Grunewald 1934.

Gaarder, K., Innføring i Internasjonal privatrett (Introduction to Private International Law). Oslo, Bergen, Tromsø 1975.

Gamillscheg, F., Doppelehe und hinkende Ehe im internationalen Privatrecht: Göttinger Festschrift für das Oberlandesgericht Celle (Göttingen 1961) 61-78.

Gamillscheg, F., Die Grundrechte bei der Anwendung ausländischen Rechts: Festschrift Nipperdey I 323-350.

Gamillscheg, Kommentar. See Staudinger.

Garland, P.G., American-Brazilian Private International Law. New York 1959.

Giardina, A., L'eguaglianza dei coniugi nel diritto internazionale privato: Riv. dir. int. proc. 1974, 5-31.

La giurisprudenza italiana di diritto internazionale privato e processuale. Repertorio 1942-1966. By F. Capotorti and others. Bari 1967. (Cited Giur. It. D.I.P. (1942/66)).

Götz. See Berner Kommentar.

Goldman, B., La protection internationale des droits de l'homme et l'ordre public international dans le fonctionnement de la règle de conflit de lois: René Cassin Amicorum Discipulorumque Liber I (Paris 1969) 449-466.

Goldschmidt, W., and Rodriguez-Novás, J., American-Argentine Private International Law. Dobbs Ferry, N.Y., 1966.

Goodrich, H.F., and Scoles, E.F., Handbook of the Conflict of Laws. Ed. 4. St. Paul, Minn., 1964.

Gotlieb, A.E., The Incidental Question in Anglo-American Conflict of Laws: 33 Can. Bar Rev. 523-555 (1955).

Graulich, P., Principes de droit international privé. Paris 1961.

Graveson, R.H., Conflict of Laws. Private International Law. Ed. 7. London 1974.

Graveson, R.H., The Doctrine of Evasion of the Law in England and America: J. Comp. Leg. 19 (1937) I 21-31.

Grodecki, J.K., Intertemporal Conflict of Laws: Encyclopedia III:8 Tübingen, The Hague, Paris 1976.

Guradze, H., Die Europäische Menschenrechtskonvention. Berlin & Frankfurt a.M. 1968.

Habermalz, W., Das Ehehindernis der Rassenzugehörigkeit in ausländischen Rechtsordnungen und seine Anwendung im deutschen IPR. Thesis, Göttingen 1963.

Hahlo, H.R., The South African Law of Husband and Wife with an Appendix on Jurisdiction and Conflict of Laws by E. Kahn. Ed. 3. Cape Town, Wynberg, Johannesburg 1969; ed. 4, 1975. (Cited *Hahlo (-Kahn)*; references are to the third edition).

Hainzl, A., Die Prüfung der Ehefähigkeit bei Ausstellung eines Ehefähigkeitszeugnisses zur Heirat im Auslande: ÖStA 18 (1964) 17-21.

Hakulinen, Y.J., Das Eherecht Finnlands: Leske and Loewenfeld 337-368.

Hambro, E.I., Ordre Public and Fraus Legis in Norwegian Conflict Law: IntRDipl. 1957, 315-326.

Hamilton, E. (ed.), Solución de conflictos de leyes y jurisdicción en Chile (Derecho internacional privado). Trabajo collectivo. Santiago de Chile 1966.

Hartley, T.C., Bigamy in the Conflict of Laws: 16 I.C.L.Q. 680-703 (1967).

Hartley, T.C., The Policy Basis of the English Conflict of Laws of Marriage: 35 M.L.R. 571-583 (1972).

Henrich, D., Wann verbietet der deutsche ordre public die Anwendung ausländischen Rechts?: StAZ 1966, 301-308.

Hoffmann and Stephan, Ehegesetz nebst Durchführungsverordnungen. Kommentar begründet von E. Hoffmann und W. Stephan, neu bearbeitet und fortgeführt von W. Appell, K. Johannsen und W. Stephan. Ed. 2 Munich 1968.

von Hoffmann, B., and Ortiz-Arce, A., Das neue spanische internationale Privatrecht: RabelsZ 39 (1975) 647-691.

Holder, W.E., Public Policy and National Preferences – The Exclusion of Foreign Law in English Private International Law: 17 I.C.L.Q. 926-952 (1968).

Holleaux, G., Ehescheidung und Ehetrennung (Voraussetzungen). A. Französisches Recht: IntFamR 149-171.

Holleaux, G., Ehescheidung und Ehetrennung (Wirkungen). A. Französisches Recht; C. Rechtsvergleichung: IntFamR 195-212, 227-234.

Holmøy. See Ekteskapslovgivningen.

Holt, H.W., Die Gültigkeit der Ehe im Kollisionsrecht der Vereinigten Staaten von Amerika: RabelsZ 21 (1956) 21-35.

Hooper, A., A New Rule for Recognition of Foreign Divorces?: 27 M.L.R. 727-733 (1964).

Hornslet, M., Danielsen, S., and Hermann, J., Aegteskabsloven (The Danish Marriage Act). Copenhagen 1970.

Hoyer, H., Die Anerkennung ausländischer Eheentscheidungen in Österreich. Vienna 1972.

Hoyer, V., Scheidung eines Ausländers durch inländische Gerichte und Frage der Ehefähigkeit des Ausländers. Ein Lösungsvorschlag: ÖStA 27 (1973) 19-22.

Hoyer, V., Zur Frage der Wiederverehelichung im Inland geschiedener Ausländer: ÖJZ 1965, 617-621.

Hudson, M.O., (ed.), International Legislation. Vol. VIII (1938-1941). Washington 1949.

Inglis, B.D., Conflict of Laws. Wellington, N.Z., 1959.

International Encyclopedia of Comparative Law. Under the auspices of the International Association of Legal Science. Vol. III: Private International Law. Tübingen etc. (other places of publication vary with different contributions) 1972-. (Pattern of citation: Encyclopedia III:16, meaning vol. III, chapter 16).

Das internationale Familienrecht Deutschlands und Frankreichs in vergleichender Darstellung (collective work). Tübingen & Paris 1955. (Cited IntFamR).

Ius et Lex. Festgabe zum 70. Geburtstag von Max Gutzwiller. Basle 1959.

Ius Privatum Gentium. Festschrift für Max Rheinstein zum 70. Geburtstag am 5. Juli 1969. Vol. I. Tübingen 1969.

Jackson, J., The Formation and Annulment of Marriage. Ed. 2. London 1969.

Jagmetti, M.A., Die Anwendung fremden Kollisionsrechtes durch den inländischen Richter. Zürich 1961.

Jayme, E., Spannungen bei der Anwendung italienischen Familienrechts durch deutsche Gerichte. Bielefeld 1961.

Jessel, Christa, Eheschliessung eines Ausländers bei einer bulgarischen Behörde: WGO 18 (1976) 151-158.

Jochem, R., Eheschliessung einer geschiedenen Deutschen mit einem katholischen Spanier in Dänemark: RabelsZ 32 (1968) 727-740.

Jodlowski, J., and Ponsard, A., La Convention franco-polonaise du 5 avril 1967 relative à la loi applicable, à la compétence et à l'exequatur dans le droit des personnes et de la famille: Clunet 1970, 545-631.
Johnson, J. Philip, The Validity of a Marriage Under the Conflict of Laws: 38 N.D.L. Rev. 442-457 (1962).
Johnson, W.S., The Conflict of Laws with Special Reference to the Law of Quebec. Ed. 2. Montreal 1962.
Joppe, I.S., De Nederlandse rechtspraak inzake huwelijk in het internationaal privaatrecht 1963-1972. Leyden 1973.
Juris-Classeur de droit international. 8 vol. Paris (loose-leaf service). (Cited J.Cl.dr.int., Fasc. . . .).

Kahn, F., Abhandlungen zum internationalen Privatrecht. Herausgegeben von O. Lenel und H. Lewald. Vol. II. Munich & Leipzig 1928.
Kahn-Freund, O., General Problems of Private International Law: Rec. des Cours 143 (1974-III) 139-474.
Kahn-Freund, O., Reflections on Public Policy in the English Conflict of Laws: 39 Trans. Grot. Soc. 39-69 (1954).
Karnovs Lovsamling (Karnov's Collection of /Danish/ Statutes). Med kommentarer under redaktion af S. Hurwitz & W.E. von Eyben. Ed. 8. Copenhagen 1972 (with updating supplements).
Karsten, I.G.F., The Recognition of Divorces and Legal Separations Act 1971: 35 M.L.R. 299-305 (1972).
Katičić, N., Le droit international privé de la Yougoslavie dans le domaine des rapports familiaux et successoraux: Rec. des Cours 131 (1970-III) 393-488.
Kegel, G., Internationales Privatrecht. Ed. 4. Munich 1977.
Kegel, Kommentar. See Soergel and Siebert.
Kegel, G., Reform des deutschen internationalen Eherechts: RabelsZ 25 (1960) 201-221.
Kegel, G., and Lüderitz, A., Hindernis des Bandes für Ausländer trotz Scheidung in Deutschland?: FamRZ 1964, 57-60.
Kingsley, R., The Law of Infants' Marriages: 9 Vand. L. Rev. 593-605 (1956).
Kingsley, R., Remarriage After Divorce: 26 So. Cal. L. Rev. 280-291 (1953).
Klang and Gschnitzer. See Kommentar zum Allgemeinen bürgerlichen Gesetzbuch.
Kleinrahm, K., and Partikel, H.-Ch., Die Anerkennung ausländischer Entscheidungen in Ehesachen. Ed. 2. Göttingen 1970.
Knapp, Ch., Cent ans de mariage devant la Constitution fédérale: ZSR 71 (1952) 275-303.
Knapp, Ch., Essai sur la sauvegarde de l'ordre public et la protection des faibles en droit international privé: Mélanges François Guisan (Lausanne 1950) 189-231.
Knapp, V., and Eliáš, J., Das Eherecht der Tschechoslowakischen Sozialistischen Republik: Leske and Loewenfeld 121-169.
Köhler, H., Internationales Privatrecht. Ed. 3. Vienna & New York 1966.
Kollewijn, R.D., American-Dutch Private International Law. Ed. 2. New York 1961.
Kommentar zum Allgemeinen bürgerlichen Gesetzbuch. Herausgegeben von H. Klang und F. Gschnitzer. Ed. 2. Vol. I/1 (with the collaboration of, among others, G. Walker, A. Verdross-Drossberg, K. Satter, O. Wentzel and F. Schwind). Vienna 1964. (Cited *Klang and Gschnitzer*).

Kommentar zum Schweizerischen Zivilgesetzbuch, herausgegeben von M. Gmür. Vol. V/2: Schlusstitel, II. Abschnitt, Einführungs- und Übergangsbestimmungen. Erläutert von E. Beck. Bern 1932 (Cited *Beck*).
Korkisch, F., Neues Internationales Privatrecht in Ostmitteleuropa: RabelsZ 32 (1968) 601-650.
Koschucharoff, A., Das internationale Eherecht im bulgarischen Familiengesetzbuch: RabelsZ 36 (1972) 492-509.
Kosters, J., and Bellemans, F., Les Conventions de La Haye de 1902 et 1905 sur le droit international privé. Recueil de législation et de jurisprudence. Harlem & The Hague 1921.

Lachenal, J.-A., Le droit applicable aux mariages mixtes célébrés à l'étranger: Schw. Jb. Int. R. 14 (1957) 33-42.
Lalaguna, E., Matrimonio indisoluble y divorcio vincular en el órden jurídico español: R.D.P. 1972, 485-529.
La Pradelle, G. de, Les conflits de lois en matière de nullités. Paris 1967.
Lasok, D., Polish Family Law. Leyden 1968.
Latey, W., Conflicts of Jurisdiction in Matrimonial Causes: 14 I.C.L.Q. 845-861 (1965).
Lauterbach, W., Eingehung der Ehe. B. Deutsches Recht: IntFamR 22-36.
Leflar, R.A., American Conflicts Law. Ed. 2. Indianapolis, Kansas City, New York 1968; ed. 3, 1977. (References are to the second edition).
Les Législations de Droit International Privé. Statutory Private International Law. Published by the T.M.C. Asser Instituut. Oslo 1971. (Cited Statutory PIL).
Lemaire, W.L.G., Nederlands internationaal privaatrecht (Hoofdlijnen). Leyden 1968.
Lerebours-Pigeonnière, P., and Loussouarn, Y., Droit international privé. Ed. 9. Paris 1970.
Leske and Loewenfeld, Rechtsverfolgung im internationalen Verkehr. Ed. 3. Herausgegeben von E.H. Loewenfeld und W. Lauterbach. Vol. I: Das Eherecht der europäischen und der aussereuropäischen Staaten (collective work). Cologne, Berlin, Bonn, Munich 1963-.
Lewald, H., Das deutsche internationale Privatrecht auf Grundlage der Rechtsprechung. Leipzig 1931.
Linant de Bellefonds, Y., La jurisprudence égyptienne et les conflits de lois en matière de statut personnel: Clunet 1960, 822-857.
Lipstein, K., Conflict of Laws 1921-1971 – the Way Ahead: [1972 B] C.L.J. 67-120.
Lövold, A., Das Eherecht Norwegens: Leske and Loewenfeld 225-273.
Lombard, R.S., American-Venezuelan Private International Law. Dobbs Ferry, N.Y., 1965.
Lübchen, G.-A., Internationale Rechtshilfe in Zivil- und Familiensachen. Berlin 1969.
Luther, G., Die sogenannten Tondern-Ehen: RabelsZ 34 (1970) 679-702.
Lysyk, K., Conflict of Laws – Status – Capacity to Marry – Recognition of Prior Foreign Divorce – The Incidental Question: 43 Can. Bar Rev. 363-380 (1965).

Maddaugh, P.D., Validity of Marriage and the Conflict of Laws – A Critique of the Present Anglo-American Position: 23 U.Tor.L.J. 117-147 (1973).

Mänhardt, F., Das internationale Personen- und Familienrecht Österreichs. Munich & Salzburg 1971.
Makarov, A.N., Grundriss des internationalen Privatrechts. Frankfurt a.M. 1970.
Makarov, A.N., Kollisionsnormen in den sowjetischen "Grundlagen" des Ehe- und Familienrechts: Festschrift Rheinstein I 363-381.
Makarov, A.N., Quellen des Internationalen Privatrechts.
– Ed. 2. 2 vol. (I: Gesetzestexte, II: Texte der Staatsverträge). Berlin & Tübingen 1953-1960. (Cited *Makarov*, Quellen I and II, respectively).
– Ed. 3. 1 vol. (Nationale Kodifikation). Tübingen 1978. (Cited *Makarov*, Quellen).
Makarov, A.N., Le remariage du conjoint divorcé en droit international privé (Etude comparative): Rev.crit.d.i.p. 1967, 643-665.
Mann, M., Foreign Penal Laws and the English Conflict of Laws: 42 Trans. Grot. Soc. 133-146 (1956).
Maridakis, G.S., Les principaux traits de la récente codification hellénique touchant le droit international privé: Rec. des Cours 85 (1954-I) 107-237.
Marín López, A., La conclusión del matrimonio en derecho internacional privado español: Rev.Esp.Der.Int. 12 (1959) 31-66.
Marquardt, K.-H., Le Certificat de capacité matrimoniale en droit comparé. Paris 1965.
Massfeller, F., Ehescheidung und Ehetrennung (Voraussetzungen). B. Deutsches Recht; C. Rechtsvergleichung: IntFamR 171-188, 188-194.
Massfeller, F., Ehescheidung und Ehetrennung (Wirkungen). B. Deutsches Recht: IntFamR 212-226.
Maury, J., L'éviction de la loi normalement compétente – l'ordre public international et la fraude à la loi. Valladolid 1952.
Melchior, G., Die Grundlagen des deutschen internationalen Privatrechts. Berlin & Leipzig 1932. Reprint, Berlin & New York 1971.
Mercier, P., Conflits de civilisations et droit international privé. Polygamie et répudiation. Geneva 1972.
Mergenthaler, E., Das ausländische Ehehindernis der Religionsverschiedenheit: StAZ 1965, 134-137.
Miaja de la Muela, A., Derecho internacional privado. 2 vol. Ed. 4. Madrid 1966-1967; ed. 5, 1969-1970; ed. 6, 1972-1974; ed. 7, 1976-1977. (References are to the fourth edition).
Miele, A., Il matrimonio dello straniero in Italia. Padua 1972.
Miele, M., Diritto internazionale privato. Padua 1966.
Monaco, R., L'efficacia della legge nello spazio. Ed. 2. Turin 1964.
Morelli, G., Elementi di diritto internazionale privato italiano. Ed. 9. Naples 1968; ed. 10, 1971. (References are to the ninth edition).
Morris, J.H.C., The Conflict of Laws. London 1971.
Moser, B., Die Europäische Menschenrechtskonvention und das bürgerliche Recht. Vienna 1972.
Müller, H., Das internationale Privatrecht der Eheschliessung: Vorschläge und Gutachten 37-46.
Müller-Freienfels, W., "Spanierheiraten" Geschiedener im Meinungsstreit: Internationales Privatrecht und Rechtsvergleichung im Ausgang des 20. Jahrhunderts. Bewahrung oder Wende? Festschrift für Gerhard Kegel (Frankfurt a.M. 1977) 55-98.
Muret, A., Le mariage en Suisse des étrangers. Thesis, Lausanne 1933.

Neuhaus, P.H., Ehehindernisse der Religionsverschiedenheit und ordre public: StAZ 1965, 279-281.
Neuhaus, P.H., Europäisches Familienrecht? Gedanken zur Rechtsvergleichung und Rechtsvereinheitlichung: Festschrift Dölle II 419-435.
Neuhaus, P.H., Die Grundbegriffe des internationalen Privatrechts. Ed. 2. Tübingen 1976.
Neuhaus, P.H., Internationales Familienrecht und Grundrechte: FamRZ 1964, 609-612.
Neuhaus, P.H., Das Verhältnis von Auflösung und Annullierung der Ehe in rechtsvergleichender Sicht: Festschrift für Hans G. Ficker zum 70. Geburtstag am 20. Juli 1967 (Frankfurt & Berlin 1967) 337-361.
Neumayer, K.H., Ehescheidung und Wiedererlangung der Ehefähigkeit: RabelsZ 20 (1955) 66-85.
Niboyet, J.-P., Traité de droit international privé français. Vol. III, V, VI/1. Paris 1944, 1948, 1949.
Niederer, W., Einführung in die allgemeinen Lehren des internationalen Privatrechts. Ed. 3. Zürich 1961.
Nitsche, H., Die Voraussetzungen der Eheschliessung im internationalen Privatrecht Portugals: StAZ 1972, 270-272.
North, P.M., The Private International Law of Matrimonial Causes in the British Isles and the Republic of Ireland. Amsterdam, New York, Oxford 1977.
Norwegian Laws etc. selected for The Foreign Service. Published by the Royal Ministry of Foreign Affairs. Oslo 1963- (loose-leaf service).
Nussbaum, A., Deutsches Internationales Privatrecht. Tübingen 1932.
Nygh, P.E., Conflict of Laws in Australia. Sydney, Melbourne, Brisbane 1968; ed. 2, 1971. (References are to the first edition).

Opsahl, T., The Convention and the Right to Respect for Family Life: *A.H. Robertson* (ed.), Privacy and Human Rights (Manchester 1973) 182-254.
von Overbeck, A.E., Die "kollisionsrechtliche Relativität der Rechtskraft". Ein Fremdkörper im schweizerischen Recht?: Gedächtnisschrift Peter Jäggi (Freiburg 1977) 273-297.
von Overbeck, A.E., Le remariage du conjoint divorcé selon le projet de convention de La Haye sur la reconnaissance des divorces et selon les droits allemand et suisse: Rev. crit. d.i.p. 1970, 45-64.
von Overbeck, A.E., Le remariage du conjoint divorcé selon le projet de Rechte geschiedenen Angehörigen eines Staates der keine Ehescheidung anerkennt: ZZW 1967, 346-358.

Palmieri, A., Il matrimonio concordatario degli italiani all'estero e degli stranieri in Italia. Naples 1968.
Pålsson, L., Haltande äktenskap och skilsmässor (Limping Marriages and Divorces). Stockholm 1966.
Pålsson, L., Marriage and Divorce: Encyclopedia III:16. Tübingen & Alphen a/d Rijn 1979.
Pålsson, L., Marriage and Divorce in Comparative Conflict of Laws. Leyden 1974. (Cited *Pålsson*, Marriage).
Pap, T., Das Eherecht der Ungarischen Volksrepublik: Leske and Loewenfeld 679-752.

Pearl, D., Muslim Marriages in English Law: [1972 A] C.L.J. 120-143.
Peaslee, A.J., Constitutions of Nations. Ed. 3. Vol. III (Europe), IV (The Americas). The Hague 1968, 1970.
Petev, V., Die Rechtshilfeverträge im Internationalen Privatrecht der sozialistischen Staaten: Wissenschaftliche Zeitschrift der Friedrich-Schiller-Universität Jena 14 (1965) 603-610.
Philip, A., Dansk international privat- og procesret (Danish Private International Law). Ed. 3. Copenhagen 1976.
Philip, A., The Scandinavian Conventions on Private International Law: Rec. des Cours 96 (1959-I) 241-348.
Picone, P., La capacità matrimoniale dello straniero divorziato. Naples 1970.
Poisson, E., Les relations entre époux dans les récentes codifications du droit international privé: Rev.crit.d.i.p. 1967, 277-302.
Ponsard, A., Eingehung der Ehe. A. Französisches Recht; C. Rechtsvergleichung: IntFamR 1-22, 36-42.
Popescu, T.R., and Eliescu, M., Das Eherecht der Sozialistischen Republik Rumänien: Leske and Loewenfeld 617-678.
Portero Sánchez, L., Matrimonios de españoles en el extranjero y de extranjeros en España: An. Der. Civ. 13 (1960) 501-518.

Raape, L., Internationales Privatrecht. Ed. 5. Berlin & Frankfurt a.M. 1961. For ed. 6 see Raape and Sturm.
Raape, Kommentar. See Staudinger.
Raape, L., and Sturm, F., Internationales Privatrecht. Ed. 6. Vol. I. Munich 1977.
Rabel, E., The Conflict of Laws. A Comparative Study. Vol. I. Ed. 2 by U. Drobnig. Ann Arbor 1958.
Réczei, L., Internationales Privatrecht. Budapest 1960.
Répertoire de droit international. Publié sous la direction de Ph. Francescakis. 2 vol. Paris 1968-1969 (with updating supplements). (Cited Rép. dr. int. I and II, respectively).
Restatement. See the following two entries. (Unless otherwise indicated, references are to the Restatement Second).
Restatement of the Law of Conflict of Laws. As Adopted and Promulgated by the American Law Institute at Washington, D.C., May 11, 1934. St. Paul 1934. See also Table of Statutes, UNITED STATES.
Restatement of the Law Second. Conflict of Laws 2d. As Adopted and Promulgated by the American Law Institute at Washington, D.C., May 23, 1969. 3 vol. St. Paul, Minn., 1971. See also Table of Statutes, UNITED STATES.
Rigaux, F., Le conflit mobile en droit international privé: Rec. des Cours 117 (1966-I) 329-444.
Rigaux, F., Droit international privé. Brussels 1968. (Cited *Rigaux*, DIP).
Rigaux, F., Droit international privé. Vol. I: Théorie générale. Brussels 1977. (Cited *Rigaux*, DIP I).
Römer, G., Gesetzesumgehung im deutschen Internationalen Privatrecht. Berlin 1955.
Ryan, S., Nullity of Marriage – Jurisdiction, Choice of Law and Related Problems: 28 Can. Bar Rev. 964-993 (1950).

Samtleben, J., Wiederheirat einer in Deutschland geschiedenen Brasilianerin: StAZ 1969, 108-110.

Sasse, W., Zur Lehre vom Ehehindernisse des Ehebruchs gemäss § 1312 BGB. Kann insbesondere das Ehehindernis auch durch Feststellung des Ehebruchs in einem ausländischen Scheidungsurteil entstehen?: Gruchot 71 (1931) 208-234.

Sato, T., Japanese Conflict of Laws in Marriage, Divorce, and Parental Relations: 8 Wayne L. Rev. 319-330 (1962).

Scheftelowitz, E.E., Das religiöse Eherecht im Staat. Cologne, Berlin, Bonn, Munich 1970.

Schmitthoff, C.M., Der Einfluss ausserrechtlicher Elemente auf die Prinzipiengestaltung des englischen internationalen Privatrechts: ZfRV 11 (1970) 81-94.

Schnitzer, A.F., Handbuch des internationalen Privatrechts. Ed. 4. Vol. I. Basle 1957.

Schöppe, L., Konkordate seit 1800. Frankfurt a.M. & Berlin 1964.

Scholl, C., Ehehindernisse und Eheverbote im internationalen Privatrecht der Bundesrepublik Deutschland: StAZ 1974, 169-174.

Schwelb, E., Some aspects of the International Covenants on Human Rights of December 1966: *A. Eide and A. Schou* (eds.), International Protection of Human Rights. Proceedings of the Seventh Nobel Symposium Oslo, September 25-27, 1967 (Stockholm 1968) 103-129.

Schwind, F., Die Ehen von Griechen im österreichischen internationalen Privatrecht: Festschrift zum 60. Geburtstag von Walter Wilburg (Graz 1965) 157-180.

Schwind, F., Handbuch des Österreichischen Internationalen Privatrechts. Vienna & New York 1975.

Schwind, F., Die Nachsichterteilung bei der Eheschliessung im österreichischen IPR: ÖStA 12 (1958) 37-41.

Secrétan, P., Le mariage des étrangers devant le juge suisse. Les actions en constatation et en nullité de mariage. Thesis, Lausanne 1944.

Serick, R., Bemerkungen zum marokkanischen Recht: Ius et Lex 395-412.

Siehr, K., Heilung durch Statutenwechsel: Gedächtnisschrift für Albert A. Ehrenzweig (Karlsruhe & Heidelberg 1976) 129-182.

Soergel and Siebert, Bürgerliches Gesetzbuch mit Einführungsgesetz und Nebengesetzen. Ed. 10. Vol. VII: Einführungsgesetz, by G. Kegel. Stuttgart, Berlin, Cologne, Mainz 1970. Supplemented by vol. IX, 1975. (Cited *Kegel*, Kommentar).

Sośniak, M., Les conventions conclues entre les pays socialistes sur le droit civil international et le droit international de la famille: Rec. des Cours 144 (1975-I) 1-76.

Sośniak, M., Problems of the Conflict of Laws in the Marriage Law in Poland: Pol. Yb. Int. L. 1 (1966/67) 137-148.

Spanoghe, Eg., Examen de jurisprudence (1949 à 1952). Droit international privé: Rev. crit. belge 1954, 49-82.

Spivak, S., Die Ungültigkeit der Ehe nach dem internationalen Privatrecht der Schweiz mit Berücksichtigung der Haager Eheschliessungs-Konvention. Thesis, Zürich 1928.

Statutory PIL. See Les Législations de Droit International Privé.

Staudinger, J.v., Kommentar zum Bürgerlichen Gesetzbuch und dem Einführungsgesetz. Ed. 9. Vol. VI/2: Art. 7-31 Einführungsgesetz (Internationales Privatrecht). Erläutert von L. Raape. Munich, Berlin, Leipzig 1931. (Cited *Raape*, Kommentar).

Staudinger, J.v., Kommentar zum Bürgerlichen Gesetzbuch mit Einführungsgesetz und Nebengesetzen. Ed. 10/11.
– Vol. IV/1: Familienrecht. §§ 1297-1362 /BGB and/ §§ 1-80 EheG. Erläutert von R. Dietz und H. Hübner. Berlin 1975. (Cited *Dietz*).
– Einführungsgesetz zum Bürgerlichen Gesetzbuch. Teil 2 a, Lieferung 1: Einleitung, Art. 7-9, 11. Bearbeitet von F. Korkisch, G. Beitzke, H. Coing, G. Weick, K. Firsching. Berlin 1970. (Cited *Beitzke*, Kommentar).
– Einführungsgesetz zum Bürgerlichen Gesetzbuch. Teil 3: Art. 13-17 (Internationales Eherecht), §§ 606-606 b, 328 ZPO (Internationales Verfahrensrecht in Ehesachen). Erläutert von F. Gamillscheg. Berlin 1973. (Cited *Gamillscheg*, Kommentar).

Stauffer, W., Praxis zum NAG. Textausgabe mit Hinweisen auf die wichtigsten Gerichts- und Verwaltungsentscheide sowie auf die vorbehaltenen Staatsverträge. Zürich 1975. Supplemented by *idem*, Nachtrag 1977 zur Praxis zum NAG. Zürich 1977.

Steinle, K., Die zweiseitigen Ehehindernisse im internationalen Privatrecht. Thesis, Munich 1939.

Stimson, E.S., Law Applicable to Marriage: 16 U. Cinc. L. Rev. 81-116 (1942).

Stöcker, H.A., Art. 30 EGBGB im Spannungsfeld zwischen Religion und Vernunft: StAZ 1968, 33-42.

Stöcker, H.A., Der internationale ordre public im Familien- und Familienerbrecht: RabelsZ 38 (1974) 79-127.

Storke, F.P., Annulment in the Conflict of Laws: 43 Minn. L. Rev. 849-873 (1959).

Storke, F.P., The Incestuous Marriage – Relic of the Past: U. Colo. L. Rev. 473-499 (1963/64).

Story, J., Commentaries on the Conflict of Laws. Ed. 7 by E.H. Bennett. Boston 1872.

Stumberg, G.W., Principles of Conflict of Laws. Ed. 3. Brooklyn 1963.

Sturm, F., Scheidung und Wiederheirat von Spaniern in der Bundesrepublik: RabelsZ 37 (1973) 61-79.

Süss, Th., Die Anerkennung ausländischer Urteile: Beiträge zum Zivilprozessrecht. Festgabe zum siebzigsten Geburtstag von Leo Rosenberg (Munich & Berlin 1949) 229-271.

Svenné Schmidt, T., International skilsmisse- og separationsret (Divorce and Separation in Private International Law). Copenhagen 1972.

Sveriges Rikes Lag (The Statutes of Sweden). Ed. 100 by T. Nordström. Stockholm 1979.

Swan, J., A New Approach to Marriage and Divorce in the Conflict of Laws: 24 U. Tor. L.J. 17-62 (1974).

Sykes, E.I., The Essential Validity of Marriage: 4 I.C.L.Q. 159-169 (1955).

Sykes, E.I., A Textbook on the Australian Conflict of Laws. Sydney, Melbourne, Brisbane 1972.

Szászy, I., Private International Law in the European People's Democracies. Budapest 1964.

Taintor, Ch.W., Marriage in the Conflict of Laws: 9 Vand. L. Rev. 607-632 (1955/56). (Cited *Taintor*, Marriage).

Taintor, Ch.W., Marriage to a Paramour After Divorce – The Conflict of Laws: 43 Minn. L. Rev. 889-898 (1959). (Cited *Taintor*, Marriage to a Paramour).

Tchirkovitch, S., Les dispositions du droit international privé du Code de la famille Yougoslave: Rev. crit. d.i.p. 1952, 221-239.

Travers, M., La Convention de la Haye relative au mariage. 2 vol. Paris 1912.

Tsai, Pi-Song, Ehescheidung, Anerkennung ausländischer Ehescheidungen und Wiederverheiratung im internationalen Privatrecht. Thesis, Zürich 1975.

Tyan, E., Précis de droit international privé. Beyrouth 1966.

Undén, Ö., Internationell äktenskapsrätt enligt gällande svensk lag (The Swedish Conflicts Law of Marriage). Lund 1922.

Undén, Ö., Studier i internationell äktenskapsrätt särskilt med hänsyn till Haag-konventionerna (Studies in the Conflicts Law of Marriage Particularly with Regard to the Hague Conventions). Vol. I. Lund 1913.

van Hecke, G., American-Belgian Private International Law. Dobbs Ferry, N.Y., 1968.

van Hecke, G., and Rigaux, F., Examen de jurisprudence (1953 à 1960). Droit international privé. Conflit de lois: Rev. crit. belge 1961, 357-400.

van Hecke, G., and Rigaux, F., Examen de jurisprudence (1961 à 1964). Droit international privé. Conflit de lois: Rev. crit. belge 1965, 331-369.

van Hecke, G., and Rigaux, F., Examen de jurisprudence (1965 à 1969). Droit international privé. Conflit de lois: Rev. crit. belge 1970, 269-308.

van Hecke, G., and Rigaux, F., Examen de jurisprudence (1970 à 1975). Droit international privé (Conflit de lois): Rev. crit. belge 1976, 221-267.

van Sasse van Ysselt, Die wesentlichen Merkmale des niederländischen Personenstands-, Ehe- und Kindschaftsrechts und dessen Berührungspunkte zum deutschen Recht: StAZ 1966, 189-198.

Vaucher, R.F., Le statut des étrangers en Suisse. Basle 1967.

Vernier, C.G., American Family Laws. Vol. I, II. Stanford, Cal., 1931, 1932.

Vincent, J., and Ponsard, A., Formation du mariage. Introduction générale. Conditions de fond du mariage: J. Cl. dr. int., Fasc. 546-A.

Vischer, F., Internationales Privatrecht. Basle & Stuttgart 1969. Unveränderter Nachdruck aus "Schweizerisches Privatrecht" herausgegeben von Max Gutzwiller u.a., Band I (1969).

Vischer, F., "Mariage mixte" und Ehescheidung im internationalen Privatrecht der Schweiz: Ius et Lex 413-428.

Vischer, F., Der ordre public im Familienrecht: ZZW 1969, 324-334.

Vitta, E., Diritto internazionale privato. Vol. I, II. Turin 1972, 1973.

Vom Deutschen zum Europäischen Recht. Festschrift für Hans Dölle. Vol. II. Tübingen 1963.

von Hoffmann and Ortiz-Arce. See under initial H.

von Overbeck. See under initial O.

Vorschläge und Gutachten zur Reform des deutschen internationalen Eherechts vorgelegt im Auftrag der Eherechtskommission des deutschen Rates für internationales Privatrecht von W. Lauterbach. Berlin & Tübingen 1962.

Walker, G., Internationales Privatrecht. Ed. 5. Vienna 1934.
Webb, P.R.H., "Shot-Gun" Marriages and the Conflict of Laws: 22 M.L.R. 198-204 (1959).
Webb, P.R.H., Some Thoughts on the Place of English Law as *Lex Fori* in English Private International Law: 10 I.C.L.Q. 818-845 (1961).
Webb, P.R.H., and Davis, J.L.R., A Casebook on the Conflict of Laws of New Zealand. Wellington 1970.
Weintraub, R.J., Commentary on the Conflict of Laws. Mineola, N.Y., 1971.
Wengler, W., The General Principles of Private International Law: Rec. des Cours 104 (1961-III) 273-469.
Wengler, W., Gutachten zum internationalen und ausländischen Familien- und Erbrecht. Vol. I. Berlin 1971.
Wengler, W., Nouvelles réflexions sur les "questions préalables": Rev. crit. d.i.p. 1966, 165-215.
Wengler, W., Skizzen zur Lehre vom Statutenwechsel: RabelsZ 23 (1958) 535-572.
Wengler, W., Die Vorfrage im Kollisionsrecht: RabelsZ 8 (1934) 148-251.
Wolff, M., Das internationale Privatrecht Deutschlands. Ed. 3. Berlin, Göttingen, Heidelberg 1954.
Wolff, M., Private International Law. Ed. 2. London 1950.
Woodhouse, J.T., Lack of Consent as a Ground for Nullity and the Conflict of Laws: 3 I.C.L.Q. 454-465 (1954).
Wuppermann, M., Die deutsche Rechtsprechung zum Vorbehalt des ordre public im Internationalen Privatrecht seit 1945 vornehmlich auf dem Gebiet des Familienrechts. Frankfurt a.M. 1977.

Zepos, P.J., Das Eherecht Griechenlands: Leske and Loewenfeld 985-1046.

LIST OF ABBREVIATIONS

Note. This list is in the main limited to abbreviations, used in the book, of (1) legal periodicals and other series of legal publications, (2) states or provinces of federal units, and (3) judicial and other bodies. For abbreviations of books and articles cited in this work see Bibliography.

Periodicals which, to the author's knowledge, have been discontinued are marked by an asterisk (*). The same symbol is used after the name of courts or divisions of courts which have been abolished or which no longer exist under that name.

A.	Atlantic Reporter (USA)
ABGB	Allgemeines Bürgerliches Gesetzbuch. See Table of Statutes, AUSTRIA.
A.C.	Appeal Cases (Law Reports; England)
AcP	Archiv für die civilistische Praxis ([West] Germany)
AG	Amtsgericht ([West] Germany)
A.L.R.	American Law Reports Annotated; Australian Law Reports
Act. Doc. La Haye	Conférence de La Haye de droit international privé. Actes et Documents de la . . . session
Act. La Haye	Conférence de La Haye de droit international privé. Actes de la . . . session* (since the ninth session (1960) united with Doc. La Haye to form Act. Doc. La Haye)
Ala.	Alabama; Alabama Reports
All E.R.	All England Law Reports
All E.R. Rep.	All England Law Reports Reprint (1558-1935)
Alta.	Alberta
Am. Dec.	American Decisions* (1760-1869)
Am. J. Comp. L.	American Journal of Comparative Law
Am. Rep.	American Reports* (1868-1887)
An. D.G.R.N.	Anuario de la Dirección General de los Registros y del Notariado (Spain)
An. Der. Civ.	Anuario de Derecho Civil (Spain)
Annal. Dir. Int.	Annali di Diritto Internazionale* (Italy)
Annot.	Annotation
App.	Corte di Appello (Italy)
App. Cas.	Appeal Cases* (Law Reports, 1875-1890; England)
App. Ct.	Appellate Court (Illinois)
App. Div.	Supreme Court, Appellate Division (New York)
AppG	Appellationsgericht (Canton of Basle-Town, Switzerland)
AppH	Appellationshof (Canton of Bern, Switzerland)
Aranzadi Jur.	Repertorio de Jurisprudencia (Aranzadi) (Spain)
Ariz.	Arizona
Ark.	Arkansas

B.C.	British Columbia
B.D.I.L.	A British Digest of International Law. See Bibliography.
BG	Bundesgericht (Switzerland)
BGBl	Bundesgesetzblatt (West Germany); Bundesgesetzblatt für die Republik Österreich
BGE	Entscheidungen des Schweizerischen Bundesgerichtes, Amtliche Sammlung
BGH	Bundesgerichtshof (West Germany)
BGHZ	Entscheidungen des Bundesgerichtshofes in Zivilsachen (West Germany)
BJM	Basler Juristische Mitteilungen (Switzerland)
BMA	Basic Marriage Act. See Table of Statutes, YUGOSLAVIA.
BMfJ	Bundesministerium für Justiz (Austria)
B. Mon.	Ben. Monroe's Reports* (1840-1857; Kentucky)
B. Of.	Buletinul Oficial al Marii Adunări Nationale a R.P.R. (Rumania)
B.U.L. Rev.	Boston University Law Review (USA)
BVerfG	Bundesverfassungsgericht (West Germany)
BVerfGE	Entscheidungen des Bundesverfassungsgerichts (West Germany)
BadRpr.	Badische Rechtspraxis und Annalen der Badischen Gerichte* (Gemany)
Baxt.	Baxter's Reports* (1872-1878; Tennessee)
BayObLG	Bayerisches Oberstes Landesgericht (/West/ Germany)
BerGesVR	Berichte der Deutschen Gesellschaft für Völkerrecht (West Germany)
BezG	Bezirksgericht (Switzerland)
Brit. YB. Int. L.	British Year Book of International Law
Bull. Czech. L.	Bulletin of Czechoslovak Law
Bull. dr. tchécosl.	Bulletin de Droit Tchécoslovaque
Bull. I.I.I.	Bulletin de l'Institut Intermédiaire International* (1919-1933), Bulletin de l'Institut Juridique International* (1934-1940) (The Netherlands)
Bush	Bush's Reports* (1866-1879; Kentucky)
C.A.	Court of Appeal (England and certain other common law jurisdictions)
CC	Civil Code (Bürgerliches Gesetzbuch, Code Civil, Codice Civile, etc.)
C.C.A.	Court of Criminal Appeal* (now Criminal Division of Court of Appeal) (England)
CC Fed.	Civil Code for the Federal District and Territories. See Table of Statutes, MEXICO.
CCP	Code of Civil Procedure (Code de procédure civile, Codice di procedura civile, Zivilprozessordnung, etc.)
CIC	Codex Iuris Canonici. See Table of Statutes, CANON LAW
C.I.E.C.	Commission Internationale de l'Etat Civil. See also Bibliography.
C.J.	Chief Justice
C.L.J.	Cambridge Law Journal (England)

C.L.R.	Commonwealth Law Reports (Australia)
C.S.	/Les Rapports Judiciaires de Québec/ Cour Supérieure
C. Supr.	Corte Suprema (Chile)
Cal.	California
Cal. Rptr.	California Reporter
Can. Bar Rev.	Canadian Bar Review
Cass.	Corte di Cassazione (Italy); Cour de Cassation (Belgium)
Cass. civ.	Cour de Cassation, Chambre civile (France)
Cass. req.	Cour de Cassation, Chambre des requêtes* (France)
Cass. soc.	Cour de Cassation, Chambre civile, section sociale (France)
Ch.	Chancery Division (/Law Reports/England); Court of Chancery* (now Chancery Division of the Superior Court) (New Jersey)
Ch. App.	Court of Chancery Appeals* (now Court of Appeals) (Tennessee)
Cir.	United States Court of Appeals for the . . . circuit
Civ.	Tribunal civil (Belgium)
Civ. App.	Court of Civil Appeals (Texas)
Cl. & F.	Clark & Finnelly* (Law Reports, 1831-1846; England)
Clunet	Journal du Droit International /privé et de la jurisprudence comparée/ (France)
Colo.	Colorado
Colum. L. Rev.	Columbia Law Review (USA)
Com. PI.	Court of Common Pleas (Pennsylvania)
Comm. App.	Commission of Appeals (Texas)
Conn.	Connecticut
Cornell L.Q.	Cornell Law Quarterly (USA)
Corr.	Tribunal correctionnel (Belgium)
Cour	Cour d'appel (Algeria, Belgium, France, Morocco)
Crim. App.	Court of Criminal Appeals (Oklahoma)
Ct. App.	Court of Appeal/s/ (various states of the USA)
Ct. Err. App.	Court of Errors and Appeals* (now Supreme Court) (New Jersey)
D..../J./	Recueil Dalloz de doctrine, de jurisprudence et de législation, . . . /Jurisprudence/* (since 1965 united with Recueil Sirey to form Recueil Dalloz Sirey) (France)
DA	Dienstanweisung für die Standesbeamten und ihre Aufsichtsbehörden. See Table of Statutes, [WEST] GERMANY
D.C.	District of Columbia; United States District Court for the District of (state)
D.D.C.	United States District Court for the District of Columbia
D.G.R.N.	Dirección General de los Registros y del Notariado (Spain)
D.L.R.	Dominion Law Reports (Canada)
D.P.	Dalloz. Recueil périodique et critique de jurisprudence, de législation et de doctrine* (France)
D.S..../Jur./	Recueil Dalloz Sirey, . . . /Jurisprudence/ (France)
DVO	Vierte Durchführungsverordnung zum Ehegesetz. See Table of Statutes, AUSTRIA.

Del.	Delaware
Dem.	Demarest's Surrogate Reports* (1882-1888; New York)
Dir. eccles.	Diritto Ecclesiastico (Italy)
Dir. Int.	Diritto Internazionale* (Italy)
Disp. prel.	Disposizioni sulla legge in generale. See Table of Statutes, ITALY
Dist. Ct. App.	District Court of Appeal (California)
Div. Ct.	Court for Divorce and Matrimonial Causes (Nova Scotia)
Doc. La Haye	Conférence de La Haye de droit international privé. Documents relatifs à la . . . session* (since the ninth session (1960) united with Act. La Haye to form Act. Doc. La Haye)
Dom. Rel. Ct.	Domestic Relations Court (New York)
E.D.	United States District Court for the Eastern District of (state)
EFSlg	Ehe- und familienrechtliche Entscheidungen, herausgegeben von Hluze-Litzlfellner (Austria)
EGBGB	Einführungsgesetz zum Bürgerlichen Gesetzbuch. See Table of Statutes, [WEST] GERMANY.
EGFGB	Einführungsgesetz zum Familiengesetzbuch der Deutschen Demokratischen Republik. See Table of Statutes, EAST GERMANY.
EheG	Ehegesetz. See Table of Statutes, [WEST] GERMANY.
Eng. Rep.	English Reports (1220-1865)
EvBl	Evidenzblatt der Rechtsmittelentscheidungen (forming part of Österreichische Juristen-Zeitung)
F.	Federal Reporter (USA)
FC	Family Code. See Table of Statutes, BULGARIA, SENEGAL.
F.C.	Full Court
F.L.R.	Federal Law Reports (Australia)
F. Supp.	Federal Supplement (USA)
Fam.	Family Division (/Law Reports/ England)
Fam. L.Q.	Family Law Quarterly (USA)
FamRZ	Zeitschrift für das gesamte Familienrecht (1954-1960 published as: Ehe und Familie im privaten und öffentlichen Recht) (West Germany)
Fasc.	Fascicule (of J. Cl. dr. int.; see this abbreviation)
Fla.	Florida
Ford. L. Rev.	Fordham Law Review (USA)
Foro it.	Foro Italiano
Foro nap.	Foro Napoletano (Italy)
Foro pad.	Foro Padano (Italy)
G.A. Res.	Resolution of the General Assembly of the United Nations
GBl DDR	Gesetzblatt der Deutschen Demokratischen Republik
G.P.	Gazette du Palais (France)
G.T.	Gaceta de los Tribunales (Chile)
G.U.	Gazzetta Ufficiale (Italy)

Ga.	Georgia
Giur. Comp. D.I.P.	Giurisprudenza Comparata di Diritto Internazionale Privato* (1937-1956; Italy)
Giur. Compl. Cass. Civ.	Giurisprudenza Completa della Corte Suprema di Cassazione, Sezioni Civili (Italy)
Giur. it.	Giurisprudenza Italiana
Giur. It. D.I.P. (1942/66)	La giurisprudenza italiana di diritto internazionale privato e processuale. See Bibliography.
Giur. sic.	Giurisprudenza Siciliana (Italy)
Giur. tosc.	Giurisprudenza Toscana (Italy)
Giust. civ.	Giustizia Civile (Italy)
Gruchot	Beiträge zur Erläuterung des Deutschen Rechts*
H.C.	High Court (various common law jurisdictions)
H.C.A.	High Court of Australia
HD	Högsta domstolen (Sweden); Høyesterettsdom (Norway)
H.L.	House of Lords (United Kingdom)
H.L.C.	House of Lords Cases* (1847-1866; England)
Hag. Con.	Haggard Consistory* (Law Reports, 1789-1821; England)
Harv. L. Rev.	Harvard Law Review (USA)
Hof	Gerechtshof (The Netherlands)
Hun	Hun's Reports* (1874-1895; New York)
I.C.L.Q.	International and Comparative Law Quarterly (England)
I.L.Q.	International Law Quarterly* (1947-1951, then united with J. Comp. Leg. to form I.C.L.Q.) (England)
I.L.R.	International Law Reports (1919-1949 published as: Annual Digest and Reports of Public International Law Cases) (England)
IPG	Gutachten zum internationalen und ausländischen Privatrecht (West Germany)
IPRspr.	Die deutsche Rechtsprechung auf dem Gebiete des internationalen Privatrechts im Jahre (in den Jahren) . . .
Ill.	Illinois
Ill. App.	Illinois Appellate Court Reports
Ill. L. Rev.	Illinois Law Review, since 1952/53 published as: Northwestern University Law Review (USA)
Ind.	Indiana
IntFamR	Das internationale Familienrecht. See Bibliography.
IntRDipl.	Internationales Recht und Diplomatie (West Germany)
Iowa L. Rev.	Iowa Law Review
Ired.	Iredell's Law Reports* (1840-1852; North Carolina)
J.	Judge; (Mr.) Justice
J.A.L.	Journal of African Law (England)
JBl	Juristische Blätter (Austria)
J.C.P.	Juris Classeur Périodique. La Semaine Juridique (France)
J. Cl. dr. int.	Juris-Classeur de droit international. See Bibliography.
J. Comp. Leg.	Journal of Comparative Legislation and International Law* (1896-1951, then united with I.L.Q. to form I.C.L.Q.) (England)

J.T.	Journal des Tribunaux (Belgium)
JW	Juristische Wochenschrift* (1872-1939; Germany)
JZ	Juristenzeitung (West Germany)
JuS	Juristische Schulung (West Germany)
Jur. Liège	Jurisprudence de la Cour d'appel de Liège et des juridictions de son ressort (Belgium)
Jur. Rev.	Juridical Review (Scotland)
K.B.	King's Bench (/Law Reports/ England: certain other Commonwealth countries)
KG	Kammergericht ([West] Germany)
KGJ	Jahrbuch für Entscheidungen des Kammergerichts in Sachen der freiwilligen Gerichtsbarkeit, in Kosten-, Stempel- und Strafsachen* (Germany)
KRABl	Amtsblatt des Kontrollrats in Deutschland* (1945-1948)
Kan.	Kansas
Kan. L. Rev.	University of Kansas Law Review (USA)
KrG	Kreisgericht (Austria)
Ky.	Kentucky
LG	Landesgericht (Austria); Landgericht ([West] Germany)
LNTS	League of Nations Treaty Series*
L.Q.R.	Law Quarterly Review (England)
L.R....H.L.	English and Irish Appeals* (Law Reports, 1866-1875)
L.T.	Law Times Reports* (1859-1947, then incorporated in All E.R.) (England)
LZ	Leipziger Zeitschrift für Deutsches Recht* (1907-1933)
La.	Louisiana
MDR	Monatsschrift für Deutsches Recht (West Germany)
M.L.R.	Modern Law Review (England)
Magis. Ct.	City Magistrate's Court (New York)
Man.	Manitoba
Marq. L. Rev.	Marquette Law Review (USA)
Mass.	Massachusetts; Massachusetts Reports
Mass. Gen. Laws	Massachusetts General Laws. See Table of Statutes, UNITED STATES.
McGill L.J.	McGill Law Journal (Canada)
Md.	Maryland; Maryland Reports
Md. L. Rev.	Maryland Law Review
Me.	Maine
Mich.	Michigan
Mich. L. Rev.	Michigan Law Review
Minn.	Minnesota
Minn. L. Rev.	Minnesota Law Review
Miss.	Mississippi
Mo.	Missouri
Mont.	Montana
Mont. Co. L. Rep.	Montgomery County Law Reporter (Pennsylvania)
Mun. Ct. App.	District of Columbia (Municipal) Court of Appeals

N	Natal Provincial Division (of the Supreme Court of South Africa)
NAG	Bundesgesetz betreffend die zivilrechtlichen Verhältnisse der Niedergelassenen und Aufenthalter. See Table of Statutes, SWITZERLAND.
N.C.	North Carolina; North Carolina Reports
N.C.L. Rev.	North Carolina Law Review
N.D.	North Dakota
N.D.L. Rev.	North Dakota Law Review
N.E.	North Eastern Reporter (USA)
N.H.	New Hampshire; New Hampshire Reports
N.I.	Northern Ireland Law Reports
N.J.	Nederlandse Jurisprudentie; New Jersey
NJA	Nytt Juridiskt Arkiv (Sweden)
NJW	Neue Juristische Wochenschrift (West Germany)
N.L.R.	Natal Law Reports (New Series)* (1879-1932: South Africa)
NRt	Norsk Retstidende (Norway)
N.S.	Nova Scotia
N.S.W.	New South Wales
N.T.I.R.	Nederlands Tijdschrift voor Internationaal Recht; since 1975 published as: Netherlands International Law Review
N.W.	North Western Reporter (USA)
N.Y.	New York; New York Reports
N.Y.S.	New York Supplement
Neb.	Nebraska
NiemeyersZ	/Niemeyers/ Zeitschrift für Internationales Recht* (1891-1937/1891-1909 published under other titles/; Germany)
Notre Dame Law.	Notre Dame Lawyer (USA)
Nouv. Rev. d.i.p.	Nouvelle Revue de Droit International Privé* (France)
OER	Osteuropa-Recht (West Germany)
OGH	Oberster Gerichtshof (Austria; Liechtenstein)
OLG	Oberlandesgericht (Austria; [West] Germany)
OLGR	Die Rechtsprechung der Oberlandesgerichte auf dem Gebiete des Zivilrechts* (1900-1928; Germany)
O.R.	Ontario Reports
ObG	Obergericht (Switzerland)
ÖJZ	Österreichische Juristen-Zeitung
ÖStA	Österreichisches Standesamt
Öst. H. int. R.	Österreichische Hefte für die Praxis des internationalen und ausländischen Rechts* (1956-1959)
Ohio St. L.J.	Ohio State Law Journal
Okl.	Oklahoma
Ont.	Ontario
Or.	Oregon
P.	Pacific Reporter (USA); Probate, Divorce and Admiralty Division* (/Law Reports/ 1891-1971, now Family Division) (England)

P.D.	Probate Division* (Law Reports, 1875-1890; England)
Pa.	Pennsylvania; Pennsylvania State Reports
Pa. D. & C.	Pennsylvania District and County Reports
Pa. Super. Ct.	Pennsylvania Superior Court Reports
Pas.	Pasicrisie belge
Pick.	Pickering's Reports* (1822-1839; Massachusetts)
Pol. Yb. Int. L.	Polish Yearbook of International Law
Pres.	President (of OLG, see this abbreviation)
Q.B.	Queen's Bench (/Law Reports/ England; certain other Commonwealth countries)
Qd. R.	Queensland Reports
RAG	Rechtsanwendungsgesetz. See Table of Statutes, EAST GERMANY.
R.B.D.I.	Revue Belge de Droit International
R.D.P.	Revista de Derecho Privado (Spain)
R. du B.	Revue du Barreau de la Province de Québec
RG	Reichsgericht* (Germany)
RGBl	Reichsgesetzblatt* (Germany)
RGZ	Entscheidungen des Reichsgerichts in Zivilsachen* (1880-1945; Germany)
R.I.	Rhode Island
R.L.n.s.	Revue Légale (nouvelle série) (Quebec)
R.R.S.J.	Revue Roumaine des Sciences Sociales – Série de Sciences Juridiques
RW	Rechtskundig Weekblad (Belgium)
RabelsZ	/Rabels/Zeitschrift für ausländisches und internationales Privatrecht ([West] Germany)
Rb.	Burgerlijke Rechtbank (Belgium); Rechtbank (The Netherlands)
Rec. des Cours	Académie de Droit International de la Haye, Recueil des Cours
Rép. dr. int.	Répertoire de droit international. See Bibliography.
Rev. crit. belge	Revue Critique de Jurisprudence Belge
Rev. crit. d.i.p.	Revue Critique de Droit International Privé (1905-1921 published as: Revue de Droit International Privé et de Droit Pénal International; 1922-1933: Revue de Droit International Privé; 1934-1946: Revue Critique de Droit International) (France)
Rev. Der. Santiago	Revista de Derecho, Jurisprudencia y Ciencias Sociales (Chile)
Rev. dr. fam.	Revue de Droit Familial (Belgium)
Rev. Egypt.	Revue Egyptienne de Droit International
Rev. Esp. Der. Int.	Revista Española de Derecho Internacional
Rev. Gen.	Revista General de Legislación y Jurisprudencia (Spain)
Rev. Hell.	Revue Hellénique de Droit International
Rev. int. dr. comp.	Revue Internationale de Droit Comparé (France)
Rev. trim. dr. civ.	Revue Trimestrielle de Droit Civil (France)
Rev. tunis. dr.	Revue Tunisienne de Droit
Riv. dir. int.	Rivista di Diritto Internazionale (Italy)

Riv. dir. int. proc.	Rivista di Diritto Internazionale Privato e Processuale (Italy)
Riv. dir. matr.	Rivista del Diritto Matrimoniale Italiano e dei Rapporti di Famiglia* (1934-1954), Rivista del Diritto Matrimoniale e dello Stato delle Persone (Italy)
Riv. dir. proc.	Rivista di Diritto Processuale (Italy)
S.	Recueil Sirey* (since 1965 united with Recueil Dalloz to form Recueil Dalloz Sirey) (France)
S.A.	South African Law Reports
S.A.S.R.	South Australian State Reports
S.C.	Session Cases (Scotland); Supreme Court (various common law jurisdictions)
S.C.C.	Supreme Court of Canada
S.C.L.Q.	South Carolina Law Quarterly
S.D.	South Dakota; United States District Court for the Southern District of (state)
S.E.	South Eastern Reporter (USA)
SFS	Svensk Författningssamling (Sweden)
S.I.	Statutory Instrument (United Kingdom)
S.J.	Solicitors' Journal (England)
SJZ	Schweizerische Juristen-Zeitung
S.L.T.	Scots Law Times
SÖFM	Sveriges Överenskommelser med Främmande Makter (Sweden)
S.R. (N.S.W.)	State Reports, New South Wales
S.W.	South Western Reporter (USA)
SZ	Entscheidungen des Österreichischen Obersten Gerichtshofes in Zivil- und Justizverwaltungssachen
Sask.	Saskatchewan
Schw. Jb. Int. R.	Schweizerisches Jahrbuch für internationales Recht
Sh.Ct.	Sheriff Court (Scotland)
So.	Southern Reporter (USA)
So. Cal. L. Rev.	Southern California Law Review
StAZ	Zeitschrift für Standesamtswesen* (1921-1944), since 1948 continued by Das Standesamt (1948 published under other title) ([West] Germany)
St. John's L. Rev.	St. John's Law Review (USA)
Sup. Ct.	Supreme Court (various jurisdictions of the British Commonwealth and the USA)
Supp. Ct. App.	Supreme Court of Appeals (Virginia, West Virginia)
Sup. Ct. Err.	Supreme Court of Errors (Connecticut)
Sup. Jud. Ct.	Supreme Judicial Court (Maine, Massachusetts)
Super. Ct.	Superior Court (various states of the USA)
Surr. Ct.	Surrogate's Court (New York)
Sw. & Tr.	Swabey and Tristram* (Law Reports, 1858-1865; England)
Syracuse L. Rev.	Syracuse Law Review (USA)
T.L.R.	Times Law Reports* (1884-1952; England)
T.S.	Tribunal Supremo (Spain)

Temi	Temi/Emiliana/. Rivista di giurisprudenza italiana
Temi nap.	Temi Napoletana (Italy)
Temi rom.	Temi Romana (Italy)
Tenn.	Tennessee; Tennessee Reports
Tex.	Texas
Trans. Grot. Soc.	Transactions of the Grotius Society* (1915-1959; England)
Trav. Com. fr. d.i.p.	Travaux du Comité français de droit international privé
Trib.	Tribunal civil*, tribunal de grande instance (France); tribunale (Italy)
Trib. corr.	Tribunal correctionnel (France)
U. Cinc. L. Rev.	University of Cincinnati Law Review (USA)
U. Colo. L. Rev.	University of Colorado Law Review (USA)
UN Doc.	United Nations Document
UNTS	United Nations Treaty Series
U. Pa. L. Rev.	University of Pennsylvania Law Review (USA)
U.S.	United States Reports
U. Tor. L.J.	University of Toronto Law Journal (Canada)
V.L.R.	Victorian Law Reports* (1875-1956)
V.R.	Victorian Reports
V.R. (I.E. & M.)	Victorian Reports (Insolvency, Ecclesiastical, & Matrimonial Cases)* (1870-1872)
Va.	Virginia
Va. L. Rev.	Virginia Law Review
Vand. L. Rev.	Vanderbilt Law Review (USA)
VerwG	Verwaltungsgericht (West Germany)
Vt.	Vermont
VwGH	Verwaltungsgerichtshof (Austria)
W.	Weekblad van het Recht* (The Netherlands)
WGO	Die wichtigsten Gesetzgebungsakte in den Ländern Ost-, Südosteuropas und in den ostasiatischen Volksdemokratien (West Germany)
W.L.D.	Witwatersrand Local Division (of the Supreme Court of South Africa)
W.L.R.	Weekly Law Reports (England)
W.N.	Weekly Notes* (Law Reports, 1866-1952; England)
W. Va.	West Virginia
W.W.R.	Western Weekly Reports (Canada)
Wash.	Washington
Wayne L. Rev.	Wayne Law Review (USA)
Wis.	Wisconsin
Wyo.	Wyoming
Wyo. L.J.	Wyoming Law Journal
YB Human Rights	Yearbook of the European Convention on Human Rights
Yale L.J.	Yale Law Journal (USA)
ZBJV	Zeitschrift des Bernischen Juristenvereins (Switzerland)

ZfRV	Zeitschrift für Rechtsvergleichung (Austria)
ZGB	Zivilgesetzbuch (Switzerland)
Z. osteur. R.	Zeitschrift für osteuropäisches Recht* (Germany)
ZPO	Zivilprozessordnung ([West] Germany)
ZR	Blätter für Zürcherische Rechtsprechung (Switzerland)
ZSR	Zeitschrift für Schweizerisches Recht
ZZP	Zeitschrift für Zivilprozess ([West] Germany)
ZZW	Zeitschrift für Zivilstandswesen (Switzerland)
ZivG	Zivilgericht (Switzerland)

I. Introductory

1. *Terminology and Scope of the Work.* The substance, or substantive conditions, of marriage (*les conditions de fond du mariage; die materiellen Ehevoraussetzungen*) will here be taken to include all matters pertaining to the conclusion and validity of marriage, in so far as they do not relate to form or proof.[1] Within this broad category four classes of requirements for or impediments to marriage may be distinguished: (1) general capacity to marry (including, for example, the question of marriageable age); (2) prohibitions or conditions of marriage applying to persons of a certain class (for instance, a prohibition on priests marrying or the requirement of parental consent for the marriage of infants); (3) relative incapacity applicable to marriage between certain persons only (for example, because of consanguinity or difference of religion); (4) the true consent of the parties to marry each other.[2]

The terms *capacity to marry* and *right to marry* do not cover the whole of this concept.[3] Nevertheless, in literature on the conflict of laws they are often used as synonymous with substantive conditions of marriage. For reasons of convenience this usage will be followed here, except where otherwise indicated.

Another distinction commonly drawn in municipal law is that between conditions or prohibitions of marriage which do and those which do not affect the validity of the union. Some impediments are *mandatory* or *irritant* (*impedimenta dirimentia*), rendering an infringing marriage invalid or liable to annulment. Other conditions or prohibitions are merely *directory* (*impedimenta impedientia*) in the sense that they do not purport to impair the validity of a marriage entered into in violation of them.

1. Cf. *Pålsson*, Marriage, s. 264, 405-417.
2. See on this and other divisions adopted in municipal law, for example, *Dölle*, Familienrecht 89-91.
3. See *Rabel* 263; *Vitta* II 174.

To some extent the distinctions referred to above, as well as certain other divisions sometimes made in municipal law, are also relevant in the conflict of laws. It has, nevertheless, been thought preferable to deal with all conflicts problems coming within the notion of substance of marriage, as defined above, in one chapter. This delimitation of the subject-matter and the terminology adopted here is in no way intended to prejudge the question of whether a single conflicts regime applies or should apply over the whole area.

2. *Main Conflicts Principles.* The conflicts rules governing our subject-matter are based on two different principles, which reflect the fundamental opposition between territoriality and extraterritoriality in private international law. According to one principle, the substantive aspects of marriage, like its form, are referred to the *lex loci celebrationis.* According to the other, *the personal law of the parties* applies. The latter principle, in its turn, resolves itself into two, according to whether the personal law is determined by domicile or by nationality.

The problems are, however, far more complex than might appear from these fairly simple leading principles, and the fact that one or the other of them prevails in a given legal system often does not take the matter very far. On the one hand, the solutions of specific problems may differ considerably between legal systems adopting the same basic principle in this field. On the other hand, the answers to such questions may tend to converge despite the points of departure, in terms of basic principles, of the legal systems compared being radically different.

One reason for this is that there is no universally accepted definition of the concept of substance of marriage. Not infrequently this notion is undeveloped and ill-defined. This is particularly true for countries adhering to the principle of the *lex loci celebrationis,* for example the United States. To that extent, it is true, the lack of a precise concept is not very important for practical purposes, since the choice of law will normally be the same whether a given question is classified as going to the substance of marriage or to its form. From the point of view of countries in which the substantive conditions of marriage are referable to the personal law, on the other hand, the delimitation of this concept is a matter of vital significance. In several of these countries too, particularly in England and other common law countries, the concept is rather uncertain and often understood in a narrow sense covering only the "core" of the subject-matter under review. The national variations of the concept necessarily lead to differences as to the scope of the conflicts rules governing the matter.

Secondly, there is hardly a single country in which a single principle is followed for all questions held to come within the substance of marriage or in all situations in which such questions may arise. Different conflicts rules are often applied, for example, according as a local or a foreign celebrated marriage is in issue, or according as the parties are local or foreign nationals (domiciliaries). In so far as a single rule prevails in principle, it is invariably made subject to certain exceptions, which may be more or less specific and more or less far-reaching, if not on other grounds then at least where the rule would lead to results which are incompatible with the public policy of the forum. In practice, this amounts to much the same as if different rules had been laid down for different situations.

One important distinction is that between a marriage which is to be celebrated locally and a marriage which has already been entered into – whether locally or in some foreign country – and whose validity is to be examined *ex post*. Differences often exist between, respectively, the *direct* and the *indirect* regulation of the choice of law governing the substantive conditions of marriage in these two situations.[4] This is mainly because the policy of validation comes into play once a marriage has been created and because the analogy with divorce makes itself felt in annulment cases. As a consequence, a marriage contracted in violation of some of the substantive conditions prescribed by the law which (in the eyes of the forum) should have been observed will nevertheless often be upheld.[5]

Although neither of the two principles referred to above seems ever to have been adopted in its "pure" form, it will be convenient for the purpose of our exposition to distinguish according as to whether one or the other of them preponderates in various legal systems. The first principle to be examined is that of the *lex loci celebrationis* (II), the second that of the personal law (III).

4. On the terms "direct" and "indirect" regulation of the choice of law see *Pålsson*, Marriage, s. 265.

5. Cf. as regards the form of marriage *ibid.* s. 402-404.

II. The Principle of the Lex Loci Celebrationis

A. General Introduction

3. *Sphere of Application.* The principle that all aspects of the formation and validity of marriage, including the substantive conditions to be satisfied by the parties, are governed by the law of the place of celebration is the older system, strongly impregnated by the notion of territoriality. It once prevailed in the law of contracts generally and has survived with regard to marriage in certain countries, chiefly in the Western hemisphere.[6] The *lex loci celebrationis* thus applies, as the main rule for determining capacity to marry, in the *United States* as well as in most countries of *Latin America.* As regards other parts of the world, the principle is today accepted only in some scattered countries, including the *Soviet Union, Denmark* and *South Africa.* It has also been adopted, with certain modifications, in the *Scandinavian Convention* of 1931 on the Private International Law of Marriage, Adoption and Guardianship.

4. *Rationale.* To a very large extent this principle fits in with basic preferences for territoriality in the conflict of laws generally in the countries mentioned.[7] Particularly in American law, the theory of marriage as a contract has contributed to the preservation of the traditional rule. Sociological and demographic factors have tended to reinforce that rule, at any rate in the Western hemisphere. It has enabled immigrants into the United States and Latin American countries to marry under the local law without regard to impediments laid down by the laws of their former home countries. As regards the United States, the great mobility of the people within the union has probably been an even more important factor tending in the same direction. There is in a society of the American type an obvious need for clear, simple and uniform solutions of problems relating to the validity of marriages. It should be noted here that the American conflicts rules on marriage have developed essentially through decisions in interstate rather than international conflicts cases and that cases involving the latter type of conflict are comparatively rare.

6. For comparative surveys see *Gamillscheg,* Kommentar, art. 13 no. 34-38; *Rabel* 267-280; *Wolff,* PIL 324-325.

7. Cf. the survey of sources given by *Pålsson,* Marriage, Chapter 2, particularly for DENMARK s. 24, for LATIN AMERICA s. 40 and 75, for the SOVIET UNION s. 27 and for the USA s. 48.

Reliance on the *lex loci celebrationis* provides a seductively simple solution of the present problems. It greatly facilitates the task of marriage officials, since it relieves them of the burden of inquiring into and applying foreign law to test the capacity of the parties to marry. The same advantage accrues to courts of the *forum celebrationis* when called upon to pass judgment on the validity of marriages. This is probably one of the most powerful reasons for the success of the rule. The principle also favours legal certainty and predictability. Its technical advantages are considerable because all aspects of marriage will be governed by a single law. Thereby the rule avoids the thorny distinctions which are necessary in any system referring the substance of marriage, as opposed to other aspects of it, to the personal law, as well as the many intricate problems arising in the course of the application of such a system, for example in cases where the parties are subject to different personal laws. Finally, since marriages usually do conform to the requirements of the *lex loci celebrationis* (for their celebration is unlikely to be permitted otherwise), the application of that law to test their validity will tend to result in the upholding of marriages. The rule is thus in excellent keeping with the policy of validation prevailing with particular force in American law.

On the other hand, such a system also has manifest weaknesses. In the first place, it invites evasion since it enables the parties by the mere crossing of a border to throw off marriage impediments resulting from the law of the community to which they belong. The requirements of that law may thus be rendered more or less illusory. Secondly, in so far as the place of celebration has not been deliberately chosen by the parties with a view to avoiding marriage impediments imposed by their personal law, that place will often be accidental and little or not at all related to the situation of the parties. Where the parties do not intend to establish their matrimonial home in the country in which they marry, the interest of that country in the marital status is merely transient. Surely the interests of the country with which the parties are more permanently connected, whether by domicile or by nationality, are more strongly involved.

Furthermore, the advantages of relying on the *lex loci celebrationis* are largely relative, being in the last resort dependent on the general acceptance of the system. This condition, however, is only fulfilled to a limited extent. In most countries the substantive validity of marriages is tested by the personal law rather than by the *lex loci celebrationis*. This means that the uniformity of decisions as well as the validating effects supposed to result from applying the rule of the *lex loci celebrationis* will only be very incompletely attained. Those effects are further endangered by the far-reaching exceptions to which the rule, in so far as it is recognised in principle, is usually made subject as concerns foreign marriages. These exceptions also tend to complicate the system, thereby largely depriving it of the advantage of simplicity and predictability.

The rule of the *lex loci celebrationis* appears to have its most appropriate place in relations between legal systems which are sufficiently similar to each other to be easily interchangeable. The most typical example is perhaps supplied by the inter-Scandinavian relations governed by the above-mentioned convention of 1931. The rule may also work satisfactorily within a political unit like the United States, where interstate relations play a far more important role than international ones. Even there, however, the rule cannot operate without strains or be upheld without exceptions because of the considerable differences sometimes existing between the municipal laws of the states involved.

5. *Local and Foreign Marriages Distinguished.* The doubts expressed above as to the appropriateness of the *lex loci* test are rarely allowed to prevail in so far as the marriage is celebrated in the local form of the forum country. Here the practical advantages of applying the *lex loci celebrationis,* coinciding with the *lex fori,* are normally held to outweigh other considerations. In consequence, marriage impediments imposed by the law of the domicile or nationality of the parties are disregarded, and so is the fact that the place of celebration may have been chosen for the sole purpose of evading such impediments. Generally speaking, this holds true both of the direct regulation of the choice of law to govern the marriage at the stage of its celebration and as concerns the indirect regulation of the matter relevant if the validity of the union is subsequently brought into question in the *forum celebrationis.*

A different yardstick is often applied with regard to foreign marriages, especially when the parties are local nationals and/or domiciliaries. Here it is usually thought that the parties must be bound, at least to a certain extent, by the law of the community to which they belong and that they should not be able to evade prohibitions of that law by marrying in another country which is more complaisant to their wishes. In consequence, a marriage which meets the requirements of the foreign *lex loci celebrationis* will not always be recognised as valid if it contravenes the law of the country to which the parties belong by domicile or by nationality, respectively. On the other hand, a validating role is sometimes assigned to the latter law in the sense that it is applied to sustain a marriage which is invalid by the foreign *lex loci celebrationis.*

In what follows these and other problems relating to the application of the principle of the *lex loci celebrationis,* as well as the exceptions and modifications to which it is made subject, will be more closely examined. The first part of our exposition will be devoted to the law of the United States, where the amplest material by far bearing on these questions is to be found (B). Attention will then be directed to other countries whose conflicts rules are based on the same principle (C).

B. United States

a. *General Matters*

6. *Survey of Problems and Characteristic Features.* The great bulk of American litigation raising conflicts problems as to the substantive conditions of marriage concerns interstate, rather than international, situations. This fact will, naturally, be reflected in our exposition of American law. The relatively few cases involving conflicts of an international nature sometimes give rise to special problems (the recognition of polygamous marriages may be cited as an example) which are not likely to occur in interstate relations within the United States. No significant differences seem to exist, however, as to the approach and the solutions adopted in the two types of situation, which may therefore conveniently be treated together.

In the main, the attention of American courts and writers has been directed to problems concerning the validity of a marriage which has been entered into in one state (*C*) and which is later questioned in another (*F*) where the spouses are, or at least one of them is, domiciled, both *C* and *F* being within the United States. In particular, the discussion is focused on the following type of case, which occurs frequently in practice: parties domiciled and intending to remain domiciled in state *F*, but forbidden by the law of that state to marry each other, or to marry at all, go to state *C*, where they get married in accordance with the local law but contrary to, and typically in deliberate evasion of, the prohibition imposed by the law of *F*. Immediately after the ceremony has been performed the parties return to *F* to live there as man and wife. Will such a marriage be recognised as valid in *F*?

In general, this question has been answered in the affirmative. Whatever the domicile of the parties and whether or not, by marrying in state *C,* they intentionally evaded one law or the other, the rule is that a marriage valid where entered into is valid "everywhere", that is to say, in every jurisdiction of the United States.[8] To that extent the *lex loci celebrationis* prevails (*infra* s. 9).

On the other hand, it is generally recognised that state *C* does not, for the sole reason that the marriage was celebrated there (that is to say, if the parties have no other connection with that state), have a vital interest in seeing its law applied to the marriage, except as regards the formalities of the ceremony. The state primarily concerned and having the dominant interest in the existence of the marital status, it is commonly thought, is that where the parties live or intend to live as husband and wife, *i.e.* the state of their (intended) domicile, sometimes referred to as "the state of the most significant relationship".[9] It follows that the law of the domicile has a part to play in the matter. That law may (as a matter of constitutional law), and sometimes will, be applied, in preference to the *lex loci celebrationis,* to test the substantive validity of a marriage.

One situation of this kind is where, contrary to the more typical case mentioned above, the marriage is invalid by the *lex loci celebrationis* but meets the requirements of the law of the domicile. In such situations the latter law may be relied on to validate the marriage (*infra* s. 10). This solution accords with the desideratum of upholding marriages whenever possible, which is a basic policy everywhere in the United States.[10] The impact of the policy of validation on the development of American conflicts law of marriage has been very strong indeed and is perhaps its most distinctive feature. The influence of this policy is by no means

8. See Restatement § 283(2) with Comment *h* and Reporter's Note (p. 243); *Ehrenzweig*, Conflict 376-377; *Goodrich and Scoles* 228, 232; *Leflar* 532-535; *Stimson* 91-98; *Stumberg* 279-280; *Weintraub* 168.

9. This term is used in the Restatement (Second), see § 283 with Comments *i-k* and Reporter's Note (p. 244-246). For general discussion of the weighing of state interests and of the controlling effect of the law of the domicile in determining the validity of a marriage see further: *Beale* and others, Marriage and the Domicil: 44 Harv. L. Rev. 501-529 (1930/31); *Cook* 442-456; *Goodrich and Scoles* 226-227, 230-233; *Leflar* 529, 531-538; *Stumberg* 279-281, 286-289; *Taintor*, Marriage 610-614, 631-632; *Weintraub* 168-170.

10. See, e.g., Restatement § 283 Comments *b* and *h-j*; *Ehrenzweig,* Conflict 376-379; *Goodrich and Scoles* 226-227; *Leflar* 531; cf. *Weintraub* 171-173.

limited to the framing and application of conflicts rules proper, but is also reflected in a number of other rules and devices, such as the presumption that a purported marriage is valid and the doctrine of common law marriage (*infra* s. 11). Although these rules and devices do not have specific reference to situations involving multistate elements, they often affect the decision in such cases too, operating either to preclude any conflicts problem as to the validity of a marriage from arising or to "neutralise" the effect of invalidating rules of the applicable law.

Sometimes, however, the policy of validation comes into conflict with the policy pursued by "the state of the most significant relationship". This is problematic where a marriage has been entered into in violation of the law of the domicile. Normally, the policy of validation prevails in such situations, if the marriage complies with the *lex loci celebrationis*. By way of exception, however, the state of the domicile will refuse to recognise or to give effect to such a marriage if it contravenes a local prohibition representing a public policy strong enough to outweigh the general policy of validation (*infra* s. 12-13). The policy-weighing approach adopted by the courts in drawing the borderline between the rule and its exceptions is another characteristic feature of American law.

Further exceptions from the rule of the *lex loci celebrationis* are sometimes prescribed by statute, in particular by marriage evasion statutes which, partly on the model of the Uniform Marriage Evasion Act of 1912, have been adopted in certain states (*infra* s. 15-16). The effect of such statutes is, in certain circumstances, to prevent the recognition of an out-of-state marriage entered into by a local domiciliary in violation of the law of his domicile.

The role thus assigned to the law of the domicile raises certain fresh problems. In the first place, it is necessary to specify the relevant domicile, *i.e.* the domicile considered to have such a significant interest in the marriage as to justify application of its law in preference to the *lex loci celebrationis*. In particular: what is the position when the parties do not have a common domicile at the time of the marriage, or when the (intended) matrimonial domicile does not coincide with the premarital domicile of one or both of them? These questions may have to be answered differently, according as the law of the domicile is invoked to validate or to invalidate a marriage (*infra* s. 10, 14).

In most cases where a choice has to be made between the law of the domicile and the *lex loci celebrationis*, the former law coincides with the *lex fori.* The reason is that problems concerning the validity of a marriage usually come before the courts of the (first) matrimonial domicile. Sometimes, however, especially when there has been a subsequent change of domicile, the question arises in a third state. The position to be taken by such a forum requires special consideration (*infra* s. 17).

To some extent decisions of American courts on the validity of a marriage have very probably been influenced by the purpose for which the question was relevant, *i.e.* by the nature of the incident involved, in the particular case. In a few instances the enjoyment of a claimed incident of marriage seems even to have been treated as an independent question, which could be decided without regard to the validity of the marriage for other purposes. These are basic problems as to which, however, much uncertainty exists (*infra* s. 18).

All of the problems outlined above relate to situations in which the validity of a marriage is examined after the event. This is almost invariably the type of situation envisaged by American courts and writers. Very little attention has been given to questions of the choice of law to govern the substantive conditions of marriage at the "preventive" stage, *i.e.* the law to be applied by licensing or other officials charged with the task of determining whether any legal impediment exists to the solemnisation of the proposed union. This, however, is where the problem arises in the first instance, at least as regards ceremonial marriages. Although this part of American law is strikingly undeveloped, it will therefore be the first to be considered in what follows (*infra* s. 7-8). Indeed, the multitude of problems arising at a later stage, when the validity of a marriage is questioned *ex post facto,* can hardly be understood without this background.

aa. *Local Marriages: Celebration*

7. *Local Law Prevails.* In general, when a marriage is performed in the United States, the local law of the state of celebration alone will be applied, not only as regards the form of the ceremony but also in matters of substance.[11] Even if both parties are domiciled elsewhere and have no relation whatsoever to the state of celebration, foreign law will not normally be taken into account in testing their capacity to marry. Whether the marriage will or will not be

11. See *Dyer Report* 34; *Ehrenzweig and Jayme* 146; cf. *Ehrenzweig,* Conflict 177.

recognised as valid in other states, in particular in the state of the domicile of the parties, is treated as immaterial.

How is this rather primitive system to be explained? One reason which has been suggested is that licensing officials and celebrants of marriages are generally local people, who can properly be required only to know and to comply with their own laws and who are not even likely to be conscious of the possibility that any other law might be applicable.[12] Another, at least equally important, factor seems to be the lack of an adequate machinery for the interstate exchange of legal requirements and personal records.[13]

The fact that requirements and prohibitions imposed by foreign law are virtually ignored at the stage of celebration of marriages is at the root of the many problems of evasion encountered in American law. This is so because it enables intending spouses to escape from the law of their domicile by marrying in a state with "easier" requirements. The absence of an effective prior control seems also to explain the relatively large number of cases in which the validity of evasionary and other marriages contracted in violation of the law of the domicile is questioned afterwards.

8. *Effect of Marriage Evasion Statutes.* An attempt to curb evasions of the law of the domicile was made by the Uniform Marriage Evasion Act of 1912. As regards local marriages, s. 2 of that Act provided that:

> No marriage shall be contracted in this state by a party residing and intending to continue to reside in another state or jurisdiction, if such marriage would be void if contracted in such other state or jurisdiction, and every marriage celebrated in this state in violation of this provision shall be null and void.

In a state which has enacted this provision, the law of the domicile (for which "residence" is used as a synonym in the Act) of each of the parties must be taken into account in judging their capacity to marry, not only when the validity of a local marriage is questioned *ex post facto* but also, and even in the first place, at the stage of its celebration. The local authorities, it seems, must refuse to lend their cooperation to the solemnisation of a union which would be void by the law of the domicile of either of the intending spouses.[14]

12. *Taintor,* Marriage 609. Although this statement is made in the context of a discussion of the form of the ceremony, it seems mainly to be of interest as regards capcity to marry. See also Act. Doc. La Haye 13 (1976) III 75-76.

13. See *Ehrenzweig and Jayme* 139, 145-146; *Rabel* 264, 313.

14. But the provision does not require effect to be given to prohibitions of the relevant foreign law to the extent that they are merely directory or

continued on page 12

This, it should be noted, is to be determined as if the marriage had been contracted in the foreign state itself whose law is to be taken into account, that is to say, as if the marriage was, *from the point of view of that law,* a local one. The fact that, in the particular case, the contemplated place of celebration is in another state must thus be disregarded. In practice, this means that the authorities of the (intended) state of celebration may in certain cases have to enforce a prohibition of the law of the domicile which, in the view of the courts of the state of the domicile itself, is limited to local marriages and therefore would be inapplicable to the proposed union.[15] To that extent the state of celebration must give extraterritorial force to a rule of foreign law for which the foreign state concerned does not itself claim such effect.[16]

Specifically with regard to the procedure to be followed at the stage of the prior examination of the capacity of the parties to marry, s. 3 of the Uniform Marriage Evasion Act further provided that:

> Before issuing a license to marry to a person who resides and intends to continue to reside in another state the officer having authority to issue the license shall satisfy himself by requiring affidavits or otherwise that such person is not prohibited from intermarrying by the laws of the jurisdiction where he or she resides.

The above two provisions of the Uniform Act, however, were only adopted by a small number of states and seem to have had even less influence in practice.[17] In particular, the practice known from

---

continued from page 11

make an infringing marriage voidable (as opposed to void); cf. *Clark* 76 n. 48, 84-85; *Rabel* 274; *Vernier* I 210.

15. This is another way of saying that the reference to the law of the domicile does not include the conflicts rules of that law, or that the doctrine of *renvoi* does not apply in the present connection. Cf. *infra* s. 16.

16. This consequence of the Uniform Act has been much criticised and seems largely to explain why this part of the Act had little success, even as compared with other provisions of the same Act, in being adopted by state legislatures. See, e.g., *Taintor*, Marriage 630 n. 119; *Weintraub* 173 n. 27 (characterising s. 2 of the Act as "intolerably officious").

17. Only five states (Illinois, Louisiana, Massachusetts, Vermont and Wisconsin) enacted the substance of the whole Act. Marriage evasion statutes were also adopted in a number of other states, but with one exception (Wyoming) they do not seem to cover the case of a local marriage contracted or to be contracted by a party domiciled elsewhere, but only the converse situation of an out-of-state marriage entered into by a local domiciliary. See *Rabel* 274-276; *Vernier* I 209-213; cf. *Pålsson*, Marriage, s. 48 (at n. 81) and 289 (at n. 80), *infra* s. 15.

certain European countries that compliance with the requirements of the relevant foreign law is ascertained, and that party allegations with regard to such questions are verified by the local authorities of their own motion, has not been followed in the United States.[18] Nor, as noted earlier, has any machinery been created to ensure a smooth interstate exchange of information on legal requirements for marriage and of personal records. In the main, therefore, the provisions in question failed to attain their objective, and the Act of which they formed part was long ago withdrawn from the list of recommended legislation.[19]

ab. *Local and Foreign Marriages: Validity*

aba. Rules Tending to Support Validity of Marriage

9. *Validation under Lex Loci Celebrationis.* The general rule that a marriage valid where entered into is recognised as valid everywhere in the United States is supported by an abundant body of case law.[20] In several states it has been enacted by statutes providing that a marriage valid where contracted is valid in the enacting state.[21] Historically, this rule derives its origin from early English law, where a marriage was held to be governed in its entirety by the *lex loci celebrationis.*[22] Its policy basis in American law seems to lie in the need for protecting the expectations of the parties – thereby also furthering the values of certainty, predictability and uniformity of result – and in the desire to uphold marriages, as well as the legitimacy of children born of the union, as far as possible.[23] These policies are common to all American states.

The rule in question has been coined, primarily, for cases

18. See *Ehrenzweig and Jayme* 145-146; *Rabel* 276, 313.

19. This was done in 1943. The reason given for the withdrawal was that the Act "can be effective only if it has widespread adoption; otherwise it merely tends to confuse the law." See [1943] Handbook of the National Conference of Commissioners on Uniform State Laws 64.

20. For illustrations see *infra* n. 134-138, 195-196, 210, 223, 232. Further references are given by the writers cited *supra* n. 8.

21. For lists of such statutes see Reporter's Note on Restatement § 283 (p. 243); *Clark* 76 n. 50.

22. This was the position of ENGLISH law at least until the middle of the nineteenth century. See *Ehrenzweig,* Conflict 376-377 and *infra* s. 64.

23. For elaborate discussion of the underlying policies see: Restatement § 283 Comments *b* and *h*; *Ehrenzweig ibid.*; *Goodrich and Scoles* 226-228; *Leflar* 531-532. Some writers, while appreciating the motives that have led courts and writers to adopt the rule of the *lex loci celebrationis,* suggest that

continued on page 14

involving the validity of a marriage contracted in a state or country other than that of the forum, that is to say, where the *lex loci celebrationis* is a foreign law.[24] In this situation, as always when the conflicts rules of the forum refer to foreign law, a problem of *renvoi* may present itself. In theory at least, it must be specified whether the reference to the *lex loci celebrationis* is limited to the local law of the state of celebration or whether it points to "the whole law" of that state, including its conflicts rules. In practice, however, this question is usually passed over in silence. Normally, the courts look to the local rules alone of the foreign law concerned, and are prepared to sustain a marriage which complies with those rules, without further inquiries into or discussion of conflicts problems. The implicit assumption that the "law" of the state of celebration is known once its domestic rule is known has been criticised on the ground that it disregards the presence, from the point of view of that state, of foreign elements which would have raised a conflicts problem had the case at bar come before the *forum celebrationis.*[25] The approach usually adopted by the courts means that the problem of *renvoi* is not even posed. It must not be concluded, however, that this doctrine is implicitly ruled out in relation to conflicts rules referring to the *lex loci celebrationis*. Before going further into this question, it is necessary to determine whether and to what extent an issue of *renvoi* is truly involved (in the sense that it affects or may affect the choice of the law ultimately to be applied) in this type of case.

This, in its turn, depends on the standing of the *lex loci celebrationis* in the state of celebration itself. Relatively little attention has been given to this question, apparently because conflicts problems as to the validity of a marriage are rarely encountered in the *forum celebrationis.*[26] Almost invariably, cases decided by the courts of the state of celebration have some additional connection

continued from page 13

this conflicts technique is based on insufficient analysis and that other and more adequate means should be used to achieve the results sought. For a particularly incisive criticism of the usual type of reasoning see *Cook* 442-456, who argues in favour of the law of the domicile (more specifically, the local law of the state of the intended family domicile; see *infra* s. 14). See also *Baade* 354-361, 364-381; *Maddaugh* 132-134; and *Weintraub* 171-173, who speaks of the "pseudo-conflicts analysis" underlying the rule of the *lex loci celebrationis.*

24. Cf. In re Ommang's Estate, 235 N.W. 529, 531 (Minn. Sup. Ct. 1931).

25. For a penetrative critical analysis see *Cook* 442-456.

26. Cf. In re Palmer's Estate 79 N.Y.S.2d 404, 408 (Surr. Ct. 1948); *Cook* 446.

to that state, usually the fact that the spouses are, or that one of them is, domiciled there. The situation will then either be a purely domestic one or, at most, only present weak foreign contacts, so that the local law will be applied more or less as a matter of course. In these circumstances it is a matter of some speculation what law governs when the fact of celebration of the marriage is the only link with the forum state. Nevertheless, there seems to be little doubt that the local law would be applied in such cases too, as a rule, to validate a marriage complying with that law.[27] Since the *lex loci celebrationis* coincides with the *lex fori,* it probably even applies with added force as compared with cases involving a foreign marriage.[28] In so far as this holds true, the courts of other states whose conflicts rules refer to the *lex loci celebrationis* will reach the same result, whether or not they adopt the doctrine of *renvoi.* To that extent the problem my be avoided, at least for practical purposes. Only in some rather exceptional cases, where the local law cannot be expected to prevail in the state of celebration, does a true issue of *renvoi* arise (*infra* s. 16).

10. *Validation under Law of Domicile.* Whether the rule of the *lex loci celebrationis* may be generalised so as also to mean that "a marriage invalid where contracted is invalid everywhere", is a much more doubtful question. Since marriages usually do comply with the *lex loci celebrationis,* cases presenting this problem are relatively rare in practice. True, a considerable number of court opinions state, by way of *dictum,* that (subject to certain exceptions) the validity of a marriage must be determined by the *lex loci celebrationis,* without distinguishing as to whether the effect of the rule is to uphold or to defeat the marriage.[29] Such a general

27. For a different view see *Cook* 442-456, who suggests that capacity to marry should be determined by the law of the intended family domicile (which is assumed not to refer back or on to any other law and so to exclude any problem of *renvoi*), rather than by the *lex loci celebrationis,* whether the question arises in the state of celebration or elsewhere in the USA.

28. For a judicial opinion lending some support to this view see In re Ommang's Estate, 235 N.W. 529, 531 (Minn. Sup. Ct. 1931), noted in 16 Minn. L. Rev. 172 (1931/32). In that case too, however, there was additional connection to the *forum celebrationis,* the spouses having become domiciled there at the time of the suit (though they were not so domiciled at the time of the marriage); cf. *infra* n. 143.

29. For examples of statements to this effect see: Derrell v. United States, 82 F. Supp. 18, 20-21 (E.D. Miss. 1949); Commonwealth v. Lane, 113 Mass. 458, 463 (1873); King v. Klemp, 57 A.2d 530, 534 (N.J.Ch. 1947); In re May's Estate, 114 N.E.2d 4, 6 (N.Y. Ct. App. 1953); Lederkremer v. Lederkremer, 18 N.Y.S.2d 725, 728 (Sup. Ct. 1940); Incuria v. Incuria, 280 N.Y.S.

continued on page 16

rule has also been advocated by influential writers.[30] In nearly all cases, however, where the *lex loci celebrationis* has been relied on to invalidate a marriage, the result would have been the same under any law involved, so that no true conflict existed.[31] Actual decisions holding a marriage invalid (for reasons not relating to its form) on the strength of the *lex loci celebrationis,* in circumstances where it was good by the law of the domicile of the parties, are very rare.[32]

The better view seems indeed to be that a marriage should be sustained if it is valid by the (local) law of the domicile, even though it does not satisfy the substantive requirements of the *lex loci celebrationis.* Such validation is supported by relevant policy considerations and favoured by the prevailing trend of opinion in American law.[33] On the one hand, it serves to imple-

---

continued from page 15

716, 720-721 (Dom. Rel. Ct. 1935); Mazzolini v. Mazzolini, 155 N.E.2d 206, 208 (Ohio Sup. Ct. 1958); Huard v. McTeigh, 232 P. 658, 661 (Or. Sup. Ct. 1925); Jewett v. Jewett, 175 A.2d 141, 142 (Pa. Super. Ct. 1961); Ex parte Chace, 58 A. 978, 979-980 (R.I. Sup. Ct. 1904); Spradlin v. State Comp. Comm., 113 S.E.2d 832, 834 (W.Va. Sup. Ct. App. 1960). See further *infra* n. 31 and *Beale* 669-670, 673-674.

30. For instance by *Story* and *Bishop* in the last, and by *Beale* in the present century. See *Beale ibid.* (whose view is reflected in the 1934 Restatement § 122); *Bishop*, New Commentaries on Marriage, Divorce and Separation I (Chicago 1891) 359-369; *Story (-Bennett)* 93-94, 146, 164. For a detailed account and a critical assessment of these writings see *Ehrenzweig*, Miscegenation 669-672.

31. For illustrative cases see: Marek v. Flemming, 192 F. Supp. 528 (S.D. Tex. 1961); Vaughan v. Gideon, 132 P.2d 529 (Cal. Dist. Ct. App. 1942); Anderson v. Anderson, 238 A.2d 45 (Conn. Super. Ct. 1967); Canale v. People, 52 N.E. 310 (Ill. Sup. Ct. 1898); McIlvain v. Scheibley, 59 S.W. 498 (Ky. Ct. App. 1900); Damaskinos v. Damaskinos, 89 N.E.2d 766 (Mass. Sup. Jud. Ct. 1950); Von Felden v. Von Felden, 2 N.W.2d 426 (Minn. Sup. Ct. 1942); De Fur v. De Fur, 4 S.W.2d 341 (Tenn. Sup. Ct. 1928); Kitzman v. Kitzman, 166 N.W. 789 (Wis. Sup. Ct. 1918). See also *Goodrich and Scoles* 228.

32. For such cases see: In re Estate of Levie, 123 Cal. Rptr. 445 (Ct. App. 1975) (see *infra* n. 239); Cruickshank v. Cruickshank, 82 N.Y.S.2d 522 (Sup. Ct. 1948) (see *infra* at n. 219). Other instances are, possibly, Rhodes v. Rhodes, 96 F.2d 715 (D.C. Cir. 1938), cert. denied 305 U.S. 632 (1938); and Blaisdell v. Bickum, 1 N.E. 281 (Mass. Sup. Ct. 1885), cf. *infra* n. 239. See also the Illinois and Pennsylvania cases cited *infra* n. 151 and 152, in some of which the courts held against marriages contravening a prohibition of the *lex loci celebrationis* on remarriage after divorce, notwithstanding that the divorce had been granted and the parties to the second union were domiciled elsewhere.

33. See: Restatement § 283 Comment *i* with Reporter's Note (p. 244-245); *Baade* 356, 357, 364-381; *Clark* 74-75, 77, 86; *Goodrich and Scoles* 227-231;

ment the policy of the state which has the dominant interest in the existence of the marital status. On the other, the normal policy basis for applying the *lex loci celebrationis,* namely, the desire to protect the expectations of the parties by upholding the marriage, fails where that law would lead to invalidation. Although judicial authority clearly relying on the law of the domicile to sustain a marriage in the teeth of the *lex loci celebrationis* is scarce, this position has been adopted in what seems to be the majority of cases raising the issue.[34]

All cases so holding have been decided in the state of the domicile itself, more particularly in a state where at least one of the parties was domiciled at the time of the marriage and where both made their home afterwards.[35] On policy grounds it seems that a marriage having this degree of connection to a validating law should be upheld wherever the question arises in the United States, for example in a state where the spouses have later acquired a new domicile. Furthermore, it is conceivable that the law of the domicile will be applied to validate a marriage even if the domiciliary connection does not reach the same strength as in the cases so far decided. It is, however, doubtful how far the courts will be prepared to go in this direction. Probably the rule proposed by Professor *Ehrenzweig* represents the maximum length to which validation under the law of the domicile might be carried. Accord-

---

Leflar 535; *Taintor,* Marriage 610-611; *Weintraub* 172 n. 21; and the references *infra* n. 36. It should be noted in this connection that statutes of the type enacted in several states, which provide for the application of the *lex loci celebrationis* (*supra* n. 21), are confined to situations where the effect is to validate the marriage; see *Ehrenzweig,* Miscegenation 671.

34. E.g., Succession of Hernandez, 15 So. 461 (La. Sup. Ct. 1894) (New York statute forbidding the guilty party to a divorce for adultery to marry again could not be invoked to invalidate a New York marriage between parties who made their marital domicile in Louisiana and who were free to marry by the law of that state); Wilcox v. Wilcox, 46 Hun 32 (N.Y. Sup. Ct. 1887) (marriage in Quebec, between parties domiciled and intending to remain domiciled in New York, upheld on the strength of New York law, although it was void by the law of Quebec because the wife had been previously married to another man who did not by the evidence appear not to have been living at the time of her remarriage). Other possibly relevant cases are cited *infra* n. 147, 149 (prohibitions on remarriage after divorce), 198 (consent of parties), 220 (nonage) and 226 (parental consent). For further references see Restatement § 283, Reporter's Note on Comment *i* (p. 244-245); *Ehrenzweig,* Conflict 384 n. 41; *Goodrich and Scoles* 230-231 n. 26-27.

35. This is "the state of the most significant relationship", see *infra* s. 14. For a statute in Montana providing for validation in the same circumstances see *Clark* 76 n. 51.

ing to this proposal, a marriage should be upheld, not only where it is valid by the *lex loci celebrationis* but also if it is good either by the law of the domicile of at least one of the parties at the time of the marriage or by the law of the state in which both spouses were domiciled at the time when suit was commenced to test its validity, always provided that it is not offensive to an overriding policy of the forum.[36]

11. *Other Validating Rules.* Several other rules and devices operating to validate marriages, both in purely local and in conflicts cases, exist in American law. In the first place, there are certain *presumptions in support of marriage.*[37] "The law presumes morality, and not immorality; marriage, and not concubinage; legitimacy, and not bastardy."[38] Once it is shown that a marriage has been celebrated or that the parties have cohabited as man and wife, it will therefore be presumed, not only that the marriage was entered into in proper legal form but also that the parties had the capacity to contract it and that all other conditions of validity were satisfied. There is also a presumption that a marriage, once contracted, continues in force.

Although these presumptions are rebuttable, their effect is that whoever asserts that a marriage is invalid or that it has been dissolved bears the burden of proving his contention.[39] The strength of the presumption in favour of validity and, in consequence, the nature and the amount of evidence necessary to overthrow it, vary with a number of factors. In general, however, this presumption is given considerable force, and it has been characterised as one of the strongest known to the law.[40] This seems particularly to be true for marriages of long standing or when children have been born of the union.[41]

36. See *Ehrenzweig*, Conflict 378-379, 383-384, and for a more detailed study *idem*, Miscegenation 669-678.

37. See *Clark* 66-70. For cases see Annots., 34 A.L.R. 464 (1925) and 77 A.L.R. 729 (1932).

38. Hynes v. McDermott, 91 N.Y. 451, 459 (1883).

39. This, however, does not apply in respect of a prior marriage which has been followed by remarriage; see *infra* s. 24.

40. See, for instance, Gee Chee on v. Brownell, 253 F.2d 814, 817 (5 Cir. 1958); Schmeizl v. Schmeizl, 42 A.2d 106, 109 (Md. Ct. App. 1945); and the cases cited *infra* n. 157.

41. See *Clark* 69 with references. Even in a case where suit for annulment (on grounds of duress) was brought on the day following the celebration of the marriage, however, the court insisted on the necessity of "strong, clear, and convincing" proof before a decree could be granted: Worthington v. Worthington, 352 S.W. 2d 80, 82 (Ark. Sup. Ct. 1961).

Another doctrine of importance in the present connection is that of *common law marriage,* which is still accepted in large parts of the United States.[42] This doctrine is often relied on to validate a marriage which was initially invalid (for example on the ground that one of the parties was bound by a prior undissolved marriage), but where the impediment to its validty has subsequently been removed (for example by a divorce ending the prior marriage) and where the parties continue thereafter to live as man and wife in a state authorising common law marriages.[43]

Both of the doctrines referred to above are of special practical significance in cases involving the validity of a second marriage entered into at a time when the prior union had not been dissolved, or cannot be proved to have been so, and will be further discussed in relation to that particular situation (*infra* s. 24-25). In the same connection attention will be drawn to some other devices, which have specific reference to impediments based on a prior marriage and which may at times be used as means of validating a later union (*infra* s. 26-27).

abb. Invalidating Exceptions Based on Law of Domicile or Forum

12. *Policy-Weighing Approach.* By way of exception to the general rule, a marriage which complies with the *lex loci celebrationis* will sometimes be struck down if it does not meet the substantive requirements of the (local) law of the domicile of the spouses. Aside from marriage evasion statutes and the like (*infra* s. 15), such exceptions occur where the state of the domicile has a distinctive public policy, embodied in the violated rule of its law, against the marriage. In the Restatement Second of the Conflict of Laws this idea is expressed as follows:[44]

> A marriage which satisfies the requirements of the state where the marriage was contracted will everywhere be recognized as valid unless it violates the strong public policy of another state which had the most significant relationship to the spouses and the marriage at the time of the marriage.

This and other general formulas encountered in American court opinions and writings raise a number of problems. To facilitate the

42. See *Pålsson*, Marriage, s. 267 with references.

43. See *Clark* 51-54. Cases on the effect of continued cohabitation after the removal of an impediment are collected in Annot., 104 A.L.R. 6 (1936).

44. § 283(2).

discussion, it will for the moment be assumed, firstly, that both spouses are, and have at all material times been, domiciled in one state (*D*) – so that no doubt exists as to the determination of "the state of the most significant relationship" – and, secondly, that that state is also the forum (*F*) where the validity of the marriage comes in question. This is in fact the typical situation occurring in American practice and the one usually canvassed by courts and writers. The additional difficulties which may arise when the domiciliary connections are divided between two or more states, or when state *D* does not coincide with state *F*, will be considered separately later on (*infra* s. 14, 17).

The concept of a "strong" or "distinctive" public policy, of course, does not provide any exact criterion for the delimitation of the exceptions to the general rule. Rather, it points to the approach adopted by the courts in deciding such questions. This approach is directed to an evaluation of the strength of the peculiar local policy underlying the domiciliary rule which has been violated in the case at bar, and to a weighing of this policy against the basic policy, common to all of the United States, of upholding marriages.[45]

In determining whether a requirement of the law of state *D* does or does not represent a strong public policy, the courts have had regard to a variety of factors. This will be illustrated in what follows. A systematic account of the results reached with regard to particular requirements will be given at a later stage (*infra* s. 19-32).

13. *Concept of Strong Public Policy.* One important criterion is the *sanction* imposed by the law of state *D* for violation of the rule in question in the case of a locally celebrated marriage. No true problem occurs where the rule is merely directory, forbidding the marriage or declaring it unlawful, but not rendering it void or voidable. In these cases no basis exists for invalidating the marriage, wherever celebrated.[46] Examples are afforded by cases in which a marriage, validly entered into under the *lex loci celebrationis,* was impugned on the ground that the parties had failed to obtain the consent of their parents, as required by the law of state *D*. Since such requirements (at least as a rule) are only directory in American law, the courts have had no difficulties in rejecting the attack.[47]

The same result is usually reached where, under the law of state

45. See generally: Restatement § 283 Comments *j* and *k*; *Beale* 678; *Cavers* 241-243; *Goodrich and Scoles* 232-233; *Leflar* 531-532, 534-535; *Stimson* 98-116; *Stumberg* 279-281, 286-287; *Weintraub* 168-170.

46. See, for instance, *Taintor*, Marriage 622-623, 625.

47. See *infra* s. 30.

D, the defect in question only renders the marriage voidable, as opposed to void. Such a marriage is valid until annulled and can only be attacked in direct proceedings for annulment instituted by one of the spouses against the other.[48] A decree will rarely be given if the marriage has been celebrated outside the state and is valid by the relevant foreign law. The courts are inclined to say that a local requirement or prohibition which is only sanctioned by voidability does not indicate a public policy strong enough to justify extraterritorial application.[49] Collateral attacks on a voidable marriage, for example in an inheritance suit arising after the death of one of the spouses, are excluded even in purely local cases. This holds equally good for cases where the marriage has been celebrated in another state.[50]

It should be noted here that American statutes forbidding a certain type of marriage often do not specify whether a violating marriage is valid, voidable or void.[51] Some statutes are self-contradictory, saying at one point that the marriage is voidable, but at another that it is void.[52] In such cases the courts tend to construe the statute as not impairing the validity of the marriage, or as making it voidable only, and (where the marriage has been celebrated elsewhere in accordance with the *lex loci celebrationis*) to infer that no distinctive local policy is involved.[53] Occasionally, this construction has been adopted even though the local statute plainly provided that a violating marriage would be "null and void" or "absolutely void".[54]

48. See *Clark* 34-35, 76-77, 81-82, 90, 98, 100-101, 120-121, 128-129; *Storke*, Annulment 850-851. Cases dealing with the right to attack the validity of a marriage after the death of one of the parties are collected in Annots., 76 A.L.R. 769 (1932) and 47 A.L.R.2d 1393 (1956).

49. Several examples are afforded by the nonage cases cited *infra* n. 210. For exceptions see Cunningham v. Cunningham, 99 N.E. 845 (N.Y. Ct. App. 1912) (nonage); Martin v. Martin, 46 S.E. 120 (W.Va. Sup. Ct. App. 1903) (aunt-nephew marriage).

50. For illustrative cases see Stevenson v. Gray, 17 B. Mon. 193 (Ky. Ct. App. 1856); Harrison v. State, 22 Md. 468, 85 Am. Dec. 658 (1863).

51. See, for example, as regards statutes prohibiting remarriage after divorce, *Kingsley*, Remarriage 284-286.

52. See *Clark* 82.

53. For examples of such reasoning see: Griswold v. Griswold, 129 P. 560, 564-566 (Colo. Ct. App. 1913); Farrell v. Farrell, 181 N.W. 12, 15 (Iowa Sup. Ct. 1921); Mangrum v. Mangrum, 220 S.W.2d 406 (Ky. Ct. App. 1949); Hoagland v. Hoagland, 193 P. 843 (Wyo. Sup. Ct. 1920).

54. For a nonage case where the words "absolutely void" were construed to mean "voidable" and therefore not to enshrine a strong public

continued on page 22

Where, on the other hand, the law of state *D* admittedly declares the marriage (if celebrated locally) to be void, opinion is more divided.[55] In the majority of cases such provisions, too, have not been held to enshrine a public policy strong enough to warrant invalidation of a foreign marriage which was good by the *lex loci celebrationis*. But in a fairly substantial number of cases the courts have held otherwise, refusing to recognise such a marriage because the local policy against it was found to be fundamental. This position has especially been taken when the local statute, in addition to rendering void a marriage contracted in defiance of the prohibition, imposed a criminal penalty for violation, or for cohabitation under a violating marriage, as in cases involving bigamy, incest or (in the past) miscegenation.[56] In the opinion of courts so holding, it would have been anomalous to sustain a marriage so violently in conflict with the local policy as to expose the parties to punishment for contracting it or for cohabiting. Nevertheless, even in such circumstances many courts have upheld the marriage in reliance on the *lex loci celebrationis*.[57]

Besides the sanctions envisaged by the prohibitory statute (or the absence of sanctions), the terms of the statute may contain other elements pointing to a more or less intense local policy. Where, for example, the statute provides for the possibility of an exemption from the prohibition in certain circumstances, or in the discretion of the court, its policy is likely to be less strong than where the prohibition is unconditional.[58] Statutes restricting the right of remarriage after divorce afford another illustration. Where such a restriction is only directed to the guilty party to the divorce, the courts are more inclined than in the case of a prohibition run-

---

continued from page 21

policy, see State v. Graves, 307 S.W.2d 545 (Ark. Sup. Ct. 1957); cf. the dissent by Harris, C.J., who said (at 550) he could conceive of no stronger words than "absolutely void" to express the vigour of the policy set forth in the statute.

55. See *Taintor*, Marriage 625-628, 631.

56. See the cases cited *infra* n. 104-105, 234 and 242.

57. See, for example, the cases on consanguinity cited *infra* n. 232.

58. See, for instance, In re Palmer's Estate, 79 N.Y.S.2d 404, 411 (Surr. Ct. 1948), holding *inter alia* that an out-of-state marriage in defiance of the local statute forbidding the guilty party to a divorce for adultery to marry again during the life of the innocent spouse did not offend the public policy of New York. In so holding the court emphasised that the statute provided that the divorcee, after the lapse of a certain time, could apply for permission to remarry and that no limitation was placed upon such permission.

ning equally against both parties to regard it as penal in nature and to infer that it cannot have extraterritorial force.[59]

In many cases the courts have referred to the *legislative intent* behind the local prohibition as a means of throwing light on the strength of the policy involved. As pointers to that intent the courts have relied on the language of the statute, including the sanctions imposed for violation, but also on other factors, such as the legislative history of the prohibition, its systematic context and its relation to similar rules in the same or in other states. The result of such inquiries, however, seems rarely, if ever, to be conclusive. In most cases a prohibitory statute which was silent on its sphere of application has been construed to be limited to local marriages. Courts adopting this construction often reason that if it had been the intention of the legislature to extend the prohibition to marriages solemnised in another state, it would have said so expressly.[60] In a minority of cases, however, the argument runs the opposite course: since the prohibition does not, in express terms or by necessary implication, contain any limitation as to where the marriage occurred and since it must be applied to out-of-state marriages of local domiciliaries if its policy is to remain meaningful, it is inferred that the statute was intended to be so applied.[61] In one case, which involved a local statute forbidding divorced persons to marry again within a certain time from the grant of the divorce, the court used strong language to express this view:[62]

> To say that the Legislature intended such a law to apply only while the parties are within the boundaries of the state, and that it contemplated that by crossing the state line its citizens could successfully nullify its terms, is to make the act

59. See *infra* s. 23. Prohibitions against marriage imposed by way of penalty must be distinguished from those which are not themselves of this nature but where the sanction of invalidity is "fortified" by criminal penalties; cf. *supra* at n. 56.

60. For cases where this type of reasoning appears very clearly see: Putnam v. Putnam, 8 Pick. 433, 435 (Mass. Sup. Jud. Ct. 1829); In re May's Estate, 114 N.E.2d 4 (N.Y. Ct. App. 1953); Van Voorhis v. Brintnall, 86 N.Y. 18 (1881); Schofield v. Schofield, 51 Pa. Super. Ct. 564, 576-579 (1912).

61. For cases exemplifying this model of reasoning see: Wilson v. Cook, 100 N.E. 222 (Ill. Sup. Ct. 1912); Wilkins v. Zelichowski, 140 A.2d 65 (N.J. Sup. Ct. 1958); In re Stull's Estate, 39 A. 16 (Pa. Sup. Ct. 1898); Lanham v. Lanham, 117 N.W. 787 (Wis. Sup. Ct. 1908).

62. Lanham v. Lanham, *ibid.* at 789.

essentially useless and impotent, and ascribe practical imbecility to the lawmaking power.

If this opinion is to be believed, most courts have not hesitated to ascribe "practical imbecility" to their respective legislatures, for in the majority of cases this type of prohibition has been held to be confined to local marriages even though its purpose was thereby thwarted.[63] A more plausible explanation of such differences seems to be that the courts, while purporting to ascertain and to give effect to the legislative intent, form their own views as to which solution ought to prevail and that the attribution of one intention or the other to the legislative body is in reality little or nothing more than a cloak for the shifting evaluations made by the courts themselves.

In the final analysis, the qualitative test inherent in the policy-weighing approach necessarily leaves the courts a wide margin of appreciation. The notions of the courts as to the demands and "the limit of toleration" of local policy vary considerably from one state to another and may change from time to time within a single state. On the whole, however, the courts have been restrictive in admitting invalidation of a marriage on such grounds. Some courts have expressed themselves in terms which go very far indeed in this direction. Thus, according to one famous *dictum*, exceptions to the general rule – where not based on express statutory provisions – should be limited to "marriages which are deemed contrary to the law of nature as generally recognized in Christian countries."[64] This class would only include polygamous and certain incestuous marriages. Since such unions are prohibited and void everywhere in the United States, very few cases would come within an exception so defined. Most courts, however, have not found it possible to keep the exceptions within such extremely narrow limits. In some cases it has been said, for example, that the state of the domicile cannot recognise a foreign marriage which "offends against the prevailing sense of good morals among the

63. See the references *infra* n. 134-136.

64. Commonwealth v. Lane, 113 Mass. 458, 463 (1873), quoted with approval in In re Miller's Estate, 214 N.W. 428, 429 (Mich. Sup. Ct. 1927); to the same effect see Van Voorhis v. Brintnall, 86 N.Y. 18, 26 (1881). Cf. the early case of Medway v. Needham, 16 Mass. 157, 161 (1819), where a distinction was drawn between marriages prohibited merely on account of "political expediency" and those which would "tend to outrage the principles and feelings of all civilized nations"; while, in the opinion of the court, the former will be tolerated if valid by the *lex loci celebrationis*, the latter will not be countenanced.

people there dwelling," or which has been contracted in disregard of a statute enacted "by reason of a positive policy of the state for the protection of the morals and good order of society against serious social evils."[65] These and other similar formulas, however, are too vague to be of much assistance; they circumscribe rather than specify the notion of a "strong public policy".

As a result of the lack of precise criteria, it is often uncertain whether a given prohibition does or does not show a strong public policy in any single state, as long as the point has not been decided by the courts of that state. Furthermore, the local variations of this notion frequently lead to conflicting decisions in the sense that identical or essentially similar prohibitions are treated differently from one state to another. An uncle-niece marriage, for instance, if validly entered into under the *lex loci celebrationis,* may well be upheld if the parties are domiciled in New York, but be struck down if the domicile is in New Jersey, although the statutes of both states declare such marriages to be incestuous and void.[66]

Nevertheless, a "common core" of distinctive public policy, which prevails everywhere in the United States, is identifiable. In this class are the impediments of a prior undissolved marriage (bigamy and polygamy) and of consanguinity between the parties in the direct line of ascent and descent or as brother and sister. A foreign marriage contrary to one of these impediments will not be recognised anywhere in the United States, even if it is valid by the *lex loci celebrationis.*[67] Furthermore, it is possible to enumerate those prohibitions and vices as to which a division of opinion exists and which have at least occasionally been held to require an exception to the general conflicts rule. This category includes prohibitions on remarriage after divorce, fraud, duress, insanity and similar defects vitiating the consent of the parties, non-age and lack of parental consent, as well as certain degrees of consanguinity (more remote than those mentioned above) and of affinity between the parties; in the past, difference of race (miscegenation) was also

65. In re Stull's Estate, 39 A. 16, 18 (Pa. Sup. Ct. 1898), and Wilson v. Cook, 100 N.E. 222, 223 (Ill. Sup. Ct. 1912), respectively.

66. See In re May's Estate, 114 N.E.2d 4 (N.Y. Ct. App. 1953), and Bucca v. State, 128 A.2d 506 (N.J. Super. Ct. 1957), respectively. Cf. *infra* s. 31.

67. Even a polygamous marriage, however, is usually given certain effects, and a bigamous marriage may in certain circumstances become valid if the impediment of the prior marriage is subsequently removed; see *infra* s. 20 and 25-26, respectively.

problematic. To give a more detailed picture of the situation it is necessary to examine each of the above-mentioned impediments and defects separately (*infra* s. 19-32).

Finally, it must be noted that the force behind the policy of a particular prohibition may vary, even within a single state, with the fact situation and the legal issue involved in each case. This aspect of the problem will be adverted to later on (*infra* s. 18).

14. *Relevant Domicile.* Some further questions arise if the parties were, at the time of the marriage, domiciled in different states or if there has been a change of domicile at one time or another. Which is in such situations "the state of the most significant relationship", whose strong public policy may be relied upon to invalidate a marriage complying with the *lex loci celebrationis*?

No doubt seems to exist when the parties have, or one of them has, changed domicile *before the marriage.* Such a change operates to exclude the law of the prior domicile from consideration. Suppose, for instance, that one of the parties, while domiciled in state *A*, has obtained a divorce in that state and that by the law of *A* he is forbidden to marry again within a specified period of time. Before the lapse of the prescribed time he leaves *A*, acquires a new domicile in state *D* and remarries there in defiance of *A*'s prohibition but in accordance with the law of *D*. In this situation the second marriage will be recognised as valid everywhere in the United States, even though state *A* would have declared it void if the remarrying party had remained domiciled in that state.[68]

A more difficult problem is encountered if the domicile of /one of/ the parties is changed *immediately after the marriage.* Suppose that one of the parties was domiciled in state *A* and the other in state *B* at the time of the marriage and that they intended to make, and have in fact made, their common domicile after the marriage in state *D*. Which is, here, the relevant domicile? According to one view, which was adopted in the Conflicts Restatement of 1934, each of the states *A* and *B* – that is to say, the premarital domicile of each of the parties – has a sufficient interest in the marital status to justify application of its invalidating rule, where required by its strong public policy.[69] This proposal, however, has not found much response among courts and writers. There does not seem to exist a single American case in which an otherwise valid marriage has been held invalid on the strength of the law of a state whose only relation to the spouses was that one of them had

68. See the references *infra* n. 143-144.
69. Restatement of 1934, § 132.

been domiciled there at the time of (*i.e.*, immediately before) the marriage. Some decisions are directly inconsistent with such a rule.[70] Even if both parties were domiciled in *A* at the time of the marriage but have then made their domicile in *D*, it is at least very doubtful whether the law of *A* would be applied to defeat the marriage.[71] This seems only conceivable, if at all, where the question arises within a very short time after the conclusion of the marriage.[72]

Instead, the view has come to prevail, especially among writers, that the state most significantly concerned is that where the parties intended to make, and have in fact made, their home and where they live as man and wife after the solemnisation of the marriage (*the intended matrimonial domicile*, also referred to as *the intended family domicile*).[73] That state, it is considered, is the only one whose law may be applied to strike down a marriage which is valid by the *lex loci celebrationis*, always provided that its strong public policy so dictates.

This opinion is in keeping with the actual decisions of the courts, if not always with their language, which is often ambiguous or seems to point to the law of the premarital domicile of /one of/ the spouses. In all cases where the domiciliary law has been relied

70. E.g., Mpiliris v. Hellenic Lines Ltd., 323 F. Supp. 865, 876-879 (S.D. Tex. 1970), aff'd 440 F.2d 1163 (5 Cir. 1971); People ex rel. Schutt v. Siems, 198 Ill. App. 342 (1916); Reid v. Reid, 129 N.Y.S. 529 (Sup. Ct. 1911), aff'd 131 N.Y.S. 1140 (App. Div. 1911); State v. Ross, 76 N.C. 242, 22 Am. Rep. 678 (1877).

71. This type of situation is seldom presented in practice. One of the very few cases in point is Garrett v. Chapman, 449 P.2d 856 (Or. Sup. Ct. 1969). Here it was assumed that a Montana statute restricting the right of remarriage after divorce did not apply to an out-of-state marriage of parties whose common premarital domicile was in Montana but who intended to, and did, make their matrimonial domicile in Oregon. This conclusion was reached on the basis of an express statute in Montana regulating the validity of foreign marriages in accordance with the view set forth *infra* at n. 73-75. For a decision relying on an earlier Montana statute which referred to the law of the premarital domicile alone, see In re Takahashi's Estate, 129 P.2d 217 (Mont. Sup. Ct. 1942) (in this case, however, as in almost all others, the premarital domicile remained unchanged after the marriage).

72. See *Goodrich and Scoles* 239.

73. See: *Cook* 447-455; *Goodrich and Scoles* 227, 233, 238-239; *Philip Johnson* 444, 456-457; *Leflar* 532-533; *Stumberg* 287-289; *Taintor*, Marriage 611-614, 631-632. The emphasis placed on intention is a weak point in this doctrine, especially where the parties have changed their mind or where they have not yet put their intention into practice. See for criticism on this and other grounds: *Beale* 692-693; *Ehrenzweig*, Miscegenation 663-669; *Storke*, Annulment 869-870.

on to invalidate a marriage, it has in fact been the law of the common domicile of the spouses after the marriage.[74] Express support for the view that the policy of the intended matrimonial domicile is decisive, thus confirming the prevailing trend of opinion among writers, is to be found in a relatively limited, but growing, number of cases.[75]

This position, it should be noted, is in contrast with the traditional view prevailing in European and other countries where capacity to marry is determined by the personal law of the parties, whether identified as their *lex patriae* or as their *lex domicilii.* In those countries it is usually required that each of the parties must satisfy the substantive conditions of his personal law at the time of the marriage, regardless of the intended matrimonial home (*infra* s. 48, 53). The main reason why a rule of this type – although proposed by the Conflicts Restatement of 1934 – has never been accepted by the American courts is probably that it requires a double hurdle to be overcome and therefore would be apt to increase the number of invalid marriages. Such a rule would be at variance with the American policy of sustaining marriages whenever possible. The American position seems, indeed, to have better foundation in social realities, for no premarital domicile can properly be said to be as intimately concerned with the validity of a marriage as the state in which the parties make their matrimonial home. The objections that may be raised against a rule of the American type will be taken up in the discussion of a similar proposal which has been put forward for English law (*infra* s. 55).

Once it has been accepted that the matrimonial domicile is decisive, a further problem arises as to the relevance of a *subsequent change of that domicile.* Can the validity of the marriage be affected by the law of the new matrimonial domicile? Since such questions normally come before the courts of the new domicile itself, they will be considered in connection with the problem of the position to be taken by a third state, *i.e.* a state which is not the first matrimonial domicile (*infra* s. 17).

74. See Restatement § 283 Comments *j* and *k* with Reporter's Note (p. 246); *Goodrich and Scoles* 239; *Philip Johnson* 445.

75. Mpiliris v. Hellenic Lines, Ltd., 323 F. Supp. 865, 876-879 (S.D. Tex. 1970); Bucca v. State, 128 A.2d 506, 509-510 (N.J. Super. Ct. 1957). For other cases lending some support to the same rule see: People ex rel. Schutt v. Siems, 198 Ill. App. 342 (1916); People v. Steere, 151 N.W. 617 (Mich. Sup. Ct. 1915); Reid v. Reid, 129 N.Y.S. 529 (Sup. Ct. 1911); State v. Ross, 76 N.C. 242, 22 Am. Rep. 678 (1877). See also the Montana statute applied in Garrett v. Chapman, 449 P.2d 856, 859 (Or. Sup. Ct. 1969).

15. *Evasion of Laws.* Most problems relating to the validity of an out-of-state marriage contracted in violation of the law of the domicile arise in the context of evasion, the parties having chosen the place of celebration for the specific purpose of escaping the effect of a domiciliary prohibition. The presence of this element has frequently been alluded to in the opinions of the courts, but it has usually not been decisive for the results reached. This is obvious in those cases, constituting a large majority, in which an evasionary marriage has been upheld in reliance on the *lex loci celebrationis.*[76] The prevailing view, which has been expressly stated in many such decisions, is that the existence of a motive of evasion in the minds of the parties – *i.e.,* their knowledge of the domiciliary prohibition and their intention to marry in spite of it – is immaterial in determining the validity of the marriage and does not change the operation of the usual conflicts rule.[77] The real question, here too, is whether the circumvented prohibition is important enough to warrant extraterritorial application. If the answer is no, the fact that the parties were aware of the impediment does not make their marriage more odious to the local conceptions of the domicile.

Even in the minority of cases where an evasionary marriage was struck down, the language used by the courts in referring to the subjective state of mind of the parties is hardly conclusive.[78] The true *ratio decidendi* of these cases is probably that the domiciliary prohibition was based on a strong public policy, which would in itself (*i.e.*, regardless of any subjective intention to evade) have been sufficient to compel invalidation of the marriage.[79]

76. Illustrations are afforded by most of the cases cited *infra* n. 134-138, 210, 223 and 232.

77. For court language to this effect see: Horton v. Horton, 198 P. 1105, 1106 (Ariz. Sup. Ct. 1921); McDonald v. McDonald, 58 P.2d 163, 164 (Cal. Sup. Ct. 1936); Norman v. Norman, 54 P. 143, 145 (Cal. Sup. Ct. 1898); Commonwealth v. Lane, 113 Mass. 458, 464-465 (1873); State v. Hand, 126 N.W. 1002 (Neb. Sup. Ct. 1910). And see Restatement of 1934, § 129; *Ehrenzweig*, Conflict 387; *Rabel* 273-274; *Stimson* 113-114; *Taintor*, Marriage 629-630.

78. The intent to evade the domiciliary law was relied on in most of the cases cited *infra* n. 140-141, 214, 234 and 242.

79. An illustrative comparison may be made between the Pennsylvania cases of In re Stull's Estate, 39 A. 16, 18 (Pa. Sup. Ct. 1898), and Maurer v. Maurer, 60 A.2d 440, 441 (Pa. Super. Ct. 1948). In both of these cases a foreign marriage was held invalid because it was in violation of the local statute forbidding the guilty party to a divorce for adultery to marry his paramour. But while the fact of intended evasion was made one of the

continued on page 30

These problems have also been approached by statute. A restrictive attitude to the recognition of foreign evasionary marriages was taken by the Uniform Marriage Evasion Act of 1912, s. 1 of which provided as follows:

> If any person residing and intending to continue to reside in this state who is disabled or prohibited from contracting marriage under the laws of this state shall go into another state or country and there contract a marriage prohibited and declared void by the laws of this state, such marriage shall be null and void for all purposes in this state with the same effect as though such prohibited marriage had been entered into in this state.

Although the Uniform Act as a whole was only adopted by five states, this particular provision of the Act has been followed, in the same or in some modified form, in a considerably larger number of states.[80] The effect of these *marriage evasion statutes* is to give extraterritorial force to a more or less extensive category of local prohibitions.[81]

Like the above-cited model provision, most of the statutes in question cover all prohibitions the violation of which would render the marriage void if celebrated locally.[82] Some statutes, however, have a more limited scope, applying only to certain specified types of defective marriages (for example, those regarded as incestuous). The prohibitions coming within the terms of the respective statutes follow a local domiciliary wherever he marries, though only if he intends to remain domiciled in the enacting state after the marriage.[83] Hence, if the parties intend to make their

---

continued from page 29

grounds of decision in the earlier case, it was expressly stated in the more recent case that the result did not depend upon the intention of the parties. To this effect see also State v. Kennedy, 76 N.C. 251, 22 Am. Rep. 683, 684 (1877).

80. See the references *supra* n. 17.

81. See: *Beale* 681-683; *Goodrich and Scoles* 237; *Graveson*, Evasion 21-26; *Philip Johnson* 453-454; *Rabel* 274-277; *Stimson* 114-116; *Taintor*, Marriage 629-630. For decisions applying such statutes to invalidate a foreign marriage see *infra* n. 139, 235, 242.

82. The limitation to void marriages is important, for many defective marriages are only voidable and therefore fall outside the reach of such statutes. The statute enacted in Wisconsin has a broader scope, covering marriages which are either prohibited or declared void by the local law. This, however, has not prevented the Wisconsin courts from placing a restrictive interpretation on the statute; see the cases cited *infra* n. 87.

83. The term "residence" used in nearly all statutes, as well as in the

matrimonial home in another state, the marriage is not caught by such statutes.[84] In this respect the position is essentially the same as in states which do not have a marriage evasion statute: the law of the premarital domicile alone will not be applied to strike down a marriage (cf. *supra* s. 14). The only relevant intention under such statutes is usually that of returning to live in the state of the premarital domicile. It is thus immaterial whether the subjective state of mind of the parties was directed to evading a domiciliary prohibition. A few statutes, however, differ from this pattern and impose, or have been construed to impose, such a subjective test, in addition to the requirement of an intention to return.[85]

The enactment of a marriage evasion statute, whatever its exact scope, marks the adoption of a stricter policy with regard to the violation of domiciliary prohibitions than that usually prevailing otherwise. On the face of it, such statutes relieve the courts of their normal task of weighing the strength of each particular prohibition against the general policy of validation. In practice, however, the courts have found means permitting them to preserve a large amount of control over such questions. In general, they have tended to put a narrow construction on statutes of the present type, sometimes even to the point of distorting their plain meaning.

One technique used to this end is to construe the domiciliary prohibition as making a defective marriage voidable only. Since, in many cases, the distinction between void and voidable marriages is blurred, there is often scope for the courts to adopt this construction and, thereby, to keep the marriage outside the reach of an evasion statute limited to void marriages.[86] Even where a mar-

above-cited provision of the Uniform Act, means "domicile". See, e.g., Sweeney v. Kennard, 120 N.E.2d 910, 913 (Mass. Sup. Jud. Ct. 1954); Levanosky v. Levanosky, 42 N.E.2d 561, 563 (Mass. Sup. Jud. Ct. 1942); Atwood v. Atwood, 8 N.E.2d 916, 918 (Mass. Sup. Jud. Ct. 1937). Cf. *Graveson*, Evasion 26.

84. See, e.g., People ex rel. Schutt v. Siems, 198 Ill. App. 342 (1916); Bell v. Bell, 8 S.E.2d 183 (W.Va. Sup. Ct. App. 1940); and the cases cited *infra* n. 145.

85. For an example see the West Virginia statute involved in Bell v. Bell, *ibid.* And see for Massachusetts cases adopting the same view, as a matter of construction of an earlier Massachusetts statute, *infra* n. 139.

86. See, e.g., Horton v. Horton, 198 P. 1150 (Ariz. Sup. Ct. 1921); Boysen v. Boysen, 23 N.E.2d 231 (Ill. App. Ct. 1939); Levy v. Downing, 100 N.E. 638 (Mass. Sup. Jud. Ct. 1913); Lyannes v. Lyannes, 177 N.W. 683 (Wis. Sup. Ct. 1920); In re Jansa's Estate, 171 N.W. 947 (Wis. Sup. Ct. 1919). Cf. *supra* at n. 53-54. Another means of enabling the court to avoid applying such statutes is to find that the party concerned was not, or did not intend

continued on page 32

riage was, in express terms, declared to be void by the law of the domicile, the courts have sometimes felt free to hold that the violated requirement had no extraterritorial effect and that the evasion statute therefore did not apply.[87] The reasons given by the courts in such cases are hardly comprehensible, but the real motive is clearly to be found in a dissatisfaction with the legislative policy expressed in the statute and in a desire to uphold marriages even at the cost of defeating unambiguous statutory language.[88] This attitude on the part of the courts has impaired the effectiveness of the statutes as a means of combating evasion. On the whole, this legislation has had limited influence and not been able to reverse the general trend in favour of validation.

16. *Invalidating Renvoi to Law of Domicile.* A question of the extraterritorial application of a domiciliary prohibition may be presented even if the state of the domicile does not itself have a strong public policy or a statute requiring such application, but is prepared to sustain the marriage if valid by the *lex loci celebrationis.* This occurs in the relatively rare situation where the conflicts rules of the latter law refer the matter back to the law of the domicile, thereby raising a problem of *renvoi* (*supra* s. 9). The main, if not the only, instance is where the state of celebration has a marriage evasion statute of the type applying to local marriages and requiring the courts (and marriage officials) to give effect to invalidating rules of the law of the domicile of /either of/ the parties (*supra* s. 8). A marriage contravening such a statute is bad in the state of celebration, even though it complies with the local law of that state. Should the courts of the domicile follow suit when directed by their conflicts rules to apply the *lex loci celebrationis?*

An affirmative answer to this question has been given in practice. Most cases raising the problem concern the validity of a foreign marriage contracted in defiance of a domiciliary restriction on remarriage after divorce. While conceding that the restriction did not in itself have extraterritorial effect, the courts of the domicile have given it such effect when faced with a statute of the above-

---

continued from page 31

to remain, domiciled in the enacting state; cf. *supra* at n. 84. In In re Campbell's Estate, 51 N.W.2d 709 (Wis. Sup. Ct. 1952), the court partly relied on the presumption (held not to be overcome by the evidence in the case) that the parties had capacity to marry, cf. *supra* s. 11.

87. See for such cases: Korf v. Korf, 157 N.W.2d 691 (Wis. Sup. Ct. 1968); In re Ferguson's Estate, 130 N.W.2d 300 (Wis. Sup. Ct. 1964).

88. See the dissent by Gordon, J., in In re Ferguson's Estate, *ibid.* at 303.

mentioned type in the *lex loci celebrationis.*[89] In the end, therefore, they applied their own law to invalidate the marriage when it came within the terms of such a statute.[90] Although this amounts to acceptance of *renvoi,* the problem has been little discussed in the opinions of the courts. Apparently, it was assumed without further analysis that the reference to "the law" of the state of celebration was to "the whole law" of that state. Nevertheless, it is rather remarkable, both that the state of celebration should insist on giving extraterritorial force to a domiciliary prohibition "against the will" of the state of the domicile and, perhaps even more so, that the latter state should feel compelled to "change its mind" in the face of this attitude on the part of the other state.

17. *Position of Third States.* The questions treated above become more complicated when they arise in a state (*F*) other than that of the first marital domicile (*D*).[91] Suppose, for instance, that the intending spouses are first cousins, domiciled in state *D.* They are forbidden to marry each other in *D,* the law of which declares marriages between first cousins incestuous and void. The parties therefore get married in state *C,* where such marriages are permitted. They return to make their marital domicile in *D* where they remain for a year, and then move to state *F* where they live as man and wife for many years. One of them dies intestate, and the surviving partner claims a spouse's share in the estate. This claim is contested by other relatives, who contend that the violation of *D*'s law makes the marriage invalid. What is, or what should be, the approach of a court in *F* with regard to this question?[92]

It has often been argued, especially by writers, that the validity of a marriage ought not to be subject to redetermination solely because the parties have moved from one state to another and

89. See the cases cited *infra* n. 154. For a case involving another type of prohibition (epilepsy) see In re Canon's Estate, 266 N.W. 918 (Wis. Sup. Ct. 1936).

90. But see for a case in which the marriage (between first cousins) was held not to be void by the *lex fori et domicilii* and therefore to escape the reach of the relevant foreign statute, Mazzolini v. Mazzolini, 155 N.E.2d 206 (Ohio Sup. Ct. 1958). Cf. *supra* at n. 14 and 86-87.

91. The term "third state" is used here to denote all such states, including the state of celebration (*C*). State *F* may thus coincide with state *C.* A different terminology is used in connection with the problems of remarriage after divorce (*infra* s. 21, 23), where a distinction is drawn between the divorce state, the state of celebration and third states (*i.e.*, states other than the first two).

92. Cases on this type of problem are collected in Annot., 51 A.L.R. 1412 (1927).

that the possibility of the marriage being treated as valid in one state but as invalid in another must be avoided. Uniformity of result is thus made a prime objective to be attained. On principle, therefore, the position taken in state *D*, which originally had the most significant relationship to the spouses, should be recognised as decisive for all other states which subsequently become involved.[93] It follows that the inquiry of the court in *F* should be directed to the effect of the infringement of *D*'s prohibition under *D*'s law, including its conflicts rules. If (and only if) those rules would have led to invalidation of the particular marriage in *D*, had the courts of that state been confronted with the question, the court in *F* should also refuse to recognise it. This approach has been adopted by the courts in a few cases where *D* had a marriage evasion statute or where it was otherwise clear that the policy of that state required extraterritorial application of its invalidating rule.[94]

It may, however, be difficult for a court in *F* to apply such a hypothetical test, especially if the strength of *D*'s policy is not evinced by explicit statutory provisions applicable to foreign marriages or by prior decisions on the particular point involved. In the absence of clear authority requiring invalidation in state *D*, courts of other states are unlikely to anticipate such a construction of its law.[95] Furthermore, even if there should be no doubt that the particular marriage would be held bad in *D*, the *F* court may not always be prepared to follow suit. At the time when the issue is put to the test, the parties will often (as in the above example) have left their original domicile and made their home in *F*. This tends to weaken the interest of *D* in seeing its invalidating rule applied and at the same time to give *F* a significant interest of its own in the matter. Unless the marriage happens also to be deeply

93. See: Restatement § 283 Comment *k* with Reporter's Note (p. 245) (where, however, the principle has been considerably modified in comparison with the corresponding rule in the Restatement of 1934, § 132); *Beale* 695-698; *Griswold*, Renvoi Revisited: 51 Harv. L. Rev. 1165, 1199-1200 (1937/38); *Leflar* 532-533, 535, 537; *Storke*, Annulment 870-871; *Stumberg* 289; *Taintor*, Marriage 632.

94. People v. Steere, 151 N.W. 617 (Mich. Sup. Ct. 1915); Meisenhelder v. Chicago & N.W. Ry. Co., 213 N.W. 32 (Minn. Sup. Ct. 1927); Hall v. Industrial Comm., 162 N.W. 312 (Wis. Sup. Ct. 1917). Such application of the law of *D* is also required where the question arises in state *C*, if that state has a marriage evasion statute of the type embracing local marriages; see *supra* s. 8 and 16.

95. See Restatement § 283 Comment *k* (p. 239-240).

offensive to *F*'s conceptions, therefore, it may well be upheld on the strength of the *lex loci celebrationis.*[96] In any event, this is the result arrived at by the courts in most cases.[97] In some of these, it is true, the decision is based on a finding that a court in *D* would not itself apply its rule to an out-of-state marriage.[98] In others, however, there is no indication that the court directed its attention to this question. Although the ground of decision is not always explicit, the court seems rather to have determined, as a matter of *F*'s own policy, that it would not accord extraterritorial effect to *D*'s rule, whether or not the law of *D* claimed such effect.[99]

Where, in contrast to the situations so far considered, the marriage is valid both by the *lex loci celebrationis* and by the law of state *D,* it will normally also be recognised, more or less as a matter of course, in any other state where the parties may subsequently have become domiciled or where the validity of the union is otherwise drawn into question.[100] This holds true even if the marriage is contrary to the *lex fori* and perhaps regarded as highly distasteful by that law, so that it would have been held bad if the parties had been local domiciliaries at the time of celebration

96. See: Restatement § 283 Comments *k-m* (p. 240-242); *Ehrenzweig,* Conflict 378-379, 383, 385 n. 45; *Goodrich and Scoles* 233, 237-238; *Weintraub* 170.

97. See, for example, for cases involving a restriction on the right of remarriage after divorce imposed by the law of *D,* but disregarded by the courts of other states, *infra* n. 135-137.

98. For an example see In re Winder's Estate, 219 P.2d 18, 25-26 (Cal. Dist. Ct. App. 1950). It must also be noted that some other decisions refusing to give effect to a restriction on remarriage imposed by the divorce state may be explained on the ground that the party concerned was no longer domiciled in that state at the time of the remarriage, or did not intend to continue to be so domiciled; see *supra* n. 68, 84 and *infra* n. 143-145.

99. For decisions clearly so holding see Boehm v. Rohlfs, 276 N.W. 105 (Iowa Sup. Ct. 1937); In re Ommang's Estate, 235 N.W. 529 (Minn. Sup. Ct. 1931). In both of these cases the *F* court applied the *lex loci celebrationis* to sustain a marriage which came within the terms of a marriage evasion statute of state *D.* In In re Ommang's Estate, *ibid.* at 531, the court partly relied on the fact that the parties had become domiciled in *F* at the time of the suit. For another example see Dannelli v. Dannelli's Adm'r, 4 Bush 51 (Ky. Ct. App. 1868), upholding a marriage contracted in Switzerland, between parties domiciled in the then Austrian province of Lombardy and within the prohibited degrees of affinity by AUSTRIAN law, in the absence of proof that it was invalid by SWISS law.

100. See *Goodrich and Scoles* 239; *Stimson* 82-91; and the references given *supra* n. 93. Cases on this type of situation are collected in Annot., 127 A.L.R. 437 (1940).

and made their first marital domicile in *F*.[101] Indeed, if the parties are American citizens who have married in the state of their then domicile in the United States, in accordance with the law of that state, it seems at least very doubtful, as a matter of federal constitutional law, whether the courts of another state are at liberty to deny the validity of the marriage on the strength of their own law and policy even if the parties have later moved to, and become domiciled in, that state.[102]

Nevertheless, judicial opinions often contain statements, in the nature of *dicta,* condemning certain marriages in absolute terms, the meaning of which appears to be that recognition is excluded in any circumstances, irrespective of the laws of the domicile and of the place of celebration.[103] Polygamous marriages and marriages "incestuous according to the law of nature" are the leading examples of this category of cases. Since such marriages are proscribed everywhere in the United States, these exceptions have little, if any, bearing on marriages celebrated in an American state.[104] Even as regards marriages concluded in a foreign nation, between parties domiciled there and in accordance with the foreign law

101. See for decisions sustaining a marriage regarded as incestuous and void by the *lex fori*: Sutton v. Warren, 51 Mass. 451 (1845) (aunt-nephew marriage in England); Garcia v. Garcia, 127 N.W. 586 (S.D. Sup. Ct. 1910) (marriage between first cousins in California). For a case involving a marriage below the age limit of the *lex fori* see Simmons v. Simmons, 203 N.Y.S. 215 (App. Div. 1924). The fact that the parties or one of them had been domiciled in *F* up to the time of, or until shortly before, the marriage and that they later returned to live in that state (after making their first matrimonial domicile in *D*) has been held immaterial. See, e.g., State v. Ross, 76 N.C. 242, 22 Am. Rep. 678 (1877) (South Carolina marriage contrary to miscegenation statute of the *lex fori*); Pierce v. Pierce, 109 P. 45 (Wash. Sup. Ct. 1910) (marriage in British Columbia in defiance of prohibition on remarriage after divorce imposed by the *lex fori*). Cf. *supra* at n. 68.

102. See, to the effect that so holding would run foul of the due process and the full faith and credit clauses of the U.S. Constitution, *Holt* 25-26, 30-31.

103. See *Goodrich and Scoles* 239-240; *Stumberg* 290; and the references given *supra* n. 64 and *infra* n. 114, 227.

104. But see the case of Toler v. Oakwood Smokeless Coal Corp., 4 S.E.2d 364 (Va. Sup. Ct. App. 1939), critically noted in 18 N.C.L. Rev. 130 (1939/40). That case involved a bigamous marriage in West Virginia, between parties domiciled there at the time but who afterwards came to live in Virginia. Under the law of West Virginia (state *C* and *D*), the marriage was only voidable and therefore no longer subject to attack after the death of one of the spouses. The court in Virginia (state *F*), however, refused to apply that rule for reasons of public policy and held the marriage to be void in accordance with the *lex fori.*

concerned, actual decisions declaring them invalid on grounds of the public policy of state *F* are almost non-existent.[105] Another question is whether and to what extent the public policy of *F* may cause the courts of that state to refuse the parties the enjoyment of certain *incidents* normally attached to a valid marriage (*infra* s. 18).

abc. Validity and Incidents of Marriage

18. Apart from cases where the validity of a marriage as such is involved in a suit for annulment or for a declaratory judgment that a marriage does or does not exist, the issue may be raised collaterally in a variety of other proceedings in which the rights of the parties depend on the validity of a marriage. To judge by the reasoning found in the decisions, the course normally adopted by the courts in such cases is first to examine that question and to determine it independently of the purpose for which it is relevant in the particular case and then to make the decision as to the incidents follow as an automatic consequence.[106]

This, however, is hardly the whole truth. In all probability, many decisions concerning the validity of a marriage have been affected by the incident involved in the case at bar, even if such considerations are rarely reflected in the opinions of the courts. Suppose, for instance, that an uncle-niece marriage, which is incestuous and void according to the local law of state *D* (the domicile of both parties before and after the marriage), has been entered into in state *C*, which permits such unions. This marriage may well be considered strongly offensive to the public policy of *D* if the parties attempt to cohabit in that state and therefore held invalid if attacked while such cohabitation takes place. It does not follow, however, that the same position must be taken if the validity of

105. See, however, United States ex rel. Devine v. Rodgers, 109 F. 886 (E.D. Pa. 1901), refusing to recognise a marriage lawfully entered into in Russia between an uncle (who had later become a naturalised American citizen) and his niece, who therefore was not entitled to remain in the United States as his lawful wife. The decision is based on the public policy of Pennsylvania, whose law stigmatised the union as incestuous and exposed the parties to indictment in the criminal courts. The domicile of the parties at the time of the marriage does not appear from the opinion but seems to have been in Russia. For a similar case where a foreign polygamous marriage was denied recognition see Ng Suey Hi v. Weedin, 21 F.2d 801 (9 Cir. 1927).

106. See Restatement § 283 Comment *a*; *Goodrich and Scoles* 227; *Taintor*, Marriage 607-608.

the union is questioned in an inheritance suit after the death of one of the parties, perhaps after they have lived as man and wife for decades during which the marriage has not been challenged. The issue of inheritance, as opposed to cohabitation within the state, is little related to the purpose of the invalidating rule of state *D* and therefore much less likely to evoke any strong feelings of repugnance in that state.[107]

Once it has been accepted that the determination of the validity of a marriage may vary, at least to some extent, with the purpose for which the question is relevant, it becomes natural to take one step further. This consists in recognising that a decision to permit or to deny the enjoyment of a particular incident attached to the status of marriage may be made independently of the validity of the union in other contexts.[108] In other words, a marriage may be treated as valid for some, but as invalid for other purposes.

This approach has apparently been used by the courts in certain cases, especially as concerns marriages prohibited by the *lex fori* on grounds of polygamy, incest or (in the past) miscegenation. While it has often been said, without qualification, that such marriages are invalid, the decisions are usually limited to prohibiting local cohabitation or to refusing some other incident the enjoyment of which was thought to be distinctly opposed to the public policy of the forum.[109] Such decisions probably do not

107. See *Leflar* 538; *Weintraub* 170-171, 173.

108. See: Restatement § 284 Comment *c*; *Baade* 357, 379; *Beale* 668 n. 1, 696 n. 2, 701-702; *Cavers* 243-245; *Currie*, On the Displacement of the Law of the Forum: 58 Colum. L. Rev. 964, 1022-1024 (1958); *Engdahl*, Proposal for a Benign Revolution in Marriage Law and Marriage Conflicts Law: 55 Iowa L. Rev. 56-116 (1969/70); *Goodrich and Scoles* 239-243; *Philip Johnson* 455; *Leflar* 530-531; *Maddaugh* 142-145; *Stumberg* 290; *Swan*; *Taintor*, Marriage 607-608, 614-616; *Weintraub* 170-171, 173. Cf. Act. Doc. La Haye 13 (1976) III 74-75.

109. See for cases holding local cohabitation to constitute an indictable offense, without regard to the fact that the parties were validly married under the relevant foreign law: State v. Brown, 23 N.E. 747 (Ohio Sup. Ct. 1890) (incestuous marriage); State v. Bell, 7 Baxt. 9, 32 Am. Rep. 549 (Tenn. Sup. Ct. 1872) (miscegenous marriage); cf. State v. Nakashima, 114 P. 894 (Wash. Sup. Ct. 1911) (incestuous marriage). For decisions refusing to give other incidents to a foreign marriage see Olverson v. Olverson, 293 F. 1015 (D.C.Cir. 1923), and Palmer v. Palmer, 163 N.E. 879 (Mass. Sup. Jud. Ct. 1928). In both of these cases the court was prepared to treat a foreign marriage, contracted in violation of a local prohibition on remarriage after divorce but in accordance with the *lex loci celebrationis*, as valid for certain purposes, but it declined to do so to the extent of permitting the party who had defied the local rule to obtain matrimonial relief, or of enforcing the obligations of the marital status if such enforcement would result in benefit to that party only.

imply a denial of the possibility of extending other incidents, less directly related to the object of the invalidating rule, to the foreign marriage (when valid by the *lex loci celebrationis*). This is confirmed by other cases in which similar marriages were recognised for purposes such as the legitimacy of the issue of the union or the right to intestate succession by the surviving spouse.[110]

b. *Specific Problems*

ba. *Prior Marriage*

19. *Survey of Problems.* The most common source of problems in conflicts cases, no less than in purely local cases, involving the substantive validity of marriage is that the parties have, or that one of them has, been married before. These problems are of a variety of types.

The natural starting point for our discussion is the principle of monogamy, which prevails everywhere in the United States.[111] As long as a prior marriage subsists, therefore, neither of the spouses can marry again; such second marriage, if attempted, would be invalid for bigamy. This, of course, does not apply if the prior marriage was itself void *ab initio*. Nor does the principle prevent a limited recognition of polygamous marriages validly entered into in accordance with the relevant foreign law (*infra* s. 20). Apart from these cases, a prior marriage constitutes an impediment until it ends, whether by the death of one of the spouses, by divorce or ortherwise. It is essential that such termination has taken place before the remarriage of either spouse; a subsequent dissolution, as a rule, is not sufficient to validate the second marriage.

In practice, most problems arise in connection with remarriage

110. See as regards polygamous marriages *Pålsson,* Marriage, s. 256-259 and *infra* s. 20. For decisions recognising a miscegenous marriage to the extent of permitting the surviving spouse to inherit intestate property left in the forum state see: Whittington v. McCaskill, 61 So. 236 (Fla. Sup. Ct. 1913); Miller v. Lucks, 36 So.2d 140 (Miss. Sup. Ct. 1948). But see for other cases involving miscegenous marriages: Stevens v. United States, 146 F.2d 120 (10 Cir. 1944) (sitting in Oklahoma; marriage held ineffective to revoke deceased party's will relating to property in forum); In re Takahashi's Estate, 129 P.2d 217 (Mont. Sup. Ct. 1942) (denying surviving partner's claim to be appointed administrator of deceased's estate).

111. See *Clark* 61-66. For an exception formerly admitted with regard to Indian tribal marriages contracted within Indian territory see the references given by *Pålsson*, Marriage, s. 247 (n. 12 and 13) and 250 (n. 24).

after divorce. One is that not all so-called divorces have the effect of ending the marriage. Apart from "limited divorce", which is only a form of legal separation, the laws of several states provide for an interlocutory decree system. Under this system it is necessary to distinguish between interlocutory decrees, which are only a preliminary step to divorce, and final decrees, by which alone the marriage bond is dissolved (*infra* s. 21). Another question, which usually relates to a foreign divorce (including divorces pronounced in a sister state), is the validity of the decree, in particular whether it was granted by a court of competent jurisdiction (*infra* s. 22). Finally, even where it is clear that the prior marriage has been finally and validly dissolved by divorce, the right of the divorced parties, or of one of them, to marry again may be restricted in one way or another. Statutory provisions to this effect, which exist in many of the United States, often give rise to conflicts problems (*infra* s. 23).

On the other hand, there are several rules and devices which tend to support a later marriage although a prior union still subsists or cannot be proved to have ended, or where one party is (or both of them are) divorced but forbidden to marry again, or where such obstacles have only been removed after the occurrence of the remarriage. One means which is frequently used to validate the second marriage in such circumstances is the presumption, recognised by American law, in favour of the latest of successive marriages (*infra* s. 24). Another is the doctrine of common law marriage, which often plays a role when a prior marriage has only been dissolved, or a prohibition on remarriage ceased to apply, after the second marriage was entered into (*supra* s. 11, *infra* s. 25). Sometimes the same result is reached on the strength of a statute providing, in certain circumstances, for the validation of a second marriage, once the impediment based on the prior union has been removed (*infra* s. 25). In some of the states which have an interlocutory decree system the final decree may be given retroactive effect, thereby validating an intervening second marriage (*nunc pro tunc* orders: *infra* s. 26). Where, finally, one or both of the parties to a divorce have married again although the divorce was admittedly invalid or had not become final, the remarriage will often raise an estoppel, which operates to preclude attacks on the defective divorce and, thereby, also to protect the second marriage (*infra* s. 27).

The rules and principles now referred to form part of the local law, rather than of the conflict of laws, of the respective states, and do not specifically envisage situations involving foreign elements. To a varying extent, however, all of them are also relied on in such situations and may affect the solution of, and themselves give rise to, conflicts problems.

baa. Second Marriage Barred

20. *Polygamous Marriages.* The principle that a person cannot marry again as long as he is bound by a prior marriage prevents any remarriage in the United States, even though the parties are domiciled in a foreign country sanctioning polygamy. It makes no difference if the prior union was entered into abroad, provided that it is valid under the relevant foreign law. Even if it is "potentially polygamous" according to that law, it seems to be recognised as a bar to a second marriage in the United States.[112]

Where, on the other hand, the second marriage has been lawfully contracted in a foreign country permitting polygamy, the question of its recognition may come before American courts. This type of problem is unlikely to arise unless the parties have later moved to, or want to enter, the United States, and it has in fact rarely occurred.

It is generally agreed that such cases form an exception to the conflicts rule of the *lex loci celebrationis.*[113] American courts have often stated, *obiter,* that polygamous unions come within the class of marriages "which are deemed contrary to the law of nature as generally recognized in Christian countries."[114] Although such broad language seems to imply that a polygamous marriage cannot be recognised at all, even if it is valid by the law of the country in which it was celebrated and in which the parties were then domiciled, in the relatively few cases actually involving such marriages they have usually been given certain effects. This is so, for instance, as regards succession to property in the forum by the surviving spouse or spouses and for the purpose of claims under workmen's compensation acts. As these questions have already been considered

112. Application of Sood, 142 N.Y.S.2d 591 (Sup. Ct. 1955); cf. *Pålsson*, Marriage, s. 258 (at n. 52).

113. See, for example, the cases cited in the following notes and the American writers referred to in *Pålsson*, op. cit., s. 256 n. 48.

114. Commonwealth v. Lane, 113 Mass. 458, 463 (1873), cited with approval in In re Miller's Estate, 214 N.W. 428, 429 (Mich. Sup. Ct. 1927). Other *dicta* containing similar language are collected in Annot., 74 A.L.R. 1533 (1931). See also Bucca v. State, 128 A.2d 506, 510 (N.J. Super. Ct. 1957); Incuria v. Incuria, 280 N.Y.S. 716, 721 (Dom. Rel. Ct. 1935); People v. Kay, 252 N.Y.S. 518, 522-523 (Magis. Ct. 1931).

by the author (see *Pålsson*, Marriage, s. 256-259), they will not be further treated here.

21. *Remarriage After Divorce: Finality of Divorce.* The requirement that the prior marriage must have ended before the remarriage is of particular importance in relation to the system of interlocutory divorce decrees adopted in some of the United States.[115] Under this system a divorce comes about in two phases. In the first of these the court, at the end of the trial, enters a preliminary decree, which is usually referred to as an interlocutory decree or a decree *nisi.* That decree determines the right to divorce, and sometimes settles ancillary questions concerning the custody of children, the right to support, etc. It does not, however, sever the marriage tie and therefore confers no right of remarriage. In the second phase, after a statutory period of time, the length of which ranges from three months (for example in New Jersey) to six months (in California), the decree becomes or is made final, thereby restoring the parties to the status of single persons. Under most statutes this takes place automatically at the expiry of the prescribed time (unless an affirmative move has been made by the parties or by the court to set the decree aside). In a few states (including California), however, the statute requires further proceedings to be taken and a separate final decree to be entered by the court to end the marriage.

In purpose and function this system is to some extent similar to that, adopted in certain European countries, whereby a divorce must normally be preceded by a decree of legal separation coupled with a waiting period, or by a waiting period alone, during which the parties are considered still to be married.[116] The interlocutory system is partly intended to give the spouses time for consideration of their action and to facilitate reconciliation, partly to frustrate any hope for a quick remarriage and thereby, it is claimed, to discourage the parties from seeking divorce.[117] In either case the ultimate objective is to strengthen marriage as an institution.

115. Statutes providing for such decrees in seven states are cited by *Clark* 402 n. 2. Cases involving some of these, as well as certain other statutes which have been construed to the same effect, are cited *infra* n. 120 and 124-126. See *Kingsley*, Remarriage 280-282; *Vernier* II 151-156; Note, Interlocutory Decrees of Divorce: 56 Colum. L. Rev. 228-250 (1956).

116. See, for example, *Dölle*, Familienrecht 551-553, 654-655.

117. Apparently, however, the system has not been very successful in promoting these ends. See *Clark* 403; *Kingsley*, Remarriage 281; Note, Interlocutory Decrees (*supra* n. 115) 249-250.

Another aim of the interlocutory period is possibly to prevent confusion of paternity (*turbatio sanguinis*).

The main legal problem in this connection is not one of conflict of laws, but of determining whether a given divorce decree is or is not final.[118] This is not always clear either from the decree itself or from the statute by reference to which it was granted. Difficulties and some confusion have occurred, in particular, with regard to provisions which declare both parties incapable of marrying again during the time allowed for appeal from, or for some other form of attack on, the decree.[119] Sometimes such provisions, or other provisions which do not expressly specify the nature of the decree, have been construed to postpone the termination of the marriage, at least for the purpose of remarriage, until the lapse of the stated time, the decree being thereby treated as interlocutory only.[120] More often, however, provisions of this type, even where according to their language the decree was not to become absolute or to take effect until the expiry of the prescribed time, have been held not to affect the finality of the decree but only to impose a prohibition on remarriage within that time.[121] In either alternative the parties are prevented from marrying again, during the given period, in the divorce state itself, but the choice between them is often of practical importance because a restriction on remarriage

118. See: *Beale* 684-685; *Goodrich and Scoles* 234; *Kingsley*, Remarriage 282; *Taintor*, Marriage 625-626. Cases on this problem are collected in Annot., 32 A.L.R. 1116, 1125-1129 (1924).

119. For provisions of this type see *Vernier* II 163-168, 172-178.

120. Oliver v. Oliver, 185 F.2d 429 (D.C. Cir. 1950); Brand v. State, 6 So.2d 446 (Ala. Sup. Ct. 1941) (but see Schurink v. United States, 177 F.2d 809 [5 Cir. 1949], construing the same Alabama statute); Holmberg v. Holmberg, 184 N.W. 134 (Neb. Sup. Ct. 1921); McLennan v. McLennan, 50 P. 802 (Or. Sup. Ct. 1897); Heflinger v. Heflinger, 118 S.E. 316 (Va. Sup. Ct. App. 1923); In re Smith's Estate, 30 P. 1059 (Wash. Sup. Ct. 1892) (but see Willey v. Willey, 60 P. 145 [Wash. Sup. Ct. 1900], and later Washington cases cited *infra* n. 140, 144). Many of the statutes involved in the cases cited in this and the following footnotes have since been changed, and the cases therefore often do not reflect the law as it stands today in the respective states.

121. A Kansas statute, for instance, which provided that "the decree does not become absolute and take effect until the expiration of six months" from the date when the judgment was rendered, was so construed: Durland v. Durland, 74 P. 274 (Kan. Sup. Ct. 1903). For cases involving statutes which are or were in force in other states see: Horton v. Horton, 198 P. 1105 (Ariz. Sup. Ct. 1921); In re Wood's Estate, 69 P. 900 (Cal. Sup. Ct. 1902); Griswold v. Griswold, 129 P. 560 (Colo. Ct. App. 1913); In re Smith, 37 P. 1099 (Okl. Sup. Ct. 1894); Willey v. Willey, 60 P. 145 (Wash. Sup. Ct. 1900).

after divorce, as distinct from the impediment of a prior subsisting marriage, usually has no effect outside the state which imposed it (*infra* s. 23). It seems clear that whichever of the two constructions is adopted by the courts of the state where the divorce was granted must be followed by the courts of other states and by federal courts having to pass on the validity of a second marriage entered into within the critical time.[122]

Once it has been established that the decree is interlocutory only, there will not normally be any further problem. Since the decree does not end the marriage even in the state where it was rendered, it will not be held to have done so in other states or countries either. It follows that any remarriage during the interlocutory period, wherever celebrated and wherever the parties may be domiciled (as long as the relevant laws are based on monogamy), is invalid for bigamy.[123] This position has been taken in numerous American cases involving such marriages, celebrated out of the divorce state (usually to evade its laws), not only where the question arose in that state,[124] but also where it came before the courts of the

122. This view has been accepted in nearly all cases. See, for example, for decisions construing the Kansas statute mentioned in the preceding note to make the decree final, in accordance with the interpretation placed upon it by the Kansas Supreme Court: Wheelock v. Freiwald, 66 F.2d 694, 700 (8 Cir. 1933); Bauer v. Abrahams, 216 P. 259 (Colo. Sup. Ct. 1923); Pickard v. Pickard, 45 N.W.2d 269 (Iowa Sup. Ct. 1950); King v. Klemp, 57 A.2d 530 (N.J. Ch. 1947). In the same way, the interpretation of the decree as interlocutory, where adopted by the courts of the state of rendition, has been followed by other courts; see the cases cited *infra* n. 125-126. An exception is the New York case of In re Peart's Estate, 97 N.Y.S.2d 879 (App. Div. 1950), construing the Virginia statute as making the decree final, contrary to the decision of the Virginia court in Heflinger v. Heflinger, 118 S.E. 316 (Va. Sup. Ct. App. 1923).

123. See: Restatement § 283 Comment *l*; *Beale* 683-684; *Goodrich and Scoles* 234; *Kingsley*, Remarriage 281; *Leflar* 536; *Stumberg* 285; *Taintor*, Marriage 626. But see Gibson v. Hughes, 192 F. Supp. 564 (S.D.N.Y. 1961), which involved a second marriage celebrated in French Morocco before a District of Columbia divorce dissolving the man's prior marriage had become final and where FRENCH law was applied, as the *lex loci celebrationis* and the *lex domicilii* of the spouses of the second marriage, to validate that union as a putative marriage, so as to entitle the surviving wife to compensation under a workmen's compensation act. For other devices sometimes used to validate the second marriage once the divorce becomes final, see *infra* s. 25-27. Cf. *Ehrenzweig*, Conflict 385.

124. Hendrich v. Anderson, 191 F.2d 242 (10 Cir. 1951) (applying Utah law); Oliver v. Oliver, 185 F.2d 429 (D.C. Cir. 1950); Ex parte Soucek, 101 F.2d 405 (7 Cir. 1939) (applying Wisconsin law); Sullivan v. Sullivan, 28 P.2d 914 (Cal. Sup. Ct. 1934); Scott v. Scott, 46 N.W.2d 627 (Neb. Sup. Ct. 1951); Pettit v. Pettit, 93 N.Y.S. 1001 (App. Div. 1905); Sherman v.

state of celebration[125] or of a third state.[126] Since the result was almost invariably the same under all laws involved, conflict of laws problems have rarely been raised.[127] This practice, therefore, is by no means to be regarded as an exception to the general conflicts rule of the *lex loci celebrationis*.

22. *Remarriage After Divorce: Validity of Divorce.* A remarriage after divorce may fail because the divorce decree is invalid or, though valid where granted, not recognised in the state in which the second marriage is challenged. Such may, in particular, be the case if the decree was rendered by a court without jurisdiction. The rather complex rules of American law governing this matter will not be examined here. It should be noted, however, that the

---

Sherman, 213 N.Y.S.2d 216 (Sup. Ct. 1961) (involving an interlocutory decree of annulment of the prior marriage); Atkeson v. Sovereign Camp, 216 P. 467 (Okl. Sup. Ct. 1923); In re Ott's Estate, 238 P.2d 269 (Or. Sup. Ct. 1951); Sanders v. Industrial Comm., 230 P. 1026 (Utah Sup. Ct. 1924); Heflinger v. Heflinger, 118 S.E. 316 (Va. Sup. Ct. App. 1923); Roddis v. Roddis, 118 N.W.2d 109 (Wis. Sup. Ct. 1962); In re Van Schaick's Estate, 40 N.W.2d 588 (Wis. Sup. Ct. 1949); State v. Grengs, 33 N.W.2d 248 (Wis. Sup. Ct. 1948); White v. White, 168 N.W. 704 (Wis. Sup. Ct. 1918).

125. Jones v. Jones, 5 Cal. Rptr. 803 (Dist. Ct. App. 1960) (Oregon divorce); Mosholder v. Industrial Comm., 160 N.E. 835 (Ill. Sup. Ct. 1928) (Wisconsin divorce); Johnson v. State Compensation Comm'r, 179 S.E. 814 (W.Va. Sup. Ct. App. 1935) (Virginia divorce). See also Smith v. Smith, 111 A.2d 531 (N.H. Sup. Ct. 1955) (Massachusetts divorce) where, however, the second marriage was held to be valid on another ground (*infra* at n. 168).

126. Marek v. Flemming, 192 F. Supp. 528 (S.D. Tex. 1961) (applying Arkansas law, which referred to Missouri law as the *lex loci celebrationis*; Missouri marriage after Virginia divorce which, under Virginia statute as interpreted by Virginia courts, was not final, held invalid on assumption that Missouri would follow that interpretation); Means v. Means, 104 P.2d 1066 (Cal. Dist. Ct. App. 1940) (remarriage in Arizona before Wisconsin divorce became final); Jordan v. Missouri & Kansas Teleph. Co., 116 S.W. 432 (Mo. Ct. App. 1909) (remarriage in New Jersey before New York decree annulling prior marriage became final); Earle v. Earle, 126 N.Y.S. 317 (App. Div. 1910) (remarriage in Italy, between New York domiciliaries, held void because FRENCH divorce decree dissolving prior marriage of one party had not been properly transcribed, as required by FRENCH law, and therefore was not effective). For other cases where, however, the second marriage was validated on other grounds (*infra* at n. 162, 168) once the divorce became final, see Henderson v. Henderson, 87 A.2d 403 (Md. Ct. App. 1952) (remarriage in Iowa before Virginia divorce became final), and La Plant v. La Plant, 111 A.2d 325 (N.H. Sup. Ct. 1955) (remarriage in Oklahoma before Massachusetts divorce became final).

127. One of the few cases in which the pertinent laws were found to differ is Gibson v. Hughes, 192 F. Supp. 564 (S.D.N.Y. 1961), where the foreign *lex loci celebrationis* was applied to sustain the second marriage (*supra* n. 123).

jurisdiction of American courts, in divorce as in other types of litigation, ultimately depends on the due process of law and the full faith and credit clauses of the Federal Constitution, as interpreted by the Supreme Court of the United States.[128] The relevant tests of constitutionally permissible jurisdiction include not only the necessary connection to the state of rendition (in divorce cases normally constituted by the domicile of at least one of the spouses in that state) but also certain requirements that the respondent was given proper notice of the proceeding and that he had a fair opportunity to be heard.[129] As a general principle, a judgment (given by an American court) which fails to satisfy those tests is void and open to collateral attack even in the state where it was rendered, and not entitled to recognition elsewhere in the United States.[130]

To a very large extent, however, the jurisdictional requirements for the validity and recognition of divorces are "neutralised" by other principles, mainly those of *res judicata* and estoppel, which in certain circumstances bar collateral attacks on invalid divorce decrees.[131] In practice, the effect is that many divorces which would otherwise be void for lack of jurisdiction are treated as valid. This is especially so when a divorce has been followed by remarriage, this being one of the main grounds for applying the doctrine of estoppel (*infra* s. 27).

23. *Prohibitions on Remarriage After Divorce.* Statutes in many of the United States limit the right of divorced persons to

128. The federal concept of jurisdiction must be distinguished from the question of the authority of the court under its own local law. The limitations imposed on the power of the court as a matter of local policy are additional to the minimum requirements for jurisdiction derived from the Federal Constitution. See generally: Restatement, before § 24 (p. 100-102) and § 92-93, 105 with Comments and Reporter's Notes; *Ehrenzweig,* Conflict 71; *Goodrich and Scoles* 101-102, 390-397; *Leflar* 34-39, 99-100, 187-188.

129. Specifically for jurisdiction in divorce see, for example, Restatement § 69-72 with Comments and Reporter's Notes; *Clark* 287-291; *Goodrich and Scoles* 255-258, 261-266; *Leflar* 539-547.

130. See Restatement, before § 24 (p. 100-101), § 69 Comment *a,* § 92 Comments *e, f, h* and *i; Clark* 295; *Leflar* 34, 184-185. The recognition of divorces granted in a foreign nation is governed by the laws of the different states; on these questions see, e.g., *Clark* 294-295; *Ehrenzweig,* Conflict 245-248.

131. On the role of the doctrine of *res judicata* in divorce cases see Restatement § 73 with Comment and Reporter's Note; *Clark* 291-294; *Goodrich and Scoles* 258-259; *Leflar* 541-543.

marry again, or confer power on the divorce court to impose such limitations.[132] Under most of these statutes both parties to a divorce are, or may be, forbidden to remarry (except to each other) within a stated time after the divorce is granted. Such bilateral prohibitions have sometimes been construed to imply that the prior marriage is not completely dissolved (*supra* s. 21). In what follows, however, it will be assumed that the divorce decree is final.

The policy basis of bilateral prohibitions against remarriage is in part similar to that underlying the system of interlocutory divorce decrees. The main purpose to be served by such restraints is apparently to discourage divorce and to promote reconciliation and, thereby, to protect existing marriages (the theory being that the desire to marry again is one of the prime motives for seeking divorce). It is also sought to avoid doubts as to the paternity of any child born by the wife within a short time after the divorce (*turbatio sanguinis*). Finally, as regards restrictions which are coterminous with the time allowed for appeal from the divorce decree, the rationale is a desire to prevent the complications which might arise from a second marriage in case the decree is reversed on appeal.

Another type of prohibition, known to a few states, is only directed against the remarriage of one of the parties to the divorce, usually the guilty party against whom the divorce was pronounced for a matrimonial offence. Such unilateral restrictions are imposed by way of punishment, discipline or example and have a penal connotation. Some of them apply, either for a term of years or permanently, to any remarriage by the party in fault. Other statutes only forbid the intermarriage of the guilty party to a divorce for adultery and his or her paramour, usually during the lifetime of the injured spouse.

Conflicts problems involving one or the other type of restriction are quite frequent in practice.[133] The most commonly occurring

132. See: *Clark* 405; *Kingsley*, Remarriage 280, 283-286; *Taintor*, Marriage to a Paramour; *Vernier* II 172-179; Note, 36 Va. L. Rev. 665-673 (1950).

133. For writings on these questions see: Restatement § 283 Comment *l* and Reporter's Note (p. 247); *Beale* 685-686, 692; *Clark* 405-406; *Ehrenzweig*, Conflict 265, 384-385, 387; *Goodrich and Scoles* 233-235; *Philip Johnson* 451-452; *Kingsley*, Remarriage 286-291; *Leflar* 536-537; *Stumberg* 284-285; *Taintor*, Marriage 624-626; *idem*, Marriage to a Paramour 890-898; Comments in 30 Marq. L. Rev. 108-116 (1946/47), 32 Marq. L. Rev. 205-212 (1948/49) and 33 Yale L.J. 426, 429-431 (1923/24); Note, 36 Va. L.

continued on page 48

situation is where a divorcee seeks to avoid a prohibition imposed by the divorce state by going into another state and remarrying there within the forbidden time, both parties to the new marriage being and intending to remain domiciled in the former state. Does the prohibition apply in such cases, so as to defeat the marriage?

In the majority of cases involving a bilateral prohibition, whether or not it had been evaded on purpose (and once it had been determined that the finality of the divorce decree was not affected), such prohibitions have not been thought to express a local policy strong enough to justify extraterritorial application. In consequence, where the marriage was valid under the *lex loci celebrationis* it has been upheld, whether it was challenged in the prohibiting state itself,[134] in the state of celebration,[135] or in a third state.[136]

---

continued from page 47
Rev. 665, 669-671 (1950). Cases are collected in Annots., 32 A.L.R. 1116 (1924) and 51 A.L.R. 325 (1927).

134. Horton v. Horton, 198 P. 1105 (Ariz. Sup. Ct. 1921); Mohn v. Tingley, 217 P. 733, 736 (Cal. Sup. Ct. 1923); In re Wood's Estate, 69 P. 900 (Cal. Sup. Ct. 1902); Loth v. Loth's Estate, 129 P. 827 (Colo. Sup. Ct. 1913); Griswold v. Griswold, 129 P. 560 (Colo. Ct. App. 1913); Farrell v. Farrell, 181 N.W. 12 (Iowa Sup. Ct. 1921); Dudley v. Dudley, 130 N.W. 785 (Iowa Sup. Ct. 1911); In re Kinkead's Estate, 57 N.W.2d 628, 632-635 (Minn. Sup. Ct. 1953); Hoagland v. Hoagland, 193 P. 843 (Wyo. Sup. Ct. 1920).

135. Wheelock v. Freiwald, 66 F.2d 694, 699-700 (8 Cir. 1933) (sitting in Missouri); Smiley v. Smiley, 448 S.W.2d 642, 645 (Ark. Sup. Ct. 1970); Criss v. Industrial Comm., 180 N.E. 572, 574 (Ill. Sup. Ct. 1932); Pickard v. Pickard, 45 N.W.2d 269 (Iowa Sup. Ct. 1950); Webster v. Modern Woodmen, 186 N.W. 659 (Iowa Sup. Ct. 1922); In re Ommang's Estate, 235 N.W. 529 (Minn. Sup. Ct. 1931); Olsen v. Olsen, 209 N.Y.S.2d 503 (Sup. Ct. 1960).

136. In re Sander's Estate, 305 P.2d 655 (Cal. Dist. Ct. App. 1957) (remarriage in Arizona after divorce in Oklahoma); In re Winder's Estate, 219 P.2d 18, 25-26 (Cal. Dist. Ct. App. 1950) (remarriage in Iowa after divorce in Colorado); People v. Woodley, 136 P. 312 (Cal. Dist. Ct. App. 1913) (remarriage in Oregon after divorce in Washington); Bauer v. Abrahams, 216 P. 259 (Colo. Sup. Ct. 1923) (remarriage in New Mexico after divorce in Kansas); Green v. McDowell, 242 S.W. 168 (Mo. Ct. App. 1922) (remarriage in Tennessee after divorce in Oklahoma); King v. Klemp, 57 A.2d 530 (N.J. Ch. 1947) (remarriage in New York after divorce in Kansas); In re Peart's Estate, 97 N.Y.S.2d 879 (App. Div. 1950) (remarriage in Maryland after divorce in Virginia); Goodwin v. Goodwin, 142 N.Y.S. 1102 (App. Div. 1913) (remarriage in Illinois after divorce in Colorado): Marzano v. Marzano, 154 N.Y.S.2d 507 (Sup. Ct. 1956) (remarriage in Virginia after divorce in Alabama); In re Anonymous, 237 N.Y.S.2d 5 (Surr. Ct. 1963) (remarriage in Mexico after divorce in Oregon); Garrett v. Chapman, 449 P.2d 856 (Or. Sup. Ct. 1969) (remarriage in Idaho after divorce in Montana); Fisch v. Marler, 97 P.2d 147, 151-152 (Wash. Sup. Ct. 1939) (remarriage in Montana

This tendency is even more pronounced in cases involving a unilateral prohibition running against the guilty party alone. Inhibitions of this type are usually narrowly construed and denied any extraterritorial effect because they are in the nature of a penalty.[137] In New York, for example, it was held in a long series of decisions that the local prohibition against remarriage by the guilty party to a divorce for adultery was inapplicable when the second marriage had occurred in another state, even if the parties went there for the sole purpose of evading the New York statute.[138]

In a sizeable minority of cases, nevertheless, the courts have

after divorce in Idaho). The reasons of these decisions are not always clear. In several cases the courts either construed the prohibitory statute as not purporting to have extraterritorial effect or found that it would not be given such effect by the *lex loci celebrationis*. Sometimes, however, the only reason given is that the prohibition "could" not have extraterritorial force, or that the policy of favouring marriage must prevail. Although such formulas do not specify the relevant law, the policy of the *lex fori* probably was the decisive factor; cf. *supra* at n. 98-99.

137. See for cases decided in the divorce state itself, where the prohibition had been imposed: Loughran v. Loughran, 292 U.S. 216 (1934) (applying District of Columbia law), noted in 48 Harv. L. Rev. 123 (1934/35) and 33 Mich. L. Rev. 438 (1934/35); Smith v. Goldsmith, 134 So. 651 (Ala. Sup. Ct. 1931); Bituminous Casualty Corp. v. Wacht, 66 S.E.2d 757 (Ga. Ct. App. 1951); Montgomery v. Gable, 7 S.E.2d 426 (Ga. Ct. App. 1940); Commonwealth v. Lane, 113 Mass. 458 (1873); Putnam v. Putnam, 8 Pick. 433 (Mass. Sup. Jud. Ct. 1829); Ex parte Crane, 136 N.W. 587 (Mich. Sup. Ct. 1912); Patterson v. Modern Woodmen, 95 A. 692, 697 (Vt. Sup. Ct. 1915); State v. Shattuck, 38 A. 81 (Vt. Sup. Ct. 1897); and the New York cases cited *infra* n. 138. *A fortiori*, the same applies where the question arises in other states. See for cases decided in the state of celebration of the second marriage: Wilson v. Holt, 3 So. 321, 328 (Ala. Sup. Ct. 1887); Fuller v. Fuller, 40 Ala. 301, 306 (1866); Phillips v. Madrid, 22 A. 114 (Me. Sup. Jud. Ct. 1891); Van Storch v. Griffin, 71 Pa. 240 (1872); Frame v. Thormann, 79 N.W. 39 (Wis. Sup. Ct. 1899), aff'd 176 U.S. 350 (1900). And see for cases decided in a third state: Dimpfel v. Wilson, 68 A.561 (Md. Ct. App. 1908) (remarriage in District of Columbia after divorce in New York); Stephenson v. Stephenson, 298 S.W.2d 36 (Tenn. Ct. App. 1956) (remarriage in Georgia after divorce in Alabama); Wingo v. Rudder, 120 S.W. 1073 (Tex. Civ. App. 1909) (remarriage in Georgia after divorce in Alabama).

138. A leading case is Van Voorhis v. Brintnall, 86 N.Y. 18 (1881). For other cases see: Fisher v. Fisher, 165 N.E. 460 (N.Y. Ct. App. 1929); Thorp v. Thorp, 90 N.Y. 602 (1882); Lieblein v. Charles Chips, Inc., 301 N.Y.S.2d 743 (App. Div. 1969); D'Arcangelo v. D'Arcangelo, 91 N.Y.S.2d 101 (Sup. Ct. 1949); Taegen v. Taegen, 61 N.Y.S.2d 869 (Sup. Ct. 1946), aff'd 72 N.Y.S.2d 402 (App. Div. 1947); Brooks v. Brooks, 38 N.Y.S.2d 224 (Sup. Ct. 1942); In re Newins' Will, 213 N.Y.S.2d 255, 261 (Surr. Ct. 1961); In re Singer's Estate, 138 N.Y.S.2d 740 (Surr. Ct. 1955); In re Green's Estate, 280 N.Y.S. 692, 695-696 (Surr. Ct. 1935).

held otherwise, refusing to recognise or to give effect to an out-of-state remarriage on the ground that it was contrary to (and in evasion of) a prohibition imposed by the state where the divorce had been pronounced and where the parties to the new marriage were and intended to (and did) remain domiciled. Several of these decisions rely on a marriage evasion statute forming part of the law of the domiciliary state.[139] In others, the violated prohibition was in itself held to indicate a distinctive public policy compelling an exception to the rule of the *lex loci celebrationis*. Most cases within this latter group involve a restriction applying equally to both parties to the divorce.[140] In a few states, however, the same position has been taken with regard to unilateral prohibitions, running against the marriage between the guilty party to the divorce and his or her accomplice in adultery.[141] Nearly all

139. For a case where such a statute was applied to enforce a bilateral prohibition on remarriage see Cummings v. United States, 34 F.2d 284 (D. C. Minn. 1929) (applying Wisconsin law). For cases involving a unilateral prohibition directed to the party against whom the divorce had been pronounced see: Gerrig v. Sneirson, 183 N.E.2d 131 (Mass. Sup. Jud. Ct. 1962); In re Van Bibber's Case, 179 N.E.2d 253, 259 (Mass. Sup. Jud. Ct. 1962); Wright v. Wright, 162 N.E. 894 (Mass. Sup. Jud. Ct. 1928); Witherington v. Eldredge, 162 N.E. 300 (Mass. Sup. Jud. Ct. 1928); Murphy v. Murphy, 144 N.E. 394 (Mass. Sup. Jud. Ct. 1924); Wheelock v. Wheelock, 154 A. 665 (Vt. Sup. Ct. 1931). In Massachusetts, an earlier marriage evasion statute was construed to be limited to cases where both parties knew of the impediment to their marriage in Massachusetts and, in going to another state to get married, acted with the purpose of evading the local law (cf. *supra* at n. 85). For a case where this requirement was held to be satisfied see Tyler v. Tyler, 48 N.E. 1075 (Mass. Sup. Jud. Ct. 1898). But see for cases where one of the spouses was found to be in good faith and where the statute therefore had no application: Whippen v. Whippen, 51 N.E. 174 (Mass. Sup. Jud. Ct. 1898); Commonwealth v. Lane, 113 Mass. 458 (1873).

140. Brand v. State, 6 So.2d 446 (Ala. Sup. Ct. 1941); Wilson v. Cook, 100 N.E. 222 (Ill. Sup. Ct. 1912); Lincoln v. Riley, 217 Ill. App. 571 (1920); Nehring v. Nehring, 164 Ill. App. 527 (1911); Peters v. Peters, 276 P.2d 302 (Kan. Sup. Ct. 1954), noted in 4 Kan. L. Rev. 122 (1955/56); Atkeson v. Sovereign Camp, 216 P. 467 (Okl. Sup. Ct. 1923); Harvey v. State, 238 P.862 (Okl. Crim. App. 1925); Wright v. Kroeger, 345 P.2d 809 (Or. Sup. Ct. 1959); In re Kienstra, 276 P. 294 (Wash. Sup. Ct. 1929); Knoll v. Knoll, 176 P. 22 (Wash. Sup. Ct. 1918); Lanham v. Lanham, 117 N.W. 787 (Wis. Sup. Ct. 1908).

141. Succession of Gabisso, 44 So. 438 (La. Sup. Ct. 1907); Williams v. Oates, 5 Ired. 535 (N.C. Sup. Ct. 1845); In re Stull's Estate, 39 A. 16 (Pa. Sup. Ct. 1898); Maurer v. Maurer, 60 A.2d 440 (Pa. Super. Ct. 1948); Pennegar v. State, 10 S.W. 305 (Tenn. Sup. Ct. 1889); Bennett v. Anderson, 101 S.W.2d 148 (Tenn. Ct. App. 1936); Newman v. Kimbrough, 59 S.W. 1061 (Tenn. Ch. App. 1900). For cases in which a marriage evasion statute was

cases in which a restraint on remarriage was held to require extraterritorial application have been decided by the courts of the divorce state itself. Only in some very few instances has the same result been reached by courts in other states.[142]

The problem is simpler in another group of cases, where the party who had remarried out of the divorce state in the teeth of a prohibition imposed by that state never was, or was no longer at the time of the remarriage, domiciled there, or where both parties to the new marriage intended to (and did) make their family domicile elsewhere. In these circumstances it is generally agreed that the prohibition must be disregarded and that the marriage must be upheld if it is valid by the *lex loci celebrationis.*[143] This

---

relied on to invalidate an out-of-state remarriage in defiance of a prohibition directed to the guilty party alone see the references *supra* n. 139.

142. People v. Steere, 151 N.W. 617 (Mich. Sup. Ct. 1915) (remarriage in Michigan, between parties at all times domiciled in Illinois, after divorce in Illinois; effect given to Illinois prohibition); Hall v. Industrial Comm., 162 N.W. 312 (Wis. Sup. Ct. 1917) (remarriage in Indiana, between Illinois domiciliaries who later came to live in Wisconsin, after Illinois divorce; effect given to Illinois prohibition, which was based on a policy similar to that of Wisconsin). Cf. Huard v. McTeigh, 232 P. 658 (Or. Sup. Ct. 1925) (remarriage in British Columbia, between Washington domiciliaries who later removed to Oregon, contrary to prohibition attendant on Washington divorce) where, however, the marriage was assumed to be invalid, not only by the law of the divorce state but also by the *lex loci celebrationis.* The decisions cited here must be distinguished from certain other cases in which the forum applied *its own* statute to invalidate a second marriage celebrated outside the divorce state, see *infra* n. 150-152.

143. Most cases so holding have been decided in the state of celebration of the second marriage or in a third state where the parties had made thei marital domicile. The Wisconsin case of Owen v. Owen, 190 N.W. 363 (Wi. Sup. Ct. 1922), is particularly illustrative. It involved a remarriage in Michigan in violation of a prohibitory statute of Illinois, where the divorce had been granted. In ignoring the prohibition and upholding the marriage the court distinguished its earlier decision in Hall v. Industrial Comm. (preceding note) where the same statute had been given extraterritorial effect, on the ground that in the instant case the divorcee was no longer domiciled in Illinois (but, together with the second spouse, in Wisconsin, the state of the forum) at the time of the remarriage. The *Owen* case was followed in Fitzgerald v. Fitzgerald, 246 N.W. 680 (Wis. Sup. Ct. 1933) (upholding a second marriage in Indiana, which was contrary to the same Illinois prohibition). Several of the cases cited *supra* n. 135-137 may also be explained on this footing, although it is not always clear whether or to what extent the result was affected by the fact that the domicile was outside the prohibiting state. See Smiley v. Smiley, 448 S.W.2d 642, 645 (Ark. Sup. Ct. 1970); King v. Klemp, 57 A.2d 530 (N.J. Ch. 1947); Garrett v. Chapman, 449 P.2d 856 (Or. Sup. Ct. 1969); Stephenson v. Stephenson, 298 S.W.2d 36 (Tenn. Ct. App. 1956); Wingo v.

continued on page 52

holds true even in those relatively few cases where the question has come before the courts of the divorce state itself and even if that state otherwise insisted on the extraterritorial force of its prohibition.[144] The reason is that, here, the restricting state is not considered to be sufficiently concerned with the relationship to warrant application of its invalidating rule (*supra* s. 14). It makes no difference if that state has a marriage evasion statute, since such statutes do not apply to parties domiciled or intending to make their domicile in another state.[145]

The validity of an out-of-state remarriage is generally not affected by such restrictions on the right to marry again as may exist in *states other than the divorce state,* in particular in the

---

continued from page 51

Rudder, 120 S.W. 1073 (Tex. Civ. App. 1909); Frame v. Thormann, 79 N.W. 39 (Wis. Sup. Ct. 1899). See also People v. Steere, 151 N.W. 617, 619 (Mich. Sup. Ct. 1915) (*dictum*), and In re Ommang's Estate, 235 N.W. 529 (Minn. Sup. Ct. 1931) (upholding second marriage in Minnesota against Wisconsin prohibitory statute), noted in 16 Minn. L. Rev. 172 (1931/32). In the last-cited case, where the parties were local residents at the time of the suit (though not at the time of the marriage) the court, in relying on the *lex loci celebrationis,* said (at 531) that "this majority rule applies with added force where the marriage is questioned in the state where it was performed and at a time when the parties thereto are residents of that state."

144. See for such cases (to be contrasted with those cited *supra* n. 140-141): Loughran v. Loughran, 292 U.S. 216, 224-225 (1934) (applying District of Columbia law); Nelson v. Nelson, 200 Ill. App. 584 (1916); Newman v. Kimbrough, 59 S.W. 1061, 1064 (Tenn. Ch. App. 1900) (*dictum*); Pierce v. Pierce, 109 P. 45 (Wash. Sup. Ct. 1910); State v. Fenn, 92 P. 417 (Wash. Sup. Ct. 1907); Willey v. Willey, 60 P. 145 (Wash. Sup. Ct. 1900).

145. Under a Georgia statute, for instance, a foreign marriage conforming to the requirements of the *lex loci celebrationis* was to be recognised as valid "provided the parties acted in good faith and did not go to the foreign state for the mere purpose of evading the provisions of the Georgia law." This condition was held to be satisfied, and the Georgia restriction on the right of remarriage after a local divorce therefore to be inapplicable, when the parties to an out-of-state marriage did not intend to reside in Georgia: Montgomery v. Gable, 7 S.E.2d 426 (Ga. Ct. App. 1940); see also Bituminous Casualty Corp. v. Wacht, 66 S.E.2d 757 (Ga. Ct. App. 1951). And see for cases in which the Massachusetts marriage evasion statute was brushed aside because the party prohibited from remarrying (after a local divorce pronounced against that party) was not, or did not intend to continue to be, domiciled in Massachusetts at the time of the out-of-state remarriage: Sweeney v. Kennard, 120 N.E.2d 910 (Mass. Sup. Jud. Ct. 1954); Atwood v. Atwood, 8 N.E.2d 916 (Mass. Sup. Jud. Ct. 1937); Palmer v. Palmer, 163 N.E. 879 (Mass. Sup. Jud. Ct. 1928), noted in 9 B.U.L. Rev. 215 (1929), 29 Colum. L. Rev. 359 (1929), 42 Harv. L. Rev. 701 (1928/29) and 27 Mich. L. Rev. 809 (1928/29). For an Illinois case involving an Indiana statute see Powell v. Powell, 207 Ill. App. 292 (1917).

state of celebration or in a third state where the parties are or later become domiciled.[146] Statutory provisions against remarriage, where existing, form part of the local law relating to divorces decreed by the local courts and are usually construed to be inseparable from that law and, therefore, to have no reference to divorces granted in another state on the basis of the law of that other state.[147] Hence, if the divorce state itself does not restrict the right of remarriage, or if a restriction imposed by that state is denied extraterritorial effect (generally or in the circumstances of the particular case), the marriage will not normally come within the reach of any such restriction. Illustrations are afforded by some New York cases where, following a New York divorce for adultery, the guilty party had married his paramour in Pennsylvania, a state which forbids such intermarriage during the life of the non-offending spouse. Both parties to the Pennsylvania marriage were and intended to remain New York domiciliaries. In sustaining the marriage the courts held, first, that the New York statute prohibiting the guilty party from marrying again had no extraterritorial effect and therefore did not come into consideration[148] and, secondly, as a matter of construction of the Pennsylvania statute just referred to, that that statute was inapplicable to parties divorced in another state.[149]

146. See *Clark* 406; *Kingsley*, Remarriage 287; *Taintor*, Marriage to a Paramour 895-898.

147. Smith v. Goldsmith, 134 So. 651 (Ala. Sup. Ct. 1931) (construing Tennessee statute); People v. Woodley, 136 P. 312, 315 (Cal. Dist. Ct. App. 1913) (construing Oregon statute); Pickard v. Pickard, 45 N.W.2d 269 (Iowa Sup. Ct. 1950); Webster v. Modern Woodmen, 186 N.W. 659 (Iowa Sup. Ct. 1922); Dudley v. Dudley, 130 N.W. 785 (Iowa Sup. Ct. 1911) (construing Nebraska statute); Sparks v. Sparks, 284 S.W. 1111, 1113 (Ky. Ct. App. 1926) (construing Indiana statute); Phillips v. Madrid, 22 A. 114 (Me. Sup. Jud. Ct. 1891); Dimpfel v. Wilson, 68 A. 561 (Md. Ct. App. 1908) (construing District of Columbia statute); In re Kinkead's Estate, 57 N.W.2d 628, 631-632 (Minn. Sup. Ct. 1953) (construing Iowa statute); Reger v. Reger, 293 S.W. 414, 424-426 (Mo. Sup. Ct. 1927) (construing Kansas statute); State v. Bentley, 53 A. 1068 (Vt. Sup. Ct. 1903) (construing New York statute); Fitzgerald v. Fitzgerald, 246 N.W. 680 (Wis. Sup. Ct. 1933).

148. See *supra* at n. 138.

149. Lembcke v. United States, 181 F.2d 703 (2 Cir. 1950) (sitting in New York); Petrello v. Petrello, 116 N.Y.S.2d 385 (Sup.Ct. 1952); In re Palmer's Estate, 79 N.Y.S.2d 404 (Surr. Ct. 1948), aff'd on other grounds 90 N.Y.S.2d 179 (App. Div. 1949); Stack v. Stack, 6 Dem. 280 (N.Y. Surr. Ct. 1887). The opposite conclusion had been reached by trial courts in Pennsylvania (*infra* n. 152), but the Circuit Court deciding the *Lembcke* case expressed its belief that the construction put upon the Pennsylvania

continued on page 54

The construction thus adopted by most American courts may be justified on the policy consideration that a state whose only contact with the marriage is that the ceremony was performed there does not have a significant interest in seeing its invalidating statute applied to the marriage.[150] Nevertheless, there is some doubt and dissent on this point.[151] As regards Pennsylvania, for instance, it seems very doubtful whether the construction placed upon its statute by the courts of New York would be accepted by the local courts.[152]

A somewhat related, but different, question is whether the

---

continued from page 53
statute in those cases would not be approved by the Supreme Court of Pennsylvania.

150. Cf. *supra* s. 6 and 10. A stronger case for applying such a statute of the state of celebration exists if the parties are and intend to remain domiciled in that state. This was the situation in In re Mayall's Naturalization, 154 F. Supp. 556 (E.D. Pa. 1957), where the court, disagreeing with the construction of the Pennsylvania statute adopted in Lembcke v. United States (preceding note), said (at 560) that it earnestly believed that a Pennsylvania court of statewide jurisdiction would apply the statute to all marriages in Pennsylvania between the guilty party to a divorce and his or her accomplice in adultery, regardless of where the divorce was obtained. Apparently, however, this conclusion was reached independently of the fact that the parties were Pennsylvania domiciliaries. In one Illinois case the local prohibitory statute was applied to invalidate a second marriage, between parties domiciled in Illinois, although not only the divorce but the remarriage, too, had occurred in other states neither of which restricted the right of divorcees to marry again: Stevens v. Stevens, 136 N.E. 785 (Ill. Sup. Ct. 1922) (remarriage in Indiana after divorce in Arkansas), noted in 17 Ill. L. Rev. 449 (1922/23).

151. In the past it was assumed, in particular, by Illinois courts that a prohibitory statute of the state of celebration would apply to an out-of-state remarriage of a person divorced in Illinois: Lincoln v. Riley, 217 Ill. App. 571, 575 (1920); Nehring v. Nehring, 164 Ill. App. 527, 530-531 (1911). Similarly, the corresponding Illinois statute was considered applicable to a local remarriage of a person divorced elsewhere: Mosholder v. Industrial Comm., 160 N.E. 835 (Ill. Sup. Ct. 1928) (alternative ground of decision); see also Criss v. Industrial Comm., 180 N.E. 572 (Ill. Sup. Ct. 1932), and Powell v. Powell, 207 Ill. App. 292 (1917), aff'd 118 N.E. 786 (Ill. Sup. Ct. 1918), where the local prohibition was found to have no application, but only because the divorce obtained in the other state was not for a cause mentioned in the Illinois statute. And see Stevens v. Stevens (preceding note) applying the local prohibition in circumstances where both divorce and remarriage were in other states.

152. In at least one decision by a Pennsylvania trial court the statute in question was applied to invalidate a local remarriage of a person divorced for adultery in New York: Kalmbacher v. Kalmbacher, 63 Pa. D. & C. 195 (Com. Pl. 1945). The opinion to the contrary held in Lembcke v. United States (*supra* n. 149) was, in its turn, disapproved in In re Mayall's Naturalization (*supra* n. 150).

extraterritorial application of a prohibition against remarriage *imposed by the divorce state* will be affected by the existence of an identical or similar prohibition in another state where the validity of a marriage, contracted out of the divorce state in defiance of its restriction, is challenged. The "affinity of policy" which may be disclosed by such identity or similarity of the statutes of the two states concerned has doubtless been a factor of importance in a few cases where a second marriage was invalidated by the forum on the strength of the statute of the divorce state.[153] It is indeed natural that the courts of a state should be more favourably disposed than otherwise towards enforcing and giving extraterritorial effect to the policy of another state when it coincides with, or is similar to, the local policy.

A special situation occurs, finally, where the state of celebration has a marriage evasion statute directed against marriages within the state in evasion of the law of another state (*supra* s. 8). Under statutes of this type, domiciliary prohibitions on remarriage after divorce, which in themselves were confined to marriages within the state of the domicile, have been given extraterritorial effect by way of *renvoi* (*supra* s. 16). Illustrations are afforded by certain New York cases where local domiciliaries, one of whom was forbidden to marry again by a New York divorce decree pronounced against him, had married in another state, for example in Massachusetts, which had a marriage evasion statute declaring the union to be void on the ground that it would be so held in New York if it had been celebrated there. The New York courts, directed by their conflicts rules to apply the *lex loci celebrationis* and accepting this reference back to their own law, held the marriage to be void, notwithstanding that the local prohibition otherwise only applied to marriages solemnised within the state.[154]

153. The best example is Hall v. Industrial Comm., 162 N.W. 312 (Wis. Sup. Ct. 1917), where the court, sitting in a third state, enforced a prohibitory statute of the divorce state (*supra* n. 142). In so doing the court (at 314) expressly invoked the similarity of the public policy declared by the foreign statute to the policy pursued by the corresponding local statute. For a case decided by a Pennsylvania trial court see Wagner v. Wagner, 58 Mont. Co. L. Rep. 18 (Com. Pl. 1941), where the facts were very similar to those in Kalmbacher v. Kalmbacher (preceding note) but where the court (at 23-24) relied on the New York rather than on the local prohibition, giving as reason that the public policies of the two states were identical.

154. Stolz v. N.Y. Central R.R. Co., 180 N.Y.S.2d 88 (App. Div. 1958), rev'd on other grounds 164 N.E.2d 849 (Ct. App. 1959); Canwright v. Canwright, 76 N.Y.S.2d 10 (App. Div. 1947); Beaudoin v. Beaudoin, 62 N.Y.S. 2d 920 (App. Div. 1946); La Rock v. La Rock, 85 N.Y.S.2d 654 (Sup. Ct.

continued on page 56

bab. Rules Supporting Second Marriage

24. *Presumption Favouring Latest Marriage.* American law recognises a presumption that the latest of successive marriages is valid.[155] This is a variant of the usual presumption that a marriage, once contracted, is valid and continues in force (*supra* s. 11). Although that presumption applies to all marriages, it engenders a conflict when there have been two or more successive marriages. This conflict is resolved in favour of the latest union. Thus, once it is proved that successive marriages have occurred, the presumption that the latest of them is valid prevails over, and reverses, the presumption as to the validity and continuance of any prior marriage. In the absence of sufficient evidence to the contrary, it will therefore be presumed that the prior union was invalid or that it had been dissolved, whether by the death of the other spouse or by divorce, at the time of the remarriage of one of the spouses.[156] The main policy basis for this rule is that it normally accords with and protects the expectations of the parties.

Like the general presumption in support of marriage, the presumption in favour of the latest union is predominantly considered one of the strongest known in law, to be rebutted only by cogent and conclusive evidence that the prior marriage subsisted at the time of the remarriage.[157] Nevertheless, different views have been voiced by courts and writers as to the intensity, as well as the

continued from page 55
1949); Boura v. Haskell, 43 N.Y.S.2d 877 (Sup. Ct. 1943). These decisions rely on marriage evasion statutes in Louisiana, Massachusetts and Vermont.

155. See *Clark* 67-70 with references. Cases on this presumption are collected in Annot., 14 A.L.R.2d 7 (1950).

156. Most cases involve the "presumption of divorce", which seems to be peculiar to American law. In several cases, however, a presumption that the prior marriage was invalid has been relied on (alone or as an alternative to the presumption that it no longer subsisted) to validate a second marriage. See, e.g., Williamson v. Williamson, 101 A.2d 871 (Del. Super. Ct. 1954); Schaffer v. Krestovnikow, 102 A. 246 (N.J. Ch. 1917); Apelbaum v. Apelbaum, 183 N.Y.S.2d 54 (App. Div. 1959).

157. For examples of cases containing language to this effect see: O'Rourke v. Merry Queen Transfer Corp., 370 F.2d 781, 783 (2 Cir. 1967) (New York law); Harsley v. United States, 187 F.2d 213 (D.C. Cir. 1951); Estes v. Merrill, 181 S.W. 136, 138 (Ark. Sup. Ct. 1915); Williamson v. Williamson, 101 A.2d 871 (Del. Super. Ct. 1954); Reed v. Reed, 43 S.E.2d 539, 542-543 (Ga. Sup. Ct. 1947); Mauldin v. Sunshine Mining Co., 97 P.2d 608, 612 (Idaho Sup. Ct. 1940); Whitman v. Whitman, 41 So.2d 22, 25 (Miss. Sup. Ct. 1949); Kopit v. Zilberszmidt, 35 N.Y.S.2d 558, 566-567 (Sup. Ct. 1942); Smith v. Smith, 131 P.2d 447 (Or. Sup. Ct. 1942); Troxel v. Jones, 322 S.W.2d 251, 257 (Tenn. Ct. App. 1958); Anderson v. Anderson, 240 P.2d 966 (Utah Sup. Ct.

detailed conditions of application, of the presumption.[158] These differences need not be examined here. It suffices to note that the presumption has been applied to uphold a later marriage in many cases where it seems highly improbable that the prior union had in fact ended.

In so far as a subsequent marriage is sustained on the strength of the presumption, the effect is to foreclose any conflict of laws question which might otherwise arise in cases involving foreign elements. As to the law governing the presumption itself, the prevailing view seems to be in favour of applying the *lex fori.*[159]

25. *Doctrine of Common Law Marriage.* This doctrine often comes into consideration when a second marriage, whether ceremonial or based on common law, is initially invalid because it admittedly occurred before the impediment resulting from a prior marriage was removed. The problem is whether a valid common law marriage automatically comes into existence, once the prior marriage (or the statutory period of a prohibition on remarriage) ends, if the parties continue to live together as man and wife after that time in a state authorising such marriages.[160]

In a substantial number of cases a negative answer has been given to this question, usually on the ground that a relationship which has begun meretriciously cannot ripen into a valid common law marriage unless it is proved that a new agreement of marriage has been explicitly made by the parties after the removal of the impediment (which is in practice nearly always impossible).[161] In

---

1952); Spradlin v. State Comp. Comm., 113 S.E.2d 832, 835 (W.Va. Sup. Ct.App. 1960).

158. See *Clark* 68-70 with references.

159. See Headen v. Pope & Talbot, 252 F.2d 739, 742-743 (3 Cir. 1958); Schmeizl v. Schmeizl, 42 A.2d 106 (Md. Ct. App. 1945); *Ehrenzweig*, Conflict 386. But see Derrell v. United States, 82 F.Supp. 18, 20-22 (E.D. Miss. 1949), apparently relying on Arkansas law as the *lex loci celebrationis* of the second marriage.

160. See *Clark* 51-54. The problem is analogous to that encountered when the parties have begun living together in a state which does not recognise common law marriages, but have later moved to or visited another state which does recognise them; see *Pålsson*, Marriage, s. 308-310. Cases on the present problem are collected in Annot., 104 A.L.R. 6 (1936). See also Note, 18 Minn. L.Rev. 86 (1933/34).

161. Tatum v. Tatum, 241 F.2d 401, 407-410 (9 Cir. 1957); Rittgers v. United States, 154 F.2d 768 (8 Cir. 1946); Lester v. Celebrezze, 221 F. Supp. 607 (E.D. Ark. 1963); Green v. Ribicoff, 201 F. Supp. 721 (S.D. Miss. 1961); Marek v. Flemming, 192 F. Supp. 528, 533 (S.D. Tex. 1961), vacated and remanded 295 F.2d 691 (5 Cir. 1961); Ponzi v. Ponzi, 321 P.2d 847 (Cal.

continued on page 58

another group of cases, however, the courts have found in favour of a valid common law marriage without requiring any further agreement or ceremony.[162] This conclusion has particularly often been reached when the parties, or at least one of them, had contracted the second marriage in good faith, being ignorant of the existence of the impediment.[163] Where this condition was fulfilled,

continued from page 57

Dist. Ct. App. 1958); Brown v. Sheridan, 64 S.E.2d 636 (Ga. Ct. App. 1951); Brinson v. Brinson, 96 So.2d 653 (La. Sup. Ct. 1957); In re Binger's Estate, 63 N.W.2d 784 (Neb. Sup. Ct. 1954); Seagriff v. Seagriff, 195 N.Y.S.2d 718 (Dom. Rel. Ct. 1960); Maiorana v. Salerno, 133 N.Y.S.2d 521 (Sup. Ct. 1954); Taegen v. Taegen, 61 N.Y.S.2d 869 (Sup. Ct. 1946), aff'd 72 N.Y.S.2d 402 App. Div. 1947); Blodgett v. Blodgett, 187 P. 340 (Wash. Sup. Ct. 1920); Hall v. Industrial Comm., 162 N.W. 312, 314 (Wis. Sup. Ct. 1917). Occasionally, the same position has been taken on the ground that the forum state would not recognise a common law marriage, even if validly created under the law of another state, between parties domiciled in the former state. See Metropolitan Life Ins. Co. v. Chase, 294 F.2d 500 (3 Cir. 1961) (sitting in New Jersey; refusing to recognise a common law marriage of local domiciliaries, which was alleged to have resulted from temporary visits to the District of Columbia made after the impediment to the marriage was removed); cf. *Pålsson*, Marriage, s. 299, 311.

162. A leading case adopting this view is Matthews v. Britton, 303 F. 2d 408 (D.C. Cir. 1962). For other examples see: Albina Engine and Machine Works v. O'Leary, 328 F.2d 877 (9 Cir. 1964), cert. denied 379 U.S. 817 (1964) (Oregon law); McVicker v. McVicker, 130 F.2d 837 (D.C. Cir. 1942); Walls v. Celebrezze, 215 F.Supp. 414 (S.D. Tex. 1963); Darling v. Dent, 100 S.W. 747 (Ark. Sup. Ct. 1907); Thomey v. Thomey, 181 P.2d 777 (Idaho Sup. Ct. 1947); Henderson v. Henderson, 87 A.2d 403 (Md. Ct. App. 1952) (District of Columbia law); Boltz v. Boltz, 92 N.E.2d 365 (Mass. Sup. Jud. Ct. 1950); In re Sokoloff's Estate, 2 N.Y.S.2d 602 (Surr. Ct. 1938); Olinghouse v. Olinghouse, 265 P.2d 711 (Okl. Sup. Ct. 1954); Holgate v. United Electric Rys., 133 A. 243 (R.I. Sup. Ct. 1926); Consolidated Underwriters v. Kelly, 15 S.W.2d 229 (Tex. Comm. App. 1929); Willey v. Willey, 60 P.145 (Wash. Sup. Ct. 1900) (California law). In some cases the courts have held the same way while still paying lip service to the requirement of a renewed exchange of consents, which was found on the slightest evidence. See, e.g., Schaffer v. Krestovnikow, 102 A. 246, 248 (N.J. Ch. 1917); Taylor v. Taylor, 71 N.Y.S. 411 (App. Div. 1901); In re Stauffer's Estate, 94 A.2d 726 (Pa. Sup. Ct. 1953). Cf. *Pålsson*, Marriage, s. 298, 308-309.

163. For decisions stressing the importance of this fact see: Parrella v. Parrella, 120 F.2d 728 (D.C. Cir. 1941); Metropolitan Life Ins. Co. v. Holding, 293 F. Supp. 854 (E.D. Va. 1968); Krug v. Krug, 296 So.2d 715 (Ala. Sup. Ct. 1974); King v. King, 114 So.2d 145 (Ala. Sup. Ct. 1959); Hackmeyer v. Hackmeyer, 106 So.2d 245 (Ala. Sup. Ct. 1958); Jones v. Jones, 161 So. 836 (Fla. Sup. Ct. 1935); In re Walls' Estate, 99 N.W.2d 599 (Mich. Sup. Ct. 1959); Hess v. Pettigrew, 247 N.W. 90 (Mich. Sup. Ct. 1933); Sims v. Sims, 85 So. 73 (Miss. Sup. Ct. 1920); In re Haffner's Estate, 172 N.E. 483 (N.Y. Ct. App. 1930); Sorensen v. Sorensen, 220 N.Y.S. 242 (App. Div. 1927); Mortensen v. Mortensen, 225 N.Y.S.2d 323 (Sup. Ct. 1962) (Georgia law);

a valid marriage has occasionally even been held to result, once the impediment was removed, from continued marital conduct in a state which had abolished common law marriages by statute.[164] In most cases the fact paving the way to the creation of a common law marriage was that the other spouse in the prior marriage died or that a divorce was granted or became final after the remarriage. The same device has been used, however, when the subsequent event removing the obstacle to the second marriage was the expiry of a statutory prohibition on remarriage after divorce.[165]

In a few states the validation of a subsequent marriage, in circumstances substantially similar to those in which the doctrine of common law marriage has been relied on in other states, is assured by statute.[166] The relevant Massachusetts statute, for instance, provides that a second, initially bigamous, marriage becomes valid from the time when the prior union is dissolved, if it was entered into by one of the parties in good faith and if the parties live together as husband and wife and continue to do so after the removal of the impediment.[167] This statute (or its predecessor) has been invoked, both by Massachusetts and by other courts, in many cases where a marriage of Massachusetts domiciliaries had been celebrated in another state (which had no similar statute) after a Massachusetts divorce of one of the parties, but before the decree became final,[168]

Skinner v. Skinner, 150 N.Y.S.2d 739 (Sup. Ct. 1956) (District of Columbia and Pennsylvania law); Johnson v. Wolford, 157 N.E. 385 (Ohio Sup. Ct. 1927); In re Dearborn's Estate, 2 P.2d 93 (Okl. Sup. Ct. 1931); Troxel v. Jones, 322 S.W.2d 251, 256-257 (Tenn. Ct. App. 1958) (Michigan law); Gorman v. Gorman, 166 S.W.123 (Tex. Civ. App. 1914); In re Gallagher's Estate, 213 P.2d 621 (Wash. Sup. Ct. 1950) (Michigan law).

164. Reger v. Reger, 177 N.E.2d 901 (Ind. Sup. Ct. 1961).

165. E.g., Mock v. Chaney, 87 P. 538 (Colo. Sup. Ct. 1906); Harper v. Atlanta & W.P.R. Co., 125 S.E. 885 (Ga. Ct. App. 1924); Lee v. Lee, 130 N.W. 128 (Iowa Sup. Ct. 1911); Weisel v. National Transp. Co., 218 N.Y.S. 2d 725 (App. Div. 1961) (Florida law); In re Crandall's Estate, 212 N.Y.S. 210 (App. Div. 1925); Harvey v. State, 238 P. 862 (Okl. Crim. App. 1925).

166. Cases on this type of statute are collected in Annot., 95 A.L.R. 1292 (1935).

167. Mass. Gen. Laws, c. 207 § 6. This statute has been liberally construed; see, besides the cases cited *infra* n. 168-169 and 171, Hopkins v. Hopkins, 192 N.E. 145 (Mass. Sup. Jud. Ct. 1934).

168. Fraser v. Fraser, 147 N.E.2d 165 (Mass. Sup. Jud. Ct. 1958) (Rhode Island marriage); Vital v. Vital, 65 N.E.2d 205 (Mass. Sup. Jud. Ct. 1946) (do.); Gardner v. Gardner, 122 N.E. 308 (Mass. Sup. Jud. Ct. 1919) (New York marriage); Smith v. Smith, 111 A.2d 531 (N.H. Sup. Ct. 1955) (New Hampshire marriage); La Plant v. La Plant, 111 A.2d 325 (N.H. Sup. Ct. 1955) (Oklahoma marriage). And see for a similar decision based on a corres-

continued on page 60

or while the divorced party was forbidden to marry again.[169] Provided that one of the spouses was in good faith and that the other requirements of the statute in question are satisfied, a foreign marriage is validated even if it would otherwise come within the terms of the Massachusetts marriage evasion statute, the effect of which is "neutralised" to that extent.[170] In a few cases, decided by courts outside Massachusetts, the validating statute has been given even wider extraterritorial reach. In those cases the statute was applied, although the parties had not only married outside Massachusetts but had left that state permanently and become domiciled elsewhere (in the state of the respective forum) when the Massachusetts divorce became final.[171] The better view, however, which has been adopted in other cases, including one Massachusetts decision, seems to be that the statute is ineffective to validate the marriage in such circumstances and that it only applies if the parties live together as man and wife in Massachusetts at the time when the invalidating flaw disappears.[172]

continued from page 59
ponding statute in Wisconsin, Hoffman v. Hoffman, 7 N.W.2d 428 (Wis. Sup. Ct. 1943) (Illinois marriage).

169. An older case held that the statute was inapplicable to a marriage contravening a prohibition on remarriage, as distinct from a still subsisting prior marriage: Wright v. Wright, 162 N.E. 894 (Mass. Sup. Jud. Ct. 1928). But this decision can no longer stand; see Vital v. Vital (preceding note) and In re Van Bibber's Case, 179 N.E.2d 253 (Mass. Sup. Jud. Ct. 1962) (applying the statute to validate a marriage in New Hampshire, entered into within the prohibited time of two years from the husband's Massachusetts divorce).

170. Cf. *supra* n. 139. The crucial question has often been whether the non-divorced party could properly be said to have been in good faith as to the lawfulness of an out-of-state marriage contracted in evasion of the law of the domicile. For cases where, in contrast to those cited *supra* n. 168-169, this question was answered in the negative see, e.g., Fraser v. Fraser, 133 N.E. 2d 236 (Mass. Sup. Jud. Ct. 1956); Levanosky v. Levanosky, 42 N.E.2d 561 (Mass. Sup. Jud. Ct. 1942).

171. Arcand v. Flemming, 185 F. Supp. 22 (D.C. Conn. 1960), extending the statute to a Connecticut marriage (celebrated at a time when the husband's Massachusetts divorce was not yet final) the parties to which remained in Connecticut after the marriage and had no subsequent connection with Massachusetts (but this decision was rendered on a postulation of what a Connecticut state court would do, in the absence of any applicable local precedent, and has since been supplanted, as a statement of Connecticut law on the subject, by the decision to the contrary cited *infra* n. 172). For a similar decision in New York see Russo v. Art Steel Co., 251 N.Y.S.2d 238 (App. Div. 1964), involving a New York marriage between parties living in that state.

172. See Commonwealth v. Stevens, 82 N.E. 33 (Mass. Sup. Jud. Ct. 1907), where the court refused to apply the statute to validate a Georgia marriage

26. *Retroactive Operation of Final Divorce Decree.* A second marriage entered into in reliance on an interlocutory divorce decree, which has only been made final after the remarriage, may sometimes be "saved" by giving the final decree retroactive effect from the date mentioned in the decree (*nunc pro tunc* orders). Statutes authorising the divorce court to make such orders exist in a few states which have adopted a system of interlocutory divorce decrees of the type requiring a separate final decree to end the marriage.[173] In California, for example, the relevant statute provides that the court, on the motion of either party or upon its own motion, may cause a final judgment to be entered granting the divorce "as of the date when the same could have been given or made by the court if applied for", that is to say, as of the time of the expiry of the minimum period which must have elapsed from the grant of the interlocutory decree.[174] This power vests in the court where "by mistake, negligence or inadvertence" the final decree has been delayed beyond that date. The typical situation for which this provision creates a remedy seems to be where the parties to the divorce were ignorant of the need for taking further action after the first decree, believing that it would automatically dissolve their marriage after the lapse of the prescribed interlocutory period. If the parties have, or if one of them has, married again on the strength of that belief, a subsequent *nunc pro tunc* decree operates to validate the remarriage retroactively, provided of course that it was celebrated after the day to which the decree relates back.[175] The desire to achieve such validation seems indeed to be the main rationale of statutes permitting this type of order to be made.

A second marriage so validated by the divorce state will normally be recognised everywhere in the United States. The simplest case is where the remarriage occurred in the divorce state itself and

(celebrated before the husband's Massachusetts divorce became final) on the ground that the parties had moved to Georgia and continued to reside there until long after the impediment was removed. The fact that the parties had later returned to live in Massachusetts was treated as immaterial. For other decisions taking the same view see: Parker v. Parker, 270 A.2d 94 (Conn. Super. Ct. 1970) (involving facts indistinguishable from those of the *Arcand* case cited in the preceding note and expressly overruling the decision in that case); Fowler v. Fowler, 79 A.2d 24 (N.H. Sup. Ct. 1951).

173. See Restatement § 283, Reporter's Note on Comment *l* (p. 246-247).

174. CC § 4515 (formerly § 133). This provision has recently been changed, and the wording cited in the text is no longer that in force today.

175. Cases on this aspect of divorce decrees entered *nunc pro tunc* are collected in Annot., 19 A.L.R.3d 648, 678-680 (1968).

where, in consequence, the *lex loci celebrationis* governing capacity to marry coincides with the law on which the *nunc pro tunc* decree is based.[176] In this situation the recognition by other states that the decree has had the effect of validating the marriage does not raise any question of the extraterritorial reach of the decree.[177] The position is more doubtful where the second marriage was celebrated in another state, which may be that of the forum or a third state. In part the problems encountered here have been approached in terms of constitutional law, as a question of the right of the *nunc pro tunc* state to exercise extraterritorial control over the marital status, or of the right of other states to oppose what in their eyes may amount to an encroachment on their legislative power.[178] It seems very doubtful, however, whether these problems are governed by any provision, in particular the full faith and credit clause, of the Federal Constitution. In any event the policy of validation, which operates in favour of sustaining the second marriage, has prevailed here too, and seems likely to do so in most cases.[179] Nevertheless, there is some dissent and some uncertainty, both as to the principle itself and as to its scope and limits.[180]

176. For cases sustaining the second marriage in such circumstances see: Macedo v. Macedo, 84 P.2d 552 (Cal. Dist. Ct. App. 1938); Bannister v. Bannister, 29 A.2d 287 (Md. Ct. App. 1942), noted in 7 Md. L. Rev. 254 (1942/43); In re Kelley's Estate, 310 P.2d 328 (Or. Sup. Ct. 1957).

177. It does not seem to make any difference if the remarrying party is domiciled elsewhere at the time when the divorce is made final by the *nunc pro tunc* decree. In countries where capacity to marry is tested by the law of the domicile, by contrast, this fact may be of vital importance; cf. *infra* at n. 181 and s. 57.

178. See Graves v. Carter, 61 S.E.2d 282, 283 (Ga. Sup. Ct. 1950), and the dissenting opinion by Henriod, J., in Cahoon v. Pelton, 342 P.2d 94, 101-102 (Utah Sup. Ct. 1959).

179. Shippee v. Shippee, 66 A.2d 77 (N.H. Sup. Ct. 1949); Cahoon v. Pelton, 342 P.2d 94 (Utah Sup. Ct. 1959); Matter of Estate of Storer, 544 P.2d 95 (Wash. Ct. App. 1976).

180. In Graves v. Carter, 61 S.E.2d 282 (Ga. Sup. Ct. 1950), H had remarried in Georgia after a divorce from W(1) in California which was not made final *nunc pro tunc* until after the death of W(2). This decree was held ineffective to validate the second marriage so as to render void a will made by W(2) prior to the celebration of that union, because the retroactive effect of a *nunc pro tunc* order could not alter otherwise vested rights arising before the entry of the order (*contra*: Matter of Estate of Storer, *supra* n. 179). See also the restriction placed on the ruling in Cahoon v. Pelton, 342 P.2d 94 (Utah Sup. Ct. 1959), by Crockett, C.J. (at 100-101), and the dissenting opinion in that case by Henriod, J. (at 101-102). An Oregon curative statute of a type somewhat different from, but analogous to, that considered here was

Courts and writers in other common law countries, when confronted with similar problems, tend to emphasise the factor of domicile, in particular the question of whether the remarrying party was still domiciled in the country of the divorce court at the time when a retrospective decree or statute came into force in that country.[181] By contrast, there is no indication that this factor should have carried weight in the American cases. This difference underlines the considerably less significant part assigned in the United States, as compared with other common law countries, to the law of the domicile in determining capacity to marry.

27. *Estoppel from Attacking Defective Divorce.* The principle of estoppel has been extensively applied as a means of barring attacks on invalid divorce decrees, especially on decrees granted by a foreign court without jurisdiction.[182] Generally speaking, this principle turns on the conduct of the parties when or after the divorce was obtained. The idea is that a person will not be heard to say that the decree is ineffective if to assert so is inconsistent with a position he has previously taken. This consideration applies with particular force when new relationships, which have been formed in reliance on the divorce, would be upset by holding it invalid. The fact that a defective divorce decree has been followed by remarriage is therefore of special importance and appears to be the ground most frequently relied on to raise an estoppel against collateral attacks on such decrees.

An estoppel lies, in the first place, against the spouse who has procured the divorce. At least as a rule, that spouse will be precluded from contesting the validity of the decree in subsequent proceedings, for example in order to escape obligations under a

---

denied extraterritorial effect in Jones v. Jones, 5 Cal. Rptr. 803, 808 (Dist. Ct. App. 1960).

181. See the CANADIAN case of Ambrose v. Ambrose (1961), 25 D.L.R. (2d) 1 (B.C.C.A.), considered *infra* at n. 451-455.

182. See: Restatement § 74 with Comment and Reporter's Note; *Clark* 295-314; *Goodrich and Scoles* 259-260; *Harper,* The Validity of Void Divorces: 79 U. Pa. L. Rev. 158-184 (1930/31); *Jacobs,* Attack on Decrees of Divorce: 34 Mich. L. Rev. 749-808, 959-978 (1936); *Leflar* 548-550; *Rosenberg,* How Void Is a Void Decree, or The Estoppel Effect of Invalid Divorce Decrees: 8 Fam. L. Q. 207-224 (1974); *Stumberg* 304-307; *Weiss,* A Flight on the Fantasy of Estoppel in Foreign Divorce: 50 Colum. L. Rev. 409-432 (1950). Cases are collected in Annots., 109 A.L.R. 1018 (1937), 122 A.L.R. 1321 (1939), 140 A.L.R. 914 (1942), 153 A.L.R. 941 (1944) and 175 A.L.R. 538 (1948).

second marriage.[183] The same holds true of the other spouse if he or she has appeared or otherwise participated in the divorce proceedings or accepted some benefit (such as alimony) under the decree or, without valid reason, waited an unreasonably long time to challenge it.[184] Above all, that spouse will be estopped from attacking the decree if he or she has chosen to treat it as valid by marrying again.[185] Opinion is more divided as to the position of persons who were not parties to the divorce proceedings.[186] The usual situation is where the second spouse of one of the divorced parties attempts to question the divorce. Many cases hold that the second spouse is not permitted to do so, especially if he or she was active by inducing or aiding the other party to secure the divorce or otherwise contracted the marriage with knowledge of the circumstances in which the divorce was obtained.[187] For our purpose it is not necessary to go into further detail. It must only be noted that the application of the principle varies from state

183. Rabourn v. Rabourn, 385 P.2d 581 (Alaska Sup. Ct. 1963); Unruh v. Industrial Comm., 301 P.2d 1029 (Ariz. Sup. Ct. 1956); Rediker v. Rediker, 221 P.2d 1, 6-8 (Cal. Sup. Ct. 1950); Hensgen v. Silberman, 197 P.2d 356 (Cal. Dist. Ct. App. 1948); Krause v. Krause, 26 N.E.2d 290 (N.Y. Ct. App. 1940); Brown v. Brown, 272 N.Y.S. 877 (App. Div. 1934), aff'd 195 N.E. 186 (N.Y. Ct. App. 1935). In all these cases the moving party in the divorce proceedings had himself relied on the decree by marrying again. An estoppel also lies if that party seeks to reap some other advantage from denying the validity of the decree, for example by claiming a surviving spouse's share in the deceased respondent's estate. See, e.g., Curry v. Curry, 79 F.2d 172 (D.C. Cir. 1935); Starbuck v. Starbuck, 66 N.E. 193 (N.Y. Ct. App. 1903); In re Robottom's Estate, 288 N.Y.S. 397 (App. Div. 1936); Scoufos v. Fuller, 280 P.2d 720 (Okl. Sup. Ct. 1954).

184. In re Shank's Estate, 316 P.2d 710 (Cal. Dist. Ct. App. 1957); Lanigan v. Lanigan, 78 So.2d 92 (Fla. Sup. Ct. 1955); Dennis v. Dennis, 147 N.E.2d 828 (Mass. Sup. Jud. Ct. 1958); Langewald v. Langewald, 125 N.E. 566 (Mass. Sup. Jud. Ct. 1920).

185. E.g., Bruguiere v. Bruguiere, 155 P. 988 (Cal. Sup. Ct. 1916); Reichert v. Appel, 74 So.2d 674 (Fla. Sup. Ct. 1954); Varap v. Varap, 222 N.E.2d 77 (Ill. App. Ct. 1966); Parmelee v. Hutchins, 131 N.E. 443 (Mass. Sup. Jud. Ct. 1921); Marvin v. Foster, 63 N.W. 484 (Minn. Sup. Ct. 1895); Carbulon v. Carbulon, 57 N.E.2d 59 (N.Y. Ct. App. 1944); Packer v. Packer, 179 N.Y.S.2d 801 (App. Div. 1958).

186. See Restatement § 74 Comment *b*.

187. E.g., Goodloe v. Hawk, 113 F.2d 753 (D.C. Cir. 1940); Bowen v. Finke, 34 F. Supp. 235 (D.D.C. 1940); Spellens v. Spellens, 317 P.2d 613 (Cal. Sup. Ct. 1957); Dietrich v. Dietrich, 261 P.2d 269 (Cal. Sup. Ct. 1953); Gilb v. Gilb, 339 P.2d 176 (Cal. Dist. Ct. App. 1959); Smith v. Smith, 320 P.2d 100 (Cal. Dist. Ct. App. 1958); Apelbaum v. Apelbaum, 183 N.Y.S.2d 54 (App. Div. 1959); Sorensen v. Sorensen, 220 N.Y.S. 242 (App. Div. 1927); Kaufman v. Kaufman, 163 N.Y.S. 566 (App. Div. 1917).

to state and that controversies and conflicts of authority exist on several points, sometimes even within a single state.[188] Therefore it is not possible to formulate hard-and-fast rules.[189]

Most cases in which the doctrine of estoppel has been invoked by the courts involve a divorce decree which was invalid for lack of jurisdiction.[190] The doctrine has also been applied, however, in cases where the divorce was not final at the time of the remarriage.[191] Technically, an estoppel does not operate to cure any defect that may vitiate the divorce, but only to prevent one or more particular persons from setting up its invalidity. Other persons, who had nothing to do with the divorce and who have in no way taken advantage of it, are not affected and may still question the decree, if they are otherwise entitled to do so. Nevertheless, for most practical purposes the effect is nearly always the same as if the divorce was validated.[192] In so far as a divorce is immune from attack when it has been followed by remarriage by one or both of the parties, the second marriage, while remaining invalid in theory, will prevail over the first. It is thus recognised that the prior marriage has ended *de facto*, although not in accordance with current legal requirements, and that the legal position must be adjusted to this fact. It will be appreciated that the function of the principle of estoppel in this connection is closely analogous to that of the presumption in favour of the latest of several marriages, namely, to protect the legitimate expectations of the parties (*supra* s. 24).

bb. *Other Requirements or Impediments*

28. *Consent of Parties.* The decisions on the choice of law governing the validity of a marriage which is alleged to be void or voidable on some ground vitiating the true consent of the parties, such as duress, fraud, mistake or insanity, present a rather confused picture. Often, it seems, such issues are dealt with as questions of fact not susceptible of giving rise to conflicts problems, or are not

188. See, for instance, for the confusion presented by the New York cases *Clark* 299-302; *Rosenberg* (*supra* n. 182) 213-219.

189. Cf. the loosely formulated black-letter-rule of the Restatement § 74: "A person may be precluded from attacking the validity of a foreign divorce decree if, under the circumstances, it would be inequitable for him to do so".

190. See the examples given *supra* n. 183-185, 187.

191. Spellens v. Spellens, 317 P.2d 613, 619-620 (Cal. Sup. Ct. 1957); Smith v. Smith, 320 P.2d 100 (Cal. Dist. Ct. App. 1958).

192. See *Jacobs* (*supra* n. 182) 759.

properly distinguished from the problem of jurisdiction.[193] This approach, which in effect favours the application of the *lex fori,* may be unobjectionable as long as the laws involved are virtually uniform in substantive content. In fact, however, differences of practical significance exist among the laws of the United States, for example as to what constitutes fraud as a ground for annulment of a marriage or what defences are available in an action based on this ground.[194]

In so far as the courts have expressed an opinion on the applicable law, different views have been adopted. In one group of cases reliance has been placed on the *lex loci celebrationis,* in accordance with the "orthodox" rule. Most of these cases concern fraud and/or duress, which are the most frequently pleaded grounds of annulment within the present category.[195] A few other decisions endorsing the same conflicts rule involve marriages claimed to be invalid for reasons of sham because they were entered into in jest or for a limited purpose (for example in order to legitimise a child) on the understanding that no cohabitation was to occur and that none of the usual incidents of marriage were to be assumed.[196] Apparently, however, the result reached in all these cases, whether a decree of annulment was denied or granted, would have been the same under the *lex fori* coinciding with the *lex domicilii* of both parties.

A number of other decisions expressly rely on the *lex fori,* held to be applicable either in that capacity or *qua* the law of the

193. Cf. *Ehrenzweig,* Conflict 381-382.

194. For a survey and critical analysis of the grounds on which a marriage may be invalidated for lack of mutual consent in American law see *Clark* 94-118.

195. Nullity decree *granted*: Osborne v. Osborne, 134 A.2d 438 (D.C. Mun. Ct. App. 1957); Damaskinos v. Damaskinos, 89 N.E.2d 766 (Mass. Sup. Jud. Ct. 1950). Decree *denied*: McConnell v. McConnell, 99 F. Supp. 493 (D.D.C. 1951); Worthington v. Worthington, 352 S.W.2d 80 (Ark. Sup. Ct. 1961); Riedl v. Riedl, 153 A.2d 639 (D.C. Mun. Ct. App. 1959); Levy v. Levy, 34 N.E.2d 650 (Mass. Sup. Jud. Ct. 1941); Hanson v. Hanson, 191 N.E. 673 (Mass. Sup. Jud. Ct. 1934); Jewett v. Jewett, 175 A.2d 141 (Pa. Super. Ct. 1961); Wells v. Talham, 194 N.W. 36 (Wis. Sup. Ct. 1923). See *Clark* 107-108.

196. Schibi v. Schibi, 69 A.2d 831 (Conn. Sup. Ct. Err. 1949) (New York marriage of Connecticut domiciliaries, entered into solely "to give the child a name", held valid under New York law); Davis v. Davis, 175 A. 574 (Conn. Sup. Ct. Err. 1934) (New York marriage of Connecticut domiciliaries held void under New York law because entered into in jest, as the result of a dare). For another case involving a sham marriage which was upheld on the strength of the *lex loci celebrationis,* see *infra* n. 203.

common domicile of the parties. In one of these cases the marriage was annulled for fraud, although the ground invoked was assumed to be insufficient under the *lex loci celebrationis.*[197] Conversely, in a few other fraud cases the court refused a decree in accordance with its own law, although a ground for annulment probably existed under the *lex loci celebrationis.*[198] It is hard to see any tenable distinction between the decisions relying on the *lex fori,* on the one hand, and those holding annulment for fraud to be governed by the *lex loci celebrationis,* on the other. A similar confusion exists in cases involving insanity or other forms of mental incompetence as grounds for annulment.[199]

In a special class, finally, are cases concerning sham marriages entered into as a means of circumventing United States immigration laws.[200] In these cases an alien and an American citizen had gone through a marriage ceremony for the sole purpose of securing the former party's entry into, or of preventing his deportation from,

197. Lederkremer v. Lederkremer, 18 N.Y.S.2d 725 (Sup. Ct. 1940).

198. Anonymous v. Anonymous, 85 A.2d 706, 715-716 (Del. Super. Ct. 1951), aff'd on other grounds *sub nom.* Du Pont v. Du Pont, 90 A.2d 468, 473 (Del. Sup. Ct. 1952), cert. denied 344 U.S. 836 (1952). In this case, which involved a New York marriage and where the matrimonial domicile was established in Delaware, the court below, while reserving its attitude with regard to a marriage void where contracted, took the view that the annulment of a marriage which was merely voidable under the *lex loci celebrationis* must be governed by the *lex fori.* The Supreme Court of Delaware rejected this distinction and held that the *lex fori* applied in either case, the reason being that jurisdiction for annulment was exclusively statutory and that the court therefore lacked power to give a decree otherwise than in accordance with the grounds set forth in the relevant statute of the *lex fori.* For other cases in which a decree was refused on the forum's own law see: Samluk v. Gorecki, 265 A.2d 46 (Del. Super. Ct. 1970); Lyon v. Lyon, 82 N.E. 850 (Ill. Sup. Ct. 1907); Chipman v. Johnston, 130 N.E. 65 (Mass. Sup. Jud. Ct. 1921); Capasso v. Colonna, 122 A. 378 (N.J. Ch. 1923), aff'd 124 A. 760 (N.J. Ct. Err. App. 1924); Lyannes v. Lyannes, 177 N.W. 683, 689 (Wis. Sup. Ct. 1920).

199. For decisions relying on the *lex loci celebrationis* see: Henderson v. Ressor, 178 S.W. 175 (Mo. Sup. Ct. 1915), writ of error dismissed 248 U.S. 536 (1918); Storf v. Papalia, 46 A.2d 907 (N.J. Ch. 1946); In re Reeves' Estate, 7 S.W.2d 683 (Tex. Civ. App. 1928); In re Gallagher's Estate, 213 P.2d 621, 624-627 (Wash. Sup. Ct. 1950); Kitzman v. Kitzman, 166 N.W. 789 (Wis. Sup. Ct. 1918). For cases where preference was given to the *lex fori et domicilii* see: Beddow v. Beddow, 257 S.W.2d 45 (Ky. Ct. App. 1952); Davis v. Seller, 108 N.E.2d 656 (Mass. Sup. Jud. Ct. 1952); True v. Ranney, 21 N.H. 52, 53 Am. Dec. 164 (1850); Johnson v. Johnson, 104 N.W.2d 8 (N.D. Sup. Ct. 1960); First National Bank v. North Dakota Work. Comp. B., 68 N.W.2d 661 (N.D. Sup. Ct. 1955).

200. See *Clark* 116-118; *Ehrenzweig and Jayme* 159. Cf. on proxy marriages *Pålsson*, Marriage, s. 315 n. 180.

the United States. It had been expressly agreed that the parties would never live together as man and wife, and there was no consummation. Such unions have usually come in issue in criminal proceedings brought against the parties (or against a lawyer who had arranged the marriage) who, when charged with false representation of marital status to the immigration authorities, defended on the ground that the marriage was valid under the *lex loci celebrationis* and that, therefore, no misrepresentation had been made.

The decisions in these cases are in disagreement and little conclusive as to questions of choice of law. No less than three different approaches have been adopted by the courts. In one case, where the marriage ceremony had been performed in New Jersey, it was held that the parties were never married at all, since they had not assented to enter into the marriage relation as it is ordinarily understood.[201] In the opinion of the court, this was the law in New Jersey as well as elsewhere, so that no choice of law had to be made. In a subsequent case, which is the leading authority on the matter, the Supreme Court of the United States found it unnecessary to pass on the validity of the marriages alleged in that case, but held that a marriage within the meaning of the applicable federal statute had not occurred.[202] The difference from the previous case is apparently that the decision of the Supreme Court is confined to the particular incidents of marriage envisaged by the relevant immigration statute and that it leaves the question open for other purposes. In a still later case, where the earlier decisions were distinguished on tenuous grounds, the view invoked by the defense was accepted and a conviction reversed because the marriage was valid (or, more exactly, because it had not been shown to be void) under the *lex loci celebrationis,* which was the law of New York.[203] The reason for the confusion thus to be found in the decisions under review seems to be that there is a tension between the desire to implement immigration policy and considerations relevant to the law of marriage.[204] Where the question arises in a context not involving the former policy, a marriage of the

201. United States v. Rubenstein, 151 F.2d 915, 918-919 (2 Cir. 1945).

202. Lutwak v. United States, 344 U.S. 604, 610-613 (1952). Followed in United States v. Pantelopoulos, 336 F.2d 421 (2 Cir. 1964). See also Scott v. Immigration and Naturalization Service, 350 F.2d 279, 282 (2 Cir. 1965) (a deportation case not involving any criminal statute).

203. United States v. Diogo, 320 F.2d 898 (2 Cir. 1963).

204. See *Baade* 369-370; *Clark* 117.

present type will more readily be recognised as valid in American law.[205]

By way of conclusion, the approach adopted with regard to the choice of law in consent cases is neither uniform, nor very clear. To some extent, no doubt, the relevant policies vary with the grounds of invalidity asserted in each case. Obviously, for instance, sham marriages invoked for immigration purposes form a group of their own, where the decision is likely to be dominated by considerations normally extraneous to the law of marriage. It is submitted that the preferable approach in these cases is that taken by the Supreme Court of the United States, treating the matter as a claim to an incident and refusing to decide on the validity of the marriage for other purposes.

Apart from this special group of cases, the overall impression is that the *lex fori/lex domicilii* prevails, especially where the marriage is valid by that law. Some decisions sustain a marriage in reliance on the *lex fori,* although a ground for annulment seems to have existed under the *lex loci celebrationis* (*supra* n. 198), whereas the latter law has apparently never been applied to invalidate a marriage which was valid by the *lex fori.* The state of the forum presumably sees no need to protect itself or its domiciliaries when the defect alleged to vitiate the consent of the parties is not a sufficient ground for annulment under its own law. In particular, this holds true where annulment is unusually easy in the state of celebration – perhaps for the reason that a divorce is difficult to obtain in that state and that annulment functions as a partial substitute (as used to be the case in New York) – but is subject to stricter rules in the forum, where divorce is the normal method of ending unsuccessful marriages.[206] On the other hand, probably no court would hesitate to strike down a foreign marriage where, in the eyes of its own law, the consent of one of the parties suffered from a fundamental defect, such as duress or insanity, whether or not a nullity decree would be obtainable under the *lex loci celebrationis.*

29. *Marriageable age.* The minimum age for marriage, which is now fixed by statute nearly everywhere in the United States,

205. In Mpiliris v. Hellenic Lines, Ltd., 323 F. Supp. 865, 879-882 (S.D. Tex. 1970), a local marriage entered into solely to enable the man to gain entry into the United States was attacked collaterally but upheld by the court. Cases of the type cited *supra* n. 201-202 were distinguished on the ground that the case at bar did not involve any prosecution for criminal offences.

206. See *Taintor,* Marriage 622.

varies considerably in different states, ranging from fourteen for males and twelve for females in states where the common law rule remains in force to twenty-one for men and eighteen for females in a few states.[207] Many variations also exist as to the legal consequences of non-compliance with such requirements, for example as to whether want of age renders a marriage void or only voidable and by what acts or conduct it may be ratified so as to become valid.[208]

Conflicts problems concerning age requirements occur with some frequency.[209] The typical case is that domiciliaries of state *D*, who are (or one of whom is) below the prescribed age according to the law of that state, go to state *C* and get married there, taking advantage of its lower age limit, and then promptly return to live in *D*, where the validity of the union comes into litigation.

In the great majority of such cases the courts of *D* have upheld the marriage once it was found to be valid by the *lex loci celebrationis.*[210] This result has been reached whether or not an element of evasion was present, and even where *D* had a marriage evasion statute for foreign marriages of local domiciliaries. Sometimes the courts have adopted a predominantly jurisdictional approach, holding that they lacked power to annul a marriage solemnised in another state.[211] In other cases, where (as is the general rule) jurisdiction for annulment was entertained by the courts of *D*, a variety of reasons have been given to sustain the

207. See *Clark* 77-80; *Kingsley,* Infants' Marriages 593-594; *Vernier* I 115-119. A survey of various age requirements is also given by *Beyer and Musso,* Gesundheitszeugnisse, Alterserfordernis, Einwilligung des gesetzlichen Vertreters zur Eheschliessung nach dem Recht der Vereinigten Staaten von Amerika: StAZ 1966, 180-183.

208. See *Clark* 80-84; *Kingsley,* Infants' Marriages 596-603.

209. See on these problems: *Beale* 679-680; *Clark* 84-86; *Ehrenzweig,* Conflict 382-384; *Goodrich and Scoles* 236-237; *Philip Johnson* 452-453; *Kingsley,* Infants' Marriages 604; *Leflar* 537-538; *Stumberg* 282; *Taintor,* Marriage 623-624. Cases are collected in Annot., 71 A.L.R.2d 687 (1960).

210. State v. Graves, 307 S.W.2d 545 (Ark. Sup. Ct. 1957); McDonald v. McDonald, 58 P.2d 163 (Cal. Sup. Ct. 1936); Spencer v. People, 292 P.2d 971 (Colo. Sup. Ct. 1956); Payne v. Payne, 214 P.2d 495 (Colo. Sup. Ct. 1950); Mangrum v. Mangrum, 220 S.W.2d 406 (Ky. Ct. App. 1949); Hilliard v. Hilliard, 209 N.Y.S.2d 132 (Sup. Ct. 1960) (a case where only one of the parties was a local domiciliary); Keith v. Pack, 187 S.W.2d 618 (Tenn. Sup. Ct. 1945).

211. Levy v. Downing, 100 N.E. 638 (Mass. Sup. Jud. Ct. 1913) (marriage voidable under the *lex loci celebrationis,* in the discretion of the foreign court); Bell v. Bell, 8 S.E.2d 183 (W.Va. Sup. Ct. App. 1940). In both cases the result of the refusal by the forum to assume jurisdiction was that the marriage remained valid until annulled by a court of the *forum celebrationis.*

marriage. One is that the relevant statutes of *D* provided, or were construed to mean, that nonage only made a marriage voidable and therefore, in the opinion of the court, could not possibly enshrine a particularly strong public policy against such unions (nor come within the terms of an evasion statute limited to void marriages).[212] Whatever such statutory language or construction may imply, the fact is that the courts of most states have taken the view that "this type of vice does not reach the dignity of making the marriages odious to the people of the domicile".[213] In a comparative law perspective this degree of liberality is rather remarkable, especially in view of the relatively wide variations in the age limits established in the different laws of the United States. The explanation may be that these variations largely depend on historical accident rather than reflect sharp clashes of well considered social policy.

In some cases of the present type, nevertheless, the courts of state *D*, relying on their own law, have refused to recognise the marriage.[214] In these cases it was inferred, usually from the language of the local statute concerned, that the policy expressed in *D*'s age limit was strong enough to demand invalidation of an infringing foreign marriage contracted by local domiciliaries. A common feature of these cases is that the question arose in annulment proceedings instituted within a short time of the celebration of the marriage and of the return of the parties to state *D*. In such circumstances the policy of validation was probably considered to carry less weight than otherwise, and the decisions are therefore hardly conclusive as to nonage cases involving different sets of facts or legal issues.[215] It seems quite possible, even in states where

212. At times this construction of the statute involved seems to have been rather strained; see *supra* n. 54.

213. *Taintor*, Marriage 624.

214. Wilkins v. Zelichowski, 140 A.2d 65 (N.J. Sup. Ct. 1958); Cunningham v. Cunningham, 99 N.E. 845 (N.Y. Ct. App. 1912), critically noted in 26 Harv. L. Rev. 253 (1912/13); Holland v. Holland, 212 N.Y.S.2d 805 (Sup. Ct. 1961); Mitchell v. Mitchell, 117 N.Y.S. 671 (Sup. Ct. 1909); Ross v. Bryant, 217 P. 364 (Okl. Sup. Ct. 1923), noted in 23 Colum. L. Rev. 782 (1923). See also Sirois v. Sirois, 50 A.2d 88 (N.H. Sup. Ct. 1946), where the *lex fori* was applied to annul the marriage but where the result would have been the same under the other law.

215. In Wilkins v. Zelichowski, 140 A.2d 65 (N.J. Sup. Ct. 1958), for example, the court took care to point out (at 69) that it was not concerned with a collateral attack on an out-of-state marriage but with a direct proceeding for annulment. In Cunningham v. Cunningham, 99 N.E. 845 (N.Y. Ct. App. 1912), the parties had not cohabited, and this fact apparently carried some weight with the court.

a nullity decree was granted in the above circumstances, that the scales would be tipped in favour of validity if, for instance, the parties had been living for a long time as man and wife in *D* and if the question came up in a suit for divorce and alimony brought by one of them against the other.[216]

Even if the marriage would be struck down for lack of age in state *D,* it will not necessarily be held bad in third states (*supra* s. 17). This is illustrated by an Iowa case involving the validity of a Minnesota marriage between Wisconsin domiciliaries, which was challenged on the ground that one of the parties had been under age according to the law of Wisconsin. Although Wisconsin had a marriage evasion statute applying to foreign marriages of local domiciliaries, the Iowa court decided to apply Minnesota law as the *lex loci celebrationis,* which was similar to the *lex fori* in substantive content, and sustained the marriage in reliance on that law.[217]

Where, on the other hand, the policy of the forum was hostile to the marriage, that policy has never been extended to third state situations. This type of problem may be exemplified by a New York case, which involved a marriage celebrated in the British West Indies, validly under the local law, between parties domiciled there at the time. By the law of New York, where the parties had meanwhile become domiciled, the marriage was subject to annulment for nonage, but the court refused to apply this rule and upheld the marriage in accordance with the relevant foreign law.[218]

A division of opinion exists as to cases where, in contrast to those considered so far, the marriage does not meet the age requirements of the *lex loci celebrationis* but is valid by the law of the domicile of the parties. In one New York case the former law was applied to annul a California marriage of a New York domiciliary because of non-age and lack of parental consent,

216. See, for instance, the points of view advanced by *Clark* 85 and by *Leflar* 538.

217. Boehm v. Rohlfs, 276 N.W. 105 (Iowa Sup. Ct. 1937).

218. Simmons v. Simmons, 203 N.Y.S. 215 (App. Div. 1924). See also Reid v. Reid, 129 N.Y.S. 529 (Sup. Ct. 1911), aff'd 131 N.Y.S. 1140 (App. Div. 1911), where the female party was domiciled in New York at the time of the marriage and under the age of consent according to the law of that state, but where the intended matrimonial domicile was in Maryland and the place of celebration in the District of Columbia; the marriage was sustained in reliance on the *lex loci celebrationis* alone but seems also to have been valid by the law of the intended matrimonial domicile. Note that the contrary result has been reached in New York where both parties were local domiciliaries at the time of the marriage (*supra* n. 214).

although the union was valid by the law of New York where both parties made their domicile after the marriage.[219] In other cases, however, the courts have refused to enforce by nullity decree a statute of the *locus celebrationis* rendering the marriage voidable for want of age of one of the parties.[220] This position accords with the weight of extrajudicial opinion, which is in favour of applying the *lex fori/lex domicilii* when the effect is to validate the marriage (*supra* s. 10).

30. *Parental Consent.* In addition to establishing a minimum age for marriage, the statutes of nearly all of the United States prescribe that the consent of parents (or of other persons standing *in loco parentis,* such as a guardian) must be obtained for the marriage of minors below a certain age.[221] In most states this age limit is fixed at twenty-one for males and eighteen for females, but variations exist on this as well as on many other details of the rules. Almost invariably, however, requirements of parental con-

219. Cruickshank v. Cruickshank, 82 N.Y.S.2d 522 (Sup. Ct. 1948). For adverse comments on this case see *Clark* 86 n. 83; *Ehrenzweig,* Conflict 384 n. 41; and note in 49 Colum. L. Rev. 693 (1949). There are a few other cases in which the *lex loci celebrationis* was invoked to invalidate a marriage for nonage; see Vaughan v. Gideon, 132 P.2d 529 (Cal. Dist. Ct. App. 1942), and Canale v. People, 52 N.E. 310 (Ill. Sup. Ct. 1898). In the former of these cases, however, the result would have been the same under the *lex fori et domicilii,* and in the latter the *lex loci celebrationis* coincided with the *lex domicilii* (at the time of the marriage); in neither case, therefore, was a true conflict present.

220. Capasso v. Colonna, 122 A. 378 (N.J. Ch. 1923), aff'd 124 A. 760 (N.J. Ct. Err. App. 1924); Portwood v. Portwood, 109 S.W.2d 515 (Tex. Civ. App. 1937). And see Jimenez v. Jimenez, 116 A. 788 (N.J. Ch. 1922), where an annulment was refused, although the petitioning party was under age both by the *lex fori* and by the *lex loci celebrationis* (New York law), on the ground that the marriage had been confirmed by marital cohabitation in New York after that party had attained full age according to the *lex fori* (though not according to the other law). A similar case is Parks v. Parks, 10 S.E.2d 807 (N.C. Sup. Ct. 1940) where, however, the cohabitation occurred in the state of the forum. See also Duley v. Duley, 151 A.2d 255 (D.C. Mun. Ct. App. 1959), where the parties were under marriageable age both by the *lex fori* and by the *lex loci celebrationis,* but where the court refused to annul the marriage in the exercise of the discretion vested in it under the former law. Cf. Levy v. Downing, 100 N.E. 638 (Mass. Sup. Jud. Ct. 1913), where the court held that it lacked jurisdiction to annul the marriage, which was voidable for nonage under the foreign *lex loci celebrationis,* on the ground that the grant of a decree was, in the eyes of that law, in the discretion of the foreign court. For writers supporting validation in the situation envisaged in the text see *Clark* 86; *Ehrenzweig,* Conflict 384.

221. See *Beyer and Musso* (*supra* n. 207); *Clark* 79; *Vernier* I 119-128.

sent, as opposed to those of marriageable age, are only laid down as a condition for issuing a marriage license and are held to be merely directory. Except where otherwise specifically provided, the purpose of the relevant statutes, as construed by the courts, is to prevent, as far as possible, the formation of unions without the requisite consent, but not to invalidate them if they are once entered into.[222]

This facilitates the treatment of such requirements in the conflict of laws. There are many cases in which a foreign marriage has been attacked, either directly in proceedings for annulment or collaterally in other proceedings, for failure by the parties or by one of them to secure the parental consent required by the *lex fori et domicilii*. Like the nonage cases proper, these cases are often coloured by evasion, the parties having deliberately taken advantage of the more favourable rules, or misrepresented their age to the licensing official, of the other state in order to get married there. Whether or not this was so, the marriage has been sustained in all cases where lack of parental consent was the only ground invoked against it (the parties having attained marriageable age) and where the union was lawful or, while prohibited, not invalid by the *lex loci celebrationis*.[223] In most cases the courts have specified that the question must be determined by that law, but they have often added that the result was the same under the *lex fori*. Sometimes the choice between the two laws has been left open.[224] Occasionally, the courts have adduced supplementary reasons for refusing to annul a marriage on the present ground. In one case it was said that the petitioner, who (by marrying elsewhere without the requisite consent) "deliberately sought to and did circumvent the

222. See, for instance, Browning v. Browning, 130 P. 852, 853 (Kan. Sup. Ct. 1913).

223. Castor v. United States, 174 F.2d 481 (8 Cir. 1949) (sitting in Missouri); Hitchens v. Hitchens, 47 F.Supp. 73 (D.D.C. 1942); McDonald v. McDonald, 58 P.2d 163 (Cal. Sup. Ct. 1936); Reifschneider v. Reifschneider, 89 N.E. 255 (Ill. Sup. Ct. 1909); Commonwealth v. Graham, 31 N.E. 706 (Mass. Sup. Jud. Ct. 1892); Noble v. Noble, 300 N.W. 885 (Mich. Sup. Ct. 1941); Cross v. Cross, 102 P.2d 829 (Mont. Sup. Ct. 1940); Sturgis v. Sturgis, 93 P. 696 (Or. Sup. Ct. 1908) (marriage of a spendthrift without the consent of his guardian); Ex parte Chace, 58 A. 978 (R.I. Sup. Ct. 1904); Lyannes v. Lyannes, 177 N.W. 683, 687-688 (Wis. Sup. Ct. 1920); and cases cited *infra* n. 224-225. See further Annot., 71 A.L.R.2d 687 (1960); *Taintor,* Marriage 622-623.

224. For instance, Needam v. Needam, 33 S.E.2d 288 (Va. Sup. Ct. App. 1945).

Laws of this State", had not come into court with clean hands.[225] The fact of evasion was thus turned against the petitioner in a rather unusual way, being used as an argument to support the validity of the union.

Cases in which, conversely, the marriage was, or possibly was, invalid for lack of parental consent according to the *lex loci celebrationis* but valid by the *lex fori et domicilii* have seldom occurred in practice.[226] On this point reference may be made to what has been said on the corresponding problem with regard to nonage (*supra* s. 29).

31. *Consanguinity and Affinity*. It has frequently been affirmed by American courts and writers that no recognition can be accorded to marriages which "by the general consent of all Christendom are deemed incestuous", or which would involve "incest in a degree regarded generally as within the prohibition of natural law", even though such unions should be valid by the *lex loci celebrationis.*[227] Different views have been advanced, however, as to what relationships fall within this category. At least at the present day, a common consent in American law is only to be found for marriages in the direct line of ascent and descent and between brother and sister, which must probably be denied all recognition.[228] This does not take the matter very far, for marriages within these degrees of consanguinity are unlawful, not only all over the United States but almost everywhere else, and seem never to have given rise to conflicts problems.

In practice, such problems have chiefly been presented by marriages between uncle and niece or between aunt and nephew, which are forbidden in the great majority of the United States, and between first cousins, which are forbidden in a substantial

225. Carr v. Carr, 104 N.Y.S.2d 269, 272 (Sup. Ct. 1951).

226. For a decision refusing to annul the marriage in such circumstances see Bays v. Bays, 174 N.Y.S. 212 (Sup. Ct. 1918), noted in 4 Cornell L.Q. 200 (1918/19). Here the court relied on equitable principles, saying (at 220) that "the plaintiff has not come into court in good conscience and with clean hands" (cf. Carr v. Carr, preceding note). But this case was distinguished, on what seems to be dubious grounds, in Cruickshank v. Cruickshank, 82 N.Y.S. 2d 522 (Sup. Ct. 1948), where the *lex loci celebrationis* was applied to defeat the marriage of an infant without parental consent; see *supra* at n. 219.

227. See *Story(-Bennett)* 150 and In re May's Estate, 114 N.E.2d 4, 6 (N.Y. Ct. App. 1953), respectively. Cf. *supra* at n. 64, 103.

228. See, e.g., Dannelli v. Dannelli's Adm'r, 4 Bush 51, 58 (Ky. Ct. App. 1868); Commonwealth v. Lane, 113 Mass. 458, 463-464 (1873) (*dictum*); *Ehrenzweig and Jayme* 160.

number of states.[229] In addition, marriages between persons related by affinity, for example between a man and his deceased wife's sister or his deceased brother's widow, which are or formerly were proscribed by certain American and foreign laws, have been in issue in a few conflicts cases.[230] The decisions are at considerable variance.[231] Although the courts have often spoken in terms of "divine" or "natural" law, the disagreement ultimately turns on differing degrees of force, or different conceptions of the force, behind the prohibitions of the respective states.

Most cases involve evasionary marriages contracted in a sister state where the union was lawful, between parties within the prohibited degrees of relationship according to the law of their domicile. The balance of authority, especially as represented by more modern decisions, is in favour of upholding such unions in reliance on the *lex loci celebrationis.*[232] This view has prevailed whether or not the parties went to the other state with the intention of avoiding the domiciliary prohibition. *A fortiori,* the same solution has been adopted in cases where the marriage was valid both by the *lex loci celebrationis* and by the law of the domicile

229. For a general discussion of, and for details concerning, the prohibitions based on consanguinity and affinity in American law see *Clark* 70-74; *Storke,* Incestuous Marriage 473-478; *Vernier* I 173-187.

230. See, for instance, Dannelli v. Dannelli's Adm'r, 4 Bush 51 (Ky. Ct. App. 1868); Commonwealth v. Lane, 113 Mass. 458, 467-471 (1873) (*dictum*). For a comparative survey of the law relating to such unions see *Dölle,* Familienrecht 105-106.

231. For a comprehensive study on these conflicts problems see *Storke,* Incestuous Marriage 478-499. Among other writers see: *Beale* 687-691; *Clark* 74-77; *Ehrenzweig and Jayme* 160-161; *Goodrich and Scoles* 236; *Holt* 25-32; *Philip Johnson* 446-447; *Leflar* 535-536; *Stumberg* 283-284; *Taintor,* Marriage 626-627. Cases are collected in Annot., 117 A.L.R. 186 (1938).

232. *Uncle and niece*: Fensterwald v. Burk, 98 A. 358 (Md. Ct. App. 1916); In re May's Estate, 114 N.E.2d 4 (N.Y. Ct. App. 1953), noted in 34 B.U.L. Rev. 82 (1954), 22 Ford. L. Rev. 302 (1953), 67 Harv. L. Rev. 1068 (1953/54), 29 Notre Dame Law. 115 (1953/54), 15 Ohio St. L.J. 220 (1954), 28 St. John's L. Rev. 113 (1953/54), and 5 Syracuse L. Rev. 120 (1953/54); Campione v. Campione, 107 N.Y.S.2d 170 (Sup. Ct. 1951). *First cousins*: In re Miller's Estate, 214 N.W. 428 (Mich. Sup. Ct. 1927), noted in 26 Mich. L. Rev. 327 (1927/28) and 12 Minn. L. Rev. 70 (1927/28); Toth v. Toth, 212 N.W.2d 812 (Mich. Ct. App. 1973); Mazzolini v. Mazzolini, 155 N.E.2d 206 (Ohio Sup. Ct. 1958) (this case involved a reference back to the *lex fori*; cf. *supra* at n. 90); Leefeld v. Leefeld, 166 P. 953 (Or. Sup. Ct. 1917) (under peculiar wording of local statute); Schofield v. Schofield, 51 Pa. Super. Ct. 564 (1912), noted in 61 U. Pa. L. Rev. 490 (1912/13). See also Restatement § 283 Comment *k* and Reporter's Note (p. 246).

of the parties at the time of the marriage, although it was contrary to the *lex fori* and would have been void if celebrated locally.[233]

In a relatively substantial number of cases, however, the courts have been less tolerant. In these cases a foreign marriage between uncle and niece (aunt and nephew) or between first cousins, although valid by the *lex loci celebrationis,* was struck down, as incestuous, in the state of the domicile.[234] Some decisions so holding rely on a marriage evasion statute.[235] In the other cases the policy evinced by the local prohibition was, even without such support, held to be so vigorous as to require extraterritorial application. In some of the cases under review only one of the parties was a local domiciliary at the time of the marriage.[236] In all except one, however, the state of the forum was also that of the intended matrimonial domicile of the spouses (cf. *supra* s. 14). The one exception relates to a third state situation: a Kentucky marriage of first cousins domiciled in Illinois, which was valid in Kentucky but void by the law of Illinois, was held invalid by the court of Minnesota on the strength of the Illinois policy (as expressed in a marriage evasion statute).[237]

These exceptions to the rule of validation under the *lex loci celebrationis* seem now to be losing in importance. The present-day tendency is to look upon "incestuous" marriages more soberly and with more tolerance than in earlier days, at least when they do not involve members of the nuclear family. This is notably so for

233. Sutton v. Warren, 51 Mass. 451 (1845); Garcia v. Garcia, 127 N.W. 586 (S.D. Sup. Ct. 1910); cf. *supra* at n. 101. But see United States ex rel. Devine v. Rodgers, 109 F. 886 (E.D. Pa. 1901). This case is difficult to explain and of dubious authority; cf. *Beale* 698-699 and *supra* at n. 105.

234. *Uncle and niece or aunt and nephew*: Osoinach v. Watkins, 180 So. 577 (Ala. Sup. Ct. 1938); Catalano v. Catalano, 170 A.2d 726 (Conn. Sup. Ct. Err. 1961); Sclamberg v. Sclamberg, 41 N.E.2d 801 (Ind. Sup. Ct. 1942); Bucca v. State, 128 A.2d 506 (N.J. Super. Ct. 1957); Martin v. Martin, 46 S.E. 120 (W.Va. Sup. Ct. App. 1903). *First cousins*: In re Mortenson's Estate, 316 P.2d 1106 (Ariz. Sup. Ct. 1957), noted in 10 S.C.L.Q. 505 (1957/58); Weinberg v. Weinberg, 242 Ill. App. 414 (1926); Johnson v. Johnson, 106 P. 500 (Wash. Sup. Ct. 1910). See also, for a case involving a marriage between *stepfather and stepdaughter,* Rhodes v. McAfee, 457 S.W.2d 522 (Tenn. Sup. Ct. 1970).

235. In re Mortenson's Estate and Weinberg v. Weinberg, *ibid.*

236. See the uncle-niece cases of Catalano v. Catalano, Sclamberg v. Sclamberg and Bucca v. State, cited *supra* n. 234. In each of those cases the parties were married in a foreign country which was at the time the domicile of the wife.

237. Meisenhelder v. Chicago & N.W. Ry. Co., 213 N.W. 32 (Minn. Sup. Ct. 1927), approvingly noted in 26 Mich. L. Rev. 327 (1927/28).

marriages between first cousins, which today certainly are not, as was once assumed, "prohibited in nearly all civilized countries".[238]

The courts have seldom had occasion to consider the converse case of a marriage valid by the law of the domicile but invalid, on grounds of consanguinity or affinity, by the *lex loci celebrationis.* As in other cases of this type, however, the weight of extrajudicial opinion is in favour of sustaining such a marriage.[239]

32. *Miscegenation.* Until some time ago marriages between white persons and negroes, as well as various other kinds of interracial marriage, were forbidden by "anti-miscegenation" statutes in a considerable number (at one time even in a majority) of the United States.[240] This prohibition engendered conflicts problems similar to those treated in the preceding sections.[241] In several states, chiefly in the South, where interracial marriages were considered particularly odious, the local statute against such unions was given extraterritorial force. An out-of-state marriage in violation of the statute was therefore declared void, without regard to the *lex loci celebrationis,* if the parties were local domiciliaries who had gone to the other state only in order to have the ceremony performed, returning afterwards to live in the forum state.[242] The

238. Johnson v. Johnson, 106 P. 500, 501 (Wash. Sup. Ct. 1910). For the modern view see, for example, *Ehrenzweig,* Conflict 386; *Storke,* Incestuous Marriage 477, 499.

239. See *Clark* 75, 77 and other references given *supra* n. 33. *Contra*: In re Estate of Levie, 123 Cal. Rptr. 445 (Ct. App. 1975) (Nevada marriage of first cousins domiciled in California held void by virtue of Nevada law, although it was valid by California law). See also Blaisdell v. Bickum, 1 N.E. 281 (Mass. Sup. Ct. 1885) (uncle-niece marriage held void in accordance with the foreign *lex loci celebrationis*; but it does not appear from the report of this case whether a true conflict was involved).

240. No less than 40 states seem at one time to have had such statutes; 16 of these survived until 1967 when they were declared unconstitutional (*infra* n. 245). See: *Clark* 91-94; *Foster,* A Study of the Wyoming Miscegenation Statutes: 10 Wyo. L.J. 131-138 (1955/56); *Habermalz* 21-26, 93-102; *Riley,* Miscegenation Statutes – A Re-evaluation of their Constitutionality in Light of Changing Social and Political Conditions: 32 So. Cal. L. Rev. 28-48 (1958); *Vernier* I 204-209; Note, Constitutionality of Anti-Miscegenation Statutes: 58 Yale L.J. 472-482 (1948/49).

241. See: *Beale* 691; *Ehrenzweig,* Miscegenation; *Goodrich and Scoles* 235-236; *Habermalz* 27-29; *Holt* 33-35; *Philip Johnson* 445-446; *Stumberg* 286; *Taintor,* Marriage 627-629. Cases are collected in Annot., 3 A.L.R.2d 240 (1949).

242. Stevens v. United States, 146 F.2d 120 (10 Cir. 1944) (applying Oklahoma law); State v. Kennedy, 76 N.C. 251, 22 Am. Rep. 683 (1877); Baker v. Carter, 68 P.2d 85 (Okl. Sup. Ct. 1937); Eggers v. Olson, 231 P. 483 (Okl. Sup. Ct. 1924). In some other cases the same result was reached

main concern of courts so holding was to prevent marital cohabitation, between parties caught by the local prohibition, within the borders of the state. Where local cohabitation was not involved, the courts did not shrink from recognising a violating marriage when it was valid by the foreign *lex loci celebrationis*. Illustrations are afforded by cases where the parties had established their marital domicile in the other state and continued to live in that state all through their married life and where the sole question to be decided was the effect of the marriage on the distribution of property in the forum state on the death intestate of one of the spouses.[243] Even for the purpose of local cohabitation the courts were inclined to recognise a miscegenous marriage, where valid by the relevant foreign law, if the parties had been domiciled in the foreign state at the time of celebration and had only later moved or returned to the state of the forum.[244]

These problems, however, now belong to the past. By a decision of the Supreme Court of the United States, which was handed down in 1967, the miscegenation statute then in force in Virginia was held to violate both the equal protection and the due process clauses of the Fourteenth Amendment to the Federal Constitution.[245] Inferentially, this decision invalidates, for the whole of the United States, all restrictions on the right to marry which are based on racial criteria. Such restrictions, therefore, can no longer be applied to marriages celebrated anywhere in the United States.

under marriage evasion statutes: State v. Tutty, 41 F. 753 (S.D. Ga. 1890); In re Takahashi's Estate, 129 P.2d 217 (Mont. Sup. Ct. 1942); Naim v. Naim, 87 S.E.2d 749 (Va. Sup. Ct. App. 1955), vacated and remanded 350 U.S. 891 (1955), decision adhered to 90 S.E.2d 849 (1956), app. denied 350 U.S. 985 (1956). For an early decision to the contrary, holding the local statute to be inapplicable to an extrastate ceremony even where it had been deliberately evaded, see Medway v. Needham, 16 Mass. 157 (1819).

243. Whittington v. McCaskill, 61 So. 236 (Fla. Sup. Ct. 1913); Miller v. Lucks, 36 So.2d 140 (Miss. Sup. Ct. 1948). Cf. *supra* s. 18.

244. State v. Ross, 76 N.C. 242, 22 Am. Rep. 678 (1877). But see State v. Bell, 7 Baxt. 9, 32 Am. Rep. 549 (Tenn. Sup. Ct. 1872), holding that a marriage validly entered into in Mississippi, between a white man and a coloured woman apparently domiciled in that state at the time of celebration, did not protect the parties from criminal prosecution for miscegenous cohabitation in Tennessee.

245. Loving v. Virginia, 388 U.S. 1 (1967). For an earlier state decision holding the local (California) miscegenation statute to be unconstitutional see Perez v. Lippold, 198 P.2d 17 (Cal. Sup. Ct. 1948).

C. Other Countries

33. *Latin America.* The principle of the *lex loci celebrationis* is widely accepted in Latin America.[246] It has found expression in the *Montevideo Treaties* of 1889 and 1940, according to which capacity to marry is governed, along with other aspects of the validity of marriage, by the law of the place of celebration.[247] The rule has also been adopted in many national codifications, for example in those of *Argentina* and *Chile.*[248]

A characteristic feature of Latin American law is, however, that the *lex loci celebrationis* applies fully only as concerns local marriages. In so far as the rule is recognised at all in respect of foreign marriages, it is heavily qualified by exceptions and riders, usually in favour of the *lex fori.* This is particularly true when the parties are local nationals or domiciliaries, as the case may be. Furthermore, these qualifications of the principle are more rigidly fixed by statutory law, leaving less room for policy-weighing by the courts in individual cases, than in the United States.

The most common type of modification of the principle is that whereby a total or partial *cumulation* of two laws is required: the conditions of capacity to marry laid down by the *lex fori,* or at least a substantial part of those conditions, must be satisfied in addition to the requirements of the foreign *lex loci celebrationis.* Under the Montevideo Treaties, for instance, the signatory States are not bound to recognise a marriage which, though validly performed in one of those States, is vitiated by any of the following impediments: (*a*) want of age of either of the contracting parties, the minimum age required for a male being fourteen years and for a female twelve years; (*b*) kinship in a direct line by consanguinity or affinity, whether legitimate or illegitimate; (*c*) kinship between legitimate or illegitimate brother and sister; (*d*) the fact of having caused the death, either as principal or as accomplice, of the

246. See generally *Alfonsín* 32-36; *W. Goldschmidt,* Droit international privé latino-américain: Clunet 1973, 65, 82-84 (critically); *Rabel* 267-270. But see for BRAZIL and certain other countries *infra* s. 38.

247. Treaty of 1889, art. 11 par. 1; of 1940, art. 13 par. 1.

248. ARGENTINA: Act of 2 Nov. 1888, art. 2; *Goldschmidt and Rodriguez-Novás* 58; CHILE: CC art. 14; Act of 10 Jan. 1884, art. 15; *Etcheberry* 39; *Hamilton* 99-100. For other countries see, e.g., COLOMBIA: CC art. 18; *Caicedo Castilla* 365; *Eder* 43; ECUADOR: CC art. 13, 91; GUATEMALA: CC art. 86; Act of 25 Jan. 1936, art. 35-36; MEXICO: CC Fed. art. 12; *Bayitch and Siqueiros* 79-87; NICARAGUA: CC, Preliminary Title art. VI no. 6, art. 102-103; URUGUAY: CC art. 101, 2395; *Alfonsín* 121-122, 127-128.

spouse of one of the parties in order to marry the surviving spouse; (*e*) a prior marriage not legally dissolved.[249]

Although this provision only specifies the cases in which the Contracting States may refuse to recognise a marriage valid by the *lex loci celebrationis*, without imposing any duty on them to do so, the impediments listed seem in fact to constitute a "common core" of national public policy in those States. *Argentine* law, for example, contains a catalogue of impediments requiring extraterritorial application which very closely resembles that set out in the Montevideo Treaties.[250] A number of other countries, including *Chile* (which is not a party to the treaties in question), go even further, subjecting their nationals marrying abroad to all or nearly all prohibitions contained in their own law.[251]

The exception based on the existence of a previous, not legally dissolved marriage is of considerable practical importance. This is so because several Latin American countries, including Argentina and Chile, do not recognise, or are very restrictive in recognising, foreign divorces of their nationals or domiciliaries, as the case may be. When such a divorce has been followed by remarriage in the foreign country, therefore, these countries will often refuse to recognise the validity of the new marriage.[252] In *Chilean* practice this and certain other impediments have been held to apply even though they were only present in the person of the foreign spouse of the Chilean party.[253] Thus, a New York marriage between a divorced man of American nationality and a Chilean woman, who

249. Treaty of 1889, art. 11 par. 2; of 1940, art. 13 par. 2. For a decision by an ARGENTINE court applying the 1889 Treaty and carrying the exception provided for in art. 11 par. 2 even further than warranted by its wording see Court of First Instance of Buenos Aires 22 Sept. 1955, Rev. crit. d.i.p. 1957, 60 (relying on the *lex fori*, which was also the *lex domicilii* of the parties, to annul a marriage, celebrated in Paraguay, on the ground that the respondent suffered from leprosy) with a critical note by W. Goldschmidt.

250. Act of 2 Nov. 1888, art. 2 as compared with art. 9.

251. CHILE: Act of 10 Jan. 1884, art. 15 par. 2, cf. CC art. 15; *Etcheberry* 40; *Hamilton* 100-102; *Pescio*, Les règles de droit international privé dans le Code chilien: Rev. int. dr. comp. 40 (1963) 181, 189-191; COLOMBIA: CC art. 19; *Caicedo Castilla* 367; ECUADOR: CC art. 91 par. 2, cf. art. 14; GUATEMALA: CC art. 86; Act of 25 Jan. 1936, art. 36; NICARAGUA: CC art. 103; URUGUAY: CC art. 102; *Alfonsín* 128. Cf. *Pålsson*, Marriage, s. 40 at n. 53.

252. See, for example, on the complicated position under ARGENTINE law: *D. Geitner*, Ehescheidungs- und Ehetrennungsgründe in Lateinamerika (Thesis, Kiel 1970) 192-208; *W. Goldschmidt*, Zum argentinischen Eherecht: FamRZ 1964, 486-487; *Goldschmidt and Rodriguez-Novás* 60-61.

253. See *Etcheberry* 40; *Hamilton* 101.

had not been married before, failed to be recognised in Chile because the man, notwithstanding his divorce which was valid in New York, was regarded by Chilean law as still "tied by an undissolved matrimonial bond."[254] Similarly, Chilean law was applied to annul a marriage, celebrated in Germany, between a man of Chilean nationality and his German wife on the ground of the latter party's impotence.[255] These decisions may be compared with the doctrine of the "bilaterality" of certain marriage impediments espoused in countries which adhere to the principle of the personal law in matters of capacity to marry (*infra* s. 49-52).

The effect of provisions of the above-mentioned type is that certain foreign marriages complying with the *lex loci celebrationis* will be denied recognition under the *lex fori*. To the opposite effect is a rule of *Argentine* law, which provides in general terms that foreign laws shall not apply whenever the local laws would be more favourable to the validity of the acts in question.[256] A validating role is thus assigned to the *lex fori*. The range of this principle includes marriages. It follows that a marriage which is invalid by the *lex loci celebrationis* but which complies with the local law of Argentina will be upheld in that country.

34. *Soviet Union.* The position of Soviet law is similar to that taken by several Latin American countries. Thus, the rule of the *lex loci celebrationis* is absolute with regard to marriages celebrated in local form in the Soviet Union.[257] Even if both parties are foreigners, therefore, their capacity to marry will be tested by Soviet law alone if they choose to marry in that form.[258] As concerns foreign marriages, on the other hand, Soviet law is not

254. Court of Appeals of Valparaiso 1940 (Gazitúa Braun v. Berdeau), G.T. 1940, 81-359.

255. C. Supr. 11 Sept. 1933 (Grimmer v. Zúñiga), Rev. Der. Santiago 31 (1934) I 171.

256. CC art. 14 no. 4; see *Goldschmidt and Rodriguez-Novás* 58-59.

257. Fundamental Principles of 1968, art. 31 par. 1; cf. art. 32 par. 1, concerning marriages between Soviet citizens performed at Soviet embassies and consulates abroad. See *Makarov,* Kollisionsnormen 373-375. See also the treaty of legal assistance between the SOVIET UNION and POLAND of 28 Dec. 1957, art. 28, where the *lex loci celebrationis* has been adopted as the law governing marriage, apparently including the substantive conditions of validity; cf., however, on the difficulties of interpretation caused by this provision *Sośniak,* Conventions 30-31; *idem,* Problems 141-142.

258. Marriages between foreigners may, however, in certain circumstances be performed at foreign embassies or consulates in the Soviet Union; see Fundamental Principles of 1968, art. 31 par. 3. These marriages depend on the law, including the conflicts rules, of the respective foreign States.

content to refer to the *lex loci celebrationis* if the parties are Soviet citizens or a Soviet citizen and a foreigner. Such a union, even if valid according to the relevant foreign law, will only be recognised if there were no obstacles to it arising from the conditions for marriage laid down by the Soviet (municipal) law.[259] To that extent Soviet law, *qua* the national law of the parties or one of them, is given extraterritorial application. If, however, both parties are foreigners their marriage will be recognised without further conditions if it has been performed abroad "according to the laws of the State concerned."[260]

35. *Scandinavia: Convention of 1931.* Pursuant to this convention, the right to marry of a person possessing the nationality of one of the Scandinavian States, when tested in another of those States, is to be determined by the law of the latter State, that is to say, by the *lex loci celebrationis.*[261] This rule, however, only applies if the intending spouses are, or if one of them is, habitually resident in the country of celebration.[262] In contrast to most other conflicts rules based on the principle under review, therefore, the Scandinavian rule always presupposes a real connection with the applicable law. Where neither of the parties meets the condition of habitual residence in the country of celebration, their right to marry, in so far as it is governed by the convention, will be determined by the law of their respective nationality.[263] Hence,

259. Fundamental Principles of 1968, art. 32 par. 3. See *Makarov,* Kollisionsnormen 376; *O.M. Stone,* The New Fundamental Principles of Soviet Family Law and Their Social Background: 18 I.C.L.Q. 392, 409 (1969).

260. Fundamental Principles of 1968, art. 32 par. 4. Apparently this provision must be interpreted as referring to the law of the state of celebration, including its conflicts rules; see *Makarov ibid.*

261. Art. 1 par. 1 sent. 1 of the convention as amended in 1969. See NJA 1969 II 564-565; *Holmøy* 16, 227-229; *Hornslet, Danielsen and Hermann* 390-393; *Philip,* IPR 198-199. On the system of recognition of inquiries into marriage impediments and publication of banns performed in one of the Contracting States see *Pålsson,* Marriage, s. 280.

262. It is immaterial which of the parties is so resident. This holds true even if one of the parties is a non-Scandinavian national, although in this case the rules of the convention only apply to the Scandinavian party. See the references in the preceding note.

263. See the references given *supra* n. 261. In this case, as well as in that mentioned *infra* at n. 267, the authorities of the country of celebration may request the party concerned to prove his right to marry by a certificate issued by the competent authorities of the country of his nationality; see art. 1 par. 1 sent. 3 of the convention. The rules treated here received their present shape by an amendment of the convention made in 1969. For the position under the convention as originally adopted see *Philip,* Conventions 278-282.

for instance, if a Finnish national habitually resident in Finland and a Norwegian national habitually resident in Norway wish to marry in Sweden, their capacity will be tested by Finnish and Norwegian law, respectively.

The restriction thus placed on the operation of the *lex loci* considerably reduces the risk of evasion otherwise often incurred under this system. That risk is further minimised by the essential similarity of Scandinavian municipal laws on the matter, which indeed is the avowed *raison d'être* of the basic conflicts rule of the convention.[264] In these respects the rule operates under more favourable conditions than is usually the case elsewhere.

Nevertheless, by an amendment of the convention made in 1973, an additional safeguard against evasion was created in regard to one particular issue. Where the *lex loci celebrationis* does not require any consent to the marriage of an incompetent person by his parents or guardian, it is now provided, as regards a party habitually resident in a Contracting State other than the country of celebration, that such consent must be obtained in accordance with the law of the former State.[265] To that extent the law of the habitual residence must be taken into account in cumulation with the *lex loci celebrationis,* which remains applicable in other respects. The reason why this rider was added to the basic conflicts rule of the convention was that the requirement of parental consent had been abolished in Sweden, but not in the other Contracting States.[266] The new provision is designed to prevent the possibility of escape from such requirements by a party habitually resident in one of the latter States. This amendment of the convention further illustrates the close dependency of the *lex loci* test on the condition of uniformity in the municipal law of the countries involved.

On the other hand, the convention also contains an exception of an entirely different spirit, providing that the law of a party's nationality must always be applied if the party concerned so requests.[267] This provision, which applies regardless of the habitual residence of the intending spouses, means that the parties can always "contract out" of the *lex loci celebrationis* (and also of the law of the habitual residence if that law would otherwise have to

264. See NJA 1969 II 564; *Philip,* IPR 200. Cf. generally on this and other Scandinavian conventions on private international law, *Philip,* Conventions 253-256, 281.

265. Art. 1 par. 2.

266. See NJA 1973 II 565-567.

267. Art. 1 par. 1 sent. 2; cf. NJA 1969 II 565.

be taken into account because of the above-mentioned special rule on parental consent). If, for example, a Norwegian national habitually resident in Norway and a Swedish national habitually resident in Denmark want to marry in Denmark, Danish law alone will normally apply, but each of the parties may demand that his or her right to marry be determined by his or her national law instead. This option is of practical interest where the national law permits the formation of a union which is prohibited by the normally governing law and, in such situations, favours the application of the more liberal of the laws involved. In view of the high degree of similarity of the laws of the countries concerned, such cases rarely occur in practice. In so far as they do, however, the authorities of the country of celebration are not allowed to refuse to marry the parties on the ground that the union would violate (the public policy of) the local law.[268]

36. *Denmark*. Outside the area of the inter-Scandinavian relations covered by the above convention, the conflicts problems of marriage are approached differently in the Scandinavian countries.[269] In Denmark, as the only one among those countries, the principle of the *lex loci celebrationis* prevails. Normally, therefore, a marriage celebrated in Denmark is governed by Danish law alone, regardless of the nationality and habitual residence of the parties.[270]

By way of exception to this rule, foreign law has to be taken into account in a few cases. Thus, although under Danish law a minor or other incompetent person cannot marry without the consent of his parents or guardian, no such consent is necessary if it is not required by the law of the party's habitual residence.[271] Here a permissive role is assigned to the relevant foreign law, which is on this point substituted for Danish law.

In certain other circumstances foreign law fulfills a prohibitive function. As a rule, it is provided that a marriage licence may not be issued to a party of foreign nationality and habitual residence if it is known to the Danish licensing authority that the intended

268. In the Final Protocol attached to the convention an exception is admitted in certain cases of consanguinity or affinity between the parties; see *Philip*, Conventions 280.

269. For FINLAND, NORWAY and SWEDEN see *infra* s. 38.

270. Marriage Order of 18 Dec. 1969, § 22 par. 1; *Philip*, IPR 195-196.

271. Marriage Order of 18 Dec. 1969, § 22 par. 3. This, however, only applies if the relevant foreign law is relied on and proved by the party concerned. The provision also makes it clear that no effect will be given to rules of foreign law which, conversely, establish more stringent requirements as to parental consent than those of DANISH law. See *Philip*, IPR 196.

marriage is absolutely prohibited in the country of which the party is a national or in which he has his habitual residence.[272] This means that certain impediments imposed by the relevant foreign law (determinable by an alternative test of a type which is quite unusual in the present connection) must be taken into account, in addition to the requirements of Danish law.

For several reasons, however, the practical significance of this modification of the general conflicts rule is more limited than might be expected at first sight. In the first place, the provision only applies when the prohibition in question is known to the licensing official. No system of *ex officio* investigation of foreign law is envisaged, nor is the party concerned required to prove his capacity to marry under such law. Secondly, rules of foreign law by which a general prohibition against remarriage is imposed on divorced persons are excluded from the scope of the provision, such prohibitions being disregarded in Denmark.[273] Thirdly, the marriage may be permitted in other circumstances too, despite the existence of a foreign prohibition which would normally preclude the grant of a licence, the decision being ultimately left to the discretion of the Danish Ministry of Justice.[274] In the exercise of this discretion the Ministry gives weight both to the nature of the prohibition in question, especially its compatibility with Danish public policy, and to the relationship of the parties with the foreign country and with Denmark, respectively. Public policy interferes more readily than otherwise when there is a strong connection with Denmark, but the latter factor also plays a role independently of public policy. Although the approach seems to be individualising rather than based on hard-and-fast criteria, the foreign prohibition will normally be left out of consideration, and the marriage be permitted, if one of the parties is a Danish national or if the parties intend to live as man and wife in Denmark. This last point may be illustrated by the following case:[275]

272. Marriage Order of 18 Dec. 1969, § 22 par. 2.

273. *Ibid.* Nevertheless, if to the knowledge of the licensing authority a party is subject to a prohibition of this type (imposed by the law of his nationality or habitual residence), the official must draw the attention of the parties to the fact and warn them that it is uncertain whether the marriage will be recognised abroad; see Circular Letter of the Ministry of Justice of 18 Dec. 1969, § 5.

274. Marriage Order of 18 Dec. 1969, § 22 par. 5.

275. Ministry of Justice, case L 3335/1936. See further *Hornslet, Danielsen and Hermann* 64-65; *Philip*, IPR 196-197.

> Two British nationals domiciled in Scotland wanted to marry during a temporary stay in Denmark. The man was a divorcee and the woman was the sister of his former wife. Following advertisement of the intended marriage in Scotland it became known that a union within this degree of affinity would be void by Scottish law. In view of the fact that the parties lacked any connection with Denmark and that the marriage would violate an unconditional prohibition imposed by a law as closely related to Danish matrimonial law as that of Scotland, it was held by the Ministry of Justice that Danish authorities should not lend their cooperation to the celebration of the proposed union. Later, however, at a time when the parties had become permanently resident in Denmark, the Ministry gave its permission to the marriage.

Although the ministerial practice leaves room for some uncertainty, it seems on the whole to be rather rare that effect is given to prohibitions of foreign law. This practice, in conjunction with the liberality of Danish (as generally Scandinavian) matrimonial law, has in many cases opened the way to the celebration of evasionary marriages in Denmark by foreigners who wanted to escape the effect of stricter foreign laws.[276]

37. *South Africa.* By the weight of judicial and extrajudicial opinion in South Africa, the substantive as well as the formal validity of a marriage must be determined by the *lex loci celebrationis.*[277] This rule follows the tradition of Roman-Dutch law but contrasts with the principle accepted in modern English law (and generally in the laws of British Commonwealth countries) that capacity to marry is governed by the law of the domicile.

276. In most of these cases the ground for excluding the foreign law from application was that it prohibited a divorcee from marrying again (because, in contrast with DANISH law, it did not recognise the divorce). See on the unions known as *Tondern marriages, infra* s. 63 at n. 502-504.

277. See *Hahlo(-Kahn)* 571-574, 580. The principal judicial authority is Friedman v. Friedman's Executors (1922), 43 N.L.R. 259. This case involved the validity of a marriage concluded in Natal between a man domiciled in the Transvaal and his deceased first wife's sister, who was domiciled in Natal. A union between persons so related was prohibited in the Transvaal but permitted by the local law of Natal. The latter law was applied, apparently in its capacity of the *lex loci celebrationis,* to uphold the marriage. The decision may have been influenced by the fact that one of the parties was domiciled in the country of celebration and so be open to the same explanation as the ENGLISH case of Sottomayor v. De Barros (No. 2) (1879), 5 P.D. 94 (*infra* s. 70); see *Dicey and Morris* 272 n. 77; but see *Hahlo(-Kahn)* 574 n. 2, where this interpretation is rejected.

In principle, the *lex loci celebrationis* applies whether the marriage has been celebrated in South Africa or in some foreign country. As regards foreign marriages, however, the rule is subject to several modifications and exceptions, the combined effect of which is to approach the South African system to that prevailing in England and, it seems, to place it somewhere mid-way on the scale between English and American law.

One such modification is achieved by the doctrine of *renvoi*, which probably applies when the effect is to uphold an otherwise invalid marriage (*i.e.*, a marriage which is invalid under the local law of the foreign country of celebration).[278] Other exceptions, conversely, operate to give extraterritorial force to invalidating rules of South African law, usually in circumstances where that law is the *lex domicilii* of the parties.

The first of these exceptions is based on the principle of public policy.[279] A foreign marriage, although good by the *lex loci celebrationis,* will be denied recognition if it is regarded as offensive to the fundamental notions of South African law. While the concept of public policy is ill defined, it probably only has reference to polygamous unions and to certain extreme cases of incest or want of age or consent.

Secondly, the principle of *fraus legis* espoused by South African law plays a part in the present connection.[280] This doctrine has a broader range than that of public policy, inasmuch as it enables the invalidation of any foreign marriage contracted in evasion of South African law, independently of the strength of the violated local policy. On the other hand, the principle is confined to cases where the parties are, or one of them is, domiciled in South Africa and have deliberately married elsewhere to escape a local prohibition.

Thirdly, a specific provision confers extraterritorial force on the prohibition of South African law against intermarriage between whites and non-whites ("Europeans" and "non-Europeans", in the terms of the relevant statute). A foreign marriage in contravention of that prohibition, regardless of its validity under the *lex loci celebrationis*, is declared to be void and of no effect whenever the male person is a citizen of or domiciled in the South African

278. See *Hahlo(-Kahn)* 580.

279. See *Hahlo(-Kahn)* 569, 582-584, 588.

280. See *Hahlo(-Kahn)* 569, 581-582 and *Pålsson,* Marriage, s. 289 at n. 83.

Republic.[281] This provision goes further than the exception based on *fraus legis,* firstly because it relies on an alternative test of domicile or nationality, and secondly because its application does not depend on proof of evasive intent.

III. The Principle of the Personal Law

A. General Introduction

38. *Domicile* v. *Nationality*. Marriage belongs to the core of personal status. In most countries of the world, therefore, the personal law of the parties is applied as the main rule governing the substantive conditions of marriage.[282] Moreover, as already demonstrated, even in countries espousing the principle of the *lex loci celebrationis* that principle is modified by numerous exceptions in favour of the personal law.

As usual, this brings out the fundamental opposition between the principles of domicile and nationality for determining the personal law. In addition to the general remarks on this problem already made by the author (see *Pålsson*, Marriage, Chapter 3), it may be noted that questions of capacity to marry have on the whole been comparatively resistant to the general tendency towards increasing the role of domicile and similar criteria at the expense of nationality. Although to some extent observable here too, this tendency is less pronounced than in several other matters, including divorce. One reason for this difference is that the problem as to "the proper law of the family", which is encountered with regard to the effects and the dissolution of marriage and for which the test of nationality often fails to afford an appropriate solution, does not arise at the stage of the formation of the union. The question of capacity to marry relates to each of the parties individually, so that no such difficulties stand in the way of applying the law of their respective nationality.

281. Prohibition of Mixed Marriages Act 1949, s. 1 (2) (as amended in 1968) in conjunction with s. 1 (1). See Ex parte Cathrall, 1965 (2) S.A. 505 (N); *Habermalz* 34-38; *Hahlo(-Kahn)* 63-64, 580-581; *E. Kahn*, The Prohibition of Mixed Marriages Act, 1949, and South African Conflict of Laws: 3 I.L.Q. 91-96 (1950).

282. See generally: *Alfonsín* 27-31; *Dyer Report* 25-31; *Gamillscheg*, Kommentar, art. 13 no. 10-14, 17-24, 29, 31-32; *Marín López* 35-42; *Poisson* 279-283; *Rabel* 264-265, 280-283; *Wolff*, IPR 188.

Accordingly, the rule of the *lex patriae* prevails in the majority of countries subscribing to the principle of the personal law in the present field. That rule was adopted in the *Hague Convention on Marriage* of 1902[283] and has been followed nearly everywhere in *Continental Europe,*[284] including the socialist States of Eastern Europe (though with the notable exception of the Soviet Union),[285] in two Scandinavian countries (*Finland* and *Sweden*),[286] as well as in numerous non-European countries possessing a codification inspired by Continental European models.[287] It has, too, found

283. Art. 1. See *Buzzati* 89-113; *Gamillscheg,* Kommentar, art. 13 no. 934-946; *F. Kahn* 61-69; *Travers* I 52-61.

284. AUSTRIA: DVO § 6 par. 1; *Köhler* 54-55, 58-60, 72; *Schwind,* IPR 141; BELGIUM: CC art. 3 par. 3, art. 170 *ter; Graulich* 68, 108-110; *Rigaux,* DIP 350-351; *van Hecke* 55; FRANCE: CC art. 3 par. 3, art. 170 par. 1-2; *Batiffol and Lagarde* II 35-37; *Bischoff* no. 11-14; *Vincent and Ponsard* no. 19-25; WEST GERMANY: EGBGB art. 13 par. 1; *Gamillscheg,* Kommentar, art. 13 no. 1-2, 6-11; *Kegel,* Kommentar, art. 13 no. 1-3; *Raape,* IPR 236-242; GREECE: CC art. 13; *Bendermacher-Geroussis* 1-5; *Maridakis* 214-218; *Zepos* 1043-1044; ITALY: Disp. prel. art. 17 par. 1; CC art. 115 par. 1, art. 116 par. 1; *Balladore Pallieri* 166-167; *A. Miele* 11-13; *Monaco* 156-160; *Morelli* 99-101, 105; *Vitta* II 174-177; LUXEMBOURG: CC art. 3 par. 3, art. 170; *Bernecker* 279; NETHERLANDS: Act of 15 May 1829, art. 6; *Joppe* 1-4; *Kollewijn* 45-46; *Lemaire* 92-94; PORTUGAL: CC art. 49 in conjunction with art. 31 par. 1; *Nitsche* 270-271; SPAIN: CC art. 9(1) par. 1 (as amended in 1974); *von Hoffmann and Ortiz-Arce* 664 (the rule was the same before the 1974 reform, see *Fernández Flores* 793-797; *Marín López* 51-53; *Miaja de la Muela* II 266-267; *Portero Sánchez* 503-507, 514-516); SWITZERLAND: NAG art. 7 c par. 1; *Beck,* art. 7 c no. 1-28, art. 7 d no. 1-9, art. 7 f no. 9-11; *Dutoit* 42-43; *Vischer,* IPR 584-589; TURKEY: *Ansay* 48; *Hirsch,* Die Quellen des internationalen Privatrechts in der Türkei: Festschrift Lewald 245, 253, 256.

285. Generally, *Florio* 343-344; *Korkisch* 619-620; *Szászy* 345. And see for ALBANIA: Act of 21 Nov. 1964, art. 5; *Begeja* 849; BULGARIA: FC art. 91; *Jessel* 152; *Koschucharoff* 497; CZECHOSLOVAKIA: Act of 4 Dec. 1963, § 19; *Florio* 321-323; EAST GERMANY: RAG § 18 par. 1; *FGB-Kommentar* 446-448 (on the corresponding provision of the EGFGB, which was repealed as from 1 Jan. 1976); HUNGARY: Decree-Law no. 23/1952, § 16 par. 1; *Pap* 745-746; *Réczei* 354-356, 363-365; *Szászy,* Chronique de jurisprudence hongroise de droit international privé (1945-1972): Clunet 1973, 460, 470-471; POLAND: Act of 12 Nov. 1965, art. 14; *Lasok* 244-245; *Sośniak,* Problems 137-140; RUMANIA: CC art. 2 par. 2; *Popescu and Eliescu* 675-676; YUGOSLAVIA: BMA art. 73 par. 1; *Blagojević* 116-118; *Katičić* 419-420; *Tchirkovitch* 223-225.

286. FINLAND: Act of 5 Dec. 1929, § 1, § 2 par. 1; SWEDEN: Act of 8 July 1904 (as amended in 1973) ch. 1 § 1; but cf. *infra* at n. 295.

287. For the *Islamic* countries see generally *Benattar* 58-62 and, e.g., EGYPT: CC art. 12; *El-Mikayis* 520-521; *Linant de Bellefonds* 828-831; IRAN: CC art. 6-7; IRAQ: CC art. 19 no. 1; LEBANON: *Tyan* 158-159;

expression in bilateral treaties, in particular in many treaties of legal assistance concluded between East European countries[288] but also in some treaties one of the parties to which is a West European country.[289]

The law of the domicile applies in *England* and other parts of the *United Kingdom* and *British Commonwealth.*[290] The position is similar in *Norway* where, however, the concept of domicile rather corresponds to that of habitual residence.[291] The pattern of solutions adopted in *Latin American* countries presents a rather confused picture. According to the *Bustamante Code,* which is

---

MOROCCO: *Dahir* of 12 Aug. 1913, art. 8; *Dahir* of 4 March 1960, art. 1-3; *Serick* 401; SENEGAL: FC art. 843 par. 1; SYRIA: CC art. 13; TUNISIA: Decree of 12 July 1956, art. 1, 2 and 4 no. 1; *Lescure,* L'évolution du système des conflits de lois tunisien. L'exemple du mariage: Rev. crit. d.i.p. 1959, 31, 63-68. Among other non-European countries see JAPAN: Act of 21 June 1898, art. 13 par. 1; *Sato* 320, 322; THAILAND: Act of 10 March 1938, § 19.

288. See in chronological order: CZECHOSLOVAKIA-EAST GERMANY, 11 Sept. 1956 (as amended by Protocol of 10 Dec. 1975) art. 27 par. 1; EAST GERMANY-POLAND, 1 Feb. 1957 (as amended by Protocol of 18 April 1975) art. 21 par. 1; EAST GERMANY-RUMANIA, 15 July 1958, art. 22 par. 3; HUNGARY-RUMANIA, 7 Oct. 1958, art. 22 par. 3; CZECHOSLOVAKIA-RUMANIA, 25 Oct. 1958, art. 22 par. 3; BULGARIA-RUMANIA, 3 Dec. 1958, art. 22 par. 3; HUNGARY-POLAND, 6 March 1959, art. 31 par. 2; ALBANIA-HUNGARY, 12 Jan. 1960, art. 26; POLAND-YUGOSLAVIA, 6 Feb. 1960, art. 25 par. 2; ALBANIA-RUMANIA, 12 Sept. 1960, art. 22; CZECHOSLOVAKIA-POLAND, 4 July 1961, art. 12 par. 1; CZECHOSLOVAKIA-HUNGARY, 2 Nov. 1961, art. 18 par. 1; BULGARIA-POLAND, 4 Dec. 1961, art. 22 par. 1; POLAND-RUMANIA, 25 Jan. 1962, art. 22 par. 3; CZECHOSLOVAKIA-YUGOSLAVIA, 20 Jan. 1964, art. 23 par. 1; BULGARIA-HUNGARY, 16 May 1966, art. 18 par. 3; EAST GERMANY-YUGOSLAVIA, 20 May 1966, art. 31 par. 1. See also BULGARIA-MONGOLIA, 27 Nov. 1968, art. 18 par. 3; EAST GERMANY-MONGOLIA, 30 April 1969, art. 28 par. 1. For comments see: *Drobnig,* Kollisionsnormen 171; *Lübchen* 84-86; *Sośniak,* Conventions 29; *idem,* Problems 141.

289. E.g., AUSTRIA-POLAND, 11 Dec. 1963, art. 24 par. 1; FRANCE-POLAND, 5 April 1967, art. 4 par. 2-3 (see *Bottini* 8-11; *Jodlowski and Ponsard* 565); FRANCE-YUGOSLAVIA, 18 May 1971, art. 3 par. 1. For certain other treaty provisions referring personal status generally to the *lex patriae* see *Makarov,* Quellen II no. 32-41, and the references given in *Pålsson,* Marriage, s. 78 n. 114-115.

290. ENGLAND: *Cheshire and North* 335-346; *Dicey and Morris* 258-268; *Graveson,* Conflict 256-269; SCOTLAND: *Anton* 276-283; *D.M. Walker,* Principles of Scottish Private Law I (ed. 2, Oxford 1975) 172-173, 238; AUSTRALIA: *Nygh* 403-410; CANADA: *Castel,* PIL 102-104; *Falconbridge* 700-715; see also the QUEBEC CC art. 6 par. 4 and *W.S. Johnson* 185; NEW ZEALAND: Marriage Act 1955, s. 3 (1); *Webb and Davis* 217-226, 256-257.

291. See *Gaarder* 131-136; *Holmøy* 15-16, 61; *Lövold* 267-268.

accepted by fifteen Latin American States, the parties are subject to their personal law in all matters relating to the substantive conditions of marriage, but the Code leaves each State free to decide for itself whether the personal law is to be determined by domicile, by nationality or by the aid of any other criterion.[292] While most Latin American countries, even within the group of States which have adopted the Bustamante Code, follow the *lex loci celebrationis* as the basic rule for capacity to marry (*supra* s. 33), a few of them espouse the test of domicile (*Brazil*) or even of nationality (*Venezuela*).[293] A mixed system exists, for instance, in *Peru,* where capacity to marry is governed by the law of the domicile of the respective parties, except that Peruvian nationals are always subject to Peruvian law.[294] In effect, a system of this type comes close to applying the *lex fori* as a general rule.

Another type of solution involving a compromise between the principles of domicile and of nationality is to be found in *Swedish* law. As a rule, a person who wants to marry before a Swedish authority must establish his right to marry under the law of his nationality (*supra* n. 286). By way of exception, however, if the party is habitually resident in a country other than that of his nationality and if he has been so resident for not less than two years, he may request the Swedish authority to determine his right to marry in accordance with the law of his habitual residence, provided that the other intending spouse consents.[295] This exception applies not only to foreigners habitually resident in Sweden but also to Swedish nationals habitually resident in a foreign country and to foreigners so resident in a third country. Foreign law is thus placed on an equal footing with the *lex fori.*[296]

292. Art. 36 and 7, respectively. In addition to the personal law, however identified, the *lex loci celebrationis* must be respected to a very large extent; see *infra* at n. 630.

293. See for BRAZIL: Act of 4 Sept. 1942, art. 7; *Garland* 23-28; for VENEZUELA: CC art. 9, 104, 108; *Lombard* 37-42. In both countries, however, the rule of the *lex domicilii* and of the *lex patriae,* respectively, is subject to far-reaching exceptions in favour of the *lex loci celebrationis;* see *infra* at n. 631-632. For a bilateral treaty referring capacity to marry to the *lex patriae* of the respective parties see that between COLOMBIA and ECUADOR, of 18 June 1903, art. 9.

294. CC, Preliminary Title, art. V.

295. Act of 8 July 1904 (as amended in 1973) ch. 1 § 2 par. 1-2; see NJA 1973 II 576-578.

296. Pursuant to par. 3 of the same provision, however, the Government may exceptionally (in individual cases) permit the application of SWEDISH law even in respect of a foreign national who has not been habitually resident

Further modifications of the nationality principle (and, to a considerably lesser degree, of the domicile principle), which result in a mixed system to some extent combining the two principles, are based on certain general conflicts rules and devices. Such effects are produced notably by resorting to domicile, /habitual/ residence and similar criteria as supplementary connecting factors in cases where the test of nationality fails to operate or is insufficient to indicate a specific legal system (*infra* s. 40-42), and by applying the doctrine of *renvoi* (*infra* s. 58-59).

39. *Rationale.* Reliance on the personal law has some obvious advantages over relying on the *lex loci celebrationis.* The application of the personal law, whether determined by domicile or by nationality or by a combination of both factors, secures a certain stability in the regulation of a person's capacity to marry and avoids the highly unsatisfactory consequence that this question should depend on the often accidental place of celebration. Evasion of "inconvenient" marriage laws is rendered considerably more difficult, if not impossible. Although many parties may not welcome such an attitude, their freedom to evade the law of their home country is generally not an interest worthy of legal protection.

As is usually recognised even in American law (*supra* s. 6, 10, 14), the country with which the parties are durably connected has a more significant interest than the *locus celebrationis* in controlling the creation of marital status (apart from the formalities involved). In general, therefore, the personal law is to be preferred as the law governing the substantive conditions of marriage. As long as the principle of the *lex loci celebrationis* is not universally accepted, giving effect to the personal law is more likely to prevent the creation of limping marriages, provided that that law is required to be satisfied not only when the validity of a marriage already entered into is in issue but also when a marriage is about to be celebrated.

On the other hand, the adoption of such a rule puts a heavy strain on the machinery for proving and applying foreign law in the country of celebration, especially in view of the fact that this task rests, primarily, with marriage officials who are in an even less favourable position than the courts to discharge it. This strain is only partly relieved by the widespread practice of using certificates of capacity to marry for this purpose (*infra* s. 115-116).

The principle also carries with it a number of other complica-

---

in Sweden for two years. To that extent the rule embodies a unilateral preference for the *lex fori.* See for the legislative history NJA 1973 II 578-579.

tions. The statement that "the personal law governs" is indeed a very rudimentary one and must be supplemented by details which concern many questions. These questions, beginning with the basic choice between domicile and nationality as the relevant connecting factor, are approached in a variety of ways in different countries. In what follows, a number of problems will be considered which involve the substantive details and the application of the principle (B), as well as its scope and the exceptions to which it is made subject (C). This exposition will be followed by a special part, where various types of requirement for or impediment to marriage are examined separately (D). Finally, it is proposed to deal with some predominantly administrative or procedural matters, namely, dispensations from marriage impediments and proof of foreign law (E).

B. Specification of the Principle

a. *Nationality as Connecting Factor: Problem Cases*

40. *Dual Nationality.* In so far as nationality is used as the relevant test to identify the appropriate law for capacity to marry, a problem presents itself when a party holds two (or more) nationalities. The rules adopted or recommended for the solution of such conflicts generally apply in this situation.

As usual, a considerable diversity of opinion exists in cases where both nationalities are *foreign*. One solution, which has or has had some support in Continental European countries, is to the effect that capacity to marry must be established under both national laws involved (cumulative choice of law).[297] This proposal aims at ensuring that a marriage will only be entered into if it will be recognised as valid in both home countries. The policy of preventing the creation of a limping status, which is the main desider-

297. See, e.g., AUSTRIA: *Hainzl,* Hat ein ausländischer Doppelstaater zur Eheschliessung in Österreich von beiden Staaten ein Ehefähigkeitszeugnis beizubringen?: ÖStA 24 (1970) 64-65; [WEST] GERMANY: *Beyer* 34; *Frankenstein* 69-70; ITALY: Cass. 14 March 1968, Riv. dir. int. proc. 1968, 674 (where, however, it was not necessary to decide the point; cf. the decision of the court below, App. Torino 11 July 1964, Riv. dir. int. proc. 1965, 135); App. Milano 6 Dec. 1968, Riv. dir. int. proc. 1969, 808; *A. Miele* 68-77 (but see *idem* 78-82, where the writer advocates a solution permitting the party to opt in favour of the law of one of his nationalities); SWITZERLAND: *Niederer* 159; *S. Schmidheiny,* Die privatrechtlichen Folgen der selbständigen Staatsangehörigkeit der Ehefrau (Thesis, Zürich 1958) 37-38, 40.

atum behind the rule of the national law, is thus carried to its maximum length. On the other hand, such a solution, more than any other, tends to restrict the right to marry and, if extended to situations where a marriage is attacked *ex post*, to facilitate annulment. This is contrary to the policy of favouring marriage, which carries weight everywhere. Chiefly for this reason, a cumulative application of the different laws at issue is now usually considered unacceptable.[298]

All other solutions that have been proposed are based on the principle that one law must prevail.[299] In consequence, it will always be both sufficient and necessary that the intending spouse has capacity to marry according to that law. Although the criteria used for the choice of the relevant law vary, most of them result in giving weight to the person's domicile or (habitual) residence as connecting factors supplementing nationality. This is so whether those criteria are regarded as solely decisive or whether they are taken into account within the doctrine of effective nationality, which is favoured by the prevailing trend of opinion in most countries attached to the nationality principle.[300]

The position is simpler in the more frequently occurring case where one of the competing nationalities is that of the *forum* State. The generally accepted rule is that such conflicts must be resolved in favour of the local nationality, regardless of the party's domicile and of other factors pointing to the strength of the respective nationalities.[301] This rule includes capacity to marry, which accordingly will be determined by the *lex fori* alone.[302]

298. See *Pålsson*, Marriage, s. 153 at n. 136.

299. A survey of such solutions is given *ibid.* s. 152, 154-158. See also *Gamillscheg*, Kommentar, before art. 13 no. 167-173.

300. References in *Pålsson*, Marriage, s. 157 n. 145. See also, e.g., AUSTRIA: *Schwind*, IPR 100-101, 147; FRANCE: *Bischoff* no. 16; *Vincent and Ponsard* no. 26; WEST GERMANY: *Beitzke*, Das Personalstatut des Doppelstaatlers: Liber Amicorum Adolf F. Schnitzer (Geneva 1979) 19, 28; *Gamillscheg*, Kommentar, before art. 13 no. 171, art. 13 no. 710; SWITZERLAND: *Beck*, before art. 59 no. 61, art. 7 c no. 30; *Secrétan* 43; YUGOSLAVIA: *Katičić* 420-422.

301. See *Pålsson*, Marriage, s. 159. See also *Gamillscheg*, Kommentar, before art. 13 no. 153-156.

302. Specifically with reference to capacity to marry see, e.g., AUSTRIA: *Hainzl*, Doppelstaater (*supra* n. 297) 65; FRANCE: *Bischoff* no. 16; *Vincent and Ponsard* no. 26; [WEST] GERMANY: LG Tübingen 25 July 1934, IPRspr. 1934 no. 57; AG Lübeck 7 Jan. 1955, IPRspr. 1954/55 no. 77; *Beitzke*, Doppelstaatler (*supra* n. 300) 33; ITALY: *A. Miele* 68; SWITZERLAND: *Beck*, art. 7 c no. 30, art. 7 e no. 9; *Muret* 29; *Stauffer*, art. 7 c no. 1, art. 7 e no. 2.

As noted in the general discussion of this problem, however, such automatic preference for the local nationality has in recent years been criticised as excessive by many Continental European writers.[303] These writers favour a more objective and less rigid approach, which more or less resembles that implied, in respect of conflicts between foreign nationalities, by the doctrine of effective nationality. As has been submitted earlier, this new tendency has much to commend itself. So far, however, it has only found occasional support in judicial and administrative practice involving questions of capacity to marry.[304]

41. *Statelessness.* The general rules adopted for the choice of law to govern the personal status of parties lacking any nationality extend to capacity to marry. Normally, therefore, the capacity of a stateless person must be determined in accordance with the law of his domicile or habitual residence.[305] In the absence of a domicile or habitual residence (as the case may be) in any country, reliance is placed on the law of the person's temporary residence or on the *lex fori.*[306]

303. See *Pålsson*, Marriage, s. 161. See also *Gamillscheg*, Kommentar, before art. 13 no. 157-166; *Samtleben*, Mehrstaater im internationalen Privatrecht: RabelsZ 42 (1978) 456-484; *Schwind*, IPR 100.

304. A WEST GERMAN case may be cited where the court, in judging the validity of a marriage between parties of local and foreign (Israeli) nationality, gave preference to the law of the latter nationality, as that with which the parties were more closely connected: OLG Stuttgart 5 April 1968, IPRspr. 1968/69 no. 232; see *Gamillscheg*, Kommentar, art. 13 no. 46.

305. See *Pålsson*, Marriage, s. 164. Specifically as concerns capacity to marry see also, e.g., AUSTRIA: *Köhler* 55, 58; *Schwind*, IPR 146; FRANCE: Trib. Seine 23 Feb. 1883, Clunet 1883, 388 (see also Trib. Seine 14 Feb. 1908, Clunet 1908, 813, dealing with the formalities of marriage); *Bischoff* no. 18; *Vincent and Ponsard* no. 27, 77; WEST GERMANY: LG Ulm 8 Aug. 1956, IPRspr. 1956/57 no. 101; BGH 11 June 1958, BGHZ 27, 375, IPRspr. 1958/59 no. 5; *Beitzke*, Ehevoraussetzungen 287-288; *Gamillscheg*, Kommentar, art. 13 no. 41-43, 45, cf. before art. 13 no. 126-129; *Wengler*, Gutachten no. 20; HUNGARY: *Szászy*, Chronique (*supra* n. 285) 470; NETHERLANDS: Rb. Middelburg 18 Nov. 1935, N.J. 1936 no. 142, Bull. I.I.I. 35 (1936) 225; Rb. 's-Hertogenbosch 31 July 1936, N.J. 1936 no. 860, Bull. I.I.I. 36 (1937) 41; SWEDEN: Act of 8 July 1904 (as amended in 1973) ch. 7 § 3; SWITZERLAND: *Beck*, art. 7 c no. 29, art. 7 e no. 10; *Muret* 28; *Vischer*, IPR 586; YUGOSLAVIA: *Katičić* 421-422.

306. See *Pålsson*, Marriage, s. 165. As to cases where an intending spouse possibly has a nationality but where that nationality is unspecified or cannot be determined with certainty, see the FRENCH decision of Trib. Pontoise 23 April 1969, Clunet 1969, 928, note Dayant (applying the *lex fori*, which coincided with the *lex domicilii*), and the WEST GERMAN Service Instruction of 1968, § 140(7) (such parties to be treated as if they were stateless).

Similar rules are widely accepted as regards the personal status, including capacity to marry, of *political refugees* even where such persons are still in possession of the nationality of the State from which they have escaped (statelessness *de facto*).[307]

42. *Composite Legal Systems.* The rule that capacity to marry is governed by the *lex patriae* is insufficient, and must be supplemented (or possibly replaced) by other rules, where the person concerned possesses the nationality of a State with a composite legal system. The same problem is presented by conflicts rules using domicile or other territorial criteria as connecting factors, in so far as they point to a composite legal system of personal application, *i.e.* laws of the type found in most Arab States, in Israel, India and many other countries. These problems, too, are general in nature and approached in accordance with general rules.

Thus, where the composite legal system is one of *personal* application, it is generally agreed that reliance must be placed on the rules of interpersonal (interconfessional, etc.) law to be found in that system itself.[308] If, for instance, a question of the capacity to marry of a domiciled Israeli national has to be decided in England or in West Germany, the governing law will be that of Israel, respectively, as the party's *lex domicilii* or *lex patriae*. This reference will be understood to mean the law of whichever religious community in Israel (Jewish, Muslim or Christian) the party belongs to, since this is the relevant criterion according to Israeli law.[309]

Similarly, where the composite legal system is of *territorial* application, it is common ground that recourse must be had, in the first place, to such unitary rules of interlocal conflicts law as may

307. See generally *Pålsson,* Marriage, s. 166-168 with references; *adde, Gamillscheg,* Kommentar, before art. 13 no. 135-151. Specifically as concerns the substantive conditions of marriage see also, e.g., AUSTRIA: *Köhler* 55, 58; *Schwind,* IPR 146; FRANCE: *Bischoff* no. 18; *Vincent and Ponsard* no. 27, 78; WEST GERMANY: LG Hannover 17 June 1950, IPRspr. 1950/51 no. 11; AG Bielefeld 29 Aug. 1961, IPRspr. 1960/61 no. 99; *Beitzke,* Ehevoraussetzungen 288 (but see OLG Celle 26 June 1963, IPRspr. 1962/63 no. 75, applying the *lex patriae,* HUNGARIAN law, although the party was a political refugee); SWEDEN: Act of 8 July 1904 (as amended in 1973) ch. 7 § 3; SWITZERLAND: *Götz,* art. 105 no. 25.

308. See *Pålsson,* Marriage, s. 173; also, *Gamillscheg,* Kommentar, before art. 13 no. 191-193, art. 13 no. 65; *Raape and Sturm* 385-386.
385-386.

309. See, for example, for WEST GERMAN cases involving the prohibition of JEWISH law against marriage between persons of different religion: OLG Hamm 17 Nov. 1970, IPRspr. 1970 no. 48; BGH 12 May 1971, BGHZ 56, 180, IPRspr. 1971 no. 40. See further *infra* s. 108.

exist in the composite State itself.[310] In the past, the Polish statute on interprovincial conflict of laws was perhaps the most important enactment of this type, frequently called in aid to specify a reference to the then composite legal system of Poland, *inter alia*, in cases involving capacity to marry.[311] The Soviet Union and Yugoslavia are present-day examples of countries in relation to which this method of identifying the applicable law is appropriate, both of them having a composite system of family law in conjunction with overriding rules of interlocal conflicts law.[312]

So far, however, most problems encountered in practice have concerned nationals of composite States such as Canada, the United Kingdom or the United States, which lack an overriding

310. See *Pålsson*, Marriage, s. 176; see also *Gamillscheg*, Kommentar, before art. 13 no. 188-190; *Raape and Sturm* 380.

311. See, for example, the GERMAN decisions cited by *Gamillscheg ibid.* no. 188. With the unification of POLISH family law in the years following the Second World War, this statute lost its practical importance; see *Pålsson*, Marriage, s. 178.

312. The family law of the SOVIET UNION is composite in character, though only to a limited extent. The basic rules of Soviet family law were unified by the Fundamental Principles of 1968, which apply throughout the Union. The enactment of supplementary legislation, however, falls within the competence of the various Union Republics (Fundamental Principles art. 7), and these rules differ in many details. Overriding provisions for the solution of interlocal conflicts arising from this diversity of legislation are given in art. 8 and 32 par. 2 of the Fundamental Principles. Cf. in this connection the WEST GERMAN decision of LG Stuttgart 5 Aug. 1964, IPRspr. 1964/65 no. 80, involving SOVIET law as it stood before the adoption of the Fundamental Principles and holding a rule of all-Union law to prevail over a contrary provision in the governing Family Code of one of the Union Republics. The family law of YUGOSLAVIA was unified by a number of postwar federal enactments, including the Basic Marriage Act of 1946, but has in recent years undergone a new development towards "fragmentation". This development started in 1971 when, by an amendment of the federal Constitution, exclusive legislative competence, *inter alia*, in the area of family law was vested in the constituent Republics and autonomous Provinces of Yugoslavia. Since then these units have adopted, or are preparing to adopt, their own statutes on matters of family law, which supersede the previous federal enactments. Conflict of laws, however, remains within the federal competence. This includes questions of interlocal conflicts law, which may be expected to play a major role in the future. So far no statute has been enacted on this subject, but new legislation covering both international and interlocal conflicts is being prepared. See *Bergmann(-Ferid)*, Jugoslawien; *Hepting*, Bemerkungen zur Anwendung der jugoslawischen Teilrechte in der deutschen Praxis: StAZ 1977, 99-101; *Sajko*, Die Rechtsspaltung im jugoslawischen Familien- und Erbrecht und ihre kollisionsrechtlichen Auswirkungen: StAZ 1977, 93-99.

system of rules for the solution either of interlocal or of international conflicts.[313] Various approaches have been adopted by Continental European and other courts, faced with the task of applying the *lex patriae* of such persons to determine their capacity to marry.

The method normally used is to select the law of a particular law district within the composite unit by the aid of a supplementary connecting factor designated by the conflicts rules of the *lex fori.* As regards American nationals, the criteria usually relied upon for this purpose are the party's citizenship of and/or domicile in one of the United States or, in default of that, his last American domicile.[314] In cases involving British nationals, especially United Kingdom citizens, the relevant supplementary connecting factor has often been left unspecified. Occasionally preference has been given to English law without proper investigation, apparently because the court wrongly identified that law with the law of the whole composite unit.[315] Mostly, however, the law chosen seems in fact to have been the only one (within the composite area) to which the party concerned had any relation, in particular because he was domiciled, or had had his last domicile within the composite unit, in the law district in question.[316]

313. Cf. *Pålsson,* Marriage, s. 178-179. For the present purpose AUSTRALIA is no longer a composite State, since unity of matrimonial law throughout Australia was brought about by the Matrimonial Causes Act 1959 and the Marriage Act 1961; see *Nygh* 67.

314. See generally *Pålsson,* Marriage, s. 183-184. For WEST GERMAN cases specifically relating to capacity to marry see: BayObLG 31 May 1966, IPRspr. 1966/67 no. 146 (Michigan law); OLG Karlsruhe 3 Oct. 1968, IPRspr. 1968/69 no. 69 (Texas law); AG Zweibrücken 14 May 1970, IPRspr. 1970 no. 46 (Nebraska law). Cf. *Drobnig,* PIL 84; *Gamillscheg,* Kommentar, before art. 13 no. 197-199.

315. See, for instance, the FRENCH decision of Cour Paris 23 March 1888, Clunet 1889, 638, applying ENGLISH law (though with acceptance of a reference back by the conflicts rules of that law to the *lex fori*) to determine the capacity to marry of an Irishman. Some other courts have relied on the false concept that the party concerned was of "English nationality"; see FRANCE: Trib. Grenoble 7 May 1958, G.P. 1958.2.82; ITALY: Cass. 14 March 1968, Riv. dir. int. proc. 1968, 674; cf. *Pålsson,* Marriage, s. 174, 180.

316. See, e.g., WEST GERMANY: President of OLG Hamburg 5 Aug. 1955, IPRspr. 1954/55 no. 84 (SCOTTISH law); LG Hamburg 16 Oct. 1958, IPRspr. 1958/59 no. 117 (ENGLISH law); AG Hamburg 9 and 22 Dec. 1966, IPRspr. 1966/67 no. 64 and 66, respectively (do., with *renvoi* to the *lex fori*); *Wengler,* Gutachten no. 18; ITALY: Cass. 14 March 1968, Riv. dir. int. proc. 1968, 674 (ENGLISH law).

When the problem of specifying a reference to the national law of an American or a United Kingdom citizen arises in a country which accepts the principle of *renvoi*, the two questions are usually closely interwoven.[317] In most of the above-mentioned cases the relevant law within the foreign composite system was identified primarily for the purpose of applying its conflicts rules, rather than its domestic rules, on capacity to marry. In several cases those conflicts rules were found to refer back to the *lex fori*, either because the place of celebration was in the forum country or because, at the time of the marriage, the party was domiciled there. Accepting this *renvoi*, the court in the end applied its own domestic law.[318]

The connection between the two questions is even more obvious in another group of cases, concerned with the capacity to marry of American nationals. Despite the fact that a federal conflicts law of marriage does not exist in the United States, the courts in these cases purported to rely on "American" conflicts rules (without indicating the law of any particular state), which were understood to refer either to the *lex loci celebrationis* or to the party's *lex domicilii*.[319] Although, strictly speaking, these decisions are untenable, they may perhaps be rationalised on the footing that effect was given to (what the respective courts believed to be) uniform conflicts principles (as distinct from overriding unitary rules) accepted all over the United States.[320] However this may be, such an approach seems only conceivable in countries endorsing the principle of *renvoi*. The reason is that the "American" conflicts rules on capacity to marry may well point to the law of a country outside the United States, depending on the place of celebration of the marriage or on the domicile of the parties. In fact, a reference back to the *lex fori* was found and accepted in nearly all cases within the present group.[321]

317. Cf. on these complications, and for a suggestion of how to avoid them, *Pålsson*, Marriage, s. 186.

318. See further *infra* s. 58-59 with references.

319. FRANCE: Trib. Seine 6 April 1951, Rev. crit. d.i.p. 1953, 586, note Batiffol; Trib. Seine 10 Jan. 1962, G.P. 1962.1.284; cf. *Bischoff* no. 17; *Vincent and Ponsard* no. 26, 121; [WEST] GERMANY: OLG Dresden 15 Jan. 1912, OLGR 26, 211; LG Tübingen 25 July 1934, IPRspr. 1934 no. 57; AG Zweibrücken 14 May 1970, IPRspr. 1970 no. 46.

320. For a discussion of this approach see *Pålsson*, Marriage, s. 179-180.

321. The only exception among the cases cited *supra* n. 319 is the FRENCH decision of Trib. Seine 6 April 1951, Rev. crit. d.i.p. 1953, 586, applying the law of New York as the *lex loci celebrationis*, to which the "AMERICAN" conflicts rule was held to refer.

b. *Parties Subject to Different Personal Laws*

43. *Introductory*. Whether the personal law governing capacity to marry is determined by domicile (or analogous criteria, such as habitual residence) or by nationality, a problem of some difficulty arises where, as very often happens, the parties are subject to different personal laws at the time of the marriage (assuming that time to be the relevant one; see *infra* s. 53). Several types of solution are possible and have been proposed or adopted in such situations.[322] Some of them are to the effect that the capacity of both parties falls to be tested by a single law, either one of the two personal laws involved or a third, "neutral" law (*infra* s. 44-46). The prevailing view, however, is that both personal laws must be applied, either cumulatively (so that each party must meet the requirements of both laws) or separately as to each of the parties (*infra* s. 47-48). The latter alternative, which amounts to judging each party's capacity by the standards of his own law, is the one usually accepted in principle. The difference between this approach and that requiring a cumulative application of the two laws is, however, reduced by the doctrine that certain marriage impediments are bilateral, in the sense that they extend to both parties. It will therefore be necessary to discuss that doctrine and the distinction drawn between bilateral impediments and others, which are characterised as unilateral (*infra* s. 49-52).

ba. *Solutions Requiring Choice of One Law*

44. *Preference for Male Party's Personal Law*. According to a view which enjoyed much support in the past, the future husband's personal law should prevail, and the capacity to marry of both parties should be determined by that law alone.[323] This may have been natural at a time when the husband was commonly regarded as the head of the family and the female party "married out" of her community, losing her former nationality and/or domicile through the marriage and acquiring that of the husband instead.

322. For surveys of these solutions see: *Dyer Report* 31-33; *Poisson* 280-283; *Rabel* 284-286.

323. For references see: *Gamillscheg*, Kommentar, art. 13 no. 26-27; *Rabel* 285; *G. Walker* 573 (n. 10), 574.

The husband's community could then properly be regarded as "the true seat of the marriage relation."[324]

Solutions based on a preference for the husband's law still receive, or until recently received, support in some European countries.[325] One example is the doctrine, which plays a part in *English* law, that capacity to marry is to be referred to the law of the country of the intended matrimonial home, inasmuch as that doctrine is combined with a presumption in favour of the law of the husband's antenuptial domicile (*infra* s. 54). Another illustration is afforded by the conflicts rules of *Swiss* law, as construed by the courts and appropriate administrative bodies. Basically, it is true, Swiss law provides that each of the parties is subject to his (her) *lex patriae* in matters of capacity to marry.[326] This rule applies where the parties are, or one of them is, of foreign nationality, irrespective of whether the marriage is celebrated in Switzerland or elsewhere.[327] In the case of a marriage in Switzerland between a man of Swiss and a woman of foreign nationality, it has nevertheless been suggested, and apparently held in a part of the relevant cantonal practice, that proof of the female party's capacity under her national law can be dispensed with if the requirements of Swiss (domestic) law are fulfilled.[328] A similar view

324. *von Savigny,* System des heutigen römischen Rechts VIII (Berlin 1849, reprint 1961) 325-326; *idem,* Private International Law and the Retrospective Operation of Statutes. A Treatise on the Conflict of Laws (transl. by W. Guthrie; ed. 2, Edinburgh 1880) 291.

325. Besides the references given below see for FRANCE: *Bartin* 123; for ITALY: *Vitta,* Relazione e progetto di legge sul diritto internazionale privato: Prospettive del diritto internazionale privato (Milan 1968) 1, 238 (but see *Vitta* II 176-177); for SPAIN: T.S. 29 Sept. 1961, Rev. Esp. Der. Int. 16 (1963) 611; *Portero Sánchez* 514.

326. NAG art. 7 c par. 1; see the comments on this provision cited *supra* n. 284.

327. For marriages celebrated abroad there is a "rival" conflicts provision in NAG art. 7 f par. 1, which according to its wording validates such marriages if they are "in conformity with the laws there in force"; see *infra* s. 69. It has been held by the Federal Tribunal, however, that this provision is limited to marriages between Swiss nationals and that art. 7 c, requiring compliance with the *lex patriae,* applies to foreign marriages in other cases: BG 2 Dec. 1943, BGE 69 II 342, 345; BG 11 Nov. 1954, BGE 80 I 427, 431-434; BG 3 June 1971, BGE 97 I 389, 402-403. Opinion among writers is divided on this question. See for support of the view taken by the Federal Tribunal, e.g., *Secrétan* 31-35; *Spivak* 46-49; *Vaucher* 548-551. Other writers argue that art. 7 c should be confined to marriages in Switzerland and that more liberal rules should be followed in the recognition of foreign marriages; see *Dutoit* 42-43; *Lachenal; Vischer,* IPR 588-589.

328. See: *Gamillscheg,* Kommentar, art. 13 no. 14; *Secrétan* 39-41;

prevails for mixed marriages entered into abroad. It is settled that such a marriage in order to be recognised in Switzerland must be valid by the husband's *lex patriae* if he is of foreign and the wife of Swiss nationality.[329] It is at least very doubtful, however, whether validity by the law of the female party's (premarital) nationality is prerequisite to recognition in the converse case of a marriage between a man of Swiss and a woman of foreign nationality.[330] The weight of extrajudicial opinion holds that this case must be treated as if both parties were, and had at all material times been, Swiss nationals.[331] If both parties are foreigners but of different nationality, it has similarly been suggested that recognition in Switzerland should only depend on compliance with the husband's law and that the wife's (premarital) law should be left out of consideration.[332]

On the whole, however, such a preference for the husband's personal law is today regarded as arbitrary and unjustifiable. Logically, of course, it is open to the objection that it assigns proleptic operation to the relationship of which the formation or validity is the very question to be submitted to the applicable law.[333] A second objection, which carries much more force, is that solutions of this kind are incompatible with modern views of equality between man and woman.[334]

45. *Preference for Personal Law Coinciding with Lex Fori.* Another proposal is to the effect that the *lex fori* should prevail where it is the personal law of one of the parties, whether of the man or of the woman. This solution gained some support in *France* a few decades ago under the influence of the nationalistic conflicts

---

Stauffer, art. 7 e no. 14; *Vischer,* IPR 586. The argument advanced in support of this solution is essentially that the woman acquires Swiss nationality through such a marriage and that it is of relatively little importance whether the union will be recognised as valid by the law of her premarital nationality. Cf. *Beck,* art. 7 e no. 8; *von Overbeck,* Wiederverheiratung 346 n. 3.

329. BG 11 Nov. 1954, BGE 80 I 427, 434.

330. This question was expressly left open by the decision of BG 11 Nov. 1954, *ibid.* Cf. *Lachenal* 39.

331. To this effect see *Beck,* art. 7 f no. 11, 74; *Vaucher* 549. *Contra,* see *Spivak* 68-70. As noted *supra* n. 327, foreign marriages between Swiss nationals come within the provision of NAG art. 7 f, which refers to the *lex loci celebrationis.*

332. See *Beck,* art. 7 f no. 10-11, 59, 74, 85; *Vaucher* 549.

333. See, for example, *Audinet* 181-182; *Bischoff* no. 22; *A. Miele* 60-62; *Monaco* 156-157.

334. See, for instance, *Gamillscheg,* Kommentar, art. 13 no. 25, 28; *H. Müller* 39-40.

doctrines whose chief proponent was Professor *Niboyet.*[335] Present-day examples of precedence being taken by the *lex fori* are to be found in the conflicts provisions enacted by certain Arab States. In *Egypt,* for instance, the substantive conditions of marriage are governed by Egyptian law alone (except that each party's *lex patriae* applies with regard to capacity in a narrow sense) if, at the time of the marriage, one of the parties is a local national.[336]

This type of solution, too, however, is usually considered arbitrary and rejected almost everywhere, at least as a general rule. Nevertheless, a partly similar effect is often achieved by other conflicts rules and mechanisms conducive to the application of the *lex fori.* One example of the *vis attractiva* exerted by that law is that the doctrine of public policy is more readily called in aid to defeat the application of the normally governing personal law (where foreign) of one of the parties if the other party is subject to the *lex fori* as his personal law than otherwise. This is an aspect of the tendency for reliance on public policy to depend largely on the degree of connection of the case with the forum country (*infra* s. 72). Another expression of the favour of the *lex fori* is the existence, in several countries, of unilateral conflicts rules expanding the normal scope of that law in certain situations where one of the parties is a local domiciliary or national, as the case may be.[337]

335. For decisions relying, at least in part, on the doctrine referred to here see: Trib. Seine 17 March 1948, Rev. crit. d.i.p. 1948, 112, note Niboyet; Trib. Seine 20 July 1948, Rev. crit. d.i.p. 1949, 96, note (critical on this point) G. Holleaux. In both these cases the validity of a marriage, celebrated in France, between a man of foreign and a woman of French nationality was said to be determinable by FRENCH law alone. This solution carries the doctrine of the prevalence of the local nationality even further than was claimed by its originators, who did not extend the doctrine to questions of the formation (as distinct from the effects and the dissolution) of marriage; see *Delaume,* L'influence de la nationalité française sur la solution des conflits de lois en matière des personnes: Rev. crit. d.i.p. 1949, 5, 17; *Niboyet* V 338, 360. The decisions under review are clearly inconsistent with the mainstream of FRENCH authority on the matter; see *infra* n. 342.

336. CC art. 14 as compared with art. 12; see *El-Mikayis* 521; *Linant de Bellefonds* 836-840. This rule has been followed in IRAQ (where it seems even to apply without the exception foreseen by the EGYPTIAN provision): CC art. 19 no. 5 as compared with no. 1; and in SYRIA: CC art. 15 as compared with art. 13.

337. For examples of such rules see *infra* s. 70 (ENGLAND) and n. 621 (YUGOSLAVIA).

46. *Choice of Third, "Neutral" Law.* Sometimes the more radical view is taken that neither of the personal laws, where different, should apply and that the choice of the governing law, instead, should be based on a "neutral" criterion. The law thus chosen may, of course, and in practice usually will, coincide with the personal law of one of the parties, but it may also be the law of a third country.

One solution of this type is that represented by the *English* doctrine of the intended matrimonial home (*infra* s. 54). Similar to that doctrine is the rule of *Brazilian* law according to which, in the absence of a common domicile at the time of the marriage, the law of the first marital domicile applies.[338]

In *France,* where the substantive conditions of marriage are normally governed by the *lex patriae,* occasional support may be found for a "neutral" choice of law in cases where the parties do not have a common nationality. One proposal is that recourse should be had to the *lex loci celebrationis.*[339] Another solution has been adopted by a few decisions holding that annulment, on grounds of substance, of a marriage between parties of different nationality is governed by the law of the common domicile of the spouses.[340] This solution is inspired by the analogy with divorce, for which such a rule was at the time accepted in French practice.[341] Neither of the two "neutral" approaches, however, has found much response among courts and writers. The prevailing French view is clearly in favour of applying the *lex patriae* of each of the parties to determine the substantive conditions of marriage, whether the question occurs in a suit for annulment or in any other connection.[342]

338. Act of 4 Sept. 1942, art. 7 par. 3; *Garland* 24. Cf. for a WEST GERMAN case where this provision was considered and applied within the context of the principle of *renvoi,* OLG Celle 18 Sept. 1968, IPRspr. 1968/69 no. 67. For a critical comment on this decision see *Samtleben.*

339. See *Bottini* 10. The same solution is advocated, for the SOCIALIST countries of EASTERN EUROPE, by *Petev* 605-606.

340. Trib. Melun 20 Jan. 1954, G.P. 1954.1.272; Trib. Grenoble 7 May 1958, G.P. 1958.2.82. See *Delaume* 99. In favour of such a rule see also *Audit* 36, 284, 303, 305, 315-317, 338.

341. For criticism of this extension of the rule in divorce see *Bischoff,* La compétence du droit français dans le règlement des conflits de lois (Paris 1959) 56 (n. 155), 60; *Francescakis,* Le divorce d'époux de nationalité différente: Rev. crit. d.i.p. 1954, 325, 340, 346.

342. See, e.g., Trib. Seine 5 May 1919, Rev. crit. d.i.p. 1919, 543; Trib. Seine 6 April 1951, Rev. crit. d.i.p. 1953, 586; Trib. Paris 15 March 1972, Rev. crit. d.i.p. 1973, 509, note D. Alexandre; *Batiffol and Lagarde* II 12-13, 37; *Bischoff* no. 21-26; *Vincent and Ponsard* no. 32-36, 74.

bb. *Solutions Requiring Application of Both Personal Laws*

47. *Cumulative Approach.* It has occasionally been suggested that both personal laws must be applied in cumulation.[343] If this approach were to be followed consistently, each of the parties would have to comply with all substantive conditions of marriage imposed not only by his own law but also by the law of the other party. It will be appreciated that such a solution carries the policy of preventing conflicts with the personal laws involved to its maximum length. Indeed, it goes further than warranted by the desire to prevent such conflicts, for the personal law itself to which either party is subject will not normally claim complete control over the other party. By any reasonable standard, it seems that the cumulative approach is unduly restrictive of the right to marry.[344] In its generalised form it has scarcely any adherents today. Nevertheless, as a consequence of the view that certain marriage impediments are bilateral in character, it is accepted that each party must in some respects submit to the control of both laws (*infra* s. 49-52).

48. *Each Party Subject to His Own Law.* The prevailing view in almost all countries following the principle of the personal law is that each of the parties must comply with the requirements of his own law, but not with those imposed by the law of the other party.[345] In English literature this system has been christened the *dual domicile doctrine* (of course, where the *lex patriae* is the relevant law nationality must be substituted for domicile), but it is better characterised by French writers as *le système d'application distributive des lois en conflit.*[346]

In a way this approach, too, involves a cumulative application of the two laws. This is so in the sense that a marriage can only be validly created if — in addition to meeting the requirements as to

343. See among older works: *Arminjon,* Précis de droit international privé II (ed. 2, Paris 1934) 573-575; *Lerebours-Pigeonnière,* Précis de droit international privé (ed. 2, Paris 1933) 363 (but see now *Lerebours-Pigeonnière and Loussouarn* 586); *Secrétan* 45; *Zitelmann,* Internationales Privatrecht II (Munich & Leipzig 1912) 605-607.

344. See, for example, *Poisson* 280. This position was taken as early as during the work of the First Hague Conference; see Act. La Haye I/1 (1893) 46; *Buzzati* 102-104.

345. See the references *supra* n. 283-295 and 342. For ITALY see also *A. Miele* 59-68. For the controversy in ENGLISH law between this view and the doctrine of the intended matrimonial home see *infra* s. 54-55.

346. See, for instance, *Cheshire and North* 335 and *Batiffol and Lagarde* II 13, respectively.

form laid down by the law governing that question – both parties have the capacity to contract it in accordance with their respective laws. In principle, however, the law of each party will only be taken into account as concerns that party himself. This is the distinction, of vital importance (though not brought out by the English terminology referred to above), between the present approach and that based on cumulation. Suppose, for instance, that a Swedish man, eighteen years of age, wants to marry a Greek girl who is only fifteen. According to Swedish municipal law the minimum age for marriage is eighteen years both for the male and for the female party, but Greek law is content to require fourteen years as regards the female party.[347] In all probability these parties will be able to marry validly – whether in Sweden, in Greece or in any other country where capacity to marry is cognisable by the *lex patriae* – since each of them has attained the age prescribed by his personal law.[348] By contrast, if the two laws were to be applied in cumulation, the marriage would be precluded because the Greek party does not meet the age requirement of Swedish law.

49. *Unilateral and Bilateral Marriage Impediments.* In the example just mentioned it was assumed that the requirement of Swedish law as to age of marriage had to be satisfied by the Swedish party alone, the other party's capacity to marry not being a matter for Swedish law. It is usually agreed, however, that certain conditions for or impediments to marriage forming part of the personal law of one of the parties must be treated otherwise and, in effect, apply to both. Such impediments have been termed bilateral (*zweiseitige Ehehindernisse*), in contrast with those exemplified by the Swedish rule on age of marriage, which are styled unilateral (*einseitige Ehehindernisse*).[349] This distinction has been cultivated and developed by German and other Conti-

347. See, respectively, the SWEDISH Marriage Code of 1920, ch. 2 § 1, and the GREEK CC art. 1350.

348. The conclusion may conceivably be disturbed by considerations based on local public policy. At least as regards SWEDEN, however, this is very unlikely if, as in the example, the foreign party has reached fifteen years of age; see Act of 8 July 1904 (as amended in 1973) ch. 1 § 3 no. 1 (*e contrario*) and *infra* at n. 1062.

349. For a GERMAN monograph on the problems connected with this distinction see the thesis, cited in the bibliography, by *K. Steinle.* A comparative survey of these problems is given by *Rabel* 286-295. See also, in relation to the HAGUE CONVENTION on Marriage of 1902, *Buzzati* 104-113; *F. Kahn* 62-69.

nental conflicts scholars.[350] Although not always expressed in the terms of the unilateral-bilateral dichotomy, the concept is a reality, in the sense that the problem covered by it is presented in all legal systems accepting the dual domicile (nationality) doctrine as authoritative where the parties are subject to different personal laws.[351]

The notion of a bilateral impediment, as worked out by Continental writers, implies that a person (*A*) is prevented from marrying, not only when the fact constituting the impediment in question is present in his own person but also when it exists with regard to the other party (*B*) alone. Where an impediment of this kind figures in *A*'s personal law governing his capacity to marry, it must therefore be taken into account even if, in the instant case, it only attaches to *B*'s person and even if it is unknown to *B*'s personal law governing that party's capacity. This approach, it is insisted, does not amount to saying that the question of *B*'s capacity should in any respect be submitted to *A*'s law but only that that law is construed as meaning that *A* cannot marry a person who, in the

350. See, besides the references in the preceding note, for AUSTRIA: *G. Walker* 578-579; BELGIUM: *Graulich* 108-110; *Rigaux,* case note: Rev. crit. d.i.p. 1957, 73-74; FRANCE: *Batiffol and Lagarde* II 37; *Bischoff* no. 27-32; *G. de La Pradelle* 153-155; *Niboyet* V 317-319; *Ponsard* 14-15, 39-40; *Savatier,* Cours de droit international privé (ed. 2, Paris 1953) 276-277; EAST GERMANY: *FGB-Kommentar* 447; *Lübchen* 84-85; [WEST] GERMANY: *Frankenstein* 75-76, 83; *Gamillscheg,* Kommentar, art. 13 no. 155-157; *Kegel,* IPR 346-348; *Lauterbach* 25-27; *Lewald* 80-83; *Nussbaum* 132-133; *Raape,* IPR 237-240; *Scholl* 169-174; *Wolff,* IPR 188-189; GREECE: *Bendermacher-Geroussis* 2-4; *Ehrenzweig, Fragistas and Yiannopoulos* 72-73; *Maridakis* 215-216; ITALY: *A. Miele* 65-68; SWITZERLAND: *Beck,* art. 7 c no. 20-27; *Muret* 24-27; *Secrétan* 46-47; *Spivak* 42-45; *Vischer,* IPR 585; YUGOSLAVIA: *Katičić* 419-420.

351. In ENGLAND, as well as in other common law countries, the present problem has attracted relatively scant attention. Nor are the terms unilateral and bilateral usually used in English-speaking countries to denote the distinction interesting us here (note that the meaning of the terms is not the same when employed with reference to different types of restrictions on remarriage after divorce; *supra* s. 23). Nevertheless, the reality expressed by saying that certain marriage impediments must be treated as bilateral is also part of the ENGLISH conflict of laws. Indeed, an ENGLISH decision has carried that approach further than in any other country; see *infra* at n. 364. Conceptually, the necessity of taking the other party's person into consideration is expressed by the current formula that the dual domicile rule requires each of the parties to have, according to his domiciliary law, "the capacity to marry the other"; see *Cheshire and North* 335; *Dicey and Morris* 258. Before the problem arose for decision in any ENGLISH case, it was considered, against the background of Continental experience, by *Wolff,* PIL 336-337.

eyes of *A*'s law, labours under the particular disability.[352] In other words, *A* is under a "mediate" or "reflected" incapacity. By thus, as it were, "transferring" the impediment from *B*'s to *A*'s person one avoids the bilateral approach coming into conflict with the concept that each party's capacity is exclusively governed by his own law. Nevertheless, for all practical purposes the effect of treating an impediment, imposed by *A*'s law, as bilateral is the same as if *B* was, in respect of that impediment, subject to *A*'s law; for if *A* lacks capacity to marry *B* it is of no avail that *B* may be able to marry *A*. What is considered impossible to do directly is in fact done indirectly.

Probably the most important example of an impediment usually classified as bilateral is the *impedimentum ligaminis,* which forms part of all legal systems based on the principle of monogamy.[353] Assuming that *A*'s personal law so regards this impediment, *A* will be under a double incapacity: he will neither be able to marry again if he is himself bound by a previous, valid and still subsisting marriage, nor – should *A* be a single person – to marry a person (*B*) who is so bound, and that irrespective of whether the new union is considered lawful by *B*'s personal law. Accordingly, if *B* is already married *A* cannot marry him even though *B*'s law permits polygamy.[354] A second situation, which has been quite frequent

352. See, for example, *Scholl* 169; *Steinle* 75-76, 81.

353. See in favour of the view that this impediment is bilateral, e.g., ENGLAND: Padolecchia v. Padolecchia, [1968] P. 314, 336 (*obiter*); Breen v. Breen, [1964] P. 144, as explained (alternatively) by *Lipstein,* case note: Clunet 1965, 453; *Hartley,* Bigamy 682-683; *North* 225, 378-379; FRANCE: *Bischoff* no. 29; [WEST] GERMANY: RG 22 April 1932, RGZ 136, 142, 144-145, IPRspr. 1932 no. 146; RG 8 June 1936, RGZ 151, 313, 317; RG 16 July 1936, RGZ 152, 23, 36; BGH 12 Feb. 1964, BGHZ 41, 136, 142, IPRspr. 1964/65 no. 74 (*obiter* as regards GERMAN law); *Frankenstein* 94-97; *Gamillscheg,* Doppelehe 61-62; *idem,* Kommentar, art. 13 no. 155, 243, 247; *Hoffmann and Stephan* § 5 no. 30; *Kegel,* Kommentar, art. 13 no. 33; *Scholl* 170-171; QUEBEC: Cholette v. Jones (1938), 45 R.L.n.s. 111 (C.S.); SWEDEN: *Undén,* Internationell äktenskapsrätt 19-20, 56. See also the references given *supra* n. 349-350 and *infra* n. 354-357. This view does not, however – as has sometimes been assumed; see *Makarov,* Remariage 644 – prevail everywhere. In ITALIAN law, for instance, the impediment is treated as unilateral; see *infra* n. 394. For SWISS law, where the position appears to be unsettled, see on the one hand, *Beck,* art. 7 c no. 21; on the other, *Vischer,* IPR 585. See also *infra* at n. 396-398.

354. For examples of such cases see BELGIUM: Corr. Bruxelles 12 June 1953, Clunet 1954, 438, note Abrahams, Rev. crit. d.i.p. 1954, 376, note Philonenko; FRANCE: Trib. Seine 21 June 1967, Rev. crit. d.i.p. 1968, 294, note Batiffol; Cour Lyon 21 May 1974, D.S. 1975. Jur. 9, note Guiho;

continued on page 110

in practice, is where *B*'s prior marriage has been ended by a divorce which is valid by *B*'s but not recognised by *A*'s law. This has been a source of problems especially in cases involving a Spanish national (*A*) who intended to marry, or had already married, a divorcee (*B*) possessing the nationality of another country. The reason is that Spanish law refuses to recognise foreign divorces, at least for the purpose of remarriage with a Spanish national, even if the parties to the dissolved union are foreigners and the divorce was granted, or is recognised as valid, in their home country.[355] In the eyes of Spanish law, therefore, *B*'s prior marriage continues in force (unless it has been dissolved by the death of the other spouse) so that *A*, although himself a single person, is incapacitated

---

continued from page 109

Cour Reims 19 Jan. 1976, Clunet 1976, 916, note Fadlallah; WEST GERMANY: expert opinion in IPG 1971 no. 14 (Hamburg). If neither of the two laws allows polygamy, *B*'s remarriage violates both of them. In such cases some courts rely on the provisions of both laws to annul the marriage for bigamy. See, for example, for WEST GERMAN decisions so doing: LG München 15 April 1930, IPRspr. 1930 no. 67; LG Kleve 17 Sept. 1952, IPRspr. 1952/53 no. 107; LG Stuttgart 4 Nov. 1952, IPRspr. 1952/53 no. 108. This seems to be the proper course to adopt on the view that the impediment is bilateral. Often, however, the *lex fori* alone is applied (where it is one of the two laws involved) in cases of this type, without regard to the bilateral character of the impediment under the other law. See for WEST GERMAN cases, e.g., LG München 15 Sept. 1952, IPRspr. 1952/53 no. 109; LG Ulm 27 June 1956, IPRspr. 1956/57 no. 103. For a third solution see LG Hamburg 8 Oct. 1975, IPRspr. 1975 no. 38 (giving preference to the law of the petitioner as "the injured party", the respondent being the bigamously married party). This is not a purely academic question, for the law by virtue of which a marriage is annulled will often be decisive for the effects of the annulment; cf. AG Hamburg 21 April 1966, IPRspr. 1966/67 no. 144.

355. This attitude is based on public policy and reflects the principle of indissolubility of marriage, which is a cornerstone of SPANISH matrimonial law. Considerations of this kind pervade the treatment of divorce (and remarriage) in cases presenting foreign elements, to the extent of leaving very little room for the application of "normal" conflicts rules and techniques. See on these questions, the details of which are rather complex, *Aguilar Benítez de Lugo* 239-242; *Gamillscheg*, Kommentar, art. 13 no. 271; *Jochem* 737; *Lalaguna* 509-529; *Medina Ortega*, Reconsideración del divorcio en el derecho español de conflictos: Rev. Esp. Der. Int. 15 (1962) 445, 456-458; *Miaja de la Muela* I 485-486, II 266-267; *Müller-Freienfels* 60-66; *Rull y Villar and Martinez-Agullo y Sanchis*: Rev. Esp. Der. Int. 21 (1968) 816-825. The recent (1974) reform of the Spanish conflict of laws rules apparently does not affect the law and practice on the present subject; see *von Hoffmann and Ortiz-Arce* 664, 668.

from marrying *B*.[356] Similar situations may arise under other laws, which are not generally opposed to the recognition of foreign divorces. This will be so if, in the particular case, *B*'s divorce does not meet the conditions for recognition under *A*'s law or if, where that law requires validation of foreign divorces in special exequatur proceedings, no such proceedings have taken place. Here too, from the point of view of *A*'s law, *B*'s prior marriage has not been properly dissolved, with the consequence (still assuming that *A*'s law considers this impediment to be bilateral) that *A* cannot marry *B*.[357]

As confirmed by these illustrations, the effect of treating a marriage impediment as bilateral is that it will extend, not only to the party who is subject to the law imposing it, but to the other party as well. The net result is that each party will have to comply with a *partially cumulative* test, namely, with all conditions of capacity to marry laid down by his own law and, in addition, with those requirements of the other party's law which are regarded as bilateral. To the extent that the bilateral approach is adopted, therefore, the principle of determining each party's capacity in accordance with his own law alone is in fact, if not in theory, modified so as to become indistinguishable from the principle requiring the two laws to be applied in cumulation.

The question may now be asked as to whether and, if so, how it can be justified that one of the parties (*B*) is made subject, at least in certain respects, to the other party's (*A*'s) law. It might be, and indeed sometimes has been, objected that this amounts to an

356. For cases in point see: T.S. 12 May 1944, Aranzadi Jur. 11 (1944) 669; T.S. 5 April 1966, Rev. Esp. Der. Int. 20 (1967) 305, note Pecourt García. See also D.G.R.N. 23 April 1970, Clunet 1973, 788, and T.S. 29 May 1970, considered by *Lalaguna* 513. The principle has been carried even further by a decision forbidding the remarriage (in civil form) in Spain between parties both of whom were of foreign nationality and had been divorced in their home country: D.G.R.N. 10 Sept. 1961, An. D.G.R.N. 1961, 152 (but see for more recent decisions which have gone some way to mitigate the rigour of this attitude: D.G.R.N. 18 Sept. 1971, Rev. Gen. 1971, 877, note Ortiz de la Torre, Clunet 1973, 782; D.G.R.N. 23 March 1976, R.D.P. 1976, 758). A similar position appears to be taken by MALTESE law. See the WEST GERMAN expert opinion in IPG 1974 no. 15 (Hamburg), and *Otto*, Das Eherecht von Malta: StAZ 1974, 306-307, both dealing with a marriage between a Maltese and a divorced Greek national.

357. See, e.g., FRANCE: Trib. Seine 25 July 1930, Rev. crit. d.i.p. 1930, 687; WEST GERMANY: OLG München 21 Nov. 1949, StAZ 1950, 130; AG Hamburg 24 Dec. 1969, IPRspr. 1968/69 no. 75, critically noted by *Jayme and Siehr* in StAZ 1970, 345-346; LG München 15 March 1972, IPRspr. 1972 no. 161.

encroachment by *A*'s law upon what ought to be "the exclusive domain" of *B*'s law.[358] The simplest answer is that the point at issue is not, or rather not only, whether *A* has capacity to marry in general, but whether he can enter into the particular marriage with *B*, in other words whether the parties have the capacity to marry *each other*.[359] So phrased, of course, the question cannot be resolved without mutual consideration of the other party's person. On the other hand, it is common ground that such interdependence does not exist with regard to all requirements for or impediments to marriage. This takes us to the thorny problem of the method of determining whether any particular impediment is to be treated as unilateral or as bilateral.

50. *Criteria and Implementation of This Distinction.* There is no simple and objective criterion by reference to which the distinction between the two kinds of marriage impediment can be drawn. It seems to be generally agreed, however, that each problem must be approached, primarily at least, as a question of *construction of the municipal law establishing the impediment.*[360] An impediment is classed as bilateral or as unilateral, respectively, depending on whether its policy, as deducible from the wording, context, objective and spirit of the provision enshrining it, is or is not such as to command application in respect of both parties.

In accordance with this approach, the label of *unilateral* is attached to such conditions or impediments as are exclusively, or at least predominantly, designed to protect one of the spouses or intending spouses. Requirements as to marriageable age are usually cited as a typical example.[361] While such requirements have to be satisfied by the party whose capacity is governed by the law im-

358. This is, in essence, the argument advanced by most FRENCH writers against the application of the above-mentioned rule of SPANISH law which prevents the intermarriage of a Spaniard and, for example, a French national who is validly divorced according to FRENCH law. See the references *infra* n. 794.

359. See the wording of the dual domicile rule in ENGLISH law, *supra* n. 351.

360. See the writers cited *supra* n. 349-350.

361. Continental opinion is unanimous on this point. See the references *supra* n. 349-350 and, e.g., AUSTRIA: *Schwind,* Nachsichterteilung 38; BELGIUM: *Rigaux,* DIP 350; FRANCE: *Batiffol,* case note: Rev. crit. d.i.p. 1968, 299; WEST GERMANY: *Gamillscheg,* Kommentar, art. 13 no. 195; *Hoffmann and Stephan* § 1 no. 87; *Kegel,* Kommentar, art. 13 no. 14, 32; ITALY: *Betti* 413; *Jayme* 26; SWITZERLAND: *Beck,* art. 7 c no. 21; *Knapp,* Essai 210.

posing them,[362] they do not apply to the other party.[363] On this point, however, a different position has been taken in an *English* case.[364] In that case a marriage had been entered into in Austria between a domiciled Englishman and a girl of fifteen years, whose domicile was Hungarian. Although the union was valid by Hungarian law, and also by Austrian law, the *lex loci celebrationis,* it was held to be void because English law prohibited a marriage "between persons either of whom is under the age of sixteen."[365] The decision was based on the ground that "by the law of the husband's domicile it was a marriage into which he could not lawfully enter."[366] This ground implies that the relevant English statute was construed to mean that "the incapacity to marry below a certain age includes the incapacity to marry a person below that age."[367] The effect of the decision is that if either party is domiciled in England, then both of them are subject to the English rule as to age of marriage, which is another way of saying that the rule must be treated as bilateral.[368] Unfortunately, the court reached its conclusion without any discussion of the present problem, apparently because the wording of the English statute was thought to preclude any doubt that it applied to both parties.[369]

Another group of requirements usually considered unilateral are those which relate to the true consent of the parties.[370] This cate-

362. BELGIUM: Civ. Liège 3 May 1967, Pas. 1967.III.99; FRANCE: Cour Paris 2 Dec. 1966, Rev. crit. d.i.p. 1967, 530, note Malaurie; WEST GERMANY: OLG Celle 5 June 1947, IPRspr. 1945/49 no. 17; LG Mannheim 29 Jan. 1965, IPRspr. 1964/65 no. 87; AG Hochheim 3 Jan. 1966, IPRspr. 1966/67 no. 57; ITALY: App. Roma 20 May 1963, Riv. dir. int. 1963, 656, note Cassese (recognising a foreign nullity decree based on nonage); SCOTLAND: A.B. v. C.D., 1957 S.C. 415.

363. See the SWISS decision of BG 27 Jan. 1949, BGE 75 I 82, Clunet 1952, 670, note Knapp, Schw. Jb. Int. R. 7 (1950) 222, note Knapp.

364. Pugh v. Pugh, [1951] P. 482. Noted by *Bresler,* 4 I.L.Q. 478 (1951); *O.M. Stone,* 15 M.L.R. 90 (1952); *Unger,* Capacity to Marry in the Conflict of Laws: 15 M.L.R. 88 (1952).

365. Age of Marriage Act 1929, s. 1 (1), now: Marriage Act 1949, s. 2.

366. Pugh v. Pugh, [1951] P. 482, 494.

367. *Kahn-Freund,* Problems 90.

368. See *Cheshire and North* 344; *Dicey and Morris* 264-265; *Graveson,* Conflict 264, 267 n. 48; *Latey* 847-848.

369. For pertinent criticism of the decision see *Anton* 76-77, 277; *Hartley,* Policy Basis 577-578; *Morris* 104, 116; *Schmitthoff* 89-90; *Swan* 24, 33-34. See also *Wolff,* PIL 337 (writing before this case arose).

370. For comparative surveys of these requirements see *Dölle,* Familienrecht 169-170, 265-270, 313-339; *Neuhaus,* Verhältnis 351-353. The view

continued on page 114

gory includes provisions concerning coercion, duress, error, fear, fraud, frustration, misrepresentation, etc., as grounds for annulling a marriage. Rules of this kind exist primarily in the interest of the party whose consent is alleged to have been vitiated. It is therefore natural that such issues should be determined as to each of the parties by reference to his personal law alone.[371] Nevertheless, there is a minority opinion in several countries which favours a bilateral approach making each of the parties subject to the consent requirements of both personal laws.[372]

---

continued from page 113
that they are to be treated as unilateral in the conflict of laws is generally supported by the writers cited *supra* n. 349-350. See also, e.g., AUSTRIA: *Schwind*, IPR 145; BELGIUM: *van Hecke and Rigaux* (1953 à 1960) 364-365; ENGLAND: *Cheshire and North* 403; *Dicey and Morris* 276, 279; *Graveson*, Conflict 252-253; *Morris* 116; *Webb*, "Shot-Gun" Marriages 203 (and see for AUSTRALIA *Nygh* 416); FRANCE: *Bischoff* no. 51-52; [WEST] GERMANY: *Frankenstein* 82, 87; *Gamillscheg*, Kommentar, art. 13 no. 210, 468-471; *Hoffmann and Stephan*, before § 28 no. 13; *Kegel*, Kommentar, art. 13 no. 14, 32, 36; SWEDEN: *Undén*, Internationell äktenskapsrätt 54; SWITZERLAND: *Albisetti* 49; *Beck*, art. 7 c no. 21. As concerns the HAGUE CONVENTION of 1902 see also *Travers* I 155-156.

371. For cases expressly or implicitly supporting this view see AUSTRIA: OLG Wien 22 Dec. 1971, EFSlg 8 (1971) 217 no. 15, 746; OLG Wien 15 Jan. 1974, EFSlg 11 (1974) 251 no. 22, 677; BELGIUM: Civ. Liège 3 Feb. 1966, Jur. Liège 1965/66, 203; FRANCE: Trib. Seine 4 Feb. 1918, Rev. crit. d.i.p. 1918, 112; Trib. Strasbourg 21 Dec. 1920, Clunet 1921, 933; Cour Tunis 10 March 1951, Rev. crit. d.i.p. 1953, 119; Trib. Seine 6 April 1951, Rev. crit. d.i.p. 1953, 586, note Batiffol; Cour Tunis 17 Oct. 1955, Rev. tunis. dr. 1956, 133; Cour Paris 2 Dec. 1966, Rev. crit. d.i.p. 1967, 530; [WEST] GERMANY: (cases decided under the Hague Convention of 1902) RG 6 Feb. 1930, IPRspr. 1930 no. 64; RG 15 Dec. 1930, IPRspr. 1931 no. 58; KG 18 Dec. 1933, IPRspr. 1933 no. 46; RG 7 May 1936, RGZ 151, 226; (other cases) RG 6 Oct. 1927, IPRspr. 1926/27 no. 68; RG 22 Oct. 1930, IPRspr. 1931 no. 57; BayObLG 13 May 1931, IPRspr. 1931 no. 61; RG 11 Nov. 1937, JW 1938, 108; OLG München 4 April 1950, IPRspr. 1950/51 no. 132; LG Hamburg 11 July 1973, IPRspr. 1973 no. 35; LG Hamburg 7 Nov. 1973, IPRspr. 1973 no. 37; ITALY: Cass. Torino 21 July 1883, Clunet 1884, 553; Trib. Firenze 10 March 1960, Giur. tosc. 1960, 616; App. Roma 4 July 1963, Temi rom. 1964, 22; NETHERLANDS: Hof Amsterdam 6 March 1963, N.J. 1963 no. 199, Clunet 1969, 1017, note Kollewijn; SWITZERLAND: AppH Bern 27 Oct. 1927, ZBJV 64 (1928) 185, SJZ 24 (1927/28) 235 (under the Hague Convention of 1902); BezG Zürich 22 Feb. 1952, SJZ 49 (1953) 78.

372. The position of ENGLISH law is very doubtful, and it is not even settled that issues of defective consent are referable to the personal law at all; see *infra* s. 97. For a decision, holding a marriage to be void for duress, which lends some support to the bilateral approach see Szechter v. Szechter, [1971] P. 286, 294-295 (*obiter*). And see among writers: *Webb and Davis* 246-247 (for NEW ZEALAND law); *Woodhouse* 460, 464-465. This view is shared by

A related group of provisions are those requiring the consent of parents or guardians to the marriage of minors or other incompetent persons.[373] The purpose of such prescriptions is generally to protect the incompetent party from rash and inconsiderate decisions, sometimes also to protect the interests of the parents themselves. In either case, these requirements only "concern" the party who is subject to the law imposing the incapacity to marry without parental consent, and they cannot reasonably be interpreted to affect his capacity to marry a person whose own law does not provide for that incapacity. In other words, consent requirements of this type must be classified as unilateral.[374] They are invariably so treated in Continental European and Scandinavian practice.[375]

---

some Continental European courts and writers. See for GERMANY: KG 21 Dec. 1936, JW 1937, 2039, annulling a marriage between a German and a Polish national on the ground, supplied by GERMAN law alone, that the union had been entered into by the latter party while in a state of unsound mind; see also *Hoffmann and Stephan* § 2 no. 16, invoking public policy to reach the same result (but the prevailing opinion is to the contrary, treating this impediment as unilateral; see *Gamillscheg*, Kommentar, art. 13 no. 210); GREECE: *Bendermacher-Geroussis* 5; *Maridakis* 217-218 (arguing that both spouses should be equally protected and that, therefore, the grounds for annulment based on lack of consent which are supplied by the personal law of one of them must be available to both); ITALY: Trib. Bari 20 March 1968, Riv. dir. int. proc. 1970, 63, annulling a marriage between an Italian and an American national by reason that the former party had acted under duress (ITALIAN law alone was applied in this case, but the court said, at 66, that it would have proceeded to examine the nullity grounds of AMERICAN law had a sufficient ground not existed under ITALIAN law).

373. For comparative surveys see *Dölle*, Familienrecht 170-181; *Gamillscheg*, Kommentar, art. 13 no. 215-216; *Götz*, art. 98 no. 17-18. See also the list of such requirements in StAZ 1965, 26.

374. See, besides the references *supra* n. 349-350, e.g., AUSTRIA: *Schwind*, IPR 142; FRANCE: *Bischoff* no. 54; [WEST] GERMANY: *Frankenstein* 84; *Gamillscheg*, Kommentar, art. 13 no. 217-218; *Hoffmann and Stephan* § 3 no. 96; *Kegel*, Kommentar, art. 13 no. 14, 32; SWITZERLAND: *Albisetti* 49; *Beck*, art. 7 c no. 21; *Stauffer*, art. 7 c no. 4. See also the SCANDINAVIAN Convention of 1931 (as amended) art. 1 par. 2 (*supra* at n. 265).

375. For decisions see, e.g., BELGIUM: Civ. Bruxelles 3 Jan. 1913, Clunet 1914, 633; Civ. Bruxelles 13 May 1950, Pas. 1950.III.91; Civ. Tournai 10 Oct. 1962, J.T. 1962, 716; Civ. Liège 3 May 1967, Pas. 1967.III.99; FRANCE: Trib. Seine 21 Dec. 1885, Clunet 1886, 448; Trib. Seine 10 Jan. 1917, Clunet 1918, 1192; Trib. Seine 8 March 1920, Clunet 1920, 206; Trib. Seine 17 Nov. 1926, Clunet 1928, 404; Cour Paris 2 Dec. 1966, Rev. crit. d.i.p. 1967, 530; [WEST] GERMANY: RG 20 Oct. 1898, RGZ 42, 336; RG 21 Dec. 1916, LZ 1917, 924; LG Berlin 10 March 1947, IPRspr. 1960/61 no. 89; OLG Frankfurt 31 Oct. 1950, IPRspr. 1950/51 no. 126; LG Mann-

continued on page 116

The problem is avoided in England and other countries following English law, since parental consents are held to go to the formalities of marriage cognisable by the *lex loci celebrationis*.

The class of unilateral impediments also includes certain prohibitions, directed to one of the parties alone, which are of a penal character or pertain to the area of public law. By way of examples one may cite, respectively, restrictions on the right of remarriage of the guilty party to a divorce, and requirements of consent by the Government, or by some governmental body, to the marriage of diplomats or servicemen.[376]

The *bilateral* approach prevails with regard to marriage impediments which, whether belonging to private or to public law, are predominantly founded on grounds of morality or social policy affecting the union as such, and not only one of the parties. The *impedimentum ligaminis*, which is a corollary of the principle of monogamy, has already been mentioned (*supra* s. 49). Other examples are afforded by certain rules disqualifying a person for marriage because of physical or mental incapacity.[377] Thus, prohibitions based on insanity, epilepsy and venereal or other diseases are generally considered bilateral, at least to the extent that the purpose of such rules is eugenic.[378] If, for instance, *A*'s personal law forbids a person to marry on the ground that he suffers from a contagious venereal disease, the prohibition will normally be interpreted to extend to cases where *A* is himself healthy but where the other party, *B*, whose personal law does not know this kind of incapacity, is affected by the disease. The reason is mani-

continued from page 115
heim 29 Jan. 1965, IPRspr. 1964/65 no. 87; BGH 10 Feb. 1965, IPRspr. 1964/65 no. 88; KG 22 April 1968, FamRZ 1968, 466; NETHERLANDS: Rb. Amsterdam 18 Jan. 1968, N.J. 1968 no. 338.

376. See *infra* s. 94 and 111, respectively.

377. For comparative surveys of such provisions see *Dölle*, Familienrecht 94-98, 169-170; *Gamillscheg*, Kommentar, art. 13 no. 427-428. See *infra* s. 100.

378. See among writers: *Batiffol and Lagarde* II 37; *Beck*, art. 7 c no. 23; *Bendermacher-Geroussis* 2-3; *Bischoff* no. 30; *Gamillscheg*, Kommentar, art. 13 no. 431; *Graulich* 109 n. 8; *Katičić* 419-420; *Kegel*, Kommentar, art. 13 no. 31; *Knapp*, Essai 211; *G. de La Pradelle* 153-154; *Muret* 25-26; *Neuhaus*, Grundrechte 611-612; *Rabel* 291-292; *Undén*, Internationell äktenskapsrätt 19-20; *Wolff*, PIL 336. It should be noted that the eugenic marriage prohibitions of SWEDISH law, which are often cited as examples in this discussion, have now been abolished. As regards prohibitions based on insanity, the purpose is not always eugenic; they may also be designed to ensure the true consent of the party. Where this is the only purpose of such prohibitions, they are usually classified as unilateral; see *supra* at n. 371-372.

festly that the object of the disqualifying rule cannot be attained unless both parties are made subject to it.

Whether the same applies in respect of provisions making impotence a ground for annulment is more doubtful and controversial; the answer varies with the spirit and objective of such provisions (*infra* s. 102). Differences of view exist on many other points as well, for instance as to the treatment of waiting periods, imposed on the wife alone with the object of preventing *turbatio sanguinis,* for remarriage after the dissolution of a previous marriage (*infra* s. 95).

Relative marriage impediments, which are directed against the intermarriage of persons standing in a certain relationship to each other, for example on account of consanguinity or affinity, do not usually give rise to problems in the present respect. Such impediments have been characterised as "necessarily bilateral" because, in the nature of things, the disqualifying fact attaches to both parties to the relationship.[379] At least when both of them are equally affected by the incapacity, there can be no doubt as to the proper approach in conflicts cases. If, for instance, a particular law forbids marriage between uncle and niece, it goes without saying that two persons so related are equally incapable of marrying each other. It follows that the marriage will be barred whenever one of them, whether the uncle or the niece, is subject to the prohibiting law.[380] It is immaterial that the union may be permitted by the other party's personal law, for a marriage can only be lawfully contracted if both parties have capacity to do so.

Although, in effect, this approach amounts to treating relative impediments as bilateral, the use of this terminology may seem superfluous and even somewhat confusing here. It is simpler to

379. See, e.g., *Frankenstein* 75, 83, 94; *Gamillscheg,* Kommentar, art. 13 no. 155, 235, 384; *Neuhaus,* Grundbegriffe 158-159; *Scholl* 170.

380. This is the generally accepted view with regard to impediments based on consanguinity or affinity. See the writers cited *supra* n. 349-350 and 379. For decisions holding a marriage to be barred when prohibited on such grounds by the personal law of one of the parties (though valid by the other law) see WEST GERMANY: OLG Düsseldorf 8 April 1969, IPRspr. 1968/69 no. 72; GREECE: Court of Appeals of Corfu 1932 no. 100, Clunet 1933, 1076. Several such decisions are to be found in common law countries. See for ENGLAND: Mette v. Mette (1859), 1 Sw. & Tr. 416, 164 Eng. Rep. 792; In re Paine, [1940] Ch. 46; *Cheshire and North* 341, 343-344; *Dicey and Morris* 262-264; *Falconbridge* 704-714; *Graveson,* Conflict 259-260, 263, 265; *North* 121; AUSTRALIA: Ungar v. Ungar (1967), 10 F.L.R. 467 (N.S.W. Sup. Ct.); CANADA: Rosenberg-de la Marre v. Rosenberg-de la Marre (1971), 14 D.L.R. (3d) 127 (N.S. Div. Ct.); see also Crickmay v. Crickmay (1966), 60 D.L.R. (2d) 734 (B.C.C.A.) (marriage upheld because not prohibited by either party's domiciliary law).

say that *A*, whose law contains the impediment, lacks capacity to marry *B* according to his own law.[381] Since a relative impediment is founded on a quality (a particular relationship) necessarily existing in regard to both parties, there is no question here – as otherwise implied by the notion of bilaterality – of *extending* a rule of *A*'s law to apply on grounds solely relating to *B*'s person.

Nevertheless, the distinction unilateral-bilateral has a part to play here too. Indeed, if the above approach is normally or *prima facie* the appropriate one in respect of relative impediments, it has been suggested that some impediments of this type should, conversely, be *restricted* so as only to apply to one of the parties, *i.e.* that they should be treated as unilateral. The argument is, in substance, that a prohibition against the intermarriage of two persons may properly have to be construed as addressed, solely or predominantly, to one of them.[382] In other words, the true meaning of a rule by which *A* and *B* are forbidden to marry each other may be that *A* is forbidden to marry *B*.

Most of these questions are disputed and unsettled. One example concerns prohibitions against the intermarriage of a person who has been divorced for adultery and his paramour.[383] Mostly such prohibitions are assumed to be bilateral,[384] with the consequence

381. For criticism of the use of the term bilateral in respect of impediments based on consanguinity or affinity see *Katičić* 419; *Steinle* 32-33. Many other writers do not use the term here; see, e.g., Act. La Haye 3 (1900) 169; *Bischoff* no. 27; *Graulich* 109; *Muret* 27; *Schnitzer* 341. In any event this difference is merely a verbal one which does not reflect any divergency of opinion as to the treatment of such impediments.

382. See the cases and writers cited *infra* n. 386, 1115 and 1166-1167.

383. For comparative surveys of this type of prohibition, which is steadily losing ground in modern law, see *Dölle*, Familienrecht 128-130; *Gamillscheg*, Kommentar, art. 13 no. 364-366; *Götz*, art. 101 no. 14. For AMERICAN law see also the references *supra* n. 132.

384. See *Rabel* 292-293 and, e.g., AUSTRIA: *Hainzl* 19; *Schwind*, Nachsichterteilung 39; BELGIUM: verbal note from the Foreign Office, of 25 April 1934, RabelsZ 8 (1934) 641; *Massfeller*, Das Ehehindernis des Ehebruchs bei der Eheschliessung von ausländischen Staatsangehörigen: StAZ 1934, 307, 308; *Rigaux*, case note: Rev. crit. d.i.p. 1957, 73-74; [WEST] GERMANY: Service Instruction of 1968, § 161(1), 383(2) no. 2; *Gamillscheg*, Kommentar, art. 13 no. 369; *Hoffmann and Stephan* § 6 no. 44; *Kegel*, Kommentar, art. 13 no. 33; *Luther*, Das Ehehindernis des Ehebruchs im interzonalen Privatrecht: FamRZ 1957, 6; *Nussbaum* 132-133; *Raape*, IPR 239-240; *Sasse* 211-221; *Wolff*, IPR 189; GREECE: *Ehrenzweig, Fragistas and Yiannopoulos* 72-73; NETHERLANDS: *Massfeller*, Das Ehehindernis des Ehebruchs nach niederländischem Recht: StAZ 1937, 240-241. The prohibition has now been abolished in the domestic law of most of the countries listed here.

that the marriage will be barred whichever of the two parties is subject to the prohibitory law.[385] As against that, however, it is claimed to be more consonant with the purpose and spirit of such restrictions to construe them as directed against, and as imposing a penalty upon, the adulterer and as only secondarily affecting the paramour. The inference is that the prohibition must be taken into account when the adulterer, but not when the accomplice alone, is subject to the law embodying it.[386] Similar controversies exist, *inter alia,* as to the scope of certain impediments of a religious nature (*infra* n. 1115).

51. *Discussion and Critique.* The distinction under review reflects true differences in the treatment of various marriage impediments and seems indispensable in any legal system espousing the principle of the personal law. It is hardly surprising that the drawing of the dividing line between the two categories gives rise to doubts and differences of opinion on many points, for the problems involved are rather complex and require a variety of circumstances to be taken into consideration. It is essential, however, that these problems should be approached without too much dogmatism. Assertions of the type that any particular impediment "is" either unilateral or bilateral, which tend to attribute absolute validity to the solutions proposed, are often grossly simplified and risk obscuring the fact that policy issues are at stake and that the solution of each problem depends on value judgments admitting of some relativism.

To facilitate the discussion, we shall first concentrate on situations where the problem presents itself *in the country of origin* of the debated impediment, that is to say, where it relates to a rule of the *lex fori* applicable in its capacity as the personal law of one

385. For cases see AUSTRIA: OGH 16 Dec. 1925, SZ 7 no. 398; [WEST] GERMANY: decisions by the Prussian Ministry of Justice reported in StAZ 1931, 254 and 1934, 292; LG Aachen 11 March 1931, IPRspr. 1932 no. 67 (LUXEMBOURG law); OLG Frankfurt 28 Feb. 1956, IPRspr. 1956/57 no. 5 (DUTCH law); AG Hamburg 9 and 22 Dec. 1966, IPRspr. 1966/67 no. 64 and 66, respectively; NETHERLANDS: Hof Amsterdam 25 May 1915, W. no. 9894, Clunet 1920, 764; Hof 's-Hertogenbosch 21 Dec. 1937, N.J. 1938 no. 341 (in some other cases the prohibition was even held to apply, for reasons of public policy, when both parties to a locally celebrated marriage were of foreign nationality; see *infra* n. 884).

386. BELGIUM: *Graulich* 109 n. 5; GERMANY: older opinions cited by *Sasse* 212-213; NETHERLANDS: Rb. 's-Gravenhage 1 Feb. 1935, N.J. 1935, 403, Bull. I.I.I. 34 (1936) 195; *Soelling,* Das Ehebruchshindernis des Art. 89 Niederländischen Bürgerlichen Gesetzbuchs trifft nur den geschiedenen Gatten, nicht den Teilnehmer am Ehebruch: StAZ 1927, 136-137.

of the parties. An authoritative answer to the question of whether a particular impediment does or does not "claim" to be treated as bilateral can only be given by the courts of that country. Normally, it is true, the same effect is likely to be given to it in other countries whose conflicts rules refer to the same law, but this raises some additional problems which will be postponed for the moment (see *infra* s. 52).

Assuming that one of the parties is subject to the *lex fori* as his personal law, a question concerning the unilateral or bilateral character of the requirements of that law can only be posed if the other party's capacity to marry is referable to foreign law. The question is meaningless in purely domestic cases, including cases where foreign elements are present but where those elements are insufficient to make foreign law applicable to either party; for in such cases it is a matter of course that each party must comply with all requirements of the *lex fori.* Accordingly, our problem is always linked to the context of conflict of laws.

This being so, it may seem incongruous that – as is generally taught – the solution should depend on the proper construction of the *municipal* rules involved. It might be expected that the answer to what is a question of the conflict of laws should be supplied by the *conflicts* rules on the matter. In fact, however, those rules are silent on problems of the present type (except where the point at issue happens to be covered by judicial precedent). The solutions therefore have to be worked out by courts and writers, who will normally seek guidance in the relevant municipal rules. This is no more remarkable than many other instances of the well-known tendency for conflicts rules, whether written or unwritten, to be framed so as to reflect rules and policies of municipal law.

On the other hand, the connection between rules of municipal law and their treatment in the conflict of laws is not an automatic one, but leaves considerable room for evaluation. The wording of a provision establishing a marriage impediment can scarcely be conclusive in determining whether it is or is not to be applied bilaterally in conflicts cases.[387] Presumably the rules of matrimonial law in any legal system are generally framed with a view to situations where both parties are subject to those rules and where the present problem therefore does not arise at all. A provision con-

387. That the wording carries little weight in this connection is properly emphasised by several writers. See, e.g., *Frankenstein* 94 n. 137; *Gamillscheg,* Kommentar, art. 13 no. 429; *Raape,* IPR 240.

cerning the minimum age for marriage may, for instance, prescribe that "a person may not marry until the age of eighteen", or prohibit marriages between persons "either of whom" is below that age. In either alternative, the requirement will apply to both parties if their capacity to marry is governed by the law of which it forms part. To that extent it is immaterial which formulation is chosen. It seems, furthermore, highly unlikely that the choice of words should be intended to prejudge, or have any relation whatsoever to the purposes of, the distinction in the conflict of laws between unilateral and bilateral marriage impediments. Reasonably, therefore, the wording cannot be interpreted to imply that the rule should be referred to one or the other of these categories.[388]

Rather, the inquiry must be directed to *the objective, the spirit and the policy* of the provision examined. Sometimes, perhaps, the wording may be of assistance in this respect, but other means of interpretation should normally carry more weight. Often, for example, guidance may be derived from the rules concerning the right to bring proceedings for annulment on the ground of the particular incapacity.[389] Typically, the impediment should be treated as bilateral if both spouses, or if third parties as well as the spouses themselves, are entitled to rely on it in nullity proceedings rather than if the right to do so is vested in one of them alone, and *vice versa.*[390]

There may, of course, be difficulties in identifying the objective and the policy of a particular marriage impediment. Not only may the purpose and the strength of the policy behind "the same" impediment vary from one legal system to another, but it is also possible that one prohibition has several different functions within a single legal system. A waiting period for the remarriage of a divorcee, for instance, may be in the nature of a penalty imposed upon the guilty party to the divorce, but it may also lack any such connotation and be designed to discourage divorce and, thereby, to protect existing marriages or, if it is directed against the wife alone, to avoid *turbatio sanguinis.*[391] It may, too, serve more than one of these functions at the same time.

Furthermore, even where the purpose and the policy of a

388. The decision in the ENGLISH case of Pugh v. Pugh, [1951] P. 482, is open to criticism on this ground; see *supra* at n. 364-369.

389. See *Gamillscheg,* Kommentar, art. 13 no. 156.

390. Perhaps the best illustration of this point is the treatment of impotence as a ground for annulment; see *infra* s. 102.

391. See *Dölle,* Familienrecht 135-137, 588-589; *Hartley,* Bigamy 694-699. Cf. *supra* s. 23 and *infra* s. 92-96.

particular provision laying down a disability for marriage is unequivocally ascertainable, it does not automatically follow that it must be treated either as unilateral or as bilateral in conflicts cases. This is still a matter of evaluation, which can hardly be kept distinct from other policy considerations affecting choice of law issues. In many cases the present question is virtually indistinguishable from those canvassed within the doctrine of public policy. If certain requirements of the *lex fori,* to which one of the parties is subject as his personal law, are extended to the other party, this can often be interchangeably justified by saying that public policy so demands or that the requirements in question are bilateral.[392] The only difference is that the policy basis of the decision may appear less overtly if the latter ground is invoked.

Once it is recognised that policy issues are involved, there should be no difficulty in admitting that a particular marriage impediment in a given legal system "is" not necessarily either unilateral or bilateral for all purposes and in all connections in which the question may turn up. It may well be treated one way in some circumstances, but the other way in others, because the force of the policy behind it – when weighed against countervailing considerations, especially the policy of favouring marriage – varies with different fact situations. This relativity of the distinction is no more anomalous than it is in regard to the principle of public policy, the involvement of which often depends on a variety of circumstances, *inter alia,* on the intensity of the contacts with the *lex fori.*

To illustrate this point it is proposed to return to the treatment of the *impedimentum ligaminis* (cf. *supra* s. 49). Assuming that that impediment forms part of the *lex fori* governing *A*'s capacity to marry and that *A* is himself a single person, it is generally agreed that *A* cannot marry a person, *B,* who is bound by a prior marriage, even if *B*'s personal law permits polygamy and therefore has no objection to the proposed union. This attitude is justified, sometimes by reference to the bilateral character of the impediment according to *A*'s law, sometimes on grounds of (prohibitive) public policy.[393] The same position is not always adopted, however, where *B,* according to his own law, is divorced and where the reason why *A*'s law regards him as still bound by the prior marriage is that the divorce is not recognised by *A*'s law. In *Italian* law, for example,

392. Cf. *Neuhaus,* Grundbegriffe 158 n. 447 (as concerns the impediment of a prior marriage); *Scholl* 173.

393. See the references *supra* n. 353-354 and *infra* s. 78.

the latter question is generally considered immaterial. Provided that *B*'s divorce is valid by *B*'s own *lex patriae*, the fact that it may not be recognised by Italian law, as a rule, is consequently no bar to the intermarriage of *A*, an Italian national, and *B*.[394] Thus, while the impediment of the prior marriage operates bilaterally in cases involving a foreign law which allows polygamy, it is treated as unilateral in cases turning on the validity of a foreign divorce.[395]

Furthermore, even in countries which do not recognise this

394. A leading case is Cass. 14 March 1968, Riv. dir. int. proc. 1968, 674 (affirming App. Torino 11 July 1964, Giur. it. 1965 I 2, 273, note Marazzi, Clunet 1966, 682) holding a foreigner, who was validly divorced according to his *lex patriae*, entitled to remarry an Italian national in Italy without a prior validation of his divorce by the forum. Other decisions to the same effect include: App. Napoli 30 June 1953, Dir. eccles. 1962 II 365; Trib. Napoli 25 Sept. 1955, Foro nap. 1955, 336; Trib. Roma 15 May 1961, Temi rom. 1961, 365, note Zuddas. *A fortiori*, validation of the divorce by the forum is immaterial where the remarriage has occurred in a foreign country. See: App. Roma 2 July 1959, Riv. dir. matr. 1959, 703, note Cassoni, Riv. dir. proc. 1961, 144, note Carnelutti, Clunet 1961, 852; App. Roma 17 June 1961, Foro pad. 1963 I 1272, note M. Miele, Giur. it. 1961 I 2, 683, note Cansacchi, Clunet 1964, 337; App. Napoli 24 Feb. 1965, Dir. Int. 1967 II 52. But a different position has been adopted in cases where the divorcee's prior marriage had a substantial connection with Italy, especially where the place of celebration was in that country; see *infra* n. 701-702. The problems involved in these cases, *inter alia*, that known as the incidental question, have been a fertile ground of doctrinal controversies. Despite many differences of opinion, however, it has never been held or apparently even suggested that the foreign party's divorce must be validated in Italy by reason that ITALIAN law (governing the capacity of the other party to the second marriage) regards the prior marriage as a bilateral impediment. The unilateral character of that impediment seems to be beyond doubt. See *Jayme*, Die Eheschliessung zwischen ledigen italienischen und geschiedenen deutschen Staatsangehörigen in Deutschland: StAZ 1966, 150-154; *A. Miele* 65, 67. For a comparable DUTCH decision see Rb. Dordrecht 10 April 1964, N.J. 1965 no. 218, Clunet 1969, 1019, note Kollewijn (authorising a German woman, whose prior marriage had been annulled by a German court, to marry a Dutch national on the ground that by GERMAN law the nullity decree had made her a single person, regardless of whether the decree would be recognised by DUTCH law).

395. Though ITALIAN courts and writers do not express the solutions in these terms. In the former situation the relevant foreign law is excluded on grounds of public policy, and that even if both parties are of foreign nationality; see as regards marriages in Italy CC art. 116 par. 2 in conjunction with art. 86. As to cases involving the remarriage of a divorced foreigner, the particular question discussed here seems never to have been considered a problem. In general, it may be noted, the concept of bilateral marriage impediments (which alone necessitates the use of the term unilateral as its opposite number) is undeveloped and disfavoured in ITALIAN law. See, e.g., *Balladore Pallieri* 141; *Ballarino* 132; *Vitta* II 188 n. 51.

distinction and where the remarriage would be barred in the latter type of situation, too, it is by no means excluded that a different position will be taken if the remarriage occurs in a foreign country.[396] Especially if the marriage has already been entered into and its validity is questioned later on, perhaps after many years during which the parties have lived as man and wife and been so regarded in the foreign country, the policy of validation may well prevail over any dogmatic considerations as to the bilateral nature of the impediment. A *Canadian* case may be cited in which this approach was adopted even in respect of a locally celebrated marriage.[397] In that case the Supreme Court of Canada affirmed the validity of a marriage celebrated in Ontario between a local domiciliary, who was single, and a divorced Israeli domiciliary, whose divorce was valid by Israeli law (governing that party's capacity to marry under the conflicts rules of the forum) but did not meet the conditions for recognition under Ontario law (governing the other party's capacity). The question was not even posed of whether the Ontario domiciliary had been precluded from marrying the Israeli party on the ground that, in the eyes of Ontario law, the latter party was still bound by his prior marriage, as would have been necessary according to the doctrine that this impediment is bilateral.[398]

This should be sufficient to show that caution is advisable in the face of unqualified statements that one marriage impediment or the other "is" either unilateral or bilateral. Such statements may be too rigid even if the outlook is confined to a single legal system. The same is true to a much greater extent if the perspective is broadened to comprise different legal systems containing "the same" impediment. On the other hand, it would be at least equally exaggerated to suggest that there are no rules and that each case must be decided on its own merits. As should be clear from the

396. See, for instance, for AUSTRIAN law *Hainzl* 20; cf. *Marquardt* 78.

397. Schwebel v. Ungar (1964), 48 D.L.R. (2d) 644 (S.C.C.), Clunet 1969, 746, note Castel. This decision also provides an illustration of the incidental question; see *infra* at n. 715-718.

398. See *Castel ibid.* 749-750; *Lysyk* 370; *Morris* 109. A very different approach was adopted in an earlier CANADIAN case, Miller v. Allison (1917), 33 D.L.R. 144 (B.C.S.C.), involving the validity of a marriage in Washington, USA, between a man domiciled in British Columbia and a woman divorced from her first husband in Oregon, USA, and domiciled at the time of the remarriage in Idaho, USA. In holding this marriage to be a nullity the court relied exclusively on the law of British Columbia, *i.e.* the husband's *lex domicilii*, by which the wife's divorce was invalid, without inquiring into the position under the law of Idaho, the wife's own premarital *lex domicilii.*

examples already mentioned, a pattern of *typical* solutions can be detected without too much difficulty. Most requirements for or impediments to marriage may usefully be characterised as unilateral or as bilateral, provided that it is borne in mind that the distinction cannot claim to have absolute validity.

52. *Further Discussion: Impediments Imposed by Foreign Law.* Attention will now be directed to situations where our problem comes before the courts or other authorities of a country other than that of the origin of the debated impediment, *i.e.* where it forms part of a foreign law governing the capacity of one of the parties pursuant to the conflicts rules of the forum. Two questions may be distinguished here.

The first is whether the impediment "claims" to be applied to both parties. This is a question of interpretation of the foreign *lex causae* which, like any such question, must be answered in accordance with the practice and other data existing in the foreign country itself. If the point in issue has not yet been authoritatively decided in that country, the court must proceed to place its own interpretation on the provision, acting as if it were sitting in the foreign country. To that extent the problem is the same as that considered in the preceding section.

Assuming now that the foreign provision has been found to "require" bilateral application, the second question is whether the forum is prepared to accord it such effect. The answer is usually in the affirmative. It is often said that the whole problem is one as to the proper interpretation of the *lex causae.*[399] On this view there is not even room for asking the question posed here. In any event, the proposed solution is rational inasmuch as the aim, or at least one of the aims, of the reference to the foreign law is to ensure that the marriage will be recognised as valid by that law. This aim can only be reached if the rules of the foreign law are treated the way they "claim" themselves, *i.e.* as they would be applied in their country of origin.

Nevertheless, there are some difficulties with this solution, and it is scarcely to be expected that it will prevail in all cases. In the first place, it may be recalled that even from the point of view of the foreign *lex causae* the problem is one relating to the conflict of laws. By respecting a "claim" to bilateral application of one requirement or the other laid down by that law, the forum will in effect subordinate its own conflicts rules to those of the foreign

399. See, for example, *Lewald* 80; *Maridakis* 215-216; *Niboyet* V 318; *Rabel* 286; *Steinle* 79-81; *Wolff,* IPR 189.

law. The technique bears a certain resemblance to that involved in the doctrine of *renvoi*.[400] Admittedly, this is no valid objection to the prevailing view, but rather to sweeping assertions of the type that "foreign conflicts rules are never to be applied". The argument may well carry some weight, however, in countries which are dogmatically opposed to any form of *renvoi*. Nor is it difficult to imagine situations where it seems little rational to take the view that, on the one hand, *renvoi* must be rejected and, on the other, that a "claim" to bilateral application by the foreign law must be accepted. The following hypothetical case may serve as an illustration:

> An Englishman domiciled in Greece wants to marry in that country. The other party is a Greek girl of fourteen years, the age of marriage for women according to Greek law (CC art. 1350). By the conflicts rules of Greece the capacity of each of the parties is governed by the law of their respective nationality (CC art. 13). As regards the English party, it is immaterial that the conflicts rules of English law refer back to Greek law *qua* the law of his domicile.[401] By English law the minimum age for marriage is sixteen years, and this rule applies to both parties when one of them is subject to English law (*supra* at n. 364). If the rule is accorded such effect by the competent Greek authority, the marriage will therefore be barred, notwithstanding that either party is of age by his own *lex patriae*. It is difficult to see, however, what useful purpose will be served by this solution if English law does not "claim" to be applied at all (so that the marriage would be upheld by an English court on the strength of Greek law) and comes into consideration only because Greek law refuses to accept the *renvoi* to its own domestic law.[402]

Furthermore, even where, as normally, a "faithful" application of the relevant foreign law is essential to prevent the creation of a limping marriage, the desire to achieve this goal may at times be outweighed by countervailing policies and desiderata. This may be exemplified by the aforementioned rule of Spanish law whereby,

400. See *Bischoff* no. 37-39.

401. See the GREEK CC art. 32.

402. The assumption that an ENGLISH court would sustain the marriage on the strength of GREEK law in this case is only tenable, however, if the English court would not itself accept the reference back to ENGLISH domestic law by the GREEK conflicts rule. This question is somewhat uncertain; cf. *infra* at n. 464, 474, 479.

as a consequence of the refusal by that law to recognise foreign divorces, a Spanish national is prohibited from marrying a divorced foreigner (*supra* at n. 355-356). While this prohibition has been respected in certain cases by courts outside Spain directed by their conflicts rules to test the capacity of the Spanish party by the law of his nationality, other courts have declined to do so and have permitted or upheld the second marriage in the teeth of the applicable Spanish law when the divorce was valid by the divorcee's own personal law, which usually coincided with the *lex fori* (*infra* s. 84-90). In these latter cases the claim of Spanish law to control the status of the divorcee, who lacked any connection to that law, was rejected as exorbitant and contrary to the forum's own policy in the matter. Various conflicts mechanisms, such as the doctrines of public policy, classification and the incidental question, have been called in aid to canalise such evaluations. Which conceptual tools are used is less important than the fact that the forum certainly can, and sometimes will, make an independent decision to defeat a "claim" to bilateral application raised by the relevant foreign law.[403]

It should finally be noted that issues of the present type are often avoided because they concern marriage impediments which are rejected by the forum in any case – even where imposed by the common personal law of the parties – for reasons of public policy or of their public law nature. To a very large extent this holds true of prohibitions based on race or religion as well as those of a distinctly political character (*infra* s. 107-111).

c. *The Time Factor*

ca. *Relevant Time for Ascertaining Connecting Factor*

53. *Time of Celebration Decisive.* In almost all countries adhering to the principle of the personal law it is well settled that the relevant domicile or nationality, respectively, is that possessed by each of the parties immediately before the celebration of the

403. This is one thing. An entirely different contention is that bilateral impediments imposed by foreign law can never be recognised with this effect by the forum and that they must invariably be treated as unilateral. See in this vein *Audit* 302-305 and the ITALIAN writers cited *supra* n. 395. Such general assertions must be rejected as excessively dogmatic.

marriage.[404] As a rule, any subsequent change of the connecting factor by the parties or one of them, whether brought about as a legal effect of the marriage (as may be the case with the domicile and/or nationality of the female party) or independently thereof, is immaterial for the purpose of determining the validity of the union.

This solution is based on impeccable logic. The issue is one of whether a marriage may be, or has been, validly entered into and thus depends on conditions existing at the time of the ceremony. It is very natural that the governing law should be that of the country to which the parties "belong", whether by domicile or by nationality, until the moment of the formation of the union.[405] The protection of that law, it has been argued, should not be denied to the parties, nor should the parties be allowed to frustrate the requirements of that law by anticipating a change of domicile or nationality which may be the consequence of the marriage or occur subsequently.

Nevertheless, it may be doubted whether a rigorous application of the premarital personal law is always socially appropriate and desirable. Other solutions, or at least certain modifications of the prevailing principle, have been proposed by writers or adopted by courts in several countries.

54. *Doctrine of Intended Matrimonial Home.* In *England* and elsewhere in the *British Commonwealth*, there is some support for the view that capacity to marry should be governed by the law of the country in which the parties intend to set up their matrimonial home, rather than by the law of their premarital domicile. This doctrine was in particular forcefully advocated by Professor *Cheshire.*[406] A related, though more flexible, concept which has

404. References *supra* n. 283-296 and *infra* n. 416-418, 430, 432. See also *Rabel* 295-296 and for particular countries, e.g., FRANCE: Cour Chambéry 7 Feb. 1885, Clunet 1888, 796; Trib. Seine 6 April 1951, Rev. crit. d.i.p. 1953, 586, note Batiffol; *Bischoff* no. 19; *Vincent and Ponsard* no. 36; [WEST] GERMANY: RG 20 Jan. 1928, RGZ 120, 35, 36; RG 15 Dec. 1930, IPRspr. 1931 no. 58; KG 19 Dec. 1932, IPRspr. 1932 no. 74; RG 8 June 1936, RGZ 151, 313, 314; OLG München 4 April 1950, IPRspr. 1950/51 no. 132; BGH 11 June 1958, BGHZ 27, 375, 380-381, IPRspr. 1958/59 no. 5; BGH 14 July 1966, BGHZ 46, 87, 95, IPRspr. 1966/67 no. 59 b; *Gamillscheg*, Kommentar, art. 13 no. 88-92; *Kegel*, IPR 348; *idem*, Kommentar, art. 13 no. 37; *Raape*, IPR 242-243; *Wolff*, IPR 189; GREECE: *Bendermacher-Geroussis* 4, 7; ITALY: *Betti* 414, 422; *Vitta* I 278-279; SWITZERLAND: *Beck*, art. 7 c. no. 31.

405. See, for example, for ENGLISH law *Cheshire and North* 339.

406. See *Cheshire*, PIL 276-288 (but see now *Cheshire and North* 335-347, where this view has in the main been abandoned in favour of the dual

been suggested is that of "the proper law of the contract to marry", as determined by "the most real connection", which is presumed to point to the law of the matrimonial domicile.[407]

These ideas are very close to the prevailing *American* doctrine that the creation of the marital status must ultimately be determined by the law of the intended matrimonial (family) domicile (*supra* s. 14). Like that doctrine they derive support in the main from the sociological consideration that the community most intimately concerned with the marital relation is that of the country in which the parties live as man and wife. By contrast, it is argued, the social life of the country of the antenuptial domicile is not affected by the union if the parties propose to sever their connections with that country immediately after the marriage. An additional argument which, however, has played a lesser role in the English than in the American discussion, is that the test of the intended matrimonial home avoids the double gauntlet to be passed if the law of the premarital domicile of each of the parties must be satisfied, and therefore is more likely to lead to validation of the marriage.[408] At the same time, it avoids the more or less technical difficulties involved in the combined application of two laws, for example the problem as to the unilateral or bilateral character of various marriage impediments (*supra* s. 49-52).

In view of the fact that it may be difficult to ascertain the genuine intentions of the parties, Professor *Cheshire* works with a basic presumption in favour of the law of the *husband's* domicile at the time of the marriage.[409] On this point, it seems, *Cheshire's* theory differs from other variants of the present doctrine. The consideration underlying this presumption is that it is normally in the country of the husband's domicile that the parties intend to establish their permanent home. The presumption will be rebutted if it can be inferred that the parties at the time of the marriage

---

domicile theory); *idem,* Husband and Wife 136-142. For a similar CANADIAN view see *Maddaugh* 131, 134-138, 146.

407. See *Sykes,* Essential Validity 160, 168-169; cf. *idem,* Conflict 90-92.

408. An ENGLISH decision which may serve to illustrate this argument is Radwan v. Radwan (No. 2), [1973] Fam. 35; see *infra* at n. 412. Cf. *Swan* 21-23, 36-38, suggesting that the theory should be confined to cases where its effect is to validate an otherwise invalid marriage. Another means of promoting this policy would be by upholding the marriage if it complies with the domiciliary law of *either* party. Such a rule is clearly at variance with the decided cases, but a reform of the law along these lines has been proposed by *Hartley,* Policy Basis 578.

409. *Cheshire,* PIL 277-278, 281. See also *Schmitthoff,* Validity of Marriage and the Conflict of Laws: 56 L.Q.R. 514-518 (1940).

intended to make their home elsewhere and if they have in fact done so within a reasonable time. This addition to the doctrine considerably reduces the importance of the subjective element, for in all cases where the place of the future matrimonial home is in doubt the husband's law will prevail.

It is rather uncertain whether and to what extent this doctrine forms part of English law, or of the law of other Commonwealth countries. Most of the relevant decisions are inconclusive, because the reasoning is equivocal as between the intended matrimonial home and the dual domicile theories and because the actual result would have been the same on either view.[410] Some decisions contain language, in the nature of *dicta,* indicating support for the doctrine propounded by *Cheshire.*[411] Finally, this doctrine was clearly adopted, in preference to the dual domicile rule, in one recent English case where for once the issue could not be avoided because it was essential to the decision:[412]

> A domiciled Englishwoman had entered into a polygamous marriage abroad with a domiciled Egyptian who was already married (the other marriage was dissolved later). The parties intended to and did in fact establish their joint home in Egypt. Some twenty years later, when the parties had become domiciled in England and acquired a family of eight children, the validity of the union came into question before the English court. The dual domicile doctrine would have led to invalidation since by English domestic law, the wife's premarital *lex domicilii,* she lacked capacity to contract such

410. See, e.g., ENGLAND: Mette v. Mette (1859), 1 Sw. & Tr. 416, 164 Eng. Rep. 792; Brook v. Brook (1861), 9 H.L.C. 193, [1861-73] All E.R. Rep. 493; In re De Wilton, [1900] 2 Ch. 481; In re Bozzelli's Settlement, [1902] 1 Ch. 751; Cheni v. Cheni, [1965] P. 85, 93; Ali v. Ali, [1968] P. 564, 576-577; *Cheshire,* PIL 282-285; AUSTRALIA: Hogarth v. Ray, [1958] Qd.R. 337, 341 (S.C.); CANADA: Miller v. Allison (1917), 33 D.L.R. 144 (B.C.S.C.); Dejardin v. Dejardin, [1932] 2 W.W.R. 237 (Man. K.B.); Reed (*alias* Frew) v. Reed (1969), 6 D.L.R. (3d) 617 (B.C.S.C.); Feiner v. Demkowicz (1973), 42 D.L.R. (3d) 165 (Ont. H.C.).

411. ENGLAND: Warrender v. Warrender (1835), 2 Cl. & F. 488, 535-536, 6 Eng. Rep. 1239, 1256 (H.L. on an appeal from SCOTLAND); De Reneville v. De Reneville, [1948] P. 100, 114, 121-122 (C.A.); Casey v. Casey, [1949] P. 420, 429-430 (C.A.); Kenward v. Kenward, [1951] P. 124, 144-146 (C.A.); SCOTLAND: Bliersbach v. MacEwen, 1959 S.C. 43, 55; AUSTRALIA: In the Will of Swan (1871), 2 V.R. (I.E. & M.) 47, 50.

412. Radwan v. Radwan (No. 2), [1973] Fam. 35.

a marriage.[413] The court, however, apparently inspired by the desire to uphold a long-standing union and to avoid the hardship of a decision to the contrary, held that the particular issue before it was governed by the law of the intended matrimonial home and so applied Egyptian law, by which the marriage was valid. The decision is expressly confined to the question of capacity to marry as affected by the polygamous nature of the union and does not purport to cover any other aspect of capacity (not even, it seems, in relation to polygamous marriages), such as affinity or nonage.[414] Thus, while a special conflicts rule is created for the particular question decided by the court, the general problem as to what law governs capacity to marry is left untouched.[415]

413. See also the Nullity of Marriage Act 1971, s. 1 (*d*) – added by the Matrimonial Proceedings (Polygamous Marriages) Act 1972, s. 4, and since re-enacted by the Matrimonial Causes Act 1973, s. 11 (*d*) – which provides that a polygamous marriage entered into outside England is void if either party was at the time of the marriage domiciled in that country. In the instant case the marriage had taken place before the commencement of the 1971 Act and therefore did not come within its reach. On the other hand, s. 1 (*d*) of the Act had clearly been enacted on the understanding that the dual domicile rule formed part of the ENGLISH common law and that the provision only codified that rule. In the opinion of the court, however, this assumption was erroneous, inasmuch as capacity to enter into a polygamous marriage by the common law depended upon the law of intended matrimonial residence. Furthermore, the court took the view that the position remained unaltered even after the coming into force of the 1971 Act (July 31, 1971), so that, apparently, the decision would have been the same if the marriage had been celebrated after that date. This conclusion was reached on the basis of s. 4 (1) of the 1971 Act (since re-enacted by s. 14 (1) of the 1973 Act) which, *inter alia*, exempts from the operation of s. 1 of the Act (now s. 11 of the 1973 Act) marriages governed by foreign law in accordance with the rules of private international law applicable apart from the Act. The effect of this saving clause, as construed by the court, is to preserve the common law rule referring (as was held by the court) capacity to contract a polygamous marriage to the law of the intended matrimonial home, even though that rule is inconsistent with the statutory rule in s. 1 (*d*) of the Act (s. 11 (*d*) of the 1973 Act), thus depriving the latter rule of all meaning. See Radwan v. Radwan (No. 2), *ibid.* at 52. This reasoning has been massively criticised; see the references *infra* n. 415.

414. Radwan v. Radwan (No. 2), *ibid.* at 54.

415. The decision has been heavily attacked by writers. See *Cheshire and North* 354-355; *Dicey and Morris* 288-289; *Graveson*, Conflict 267-269; *Karsten*, Capacity to Contract a Polygamous Marriage: 36 M.L.R. 291-297 (1973); *North* 123-124; *Pearl*, Capacity for Polygamy: [1973] C.L.J. 43-46; *Wade*, Capacity to Marry–Choice of Law Rules and Polygamous Marriages: 22 I.C.L.Q. 571-575 (1973). But see for an approving comment *P.B. Carter* (1972-1973) 436-437.

Apart from this much-criticised decision with its narrow *ratio decidendi*, however, the weight of judicial and extrajudicial opinion is in favour of the "orthodox" approach requiring application of the premarital domiciliary law or laws of the parties (the dual domicile doctrine). Several decisions have expressly approved, or seem clearly to lean towards, this rule.[416] On the facts, it is true, most of these cases, too, can be reconciled with the doctrine of the intended matrimonial home, but that test appears to have been plainly rejected as the basis of decision.[417] Moreover, a growing number of statutory provisions dealing with various conflicts questions of capacity to marry have been enacted in recent years, both in England and in other parts of the Commonwealth. All of these enactments seem either to follow the dual domicile rule or, where they depart from that rule, to recognise its existence at common law.[418]

416. ENGLAND: In re Paine, [1940] Ch. 46; Pugh v. Pugh, [1951] P. 482, 494 (cf. the notes of this case cited *supra* n. 364); Padolecchia v. Padolecchia, [1968] P. 314, 336; R. v. Brentwood Marriage Registrar, [1968] 2 Q.B. 956, 968; SCOTLAND: Lendrum v. Chakravarti, 1929 S.L.T. 96, 103 (*obiter*); AUSTRALIA: Ungar v. Ungar (1967), 10 F.L.R. 467 (N.S.W. Sup. Ct.); Stankus v. Stankus (1974), 9 S.A.S.R. 20 (S.C.); CANADA: Schwebel v. Ungar (1964), 48 D.L.R. (2d) 644 (S.C.C.), Clunet 1969, 746, note Castel; Crickmay v. Crickmay (1966), 60 D.L.R. (2d) 734, 735 (B.C.C.A.). And see among writers, most of whom proceed by an analysis of the relevant ENGLISH cases: *Anton* 276-278; *Baty* 444-451 (especially at 447 n. 11); *Castel,* PIL 102-104; *Dicey and Morris* 258-268; *Falconbridge* 700-715; *Graveson,* Conflict 256-269; *Inglis* 260-262; *North* 119-129; *Nygh* 403-410; *Sykes,* Conflict 83-89; *Wolff,* PIL 332-337.

417. In two of the cases cited in the preceding note the premarital *lex domicilii* of one of the parties was applied although it did not coincide with the law of the intended matrimonial home; see Padolecchia v. Padolecchia and Schwebel v. Ungar, *ibid.*; cf. on the latter case *Lysyk* 368-369. The decisions in those cases seem to be incompatible with any other rule than that of the dual domicile doctrine. For other ENGLISH cases see Shaw v. Gould (1868), L.R. 3 H.L. 55; Sottomayor v. De Barros (No. 1) (1877), 3 P.D. 1 (C.A.) (the decision in this case supports the application of the law of the premarital domicile where it is common to the parties and, to that extent, seems to exclude the law of the intended matrimonial home). Cf. *Morris* 102, 106; *Nygh* 406-408; *Sykes,* Conflict 84-87.

418. ENGLAND: Marriage (Enabling) Act 1960, s. 1 (3) (concerning marriage between persons within certain degrees of affinity; see *Morris* 104; *O.M. Stone,* The Last of the "In-Laws": 23 M.L.R. 538-540 (1960)); Matrimonial Causes Act 1973, s. 11 (*d*) (dealing with polygamous marriages entered into abroad; cf. *supra* n. 413); AUSTRALIA: Marriage Act 1961, s. 10 (2) (b) (age of marriage); see *Nygh* 409; *Sykes,* Conflict 92; NEW ZEALAND: Marriage Act 1955, s. 3 (1) (all provisions of the Act, so far as they relate to capacity of marry, apply to the marriage of any person domiciled in New

55. *Discussion.* One of the main objections advanced against the doctrine of the intended matrimonial home is that it enables the parties or (in practice usually) one of them to escape the protection afforded and the restraints imposed by the law of their domicile up to the moment of the marriage.[419] This consideration must be weighed against the undeniable social concern of the country of matrimonial residence and against the policy of validation, which will normally militate in favour of the law of the latter country. On this point it is probably impossible to make any evaluation in the abstract which will win general approval. Even if it is recognised that the interest of a country whose only contact with the marriage is that one of the parties was domiciled there until the time of celebration is less significant than that of the country of the matrimonial home, however, it is hardly realistic to expect that the former country will be prepared to give up all claim to control, at all events if the question arises in that country itself. At least as regards certain requirements, for example those concerning age of marriage, it seems much more likely that they will be conceived as following and protecting a local domiciliary wherever the parties intend to live, and even at the cost of defeating a marriage which conforms to the standards of the law of the matrimonial home or residence.[420] In this respect, perhaps, "the legal atmosphere" in a country like England is different from that of the United States, where the problem usually occurs in the context of an interstate rather than international conflict and where the policy of validation seems more easily to be allowed to prevail over other considerations.

Another criticism made of *Cheshire's* doctrine is that it places too much emphasis on the subjective test of intention. Such an element fits badly into a system of which the main intrinsic merit is supposed to lie in its foundation in social reality. In the first place, there may be cases where the parties, at the time of the marriage, genuinely intend to make their home in a particular country but where they change their mind afterwards and never carry out their original intention. In this situation, social considerations would surely seem to call for the application of the law

---

Zealand at the time of the marriage, wherever the marriage is solemnised), cf. Matrimonial Proceedings Act 1963, s. 7 (1) (a); see *Webb and Davis* 217-226, 256-260.

419. See, e.g., *Cheshire and North* 338, 340; *Dicey and Morris* 260. Cf. from the point of view of WEST GERMAN law *H. Müller* 39.

420. See, e.g., *Morris* 98-99; *Nygh* 409.

of the *actual,* rather than the intended, matrimonial residence.[421] Secondly, it may be uncertain at the time of the marriage where the parties intend to set up their home because they have not yet made up their mind on the question. In such cases the law to determine their capacity to marry cannot be definitely identified at that point of time, so that the validity of the union may remain in doubt for a more or less protracted period after it has been entered into.[422] Besides, the proposed test fails entirely in those, admittedly exceptional, cases in which the parties do not contemplate living together as husband and wife (sham marriages).[423]

To this, it is true, it may be replied that all such doubtful cases are covered by the presumption, suggested by *Cheshire,* that the matrimonial home will coincide with the husband's antenuptial domicile. This part of the doctrine, however, appears somewhat arbitrary and difficult to justify. To rely on presumed intentions is scarcely an appropriate element, even less than reliance on actual intentions, in a system claiming superiority on account of its touch with social realities. Moreover, the preference given to the husband's law is in glaring inconsistency with the principle of equality of the sexes (*supra* s. 44).

A striking feature of the Anglo-American discussion of these questions, at least from the viewpoint of a Continental or Scandinavian lawyer, is its almost exclusive concern with situations in which the validity of a marriage is examined by the courts *ex post,* whether in direct proceedings for annulment or incidentally in other proceedings. The underlying assumption, apparently shared by the opponents of doctrines of the type propounded by *Cheshire,* is that the question of what law governs capacity to marry seldom if ever arises at the time of the marriage.[424] This, of course, is not true if the "preventive" stage is taken into account, that is to say, if the problem is posed of what conditions must be satisfied by the parties before they can be allowed to get married. Surely this aspect of the matter is worth some attention, the more so as the cases in which the validity of a marriage presenting foreign ele-

421. See *Sykes,* Essential Validity 166-167. This seems to be the main point on which the test of "the proper law of the contract" proposed by that author (*supra* at n. 407) differs from *Cheshire's* view. See also *Maddaugh* 136-137.

422. See, for instance, *Dicey and Morris* 261.

423. For illustrative ENGLISH cases see *infra* n. 973; cf. *Woodhouse* 455, 458, 460, 462. For AMERICAN cases of this type see the references *supra* n. 201-205.

424. See, for instance, *Cheshire,* Husband and Wife 139; *Maddaugh* 137.

ments (however those elements are more exactly defined) is questioned *ex post* represent but the tip of an iceberg as compared with the total number of such marriages contracted or attempted to be contracted in local form.

It is almost too clear for argument that neither the future matrimonial home, nor the intentions of the parties in that respect can provide a workable test for the choice of law to govern capacity to marry at the stage of the formation of the union. Those criteria are too uncertain to be relied upon by the registrars of marriages and similar functionaries who, primarily, administer this part of the law and who are not in the favourable position, enjoyed by the courts when faced *ex post* with problems of the present kind, of knowing what course events will take after the ceremony has been performed. Any "prospective" test for the choice of law, such as that based on the intentions of the parties, is bound to leave plenty of scope for guesswork and to open the gate to easy evasion. In practice, the preventive function of the law governing capacity to marry can only be fulfilled if that law is identified by reference to the domicile (or whatever is the relevant connecting factor) existing at the time of the marriage.

This, on the other hand, does not in itself rule out the possibility of applying a different law if the question is raised at a later stage, in judicial or other proceedings involving the validity of the marriage. Even if, in the eyes of the forum, the parties lacked capacity to contract the marriage because it contravened the law of their premarital domicile, it may well be appropriate on policy grounds to sustain the union, once it has come into existence, if it complies with the law of the country in which the parties have meanwhile established their joint home. This question is very similar to that discussed, from the viewpoint of certain Continental European countries, in the following section.

56. *Validation under Personal Law at Time of Proceedings.* An exception to the rule that the time of marriage is decisive is often admitted by Continental courts and writers in circumstances where the marriage is bad by the relevant premarital *lex patriae* but good by the law of the present nationality of the spouses, *i.e.* their personal law at the time when suit is brought to test the validity of the union. The best known example is a *German* case, decided by the Supreme Court of the *Reich* in 1931:[425]

425. RG 16 May 1931, RGZ 132, 416, IPRspr. 1931 no. 59.

A man of Austrian nationality and of Christian religion married a woman of Russian nationality and of Jewish religion. The celebration took place in Russia in 1918. The parties lived in the Trieste region of Austria and acquired Italian nationality when Trieste went to Italy after the First World War. Subsequently they settled in Germany, where the husband brought proceedings for annulment on the ground that by Austrian law, his premarital *lex patriae,* marriages between Christians and non-Christians were prohibited (the impediment of *disparitas cultus*). Although that law was applicable in principle under the German conflict of laws rules, the *Reichsgericht* sustained the marriage in reliance on Italian law where this prohibition would be disregarded as contrary to Italian public policy.[426] The court declared that it saw no good reason to annul a marriage which would be treated as valid in the present home country of the spouses.

This decision has been followed by other [West] German courts and been approved by the majority of writers.[427] Such a validating application of the new *lex patriae* also receives support in a number of other Continental countries.[428] In addition, similar results are often reached by other means, in particular by conflicts rules requiring, generally or in certain cases, that a ground for annulment must exist not only according to the premarital personal law but also according to some other law, such as the *lex fori* or the *lex loci celebrationis* (*infra* s. 69-71).

It will be appreciated that the view referred to here has certain features in common with the English theory of the intended matrimonial home. Under both of them the validity of a marriage may have to be reassessed by reason of a change of the relevant

426. Cf. *infra* at n. 1129.

427. For *obiter dicta* supporting this view see: KG 5 Aug. 1937, JW 1938, 855, note Massfeller; BGH 11 June 1958, BGHZ 27, 375, 380, 382, IPRspr. 1958/59 no. 5; LG Stuttgart 12 July 1967, IPRspr. 1966/67 no. 75; KG 30 Nov. 1970, IPRspr. 1970 no. 57. See also the expert opinion in IPG 1965/66 no. 23 (at 244) (Hamburg) and among writers (who differ on several points of detail): *Dölle,* IPR 114; *Frankenstein* 188-190; *Gamillscheg,* Kommentar, art. 13 no. 103-124; *Neuhaus,* Grundbegriffe 299-300; *Nussbaum* 135; *Raape,* IPR 243-244, 263; *Siehr* 137; *Wolff,* IPR 196-197 (but cf. 189).

428. See *Rabel* 296; *Rigaux,* Conflit mobile 427-431; *idem,* DIP I 308-309; and, e.g., for BULGARIA: *Koschucharoff* 498; GREECE: *Maridakis* 131-132, 217; ITALY: *Betti* 422-423; SWITZERLAND: *von Overbeck,* Wiederverheiratung 350 n. 18; *Spivak* 40-41; *Vischer,* IPR 593; YUGOSLAVIA: *Katičić* 428-429.

connecting factor occurring at or after the time of celebration. The policy grounds underlying the two doctrines are partly the same, and their merits and demerits may be discussed along similar lines.

On the other hand, aside from the fact that the personal law is normally determined by nationality rather than by domicile, the Continental concept differs in some respects from its English counterpart. In the first place, it always presupposes an actual change of the relevant connecting factor and does not rely on the (presumed) intentions of the parties. Secondly, since the relevant date is that of the proceedings, the choice of law to govern the validity of the marriage may be affected more than once if there have been successive changes of the connecting factor. In such cases the last change, rather than the first, will be decisive.[429] Thirdly, the Continental doctrine only operates to validate an initially defective marriage. The authorities cited above in no way support the proposition that the personal law at the time of the proceedings should prevail in the converse situation where a marriage which complies with the premarital law or laws would be struck down by the new law. It is generally agreed that the marriage remains valid in such cases (*semel validum, semper validum*).[430] This is not always true of the doctrine of the intended matrimonial home. Although that doctrine, too, generally favours validation, it may in certain circumstances have the opposite effect.[431]

429. See *Gamillscheg*, Kommentar, art. 13 no. 124 (who points out that this is of importance chiefly for stateless persons and refugees who may often have to move from one country to another and whose personal status is subject to the law of their /habitual/ residence). But cf. *Siehr* 178-180.

430. See the references *supra* n. 404 and *infra* n. 432. *Adde,* FRANCE: Cass. civ. 19 Feb. 1963, Clunet 1963, 986, note Ponsard, Rev. crit. d.i.p. 1963, 559, note G. Holleaux; Trib. Lyon 20 Nov. 1975, Rev. crit. d.i.p. 1976, 477, note P. Lagarde. These two cases are particularly illustrative because, there, the validity of actually polygamous marriages, lawfully contracted under the personal law at the time of celebration, was treated as unaffected by the fact that the husband had subsequently acquired French nationality. [WEST] GERMANY: RG 23 June 1930, IPRspr. 1930 no. 65; RG 24 Jan. 1941, RGZ 165, 398, 403; KG 30 Nov. 1970, IPRspr. 1970 no. 57; expert opinion in IPG 1967/68 no. 21 (at 246-249) (Cologne); *Gamillscheg*, Kommentar, art. 13 no. 94-102 (with some modifications); GREECE: *Maridakis* 216-217. For the position in ISRAEL see *Bentwich,* The Legal System of Israel: 13 I.C.L.Q. 236, 247 (1964); *Scheftelowitz* 179.

431. See the CANADIAN case of Schwebel v. Ungar (1964), 48 D.L.R. (2d) 644 (S.C.C.), where the marriage was upheld in reliance on the law of the premarital domicile but where the test of the intended matrimonial home would probably have led to invalidation.

As in England, so in the countries of Continental Europe, however, opinions are divided on the present matter. Some writers contend that the validity of a marriage must be determined once and for all by reference to the law of the premarital nationality of the parties and that there is no need or justification for an exception to the effect referred to above.[432] In some countries this is clearly the prevailing view.[433] It is indeed common ground in Continental countries (in contrast with England) that capacity must be tested by the premarital personal law or laws alone when the question arises at the stage of the *formation* of the marriage. Consistency may then seem to demand that the choice of law should be the same when the validity of the union is questioned at a later stage.

This argument, however, is not conclusive. The relevant policies do not fully coincide, nor does one policy always pull in the same direction, in the two situations. The most important difference is that the policy of validation, which is without significance at the stage of celebration, comes into consideration once the union has been formed.[434] The policy of promoting international uniformity of decision, on the other hand, carries more weight at the former than at the latter stage. The most effective means of achieving such uniformity is by refusing to create a marriage which would not be recognised as valid in the home country of the parties or one of them. When the marriage has already come into existence it may well be impossible to reach this aim, however much the forum so desires. Often the choice will lie between siding with a validating or with an invalidating law. If, in this situation, the former law is that of the present nationality of the spouses, it seems eminently sensible to opt in favour of that law. Not only is this solution consonant with the policy of validation, but it is also the best way in which the forum can further international uniformity of decision. On the latter score it is surely more important to look to the country with which the parties are now (in the eyes of the forum) most closely connected than to any other country, including that of their premarital nationality to which they no

432. See, e.g., WEST GERMANY: *Kegel*, Kommentar, art. 13 no. 38; *Letzgus*, Die Ehescheidung im deutschen internationalen Privatrecht: AcP 145 (1939) 295, 296; GREECE: *Bendermacher-Geroussis* 4; SWITZERLAND: *Beck*, art. 7 f no. 134.

433. See for AUSTRIA: *Köhler* 59 n. 13; *Mänhardt* 34 n. 54; *Schwind*, IPR 141. The same view is apparently taken by FRENCH courts and writers; see the references *supra* n. 404; but cf. *Bartin* 122.

434. Cf. *Hartley*, Policy Basis 577-578, 582.

longer have any relation. In the already mentioned German case (*supra* at n. 425), for example, it is very difficult to see what useful purpose would have been served by applying the invalidating rule of Austrian law, with which neither of the spouses had any connection at the time of the suit. Certainly the approach adopted by the *Reichsgericht* in asking how the marriage would be treated in Italy, the country of their common nationality at that time, was more realistic.

In conclusion, therefore, it may be stated that the present doctrine rests on a sound policy basis. Nevertheless, doubts may be raised as to various details concerning the scope of the doctrine.[435] One question is whether a distinction should be drawn according to the circumstances in which the change of nationality took place. In particular, it may be doubted whether it is appropriate that a ground for annulment existing under the wife's premarital law should be extinguished by a change of nationality on her part which is an automatic legal effect of the marriage.[436] Another possible ground of distinction is that of the degree of reliance placed on the validity of the union. Clearly, for instance, there is better reason to uphold a marriage on the ground envisaged here if the parties have at all times treated it as valid and still live together as man and wife, especially if their matrimonial home is in the country of their new nationality, than if they have separated.[437] It is very difficult to draw an exact borderline which does justice to such variable circumstances. Obviously, however, a marriage cannot be "resurrected" by a change of nationality occurring after a nullity decree, which is valid in the forum country, has been secured on the basis of the "old" law.[438]

435. Particularly elaborate patterns of solution, which include certain distinctions not mentioned here, have been proposed by *Gamillscheg*, Kommentar, art. 13 no. 109-124, and by *Siehr* 136-164.

436. See, e.g., FRANCE: Trib. Seine 6 April 1951, Rev. crit. d.i.p. 1953, 586; [WEST] GERMANY: KG 5 Aug. 1937, JW 1938, 855; *Frankenstein* 187; *Nussbaum* 132. And see the decision of BGH 11 June 1958, BGHZ 27, 375, 382, according to which only a change of nationality by both spouses is relevant for the present purpose. For an approving note of this case see *Beitzke:* JZ 1959, 123, 124-125. But see for more refined views: *Gamillscheg*, Kommentar, art. 13 no. 112-113, 119, 123; *Siehr* 146-148.

437. Cf. *Gamillscheg*, Kommentar, art. 13 no. 114-115; *Siehr* 150-153; *Vischer*, IPR 593.

438. Cf. the GERMAN case decided by KG 10 July 1933, IPRspr. 1933 no. 100, aff'd RG 2 July 1934, RGZ 145, 74, IPRspr. 1934 no. 129.

cb. *Subsequent Changes in Lex Causae*

57. A problem analogous to that arising in relation to the form of marriage may be posed if, after the celebration of the marriage but before its validity is called in question, the content of the personal law governing the capacity of one or both of the parties has been changed. Can such alterations in the *lex causae* affect the validity of the union? This can only be a problem if two conditions are met.[439] The first is that the new law itself claims to have retroactive effect so as to interfere with the validity of marriages entered into before it came into force. Secondly, since it is obvious that such legislation must be enforced in accordance with its own terms where it forms part of the *lex fori* (assuming that the subject-matter is governed by that law), it must be presupposed that the *lex causae* is a foreign law, referred to by the conflicts rules of the forum.[440] In other words, the question of applying the retrospective statute must be raised in a forum outside the State of enactment itself.

The overwhelming weight of opinion as to problems of this type generally is in favour of applying the relevant foreign law as it stands at the time of the proceedings, including its transitional provisions.[441] It follows that effect must be given to such retrospective changes as that law may have undergone since the time of the (attempted) creation of the relationship involved. Although decisions covering the issue specifically in respect of capacity to marry are scarce, so that much room is left for speculation, there appears to be no good reason why this sound principle should not be followed, as a rule, here too.[442] No valid objection can be

439. Cf. *Pålsson*, Marriage, s. 398.

440. For an example of validation under the *lex fori*, which was applicable *qua* the law of the domicile of both parties, see the ENGLISH case of R. v. Dibdin, [1910] P. 57 and 101 (C.A.). Note, however, that there may be cases where the *lex causae* coincided with the *lex fori* at the time of the marriage but where it no longer does at the time of the proceedings. This is possible if there has meanwhile been a change of the connecting factor affecting the choice of law for capacity to marry (*supra* s. 54-56). In this situation changes in the content of the *lex fori* must be disregarded since that law is no longer relevant at all. See *infra* n. 449.

441. See *Pålsson*, Marriage, s. 399. See also *Castel*, Conflict 177-196; *Gamillscheg*, Kommentar, before art. 13 no. 370-372; *Grodecki* 13-16; *Rigaux*, DIP I 377-378.

442. For a comparative survey see *Grodecki* 17-20. And see for FRANCE: *Bischoff* no. 19; *Vincent and Ponsard* no. 30; for WEST GERMANY: *Gamillscheg*, Kommentar, art. 13 no. 152-153; *Kegel*, IPR 11, 180, 348; *idem*,

derived from the fact that the conflicts rules on capacity to marry usually provide for the application of a person's *lex domicilii* or *lex patriae,* respectively, "at the time of the marriage" (*supra* s. 53). As has often been demonstrated, the purpose of such a time reference in a choice of law rule is only to fix the moment for the selection of the connecting factor used to identify the country of the *lex causae.* It clarifies that the relevant domicile or nationality is that at the point of celebration, but it does not purport to "petrify" the rules of the designated law as they were at that time.[443]

Accordingly, it seems that effect will normally be given to retrospective rules of the *lex causae,* at least to the extent that they operate to *validate* a marriage which was invalid by that law as it stood at the time of celebration.[444] The converse case of a retrospective *invalidation* of an initially valid marriage is more doubtful. In that type of situation, which is very rare in practice, many courts, moved by considerations of public policy and by the *favor matrimonii,* would probably hesitate and possibly refuse to apply a foreign law so stipulating.[445]

Even as regards validating changes, the prevailing principle can scarcely be accepted without some reservations similar to those appropriate in respect of the form of marriage. Such a reservation is called for, in the first place, where either party has obtained a nullity decree, based on lack of capacity according to the *lex causae* as it then stood and granted or recognised by the forum, before the retrospective validation purported to take effect. Here it seems clear that the parties must be able to rely on the finality

---

Kommentar, art. 13 no. 37; but cf. *Makarov,* Grundriss 91. For the treatment of similar problems in AMERICAN law see *supra* s. 26.

443. See, e.g., *Castel,* Conflict 183-186; *Dicey and Morris* 43; *Eek* 151-155; *Grodecki* 19; *F.A. Mann,* The Time Element in the Conflict of Laws: 31 Brit. YB. Int. L. 217, 232-236 (1954).

444. See the references *supra* n. 441-442 and, e.g., AUSTRALIA: *Nygh* 290; ENGLAND: Re Pozot's Settlement, [1952] 1 All E.R. 1107, 1109 (C.A.) (badly reported on this point); *Dicey and Morris* 262; [WEST] GERMANY: KG 21 March 1932, IPRspr. 1932 no. 82; cf. BGH 14 July 1964, BGHZ 42, 99, 100; *Wengler,* Skizzen 558-559. But cf. the FRENCH decision of Cour Chambéry 7 Feb. 1885, Clunet 1888, 796. For the corresponding problem as to the form of marriage see *Pålsson,* Marriage, s. 400.

445. Cf. *Pålsson,* Marriage, s. 401. See also *Gamillscheg,* Kommentar, before art. 13 no. 371, art. 13 no. 152. But see for WEST GERMAN cases where the courts were apparently prepared to apply such rules in the *lex causae*: OLG München 4 April 1950, IPRspr. 1950/51 no. 132; LG Mannheim 21 May 1965, IPRspr. 1964/65 no. 109.

of the decree annulling the marriage (for example for the purpose of remarriage) and that the union cannot be "resurrected" by subsequent changes in the *lex causae.*[446] A second situation which may justify a departure from the rule is where one of the parties has remarried, without a nullity decree but in reliance on the invalidity of the prior union (it must be presupposed that that union was void rather than voidable), before the validating legislation came into force or took effect. Here, too, recognising the retroactive change of status brought about under the relevant foreign law is likely to produce more harm than good, since to do so would compel the forum to invalidate the second marriage, which is presumably the "living" one.[447] With regard to the corresponding problem as to formal validity, it will be recalled, this point was expressly left open by the leading *English* authority on the matter, the *Starkowski* case decided by the House of Lords in 1954.[448]

These problems become particularly intricate if there has also been a *change of the relevant connecting factor.* Such is the case when, prior to the coming into effect of the foreign retrospective law, the party who is subject to that law has acquired a new (and lost his old) domicile or nationality, respectively. With regard to this type of situation it must first be recalled that a change of the connecting factor may be relevant so as thenceforth to exclude the application of the former personal law and to make the party subject to the new law instead. This possibility exists both under the English doctrine of the intended matrimonial home and under the Continental doctrine of validation under the new personal law (*supra* s. 54-56). To that extent a subsequent amendment of the earlier personal law must clearly be disregarded since, *ex hypothesi,* it is no longer the relevant law to determine capacity to marry.[449]

Apart from this, however, even where capacity to marry remains subject to the premarital personal law, a change of the connecting factor may make the courts more reluctant than otherwise to accept the effect of a subsequent retrospective modification of

446. See *Castel,* Conflict 193; *Gamillscheg,* Kommentar, art. 13 no. 152; and the references given in *Pålsson,* Marriage, s. 400 n. 515.

447. See *Pålsson, ibid.* at n. 513. But see *Grodecki* 19.

448. Starkowski v. Att.-Gen., [1954] A.C. 155, 168, 172, 176, 182 (H.L.).

449. This holds true even where the earlier personal law, which has since been superseded by another law, was the *lex fori.* See *Gamillscheg,* Kommentar, art. 13 no. 154.

that law.[450] An illustration is afforded by the Canadian case of *Ambrose* v. *Ambrose,* which involved much the same issue as the *Starkowski* case but where that case was distinguished:[451]

> W obtained an interlocutory decree of divorce from H(1) in California, where they were domiciled, in 1930. The decree did not dissolve the marriage, and therefore did not entitle either party to remarry, until it was made final. This could have been done at the expiration of one year, but it was not in fact done until 1939 when the order was made (without retroactivity) by the court on its own motion. Meanwhile in 1935, while still domiciled in California, W went through a ceremony of marriage in the state of Washington with H(2), who was at all times domiciled in British Columbia. W and H(2) then lived together as man and wife in that province until 1956 when they separated. In 1958, when W had discovered the true state of her divorce, she took advantage of a California statute, originally enacted in 1941, to secure a *nunc pro tunc* order in the California court whereby the 1939 judgment was backdated to 1931, the earliest time when it could have been entered. The order thus purported to confer retroactively on W the capacity to have remarried in 1935 so as to validate that marriage. H(2), however, brought a petition for nullity before the British Columbia court on the ground that their marriage was bigamous. The court, holding that the California statute and the order made under it in 1958 could not be recognised in British Columbia, granted a decree.

The court distinguished the *Starkowski* case on two grounds. Firstly, the defect vitiating the marriage and cured by retrospective legislation in that case was a matter of form referable

450. See on these problems: *Gamillscheg,* Kommentar, before art. 13 no. 372, art. 13 no. 154; *Graulich,* Conflit de lois dans le temps (Rép. dr. int. I) no. 109-110; *Rigaux,* Conflit mobile 405-409; *Wengler,* Skizzen 560-563, 568-569.

451. Ambrose v. Ambrose (1961), 25 D.L.R. (2d) 1 (B.C.C.A.), Clunet 1964, 864, with a critical note by Castel. For other critical voices see: *Castel,* Comment: 39 Can. Bar Rev. 604-624 (1961); *Grodecki* 19-20; *Hartley,* Bigamy 700-703. For comments in a positive vein see *Giardina,* Les lois étrangères rétroactives en matière de mariage et de régimes matrimoniaux: Rev. crit. d.i.p. 1972, 401, 416 n. 2; *Knittel,* The Temporal Dimension in the Conflict of Laws Rules: 40 Brit. YB. Int. L. 105, 124-125 (1964). On the CALIFORNIA system of interlocutory divorce and retroactive final decrees involved in the case see *supra* s. 21 and 26, respectively.

to the *lex loci celebrationis,* whereas the case at bar dealt with W's capacity to marry, as to which the proper law to apply was that of her domicile; and while W had been domiciled in California when she married H(2), her domicile from 1939 was at all times in British Columbia.[452] In the opinion of the court, therefore, she was not subject to the law of California when the validating statute and order came about in that state. Secondly, in the *Starkowski* case the validation of the prior union occurred before the remarriage, whereas in the instant case the remarriage preceded the validation of the divorce in the prior marriage.

The first of these distinctions is a hard nut to crack. It is by no means apparent that, in the event of a change of domicile, matters of capacity to marry must be treated differently from matters of form for the present purpose, solely because the former are governed by the *lex domicilii* and the latter by the *lex loci celebrationis.* In excluding that the wife's capacity could be affected by California legislation once she had become domiciled in British Columbia, the court seems in fact to have treated a problem of conflict of laws in time (concerning the applicable rules in the governing California law) as one involving a *conflit mobile* (*i.e.,* as a question of the choice of law as affected by a change of the relevant connecting factor).[453] Even within the framework of the former problem, it is true, a change of domicile may strengthen the case for rejecting a retrospective modification of the *lex causae.* In this respect, however, it is difficult to see why the position should differ according to whether the substantive or the formal conditions of marriage are in issue.

The second point of distinction made by the court is more interesting. Here the decision provides support for the conclusion that a retrospective validation under the relevant foreign law cannot be recognised when it takes effect after the remarriage of one of the parties to the prior union.[454] As mentioned earlier, this exception is easily justified where it is the prior marriage which is so validated and where recognition by the forum would be bought at the cost of destroying the fresh marriage. Actually, however, the *Ambrose* case was far from involving a situation of this type. What the California legislation and *nunc pro tunc* order purported to achieve, and what the British Columbia court refused to recog-

452. Cf. *Dicey and Morris* 50 n. 65.
453. See *Castel,* Conflict 181-188.
454. See *Dicey and Morris* 50, 256.

nise, was that the divorce in the prior union was made retroactive and, indirectly, that the second marriage was validated. The court was indeed concerned with the opposite of upholding that marriage, namely, with protecting a "vested right in annulment". This seems not only difficult to reconcile with the *Starkowski* case but also very dubious on policy grounds.[445]

d. *Renvoi*

58. *Current Solutions.* The doctrine of *renvoi* has been of practical significance mainly in those Continental countries where capacity to marry is governed by the law of the nationality of the parties. In most of these countries a *renvoi* from the *lex patriae* to the *lex domicilii* or the *lex loci celebrationis* is accepted in accordance with general rules on the matter.[456] As a result, American or Danish nationals, for example, when marrying in *France, West Germany, Switzerland,* etc., will be subject to the conditions of the local law to which (as a rule) their national law refers back.[457] The same is true of nationals of the United Kingdom, Australia, Canada, Brazil, Norway, etc., in so far as they are domiciled in the country of celebration.[458] Even the Hague Convention on

455. See *Hartley,* Bigamy 702-703; *Swan* 23 n. 27.

456. For general rules on *renvoi* see *Pålsson,* Marriage, s. 189 and 192. Specifically as regards capacity to marry see *Rabel* 283-284 and, e.g., AUSTRIA: LG Salzburg 1 March 1974, ZfRV 16 (1975) 48, note H. Hoyer; *Gamillscheg,* Kommentar, art. 13 no. 55-59; *Schwind,* IPR 146; BULGARIA: *Jessel* 152; *Koschucharoff* 498, 502; FRANCE: *Niboyet* V 337, 340-341; *Vincent and Ponsard* no. 76; WEST GERMANY: *Gamillscheg ibid.* no. 48-54, 61-71; *Kegel,* Kommentar, art. 13 no. 106-108; *Raape,* IPR 69, 237; HUNGARY: *Réczei* 356; SWITZERLAND: *infra* n. 467; YUGOSLAVIA: *Katičić* 424-425, 429; *Tchirkovitch* 224-225.

457. For cases involving American nationals see FRANCE: Trib. Seine 10 Jan. 1962, G.P. 1962.1.284 (see *infra* at n. 477); [WEST] GERMANY: LG Tübingen 25 July 1934, IPRspr. 1934 no. 57; BayObLG 31 May 1966, IPRspr. 1966/67 no. 146; OLG Karlsruhe 3 Oct. 1968, IPRspr. 1968/69 no. 69; AG Zweibrücken 14 May 1970, IPRspr. 1970 no. 46. For older GERMAN practice in cases involving AUSTRIAN law, which raised difficult questions as to the interpretation of § 4 of the ABGB, see RG 15 Feb. 1912, RGZ 78, 234; BayObLG 18 Jan. 1918, *Kosters and Bellemans* 101; *Gamillscheg,* Kommentar, art. 13 no. 57-59.

458. See, e.g., FRANCE: Cour Paris 23 March 1888, Clunet 1889, 638 (ENGLISH law); WEST GERMANY: AG Hamburg 9 and 22 Dec. 1966, IPRspr. 1966/67 no. 64 and 66, respectively (do.); OLG Celle 18 Sept. 1968, IPRspr. 1968/69 no. 67 (BRAZILIAN law, see *infra* n. 469). Sometimes the

continued on page 146

Marriage of 1902, which is generally hostile to *renvoi,* endorses the doctrine where the *lex patriae* designated in the first instance "expressly" refers to another law.[459] This provision, however, has been of little, if any, practical importance since the rule of the *lex patriae* prevails in all or nearly all countries which are or have been parties to the convention. The one possible exception was *Switzerland* (which has now left the convention), whose conflicts rules refer to the *lex loci celebrationis* the validity of marriages between Swiss nationals entered into abroad.[460]

In so far as a *renvoi* by the *lex patriae* is accepted, this usually covers not only a reference back to the *lex fori* (remission) but also a further reference to the law of a third country (transmission).[461] Nevertheless, the latter type of *renvoi* is rejected in a few

continued from page 145

conflicts rules of AMERICAN law, or of the law of a particular state of the USA, have been construed to the same effect, being held to refer back to the *lex fori* in its capacity as the party's *lex domicilii,* rather than because it was the *lex loci celebrationis,* or alternatively on both grounds. See FRANCE: Trib. Seine 10 Jan. 1962, G.P. 1962.1.284; [WEST] GERMANY: OLG Dresden 15 Jan. 1912, OLGR 26, 211; AG Zweibrücken 14 May 1970, IPRspr. 1970 no. 46; cf. *Drobnig,* PIL 84. Similarly with regard to DANISH law see OLG Schleswig 21 Jan. and 7 April 1953, IPRspr. 1952/53 no. 2.

459. Art. 1. See *Travers* I 61-77 and, critically, *Buzzati* 113-170; *Frankenstein* 70-73; *F. Kahn* 70-78.

460. NAG art. 7 f par. 1. The meaning of this rule, however, seems to be that SWITZERLAND is prepared to recognise such a marriage without insisting on compliance with its own law, whenever it has been validly created in the country of celebration. So construed the provision refers to the *conflicts rules* rather than to the municipal rules of the *lex loci celebrationis.* Hence, where (as in all other States parties to the Hague Convention) the capacity of Swiss nationals is determinable by their *lex patriae* according to the conflicts rules of the country of celebration, SWISS law, far from declining this "offer of competence", accepts a marriage concluded in conformity with that law, just as it would accept any other choice of law prescribed by the foreign conflicts rules. See *infra* s. 69, especially at n. 572-573, 576-577.

461. For cases concerning capacity to marry see FRANCE: Trib. Seine 11 July 1918, Clunet 1919, 286 (upholding a New York marriage between an American man and an Argentine woman whose prior marriage had been annulled by a decree validly granted in New York but not recognised by the law of Argentina; one reason for the decision, which bears a distinct mark of the policy of validation, was that ARGENTINE law referred the question on to the law of NEW YORK, as the party's *lex domicilii,* by which the marriage was valid); WEST GERMANY: BGH 11 June 1958, IPRspr. 1958/59 no. 5 (*in fine;* general statement); LG Hamburg 16 Oct. 1958, IPRspr. 1958/59 no. 117 (ENGLISH law; question of transmission to LIBYAN law, the *lex loci celebrationis*); see *Gamillscheg,* Kommentar, art. 13 no. 54. For ENGLAND see *infra* n. 464.

countries, including *Albania* and *East Germany,* which adhere to the principle in the former situation.[462]

In countries in which capacity to marry is tested by the *lex domicilii,* problems of *renvoi* seldom materialise in practice and have been relatively little considered by writers.[463] There is, however, an *English* decision which indicates support for the doctrine in this matter, and that was so even though it involved a reference on to the law of a third country:[464] The husband was an Italian national who had obtained a divorce from his first wife in Switzerland, where they were domiciled. He then came to England on a visit and sought to marry there a spinster of Spanish nationality also domiciled in Switzerland. The registrar, whose decision was upheld by the court, refused to issue the licence required for the marriage because an impediment existed by Swiss law, which governed the question according to the English conflict of laws. The impediment was that the divorce did not entitle the husband to remarry; for the Swiss conflicts rule referred his capacity to marry to his *lex patriae,* Italian law, which (as it then stood) did not recognise his divorce.[465]

Finally, in a minority of countries applying the personal law to determine capacity to marry, the present problem does not arise at all, because *renvoi* is banished by general rules excluding the use of the principle for all purposes. This dogmatic position is taken, for instance, in *Greece, Italy, Brazil* and the *Arab countries.*[466]

59. *Discussion.* Whether *renvoi* is or is not justified with regard to capacity to marry depends on the purpose and the policy of the forum's reference to the personal law. If the objective is to prevent the creation of a limping status, the forum cannot permit the celebration of a marriage which would not be recognised as valid in the country of the *lex causae.* Since such recognition depends, in the first instance, on the conflicts rules of the relevant foreign law, those rules must be taken into account by the forum. It will

462. *Pålsson,* Marriage, s. 193. The EAST GERMAN provision on the matter is now to be found in RAG § 3.

463. For NORWEGIAN law see *Gaarder* 81, 133 (supporting the doctrine for cases where the *lex domicilii* refers to the *lex loci celebrationis*).

464. R. v. Brentwood Marriage Registrar, [1968] 2 Q.B. 956, Rev. crit. d.i.p. 1969, 491, note Wengler, See *P.B. Carter* (1968) 242-244; *Cheshire and North* 75-76; *Dicey and Morris* 59-60; *Hartley,* Policy Basis 581-582. For NEW ZEALAND law see *Webb and Davis* 248.

465. The decision in this case is also an authority on the incidental question; see *infra* at n. 746-748.

466. *Pålsson,* Marriage, s. 195. For BRAZILIAN practice in respect of marriage see *Garland* 28, 97-98, 106.

thus be necessary to accept *renvoi*. As to the validity of a marriage which has already come into existence, the same holds true if the policy basis for referring such questions to the personal law is to be found in the desire to attain uniformity of decision with the foreign country concerned.[467]

The position is different if the personal law is considered applicable solely because it is the law of the country with which, in the eyes of the forum, the party is most closely connected. If this is the basis of the rule, there seems to be no valid reason why the forum's evaluation should yield to that expressed in the conflicts rules of the *lex causae*.

Even if *renvoi* is accepted as a general principle, however, the attitude towards the doctrine seems, at least to some extent, to be influenced by the policy of *favor matrimonii*. In most cases dealing with capacity to marry which have been decided by Continental courts and in which the result was affected by *renvoi*, the doctrine operated to permit the celebration or to uphold the validity of a marriage which was, respectively, prohibited or invalid according to the municipal rules of the *lex causae*. At least in some of those cases the *favor matrimonii* probably was a motive factor behind the decision.[468] One indication of this is that the validating result was sometimes reached on a rather strained and dubious construction of the conflicts rules of the relevant foreign law.[469]

467. The purpose of avoiding collisions with the home country, and the ensuing necessity of accepting *renvoi*, in regard to the creation and validity of marriage is particularly emphasised in SWISS law. See, e.g., BG 11 Nov. 1954, BGE 80 I 427, 434; *Beck*, before art. 59 no. 102, art. 7 c no. 34; *Jagmetti* 83, 137; *Vaucher* 532; *Vischer*, IPR 529, 585.

468. This factor seems especially to carry weight in certain cases of transmission, namely, where the foreign laws involved agree to regard the marriage as valid, once their conflicts rules are taken into consideration. An example is, perhaps, the FRENCH case decided by Trib. Seine 11 July 1918, Clunet 1919, 286, cf. *supra* n. 461. Among WEST GERMAN writers see *Raape and Sturm* 166, 175, whose discussion of *renvoi* is much coloured by an imagined example of such type: Two Swiss nationals, related as uncle and niece, have married in Moscow. By SWISS domestic law this union is bad, by RUSSIAN domestic law it is good. Both countries, however, are in accord to treat it as valid, because the conflicts rules of SWISS law refer to RUSSIAN law as the *lex loci celebrationis* (*supra* at n. 460 and *infra* at n. 564), which affirms its own competence (*supra* at n. 257). It is concluded – very appropriately, it is submitted, as far as the example goes – that a WEST GERMAN court cannot reasonably hold otherwise and that it therefore must follow the reference on by SWISS law, designated in the first instance by the GERMAN conflicts rule.

469. For an example from WEST GERMANY see OLG Celle 18 Sept. 1968, IPRspr. 1968/69 no. 67. In that case a woman of Brazilian nationality

Suggestions have been put forward in certain countries that the acceptance of *renvoi* should be limited to situations of the type just mentioned and that the doctrine should be excluded as a means of prohibiting or defeating a marriage which complies with the municipal *lex causae.*[470]

A rule to this effect exists in *Portuguese* law: while generally favourable to *renvoi,* that law provides for an exception where the application of the doctrine would result in rendering unlawful an otherwise lawful status.[471] This means that a marriage will be sustained if it is good either according to the domestic rules of the *lex patriae,* designated by the Portuguese conflict of laws, or according to such other system of law as would be applied in the home country. It may be noted here that a partly similar effect can be achieved without *renvoi* if the forum's own conflicts rule permits an alternative test to be used in determining capacity to marry. On this point, too, Portuguese law affords an illustration, for while the *lex patriae* is generally the law to be applied in matters of personal status, it is added that a legal act (such as a marriage) must be recognised in Portugal if it has been celebrated in the country of the habitual residence of the parties in accordance with the law of that country, provided that the law so designated accepts its own competence.[472]

---

had remarried in Denmark after her prior marriage had been dissolved by a West German court. Although BRAZILIAN law, which governed her capacity to marry under GERMAN conflict of laws, did not recognise divorces of Brazilian nationals, the remarriage was sustained on grounds that the conflicts rules of BRAZILIAN law referred back to GERMAN law, as the *lex domicilii* of the parties to the fresh marriage, by which the divorce was valid. This interpretation of BRAZILIAN law appears to be erroneous on the particular point in issue in the case. See *Gamillscheg,* Kommentar, art. 13 no. 49; *Rabel* 535-536; *Samtleben.*

470. See for ENGLISH law *Hartley,* Policy Basis 573-574.

471. CC art. 19 par. 1 in conjunction with art. 18; see *Ferrer-Correia* 179-180 and *Pålsson,* Marriage, s. 194.

472. CC art. 31. See *Ferrer-Correia* 189-191 (favouring an extensive interpretation of this provision); *Nitsche* 271. For another example of an optional rule which, in certain circumstances, gives an intending spouse the right to submit to the law of his habitual residence instead of the normally governing *lex patriae,* see the SWEDISH Act of 8 July 1904 (as amended in 1973) ch. 1 § 2 par. 1-2, described *supra* at n. 295 (the choice left to the party by this provision is independent of *renvoi;* cf. for older law, which admitted an option where the *lex patriae* referred to some other law, *Eek* 124, 237; *Undén,* Internationell äktenskapsrätt 22-23). See also for SWISS law, where NAG art. 7 f par. 1 has been interpreted as an optional rule, *Beck,* ESchlKonv. art. 1 no. 20; *Schnitzer* 347.

In most countries endorsing the principle of *renvoi*, however, the doctrine is held to extend to cases in which it operates to prevent or to invalidate an otherwise lawful marriage.[473] One of the rare instances of *renvoi* being used to this end is the aforementioned *English* case involving the remarriage of a divorced Italian national (*supra* at n. 464). Since the divorce in that case had been granted by a Swiss court, it is clear that the remarriage would have been permitted had the English court been content to look to Swiss municipal law. The overriding policy consideration behind the decision to the contrary seems here to have been the desire to achieve harmony of decision with Switzerland, the country where both parties were and intended to remain domiciled.[474]

Such prohibiting or invalidating *renvoi* can only come into question if the reference by the relevant foreign conflicts rule back or on to the "negative" law is *compulsory*. This was the situation in the above English case, because a marriage contrary to the Italian law designated by the Swiss conflicts rule would not be recognised as valid in Switzerland (as the law then stood).[475] The position is different if the reference back or on to the other law is optional, in the sense that the courts of the foreign country are prepared to apply that law when, and only when, it is more favourable to the validity of the marriage than their own domestic law.[476] Such a reference is inoperative in all cases where the union is good by the municipal *lex causae*, and it is therefore immaterial that it does not comply with the other law. Since the *lex causae* affirms its own competence in this situation, there appears to be no conceivable basis even for raising the question of *renvoi* in the forum.

In view of this, a *French* decision which assumed and accepted a *renvoi* in such circumstances is difficult to justify.[477] In that case opposition to a proposed marriage in France was lodged by the mother of one of the parties, an American national, on grounds that the party was a minor who had not obtained parental consent to the marriage. The opposition was upheld by the court on the strength of French law, which was considered applicable by way

473. See, for instance, [WEST] GERMANY: *Gamillscheg*, Kommentar, art. 13 no. 68; *Massfeller*, Ehehindernis des Ehebruchs (*supra* n. 384) 308-309; SWITZERLAND: *supra* n. 467.

474. Cf. *Hartley*, Policy Basis 582.

475. The SWISS rule on the present point has since been changed; see *infra* at n. 799-802.

476. See *Beck*, art. 7 c no. 36; *Gamillscheg*, Kommentar, art. 13 no. 68.

477. Trib. Seine 10 Jan. 1962, G.P. 1962.1.284.

of *renvoi* from "American" law either because it was the party's *lex domicilii* or in its capacity as the *lex loci celebrationis*. It was so held notwithstanding the fact that by the relevant American (California) law, as found by the court, a marriage solemnised in France without parental consent would be recognised as valid. In other words, the foreign conflicts rule did not insist on compliance with French law. While purporting to give effect to that rule, the court in fact reached a result contrary to the hypothetical decision in the foreign country itself.

On this as well as on other points it seems too clear for argument, whatever the policy basis for applying *renvoi*, that the conflicts rules of the *lex causae* must be treated "faithfully", as closely as possible in accordance with the way in which they are administered in the foreign country itself. This is of importance, *inter alia*, as concerns the handling of the concept of domicile (where that is the relevant connecting factor under the foreign conflicts rule) and the doctrines of classification, public policy and evasion as affecting the application of those rules.[478] Logically, the attitude towards *renvoi* prevailing in the foreign country should also be taken into account. This consequence, however, seems only to be fully accepted by the English variant of the doctrine known as the foreign court theory.[479]

e. *Evasion of Laws*

60. *True Evasions: General.* The notion of evasion of laws, so far as it is of interest here, implies that a person's domicile (habitual residence, etc.) or nationality, whichever is decisive for the choice of law to govern his capacity to marry, has been "fraudulently" changed, usually before the time of celebration, with the object of escaping a prohibition of the otherwise applicable law and of

478. See, e.g., *Beck*, before art. 59 no. 104; *Gamillscheg*, Kommentar, art. 13 no. 61-63, 230; *Malaurie*, Domicile (Rép. dr. int. I) no. 74; *Maury* 170-171. For a GERMAN case in which a reference back to the *lex fori* was wrongly found and accepted through an oversight of the proper classification according to the relevant foreign law, see KG 22 March 1906, KGJ 32 (1906) A 28, 33 (marriage in England of Australian national domiciled in Germany; requirement of consent by guardian held to be governed by GERMAN law by virtue of *renvoi* from AUSTRALIAN law, although that law classified such questions as matters of form referable to the *lex loci celebrationis*). But see for a case where this point was taken into account, LG Hamburg 16 Oct. 1958, IPRspr. 1958/59 no. 117.

479. Cf. *Pålsson*, Marriage, s. 194. See also *Ferrer-Correia* 176-177.

taking advantage of another law which permits the marriage.[480] The doctrine of evasion affords a means of combating such manoeuvres, enabling the forum to disregard a point of contact so created and to prevent or to invalidate the marriage on the strength of the "old" law which was sought to be eluded. Although this is a modification of the usual method of selecting the relevant law, the principle of controlling capacity to marry by the personal law remains intact; the doctrine is only designed to protect the system from improper use.

The prevailing view in most countries applying the personal law to test capacity to marry is, however, that a doctrine of evasion is neither necessary nor desirable to complement the rule, and the role played by the doctrine in practice has on the whole been insignificant.[481] The need for such a doctrine in these countries, if it exists at all, seems indeed to be small. The main reason is that a change of domicile or nationality (as the case may be), which is the necessary condition for a true evasion of the personal law, is a rather complicated affair which normally affords considerable difficulties and entails far-reaching consequences in other respects. Such a step, particularly a change of nationality, will seldom be taken solely in order to circumvent a prohibition against marriage, especially since the obstacle can in practice often be overcome by other and less drastic means. Among these, the possibility of a "false evasion" (*infra* s. 63), which in many cases offers good chances of success, may be held out.

The position is different in countries committed to the rule of the *lex loci celebrationis* as the law governing the entire validity of marriage. That rule admits of easy evasion, inasmuch as a person can get rid of a marriage impediment merely by having the ceremony performed in a country whose law ignores the impediment in question. Very naturally, therefore, it has often been felt necessary to call in aid the doctrine of evasion (or to modify the rule in some other way) as a means of securing a certain amount of control of the substantive conditions of marriage by the law of the country to which, in the eyes of the forum, the parties "belong".[482]

480. This is at least the typical situation raising a problem of evasion in respect of capacity to marry. It is not our intention here to scrutinise the differences, existing on various points of detail, as to the definition of the concept of evasion in the conflict of laws. These questions are discussed at great length by writers on the subject; see, for example, *Römer* 59-95.

481. See *infra* s. 61-62.

482. This course has been adopted in SOUTH AFRICA (*supra* s. 37), SWITZERLAND (*infra* s. 69) and, in part, in the USA (*supra* s. 8, 15). Other

In a system based on the rule of the personal law (whether determined by domicile, nationality or otherwise), on the other hand, this function is fulfilled by the rule itself. While that rule goes further than warranted by the desire to prevent evasions alone, it is in itself sufficient, at least in principle, to make ineffectual the simple kind of evasion which consists in the mere transfer of the place of celebration (reducing such a step to a typical false evasion, *infra* s. 63). To that extent in any case, the additional safeguard of a special doctrine of evasion becomes superfluous.

61. *English Law.* Perhaps the best illustration of the tendency referred to above is afforded by the development of English law, especially as compared with that of American law. While the doctrine of evasion has gained some recognition as a method of asserting domiciliary control of marriage in American statute and case law (*supra* s. 8, 15), it has never been accepted in England.[483] The same is generally true of other countries within the British Commonwealth following the English rule that capacity to marry depends on the *lex domicilii.*[484]

Quite a few cases decided by English and other Commonwealth courts deal with marriages contracted or sought to be contracted in circumstances which suggest a deliberate evasion of the requisites either of the *lex fori* or of some foreign law. These cases may be divided into two groups:

The earliest cases were concerned with lack of parental consent and similar matters. Here the problem was disposed of by relegating such questions to the category of formalities, referable to the *lex loci celebrationis* (see *Pålsson,* Marriage, s. 409). The courts were clearly aware that this approach facilitated evasions, but they did not succumb to the temptation, if they felt one, of establishing any doctrine of evasion as a corrective. Rather, the classification

---

and more far-reaching means are used to the same end in many LATIN AMERICAN countries and in the SOVIET UNION (*supra* s. 33-34).

483. See *Audit* 308-323; *Baty* 447-448; *Graveson,* Evasion 26-31; *Wolff,* PIL 143-144; cf. *Pålsson,* Marriage, s. 289. In recent years, however, the doctrine seems to have found its way into certain other branches of ENGLISH conflict of laws; see *Graveson,* Conflict 170-174, 270-271. For an unorthodox view assigning strong weight to the factor of evasion see *Swan* 33-34, 37-39.

484. See, for example, for the common law provinces of CANADA, *Castel,* Conflict 99 (but the position is different in QUEBEC, see *idem,* Fraude).

as form seems to imply that these matters were not considered sufficiently important to warrant domiciliary control.[485]

The second group of cases involves endeavours to avoid domiciliary prohibitions against marriage within certain degrees of consanguinity or affinity or against remarriage after divorce.[486] Here too, the English courts, in contrast with several American courts, have declined recourse to any doctrine of evasion as a means of frustrating such attempts. Sometimes, it is true, they have used language indicating, in terms not unlike those found in American judgments adopting the doctrine, that the desire to forestall evasions was an important consideration behind the decision.[487] This factor, however, was not relied upon as an independent ground of decision, but only as a policy ground supporting the rule of the *lex domicilii,* which was established or confirmed in these cases. On the one hand, if the parties have married or if they seek to marry away from the country of their domicile to flout its law, the attempt will fail simply because the union does not comply with the governing law.[488] It is thus unnecessary to consider any doctrine of evasion. On the other hand, if there has been a true change of domicile (as defined by English law) before the marriage, this change will be recognised as effective to bring the union under the protection of the "new" law.[489] It is immaterial whether the change was brought about for the sole purpose of escaping a prohibition imposed by the "old" law. Indirectly, it is true, the existence of such a motive may be rele-

485. Cf. *Graveson,* Evasion 30. It should be noted, however, that the early cases on parental consent were decided at a time long before the rule of governing capacity to marry by the *lex domicilii* was recognised in ENGLISH law. The development of this rule, and of the distinction between the formal and the substantive validity of marriage, only began by the middle of the 19th century; see *infra* at n. 527-528.

486. See for ENGLISH cases dealing with foreign marriages: Brook v. Brook (1861), 9 H.L.C. 193, [1861-73] All E.R. Rep. 493; In re De Wilton, [1900] 2 Ch. 481; R. v. Dibdin, [1910] P. 57 and 101 (C.A.), aff'd *sub nom.* Thompson v. Dibdin, [1912] A.C. 533 (H.L.); In re Paine, [1940] Ch. 46. For cases concerned with (attempted) marriages in England see: Padolecchia v. Padolecchia, [1968] P. 314; R. v. Brentwood Marriage Registrar, [1968] 2 Q.B. 956.

487. See particularly Brook v. Brook (1861), 9 H.L.C. 193, 212, [1861-73] All E.R. Rep. 493, 497; R. v. Brentwood Marriage Registrar, [1968] 2 Q.B. 956, 967, 970.

488. See the cases cited *supra* n. 486.

489. For cases involving locally celebrated marriages see ENGLAND: Scott v. Att.-Gen. (1886), 11 P.D. 128; AUSTRALIA: Pezet v. Pezet (1946), 47 S.R. (N.S.W.) 45 (F.C.).

vant as tending to support the conclusion, fatal to the acquisition of a domicile of choice in a country, that the party only intended to stay there temporarily until he could accomplish his purpose. Like any other motive, however, that of enjoying a more favourable legal system does not, as such, negate the possibility of a genuine *animus manendi.*[490] In conclusion, therefore, the fact of evasion neither precludes a change of domicile, nor does it affect the normal operation of choice of law rules employing domicile as the relevant connecting factor.

62. *Continental and Scandinavian Law.* Evasion of laws (*fraude à la loi, Gesetzesumgehung, frode alla legge*) is a cherished subject of contention in Continental literature on the conflict of laws.[491] Together with divorce, marriage is usually cited as one of the main instances in relation to which this problem is likely to present itself. Nevertheless, cases involving a true evasion of the law governing capacity to marry – including a change of nationality (if, as normally, the *lex patriae* is the relevant law) effected solely to shake off an impediment existing under the "old" law – are seldom presented in practice. Besides the reasons already mentioned (*supra* s. 60), the modern tendency to restrict the catalogue of prohibitions against marriage is a factor accounting for the paucity of such cases.[492]

Almost all cases which have raised the problem involve a remarriage after divorce in circumstances where the prohibition of the evaded law was primarily directed against the divorce. In the past, a famous example of such evasions, committed on a larger scale, were the unions known as *Klausenburg marriages,* which were concluded in Hungary to avoid Austrian law.

> These cases had their background in the then provision of Austrian law (ABGB §111) which forbade divorce when one of the spouses was a Catholic. To overcome this prohibition the parties (or one of them), after obtaining a separation from bed and board in Austria, acquired Hungarian citizenship

490. See, e.g., Drexel v. Drexel, [1916] 1 Ch. 251; *Dicey and Morris* 107; *Graveson,* Conflict 172; *idem,* Evasion 29-30. Cf. *Cheshire and North* 174.

491. Among recent monographs see those by *Audit* and by *Römer,* both with extensive bibliographies. See also *Gamillscheg,* Kommentar, before art. 13 no. 210-218 (with bibliography), and for the law of QUEBEC, *Castel,* Fraude.

492. Cf. *Nussbaum,* Principles of Private International Law (New York, London, Toronto 1943) 128.

> and then took advantage of Hungarian law to secure a divorce and to marry again in Hungary. Afterwards the parties to the new marriage returned to live in Austria, where the validity of such unions arose for decision in numerous cases.

After some vacillation, these marriages were upheld by the Austrian courts, regardless of the fact that Austrian law had been flouted.[493] This solution accords with the general trend of opinion among writers in most other Continental countries and in Scandinavia. The prevailing view is that a proper application of the normal conflicts rules and devices, including that of public policy, is sufficient to deal with the rare cases in which a new nationality has been acquired for the sole purpose of defeating a marriage impediment under the "old" law.[494] This fact alone is considered insufficient to invalidate the marriage if it complies with the new *lex patriae.* There are some dissenting opinions, however, and in the almost total absence of decisions on the matter in most countries the possibility of a resort to the doctrine of evasion can scarcely be excluded in all cirumstances.[495]

In theory at least, a different position prevails in *French* law, which traditionally gives a broad scope for the doctrine of *fraude à la loi.* An early case, which is still regarded as a leading authority

493. See *Gamillscheg,* Kommentar, art. 13 no. 75, 257-258; *Römer* 108-110, 114; *G. Walker* 630-636. For an example of a decision see RG (in its then capacity as the Supreme Court of AUSTRIA) 24 Jan. 1941, RGZ 165, 398, 403-404.

494. See in this vein, e.g., AUSTRIA: *Klang and Gschnitzer* 244-245; *Schwind,* IPR 92-95; [WEST] GERMANY: *Gamillscheg,* Kommentar, art. 13 no. 72-74; *Kegel,* Kommentar, art. 13 no. 112; *Lauterbach* 25 n. 15; *Lewald* 79; *Melchior* 378-381; *Wolff,* IPR 48; cf. the decision of OLG München 22 Nov. 1909, NiemeyersZ 20 (1910) 529; ITALY: *Vitta* I 436-448; SCANDINAVIAN countries: *Eek* 212-217; *Hambro* 322-324, 326; *Philip,* Conventions 282; SWITZERLAND: *Beck,* art. 7 c no. 32, art. 7 f no. 69, 96-98; *Niederer* 331-336; *Spivak* 40.

495. For BELGIUM and FRANCE see *infra* n. 496-500. Opinions in WEST GERMANY are divided. While generally emphasising the limited importance of the problem, some writers support the doctrine – see *Römer* 113; or seem prepared to have recourse to it in special circumstances – see *Dölle,* IPR 71-74; *Gamillscheg,* Kommentar, before art. 13 no. 210-214, 216-218, art. 13 no. 91; *Kegel,* IPR 214-220; *Neuhaus,* Grundbegriffe 193-200; *Raape and Sturm* 330-331 (in addition, it is agreed that the doctrine must be taken into account, where it forms part of the governing foreign law, for the purpose of applying *renvoi;* see *Gamillscheg,* Kommentar, art. 13 no. 62; *Raape and Sturm* 331-332; cf. *supra* at n. 478). For the approach prevailing in certain countries of EASTERN EUROPE see *Katičić* 423-424; *Réczei* 119-123; *Szászy* 179-181.

on the problem and which is invariably cited in the relevant Continental literature, provides an illustration concerning divorce and remarriage.[496] That case involved the French Princess de Bauffremont who wanted a divorce from her first husband. By French law, as it stood at the time, divorce was unknown as an institution. She therefore acquired the nationality of Saxe-Altembourg and procured a divorce there in accordance with the local law. She then remarried in Prussia the Rumanian Prince Bibesco. When her divorce and second marriage came under the scrutiny of the French courts, however, both were rejected for *fraude à la loi* and held to be of no effect in France.[497] The view thus adopted by the French courts is apparently shared in some other countries, such as *Belgium,* following the tradition of French law.[498]

Even in countries accepting the doctrine, however, its impact has been limited. Cases of the type illustrated by the matrimonial affairs of Princess de Bauffremont have been very unusual, indeed to the extent of being referred to as an *hypothèse d'école.*[499] It should also be noted that the doctrine has only been applied to counter evasions of the *lex fori,* and not where a foreign law had been evaded.[500]

A related, but different, problem is that of the validity of a *sham marriage,* contracted for purposes such as the acquisition of the husband's nationality by the wife, usually with the ultimate

496. Cass. civ. 18 March 1878, S.1878.1.193, note Labbé, Clunet 1878, 505.

497. For other decisions taking the same view see: Cour Paris 30 June 1877, Clunet 1878, 268; Trib. Seine 4 Feb. 1882, Clunet 1882, 544; Cour Paris 14 March 1889, Clunet 1889, 463; Cass. civ. 25 March 1889, Clunet 1889, 642. For writings on the doctrine generally see, e.g., *Batiffol and Lagarde* I 439-445; *Francescakis,* Fraude à la loi (Rép. dr. int. II); *Maury* 43-46, 153-172; *Niboyet* III 630-669. Specifically with reference to marriage see also: *Audit* 138-142, 149-156, 288-289; *Delaume* 103; *Niboyet* V 333-334; *Vincent and Ponsard* no. 65, 106.

498. BELGIUM: Cour Bruxelles 5 Aug. 1880, Clunet 1880, 508 (a continuation of the case of Princess de Bauffremont); *Graulich* 120-122; *Rigaux,* DIP 266-269. See also for QUEBEC: CC art. 135; Cholette v. Jones (1938), 45 R.L.n.s. 111 (C.S.); *Castel,* Fraude 18-20.

499. *Audit* 289.

500. See for FRENCH law *Audit* 297-306; *Maury* 168-170; cf. the decision of Trib. Seine 12 Nov. 1965, Rev. crit. d.i.p. 1966, 624, note Decroux. This distinction has been criticised by some writers, who insist that the doctrine should be extended to cover evasions of foreign law as well; see, for example, *Louis-Lucas,* La fraude à la loi étrangère: Rev. crit. d.i.p. 1962, 1-17. For a similar view in WEST GERMAN law see *Römer* 80-85. Cf. for the law of QUEBEC, *Castel,* Fraude 7-8, 25.

objective of surmounting obstacles posed by emigration or immigration laws. While the questions treated above concern evasion as a means and marriage as an end, a sham marriage, conversely, typically involves the use of marriage as a means of evading other laws. These problems will be adverted to in the context of consent in marriage (*infra* s. 99).

63. *False Evasions.* In practice, a much more frequent situation than those considered so far is where the parties have gone abroad to escape an impediment existing under their personal law but have done so *without changing their domicile or nationality*, respectively. This possibility is very often open to the parties, if they choose for the celebration of their marriage a country where no reference is made to the personal law in ascertaining their capacity to marry, whether because such questions are in that country held to be a matter for the *lex loci celebrationis* alone or because a prohibition which the personal law regards as affecting capacity is there characterised as pertaining to form, or for any other reason.

A young French or German couple, who cannot marry in their home country for lack of parental consent, may for example go to Scotland and get married there in conformity with the local law, which is solely applicable in this matter according to the Scottish conflicts rule (*Gretna Green marriages* and the like).[501] A more recent instance of this type of evasion, which acquired its reputation in the 1960s, is supplied by the *Tondern marriages* celebrated in Denmark, usually in avoidance of the impediment of a prior marriage according to the *lex patriae* of one of the parties.[502] These cases had their background, in the main, in the then prevailing West German practice by which a divorce, even if granted by a West German court, did not entitle the ex-spouses to marry again if, in the eyes of the *lex patriae* of one of the parties to the new marriage, the divorce was not effective to dissolve the prior union (*infra* s. 85). As a result of this practice, Italian and Spanish nationals, for example, could not remarry in West Germany where they lived and where they had been divorced, because their divorces were not recognised in their respective home countries. In the case of Spanish nationals this impediment stood in their way even though they had not themselves been married before, if the intended partner was a divorcee (of any nationality).[503] In

501. Cf. *Pålsson,* Marriage, s. 409, especially at n. 543. For Continental cases of this complexion see *infra* n. 507.

502. See *Böhmer; Luther; Svenné Schmidt* 218-220.

503. Cf. *supra* at n. 355-356.

numerous instances of this type the obstacle was overcome by a trip to Denmark, where the parties could get married without regard either to their *lex domicilii* or to their *lex patriae.*[504] The use of this circuitous road to marriage, however, has since become unnecessary in most, if not all, cases because of changes, *inter alia,* in the West German practice on the present point (*infra* s. 88).

From the point of view of countries applying the personal law to test capacity to marry, cases of the kind mentioned here do not involve true evasion because the parties have not succeeded in avoiding the rules of that law. They have acted as if the *lex loci celebrationis* was the governing law, whereas in truth, once they return to their home country and the validity of the marriage is put to the test there, the apparently evaded rules of the personal law still hold their sway. In this sense the evasion is a false one (*unechte Gesetzesumgehung*).[505] If the union is void by the relevant personal law, it will be so held notwithstanding that it was celebrated in a foreign country in accordance with the law of that country.[506] Similarly, if it is voidable, it will be liable to annulment on the same conditions as if it had been celebrated locally.[507] Sometimes a voidable marriage, contracted abroad, will even be treated as invalid independently of any proceedings for annulment. In *Switzerland,* for instance, the substantive as well as the formal validity of a foreign marriage is examined as a condition for having it entered in the local registers of civil status, since such registration amounts to provisional recognition of the marriage. Registration was therefore refused in a case where a

504. Cf. *supra* s. 36, especially at n. 273 and 276.

505. See *Gamillscheg,* Kommentar, before art. 13 no. 215, art. 13 no. 78-86; *Kegel,* IPR 224-225; *Raape,* IPR 129-130, 249 n. 20 a); *Römer* 79, 100-103, 112, 119-121.

506. See, for example, the ENGLISH cases cited *supra* n. 486.

507. See, e.g., BELGIUM: Cour Bruxelles 25 Nov. 1959, Rev. crit. d.i.p. 1962, 76, note Rigaux; Cass. 8 March 1963, Pas. 1963.I.754; Rb. Brugge 3 Nov. 1965, RW 1966/67, 1339; *Verwilghen,* Un cas de mariage confessionnel contracté par des Belges à l'étranger: J.T. 1970, 57, 59; FRANCE: Trib. Seine 17 Nov. 1926, Clunet 1928, 404; *Audit* 145, 289; *Niboyet* III 644-645, V 332-333; [WEST] GERMANY: RG 20 Oct. 1898, RGZ 42, 336; RG 14 Jan. 1935, JW 1935, 1403; AG Hamburg 28 July 1964, FamRZ 1964, 532; LG Berlin 26 June 1972, IPRspr. 1972 no. 42; *Gamillscheg,* Kommentar, art. 13 no. 79; NETHERLANDS: Rb. Breda 29 Sept. 1964, N.J. 1965 no. 442; Rb. Amsterdam 18 Jan. 1968, N.J. 1968 no. 338; Hof 's-Gravenhage 8 Jan. 1970, N.J. 1970 no. 463; SPAIN: T.S. 1 March 1919, Clunet 1922, 187. In most of the cases cited here the attempt at evasion, which was foiled by the institution of proceedings for annulment, concerned requirements of parental consent imposed by the party's *lex patriae.*

foreign marriage was voidable for bigamy according to the relevant *lex patriae*, the union being held invalid although no decree of annulment had been given.[508]

These results are reached by applying the ordinary conflicts rules of the forum, which refer to the personal law of the parties. To that extent there is obviously no need to resort to any doctrine of evasion.

Nevertheless, false evasions quite often enable the parties to attain their end. In the first place, where the prohibition of the personal law which has been disregarded is merely directory, the marriage cannot be impeached once it has come into existence. Continental practice affords many examples of marriages, celebrated abroad to avoid such prohibitions of the personal law, which were upheld when questioned in the parties' home country.[509]

Secondly, where the defect existing under the personal law makes the marriage voidable only (as opposed to void), the union will normally be recognised as valid unless and until it is annulled by a court in proceedings brought for this purpose by a person entitled to do so within the time limit that may be prescribed for such proceedings.[510] In numerous cases of this type, too, the evasion was successful because the requisite action against the marriage was never taken.[511] The course adopted in *West Germany* as to the Tondern marriages mentioned above provides a typical example. Contrary to the practice in Switzerland in similar cases (*supra* at n. 508), these marriages were recognised so as to permit registration in the West German records of civil status, once it

508. BG 11 Nov. 1954, BGE 80 I 427 (the *Caliaro* case, see *infra* at n. 741). For criticism of the decision on this point see *Cermak*, case note: Öst. H. int. R. 1956, 14; *von Overbeck*, Remariage 54-55; but to that extent the Federal Tribunal has abided by its earlier position, see BG 3 June 1971, BGE 97 I 389, 402.

509. See *Rabel* 311 and, e.g., BELGIUM: Cour Bruxelles 16 Dec. 1959, J.T. 1960, 296, Clunet 1962, 1042; Civ. Bruxelles 16 Dec. 1967, J.T. 1970, 68, Clunet 1971, 864, noted by *Verwilghen* (*supra* n. 507) 57-65; WEST GERMANY: *Römer* 113; NETHERLANDS: Hoge Raad 23 May 1919, N.J. 1919, 689; *Kollewijn* 46.

510. The position taken by the SWISS Federal Tribunal (*supra* at n. 508) is an exception.

511. See, e.g., [WEST] GERMANY: RG 21 Dec. 1916, LZ 1917, 924; LG Hamburg 2 Oct. 1963, FamRZ 1964, 565; LG Mannheim 29 Jan. 1965, IPRspr. 1964/65 no. 87; AG Frankfurt 3 June 1965, IPRspr. 1964/65 no. 89 A; OLG Hamm 3 April 1968, IPRspr. 1968/69 no. 64; expert opinion in IPG 1972 no. 12 (Cologne); *Gamillscheg*, Kommentar, art. 13 no. 229; *Luther* 698-699; SWEDEN: Supreme Court of Administrative Justice 1 June 1954, Regeringsrättens Årsbok 1954 no. 33; *Eek* 239 n. 14.

had been ascertained that they were valid as to form by the *lex loci celebrationis,* Danish law.[512] Decisions granting requests for such registration have usually been based on the ground that the marriage was only voidable (*nichtig*), not void, by the *lex patriae* governing its substantive validity, so that it had to be treated as valid until it was properly annulled.[513] Nor have these marriages usually been attacked afterwards in proceedings for annulment. Moreover, in those few cases in which such proceedings have been brought in West Germany, the courts found various means permitting them to reject the attack and to uphold the marriage.[514] For all practical purposes, therefore, it seems that the device of the Tondern marriage has been a successful method of avoiding the prohibition of the *lex patriae* against remarriage and the West German conflicts rule requiring that prohibition to be taken into account. Clearly this rule, even before its scope was restricted (*infra* s. 88), was not one which the West German courts were prepared to "fight for".

There are thus many cases in which a prohibition of the govern-

512. See for cases in which the *lex patriae,* which refused to recognise the West German divorce, was SPANISH law: OLG Schleswig 16 Dec. 1966, IPRspr. 1966/67 no. 290; OLG Frankfurt 26 May 1967, IPRspr. 1966/67 no. 71; AG Hamburg 23 Feb. 1969, IPRspr. 1968/69 no. 84; LG Hamburg 23 Oct. 1969, IPRspr. 1968/69 no. 149; ITALIAN law: AG Hamburg 30 Jan. 1968, IPRspr. 1968/69 no. 129; LG Bochum 8 Jan. 1969, IPRspr. 1968/69 no. 140; expert opinion in IPG 1965/66 no. 12 (Munich); BRAZILIAN law: AG Hamburg 17 Feb. 1967, IPRspr. 1966/67 no. 154; TURKISH law: AG Hamburg 25 March 1968, IPRspr. 1968/69 no. 133. And see *Böhmer* 86-90; *Luther* 689-692; *Wuppermann* 103-104.

513. In some cases doubts have been raised as to the proper construction of the relevant foreign law on this point. While it is quite clear that, for instance, ITALIAN law treats a bigamous marriage as voidable only, the position of SPANISH law is somewhat more ambiguous. Even where the marriage was assumed to be void according to the foreign law concerned, however, the view has usually been taken that a decree of nullity must be obtained before the invalidity of the union can be asserted in WEST GERMANY. On these questions see the decisions cited *supra* n. 512, the references *infra* n. 737-739 and, e.g., expert opinion in IPG 1969 no. 27 (Hamburg); *Böhmer* 88-90; *Gamillscheg,* Kommentar, art. 13 no. 272, 482; *Jochem* 736-740; *Luther* 687-689; *Weyers,* Die Eheschliessung nach spanischem Recht (Karlsruhe 1960) 40-41.

514. See: LG Aachen 26 May 1967, IPRspr. 1966/67 no. 72; OLG Celle 18 Sept. 1968, IPRspr. 1968/69 no. 67 (cf. *supra* n. 469); LG Hamburg 26 Feb. 1969, IPRspr. 1968/69 no. 71 A. See further *infra* at n. 737-739. But a nullity decree granted by the courts of the home country will presumably be recognised in West Germany; see *Gamillscheg,* Kommentar, art. 13 no. 321.

ing law can be made illusory by parties who wish to escape from it by marrying in a suitable foreign country. This raises the question of whether it would be desirable to give teeth to such prohibitions by adopting a doctrine of evasion. Should it not be possible, at least in certain circumstances, to strike down a marriage which has been entered into abroad in avoidance of a prohibition of the relevant personal law, even though no such sanction would be available for violation of the prohibition in a purely domestic case? Some arguments may be advanced in favour of this view.[515] Within the territory of the enacting State even a merely directory prohibition will normally be effective, because it is binding on marriage officials, often under sanctions, such as a fine, coming witin the domain of administrative or criminal law. Only very exceptionally, therefore, will it happen that a marriage is celebrated at home in defiance of such prohibitions. The position is wholly different when the union is solemnised in a foreign country where the prohibition is ignored altogether. Here the prohibiting law is "defenceless" against infringements. On policy grounds it may be argued that the absence of any other sanction in these cases ought to be counterbalanced by a nullity sanction, always provided that the prohibition is considered important enough to justify its being upheld abroad. Conceivably, the doctrine of evasion might be used to supply the conceptual framework for establishing such an "extraordinary" safeguard.

A reasoning along these lines has played a part in *French* law which, again, occupies a special position. The typical situation occasioning the problem of false evasion in French practice is where young couples, of French nationality and domicile, have travelled to some foreign country for the marriage ceremony, eluding the requirements of French law as to parental consent and returning afterwards to live in France. The development of French case law concerning the validity of such unions is linked to the statutory conditions of publicity, laid down in article 170 of the French Civil Code, which is required to precede foreign marriages of French nationals. Within the framework of that provision, French courts have relied on the doctrine of *fraude à la loi* to strike down such marriages in several cases where the union was no longer open to challenge in the normal course of things.[516] A similar practice prevails in a few other countries – *Belgium, Luxembourg*

515. See, e.g., *Audit* 290-291; *Gamillscheg,* Kommentar, art. 13 no. 84-86.
516. See *Pålsson,* Marriage, s. 291.

and the Canadian Province of *Quebec* – within the sphere of influence of French law.[517]

This position seems reasonable enough in so far as it enables the forum to protect itself against evasion of requirements which it regards as essential. It may of course be doubted, especially in present-day conditions, whether parental consents, which have been the main source of problems, deserve to be ranked among the causes worth "fighting for". The main objection that may be raised against this practice is, however, the emphasis placed by the courts on the subjective test of intention. This can scarcely be a rational criterion for determining the validity of a marriage.[518] As has been pointed out earlier (*supra* s. 15), a defect which is not in itself considered serious enough to warrant invalidation of a foreign marriage should not be transformed into a fatal flaw solely because the parties knew of the impediment and acted "with a spiteful mind". Nor should a marriage which is regarded as odious be treated as less offensive solely for the reason that the parties were unaware that they violated the law.

Apart from France and the other countries mentioned here, the idea of using the doctrine of evasion as a means of strengthening the authority of the law has not proved to be attractive to the courts. In most countries it seems never to have been doubted that a marriage must be sustained if the evaded rule of the relevant personal law is not sanctioned by nullity, whether because such a sanction is not envisaged at all or because it is no longer available for lapse of time.[519] It is indeed easy to understand that courts are generally unwilling to treat the fact of evasion as a sufficient ground for resorting to such a strong measure as annulment contrary both to the letter of the law and to the usual policy of validation.[520] Some decisions, in cases where the court did not feel much sympathy with the evaded rule, even seem to suggest that the rule itself, rather than the party avoiding it, was to blame. This impression is conveyed, for instance, by certain West German cases in which a Tondern marriage following a German divorce was upheld against a petition for annulment brought upon the

517. See *ibid.*, s. 293-294.

518. For FRENCH writers sharing this view and proposing an objective approach which would exclude the question of evasive intent from consideration, see *Audit* 293-296, 307; *Niboyet* III 644-645, 657, VI/1 40-43.

519. See the references *supra* n. 509 and 511. But cf. for NORWEGIAN law *Holmøy* 17, 19.

520. Cf. *Audit* 135, 291-293.

ground that the union was voidable for bigamy according to the *lex patriae* of one of the parties.[521]

C. Limits of and Exceptions to the Principle

a. *Scope of Substance of Marriage*

64. It has so far been assumed that all questions concerning the conclusion and the validity of marriage fall within the ambit of one of the categories of form, including procedure, or substance (essentials). This is by and large the prevailing approach, particularly in those Continental European and other countries in which the personal law governing the substantive conditions of marriage is determined by the criterion of nationality. The scope of that law therefore tends to become rather wide, embracing all or nearly all questions which do not go to formalities.

Speaking in positive terms, it is generally agreed in countries applying the *lex patriae* that the substance of marriage covers the following matters: requirements as to marriageable age, physical and mental capacity, parental consents and related issues, prohibitions based on consanguinity, affinity or adoption, bigamy and various other impediments resulting from a prior (though no longer subsisting) marriage.[522] The same classification prevails with regard to the consent of the parties to marry, which is clearly outside the notion of capacity in a strict sense.[523]

A divergency of opinion exists on certain other points. Thus, while marriage impediments of a religious nature are generally regarded as substantive law, rules prescribing religious solemnisation of marriage are in a special category. Such requirements, too, are often classified as essentials in their country of origin, as for instance in *Greece* and *Spain,* but they are usually treated as matters of form in other countries (see *Pålsson,* Marriage, s. 328-329, 406).

521. References *supra* n. 514.

522. See, e.g., BELGIUM: *Graulich* 108; FRANCE: *Bischoff* no. 49; *Vincent and Ponsard* no. 41; WEST GERMANY: *Gamillscheg,* Kommentar, art. 13 no. 182-474; *Kegel,* Kommentar, art. 13 no. 3, 13-30; ITALY: *Vitta* II 177-178; SWITZERLAND: *Beck,* art. 7 c no. 6-14; *Schnitzer* 339-345. For the HAGUE CONVENTION of 1902 see *Travers* I 52-55.

523. See *infra* s. 97.

Another point of controversy concerns impediments which are in the nature of public law, for example rules whereby certain classes of public servants or servicemen are forbidden to marry without the consent of the Government, or of a governmental body, or prohibitions against marriage with an alien without such consent. In some countries, for instance in *France*, impediments of this kind are usually distinguished from those within the domain of private law, and made subject to a conflicts regime based on territoriality.[524] In other countries, for example in *(West) Germany*, this distinction is predominantly rejected.[525] Similar differences of view exist with regard to prohibitions having a penal connotation, in particular waiting periods for remarriage imposed on the guilty party to a divorce.[526] These variations in the scope of the concept of substance of marriage, however, do not always reflect true differences in the choice of law. The reason is that the personal law, where referred to in principle, is often excluded from application in the end, especially on grounds of public policy, in matters which in other countries are held to fall outside the scope of that law.

A more restrictive conception of the place to be given to the personal law prevails in *England* and in other countries following English law. This tendency is explicable against the background of the historical development of English law in this area.[527] Until the middle of the 19th century, English courts did not distinguish between form and other aspects of marriage. The principle of the common law was that the validity of a marriage depended in its entirety on the *lex loci celebrationis*. The rule that the essentials of marriage, as opposed to its form, are a matter for the personal (domiciliary) law of the parties has evolved gradually, more or less as an exception engrafted on the traditional rule.[528]

This tradition is still reflected in a basic preference for "territorialism" in the approach to several conflicts questions in

524. See *Bischoff* no. 41-43; *Niboyet* III 376, V 338-339; and *infra* s. 111.

525. See *Gamillscheg*, Kommentar, art. 13 no. 457, 461-462.

526. See *infra* s. 94.

527. See *Anton* 273-274; *Dicey and Morris* 235-236, 258; *Graveson*, Conflict 256-257; *idem*, The Comparative Evolution of Principles of the Conflict of Laws in England and the U.S.A.: Rec. des Cours 99 (1960-I) 21, 56-60; *Kahn-Freund*, Problems 336-337; *Wolff*, PIL 326-327.

528. The development of this distinction started with the decisions in Mette v. Mette (1859), 1 Sw. & Tr. 416, 164 Eng. Rep. 792, and Brook v. Brook (1861), 9 H.L.C. 193, [1861-73] All E.R. Rep. 493.

England and in other countries following English law. The rule of the *lex domicilii* is firmly established only as concerns capacity to marry in a rather narrow sense. The topics usually discussed under this head include consanguinity and affinity, age requirements and bigamy.[529] Some other questions, which are elsewhere held to affect the essential validity of marriage, are classified as pertaining to form, and as such referred to the *lex loci celebrationis*. A well-known instance is the treatment of parental consents and similar matters (*Pålsson,* Marriage, s. 409). There is *Scottish* authority for the view that this classification extends to all "prohibitive impediments", *i.e.* those which do not render the marriage void once it has been celebrated (thus including not only cases where a violative marriage is valid but also cases where it is voidable).[530] On a number of other issues the position of English law, and of other laws following it, is rather confused and uncertain. This is so, *inter alia,* as concerns want of true consent and physical incapacity as grounds of nullity. Whilte these questions are sometimes dealt with by reference to the conflicts rules governing other aspects of essential validity, they are often assigned to one or more separate categories, distinct from capacity to marry and referable to conflicts rules of their own.[531] Similar doubts exist with regard to foreign impediments of a kind unknown to the *lex fori* (for example, those founded on religious affiliation). Sometimes such impediments (or some of them) have been held to come within the category of "prohibitive law" or "illegality", which is said to affect a person's "liberty to marry", as distinct both from form and from capacity to marry, and considered exempt from the rule of domiciliary control.[532]

Again, however, such differences in the scope of the notion of

529. See, for instance, *Cheshire and North* 349-350; *Dicey and Morris* 262-267.

530. Bliersbach v. MacEwen, 1959 S.C. 43; cf. the cases cited *infra* n. 532. See, critically, *Anton* 281-282; *Anton and Francescakis* 277-285 (with reform proposals). Cf. for ENGLISH law *Wolff,* PIL 330-331, 339, suggesting that the *lex loci celebrationis* alone is decisive where the question concerns merely directory rules (of the foreign domiciliary law involved); but this, apparently, does not include prohibitions which render the marriage voidable.

531. See *infra* s. 97, 101-102.

532. See for SCOTTISH cases dealing with foreign prohibitions against the intermarriage of persons of different religion: Lendrum v. Chakravarti, 1929 S.L.T. 96, 103; MacDougall v. Chitnavis, 1937 S.C. 390, 407. Cf. the ENGLISH case of Ogden v. Ogden, [1908] P. 46, 74 (C.A.), which concerned parental consent and where a distinction was drawn between "illegality" and "capacity". For pertinent criticism of this distinction see *Baty* 444 n. 2.

substance of marriage do not necessarily correspond to true differences in the choice of law for particular questions. This is because, in countries using a wide concept, the rule of the personal law is made subject to many exceptions, under the head of public policy or otherwise, in favour of the *lex fori* or the *lex loci celebrationis.* To a certain extent this tends to lead to results similar to those reached by the use of a narrow concept of substance of marriage. This will be shown in the discussion of specific issues (*infra* s. 75-111).

b. *Exceptions to and Qualifications of the Usual Rules*

65. *Introductory.* The principle of the personal law, as set forth and specified in the preceding sections, is modified by a variety of rules, doctrines and practices. Almost invariably, these modifications operate to give a place to the *lex fori* or the *lex loci celebrationis,* as the case may be, in the matter.

In certain situations the *lex fori* is simply substituted for the personal law, so that the latter law will be ignored altogether (*ba*). This may be the result of a "lenient" practice in the enforcement of foreign law, especially at the stage of celebration of marriages (*infra* s. 66). A more special case is where the solemnisation of marriages, or jurisdiction in nullity, is vested in a religious authority; for such authorities sometimes only apply their own law, to the exclusion of any secular law (*infra* s. 67).

Another type of modification of the rule of the personal law is to the effect that the marriage is required to comply with a cumulative test: the parties must have capacity to marry, not only according to their personal law but also according to the *lex loci celebrationis,* at least where that law coincides with the *lex fori* (*bb*). The latter law may thus be invoked to prohibit or to invalidate a marriage which would be permitted or valid under the personal law (*infra* s. 68).

More frequently, a permissive or validating role is assigned to some other law, again usually the *lex fori* or the *lex loci celebrationis* (*bc*). Such other law will then be applied to allow or to uphold a marriage which does not meet the more stringent demands of the personal law. Various kinds of rules to this effect are to be found in many legal systems (*infra* s. 69-71).

Most of the rules and devices to be described in what follows are of a general character in the sense that they apply, in principle, equally to all substantive conditions of marriage. In a special category, however, is the doctrine of public policy, the application of which depends in a high degree on the particular issue involved in each case. This doctrine, which has both a validating and an invalidating function, will be examined at the end of this part of the Chapter (*bd, infra* s. 72-74).

ba. *Lex Fori Substituted for Foreign Law*

66. *Position of Foreign Law at Stage of Celebration.* In the present as well as in other branches of the conflict of laws, a certain tension exists between theory and practice, which has to do with the well-known difficulties in ascertaining and applying foreign law. To a large extent the effectiveness of the rule of the personal law depends upon the technique and the mechanisms used for this purpose. It is not possible here to go more closely into these general questions.[533] It is necessary, however, to advert to the specific problem of the application of foreign law, where it governs capacity to marry *qua* the personal law of the parties or one of them, at the stage of the formation of the union.

The usual view in *Continental European* and *Scandinavian* countries is that the relevant foreign law must be taken into account by civil registrars and similar officials of their own motion and that they must not proceed with the solemnisation of a marriage until they have been satisfied that no impediment to the proposed union exists under that law.[534] This applies both to mandatory and to directory conditions imposed by the governing law. The parties are normally required to prove the absence of impediments according to the foreign law concerned, or at least the tenor of the appropriate provisions of that law, by the production of a document of one type or another, often a certificate of capacity to marry (see *infra* s. 115-116). Although this system has its defects, it affords at least a reasonable guarantee that marriages will not be celebrated in the teeth of the governing law. In practice, this preventive application of the personal law is far more frequent and important than the application of foreign law by the courts in cases where the validity of a marriage already entered into is questioned *ex post.*

A special position is, however, taken by *French* law. This is so

533. For a comparative exposition of these problems see *Zajtay*, The Application of Foreign Law: Encyclopedia III:14 (Tübingen, Paris, New York 1972), with a comprehensive bibliography.

534. See generally *Wolff*, PIL 331. Cf. *Ehrenzweig and Jayme* 145.

because French marriage registrars, according to their instruction, are not required to take account of foreign law of their own motion but only in so far as the parties choose to invoke it and produce evidence of its contents.[535] If the parties fail to do this, or if such evidence discloses an impediment to the proposed union, the registrar must nevertheless proceed to celebrate the marriage after satisfying himself that the requirements of French domestic law are fulfilled.[536] In this way the *lex fori* may be substituted for the personal law applicable in principle, even without any examination of the foreign law concerned. The registrar must, however, warn the parties of the risk that such a marriage may subsequently be declared null by the courts. In theory at least, this risk exists even in France itself, for the French courts are not bound by the instruction issued for the registrars.

This system is open to objections and has been much criticised by French writers.[537] In practice, it amounts to stripping from the rule of the personal law an essential part of its function, indeed to the extent of reducing that rule to little more than "a courteous affirmation".[538] Even under this system, it is true, recourse to the *lex patriae* may come into question in some situations, chiefly where that law permits a marriage which is prohibited by French law.[539] Apart from such situations, however, it seems more realistic, in the light of the instruction for the registrars, to state that the *lex fori* applies as the general rule for ascertaining capacity to marry at the stage of celebration. Although this solution gives scope for evasion of the personal law (of the type known as false evasion, cf. *supra* s. 63), France has not become renowned as a

535. General Instruction of 21 Sept. 1955, no. 473.

536. *Ibid.* no. 475. See *Audit* 300-301; *Bischoff* no. 85-86.

537. See, e.g., *Batiffol and Lagarde* II 36-37; *Bischoff* no. 87-88; *C. David,* La loi étrangère devant le juge du fond (Paris 1965) 46-47; *G. Holleaux,* book review: FamRZ 1963, 635, 638; *Marquardt* 53-54; *Vincent and Ponsard* no. 47. Several critical voices were also heard in a discussion, held at a meeting of the FRENCH Committee on Private International Law in 1956, of the conflicts provisions of the Instruction; see *L'instruction générale sur l'état civil du 21 septembre 1955 et le droit international privé*: Trav. Com. fr. d.i.p. 1955/57, 41-66.

538. *Audit* 303.

539. In cases of this type, however, the application of the relevant foreign law is often likely to be barred for reasons of public policy; cf. *infra* at n. 628. For the procedure to be observed when the parties invoke a foreign law which is less exacting than French law see the Instruction of 1955, no. 474; *Bischoff* no. 84.

popular country for celebrating "runaway marriages".[540] On policy grounds the preference for the *lex fori* is defensible in those cases where the parties are domiciled and intend to make their matrimonial home in France. In such cases, on the other hand, it is anomalous that a marriage which complies with French law should be liable to annulment in France on the ground that it does not meet the conditions of the *lex patriae*. Although this is the "orthodox" solution, French courts seem likely to be slow to defeat a marriage in such circumstances.[541]

It is of interest to compare the French approach with that prevailing in *England, Scotland* and other countries within the sphere of influence of English law. As we have seen already (*supra* s. 55), the discussion of conflicts questions of marriage in those countries centres round judicial decisions, which normally concern the validity or the nullity of a marriage already celebrated and rarely deal with problems arising at the time when the union is formed. Little and fragmentary information is available as to the practice of registrars and other functionaries participating in the celebration of marriages. Nor do the statutory provisions relating to this matter shed much light on choice of law problems. The English Marriage Act, for example, provides that the certificate and the licence necessary to the solemnisation of a marriage in England shall be issued unless "any lawful impediment" to the issue of the certificate has been shown to the satisfaction of the registrar, but nothing is said on the question of what law decides whether such an impediment exists.[542]

There are some indications, however, that foreign law is frequently disregarded even where the parties are domiciled abroad. As regards parental consents and similar matters, this is a natural consequence of the view taken by the courts in these countries that such requirements are governed by the *lex loci celebrationis* and not by the *lex domicilii*. Other requirements of the foreign domiciliary law seem also to be left out of consideration, in so far as they are merely directory (prohibitive impediments).[543] Even as regards mandatory impediments imposed by the relevant foreign law, there are very few reported cases in which the registrar

540. Cf. *Anton and Francescakis* 280, pointing out that the rule whereby a foreigner who is only temporarily resident in France cannot marry there without a prefectoral authorisation (*Pålsson*, Marriage, s. 275) probably discourages parties from coming to France to marry in evasion of foreign laws.

541. Cf. *Audit* 303.

542. Marriage Act 1949, s. 32 (2) (*a*).

543. See *supra* n. 530.

refused to issue a certificate or a licence in reliance on that law and in which the question was brought before the courts (as is possible in England by way of *mandamus*).[544] This suggests, although it does not conclusively prove, that foreign law often is not effectively applied in accordance with the appropriate conflicts rules. To a certain extent this assumption is confirmed by the fact that Continental law reports afford many examples of cases in which the parties had succeeded in getting married in England despite the existence of a ground of nullity under the law of their domicile and nationality.[545]

A "lenient" practice in the enforcement of foreign law, tending to erode the rule of governing capacity to marry by the personal law, is finally to be found in certain *Latin American* countries. Civil registrars in *Brazil* and *Venezuela*, for instance, in so far as they look to foreign law at all, seem to be very little exacting in requiring proof that the conditions of that law are satisfied.[546]

67. *Religiously Solemnised Marriages.* In countries where marriages may or must be solemnised in one religious form or another, the competence of the religious authority will often exert a *vis attractiva* on the substance of the matter. The laws of many religious communities ignore the distinction, drawn in the conflict of laws of secular legal systems, between form and substance and regard the institution of marriage as an indivisible whole, for which they claim application of their own rules to the exclusion of any secular law.[547] The general question of whether and to what extent such claims are endorsed by States is beyond the range of our present inquiry. The only point to be made here is that marriages solemnised in accordance with religious law will

544. The only ENGLISH cases are: R. v. Hammersmith Marriage Registrar, [1917] 1 K.B. 634 (C.A.); R. v. Brentwood Marriage Registrar, [1968] 2 Q.B. 956; and R. v. Registrar General, ex parte Minhas, [1976] 2 All E.R. 246 (Q.B.). For examples from other common law jurisdictions see SCOTLAND: Rojas, Petitioner, 1967 S.L.T. 24 (Sh. Ct.); CANADA: In re Eaton, [1922] 1 W.W.R. 236 (B.C.S.C.).

545. See, e.g., BELGIUM: Cour Bruxelles 28 May 1955, Rev. dr. fam. 1955, 61; Civ. Bruxelles 7 July 1956, Clunet 1958, 1152; FRANCE: Trib. Seine 10 July 1901, Clunet 1901, 967; Cour Paris 15 Dec. 1948, Rev. crit. d.i.p. 1949, 113; GERMANY: RG 21 Dec. 1916, LZ 1917, 924; RG 14 Jan. 1935, JW 1935, 1403; SWITZERLAND: BG 19 Jan. 1934, BGE 60 II 1, Clunet 1938, 984; BG 11 Nov. 1954, BGE 80 I 427; cf. BG 30 Sept. 1965, BGE 91 I 364.

546. See for BRAZIL: *Garland* 24; for VENEZUELA: *Lombard* 41 n. 134.

547. Cf. *Elgeddawy* 102-103; *Scheftelowitz* 21-22, 86, 103-106.

sometimes be recognised, without further conditions (except as concerns publicity, registration or similar formalities), and endowed with civil effects even by States possessing a rule of conflict of laws by which the substantive requirements for marriage are referable to the *lex patriae* or the *lex domicilii,* as the case may be. To that extent the conflicts rule suffers a derogation in favour of the religious law in question.

An example is the role assigned to canon matrimonial law in *Italy* and *Spain.* In both of those countries marriages can be validly celebrated before ministers of the Roman Catholic Church pursuant to concordats concluded with the Holy See.[548] The solemnisation of such marriages is subject in all respects to the canon law. That law alone also applies in proceedings for annulment, for which exclusive jurisdiction is vested in ecclesiastical tribunals.[549] As regards Italy, it has been very controversial whether the concordat type of marriage is or should be available to parties of foreign nationality who want to marry in local form. The question has, however, been unambiguously affirmed in practice.[550] In Spain the canon marriage is even the sole type admitted when one of the parties is a Catholic, regardless of their nationality.[551] According to the prevailing opinion in both countries (though, as regards Italy, with many dissents among writers), the validity of these unions from the point of view of the respective States does not depend upon compliance with the usual conflicts rules, by which matters of substance are governed by the *lex patriae.*[552] The latter rules are thus brushed aside and the canon

548. ITALY: Concordat of 11 Feb. 1929, art. 34; CC art. 82; Act of 27 May 1929; SPAIN: Concordat of 27 Aug. 1953, art. XXIII-XXIV; CC art. 75-82 in conjunction with art. 42 par. 1-2.

549. See the provisions of the respective concordats, cited in the preceding note, and the SPANISH CC art. 80.

550. References are given by *Pålsson,* Marriage, s. 274 n. 22. See also *Palmieri* 101-117; *Vitta* II 223-228 (critically).

551. This principle extends not only to local marriages but also to those celebrated abroad, at least if one of the parties is of Spanish nationality; see *Pålsson,* Marriage, s. 266, 328 and 335 (n. 235).

552. For ITALIAN decisions affirming the principle that concordat marriages are exclusively governed by canon law, irrespective of the nationality of the parties, see, e.g.: Trib. Bologna 31 Oct. 1950, Annal. Dir. Int. 1951, 153; App. Trieste 17 July 1954, Riv. dir. matr. 1954, 306; Cass. 14 Dec. 1960, Giust. civ. 1961 I 421. Numerous other cases are cited by *Vitta* II 225-226 (n. 143 and 145). Most of these cases concerned the dissolution of such marriages (on this point the position of ITALIAN law has been radically changed with the adoption of the Divorce Act of 1 Dec. 1970) rather than their validity. For extrajudicial support of the view stated in the text see, e.g.,

law made to prevail. This has been justified in various ways, *inter alia* on grounds that form and substance are so tightly interwoven in the concordat system of matrimonial law as to exclude any distinction between the two aspects.[553] Whatever its true rationale may be, this exception to the conflicts rules on capacity to marry seems to be quite important, since it restricts the operation of those rules to marriages – which are relatively few in number both in Italy and in Spain – celebrated in civil form or (as concerns Italy) in some recognised religious form other than that of the concordat.[554]

Such complete "surrender" by the State is, however, not a generally accepted principle for marriages in religious form. At least in countries where this form is only optional, the substantive conditions of validity will normally be determined by secular law. To that extent the usual conflicts rules on the subject, with their reference to the personal law, have to be observed. This holds true even, for instance, in Italy if the marriage is solemnised before a minister of one of the recognised religious communities other than the Roman Catholic Church.[555]

Biscottini, Sul matrimonio concordatario degli stranieri: Foro pad. 1951 I 495-504; *M. Miele* 104-105. For voices *contra,* arguing that foreigners must comply with the substantive requirements of their *lex patriae* (as well as with those of the canon law) see, e.g., *Ballarino,* Forma degli atti e diritto internazionale privato (Padua 1970) 413-414; *Magni,* Gli effetti civili del matrimonio canonico (Padua 1948) 128-130; *Palmieri* 105-117; *Ziccardi,* Il matrimonio concordatario nel sistema legislativo italiano: Temi 1950, 312, 335-340. For SPANISH law, where the principle of the supremacy of the canon law seems to be generally recognised, see: *Aguilar Navarro* 282-283, 287-288, 291, 297-298; *Fernández Flores* 790-795; *Miaja de la Muela* II 267.

553. The validity of this argument, and of the conclusion that a concordat marriage is governed by canon law alone, is also accepted by those writers, constituting a majority in ITALY, who reject the possibility of permitting foreigners to use this form of marriage. In the opinion of those writers, the application of the canon law in regard to parties of foreign nationality is incompatible with the conflicts rules of Italian law – including art. 1 of the HAGUE CONVENTION of 1902, to which Italy is a party – which refer to the *lex patriae* in matters of substance. To avoid this inconsistency it is thought necessary to exclude foreigners from the use of the concordat form of marriage.

554. On the latter form of marriage in ITALIAN law see CC art. 83 and the Act of 24 June 1929; *Luther,* Die Formen der Eheschliessung nach italienischem Recht und ihre Bedeutung für deutsch-italienische Ehen: StAZ 1970, 33, 34, 40-41; *Vitta* II 228-233.

555. See *Vitta* II 230-231.

bb. *Prohibitive (Invalidating) Role of Lex Fori or Lex Loci Celebrationis*

68. In *English* and *Scottish* law there is some judicial and extra-judicial support for the view that the parties must have capacity to marry not only by the law of their domicile but also by the *lex loci celebrationis.*[556] In other words, an incapacity existing under the latter law may be fatal to the union even if it complies with the relevant domiciliary law or laws.

Such a rule is, of course, in keeping with the "territorialist" tradition of the English conflicts law of marriage (*supra* s. 64). Nevertheless, the standing of the rule is rather doubtful. It has never been clearly adopted as the *ratio decidendi* of English or Scottish cases, and it appears to have been plainly rejected by some decisions in other Commonwealth countries.[557] In considering this problem it is proposed to distinguish according to whether it arises in relation to a locally celebrated or to a foreign marriage.

To begin with the latter situation, the rule requiring the forum to take the foreign *lex loci celebrationis* into consideration (in addition to the personal law) has been defended on the ground that it reduces the possible occasions for limping marriages.[558] This is true, though only to the extent that the courts of the country of celebration itself insist on the application of the invalidating rule of their law. If accepted at all, the rule in question can therefore only be put on a rational basis if its operation is made subject to the principle of *renvoi.* Other arguments, however, militate against any acceptance of this rule. In the first place, it brings with it heavy complications since it requires the forum to consult yet another foreign law (including its conflicts rules), besides the domiciliary law or laws involved. Secondly, and more important, the rule tends to increase the number of invalid marriages in the forum country and is therefore in direct opposition to the policy of validation. For these reasons most writers contest the desirability of the present rule, at least where the *lex loci celebrationis* is a foreign law, and suggest that an incapacity im-

556. ENGLAND: Breen v. Breen, [1964] P. 144, Clunet 1965, 453, note Lipstein; criticised by *Unger*, Capacity to Marry and the *Lex Loci Celebrationis:* 24 M.L.R. 784-789 (1961); and by *Webb*, Foreign Marriages Following English Divorces: 11 I.C.L.Q. 251-254 (1962). SCOTLAND: Lendrum v. Chakravarti, 1929 S.L.T. 96, 103 (*obiter*); *Anton* 278-279, 290-291.

557. *Infra* n. 560, 562.

558. *Anton* 279.

posed by that law should be ignored.[559] There is *Australian* and *Canadian* authority to support this view.[560]

The position is somewhat different with regard to locally celebrated marriages. Here it is more commonly admitted, at least among writers, that the mandatory requirements of the *lex loci celebrationis,* coinciding with the *lex fori,* must be satisfied (in addition to those of the domiciliary law). While rejecting any reference to a foreign *lex loci* in the present context, Professor *Cheshire,* for instance, argues that an English registrar cannot be required to sanction a marriage if it would be void for incapacity by English law and that an English court is unlikely, for policy reasons, to uphold such a marriage.[561] If this view represents English law – which is not settled beyond doubt – it means that the *lex loci celebrationis* has the function of setting the minimum standards for locally solemnised unions. Even so confined the rule is open to objections.[562] Substantially similar results are, however, often reached in other countries either by the aid of statutory exceptions to the rule of the personal law or by an extensive use of the doctrine of (prohibitive) public policy (*infra* s. 74).

bc. *Rules Tending to Support Validity of Marriage*

69. *Validation under Lex Loci Celebrationis: Swiss Law.* The conflicts rules of Swiss law regarding capacity to marry provide an interesting example of a compromise between the principles of the personal law and of territoriality, respectively. Although these

559. See, besides the critical comments on the *Breen* case cited *supra* n. 556, *Cheshire and North* 347-349; *Hartley,* Policy Basis 576-577; *North* 121; *Nygh* 412-413; *Sykes,* Essential Validity 160-161; *Webb and Davis* 228 (for NEW ZEALAND law). Doubts as to the extension of the rule to marriages celebrated abroad are expressed by *Dicey and Morris* 271, cf. *Morris* 103-104, 110. An intermediate position is taken by *Fleming,* Marital Capacity: 4 I.L.Q. 389-393 (1951).

560. AUSTRALIA: In the Will of Swan (1871), 2 V.R. (I.E. & M.) 47; CANADA: Reed (*alias* Frew) v. Reed (1969), 6 D.L.R. (3d) 617 (B.C.S.C.), Clunet 1972, 375.

561. *Cheshire and North* 348. See also *Cheshire,* Husband and Wife 138; *Dicey and Morris* 270-272; *Graveson,* Conflict 258; *Hartley,* Policy Basis 577; *North* 379, 382; *Ryan* 988; cf. *P.B. Carter* (1968) 244. For the distinction between void and voidable marriages in ENGLISH law see, for example, *North* 132-133.

562. It is apparently rejected in CANADA even for locally celebrated marriages; see Schwebel v. Ungar (1964), 48 D.L.R. (2d) 644 (S.C.C.), Clunet 1969, 746, note Castel; cf. *Lysyk* 369-370. And see for NEW ZEALAND law *Webb and Davis* 228.

rules date a long way back in time, their approach still stands out, at least in part, as remarkably modern and broad-minded. They seek to reconcile, as far as possible, the policies of promoting international harmony of decision and of favouring the validity of marriages already entered into, though usually with a preference for the former policy in cases where a choice between them cannot be avoided.

The "orthodox" Continental rule requiring compliance with the *lex patriae* of each of the parties applies when the marriage is performed in Switzerland.[563] To that extent the desire to prevent the creation of a limping status and, thereby, to further international uniformity of decision is the prevalent consideration. A different rule obtains, however, for marriages entered into in a foreign country. Subject to certain exceptions to be spelt out below, such a marriage is recognised as valid if celebrated "in conformity with the laws there (*i.e.*, in the country of celebration) in force."[564] Under this rule, which covers the substantive as well as the formal aspects of the matter, validity by the foreign *lex loci celebrationis* is sufficient. On the other hand, if the marriage is invalid under that law, it may be declared invalid in Switzerland only if it is also invalid by Swiss law.[565] Thus a double hurdle must be overcome if the marriage is to be defeated. This amounts to much the same as an affirmative rule to the effect that the union must be upheld if it complies either with the *lex loci celebrationis* or with Swiss law.[566] To that extent the policy of validation is clearly a weighty factor underlying the system.

Although the provisions concerning foreign marriages do not contain any reference to the nationality of the parties, they have

563. NAG art. 7 c par. 1; see *supra* n. 284.

564. NAG art. 7 f par. 1. See on this provision, especially its application to the substantive conditions of marriage: *Beck*, art. 7 f no. 1-11, 50-54, 134, 136; *Gamillscheg*, Kommentar, art. 13 no. 76; *Rabel* 270-271; *Schnitzer* 346-347; *Vischer*, IPR 588-589.

565. NAG art. 7 f par. 2. See *Beck*, art. 7 f no. 51, 108-110, 133, 140-152 and ESchlKonv. art. 1 no. 20, 38; *Rabel* 280, 582-583; *Schnitzer* 347; *Spivak* 62-65.

566. By the weight of opinion, this holds true even to the extent of excluding the recognition of a foreign nullity decree based on the relevant foreign law, if the marriage complied with SWISS domestic law and therefore, pursuant to NAG art. 7 f par. 2, could not have been annulled by a Swiss court. See: AppH Bern 26 Jan. 1923, ZBJV 59 (1923) 169; *Beck*, art. 7 f no. 170-173 and ESchlKonv. art. 1 no. 20; *Schnitzer* 365; *Spivak* 63. But see *Vischer*, IPR 594. Cf. *Götz*, Vorbemerkungen zum vierten Abschnitt no. 17 (at 260-261); *Stauffer*, art. 7 f no. 13.

been construed by the courts to be confined to marriages between Swiss nationals.[567] If the parties are, or if one of them is, of foreign nationality, the rule of the *lex patriae* prevails even as to marriages celebrated abroad, so that to be recognised in Switzerland the union must be valid by that law.[568] The reason given by the Federal Tribunal is that the Swiss statute governing the matter is primarily concerned with achieving uniformity of decision with the country to which the parties belong by nationality.[569] That policy is considered strong enough to outweigh the desire to uphold marriages.[570] By contrast, when the parties are Swiss nationals who have married abroad in accordance with the law of the place of celebration, it is within the power of Swiss law itself to prevent any conflict between the two policies from arising. By recognising such marriages without insisting on compliance with its own domestic rules, Swiss law meets the demands of both policies. Naturally, however, this concession to the foreign law involved is not extended to cases in which, conversely, the marriage is invalid by that law but conforms to the standards of Swiss domestic law, which as the *lex patriae* is the basically applicable law.[571] In this case, then, the validating policy prevails over the endeavour to avoid a limping status. Such, in the main, is the rationale of the Swiss conflicts provisions with reference to foreign marriages.

The rule that foreign marriages of Swiss nationals are governed by the *lex loci celebrationis* is subject to certain qualifications and exceptions (additional to the alternative application of Swiss law to uphold the union). In the first place, this rule, as predominantly construed, refers to the *conflicts rules*, rather than the domestic rules, of the relevant foreign law.[572] Accordingly, a marriage which complies with the domestic rules of the *lex loci celebrationis* does not, for this reason alone, qualify for recognition.[573] Only in

567. See the decisions cited *supra* n. 327.

568. It is uncertain, however, whether the female party's nationality has to be taken into account. See *supra* at n. 330-332.

569. BG 11 Nov. 1954, BGE 80 I 427, 433; BG 3 June 1971, BGE 97 I 389, 403.

570. This evaluation has been criticised by some writers; see *supra* n. 327.

571. Cf. BG 2 Dec. 1943, BGE 69 II 342, 345.

572. See: BG 19 Jan. 1934, BGE 60 II 1, 6-7, Clunet 1938, 984; ObG Zürich 8 March 1939, ZR 40 (1941) 36, 39; *Beck*, art. 7 f no. 3, 5, 8, 50-53, 134, 136, 145 and ESchlKonv. art. 1 no. 15, 18-23; *Marquardt* 96-97; *Rabel* 270-271, 284; *Rathgeb*, La loi applicable aux suisses à l'étranger en vertu de l'article 28 ch. 2 de la loi fédérale du 25 juin 1891 sur les rapports de droit civil des citoyens établis ou en séjour: Festschrift Lewald 359, 370.

573. But see *Schnitzer* 346-347; *Spivak* 60-62.

this way can there be harmony with the spirit of the Swiss provision. Switzerland wants to prevent conflicts with the foreign country of celebration and is therefore prepared to recognise a marriage which is treated as valid in that country. The question whether it is so treated can only be answered by reference to the foreign conflicts rules, which in consequence necessarily come into consideration. If recognition were to be extended to marriages which conformed to the domestic *lex loci celebrationis* but which would not be sustained by the courts of the foreign country (for instance, because they would decide the question according to Swiss law, the *lex patriae*), Switzerland would indeed be creating a conflict with that country. This seems to be clearly against the purpose of the Swiss rule.[574]

Suppose, for instance, that an uncle-niece marriage, which is prohibited by Swiss law, is celebrated in West Germany, both parties being Swiss nationals.[575] Although such unions are lawful by West German domestic law, this particular marriage would (probably) be declared invalid by a West German court for the reason that Swiss law applies.[576] If this is true, then there is also no basis for recognising the marriage in Switzerland.[577] On the other hand, if the marriage was entered into in Sweden and if the parties had been habitually resident in that country long enough (two years) to be able to subject themselves to Swedish law (which, like West German law, does not know the impediment in

574. True, such a conflict is accepted where the marriage is valid by SWISS domestic law (*supra* at n. 565-566), but this is a special case.

575. For the SWISS rule prohibiting such marriages see CC art. 100 no. 1.

576. Admittedly, this conclusion stands and falls with the construction placed by the WEST GERMAN court upon the SWISS rule in NAG art. 7 f par. 1. There is a possibility that that rule, contrary to the prevailing SWISS view, will be construed as requiring (or at least as admitting) the application of the *lex loci celebrationis* even though the conflicts rules of the latter law refer, primarily, to the *lex patriae*. On this view there is a *renvoi* to WEST GERMAN law which will be accepted by the court, with the result that the marriage in our example will be upheld. Such a construction, however, is scarcely in keeping with the purpose and spirit of the SWISS conflicts rule. See *Beck*, ESchlKonv. art. 1 no. 22; *Gamillscheg*, Kommentar, art. 13 no. 16, 937. Cf. the decision of RG 6 Feb. 1930, IPRspr. 1930 no. 64, applying SWISS domestic law, as the *lex patriae* of the petitioning husband, to annul a marriage entered into in Germany without adverting to the question of whether a ground for annulment existed under GERMAN law (but the issue of *renvoi* apparently was not raised in this case; cf. *Rabel* 287 n. 87).

577. But see *Schnitzer* 347, where this very example is used to illustrate the validating effect of the rule in NAG art. 7 f par. 1.

question), then the union is regarded as lawful in Sweden and will also be recognised in Switzerland.[578]

Furthermore, the liberality of the Swiss system is tempered by two exceptions to the rule of the *lex loci celebrationis*. The first of these concerns *evasion:* a foreign marriage of Swiss nationals, although valid where celebrated, will not be recognised if the parties entered into it abroad "with the obvious intention of evading the grounds of invalidity prescribed by Swiss law".[579] This, as has been shown, is a type of safeguard often used in countries applying the test of the *lex loci* to determine capacity to marry.[580] The purpose of the Swiss provision, which is restrictively drafted, is to prevent recognition in certain circumstances where an impediment to the marriage existed by Swiss law and where there was no "legitimate" reason why the parties should be able to take advantage of a more liberal foreign law.

In practice, the operation of this clause seems to be limited to cases in which both parties were and intended to (and did) remain habitually resident in Switzerland, leaving the country only temporarily to marry abroad in contravention of a mandatory rule of Swiss law (such as the prohibition against marriage between uncle and niece or between aunt and nephew).[581] Thus, a marriage will not be caught by the above provision if the parties were, or if one of them was, habitually resident in the foreign country of celebration, or if they established their first matrimonial home in that country. In none of these cases is the contact with the place of

578. For the SWEDISH conflicts rule involved in this example see the Act of 8 July 1904 (as amended) ch. 1 § 2 par. 2 (*supra* at n. 295).

579. NAG art. 7 f par. 1. This part of the provision gives rise to various problems of interpretation, which have been canvassed by writers. See, e.g., *Beck*, art. 7 f no. 67-99; *Gubler*, Gesetzesumgehung im internationalen Eheschliessungsrecht der Schweiz (Thesis, Zürich 1941); *Rabel* 278-279; *Schnitzer* 347-348; *Spivak* 49-51, 65-68.

580. *Supra* s. 8, 15 (USA), 37 (SOUTH AFRICA), cf. s. 60.

581. The relevant grounds are listed in the SWISS CC art. 120. They include: bigamy, mental incapacity, prohibited degrees of consanguinity and affinity and certain cases where a marriage is invalid by reason of sham (because contracted solely for the purpose of enabling the woman to acquire Swiss nationality). In these cases a violative marriage is characterised as *nichtig*, that is to say, liable to annulment for reasons dictated by a public interest. In a different category are a number of other defects, which are considered less serious and which render the marriage (merely) *anfechtbar*. In these cases the marriage can only be attacked by the private parties concerned and only within certain time limits; see CC art. 123-128. The safeguard against evasion does not extend to nullity grounds of this kind, cf. *infra* n. 583.

celebration "artificial", regardless of whether the parties in choosing it were influenced by the fact that they could not get married in Switzerland. Read in this light, the provision as a whole, including both the reference to the *lex loci celebrationis* and the evasion clause, has the effect of exempting Swiss nationals marrying abroad from the requirements of Swiss law in circumstances where they are durably connected with the foreign country concerned.[582] Even if the parties did not have any "natural" link with that country, however, the recognition of their marriage in Switzerland will not be affected if the evaded prohibition was merely directory.[583] One such prohibition, which has been successfully evaded in numerous cases, is that against remarriage during a waiting period after divorce, which Swiss law requires to be imposed on the party against whom a divorce is pronounced for matrimonial offences.[584]

It may be concluded that the scope left for the evasion clause is rather narrow. Few marriages have failed to be recognised on this ground alone.[585]

The second exception to the rule of the *lex loci celebrationis,* which is not expressly mentioned by the relevant statute, is that a foreign marriage will not be recognised if to do so would be contrary to Swiss *public policy.*[586] This exception has been relied

582. The provision in question is indeed often discussed in terms suggesting that the relevant law is the *lex domicilii* rather than the *lex loci celebrationis.* While this is not literally correct, it corresponds roughly to the meaning of the rule, including the evasion clause. Cf. *Beck,* art. 7 f no. 74, 87; *Vischer,* Zum Problem der rechtsmissbräuchlichen Anknüpfung im internationalen Privatrecht: Aequitas und Bona Fides, Festgabe zum 70. Geburtstag von August Simonius (Basle 1955) 401, 407.

583. The same holds true if the marriage would be *anfechtbar* under SWISS domestic law (*supra* n. 581). See, e.g., *Beck,* art. 7 f no. 78; *Gamillscheg,* Kommentar, art. 13 no. 76; *Gubler* (*supra* n. 579) 50-67; *Schnitzer* 348; *Stauffer,* art. 7 f no. 11.

584. CC art. 150 in conjunction with art. 104. This prohibition, being in the nature of a penalty, is usually left out of consideration in other countries; see *infra* s. 94. Even if the marriage was manifestly contracted in evasion of this prohibition, it will be recognised as valid in SWITZERLAND. See, besides the references in the preceding note, *Götz,* art. 104 no. 14-15, art. 130 no. 4; *Kaschewsky,* Eine schweizerische Grundsatzentscheidung zur Strafwartefrist (Art. 104 ZGB) und Frauenwartefrist (Art. 103 ZGB) bei beabsichtigter Eheschliessung im nichtschweizerischen Ausland: SJZ 68 (1972) 250-253; and comments in SJZ 56 (1960) 180, 228, 248.

585. The only decision of the Federal Tribunal that relies on this ground, as one among others, to deny recognition is BG 19 Jan. 1934, BGE 60 II 1, 6, Clunet 1938, 984. Cf. BG 30 Sept. 1965, BGE 91 I 364, 371-372.

586. See *Beck,* art. 7 f no. 6, 55-58, 154-155; *Rabel* 279; *Schnitzer* 347.

upon in a case where a Swiss national had obtained a divorce in the foreign country of his domicile and then remarried in that country; the divorce did not meet the conditions for recognition in Switzerland (the other spouse being domiciled in Switzerland), so that, in the eyes of Swiss law, the second marriage was bigamous. Although not contracted in evasion of Swiss law, this marriage was therefore rejected as violating Swiss public policy.[587]

70. *Validation under Lex Fori et Loci Celebrationis: English Law.* Another type of validating device, very different in spirit and scope from the Swiss provision dealt with above, is encountered in English law. This device derives its origin from the decision in the case of *Sottomayor* v. *De Barros* (No. 2).[588] It was there held that a marriage celebrated in England between first cousins, the man having an English and the woman a Portuguese domicile, was valid notwithstanding that in the absence of a papal dispensation it was prohibited and invalid by Portuguese law. Chiefly on the authority of this decision, the following rule – or rather exception to the rule that capacity to marry depends on the law of the domicile of each of the parties – has been formulated in the leading English textbook on the conflict of laws: "The validity of a marriage celebrated in England between persons of whom the one has an English, and the other a foreign, domicile is not affected by any incapacity which, though existing under the law of such foreign domicile, does not exist under the law of England."[589] In other words, the application of the dual domicile rule, in so far as that rule refers to a foreign law, is limited to cases in which both parties are domiciled, or the marriage is celebrated, outside England.

Viewed in its historical context, the decision in the *Sottomayor* case (No. 2) reflects the persevering influence of the principle, which was accepted in English law until a short time before that case arose, of the supremacy of the *lex loci celebrationis* in all matters touching the validity of marriage.[590] The decision also

587. BG 13 May 1938, BGE 64 II 74, Clunet 1951, 938, note Knapp. See, critically, *Kallmann,* Anerkennung und Vollstreckung ausländischer Zivilurteile und gerichtlicher Vergleiche (Basle 1946) 254-260. Cf. BG 29 Sept. 1966, BGE 92 II 217, 222 (involving an issue of jurisdiction to annul a bigamous marriage entered into abroad).

588. (1879), 5 P.D. 94.

589. *Dicey and Morris* 272. See also *North* 119, 121.

590. Cf. *supra* at n. 527. The judgment in the *Sottomayor* case (No. 2) (*supra* n. 588) regards the distinction between form and capacity, then recently established in ENGLISH law, with disfavour and is largely based on

continued on page 182

savours of the notion of the predominance of the *lex fori* in English courts. Its policy basis seems to lie in the desire to protect English domiciliaries from the injustice alleged to result if effect had to be given to prohibitions imposed by the foreign law of the other party's domicile.[591] The protection afforded by the rule in *Sottomayor* (No. 2) is, however, confined to cases where the marriage is entered into in England.[592]

The rule in question has incurred strong and almost unanimous opprobrium among writers in England and other Commonwealth countries.[593] Some critics regret the existence of this "anomalous" rule but lean in favour of recognising it as good law.[594] Others suggest that it should be interpreted as restrictively as possible.[595] Yet other commentators flatly reject the rule as "unworthy of a place in a respectable system of the conflict of laws".[596]

The main objection voiced against the rule is that it embodies a unilateral preference for the *lex fori* and gives a nationalistic bias to English private international law. Two aspects of this tendency may be distinguished. The first is that the law of the English domicile of one of the parties is regarded as more important than the law of the foreign domicile of the other: while an incap-

---

continued from page 181

the authority of older cases – such as Scrimshire v. Scrimshire (1752), 2 Hag. Con. 395, 161 Eng. Rep. 782, and Simonin v. Mallac (1860), 2 Sw. & Tr. 67, [1843-60] All E.R. Rep. 68 (Court for Divorce and Matrimonial Causes) – which failed to draw any such distinction.

591. The idea that giving effect to the foreign law in these "divided domicile situations" might cause injustice to the party subject to English law originally appeared as an *obiter dictum* in Sottomayor v. De Barros (No. 1) (1877), 3 P.D. 1, at 6-7 (C.A.). This passage was quoted with approval by the court in Sottomayor v. De Barros (No. 2) (1879), 5 P.D. 94, at 104.

592. For discussion of an extension of the rule to marriages celebrated elsewhere than in England see *Pearl* 133; *Ryan* 989-990.

593. See the references *infra* n. 594-596, 600, 604; also, *Baty* 448-450; *Wolff*, PIL 333-334. But see for approving comments: *Graveson*, Conflict 260-263; *Webb*, Thoughts 826-827 (carrying the preference for the *lex fori* even further than the rule under review). For a positive evaluation based on a study of comparative law see *Audit* 318-320.

594. See *Dicey and Morris* 259-260, 272-273. For a judicial opinion to the same effect see *infra* n. 599.

595. See *Cheshire and North* 347, approving a suggestion put forward in the AUSTRALIAN case of Miller v. Teale (1954), 92 C.L.R. 406, 414 (H.C.A.), that the effect of the rule should be "confined to a condition imposed by the law of the domicile that a specified consent or consents should be given".

596. *Falconbridge* 711. For other writers voicing a similar opinion see *infra* n. 600.

acity imposed by the former law is fatal to the marriage without further conditions, a prohibition by the latter law will be disregarded (as to marriages celebrated in England) if it is not recognised by English law. The second aspect is that, while English law prevails when it is the *lex loci celebrationis* and the *lex domicilii* of one of the parties, no corresponding preference for the foreign law concerned is admitted when the facts are appropriately reversed. It is insufficient that a foreign marriage should comply with the law of the country of celebration even if one of the parties is domiciled in that country (or in some other country by the law of which the parties are capable of intermarriage); the validity of such a union will be negatived by an incapacity existing under the domiciliary law of the other party, at all events if that law is English.[597] Different yardsticks are thus used for the application of the *lex fori* and of foreign law, respectively.

As regards the attitude of the courts, the rule enunciated in the *Sottomayor* case (No. 2) has been followed or approved in a few English, Scottish and Australian cases.[598] Other courts, however,

597. Mette v. Mette (1859), 1 Sw. & Tr. 416, 164 Eng. Rep. 792; In re Paine, [1940] Ch. 46. See also Pugh v. Pugh, [1951] P. 482, where the situation was the same, except that the *lex loci celebrationis* and the *lex domicilii* of one of the parties were two different foreign laws, by both of which the marriage was valid. In all three cases ENGLISH law was applied, as the law of the domicile of the other party, to defeat the marriage. To the same effect see the AUSTRALIAN case of Ungar v. Ungar (1967), 10 F.L.R. 467 (N.S.W. Sup. Ct.). On the facts, though not on the reasoning, it is true, these decisions are open to the alternative explanation provided by the theory of the intended matrimonial home, cf. *supra* s. 54-55. Even the *Sottomayor* case (No. 2) is reconcilable with that theory, though only if its reasoning is completely disregarded; cf. *Cheshire,* Husband and Wife 141. For a critique of the decisions in *Mette* and *Re Paine* and a proposal to generalise the rule in *Sottomayor* (No. 2) so as to validate a marriage whenever it is valid by the *lex loci celebrationis* as well as the *lex domicilii* of one party, regardless of its invalidity by the other party's law, see *Ryan* 989-991.

598. See for ENGLAND: Ogden v. Ogden, [1908] P. 46, 74-77 (C.A.); Chetti v. Chetti, [1909] P. 67, 81-87; for SCOTLAND: MacDougall v. Chitnavis, 1937 S.C. 390, 403-404, 407. These cases, however, were primarily decided on other grounds and are therefore inconclusive. In AUSTRALIA the *Sottomayor* case (No. 2) was followed in Pezet v. Pezet (1946), 47 S.R. (N.S.W.) 45 (F.C.) (a decision since overruled on other grounds, see *infra* n. 599), and referred to but distinguished in Ungar v. Ungar (1967), 10 F.L.R. 467 at 472, 476 (N.S.W. Sup. Ct.). See also the SOUTH AFRICAN case of Friedman v. Friedman's Executors (1922), 43 N.L.R. 259. That case, however, is predominantly interpreted as supporting the much broader rule that the *lex loci celebrationis* is the proper law to govern the essentials of marriage; see *supra* n. 277.

aligning themselves with the prevailing extrajudicial opinion, have expressed criticism or scepticism of that decision.[599] The standing of the rule is therefore somewhat uncertain both in England and, even more so, in other Commonwealth countries.[600] In so far as it will be followed at all, there is a clear possibility that its scope will be restricted one way or another.[601] As concerns prohibitions based on certain degrees of affinity, such a restriction seems to result from an English statute, which is based on the assumption that the dual domicile rule applies without any qualification.[602]

Nevertheless, some degree of "respectability" may be restored to the rule in *Sottomayor* (No. 2) when it is viewed in the perspective of comparative law. The fact is in any case that similar results are often reached in other countries by one means or another, usually either by the aid of special conflicts rules for the annulment of marriage which set up an additional bar to invalidation (*infra* s. 71), or by relying on the notion of permissive public policy (*infra* s. 73).[603] Provisions of the former type sometimes go

599. It was characterised as "anomalous" in the ENGLISH case of Radwan v. Radwan (No. 2), [1973] Fam. 35, 50, and was not followed in the SCOTTISH case of Lendrum v. Chakravarti, 1929 S.L.T. 96, 102-103 (since overruled on other grounds by the decision in MacDougall v. Chitnavis, *supra* n. 598). For AUSTRALIA see Miller v. Teale (1954), 92 C.L.R. 406, 414 (H.C.A.), overruling Pezet v. Pezet (*supra* n. 598) on other grounds and questioning the decision in that case in so far as it was the result of "the dubious guidance of Sottomayor v. De Barros (No. 2) and Ogden v. Ogden".

600. See for SCOTLAND: *Anton* 280-281; AUSTRALIA: *Nygh* 411-412; *Sykes,* Conflict 87-89, cf. *idem,* Essential Validity 161-163; CANADA (QUEBEC): *W.S. Johnson* 185; NEW ZEALAND: *Webb and Davis* 227-228.

601. Cf. *supra* n. 595.

602. Marriage (Enabling) Act 1960, s. 1 (3). See *Cheshire and North* 345-347; *Dicey and Morris* 263, 273; and *supra* at n. 418.

603. As regards ENGLISH law, too, the notion of public policy has been adduced to explain the decisions under consideration. See particularly *Kahn-Freund,* Reflections 53-58, suggesting that the relevant foreign law was excluded on the ground that its application would offend against fundamental notions of the *lex fori.* This explanation has the advantage of replacing the rigid rule, which is usually thought to be deducible from the decision in *Sottomayor* (No. 2), by a flexible test requiring the court to try in each case whether the application of the foreign law would lead to a result sufficiently repulsive to warrant a departure from the ordinary rules of the conflict of laws. While the opinions in the relevant ENGLISH cases provide some support for this approach, it is nevertheless believed that public policy is insufficient to explain the whole line of decisions. In the AUSTRALIAN case of Pezet v. Pezet (*supra* n. 598), for instance, the court refused to give effect to a prohibition (against remarriage during the time allowed for appeal from a decree of divorce) of the foreign *lex domicilii,* even though the prohibition existed in exactly the same form in the *lex fori;* cf. *Sykes,* Essential Validity 162.

further than the English rule, requiring the existence of a ground of nullity under the *lex fori* even where the marriage does not have any particular connection with that law.

On policy grounds it may, of course, be argued that such rules are undesirable because they increase the number of limping marriages. As against that, however, the policy of upholding marriages in the country of the forum, at least when the parties have a reasonably close relation to that country, comes into consideration. While one may readily agree with the criticism levelled at the English rule in *Sottomayor* (No. 2) in so far as it is directed against the arbitrary preference accorded to the *lex fori*, it does not necessarily follow that one must subscribe to the conclusion usually drawn, namely, that that rule should simply be eliminated in favour of the general application of the dual domicile rule, by which an incapacity under either party's *lex domicilii* is sufficient for invalidation. From the point of view of the policy of validation, the appropriate solution rather lies in extending the rule in *Sottomayor* (No. 2) so as to allow the foreign party's domiciliary law to prevail when an English marriage is valid by that law (though not by English law) and to subject foreign marriages to the same liberal regime. In other words, instead of the validating application of English law *qua* the *lex fori et celebrationis,* it is arguable that preference should be given to whichever of the two domiciliary laws is more favourable to the validity of the marriage. While such a rule is rather far away from current English law, it does not lack adherents as a reform proposal and seems to be in keeping with modern trends of opinion in several countries.[604]

71. *Special Conflicts Rules for Annulment: Various Countries.* Whether and on what grounds a marriage may be annulled or declared invalid is, of course, a facet of the question of its validity. On principle, therefore, all such questions must be dealt with by reference to the law or laws governing the various aspects of the formation and validity of the union. On the one hand, it is or should be self-evident that a marriage which complies with the law designated by the conflicts rules of a particular country as applicable in matters of substantive validity (which is the only aspect to be considered here) cannot be invalidated in that country for reasons relating to substance.[605] Any departure from this principle

604. See for ENGLISH law *Hartley,* Policy Basis 578. Cf. *Ryan* 989-991; *Swan* 21.

605. A more difficult question, which will here only be noted in passing, is whether a *foreign* nullity decree should automatically be excluded from

continued on page 186

would amount to a *contradictio in adjecto*. Where, on the other hand, the marriage fails to meet the requirements of the proper law in this respect, it is at least very natural that it should fall to the same law to decide whether the union is valid despite the defect vitiating it (as will be the case if the violated provision was only directory) or whether it is voidable or void *ipso jure*. This is in fact the prevailing view in most countries espousing the principle that the substantive conditions of marriage are determinable by the personal law.[606]

To that extent there is obviously neither need nor justification for assigning the nullity of marriage to independent choice of law rules. Nevertheless, it is also true that such rules exist in several countries. In particular, attention must be drawn to the statutes on the conflict of laws enacted in a number of *socialist countries in Eastern Europe* and to the treaties of legal assistance concluded between those countries and, in a few cases, between one of them and an "outside" country. As regards capacity to marry, these statutes and treaties usually provide for the application of the *lex patriae* of each of the parties at the time of celebration of the marriage.[607] Their provisions on the choice of law in nullity, on the other hand, present a rather variegated picture, which reflects different degrees of technical elaboration but also certain differences of policy in the matter.[608]

The relevant *East German* and *Polish* statutes squarely endorse the principle, referred to above, of governing the nullity of marriage by the law or laws indicated as applicable with regard to the

continued from page 185

recognition in this situation. Opinions on this point are much divided in different countries. Cf. on the corresponding problem with regard to foreign nullity decrees based on want of proper form, *Pålsson*, Marriage, s. 285.

606. See generally *Rabel* 309-311, 581-582; *Wolff*, PIL 349-350. For particular countries see, e.g., AUSTRALIA: *Nygh* 453-454; AUSTRIA: *Schwind*, IPR 141, 172-173; ENGLAND: *Cheshire and North* 394-396, 399-400; *Dicey and Morris* 359-360; FRANCE: *Batiffol and Lagarde* II 55-56; *Bischoff* no. 145-148, 158; *G. de La Pradelle* 135-144; WEST GERMANY: *Gamillscheg*, Kommentar, art. 13 no. 479-484; *Kegel*, Kommentar, art. 13 no. 85-97; *Raape*, IPR 241; ITALY: *M. Miele* 118; *Monaco* 187-188; *Vitta* II 279-280; NETHERLANDS: *Lemaire* 93; SWITZERLAND: BG 2 Dec. 1943, BGE 69 II 342, 344-346; BG 11 Nov. 1954, BGE 80 I 427, 431; ObG Zürich 10 Sept. 1964, ZR 65 (1966) no. 94; *Götz*, Vorbemerkungen zum vierten Abschnitt no. 16 (at 260); *Vischer*, IPR 593.

607. See the references *supra* n. 285, 288-289. The principal exception is SOVIET law, as to which see *supra* s. 34.

608. Cf. the survey given by *Pålsson*, Marriage, s. 403. See also *Petev* 605-606.

respective aspects of its formation.[609] The same solution has been adopted in a sizeable number of treaties of legal assistance concluded between different socialist States.[610] The current tendency seems to be in favour of this "orthodox" type of rule. One pointer in this direction is a recent revision of some older treaties to which East Germany is one of the parties: in their new version, in contrast with the original one, these treaties deal with the problem of nullity of marriage by reference to the laws governing its substantive and formal conditions, respectively.[611] A clause to the same effect figures in two recent treaties concluded by Poland with West European States.[612] In all these cases the result is that each party's *lex patriae* at the time of celebration is authoritative when it is sought to annul a marriage for lack of capacity.

In a number of other East European treaties and enactments, however, a different approach is employed. The relevant *Czechoslovak* statute, for instance, subjects the nullity of marriage, whether on grounds of form or of substance, to the same conflicts regime as that concerning divorce.[613] Provisions assimilating the

609. EAST GERMANY: RAG § 20 par. 3; *FGB-Kommentar* 456-457; POLAND: Act of 12 Nov. 1965, art. 16; *Sośniak*, Problems 143. And see for RUMANIAN law *Popescu and Eliescu* 676. For a more complex, and not easily accessible, regulation see the BULGARIAN FC art. 93, elucidated by *Koschucharoff* 500-502.

610. See, in addition to the treaties cited *infra* n. 611: EAST GERMANY-RUMANIA, 15 July 1958, art. 25 par. 2; HUNGARY-RUMANIA, 7 Oct. 1958, art. 25 par. 2; CZECHOSLOVAKIA-RUMANIA, 25 Oct. 1958, art. 25 par. 2; CZECHOSLOVAKIA-POLAND, 4 July 1961, art. 15 par. 1; CZECHOSLOVAKIA-HUNGARY, 2 Nov. 1961, art. 21 par. 1; BULGARIA-POLAND, 4 Dec. 1961, art. 25 par. 1; POLAND-RUMANIA, 25 Jan. 1962, art. 25 par. 2; BULGARIA-HUNGARY, 16 May 1966, art. 21 par. 2; BULGARIA-MONGOLIA, 27 Nov. 1968, art. 21 par. 2. For comments expressing approval of this solution see: *Drobnig*, Kollisionsnormen 173; *Koschucharoff* 502-503; *Lübchen* 95-96; *Sośniak*, Conventions 32-33; *idem*, Problems 144.

611. Treaties concluded by EAST GERMANY with CZECHOSLOVAKIA on 11 Sept. 1956 (as amended by Protocol of 10 Dec. 1975) art. 27 E; and with POLAND on 1 Feb. 1957 (as amended by Protocol of 18 April 1975) art. 24 par. 1.

612. Treaties with AUSTRIA, of 11 Dec. 1963, art. 27; and with FRANCE, of 5 April 1967, art. 7. On the latter provision see *Bottini* 11; *Jodlowski and Ponsard* 566.

613. Act of 4 Dec. 1963, § 22 par. 3; see *Bystrický* 226 (critically); *Florio* 337; *Korkisch* 627-628. For a similar provision in ALBANIAN law see the Act of 21 Nov. 1964, art. 7 par. 4. This provision, however, unlike its CZECHOSLOVAK counterpart, expressly states that the relevant nationality for the purpose of determining the law applicable to the invalidation of a

continued on page 188

choice of law in nullity to that in divorce are also to be found in several treaties of legal assistance.[614] The conflicts rules for divorce, which are thus relied upon as a model, in their turn usually point to the national law of the spouses at the time of the proceedings (rather than at the time of celebration of the marriage) or, in default of a common nationality at the relevant date, to the *lex fori* alone.[615] The result is in all cases that the choice of law in nullity will be dissociated from the rules as to capacity applicable at the stage of the formation of the union.[616]

These solutions may be regarded as repercussions in the area of the conflict of laws of current tendencies in domestic law – which are by no means limited to Eastern Europe – to approach or to equate the effects of a nullity decree to those of divorce or even to

---

continued from page 187

marriage is that possessed by the parties at the time of celebration (whereas the time of the proceedings is decisive as regards divorce). Thereby the choice of law in nullity is at least partly brought into harmony with that prescribed (in art. 5 of the same Act) for capacity to marry at the stage of the formation of the union. Cf. *Korkisch* 628. The ALBANIAN type of rule is used in the treaty of legal assistance between ALBANIA and CZECHOSLOVAKIA, of 16 Jan. 1959, art. 22 par. 1.

614. EAST GERMANY-SOVIET UNION, 28 Nov. 1957, art. 23; ALBANIA-EAST GERMANY, 11 Jan. 1959, art. 24; ALBANIA-HUNGARY, 12 Jan. 1960, art. 29; CZECHOSLOVAKIA-YUGOSLAVIA, 20 Jan. 1964, art. 27; EAST GERMANY-YUGOSLAVIA, 20 May 1966, art. 36; EAST GERMANY-MONGOLIA, 30 April 1969, art. 33. See, critically, *Lübchen* 94; *Sośniak*, Conventions 33-35.

615. See *Petev* 606. A departure from this pattern is to be found in the treaties of legal assistance concluded by YUGOSLAVIA with CZECHOSLOVAKIA, art. 26, and with EAST GERMANY, art. 34-35. According to these provisions, too, the law of the common nationality of the spouses at the time of the proceedings is to be applied, but only if the proceedings are brought in the courts of the country of that nationality. In all other cases a marriage between nationals of the Contracting States can be dissolved by divorce – and, in consequence, by annulment – only on the grounds and under the conditions prescribed by the laws of both States (cumulative choice of law).

616. It should be noted here that some of the treaties of legal assistance which regulate choice of law in nullity are silent as to questions of capacity to marry; see, among the treaties cited *supra* n. 614, those concluded by EAST GERMANY with the SOVIET UNION and ALBANIA. Such gaps are filled out by having recourse to the respective national conflicts rules on the matter; cf. *Lübchen* 55, 85. Under those rules, as we have seen, capacity to marry is normally governed by each party's *lex patriae* at the time of celebration. While there are some exceptions (chiefly as regards the SOVIET UNION) to this pattern, the conflicts regime for capacity to marry is in all cases more or less different from that applicable to divorce.

merge the institution of nullity into that of divorce.[617] There are, however, some difficulties with this assimilation in the conflict of laws. At least theoretically, the result may be that a marriage must be annulled because it does not comply with the requirements as to capacity laid down by the law to be applied in nullity proceedings, although both parties were capable of intermarriage by the law or laws which governed the same question, pursuant to the forum's own conflicts rules, at the stage of the formation of the union. In other situations the principle may lead to the opposite result – which is much less objectionable – of rendering annulment more difficult than would normally be the case. The practical significance of these questions is probably rather limited in the countries of Eastern Europe, *inter alia* because of the similarity of their domestic laws and of the subordinate role they assign to nullity as compared with divorce. On principle, however, the solutions referred to here scarcely commend themselves as a model for regulating choice of law in nullity.

Certain variants of this type of solution are encountered in yet another group of East European treaties of legal assistance, which require a *cumulative* choice of law test to be met for annulment. The most common type of provison within this group of treaties is to the effect that a marriage, between nationals of one of the Contracting States and solemnised before the authorities of the other State, may only be annulled if a sufficient ground exists both by the *lex loci celebrationis* and by the law of the nationality of the spouses (at the time of the proceedings).[618] This is a rather

617. SWEDISH law may be cited as an example where this development has gone a long way. The SWEDISH rules concerning the annulment of marriage (for reasons other than want of form rendering the marriage non-existent) were abolished by an amendment of the Marriage Code made in 1973 (SFS 1973 no. 645), so that the only remaining remedy, even for initial defects vitiating the marriage, is divorce. In this connection the SWEDISH conflicts rules for annulment, which were formerly to be found in chapter 2 of the Act of 8 July 1904, were also abolished – perhaps somewhat precipitately – without being replaced by others (SFS 1973 no. 942).

618. For such provisions see the following treaties: EAST GERMANY-HUNGARY, 30 Oct. 1957, art. 29 par. 1; POLAND-SOVIET UNION, 28 Dec. 1957, art. 30; HUNGARY-POLAND, 6 March 1959, art. 33; POLAND-YUGOSLAVIA, 6 Feb. 1960, art. 27. Regardless of the place of celebration, however, the *lex fori* alone applies where the spouses are of different nationality (*i.e.*, where each of them possesses the nationality of one of the Contracting States). The position is different under the treaty between BULGARIA and EAST GERMANY, of 27 Jan. 1958, art. 25 par. 1, which – while not attaching relevance to the place of celebration – requires a ground for annul-

continued on page 190

curious combination of laws by which to decide whether a marriage is liable to annulment for lack of capacity. Indeed, while the former law is clearly appropriate in matters of formal validity and the latter is generally accepted as regards divorce, neither of them, nor the combination of the two laws, fits for determining capacity to marry under the system of the treaties concerned.[619] Technically, therefore, these provisions leave much to be desired.[620] Their policy objective is apparently to bar annulments as far as possible and, thereby, to favour the validation of marriages.

The same rationale clearly underlies various other provisions dealing with the present problem in different ways. The relevant *Yugoslav* statute, for instance, provides that if one of the spouses is a national of Yugoslavia, the marriage may be declared invalid only on the grounds sanctioned by the laws of that country, irrespective of the place and form in which it was contracted.[621] Another example of a validating role being assigned to the *lex fori* is supplied by *Finnish* law: a decree of nullity can only be granted in accordance with that law; but in addition a sufficient ground is, in certain cases, required to exist under the *lex patriae* of the parties (or of the petitioner) at the time of celebration of the marriage.[622]

---

continued from page 189

ment according to both *leges patriae.* Cf. *Drobnig,* Kollisionsnormen 173; *Koschucharoff* 503; *Lübchen* 94-95.

619. An exception is, possibly, the treaty between POLAND and the SOVIET UNION, of 28 Dec. 1957, under which capacity to marry apparently falls to the *lex loci celebrationis;* cf. *supra* n. 257. If this is the correct interpretation, the additional requirement of a ground for annulment under the *lex patriae* may be explained as an expression of the policy favouring validation.

620. Certain other treaties are better inspired in that they confine the cumulative application of the *lex loci celebrationis* and the *lex patriae* to matters of formal validity and refer questions of annulment on other grounds to the law governing capacity to marry; see *Pålsson,* Marriage, s. 403 at n. 528. Cf. the critical comments on the drafting technique put forward by *Sośniak,* Conventions 29-30, 33-35.

621. BMA art. 76. See *Blagojević* 118, 120; *Katičić* 433-434; *Tchirkovitch* 233.

622. See the Act of 5 Dec. 1929 (as amended) § 9 and § 10 par. 1; cf. § 1 and § 2 par. 1 of the same Act, referring capacity to marry to the *lex patriae* of each of the parties at the time of celebration.

bd. *Public Policy*

72. *General.* The doctrine of public policy plays a prominent part in the present context. This doctrine operates in two directions. On the one hand, an incapacity to marry imposed by the relevant foreign law will be ignored if to give effect to it would violate the public policy of the forum, so that a marriage may be allowed to be celebrated or held valid in the teeth of the foreign law (*permissive* or *validating* public policy). On the other hand, although a person has capacity to marry under the governing foreign law, the proposed union will not be allowed to be celebrated or, if this has already been done, will be declared invalid if it fails to satisfy certain requirements of the *lex fori* regarded as part of the public policy of that law (*prohibitive* or *invalidating* public policy).

The extent and the grounds of such interference with the normal operation of foreign law vary, of course, from country to country and from time to time. These questions must be examined separately for each particular issue. Generally speaking, however, much depends on the intensity and number of the contacts of the relation with, respectively, the forum and the foreign country in each case.[623] Public policy will more readily be invoked to exclude the application of foreign law when the marriage is celebrated locally than when it has been entered into abroad, and more readily when one of the parties is a national or domiciliary of the forum country than when neither of them has any such connection. Another general distinction is that between a marriage to be celebrated (in the country of the forum) and the validity of a union which has already been created (whether in the forum or in a foreign country); a marriage may be upheld in the latter case although, in the eyes of the forum, its solemnisation should never have been permitted.

73. *Permissive (Validating) Public Policy.* Generally speaking, the prevailing attitude in countries attached to the principle of the personal law in capacity to marry is that effect must be given to the requirements of the relevant foreign law when they are more stringent than those of the *lex fori.* This holds true, for instance,

623. See *Rabel* 305-306; *Rigaux,* DIP I 361-362; and, e.g., ENGLAND: *Dicey and Morris* 71-72; *Kahn-Freund,* Reflections 57-59; *M. Mann* 144-146; FRANCE: *Bischoff* no. 69-72; WEST GERMANY: *Gamillscheg,* Kommentar, art. 13 no. 143-147; *Neuhaus,* Grundbegriffe 367; *Raape and Sturm* 215-218; NORWAY: *Gaarder* 40, 134; SWITZERLAND: *Beck,* before art. 59 no. 81-88, art. 7 c no. 56-59, art. 7 f no. 61-62, 153; *Vischer,* IPR 586.

as concerns higher age limits for marriage or wider degrees of prohibited consanguinity or affinity.[624]

By way of exception, public policy is sometimes relied upon to repudiate a foreign disability or incapacity which is regarded as deeply offensive to the forum's ideas of justice and morality. In particular, such recourse to permissive or validating public policy may come into consideration where the foreign prohibition is *of a type completely unknown to the lex fori* and where the difference between the two laws can therefore be characterised as one of kind rather than of degree. Thus, for example, impediments based on race or religious affiliation will usually be denied effect in countries to whose law they are alien.[625]

Often however, it is impossible to state in terms of hard-and-fast rules that certain prohibitions, or types of prohibition, will be disregarded as contrary to public policy in a particular country. Nor can "the limits of tolerance", beyond which the forum will refuse to give effect to foreign disabilities or incapacities, be defined solely by reference to the degree of odium evoked by them in the abstract. Because of the relativity of the notion of public policy, the case will often be that a particular foreign impediment against marriage is recognised for some, but not for all, purposes or that it is applied in certain circumstances, but not in others.

Only in some very few cases will a prohibition of marriage, imposed by the governing foreign law, be overridden by public policy merely for the reason that it is regarded as invidious by the forum. As a rule, such interference of public policy presupposes, in addition, that at least one of the parties has, or that they both intend to establish, a substantial connection (usually by domicile, habitual residence or nationality, as the case may be) with the country of the forum, providing that country with an interest to defend in the case. Typically, the stronger this connection is, the more inclined will the forum become to resort to the doctrine of public policy to reject the foreign law.

Furthermore, this weapon is more likely to be used in order to protect an existing marriage, which has been entered into in contravention of the relevant foreign law, than to permit the celebration of a marriage contrary to that law. In the latter situation the

624. See *infra* at n. 1056 and 1097, respectively.

625. See *infra* s. 107-9 (religious impediments) and 110 (racial impediments).

forum, by refusing to give effect to the foreign incapacity, would be deliberately creating a limping marriage. Such a course will normally not be adopted unless there are compelling reasons to do so. The position is in some degree different when the marriage has already been celebrated, whether locally or in a foreign country, perhaps by virtue of the public policy of that (third) country. Here, inevitably, there comes into consideration the fact that it is undesirable to disturb a settled relationship. This explains why the courts will more readily be induced to rely on public policy as a means of validation. The closer the ties are with the country of the forum, the less weight is likely to be given to the question of the repulsiveness of the particular incapacity which would invalidate the marriage under the foreign law involved. Some of the rules referred to in the preceding sections, which exclude the application of the foreign law of the domicile or nationality of the parties or one of them, in certain circumstances, when the marriage is invalid by that law but valid by the *lex fori*, may be explained as "crystallised" expressions of validating public policy.[626]

The scales are turned the other way if a nullity decree, based on the defect vitiating the marriage under the relevant foreign law, has been pronounced by a foreign court. Such a decree creates a new legal situation, on which the parties are reasonably entitled to rely and which cannot be ignored by the forum. Even if the incapacity which led to the annulment would have been repudiated as repugnant to public policy, had the courts of the country invited to recognise the decree themselves been asked to invalidate the marriage, the circumstances will therefore have to be quite extreme before a foreign decree – given on the strength of the appropriate law pursuant to the conflicts rules of the forum – is refused recognition on this ground.[627]

74. *Prohibitive (Invalidating) Public Policy.* The local prohibitions against marriage are usually accorded a broad sphere of operation, by virtue of public policy, when the celebration takes place *in the country of the forum.* The role assigned to the *lex fori*

626. An example is the ENGLISH rule in Sottomayor v. De Barros (No. 2) (1879), 5 P.D. 94. See *supra* s. 70, especially n. 603.

627. Such an exceptional – and objectionable – decision has been rendered by an ITALIAN court. See App. Firenze 17 April 1953, Foro pad. 1954 I 69 with a critical note by Biscottini. Here the court refused to recognise a foreign decree annulling a marriage between a man of Israeli and a woman of Italian nationality on the ground, supplied by ISRAELI law, of difference of religion.

in such cases often tends to overshadow that of the personal law. It has indeed not been unusual to require foreign parties desiring to marry locally to comply with all, or substantially all, conditions of the local law (in addition to those of their personal law). This appears still to be the prevailing practice, for instance, in *France* and *Spain*.[628] A similar view has been voiced in *England*.[629] The same tendency can be observed in those Latin American countries in which capacity to marry is, in principle, governed by the personal law. One example is the *Bustamante Code* which, besides requiring foreigners to show that they have capacity to marry under their personal law, declares that the local legislation of the country of celebration is applicable to such parties in respect of the impediments established as "indispensable" by that legislation.[630] A comparable rule exists in *Brazilian* law which, although referring capacity to marry to the law of the domicile, prescribes that the *lex fori* must be applied with regard to "disqualifying disabilities" (a concept which is left undefined) when the marriage is celebrated in Brazil.[631] The *Venezuelan* Civil Code similarly provides that no marriage of foreigners may take place in Venezuela in violation of any of the mandatory impediments (*impedimentos dirimentes*) established by that Code, even though there may be no obstacle to the marriage under the personal law (which is here the *lex patriae*) of either party.[632]

Such far-reaching recourse to public policy has been properly criticised as excessive.[633] Some attempts have been made to restrict the scope of permissible interventions under this heading. The chief means used to this end has been to enumerate those prohibitions of the local law which have to be observed by foreign parties. This method was adopted as early as 1902, by the *Hague Convention* on Marriage which contains a specific list of prohibitions that entitle a Contracting State to prevent the celebration of a

628. For FRANCE see *Batiffol and Lagarde* II 37-40; *Bischoff* no. 61-66 (but cf. for a more liberal view, *Audit* 299-300); for SPAIN, *Portero Sánchez* 515 and (as regards Catholic marriages) the references *supra* n. 552. On the other hand, there is in both countries a tendency to disregard foreign prohibitions which are more far-reaching than those of the *lex fori* and thus to substitute that law in its entirety for the personal law; see *supra* at n. 535-538 and 552, respectively.

629. *Supra* s. 68, cf. s. 66 at n. 543-545. See also Act. Doc. La Haye 13 (1976) III 152-153, 162-163.

630. Art. 38, cf. art. 36-37.

631. Act of 4 Sept. 1942, art. 7 par. 1; see *Garland* 23-24, 42.

632. CC art. 104; see *Lombard* 41.

633. See *Rabel* 300-301.

marriage before its authorities, or to invalidate such a marriage if already performed, on grounds of its local policy.[634] This list is relatively limited and intended to be exhaustive. The check thus imposed on the operation of public policy was perhaps the most remarkable achievement of the convention.

The enumerative method has been followed in national codes and statutes in a number of *Continental European* and *Scandinavian* countries.[635] Another recent instance is the *Australian* Marriage Act of 1961, which provides for the application of certain requirements laid down by that Act to all marriages celebrated before an Australian authority.[636] In some cases the list of local impediments to be so applied is fairly comprehensive. The value of the provisions in question is further reduced by the fact that they are not always considered to preclude resort to prohibitive public policy in cases not included in the respective enumerations.[637]

In the absence of such statutory rules, the general tendency is for this mechanism to be more readily put into use when one of

634. Art. 2. See on this provision: Act. La Haye I/1 (1893) 46-47, II (1894) 48 and III (1900) 170-173; *Beck*, ESchlKonv. art. 2 no. 1-24; *Buzzati* 171-226, 248-259; *Gamillscheg*, Kommentar, art. 13 no. 947-955; *F. Kahn* 85-112; *A. Miele* 103-118; *Rabel* 297-298; *Travers* I 265-370.

635. BULGARIA: FC art. 91 par. 2-3 in conjunction with art. 9-10; see *Jessel* 152; *Koschucharoff* 497-498; *Szászy* 346-347; FINLAND: Act of 5 Dec. 1929 (as amended) § 2 par. 2; HUNGARY: Decree-Law no. 23/1952, § 16 par. 2 in conjunction with Act no. IV/1952, § 7-8; see *Réczei* 355; ITALY: CC art. 116 par. 2 in conjunction with art. 85-89; see *A. Miele* 118-141; *Vitta* II 191-194; SWEDEN: Act of 8 July 1904 (as amended) ch. 1 § 3; see NJA 1973 II 579-580; YUGOSLAVIA: BMA art. 73 par. 2; see *Blagojević* 116-117; *Katičić* 422-423; *Tchirkovitch* 223-224. Similarly, the treaties of legal assistance concluded by YUGOSLAVIA with other countries provide that certain impediments of the *lex loci celebrationis* shall or may be taken into account, in addition to those of the respective *lex patriae;* see treaties with POLAND, of 6 Feb. 1960, art. 25 par. 2; with CZECHOSLOVAKIA, of 20 Jan. 1964, art. 23 par. 2; with EAST GERMANY, of 20 May 1966, art. 31 par. 2; and with FRANCE, of 18 May 1971, art. 3 par. 2. This is a peculiarity of the YUGOSLAV treaties, which does not recur in any of the other treaties of legal assistance concluded by EAST EUROPEAN States. Most of these provide for the application of the *lex patriae* alone, thus excluding any scope for the *lex loci celebrationis* under the head of public policy or otherwise; see the references *supra* n. 288-289.

636. S. 10 (1), 22 (1); see *Nygh* 410; *Sykes*, Conflict 92-93. But cf. for CANADA and NEW ZEALAND the references given *supra* n. 562.

637. See for BULGARIA: *Jessel* 156-157; for ITALY: *Monaco* 161; *Morelli* 101-102; *Vitta* II 194. On the other hand, a very restrictive concept of prohibitive public policy sometimes prevails even without such statutory limitations. See, for example, for WEST GERMANY: *Gamillscheg*, Kommentar, art. 13 no. 143; *Stöcker*, Ordre public 105-106.

the parties holds the nationality of and/or is domiciled in the country of the forum than when no such local relation exists. On the other hand, cases in which a marriage impediment forming part of the *lex fori* was applied in regard to a party whose capacity was governed by foreign law may often be explained alternatively as expressions of public policy or on the footing that the other party was subject to the *lex fori* as his personal law and that the impediment in question, according to that law, was to be treated as bilateral (*supra* s. 49-52). No clear distinction can be drawn between these two doctrines.

Another general tendency is for public policy to interfere to forbid the solemnisation of a marriage contrary to the local law rather than to invalidate it afterwards. Such a distinction is drawn by the Hague Convention of 1902, followed by some of the national provisions mentioned above.[638] According to these provisions the celebration of a marriage may in specified cases be prevented on grounds of public policy, but those grounds may not be invoked to annul the marriage once it has come into existence even though it was entered into in the country of the forum in violation of the law of that country.[639]

This distinction, which may be regarded as another expression of the favour of validation, is of greater significance for *marriages celebrated abroad.* The courts of most countries are slow to defeat such marriages, where valid by the relevant foreign law or laws, even if reasons of public policy (or the bilateral character of a marriage impediment contained in the *lex fori*) would have been adduced to prevent local celebration of the union. This is particularly true where the parties lacked any connection with the

638. See art. 2 par. 2 of the HAGUE CONVENTION. Cf. the FINNISH and SWEDISH provisions cited *supra* n. 635, both of which are confined to the stage of celebration.

639. Under the rule of the HAGUE CONVENTION this is so in the case of the prohibitions listed in art. 2 par. 1 (absolutely prohibited degrees of relationship between the parties; absolute prohibition to marry declared against parties guilty of adultery, for which the prior marriage of one of them has been dissolved; and absolute prohibition to intermarry declared against persons condemned for having attempted to murder the husband or wife in a prior marriage of one of the parties). A different rule is laid down, however, for certain impediments specified in art. 2 par. 3 (cases in which the proposed marriage would contravene the *lex loci celebrationis* "by reason of a prior marriage, or an obstacle of a religious character"). Impediments within this category may be invoked to annul the marriage in the country of celebration, though not in any other country party to the convention. For comments on these rules see the references *supra* n. 634.

country of the forum at the time of the marriage. None of the provisions referred to above which specify the exigencies of public policy apply to foreign marriages. A remarkable deviation from usually accepted principles is, however, to be found in the *Bustamente Code,* which entitles all Contracting States (thus including countries other than that of celebration) to refuse recognition to a marriage, celebrated in any of those States, which conflicts with the provisions of the *lex fori* relative to a wide number of enumerated prohibitions and to "any other inexcusable grounds of annulment".[640] This is certainly to give too wide a scope for the demands of public policy.

D. Specific Problems

a. *Impediments Deriving from Prior Marriage*

75. *Survey of Problems.* Most conflict of laws problems of capacity to marry concern impediments which, in one way or another, have to do with a prior marriage between one of the parties and a third person. In part the problems of this type presented in countries espousing the principle of the personal law are similar to, but in part they differ from, those already considered in relation to American law (*supra* s. 19-27).

As between monogamous countries, there will rarely be any problem if the prior marriage is admittedly valid and subsisting at the time of the proposed celebration of the second. In this situation, of course, the second marriage is barred. If it is contracted nevertheless, it will normally be either void or voidable, by whichever of the laws involved the question is decided.[641]

640. Art. 40.

641. Cf. the ENGLISH case of White v. White, [1937] P. 111, where it was said (at 125) that "there cannot be any conflict of laws between different jurisdictions, because it is clear that the ceremony was bigamous, and therefore by the law of every Christian community there never was any matrimonial status common to the petitioner and the respondent." As a general statement, however, this is somewhat exaggerated. Considerable differences, which can give rise to conflict of laws problems, exist over the question whether a bigamous marriage is void or merely voidable, as well as over various details concerning the conditions and the effects of a decree of nullity. See, e.g., *Dölle,* Familienrecht 271-272, 285-288; *Gamillscheg,* Kommentar, art. 13 no. 475-536. The case may even be that a bigamous marriage is fully valid, though liable to dissolution by divorce. This is now the position of SWEDISH law; see the Marriage Code of 1920, as amended in 1973, ch. 11 § 5 par. 1 in conjunction with ch. 2 § 4.

Where, on the other hand, a legal system prescribing monogamy is confronted with one permitting polygamy, certain difficulties are bound to occur. Some of these, arising in monogamous countries, have already been dealt with by the author (see *Pålsson*, Marriage, Chapter 5). As shown there, the view once voiced, particularly in England, that polygamous marriages fall outside the notion of "Christian marriage", and therefore must be disregarded altogether, can no longer be maintained. This, however, leaves open the question of what law determines capacity to enter into such unions and of the attitude to foreign laws which affirm a person's capacity to do so. Conversely, various problems concerning the approach to foreign laws which insist on monogamy may present themselves in countries where polygamy is treated as lawful. In our discussion, however, the perspective will in the main be confined to countries where monogamy is the rule (*aa*).

As between monogamous countries, the most frequent source of conflicts problems is the fact that the validity or the subsistence of a prior union is in doubt, especially where it has been terminated by a divorce whose international recognition is questioned. In these cases the point at issue is whether the intending spouse in fact has or, if the remarriage has already taken place, whether he then had the status of a single person. The method by which such questions are to be settled is a very controversial subject, at all events in cases where foreign law governs the party's capacity to marry. The chief problem raised in such cases is whether the existence of the prior marriage is to be judged by the system of the conflict of laws of the *lex fori* or by that of the relevant foreign law. This is an instance, in practice probably the most important of all, of the general problem known as the incidental question, which plays a prominent part in the modern conflict of laws of many countries (*ab*).

Another situation which must be adverted to is where the prior marriage admittedly existed at the time of the remarriage but where it has subsequently been dissolved and where, under the relevant personal law, this dissolution operates to cure the defect of bigamy initially vitiating the second union, so that it will henceforth be immune from attack.[642] The application of

642. A special aspect of this is where the prior union is ended by a divorce purporting to have *retroactive* effect, or is invalidated with such effect, under the relevant foreign law, with the result that an intervening second marriage is validated. Situations of this type have been adverted to *supra* s. 57 and will not be further considered here.

such laws may be problematic in countries whose domestic law does not know this method of validation (*ac*).

Finally, there are in many countries various restrictions on the right to marry again even after the prior marriage has been properly dissolved, especially where it was ended by divorce. The treatment of such restrictions gives rise to not a few problems in the conflict of laws (*ad*).

aa. *Approach towards Polygamy*

76. *Introductory*. Before embarking on this subject, it must be recalled that the very notion of polygamy varies: while in most countries it is limited to actually polygamous marriages, the *English* concept (which prevails throughout the British Commonwealth) is much wider, a marriage being regarded as polygamous whenever it is *potentially* so, *i.e.* (in the case of polygyny) when the husband is by the relevant law entitled to take a plurality of wives, irrespective of whether he has in fact married more than once. By the weight of opinion in England and other parts of the Commonwealth, the law to determine the monogamous or polygamous nature of a marriage is that governing the form of the ceremony, normally the *lex loci celebrationis*, although a union which is potentially polygamous by that law as it stood at the time of celebration may subsequently be converted into a monogamous one in various ways.

Generally speaking, the modern tendency in monogamous countries is in favour of approaching, or even of equating, the legal consequences of a polygamous marriage (as defined by the *lex fori*) to those of a monogamous union (see *Pålsson*, Marriage, s. 256-263). These questions will not be further dwelt on here, except to say that this tendency is confirmed by recent statutory and judicial developments in certain countries.[643]

643. The most important of these is the enactment in the UNITED KINGDOM of the Matrimonial Proceedings (Polygamous Marriages) Act 1972. The effect of this statute is that courts in England (s. 1), Scotland (s. 2) and Northern Ireland (s. 3) are no longer precluded from granting matrimonial relief or making a declaration concerning the validity of a marriage "by reason only that the marriage in question was entered into under a law which permits polygamy", whether or not the union is actually polygamous. The provision applicable in ENGLISH courts (s. 1) has since been re-enacted by s. 47 of the Matrimonial Causes Act 1973. See *Cheshire and North* 359-361; *Dicey and Morris* 300-303; *Graveson*, Conflict 244, 280-281; *North* 108-110. As regards ENGLAND and SCOTLAND, provisions relating to the treatment of poly-

continued on page 200

The recognition extended to polygamous marriages presupposes, of course, that the union is valid as to form and that the parties had the capacity to enter into it according to the legal systems appropriate for the respective issues. What law determines capacity to contract such a marriage? In general, the answer to this question is quite simple: the law otherwise controlling capacity to marry, which as a rule is the personal law of each of the parties at the time of celebration. A different answer seems to have been given only by a rather discredited *English* decision holding that the particular issue of the lawfulness of polygamy, as distinct from other aspects of capacity to marry, is a matter for the law of the country of the intended matrimonial home.[644]

The application of foreign laws permitting the celebration or sanctioning the validity of a polygamous marriage, however, often meets with considerable difficulties in a monogamous country, *inter alia* because it may offend against the local public policy. In our discussion of these questions a distinction will be drawn between situations in which the marriage is monogamous in fact, that is to say, where the husband has not exercised, and does not attempt to exercise, his right to take more than one wife, on the one hand (*infra* s. 77), and situations involving actually polygamous marriages, on the other (*infra* s. 78).

77. *Marriages Monogamous in Fact.* This situation usually does not give rise to problems. It seems never to have been suggested that a foreigner, who is an unmarried man, should be precluded from contracting a valid marriage in a monogamous country solely because the law governing his capacity to marry recognises polygamy. In general, his right to do so will not be questioned even if the intended female partner is a national and/or domiciliary of the country of the forum, or of some other country where monogamy

---

continued from page 199

gamous marriages for the purpose of social security benefits are now contained in the Social Security and Family Allowances (Polygamous Marriages) Regulations 1975, which were made under the Social Security Act 1975, s. 162 (*b*), and the Family Allowances Act 1965, s. 12 (2) as substituted by the Social Security (Consequential Provisions) Act 1975, Sched. 2 para. 16. For some interesting new developments in WEST GERMAN case law concerning the recognition of actually polygamous marriages see *infra* n. 660.

644. Radwan v. Radwan (No. 2), [1973] Fam. 35. See *supra* at n. 412-415.

is the rule.[645] It is no doubt true that this type of mixed marriage may expose the woman to "special risks", particularly if the spouses afterwards settle in the husband's home country, where her position as a wife is likely to be inferior, in fact as well as in law, to the standards prevailing in her native country, where the husband may avail himself of his right to take additional wives and where he usually also has the right to terminate the marriage by a unilateral act of repudiation.[646] These considerations may well justify certain precautions being required to be taken, with the cooperation of the local authorities, before the parties are allowed to celebrate their marriage. The aim of these measures, if judged necessary, should be to ensure that the female party is properly informed as to her future status under the foreign law concerned and advised as to the appropriateness of regulating certain personal and proprietary rights of the spouses by an ante-nuptial agreement, etc. The *West German* Service Instruction for civil registrars directs those officials to draw the attention of the parties to such questions before solemnising a marriage between a woman of German nationality and a foreigner whose national law is founded on polygamy.[647]

Occasionally, however, the local celebration of such mixed marriages is made subject to special restrictions, which seem excessively officious and contrary to the principle of freedom of marriage as conceived in Western countries. An illustration is afforded by the administrative instruction and directives issued for the local marriage authorities in *Bulgaria*.[648] As a rule, these provisions forbid outright the intermarriage of a Bulgarian woman and a national of a State where polygamy is treated as lawful. Only exceptionally are such marriages declared to be permissible,

645. The question has been touched upon and expressly affirmed by WEST GERMAN writers. See *Gamillscheg,* Doppelehe 62; *idem,* Kommentar, before art. 13 no. 340, art. 13 no. 240-241; *Kegel,* Kommentar, art. 13 no. 111. In other countries little or no doubt has been entertained on this point. See, for instance, for ENGLISH cases involving local marriages between a domiciled Englishwoman and a foreign domiciled polygamist who was not previously married: Chetti v. Chetti, [1909] P. 67; R. v. Hammersmith Marriage Registrar, [1917] 1 K.B. 634 (C.A.); R. v. Naguib, [1917] 1 K.B. 359 (C.C.A.); Maher v. Maher, [1951] P. 342; Russ v. Russ, [1964] P. 315 (C.A.). Similarly for SCOTLAND: Lendrum v. Chakravarti, 1929 S.L.T. 96; MacDougall v. Chitnavis, 1937 S.C. 390.

646. See, for example, *Gamillscheg,* Doppelehe 62-63; and expert opinion in IPG 1965/66 no. 15 (Munich).

647. Service Instruction of 1968, § 178.

648. See *Jessel* 151, 156-157.

namely, if the relevant foreign law places special limits on the husband's right to take a fresh partner, for example by requiring the consent of the first wife, or if it is otherwise to be expected, in the light of the circumstances in the particular case, that the husband will not use his right to enter into further marriages.

As regards marriages *celebrated abroad,* it seems to be common ground that their recognition by a monogamous forum will not be affected by the fact that the law governing the capacity of the parties, or of one of them, countenances polygamy, as long as the union remains monogamous in fact.[649] It is generally also immaterial whether the place of celebration was in a monogamous or in a polygamous country.

In this last respect, however, the position of *English* law, and of other laws following the English notion of polygamy, is peculiar. This is so because a foreign marriage which is potentially polygamous by the *lex loci celebrationis* is characterised as polygamous in nature. It follows that a person whose capacity to marry is governed by English law, or presumably by any other law enjoining monogamy, cannot marry validly in the local form of a country where polygamy is legally accepted.[650] This bar exists even if it is

649. Such recognition has been tacitly afforded, as a matter of course, by ENGLISH and other COMMONWEALTH courts in numerous cases involving a marriage which, at the time of celebration, was potentially polygamous under the *lex loci celebrationis* (whether or not its nature had subsequently been changed) and valid by the personal law of both parties. Several examples are cited by *Pålsson,* Marriage, s. 253 and 258. In other countries such marriages will also be recognised without difficulty, even if the personal law of one of the parties prescribes monogamy. See, for instance, for WEST GERMANY: OLG Celle 18 Oct. 1957, IPRspr. 1956/57 no. 98 (cf. LG Hamburg 16 Oct. 1958, IPRspr. 1958/59 no. 117); *Gamillscheg,* Kommentar, art. 13 no. 242.

650. For authorities supporting this conclusion see *Pålsson,* Marriage, s. 252 n. 34. The provision of the Nullity of Marriage Act 1971 dealing with this question has since been re-enacted for ENGLAND by the Matrimonial Causes Act 1973, s. 11 (*d*). See now also *Cheshire and North* 353-355; *Dicey and Morris* 287-290, 303 (Illustration 8). But some authorities, particularly in CANADA, are incompatible with the prevailing ENGLISH view (*Pålsson, ibid.*). Note also the ENGLISH case of Radwan v. Radwan (No. 2), [1973] Fam. 35, holding that capacity for polygamy depends (at common law) on the law of the intended matrimonial residence and suggesting (at 52) that this rule still prevails, notwithstanding the above statutory provision. If, contrary to the weight of extrajudicial opinion, this view should be accepted, it means that a person of English domicile has capacity to enter into a polygamous marriage if the parties intend to (and do?) live together in a country where polygamy is lawful. See *supra* n. 413, 415.

the husband's first marriage and even if no other form of ceremony was available to the parties in the foreign country concerned.

> Suppose, for instance, that a Pakistani immigrant to England acquires an English domicile.[651] He then returns home to marry in Moslem form and brings his wife back to England with him. Although this is his only marriage, it is polygamous in the eyes of English law, since it is potentially so by Pakistani law. His capacity to contract such a marriage is determinable by English law, either because his premarital domicile was English or because England was the country of the intended matrimonial home.[652] English law, of course, does not recognise capacity for polygamy, with the result that the marriage must be treated as void in England.

This consequence of the concept of potential polygamy seems highly unsatisfactory and undesirable. No such problems are encountered in countries where the notion of polygamy is confined to actually polygamous unions.

78. *Actually Polygamous Marriages.* Where one of the parties is already bound by a prior marriage, the application of foreign laws permitting polygamy is made subject to much heavier restrictions. It is almost universally agreed in monogamous countries that a second marriage, while the former subsists, cannot be validly *celebrated locally*.[653]

651. This example has been used by writers to illustrate the unfortunate consequences of the current ENGLISH rule and the need for a reform. See *Hartley*, The Law Commission—Report on Polygamous Marriages: 34 M.L.R. 305, 306-307 (1971); *Poulter, Hyde* v. *Hyde* — A Reappraisal: 25 I.C.L.Q. 475, 504-507 (1976). Cf. *Cheshire and North* 353.

652. Cf. *supra* n. 412-415, 650.

653. See generally *Mercier* 91-93 (with some qualifications); *Rabel* 223. Conversely, the enforcement of foreign laws enjoining monogamy, in respect of foreigners subject to such a law, may be problematic in polygamous countries. An EGYPTIAN case furnishes an illustration: An Englishman, previously converted to the Moslem faith, had married a woman of Greek nationality, although (without her knowledge) he was already married to W(1). W(2) brought a petition for annulment of her marriage on this ground. Although by the relevant EGYPTIAN conflicts rule (CC art. 12) the capacity of the parties was to be referred to their respective *leges patriae,* the courts refused to grant a decree on grounds that to do so solely because the marriage was polygamous would contravene the fundamental principle of EGYPTIAN law (or rather of Moslem law, with which EGYPTIAN public policy was identified) permitting a Moslem to have more than one wife at the same time and that foreign laws conflicting with this principle must be set aside: Court

continued on page 204

As regards *England* and other countries accepting the English test for distinguishing between monogamous and polygamous marriages, the monogamous nature ascribed to marriages according to the forms of English law seems sufficient to exclude the solemnisation of an actually polygamous union.[654] It is immaterial for this purpose whether the prior marriage was celebrated by a monogamous or by a polygamous ceremony; for although in the latter case it will be regarded as polygamous in nature, such a marriage is recognised as a bar to a subsequent monogamous marriage.[655]

In other monogamous countries the doctrine of public policy is the chief means relied upon to reject foreign laws which would permit the celebration of an actually polygamous marriage. In those countries which have a "specialised public policy clause" enumerating certain impediments of the *lex fori* which must be observed, in addition to those of the foreign law normally governing capacity to marry, the existence of a prior marriage invariably figures among the impediments so specified.[656] Even in the absence of such statutory provisions, the same position is generally taken by courts[657] and writers.[658]

---

continued from page 203

of Cairo 16 Dec. 1952 and Court of Appeals of Cairo 16 May 1956, Clunet 1960, 840, critically reported by *Linant de Bellefonds;* in a critical vein see also *Elgeddawy* 156-158, 161-162, 167-171, 182-186, 189, 194-195. As pointed out by these commentators, the solution adopted by the EGYPTIAN courts is open to serious doubts, not least in view of the attitude of Moslem law towards polygamy, which is one of toleration rather than encouragement.

654. See Padolecchia v. Padolecchia, [1968] P. 314, 335-336; cf. *infra* n. 664.

655. *Pålsson,* Marriage, s. 258 at n. 52. See also Hashmi v. Hashmi, [1972] Fam. 36 (second marriage in England void, though only for the purposes of ENGLISH law and therefore not preventing the recognition of the children of that union as legitimate in accordance with the relevant foreign law, by which the union was a valid polygamous marriage).

656. References *supra* n. 631-632, 635-636, 640.

657. FRANCE: Trib. corr. Brest 18 Oct. 1949, S. 1950.2.74; Cour Paris 2 Feb. 1956, J.C.P. 1956.II.9229; Cass. civ. 15 Oct. 1958, Clunet 1959, 466, J.C.P. 1958.IV.161; Trib. Seine 21 June 1967, Rev. crit. d.i.p. 1968, 294, note Batiffol; Trib. Paris 22 Jan. 1968, Clunet 1969, 406, note Ph. Kahn; Cour Lyon 21 May 1974, D.S. 1975. Jur. 9, note Guiho; Cour Reims 19 Jan. 1976, Clunet 1976, 916, note Fadlallah; WEST GERMANY: President of OLG Hamburg 25 April 1968, IPRspr. 1968/69 no. 65.

658. E.g., AUSTRIA: *Klang and Gschnitzer* 244; *Mänhardt* 28 n. 34; BELGIUM: *Graulich* 156; *Rigaux,* DIP I 360; *van Hecke,* Le mariage polygamique devant les tribunaux belges: Rev. crit. belge 1971, 7, 10-11; FRANCE: *Batiffol and Lagarde* II 38; *Bischoff* no. 63; *Elgeddawy* 143, 239-241; *Mercier*

As an alternative to public policy, the doctrine of the bilateral character of the impediment of a prior marriage (*supra* s. 49) is sometimes invoked to prevent an actually polygamous union.[659] In contrast with public policy, this doctrine can only be used against mixed marriages, between a woman whose capacity is governed by the *lex fori*, or by any other law which insists on monogamy, and an already married man; but in this case the doctrine, if accepted, operates to bar the marriage, notwithstanding that it would be permissible by the man's personal law recognising polygamy.

There remain for consideration actually polygamous marriages which have been *performed abroad*. Such unions, where valid by the respective foreign laws applicable to the form of the ceremony and the capacity of the parties, will normally be recognised in monogamous countries, at least for certain purposes.[660] *Inter alia*,

---

32; WEST GERMANY: *Gamillscheg*, Kommentar, before art. 13 no. 340, art. 13 no. 243-244; *Hoffmann and Stephan* § 5 no. 31; *Kegel*, Kommentar, art. 13 no. 111; *Raape and Sturm* 216, 217-218 (but see for a different view: *Stöcker*, Ordre public 106; *Wiethölter*, Zur Frage des internationalen ordre public: BerGesVR 7 (1967) 133, 139, 149); GREECE: *Bendermacher-Geroussis* 3-4; SOCIALIST COUNTRIES of EASTERN EUROPE: *Szászy* 345; SWITZERLAND: *Beck*, art. 7 c no. 50-51; *Götz*, art. 101 no. 12; *Mercier* 77; *Schnitzer* 340, 344-345; *Vischer*, IPR 586.

659. References *supra* n. 353-354.

660. *Pålsson*, Marriage, s. 258 and 263. *Adde*, BELGIUM: Civ. Liège 26 June 1975, Jur. Liège 1975/76, 163; *Rigaux*, DIP I 360-361; *van Hecke and Rigaux* (1970 à 1975) 228-230; WEST GERMANY: *Gamillscheg*, Kommentar, before art. 13 no. 340, art. 14 no. 166, 240; SWITZERLAND: *Lalive*, case note: Schw. Jb. Int. R. 28 (1972) 390-391. The tendency referred to here has now also found expression in some decisions of WEST GERMAN courts. In one case a Jordanian national, while living in West Germany with W(1), married W(2) abroad, validly under the relevant foreign law, and brought her to West Germany; it was held that W(2) was entitled to reside in that country as the man's lawful spouse, that the voluntary cohabitation between the man and his two wives was compatible with the local public policy and that both wives qualified for social security benefits under the applicable WEST GERMAN legislation: VerwG Gelsenkirchen 18 July 1974, IPRspr. 1974 no. 5. Approvingly noted by *Cullmann*, Anerkennung polygamer Ehen in der Bundesrepublik Deutschland: FamRZ 1976, 313-315; and by *Jayme:* FamRZ 1975, 340. Another case involved a polygamous marriage by an Indonesian national, validly celebrated at the Indonesian embassy in West Germany; this marriage was held to be in the same category as one entered into in a foreign country and treated as valid so as to make the issue of the union legitimate: LG Frankfurt 12 Jan. 1976, IPRspr. 1976 no. 53. A strikingly more restrictive attitude has, however, been adopted in two recent FRENCH cases involving polygamous marriages validly entered into abroad.

continued on page 206

the parties are debarred from contracting a fresh marriage with a third person in a monogamous country. If, for instance, a polygamist's lawful second wife comes to a European country, she cannot remarry there without first securing a divorce from the polygamist.[661] Nor can she obtain a decree of nullity on the ground that the marriage is bigamous, since – *ex hypothesi* – the union is lawful; though there may conceivably be situations in which such annulment is compelled by the public policy of the forum.[662]

The position is different if, at the time of the marriage, the second wife was a national or a domiciliary, as the case may be, of a monogamy-insisting country, so that her capacity to marry was in the eyes of the forum subject to the law of that country. In this type of situation the second union will probably fail to be recognised by a monogamous forum, either on grounds of public policy or because the husband's prior marriage is considered a bilateral impediment precluding the woman from marrying him.

---

continued from page 205

One of them held that W(2) did not qualify as H's surviving spouse for the purpose of taking a share of his estate on his death intestate, where the right to succession was governed by FRENCH law: Trib. Paris 17 June 1972, Rev. crit. d.i.p. 1975, 62, note Fadlallah; the other, that W(2) could not claim benefits under FRENCH social security legislation: Cass. soc. 1 March 1973, Clunet 1974, 834, note G. de La Pradelle, Rev. crit. d.i.p. 1975, 54, note Graulich. Both of these decisions have incurred well-deserved criticism by the respective annotators.

661. The contrary view, by which a polygamous marriage is to be disregarded for this purpose, seems once to have been rather current – see, for instance, *Wolff,* IPR 63; critically, *Raape,* Kommentar 809 – but is scarcely acceptable today.

662. Such interference of public policy seems only conceivable if there is a strong connection with the country of the forum. For a NORWEGIAN case see HD 1 July 1977, NRt 1977, 715, annulling a polygamous marriage validly entered into in Bangladesh, between Moslem parties domiciled there at the time of the ceremony, H having previously married W(1) in Pakistan; the court emphasised that the union presented strong contacts with Norway, where H and his two wives were living and where at least H and W(2) were domiciled at the time of the proceedings. For WEST GERMAN law it has been suggested that the polygamous wife should be entitled to a decree of nullity whenever she has acquired the nationality of, or become habitually resident in, West Germany; see *Gamillscheg,* Kommentar, art. 13 no. 245. This proposition, however, which has no support in decided cases, seems to go too far. In a FRENCH case where proceedings for annulment of the second marriage were brought by the polygamous husband himself, the court refused to grant a decree – quite appropriately, it is submitted – although the petitioner had acquired French nationality in the time between the second ceremony and the proceedings: Trib. Lyon 20 Nov. 1975, Clunet 1976, 675, note Mayer, Rev. crit. d.i.p. 1976, 477, note P. Lagarde.

This, in any event, is the result arrived at in the few cases in which courts or other authorities in European countries have been faced with such issues.[663]

Sometimes the recognition of a foreign polygamous marriage may also be a problem for reasons relating to the *first* union. In this context attention must again be drawn to the *English* concept that the nature of a marriage depends on the law governing the form of the ceremony by which it came into existence. This means that a marriage in local form in England, or presumably in any other monogamous form, is impressed with a monogamous character even if the husband's personal law, or the personal law of both spouses, allows him to take two or more wives.[664] It seems to follow that if the husband avails himself of his right to marry again in a foreign country then this second union cannot be recognised in England, since to do so would violate the monogamous character of the first.[665] If this is the true position of English law, it amounts

663. BELGIUM: Corr. Bruxelles 12 June 1953, Clunet 1954, 438, note Abrahams, Rev. crit. d.i.p. 1954, 376, note Philonenko; FRANCE: Cour Reims 19 Jan. 1976, Clunet 1976, 916, note Fadlallah (annulling a polygamist's second marriage with a Frenchwoman, which had been celebrated twice, first in France and then in Senegal, the husband's home country); SWITZERLAND: administrative decision cited with an account of the case by *Mercier* 77. ENGLISH law is the same (though domicile must be substituted for nationality as the relevant connecting factor), unless the test of the intended matrimonial home is accepted in respect of capacity for polygamy; see *supra* at n. 412-415, 644, 650. In SWEDEN, however, both marriages would be treated as valid even in this situation, but the second would have to be dissolved by divorce; cf. *supra* n. 641.

664. This view is supported by the strong current of ENGLISH and other COMMONWEALTH authority. See *Pålsson*, Marriage, s. 251; *adde*, Qureshi v. Qureshi, [1972] Fam. 173; *Cheshire and North* 303-306 (who now lean in favour of the prevailing view); cf. *Lipstein* 102. Admittedly, there is some dissent, and the point has never been fully discussed or squarely decided by the courts.

665. Though whether this consequence will be accepted is not settled beyond doubt; see *Pålsson*, Marriage, s. 252 n. 35 and *infra* n. 667. From the point of view of the polygamous country concerned, it is not to be expected that the celebration of the first marriage in the monogamous form of a Western country will be treated as a bar to the husband's second marriage, where permitted by his personal law. For an illustrative ALGERIAN case, involving the relationship between FRENCH and ALGERIAN law after the accession of Algeria to independence, see Cour Oran 18 May 1965, Rev. crit. d.i.p. 1966, 230, note Verdier (rejecting the view, which had been accepted during the era of FRENCH rule, that the monogamous form of the first marriage, with a woman subject to FRENCH law in matters of personal status, implied a renunciation of polygamy on the part of the Muslim Algerian husband); discussed by *Schuster*, Das Kollisionsrecht Algeriens (Hamburg 1970) 121-123.

to saying that the husband's capacity for polygamy, although conferred on him by the appropriate law in the eyes of English conflict of laws, is frustrated by his going through a monogamous ceremony with his first wife.

The merits of this solution, it is submitted, are open to grave doubts. Not only does it create an inelegant exception to the usual conflicts rule for capacity to marry, but also it appears to give too much weight to the form of the marriage ceremony. Admittedly, cases are easily conceivable where the first wife's legitimate expectations ought in justice to be protected. The circumstances may be such as clearly to indicate that the parties had married "with a view to" monogamy and that a further marriage by the husband, despite his legal capacity for polygamy, would amount to a breach of a condition of the first.[666] It is scarcely reasonable, however, that the fact of celebration of the first marriage in monogamous form should provide the sole criterion by which to decide that the second is invalid. In the first place, there are several other factors, such as the domicile and the nationality of the parties and the intended matrimonial home, which have a valid claim to be taken into consideration in ascertaining the "true nature" of the marriage.[667] Secondly, even where a strong case is found to exist in favour of protecting the wife's "expectation of monogamy", the appropriate method of doing so is hardly by refusing to recognise the husband's second marriage. At least as a general rule, it seems that the wife's interests are more adequately safeguarded by giving her a right to divorce. Some support for this solution exists in decisions by *French* courts.[668]

666. Cf. the remarks made by way of *obiter dictum* in the ENGLISH case of Kenward v. Kenward, [1951] P. 124, 144-145 (C.A.).

667. It may be noted here that in most ENGLISH and SCOTTISH cases cited in support of the conclusion that a marriage solemnised in English (Scottish) form is monogamous in nature, regardless of the personal law of the parties, there was in fact the additional contact with England (Scotland) that the female party was a local domiciliary. An exception is Qureshi v. Qureshi, [1972] Fam. 173, where both parties to the English marriage were, and afterwards remained, foreign domiciled and subject to a personal law admitting of polygamy. Precisely in a case of this type, however, it seems anomalous that the character of the ceremony should exclude the possibility of recognising a subsequent polygamous marriage contracted by the husband in the country of his domicile (this point did not arise in the *Qureshi* case). See *Pearl* 140-142; *idem*, "I Divorce You. I Divorce You. I Divorce You": [1971] C.L.J. 40, 44; cf. *Lipstein* 102.

668. See *Mercier* 35-40; *Pålsson*, Marriage, s. 263 n. 71. Occasionally this solution has been adopted even by the courts of the country itself whose law permitted the polygamous marriage. An example is the decision of the Privy

ab. *Problems Relating to Subsistence of Prior Marriage*

79. *Introductory.* As noted already, most conflict of laws problems relating to successive marriages concern the question of whether the prior union is or was in existence at the date of the second. This question, in turn, resolves itself into two: 'Was the prior marriage validly created? If so, has it been validly dissolved before the remarriage?' Problems in the latter respect, whether of the conflict of laws or otherwise, are rare when the union has (allegedly) been ended by the death of the other spouse but all the more common where the termination was by way of divorce.[669] These problems, of course, owe their origin to the fact that different legal systems often disagree as to the validity of a marriage or a divorce, with the consequence that the remarrying party may be regarded by one of them as bound by the prior union but by another as not so bound.

This being so, the basic question, and the only one to be treated here, is that of identifying the legal system whose point of view with regard to the prior marriage is authoritative for the purpose of determining the lawfulness of the second. Once this has been done in the case at hand, it remains to find and apply the rules, including the conflicts rules, of that system to see whether it affirms or denies the validity of the prior union, or of a divorce

---

Council, on an appeal from the GAMBIA, in Drammeh v. Drammeh, 14 J.A.L. 115 (1970), where their Lordships – without pronouncing upon the validity of the second marriage (which had been made possible by a unilateral change of religion by the husband) – went to the length of characterising the relationship between the parties to that union as adulterous so far as the first wife was concerned. See *A. Phillips and H.F. Morris*, Marriage Laws in Africa (London, New York & Toronto 1971) 58. In certain circumstances the grant of a divorce seems also to be a course open to ENGLISH courts (applying their own divorce law but using the relevant foreign law as "background" or "datum" in judging whether the husband's conduct qualifies as a sufficient ground for divorce under ENGLISH law); see *Cheshire and North* 360-361; *Dicey and Morris* 302-303; *North* 110-112. Cf. *Cretney*, Immigrants' Marriages: 116 S.J. 654-655 (1972); *Lipstein* 102.

669. Analogous problems may, however, present themselves as to remarriage following a judicial declaration of death (or decree of presumption of death) of the other spouse. For a comparative survey of these questions, which will not be treated here, see *von Overbeck*, Persons: Encyclopedia III:15 (Tübingen, Paris, New York 1972) 8-12. For particular countries see further, e.g., ENGLAND: *Cheshire and North* 422-424; *Dicey and Morris* 337-339; FRANCE: *Fayon*, Absence (Rép. dr. int. I); WEST GERMANY: *Gamillscheg*, Kommentar, art. 13 no. 337-363; *Marquardt* 45-46; SWEDEN: *Eek* 235-236.

purporting to dissolve it, whichever is in issue. In our discussion, however, we shall proceed the other way round, assuming that the result of the application of the various laws involved in the particular case has been ascertained first and that it remains to decide which law is to prevail in different situations.

This issue is not really a problem in cases where both parties to the second marriage are subject to the *lex fori* as their personal law governing their capacity to marry. In this situation it cannot reasonably be doubted that the position taken by that law is decisive. Suppose, for instance, that both parties to a proposed marriage in England are domiciled locally. The man was previously married to a Frenchwoman from whom he has been divorced by a decree pronounced by a French court. It is plain that the question of whether this divorce was effective to end the prior union, so as to set the man free to marry again, depends on English law (more specifically, on its rules for the recognition of foreign divorces), which is both the *lex fori* and the *lex causae* as to the capacity of the parties to enter into the second marriage.

Where, however, the capacity of the parties, or of one of them, is determinable by foreign law, this approach is not equally self-evident. Suppose that the circumstances are the same as in the above example, except that the parties to the second marriage are and intend to remain domiciled in Spain, so that according to English conflict of laws the question of their capacity falls to Spanish law. Is recognition of the man's French divorce by English law still a relevant matter of investigation for the purpose of deciding that question? This is one possibility, but a second alternative must be considered here, namely, that reliance should be placed on the effect of the divorce according to Spanish law. Generally speaking, the problem is whether the validity and the continued existence of the prior marriage should be tested by reference to the *lex fori,* including its conflict of laws rules, or by reference to the corresponding rules of the foreign law applicable to the party's capacity to marry.[670] These are the two methods of solution envisaged by the doctrine of the incidental question (*question préalable, Vorfrage*), which is of interest here because the existence of the prior marriage is incidental in relation to the principal question of capacity to marry. The two alternatives

670. In so far as the impediment of a prior marriage is treated as bilateral, the present question can arise even if the remarrying party himself is subject to the *lex fori* in respect of capacity to marry, if foreign law applies to the intended partner's capacity. See *supra* s. 49-52 and *infra* s. 85-90.

between which the choice lies may be referred to as the *lex fori* and the *lex causae* method of solution respectively, or – as has been suggested by an English writer – as the "narrow reference approach" and the "wide reference approach", respectively.[671]

The two approaches featured here do not, however, cover all existing solutions to the present problem. A third alternative, which may come into question when a foreign divorce has been followed by remarriage by one of the parties, is to uphold that marriage by whatever law the divorce was pronounced, even though it does not meet the conditions for recognition either of the *lex fori* or of the foreign *lex causae* for capacity to marry. This solution, which amounts to giving preference to the *lex validitatis*, is rather unorthodox but, as will be seen, is endorsed by some legal systems.

In what follows we shall first advert to situations in which the prior marriage is valid and subsisting in the eyes of the *lex fori* but not so treated by some foreign law invoked in support of a party's capacity to conclude another marriage (*aba*). Then we shall turn to the converse situation, which more frequently raises the problem under review, namely, where the prior union is regarded as invalid or as validly dissolved by the *lex fori* but as valid and subsisting by the appropriate foreign law (*abb*). It is proposed to deal mainly with cases where the difference between the *lex fori* and the foreign law relates to the validity of a divorce, such cases being much more common in practice than those in which the point at issue is whether the prior marriage was validly created.

aba. Existence of Prior Marriage Affirmed by Lex Fori, Denied by Foreign Law

80. *General Rule: Remarriage Barred.* It is usually agreed or tacitly assumed that a further marriage is barred when the previous one is valid and subsisting in the eyes of the *lex fori* even if it is not so regarded by the law governing the capacity of the parties to the (proposed) second union.[672] To that extent the *lex fori*

671. The reference to the law governing the main question is said to be "wide" or "narrow" because in the former case it does, while in the latter it does not, include the incidental question. See *Hartley*, Bigamy 682.

672. See the references *infra* n. 674, 677, 680 and 683-685. Further support for this view can be derived from the authorities adopting the *lex fori* method of solution in the converse type of situation, which has been discussed at much greater length; see *infra* s. 88-90.

method of solution (the narrow reference approach) prevails for the incidental question. This is often conceded even by writers supporting the *lex causae* method in the converse type of situation to be dealt with later on.[673]

One situation of the present type is where the prior marriage has been validly created according to the forum's system of the conflict of laws, though not according to that of the relevant foreign law. Here it seems to be quite clear that neither party can marry again in the country of the forum without first securing a divorce (which must be valid by the *lex fori*) from the other spouse.[674] If contracted nevertheless in such circumstances, the second marriage must be invalidated for bigamy by the forum.[675]

Will it make any difference if a decree of nullity, or a declaration of invalidity, in respect of the prior union has been pronounced by a court in the foreign country concerned? This depends on the recognition of that decision by the forum.[676] If it is refused recognition the second marriage remains barred. The following *West German* case furnishes an illustration:[677]

673. Cf. *infra* s. 85-86.

674. See generally *Balogh* 172; *Pålsson*, Haltande äktenskap 507-508; and for individual countries, e.g., ENGLAND: *Hartley*, Bigamy 684-687; WEST GERMANY: *Dorenberg* 66-67; *Gamillscheg*, Doppelehe 64; *idem*, Kommentar, art. 13 no. 254-255; *Kegel*, Kommentar, art. 13 no. 17; SWEDEN: *Pålsson*, *ibid.* 494; SWITZERLAND: *Beck*, art. 7 c no. 87. See also the HAGUE CONVENTION on Marriage of 1902, art. 2 par. 3, entitling the Contracting States to forbid the celebration, before their own authorities, of a marriage which, although permitted by the *lex patriae*, would contravene the local law "by reason of a prior marriage". On the interpretation of this provision, which is rather disputed, see *Beck*, ESchlKonv. art. 2 no. 15-17; *Buzzati* 201-207; *Gamillscheg*, Kommentar, art. 13 no. 300, 952; *F. Kahn* 99-103; *A. Miele* 131-132; *Travers* I 323-361; *Undén*, Studier 44-50.

675. Provided the forum has jurisdiction to entertain such proceedings; cf. *Schwind*, Ehen von Griechen 166-167. Under special circumstances a spouse may conceivably be estopped from asserting this ground of invalidity; cf. *Gamillscheg*, Kommentar, art. 13 no. 255 (invoking the doctrine of *Rechtsmissbrauch*). For the position under the HAGUE CONVENTION cf. *supra* at n. 639.

676. The prevailing approach to such recognition typically differs between COMMON LAW countries, on the one side, and CONTINENTAL EUROPEAN and SCANDINAVIAN countries, on the other; see *Pålsson*, Marriage, s. 285.

677. KG 20 May 1975, IPRspr. 1975 no. 36. Cf. *Marquardt* 37; *Raape*, Die Anerkennung eines ausländischen Ehenichtigkeitsurteils mit besonderer Berücksichtigung des § 24 der 4. EheV.: MDR 1949, 586, 586-587. A similar situation is discussed from the point of view of SWEDISH law by *Undén*, Studier 31-35.

Two Yugoslav nationals had married before a West German civil registrar at a time when both were habitually resident in Yugoslavia. The marriage was valid in West Germany, but it was declared null and void for want of form by a Yugoslav court, the ground being that by Yugoslav law celebration before a consular or diplomatic representative of Yugoslavia had been compulsory in the circumstances.[678] W then sought to marry H(2) in West Germany, where she had meanwhile become habitually resident. Although no impediment existed by Yugoslav law, which as W's *lex patriae* admittedly governed her capacity to marry, the attempt failed because in the eyes of West German law W was validly married to H(1), notwithstanding the Yugoslav nullity decree. The only way to remove this impediment was by obtaining a divorce.

A similar situation occurs where the prior marriage has been dissolved by a divorce which is regarded as effective by the relevant foreign law but fails to be recognised by the *lex fori*. One case of this type is where the divorce was the outcome of some kind of extrajudicial procedure which took place in the country of the forum, in accordance with the personal law of the parties but contrary to the forum's own law. The usual rule in countries whose domestic law insists on judicial (or administrative) proceedings as the sole means by which a marriage can be validly dissolved is that this method is compulsory for all divorces granted within the country.[679] To that extent any other form of divorce which may be prescribed or permitted by the personal law of the parties is inoperative. This is so in the case of divorces effected by private act, such as a unilateral declaration of repudiation (*talak*) under Islamic law or a bill of divorcement (*ghet*) under Jewish law, or pronounced by a foreign consular officer, a religious tribunal or some other body lacking a judicial standing in the country of the forum. It follows that such a divorce, if obtained in that country, does not form a sufficient basis for remarriage even

678. See the YUGOSLAV BMA art. 26 and 75 and *Pålsson,* Marriage, s. 331 at n. 225.

679. See generally: *Bauer,* Compétence judiciaire internationale des tribunaux civils français et allemands (Paris 1965) 24-25; *Elgeddawy* 141, 208-210, 251; *Gamillscheg,* Kommentar, art. 17 no. 505-531; *Mercier* 25, 41, 72-73, 78, 98; *Pålsson,* Marriage (Encyclopedia) 154-156; *Rabel* 448-450; *Schwind,* Le divorce en droit international privé: Rec. des Cours 117 (1966-I) 445, 462. For a survey of various types of extrajudicial divorce see *North* 218-222.

if it is valid by the foreign law controlling the capacity of the parties to the (proposed) union.[680] Example:

> H and W(1), Mohammedans domiciled in Pakistan, are temporarily living in England. In 1974, while in that country, H divorces W(1) by the *talak* procedure prescribed by Pakistani law.[681] He then seeks to marry W(2), also a Pakistani Moslem, in an English registry office, invoking the *talak* in support of his contention that he has the status of a single person. By English law, however, a divorce of this type performed in England is ineffective to dissolve a marriage.[682] In the eyes of English law, therefore, the prior union is still subsisting and, *semble*, constitutes a lawful impediment to the remarriage, notwithstanding the validity of the divorce by Pakistani law which is decisive for the capacity of the parties to marry.[683]

Another case within the present category is where the divorce purporting to end the prior marriage has been validly granted in a foreign country but does not meet the conditions for recognition

680. See, e.g., FRANCE: Trib. Seine 2 June 1930, Clunet 1931, 1078; Trib. Seine 25 April 1938, Rev. crit. d.i.p. 1939, 103; [WEST] GERMANY: BayObLG 30 March 1921, OLGR 42, 87; OLG Kiel 26 Nov. 1926, IPRspr. 1928 no. 112; KG 21 March 1932, IPRspr. 1932 no. 77; OLG München 21 Nov. 1949, StAZ 1950, 130; *Albers* 145-147; *Marquardt* 42, 44; *Wengler*, Vorfrage 229.

681. On the relevant PAKISTANI law, by which the *talak* must be followed by conciliation proceedings before an arbitration council, see the ENGLISH case of Qureshi v. Qureshi, [1972] Fam. 173.

682. See the Domicile and Matrimonial Proceedings Act 1973, s. 16 (1), which provides that "no proceeding in the United Kingdom, the Channel Islands or the Isle of Man shall be regarded as validly dissolving a marriage unless instituted in the courts of law of one of those countries". Before the coming into force of this provision (on January 1, 1974) the ENGLISH rule was different and formed an exception to the principle prevailing almost everywhere else. See *Dicey and Morris* 327-330; *Graveson*, Conflict 281-282, 292, 319-322; *North* 222-224. It has been suggested that the common law rule still applies to certain extrajudicial divorces obtained in the British Isles, namely, those which are not accompanied by any formality amounting to a "proceeding" within s. 16 of the 1973 Act; see *Cheshire and North* 387; *North* 225-230, 237-238. But see for the view that "proceeding" in that Act encompasses any form of extrajudicial divorce, so as to dispose completely of the common law rule, *Jaffey*, Recognition of Extra-Judicial Divorces: 91 L.Q.R. 320-323 (1975).

683. See *Jaffey, ibid.* 322-323. Cf. R. v. Hammersmith Marriage Registrar, [1917] 1 K.B. 634 (C.A.). But the position of ENGLISH law on this point is by no means clear. See *North* 224-225, who leans in favour of the opposite view, by which the domiciliary law deciding questions of capacity to marry is to prevail over the ENGLISH rule of divorce recognition.

under the *lex fori*. Here too the usual view is that the prior union prevents a lawful second marriage even if the divorce is valid by the personal law applicable to the capacity of the parties.[684] A *French* decision may be chosen to illustrate this point:[685]

> H(1) and W had obtained a judgment of divorce in a Prussian court in 1899, when both parties were of Italian nationality. In conformity with the rules of private international law current in Prussia before the coming into force of the German Civil Code in the year 1900, the divorce had been pronounced by virtue of the *lex fori* alone. Shortly after the grant of the divorce both parties lost their Italian and acquired German nationality. W then married H(2), a Frenchman, in England. The father of H(2) brought proceedings in the French court to annul this marriage on the ground that W was still bound by her marriage to H(1). In granting a decree the court took the view that the Prussian judgment could not be recognised as validly dissolving the prior union because it had been rendered in disregard of Italian law, which did not permit divorce and which ought to have been applied pursuant to

684. See generally *Pålsson*, Haltande äktenskap 507-508. For the HAGUE CONVENTION of 1902 see the references *supra* n. 674. For individual countries see, e.g., AUSTRIA: *Hainzl* 20; ENGLAND: *Hartley*, Bigamy 684-687; *Hooper* 730-731 (but there is CANADIAN authority to the contrary; see *infra* at n. 715); FRANCE: Trib. Seine 10 July 1901, Clunet 1901, 967; cf. Cour Paris 15 Nov. 1960, Rev. crit. d.i.p. 1961, 937, note Loussouarn; *Francescakis*, Anerkennung und Vollstreckung ausländischer familienrechtlicher Urteile. C. Rechtsvergleichung: IntFamR 582, 585-586; WEST GERMANY: *Dorenberg* 137, 156-157; *Gamillscheg*, Kommentar, art. 13 no. 254-256; *Kegel*, Kommentar, art. 13 no. 26; *Raape*, IPR 312-313; *Wengler*, Vorfrage 215 (but see for a minority opinion to the contrary affecting at least certain cases of this type: *Jayme and Siehr*, case note: StAZ 1970, 345-346; *Marquardt* 38-44; *Neumayer* 80-81; *Riezler*, Anerkennung und Vollstreckung ausländischer familienrechtlicher Urteile. B. Deutsches Recht: IntFamR 567, 570-571; *Süss* 252 n. 44, 257-258 n. 55); SPAIN: cases cited *supra* n. 356; see also D.G.R.N. 3 Oct. 1952, Rev. Esp. Der. Int. 5 (1952) 933; SWEDEN: Act of 8 July 1904 (as amended) ch. 1 § 3 no. 3; *Eek* 237-238, 248; *Pålsson, ibid.* 494-495. The same solution has been adopted by SWISS courts in cases where the validity of a second marriage contracted abroad was referable to the *lex loci celebrationis* (under the rule in NAG art. 7 f par. 1; see *supra* s. 69). Such marriages have been refused recognition where the divorce of the prior union, although valid by that law, did not meet the conditions for recognition under SWISS law: BG 13 May 1938, BGE 64 II 74, Clunet 1951, 938, note Knapp; BG 11 March 1948, BGE 74 II 54, Clunet 1952, 664, note Knapp.

685. Trib. Seine 10 July 1901, Clunet 1901, 967.

> the French rules of the conflict of laws. The question was apparently not even posed of whether the result should have been different by reason of the fact that the divorce was valid by German law, which as W's *lex patriae* at the time of the remarriage was the appropriate law by which to test her capacity to marry.

The reasons why the *lex fori* method prevails in cases of the type described here are not difficult to understand. It is an elementary expression of the principle of monogamy that the right of remarriage must be denied when the prior union is valid and has not been effectively dissolved in the eyes of the *lex fori.* To hold otherwise, on the strength of the foreign *lex causae* of capacity to marry, would imply the recognition of a kind of "legal bigamy" by the forum; for the party bound by the prior marriage would have to be considered lawfully married to two persons at the same time.

It may be added that in nearly all cases where the question has arisen for decision (or would have if the answer had not been taken to be self-evident), the other party to the second union was subject to the *lex fori* in respect of capacity to marry by reason that he was a domiciliary and/or national of the country of the forum. To that extent the prevailing attitude among courts and writers is open to the alternative explanation that the impediment of the prior marriage was treated as bilateral by the *lex fori.*[686]

81. *Requirements of Validation of Foreign Divorce or Nullity Decrees.* Within the framework of the prevailing approach some special difficulties may present themselves in cases where the prior marriage has been ended by a foreign decree of divorce or annulment. In several Continental European, Scandinavian and Latin American countries there are rules requiring such decrees, generally or in certain cases, to be formally validated by a court or other authority in exequatur proceedings.[687] By *Swedish* law, for instance, an exequatur is necessary, as a rule, when a foreign

686. Cf. *supra* s. 49. This doctrine has been expressly relied upon in WEST GERMAN cases involving the issuance of a certificate of capacity to marry to a German national intending to marry abroad, where the other party to the proposed union was a previously married foreigner whose divorce had not been validated in West Germany. See the references *infra* n. 690.

687. See, e.g., AUSTRIA: DVO § 24; *H. Hoyer; Schwind,* IPR 179-183; CZECHOSLOVAKIA: Act of 4 Dec. 1963, § 67-68; *Florio* 340-341; FINLAND: Act of 5 Dec. 1929 (as amended) § 11-13; EAST GERMANY: CCP § 194; *FGB-Kommentar* 477-482; WEST GERMANY: Act of 11 Aug. 1961, art. 7; *Gamillscheg,* Kommentar, § 328 no. 468-562; *Kleinrahm and Partikel; Stein and Jonas,* Kommentar zur Zivilprozessordnung II (ed. 19, Tübingen

divorce is invoked by a party who wants to remarry in Sweden.[688] In other countries insisting on this formality it is compulsory for whatever purpose the validity of a foreign divorce (or nullity decree) is asserted.[689] This will mean that the divorce cannot produce any of its legal consequences in the country of the forum until it has received the hallmark of exequatur.

While these rules do not add anything to the substantive prerequisites of recognition of foreign divorces, they imply that exclusive jurisdiction to ascertain whether those prerequisites are met is vested in the designated exequatur authority. Hence, if a party relies on a foreign divorce decree in support of his capacity to marry again, celebrants of marriages and similar functionaries are precluded from examining the decree on their own; they must await the grant of an exequatur by the appropriate authority, pending which the proposed union cannot be solemnised.[690] Similarly, if the second marriage has already been concluded, whether locally or abroad, and if the validity of that union is challenged on the ground that there was no prior validation of the foreign divorce, the court called upon to pronounce the nullity of the marriage lacks power to go, itself, into the merits of the question of the recognition of the divorce.[691] In this situation,

1972) § 328 no. XI; POLAND: CCP art. 1145-1149; SWEDEN: Act of 8 July 1904 (as amended) ch. 3 § 8-9; NJA 1973 II 598-601. All these provisions exempt certain decrees from the requirement of validation, chiefly those emanating from the State of the common nationality of the spouses. In some other countries, however, no such exception is admitted. See for ITALY, where in principle a judgment of validation (known as *delibazione*) is necessary for all foreign judgments, CCP art. 796-799, 801, 804; *Cappelletti and Perillo* 367-386 (but see specifically with reference to remarriage after a foreign decree of divorce or annulment, *infra* s. 82). And see for BRAZIL: *Valladão,* Les effets des jugements étrangers de divorce: Rev. crit. d.i.p. 1959, 443, 449-450; VENEZUELA: CC art. 108; *Lombard* 46-51.

688. Act of 8 July 1904 (as amended) ch. 3 § 9 par. 1 (but this requirement falls away if the divorce was granted by the courts of the country of the nationality of the spouses or one of them).

689. See the references (except those concerning SWEDISH law) *supra* n. 687.

690. If the marriage is intended to take place abroad, a similar question can arise before the local authority charged with the task of issuing certificates of capacity to marry. It has been held in WEST GERMANY that this, too, must be refused as long as the foreign divorce of one of the parties has not been properly validated: AG Hamburg 24 Dec. 1969, IPRspr. 1968/69 no. 75; LG München 15 March 1972, IPRspr. 1972 no. 116.

691. This problem does not present itself under the type of rule existing in SWEDISH law (*supra* n. 688), which is confined to the stage of celebration of the fresh marriage.

however, there is some diversity of opinion as to what course should, positively, be adopted by the court.

According to one line of reasoning, the foreign divorce is totally devoid of effect until it has been properly validated and therefore must be treated as non-existent. It follows that the second marriage is invalid for bigamy. This conclusion has now and then been reached by courts in different countries.[692]

While perhaps logically attractive, this solution is open to grave objections from a practical point of view. It is unfortunate that a marriage should be declared invalid before it has been positively established that the ground for so holding (the non-recognition of the divorce in the prior union) exists, solely because the deciding court is prevented from entering upon that question. It may well turn out later that the divorce does comply with the conditions of recognition, in which case it must be accorded exequatur if and when this is sought. Furthermore, it is usually agreed that such a decision validates the foreign divorce decree retroactively, as of the date when it became effective under the foreign law concerned.[693] The basis of the forum's nullity decree in respect of the second marriage may thus be removed *a posteriori*.

These complications are avoided by another solution which, it is submitted, is much to be preferred. It consists in requiring (or at least allowing) the court before which the validity of the second marriage is in issue to stay the proceedings pending a decision as to the recognition of the divorce by the exequatur authority. The court should also have the right, where necessary, to request, or to cause the parties to request, such a decision of

692. WEST GERMANY: LG Hamburg 4 Nov. 1975, IPRspr. 1975 no. 40, pertinently criticised by *Basedow,* Auslandsscheidungen vor deutschen Gerichten und Behörden – zwei Verfahrensfragen: StAZ 1977, 6-8; ITALY: Cass. 5 Aug. 1950, Giur. it. 1951 I 1, 110, note Cansacchi, and cases cited *infra* n. 701. An illustrative VENEZUELAN case is mentioned by *Lombard* 47-48.

693. With the consequence that the second marriage, entered into before the foreign decree (of divorce or of nullity) was granted exequatur, also becomes valid retroactively. For ITALIAN decisions so holding see, e.g., Cass. 22 July 1943, Foro it. 1943 I 801; Trib. Milano 16 April 1959, Giur. it. 1960 I 2, 629, note Pagano; Cass. 22 May 1963, Foro it. 1963 I 1394; Trib. Milano 21 Jan. 1965, Riv. dir. int. proc. 1965, 349; Cass. 28 March 1973, Foro it. 1973 I 2520. On the retroactive effect of a judgment of exequatur see further, e.g., AUSTRIA: *H. Hoyer* 84-85; WEST GERMANY: *Gamillscheg,* Kommentar, § 328 no. 432, 557; *Kleinrahm and Partikel* 35; ITALY: *Cappelletti and Perillo* 369, 383, 385; *Luzzatto,* Problemi in tema di azione e di procedimento per la delibazione nella giurisprudenza italiana: Riv. dir. int. proc. 1965, 449, 470-471; VENEZUELA: *Lombard* 48 n. 164.

its own motion. A solution along these lines is supported by writers in various countries and has, in particular, been adopted in the practice of *Austrian* courts.[694]

82. *Special Position of Italian law.* Italian law occupies a special position in regard to the questions treated here. Problems concerning a foreigner's right to marry again after a decree of divorce or annulment obtained abroad have played a prominent part and been the subject of much controversy in Italian practice and legal literature. The discussion centres around the rule that foreign judgments must be formally recognised by an Italian court in the exequatur procedure known as *delibazione* before they can produce any effect in Italy.[695]

According to one view, which is or has been espoused by many writers, this requirement applies without qualification in the situation envisaged here.[696] A foreign divorce or nullity decree therefore does not pave the way to remarriage until it has been given an exequatur by the competent Italian court.[697] Such an order will only be made if the usual conditions of recognition laid down by Italian law are met, and the validity of the decree under one foreign law or another is immaterial. This approach is the same as that prevailing in other countries.

As against this, it is contended that the only relevant test is whether the prior marriage has been validly dissolved or annulled in the eyes of the *lex patriae* governing matters of family status

694. For AUSTRIAN law see: OGH 4 Nov. 1959, ÖJZ 1960, 45 EvBl no. 22; OGH 10 Oct. 1962, ZfRV 8 (1967) 157, note Scheucher; OLG Linz 12 Oct. 1966 and BMfJ 10 Jan. 1967, ZfRV 8 (1967) 168, note H. Hoyer; *H. Hoyer* 54-55, 149-155. A similar view prevails in WEST GERMAN law, except that there is no right for the court to refer the case *ex officio* to the exequatur authority. See, e.g., *Gamillscheg,* Kommentar, § 328 no. 431, 434; *Geimer,* Das Anerkennungsverfahren für ausländische Entscheidungen in Ehesachen: NJW 1967, 1398, 1401; *Kleinrahm and Partikel* 51-52, 171-172. For an ITALIAN case where, likewise, proceedings to annul the second marriage were stayed pending the decision as to the recognition of one spouse's foreign divorce, see App. Palermo 11 April 1961, Foro pad. 1963 I 1273, critical note M. Miele.

695. *Supra* n. 687.

696. At all events if the second marriage is to be, or has been, celebrated in Italy. See, e.g., *Grassetti,* Questione pregiudiziale e dottrina del rinvio: Riv. dir. int. proc. 1965, 87-89; *Monaco* 174-176. For further references see *A. Miele* 124 n. 95; *Picone* 24 n. 16; *Vitta* II 183 n. 44.

697. Once an exequatur has been granted, however, it operates to validate the foreign judgment with retroactive effect: *supra* n. 693.

according to the Italian system of the conflict of laws.[698] On this view a foreigner has the right to marry again if, and only if, the divorce or nullity decree was properly granted in the country of his nationality or, where granted elsewhere, if it is recognised in that country. Hence, there is no need to submit the decree to the procedure of *delibazione* otherwise required by Italian law. In practice, this solution comes close to that reached by adopting the wide reference approach in respect of the incidental question, although the problem has usually not been discussed in these terms by Italian writers.[699]

Judicial decisions have on the whole, if not always consistently, followed an intermediate course, which is also favoured by what now seems to be the prevailing trend of opinion among writers.[700] The courts have insisted on the necessity of a *delibazione* in cases where the marriage dissolved or annulled by a foreign court presented close contacts with Italy, usually because it had been celebrated in that country and therefore was recorded in the Italian registers of civil status.[701] In these cases, accordingly, the right of remarriage, whether in Italy or abroad, has been denied when the divorce or nullity decree had not been granted exequatur

698. See, e.g., *Rottola*, Sentenza straniera di divorzio non delibata e reato di bigamia: Riv. dir. int. proc. 1970, 611, 619-621; *Starace*, Sullo stato libero dello straniero divorziato: Riv. dir. int. proc. 1968, 843-847; *Vitta* I 476-478, II 178-186.

699. The current ITALIAN theory is indeed quite different from that represented by the wide reference approach and occasionally apt to yield different practical results; cf. *infra* at n. 705-706.

700. For a survey of ITALIAN case law see *Picone* 11-19; cf. *Marquardt* 31-34, 78. Among writers propounding a view similar to that deducible from the decisions, albeit on partly different grounds, see: *Lanfranchi*, Sull'efficacia in Italia di un atto di ripudio iraniano: Riv. dir. int. proc. 1966, 526, 539-541; *Lanzillo*, Sull'efficacia in Italia delle sentenze straniere di divorzio non delibate, ai fini dell'accertamento dello stato libero dello straniero: Riv. dir. int. proc. 1973, 396-404; *A. Miele* 123-141; *Picone* 25-61, 78-79. Further references are given by *Picone* 21 n. 13.

701. This position has especially been taken in cases where the marriage had been solemnised in concordat form. See: Trib. Napoli 2 Dec. 1961, Dir. Int. 1963 II 264, Temi nap. 1962 I 325, note Grassi; Cass. 11 Oct. 1967, Riv. dir. int. proc. 1969, 465; Cass. 29 Oct. 1971, Riv. dir. int. proc. 1972, 294 (affirming App. Milano 11 July 1969, Riv. dir. int. proc. 1969, 1043). For cases involving an Italian marriage celebrated in a form other than that of the concordat see: Trib. Palermo 6 Oct. 1958, Giur. sic. 1961, 65, 80, note M. Miele, reversed on other grounds by App. Palermo 11 April 1961, Foro pad. 1963 I 1273, note *idem;* Trib. Napoli 15 Jan. 1966, Dir. eccles. 1966 II 308, note Scordo. As to marriages contracted abroad but connected to Italy by the nationality of one of the spouses cf. *infra* n. 703.

in Italy, notwithstanding that it was valid by the foreign *lex patriae.*[702]

A different position has been adopted in cases where the prior marriage had been entered into abroad and did not have any particular relation to Italy.[703] A foreign decree of divorce or nullity in respect of such a union has been held to confer automatically on the parties the status of single persons, once the validity of the decree under their *lex patriae* was established but without requiring an exequatur procedure in Italy. In consequence, the prior marriage is no bar to remarriage in Italy in these cases, nor – *a fortiori* – to the validity of a second marriage concluded abroad.[704]

These solutions rest on an interpretation of the relevant statutory texts as well as on dogmatic considerations which are at least as controversial as the actual results. From a comparative point of view it is scarcely worth while to go into the details of these questions. Although the discussion is predominantly conducted

702. See the references in the preceding note. All these cases involved a second marriage entered into abroad by a foreigner whose prior Italian marriage had been dissolved or annulled by a foreign court. For decisions *contra* see Trib. Milano 12 June 1972, Riv. dir. int. proc. 1973, 438, and Trib. Milano 27 July 1972, Riv. dir. int. proc. 1973, 440. In both of these cases an Italian woman had married a foreigner, thereby acquiring his nationality, in concordat form in Italy. After obtaining a divorce in the country of their common nationality, the parties successfully sought a declaration in the ITALIAN court that they had acquired the status of single persons by virtue of the foreign divorce decree, which was held to produce this effect automatically within the ITALIAN legal system, thus *inter alia* paving the way to remarriage without the need for an exequatur.

703. A borderline case occurs where the female party was an Italian national at the time of the marriage (celebrated abroad) but lost that and acquired the husband's foreign nationality through the marriage. Such a connection with Italy in the past is probably insufficient to render an exequatur necessary if the marriage is dissolved by a foreign divorce decree which is valid by the law of the common nationality of the spouses at that time. See for a decision upholding a second marriage after a divorce granted in such circumstances, Trib. Roma 15 May 1961, Temi rom. 1961, 365, note Zuddas (this case also presented the peculiarity that the woman had re-acquired Italian nationality at the time of the second marriage; but this fact, too, was held to be immaterial). *A fortiori*, support for this solution can be derived from the two decisions cited in the preceding note which involved a prior marriage celebrated in concordat form in Italy. *Contra*, apparently, Trib. Milano 21 Sept. 1967, Riv. dir. int. proc. 1968, 403 (where, however, the circumstances were rather special). Cf. on this and certain other doubtful situations *Picone* 53-55.

704. See the decisions cited *supra* n. 394. All those cases involved a foreign celebrated first marriage, and in all except one (Trib. Roma 15 May 1961, see *supra* n. 703) both parties to that union were of foreign nationality.

in dogmatic terms and at a high level of abstraction, the decisions of the courts are probably also influenced by policy factors, in particular the desire to validate certain marriages contracted in defiance of the strict Italian rule as to the necessity of an exequatur for the recognition of foreign judgments.

There is no indication in Italian law that the sanction given in certain circumstances to a person's remarriage on the strength of his *lex patriae,* although the decree ending or pronouncing null his prior union has not been granted exequatur by an Italian court, should be conceived as amounting to the acknowledgment of a status of "legal bigamy" (cf. *supra* s. 80). The prevailing concept seems to be that a decree which validly confers the "liberty of status" on a person according to his national law must be recognised by Italian law for *all* purposes.[705] It is apparently not accepted that the prior marriage, while not treated as a bar to remarriage, could be regarded as still subsisting for other purposes. Rather, the position is the same as if the foreign decree had been formally recognised in an exequatur procedure. This implies that the *lex patriae* is relied upon, not because it is the law governing the party's capacity for remarriage, in relation to which the existence of the prior union is an incidental question, but because it controls his "liberty of status" generally, whether that issue appears as the main or as an incidental question.[706] In other words, the means used to uphold the second marriage consists, not in adopting the wide reference approach as to the incidental question, but in widening the basis for the recognition of foreign divorce and nullity decrees by admitting that such decrees are in certain cases effective "directly" by virtue of the *lex patriae* without having to pass the scrutiny of the Italian exequatur procedure. While this concept avoids the dilemma of "legal bigamy", the difference from the wide reference approach is probably minimal, at least if (as assumed by the prevailing opinion) such automatic recognition is limited to decrees dissolving or annulling a marriage which had

705. Expressly in favour of this view see *Picone* 9 (n. 4), 19 (with n. 12), 33, 41 (n. 39), 63, 79.

706. That this is the underlying concept appears clearly from decisions granting a declaration, general in scope and thus not limited to the purpose of remarriage, that a person enjoyed the status of a single person flowing from a foreign divorce decree; see the cases cited *supra* n. 702. Another expression of the same view is that the relevant law for determining whether a divorce is valid so as to enable the spouses in the prior union to remarry is that of their nationality at the time of the divorce and not at the time of the second marriage; see the decision of Trib. Roma 15 May 1961, Temi rom. 1961, 365, cf. *supra* n. 703.

no substantial contacts with Italy; for it is unlikely in these cases that the question of the subsistence of the prior union for purposes other than the lawfulness of the remarriage should be presented before an Italian court.

83. *Other Exceptions.* Scattered examples of cases in which, usually under the influence of the policy of validation, a second marriage has been upheld on the strength of the relevant foreign law, although the first had not been validly dissolved from the point of view of the *lex fori,* are to be found in the practice of various other countries. A rather thorny *German* case, which has been extensively commented upon, provides an illustration:[707]

> A German couple was divorced in an American court. Subsequently the husband lost his German and acquired American citizenship and remarried an American woman in the USA. Many years later W(1) petitioned the German court for a divorce, thereby raising the question of the subsistence of the first union, which in its turn depended on the recognition of the American divorce decree in Germany. This latter question was answered in the negative, *inter alia* because the American court had lacked jurisdiction in the eyes of German law. On the other hand, the court took the view that H's marriage to W(2) must be regarded as valid since it complied with the requirements of the relevant American law, the law of H's nationality at the time of that marriage. In so finding the court was impressed by the fact that the second union had existed as a valid marriage for a long period of time in the USA, the country of the parties' social environment. This situation could not be reversed by the court in any event. To avoid the necessity of concluding that H was at the same time validly married both to W(1) and to W(2), the court went on to infer that the celebration of the second marriage had had the effect of automatically dissolving the first union as from the date of the second. It followed that W(1), too, was free from the union with H and could remarry in Germany without first securing a new divorce. Her petition was therefore rejected.

This decision is clearly based on the *lex causae* approach inasmuch as the reference to the husband's *lex patriae* on the issue of his capacity for remarriage was held to include the question of the

707. KG 13 Jan. 1925, JW 1925, 2146.

validity of the divorce of the prior union. Obviously the choice of this solution was dictated, not by adherence to any dogma with regard to the incidental question but by pragmatic considerations, in particular the need felt by the court to respect the *fait accompli* created by the remarriage in the United States; it would have been vain for the court to declare that it regarded that marriage as invalid for bigamy, although this would logically have followed from the refusal of German law to recognise the divorce.[708] An at least equally interesting feature of the decision is that the court felt compelled further to hold that the prior union, while not validly ended by the divorce, had ceased to exist at the moment of the conclusion of the second. This implies that a marriage can be dissolved by one of the spouses remarrying validly in the eys of the law governing his capacity to marry, in other words that the termination of the prior union may be the effect rather than a condition of the validity of the second. Although this is quite an unorthodox approach, the decision has been approved by several commentators.[709]

A similar problem arose in somewhat special circumstances in a later German case decided by the *Reichsgericht.*[710] Here too the man had remarried, validly according to his *lex patriae* at the time of celebration, after a divorce which was effective by that law but not recognised under the conflicts rules of the forum. Litigation concerning the two marriages arose after the man, who was a civil servant, had died, when both wives claimed the right to a pension accruing to his lawful widow. As in the earlier case, the court, expressly adopting the wide reference approach, upheld the second marriage in reliance on the applicable foreign law. In contrast to the court in that case, however, the *Reichsgericht* refused to infer that the first marriage had thereby been ended but came to the

708. Cf. *Wengler,* Die Funktion der richterlichen Entscheidung über internationale Rechtsverhältnisse: RabelsZ 16 (1951) 1,27-28; *idem,* Vorfrage 226.

709. See, e.g., *Melchior* 414; *Neumayer* 80-81; *Wengler,* Principles 415-416; *idem,* Vorfrage 225-228 (cf., with regard to an analogous situation, *idem,* Nouvelles réflexions 188); *Wolff,* IPR 212; *idem,* PIL 379-380. But see for criticism: *Balogh* 167-168, 170; *Dorenberg* 156-157; *Gamillscheg,* Kommentar, art. 13 no. 259-262 (cf., however, for an approving comment *idem,* Doppelehe 76-77); *Kegel,* Kommentar, art. 13 no. 26; *Massfeller* 184-185; *Nussbaum* 164; *Raape,* IPR 312-313; *Wieruszowski,* case note: JW 1925, 2490.

710. RG 24 Jan. 1941, RGZ 165, 398. This decision was rendered by the court in its capacity as the Supreme Court of AUSTRIA during the *Anschluss* period, and it should be seen in the context of the then prevailing practice of AUSTRIAN courts. See *Klang and Gschnitzer* 245; *G. Walker* 630-636.

conclusion that both claimants had been lawfully married to the deceased at the time of his death. The sanction thus given to "legal bigamy" must be seen in the light of the fact that the proceedings took place at a time when both marriages had in any case been dissolved by the man's death. In this situation, and in view of the particular purpose of the proceedings, there was not thought to be any strong objection to treating both marriages as having been valid simultaneously; but this solution could scarcely be applied generally.[711]

There is in cases of this kind a tension between the forum's refusal to recognise the foreign divorce and its desire to sustain the new marriage. Usually, so it seems, these problems originate in an unsatisfactory state of the forum's rules for the recognition of foreign divorces which are felt to be too stringent. While the wide reference approach offers a means of avoiding invalidation of the second marriage in certain cases (namely, where the divorce is valid by the appropriate foreign law for capacity to marry), it produces too many fresh difficulties to commend itself for acceptance, except perhaps in special circumstances such as were present in the above case decided by the German *Reichsgericht*. A much more adequate remedy, enabling the cause rather than the symptom of the problem to be attacked, is by widening the forum's basis for the recognition of foreign divorces.[712] Often, it is true, this course cannot be adopted by the courts without awaiting legislative action. Sometimes, however, a satisfactory solution can be reached by the courts by means of a liberal construction of the existing rules or perhaps by "stretching" them beyond their normal limits.[713] In some cases in which the second marriage was upheld it is rather doubtful whether the court based its decision on the wide reference approach (the divorce and the remarriage being valid by the foreign *lex causae* for capacity to marry) or on a construction of the forum's own rules concerning the recognition of foreign divorces.[714] This class of ambiguous judgments includes a

711. See *Gamillscheg*, Kommentar, art. 13 no. 257-258, 261; *Wengler*, case note: Rev. crit. d.i.p. 1957, 57, 59. For critical notes of the decision see *Ferid*: Giur. Comp. D.I.P. 12 (1956) 219, and *Makarov*: Giur. Comp. D.I.P. 12 (1956) 316.

712. Cf. *Gamillscheg*, Kommentar, art. 13 no. 261; *Hartley*, Bigamy 687.

713. For an illustrative example see the DUTCH case decided by Rb. Amsterdam 21 March 1961, N.J. 1961 no. 300, Clunet 1964, 640, note Kollewijn.

714. For an example see the FRENCH decision of Trib. Seine 11 July 1918, Clunet 1919, 286 (cf. *supra* n. 461). See also the ITALIAN practice treated *supra* s. 82.

well-known *Canadian* case ultimately decided by the Supreme Court of Canada.[715]

> H(1) and W, both Jews of Hungarian domicile, decided to emigrate to Israel. While *en route* to that country, they were divorced in Italy by means of a *ghet* in accordance with Jewish law. This divorce was not recognised as bringing the marriage to an end either in Italy or in Hungary (where they were still domiciled), but it was so recognised in Israel, where both spouses arrived and became domiciled shortly after the divorce. Whilst so domiciled W married H(2) in Ontario, where she was on a temporary visit and where he was domiciled. Subsequently H(2) sought a declaration of nullity in the Ontario court on the ground that W was still married to H(1), inasmuch as that union had not been dissolved by a divorce recognised in Ontario. In rejecting the petition the court relied on Israeli law, the law of W's domicile at the time of the second marriage, by which she had had the status of a single woman free to enter into that union.

This decision apparently lends support to the wide reference approach, inasmuch as the divorce of the first marriage, being without effect according to the law of the domicile of the spouses at the time of the divorce, could not be recognised under the conflict of laws rules of the forum in Ontario, at least as those rules stood when the case at bar arose.[716] On this assumption the only possible basis for sustaining the wife's second marriage was that the divorce was valid by the foreign law governing her capacity to marry again.[717] The *ratio decidendi* is not clearly stated, however,

715. Schwebel v. Ungar (1963), 42 D.L.R. (2d) 622 (Ont. C.A.), Clunet 1964, 888, note Castel, Rev. crit. d.i.p. 1965, 321, note Wengler; aff'd (1964), 48 D.L.R. (2d) 644 (S.C.C.), Clunet 1969, 746, note Castel. For further comments on this case see *Rigaux,* Conflit mobile 421-422, 429-430; *Wengler,* Nouvelles réflexions 187-188; and *infra* n. 717-718. The decision is also of interest in respect of certain other questions of the conflicts law of marriage, *inter alia* the distinction between unilateral and bilateral marriage impediments (*supra* at n. 397-398). For a comparable DUTCH decision see Rb. Dordrecht 10 April 1964, N.J. 1965 no. 218, Clunet 1969, 1019, note Kollewijn (see *supra* n. 394).

716. The leading ENGLISH case on this point is Armitage v. Att.-Gen., [1906] P. 135; see *Dicey and Morris* 315-318. That case has been followed in CANADA on several occasions; see, for example, Re Jones (1960), 25 D.L.R. (2d) 595 (B.C.S.C.); Viccari v. Viccari, [1972] 3 O.R. 706 (H.C.).

717. See *Castel,* Conflict 55-58; *Cheshire and North* 55-57, 351; *Dicey and Morris* 35-36, 267, 268, 335, 337; *Graveson,* Conflict 77-78; *Kahn-Freund,* Problems 293; *Lysyk* 374-380; *Nygh* 237; *Swan* 49-55. Contrast the earlier

and the reasoning of the court is rather confusing. The decision is therefore alternatively open to the explanation that the court intended to lay down a novel ground for the recognition of foreign divorces by the forum.[718]

Where, as in the cases now referred to, the policy of upholding marriages is held to carry such weight as to prevail even though the divorce of a prior union does not meet the normal conditions for recognition by the forum, the question may finally be asked whether it is really appropriate to confine the operation of that policy to cases in which the divorce is good by the law applicable in respect of capacity to marry. Admittedly, this limitation is necessary if the wide reference approach is regarded as the sole conceptual tool permitting the forum to ignore the requirements of its own law for the recognition of foreign divorces. If, however, it is accepted that the true motive for such departures from the conflicts rules of the *lex fori* is to be found in the policy of validation rather than in any dogmatic view as to the treatment of the incidental question, then there is no obstacle to carrying that policy beyond the limits set by the wide reference approach. There may well be situations where those limits are hardly rational because it appears desirable to protect an existing marriage although the divorce of the prior union is invalid both by the *lex fori* and by the *lex causae* of the main issue (capacity for remarriage).[719]

CANADIAN case of Miller v. Allison (1917), 33 D.L.R. 144 (B.C.S.C.), where this factor was apparently treated as immaterial (cf. *supra* n. 398). The approach adopted in the *Schwebel* case was approved *obiter* in the ENGLISH case of Padolecchia v. Padolecchia, [1968] P. 314, 338-339. See also *North* 199-200, 268, 378, 382. Nevertheless, it seems doubtful whether this approach would be followed in ENGLAND. See for cases in which the courts, while not deciding the present issue, based their reasoning on the assumption that the validity of the divorce by the ENGLISH conflict of laws is the relevant test: Shaw v. Gould (1868), L.R. 3 H.L. 55; In re Sterling, [1908] 2 Ch. 344. And see among writers: *Hartley*, Bigamy 685-687; *Webb*, Bigamy and Capacity to Marry: 14 I.C.L.Q. 659 (1965) suggesting (at 661) that an ENGLISH court would solve the problem in the *Schwebel* case by adopting "a strictly historical approach"; cf. *Wolff*, PIL 380.

718. See *Castel*, case note: Clunet 1969, 746, 750-752; *Hartley*, Bigamy 685-687; *Hooper*; *Lysyk* 370-374; *Nygh* 437.

719. Suppose, for instance, that the facts in the GERMAN case cited *supra* n. 707 had been the same except that the husband's remarriage in the USA had preceded his change of nationality, so that according to GERMAN conflict of laws his capacity to enter into that marriage had been determinable by GERMAN law. It seems that this would in no way have altered the *fait accompli* created by the remarriage, which was the essential motive making the court acquiesce in its validity.

Statutory support for validating solutions which are independent of any particular doctrine with regard to the incidental question exists in *Finland* and *Sweden*. The relevant Finnish statute provides that a marriage entered into by a person whose prior marriage has been dissolved by a foreign divorce which is not recognised in Finland may not be annulled on this ground.[720] This apparently means that the new marriage must be held valid whenever the divorce is valid by any foreign law, regardless of whether that law coincides with the *lex causae* of capacity to marry. In contrast with this provision, which is limited to the effect of the divorce on the fresh marriage, the corresponding Swedish statute relates to the recognition of the divorce, as affected by the remarriage of either party, for all purposes: as a rule, such remarriage operates to validate a foreign divorce which does not meet the conditions for recognition otherwise imposed by Swedish law.[721] Both of these provisions bear a certain resemblance, in respect of their policy and effects, to the American doctrine that a person who has remarried in reliance on a foreign divorce decree is thereby estopped from asserting the invalidity of the decree (*supra* s. 27).

abb. Existence of Prior Marriage Denied by Lex Fori, Affirmed by Foreign Law

84. *Introductory*. This situation is much more frequent in practice than that considered in the preceding sections. It usually involves a (proposed) remarriage after a divorce validly granted by the forum but not recognised by the foreign law proper to judge the capacity of one of the parties to the fresh union.[722] If the wide reference approach is adopted here, it means that the remarriage will be barred since the prior union still subsists in the

720. Act of 5 Dec. 1929, § 49.

721. This rule applies "unless the other spouse shows that the remarried party acted manifestly unduly towards him". See the Act of 8 July 1904 (as amended in 1973) ch. 3 § 7 par. 2 and the legislative history in NJA 1973 II 595, 598. See also for the law prior to the enactment of this provision: *Eek* 247-248; *Michaeli*, Internationales Privatrecht gemäss schwedischem Recht und schwedischer Rechtsprechung (Stockholm 1948) 191, 210-211; *Pålsson*, Haltande äktenskap 495-498; *Undén*, Internationell äktenskapsrätt 56-57, 62, 93; *idem*, Studier 64-65. A similar principle enjoys some support in DANISH and NORWEGIAN practice; see *Svenné Schmidt* 369-372, 384-385, 392.

722. For comparative writings on these problems see: *Gamillscheg*, Kommentar, art. 13 no. 290-295; *Makarov*, Remariage; *Müller-Freienfels* 72-84; *Neumayer* 77-80; *Rabel* 306-307, 557-559; *Pi-Song Tsai* 207-302.

eyes of the foreign *lex causae*. Until some years ago this solution enjoyed a considerable amount of support in a number of countries, chiefly in Western Europe (*infra* s. 85-87). In describing this system special attention will be given to *(West) German* law, where our problem has played a more prominent part than in any other country and where the wide reference approach still prevails in certain cases. Generally speaking, however, the tendency has for some time now been in favour of the opposite solution based on the narrow reference approach (whether or not the problem is discussed in the terms of the incidental question). In so far as this view is accepted, the impediment of the prior marriage is held to be removed by a divorce which is valid according to the *lex fori*, regardless of the position taken by one foreign law or another (*infra* s. 88-90).

abba. Wide Reference Approach

85. *[West] German Law Until 1971.* Questions of the present type have produced an abundant body of case law and literature in West Germany. Until the picture was in part changed by a decision of the Federal Constitutional Court in 1971 (*infra* s. 88), the wide reference approach was generally adopted in the practice of courts and marriage registrars and supported by the weight of opinion among writers.[723]

One group of cases concerned an attempted remarriage by a foreigner whose prior union had ended in a divorce pronounced by a West German court but not recognised by his *lex patriae* (at the time of the proposed second marriage).[724] The typical situation in these cases was that the divorce had been obtained by the

723. See among writers: *Gamillscheg*, Kommentar, art. 13 no. 298-315; *Henrich*, Einführung in die Behandlung von Personenstandsfällen mit Auslandsberührung: StAZ 1966, 63, 65-67; *Hoffmann and Stephan* § 5 no. 28; *Lauterbach* 27; *Makarov*, Remariage 661-665; *Marquardt*, Zur Frage der Zulässigkeit der Wiederheirat eines in der Bundesrepublik geschiedenen Ausländers: StAZ 1963, 46-51; *Neuhaus*, Grundbegriffe 349-350; *Neumayer* 67-77; *Raape*, IPR 316-317; *Süss* 249-258; *Wolff*, IPR 212. For further references to cases and literature favourable to this view see *Dorenberg* 150 n. 108-109; *Gamillscheg*, *ibid.* no. 281-286. And see as to cases of a divorce granted abroad and recognised in WEST GERMANY but not in the country of the intending spouse's nationality, *Gamillscheg*, *ibid.* no. 316.

724. Although the relevant conflicts rules of WEST GERMAN law are based on the nationality principle, there are several situations in which a GERMAN court may come to grant a divorce which is not recognised by the national law of the parties or one of them. See *Gamillscheg*, Kommentar, art. 13 no. 270-280.

other spouse, who was of German nationality, on the strength of the *lex fori,* which according to West German conflict of laws applies in proceedings for divorce brought by a local national regardless of the nationality of the other spouse.[725] While there is no doubt that the German party to such a divorce is free to marry again in West Germany (his or her capacity to do so being a matter for German law), it was held that the foreigner did not have the same right since his capacity to marry remained subject to his national law by which the prior union was considered still in force. Many cases in which the German authorities therefore declined to solemnise a proposed marriage involved nationals of countries such as Italy or Spain which, as a reflection of the hostility to divorce characterising their domestic laws, refused absolutely to recognise foreign divorces of their nationals.[726] The same position was taken in cases where for some other reason the foreigner's *lex patriae* did not recognise his divorce, whether because it made such recognition subject to the condition (not met in the case at hand) that a ground for divorce existed under its own domestic rules,[727] or because it claimed exclusive jurisdiction for divorces of its own nationals or otherwise did not admit the jurisdiction of the German court.[728] Even where the divorce would in all probability be recognised by the relevant foreign law but where that law required it to be validated in special exequatur proceedings (*supra* s. 81), the divorced party was held to be precluded from marrying again until an exequatur had been granted by the appropriate foreign authority.[729]

In another group of cases the impediment existing under the foreigner's national law was based on a prior marriage of his or her

725. EGBGB art. 17 par. 1 and 3.

726. E.g., LG Weiden 28 Feb. 1953, IPRspr. 1952/53 no. 104; LG Köln 10 Jan. 1962, IPRspr. 1962/63 no. 66; OLG Karlsruhe 3 Sept. 1962, IPRspr. 1962/63 no. 70; OLG München 17 Dec. 1962, IPRspr. 1962/63 no. 72; KG 9 Dec. 1968, IPRspr. 1968/69 no. 70.

727. OLG Frankfurt 23 March 1964, IPRspr. 1964/65 no. 76; cf. OLG Hamm 15 Oct. 1951, IPRspr. 1950/51 no. 73.

728. E.g., KG 17 Oct. 1930, IPRspr. 1931 no. 62; RG 3 July 1939, RGZ 160, 396, 403 (*obiter*); President of OLG Hamburg 5 Aug. 1955, IPRspr. 1954/55 no. 84, Rev. crit. d.i.p. 1957, 50, note Wengler; OLG Celle 26 June 1963, IPRspr. 1962/63 no. 75; President of OLG Hamburg 27 Sept. 1963, IPRspr. 1962/63 no. 77.

729. OLG Bremen 16 May 1963, IPRspr. 1962/63 no. 74 (both parties to prior marriage German nationals at time of divorce; W then acquired Italian nationality and was not allowed to marry again without grant of exequatur by ITALIAN court). See also KG 9 Dec. 1968, IPRspr. 1968/69 no. 70, and the cases cited *infra* n. 789.

intended partner. Almost all these cases involved a proposed union between a Spanish national, who had not himself (herself) been previously married, and a German national divorced from his (her) first spouse by a decree of a German court but regarded by Spanish law as still bound by that marriage so as to prevent the Spanish party from marrying him (her).[730] Although Spanish law was wholly unrelated to the prior union, it was given effect, here too, so that the parties could not marry in West Germany.[731]

In both types of case referred to here the courts often found it necessary also to examine the question of whether the prior marriage had been validly created in the eyes of the relevant foreign law and to establish that the conditions of such validity were met.[732] Obviously there could otherwise not be any bar to remarriage on the present ground.

Although these solutions represented current West German law, they were a source of dissatisfaction in many instances and met with much opposition by courts and commentators arguing that remarriage must be permitted on the authority of the forum's

730. On the position of SPANISH law see *supra* at n. 355-356. The problem rarely presents itself in relation to other laws, few of which go to the length of SPANISH law in refusing to give effect to foreign divorces. Even in countries whose domestic law fails to provide for any possibility of divorce, foreign divorces of foreign nationals (or domiciliaries, as the case may be) are usually recognised when certain conditions are fulfilled. See, e.g., *Böhmer*, Die Eheschliessung geschiedener Deutscher mit ledigen Ausländern in Deutschland: StAZ 1965, 201-206; *Makarov*, Remariage 644-646; *Müller-Freienfels* 68-72; *Rabel* 535-541; *Valladão* (*supra* n. 687) 444-450. Moreover, although an existing marriage is usually classified as a bilateral impediment to remarriage, this concept is not always accepted when the union has been validly dissolved in the eyes of the divorced party's own personal law; see *supra* s. 49 and 51, particularly n. 394 (ITALIAN law), cf. the WEST GERMAN decision of BayObLG 9 Sept. 1960, IPRspr. 1960/61 no. 100 (marriage between a man of Italian and a divorced woman of German nationality held valid).

731. The leading case was BGH 12 Feb. 1964, BGHZ 41, 136, IPRspr. 1964/65 no. 74. For approving comments on this case see: *Gamillscheg*, Grundrechte 332-335; *Henrich:* NJW 1964, 2015; *Neuhaus*, Grundrechte; *Wengler*: JZ 1964, 621. For criticism see *Dieckmann*, Eheschliessung; *Fischer*: NJW 1964, 1323. See also *Abel*, Private International Law and German Matrimonial Law: 14 I.C.L.Q. 674-675 (1965).
Other decisions holding the same way include: OLG Celle 25 June 1962, IPRspr. 1962/63 no. 69; BGH 14 July 1966, BGHZ 46, 87, IPRspr. 1966/67 no. 59 b; OLG Celle 13 March 1967, IPRspr. 1966/67 no. 67; OLG Hamm 3 May 1968, IPRspr. 1968/69 no. 66.

732. See, for instance, BGH 12 Feb. 1964, BGHZ 41, 136, 141-142. Cf. *Böhmer*, Eheschliessung (*supra* n. 730) 202.

divorce decree irrespective of its recognition by any foreign law.[733] Several attempts were made to restrict the scope of the prevailing principle by introducing one distinction or the other.[734] One restriction was accepted by the courts at an early stage, namely, that the relevant foreign law, while effective to preclude the solemnisation of a new marriage in the circumstances envisaged here, could not be applied to invalidate the marriage afterwards if it had been celebrated nevertheless. The courts accordingly refused to grant a nullity decree sought on the ground that the divorce of the prior union was invalid by the foreign *lex causae.*[735] To that extent, it was considered, a German court could not ignore its own divorce decree.[736]

While this validating solution was of limited significance for locally celebrated marriages (which could only come about if the impediment existing under the *lex patriae* was disregarded inadvertently), it came to play a more prominent part in respect of

733. See the references *infra* n. 772-773. Opinions were, and still are, also divided over the question of whether a person may conclude another marriage in West Germany when his prior union has not been dissolved by divorce but where that union limps already from the outset, being invalid in WEST GERMANY but valid in the country of the party's nationality which furnishes the *lex causae* of his capacity for remarriage. For *obiter dicta* to the effect that the latter law should prevail so as to bar a remarriage see: LG Mannheim 17 March 1953, IPRspr. 1952/53 no. 96; OLG Hamm 10 March 1970, IPRspr. 1970 no. 45. See also *Beitzke*, Wiederverehelichung nach unwirksamer konsularischer Trauung: StAZ 1952, 169-171; *Dorenberg* 68-69; *Lauterbach* 27; *Raape,* IPR 242. So also in the case of a German decree of annulment of the prior marriage which is not recognised by the *lex patriae* of the party desiring to remarry in West Germany: *Jayme,* Nullità del matrimonio per difetto di assenso dei genitori e riacquisto dello stato libero in una recente vicenda matrimoniale italo-tedesca: Dir. Int. 1965 I 169-176. For views to the contrary (remarriage to be permitted) see: *Albers* 145-147, 172; *Gamillscheg*, Kommentar, art. 13 no. 265-268 (with distinctions).

734. For surveys of such proposals see *Gamillscheg,* Kommentar, art. 13 no. 296-297; *Pålsson,* Haltande äktenskap 434-438.

735. KG 13 March 1911, NiemeyersZ 23 (1913) 331 (aff'd on other grounds, RG 21 March 1912, JW 1912, 642); KG 7 March 1938, JW 1938, 1258, note Massfeller; see also LG München 6 Feb. 1948, IPRspr. 1950/51 no. 68.

736. For writers sharing this view see, e.g., *Albers,* Einzelfragen der Befreiung von der Beibringung des Ehefähigkeitszeugnisses: StAZ 1952, 49, 51; *Gamillscheg,* Doppelehe 72-73 (cf., however, *idem,* Kommentar, art. 13 no. 320, where a more reserved attitude is adopted); *Hoffmann and Stephan* § 5 no. 28; *Jayme* 38, 44-45; *Massfeller* 225-226; *Raape,* Kommentar 263, 376, 404-405; *idem,* Die hinkende Scheidung: StAZ 1958, 281, 282. Further references are given by *Dorenberg* 156 and by *Gamillscheg,* Kommentar, art. 13 no. 317-319.

marriages entered into abroad. This was especially so in the context of evasion, since the success of the devices used to escape the impediment in question (*Tondern marriages* and the like; *supra* s. 63) ultimately depended on the attitude of the West German courts. As a rule, these marriages were held to be valid in West Germany and to be liable to annulment only by the courts of the home country whose law had been infringed.[737] Some doubts existed in the case of marriages which were void *ipso jure* under the relevant foreign law.[738] Even in these cases, however, the prevailing tendency was in favour of treating the union as valid in West Germany.[739] The sanction thus given to foreign marriages entered into in violation, and usually in deliberate evasion, of the present impediment tended to weaken the case for upholding that impediment for unions celebrated in West Germany itself and

737. See the references *supra* n. 512-514. According to a rival view, such unions were also liable to annulment in a WEST GERMAN court if proceedings to this end were instituted. For a decision so holding (in a case which did not involve any element of evasion) on the strength of SPANISH law see LG Essen 28 April 1959, IPRspr. 1958/59 no. 123. And see among writers, e.g., *Gamillscheg*, Kommentar, art. 13 no. 320; *Luther* 696-697.

738. For a case involving SPANISH law where that law was so construed, with the consequence that the marriage was refused recognition even in the absence of any nullity decree, see AG Hamburg 3 Jan. 1966, FamRZ 1967, 505. Similarly in cases where the divorce had been granted by a foreign court and was followed by remarriage abroad: LG Ulm 8 Aug. 1956, IPRspr. 1956/57 no. 101 (ARGENTINE law), cf. IPG 1965/66 no. 13 (Hamburg); OLG Köln 14 July 1971, IPRspr. 1971 no. 63 (SPANISH law). See among writers favourable to this view: *Beitzke*, Prüfungsrecht und Prüfungspflicht des Standesbeamten bei Eintragung von Personenstandsfällen: StAZ 1968, 210, 212; *Hoffmann*, case note: StAZ 1967, 154; *Reuschler*, Haben Spanierinnen, die in einem Drittstaat mit einem geschiedenen deutschen Staatsangehörigen die Ehe schliessen, einen Einbürgerungsanspruch?: StAZ 1967, 216, 217-218; *Samtleben* 109-110 (for BRAZILIAN law).

739. In most cases where the marriage was, or possibly was, void *ipso jure* by the relevant foreign law, the courts – contrary to the decisions cited in the preceding note – seem to have treated it as merely voidable nevertheless. The grounds invoked in support of this practice vary: while in one line of cases the decision was based on a construction of the foreign law, other courts held, for one reason or another (*inter alia*, the demands of local public policy), that the foreign law could not be given effect on the present point since the invalidity of a marriage on grounds of substance could not be asserted until it had been established by judicial decree in proceedings for annulment, as required by GERMAN domestic law (Marriage Act of 1946, § 23). See for cases involving SPANISH and BRAZILIAN law *supra* n. 512-514. In another case confronting the court with BRAZILIAN law the marriage was upheld by means of a very dubious application of the principle of *renvoi*: OLG Celle 18 Sept. 1968, IPRspr. 1968/69 no. 67, see *supra* n. 469.

thereby contributed to paving the way for a liberalisation of this practice.

86. *Other Countries.* Solutions similar to those prevailing in West Germany were until recently supported by the weight of opinion in *Austria* and *Switzerland.*[740] The wide reference approach was clearly adopted by the Swiss Federal Tribunal in the *Caliaro* case, which was the leading Swiss authority on the matter:[741]

> H, of Italian nationality, was divorced from W(1), a Swiss national, by a decree of a Swiss court.[742] He then sought to marry W(2), also a Swiss national, both parties being domiciled in Switzerland. Aware that the projected union could not be celebrated in Switzerland the parties went to England and got married there, returning to live in Switzerland afterwards. They then applied to the appropriate cantonal authority for entry of the marriage in the Swiss registers of civil status. Their application was rejected, and the parties appealed to the Federal Tribunal. The appeal was dismissed on the ground that the marriage could not be recognised as valid in Switzerland, H's capacity to enter into it being subject to Italian law which did not recognise his divorce and therefore regarded him as still married to W(1).

This decision goes even further than the West German practice referred to above, inasmuch as a marriage already celebrated abroad was denied recognition by applying the *lex causae* of capacity to marry, although by that law the union was only voidable (*i.e.,* valid until annulled) and although no steps had been taken to annul it either in Italy or in Switzerland.[743] *A*

740. AUSTRIA: OLG Wien 14 June 1971, EFSlg 8 (1971) 213 no. 15,735; *H. Hoyer* 37-53, 62-65; *V. Hoyer,* Wiederverehelichung; *Klang and Gschnitzer* 850; *Schwendenwein,* Die eherechtliche Situation spanischer Staatsangehöriger in Österreich: ZfRV 15 (1974) 93, 95-98; *Schwind,* Ehen von Griechen 170-171, 178; SWITZERLAND: *Aubert,* book review: Rev. crit. d.i.p. 1962, 614, 617; *Beck,* art. 7 c no. 11-12, art. 7 e no. 43; *Schnitzer* 374; *Spivak* 56.

741. BG 11 Nov. 1954, BGE 80 I 427, Schw. Jb. Int. R. 13 (1956) 237 with a critical note by Lalive, Rev. crit. d.i.p. 1957, 50, note Wengler; also noted by *Reymond*: 5 I.C.L.Q. 144 (1956) (critically). For approving comments, which are few in number, see *Jagmetti* 131-134; *Vaucher* 550-552.

742. Divorces of such mixed marriages are governed exclusively by SWISS law if the petition is brought by the spouse of Swiss nationality: NAG art. 7 g par. 2. The position in this respect is the same as in WEST GERMANY (*supra* n. 725) as well as in many other countries whose conflicts rules for divorce are based on the nationality principle.

743. Cf. *supra* at n. 508.

fortiori, the decision implied a bar to the celebration of such a marriage in Switzerland.[744]

Although this decision represented the law for many years, the principle sanctioned by it seems never to have become as firmly established as it was in West Germany. It was increasingly being criticised, not always followed in the practice of the cantonal authorities administering this part of Swiss law, and eventually had to be abandoned by the Federal Tribunal.[745]

Before this happened, however, the rule in *Caliaro* came to play a role in the development of *English* law on the present point. In a case presenting facts very similar to those of *Caliaro,* the English court refused to permit an Italian national, domiciled in Switzerland and divorced from his first wife there, to marry again in England on the ground that he was unable to do so by Swiss law, which as his *lex domicilii* was the law referred to in the first instance by the English conflicts rule.[746] In so holding the

744. Regierungsrat Kanton St. Gallen 4 Feb. 1964, SJZ 64 (1968) 292; ObG Solothurn 16 March 1966, SJZ 63 (1967) 176. Nevertheless an exception was admitted where the refusal on the part of the foreign law to recognise the SWISS divorce was based on rules sanctioning distinctions of a religious nature. The typical example was supplied by LIECHTENSTEIN law which, while not prohibiting divorce (or excluding the recognition of foreign divorces of Liechtenstein nationals) generally, provided that the marriage of a person of the Catholic faith could only be dissolved by the death of one of the spouses (ABGB § 111, since repealed). It was held that no effect could be given in SWITZERLAND to the prohibition of divorce thus imposed on grounds of religion, because to do so would violate the fundamental principle of religious neutrality endorsed by SWISS law. Accordingly, Liechtenstein nationals divorced in Switzerland contrary to this prohibition were permitted to marry again: Regierungsrat Kanton Zürich 16 Oct. 1952, SJZ 48 (1952) 376, RabelsZ 19 (1954) 659, see *Vischer,* Ordre public 326-327; Conseil d'Etat Canton de Thurgovie 17 Feb. 1959, Schw. Jb. Int. R. 16 (1959) 319, Clunet 1961, 206. In the course of time, more far-reaching departures from the rule in *Caliaro* came to be accepted in the practice of several cantons; see *Götz,* Anerkennung ausländischer Zivilstandsurkunden zur Eintragung in die schweizerischen Personenstandsregister: StAZ 1969, 253, 258; *von Overbeck,* Remariage 55-56; and the account of this practice given in the decision of BG 3 June 1971, BGE 97 I 389, 397.

745. See the references *supra* n. 744 and *infra* n. 799-802.

746. R. v. Brentwood Marriage Registrar, [1968] 2 Q.B. 956, Rev. crit. d.i.p. 1969, 491, note Wengler. For discussion of this case see further: *Chesterman,* A "Limping Divorce": 32 M.L.R. 84-88 (1969); *Cohn,* Capacity to Marry – a Postscript: 90 L.Q.R. 448-452 (1974); *Dicey and Morris* 36; *Hartley,* Policy Basis 581-583; *Kahn-Freund,* Problems 292-293; *North* 130, 192, 267-268; *von Overbeck,* Relativität 295-296. Another case where the court proceeded on the same approach (although on the facts the problem

continued on page 236

court took into account that a Swiss court, following the rule in *Caliaro's* case, would probably decide the question by Italian law, which again did not recognise the divorce.[747] Although in this case the divorce had been granted by a foreign court (from the English point of view), there was no doubt that it met the conditions of recognition in England. The position was therefore essentially the same as if the divorce had been pronounced by the English court itself, and the decision in the instant case would presumably have been the same if it had.[748]

There is thus clear indication that English courts leaned in favour of the wide reference approach. In England too, however, the law has since been changed in a way which seems now to rule out this solution at least for most cases.[749]

Scattered support for solutions based on the wide reference approach is to be found, *inter alia*, in *Belgian, Dutch, French* and *Italian* case law and literature.[750] In a French case, for instance, where a man of Italian nationality had been divorced from his first wife in France and then remarried in the same country, the court granted a petition for annulment brought by the second wife on the ground that the man's divorce was invalid by his *lex patriae*.[751]

continued from page 235

under review did not arise for decision) is Padolecchia v. Padolecchia, [1968] P. 314; see *P.B. Carter* (1968) 245-246; *North* 122; *Swan* 56-58. See also for SCOTLAND: Rojas, Petitioner, 1967 S.L.T. 24 (Sh. Ct.); AUSTRALIA: Hogarth v. Ray, [1958] Qd. R. 337, 340 (S.C.).

747. On the aspect of *renvoi* involved here see *supra* at n. 464-465.

748. An earlier case lending some weight to this view is Breen v. Breen, [1964] P. 144, Clunet 1965, 453, note Lipstein. See *Cheshire and North* 351-352; *Hartley*, Bigamy 687-688; *Morris* 109-110; *North* 194, 268; and the comments cited *supra* n. 556. In favour of this solution see also *Gotlieb* 545-546, 553-554; *Wolff*, PIL 379 (but see *ibid.* 209-210).

749. See *infra* at n. 809-811. Apparently, however, the common law rule remains in force for cases where the second marriage was celebrated outside the United Kingdom, as well as in some other special situations; see *North* 192-195, 267-268.

750. See *infra* n. 751-752, 754 and 757 (DUTCH cases). At least as regards BELGIUM, FRANCE and the NETHERLANDS, however, this is a minority view which scarcely represents the law of those countries; see *infra* s. 89 at n. 794-796.

751. Trib. Seine 2 June 1942, Nouv. Rev. d.i.p. 1943, 117. Although the decision in this case accords with the wide reference approach, it is actually based on a different theory, known as *la théorie distributive* and once current in FRENCH conflict of laws, by which divorces of mixed marriages were governed as to each of the spouses separately by their respective personal laws, with the consequence that the matrimonial bond could be dissolved as to one of them but still subsist in regard to the other, whose personal law did not

Some other courts and writers denying, for the same reason, a divorced foreigner's capacity for remarriage deal with the analogous situation where (as in the above-mentioned English case) the divorce had been pronounced in a third country and was recognised under the conflicts rules of the *lex fori,* such recognition being treated as insufficient or immaterial for the present purpose.[752]

According to a view advanced by writers in several countries, a distinction should be drawn between cases of the type so far referred to, where the impediment existing under the foreign *lex causae* of capacity to marry is based on a prior marriage by the foreigner himself, and situations, typically involving the intermarriage of a divorced local national and a Spaniard, where the impediment relates to a prior union of the foreigner's intended partner: while it is considered necessary (or at least possible) that the foreign law should prevail in the former situation so as to bar another marriage, this solution is rejected in the latter because there it would amount to an encroachment by the foreign (Spanish) law upon what is held to be the sole concern of the

---

admit divorce; see *Batiffol and Lagarde* II 13-14 and, for a BELGIAN decision resting on the same peculiar theory, Cour Gand 17 June 1948, Rev. crit. belge 1949, 7, note Spanoghe, Clunet 1946/49, 82. For other countries see GREECE: *Maridakis,* Introduction au droit international privé: Rec. des Cours 105 (1962-I) 375, 442; ITALY: *A. Miele* 140 (cf., however, *Vitta* II 188-190); TURKEY: Supreme Court 5 March 1962, Clunet 1974, 183, note Sevig (but see the decision by the same court cited *infra* n. 793); and as regards certain ISLAMIC countries: *Benattar* 84-85.

752. For a DUTCH decision see Rb. Rotterdam 8 April 1968, N.J. 1969 no. 164, N.T.I.R. 18 (1971) 88. And see for ITALIAN law: *A. Miele* 141; *Picone* 6 (n. 1), 9 (n. 4), 62-77, 80; and among decisions pointing in the same direction, App. Roma 17 June 1961, Foro pad. 1963 I 1272, note M. Miele, Clunet 1964, 337 (cf. for an earlier decision in the same case, App. Roma 2 July 1959, Riv. dir. matr. 1959, 703, note Cassoni); App. Cagliari 17 March 1961, Foro it. 1961 I 682, Clunet 1964, 336. In these cases a second marriage was annulled by the ITALIAN court because the divorce of a prior union was not recognised by the relevant *lex patriae;* but the decisions are probably inconclusive since such recognition seems *ipso facto* also to have been excluded under the *lex fori,* so that the present problem was not really posed; cf. *Vitta* I 478, II 186, and *supra* s. 82. For an analogous BELGIAN case see Rb. Antwerpen 31 May 1939, RW 1938/39, 1653. The solution referred to here is also accepted by some writers insisting, in accordance with the narrow reference approach, that a remarriage must be permitted when the divorce has been pronounced by the forum itself; see *P. Lagarde,* La règle de conflit applicable aux questions préalables: Rev. crit. d.i.p. 1960, 459, 470-473 (cf. 481-482); *Rabel* 559.

divorced party's own law.[753] Occasionally, however, effect has been given to the foreign law in this type of situation also. In a *Belgian* case, for instance, a marriage between a Belgian woman, divorced from her first husband in Belgium, and a Spanish national was annulled, on her petition, on the ground that Spanish law did not recognise the divorce.[754]

Finally, attention should be drawn in this connection to the *Hague Convention on Marriage* of 1902. This convention does not provide for any exception to the rule of the *lex patriae* where that law prohibits a marriage because it does not regard a prior union of one of the parties as validly terminated.[755] It has usually been inferred from the absence of any such provision that no exception is permissible in such a case even if the divorce has been granted (or is recognised) by the forum.[756] This interpretation has been

753. See for AUSTRIA: *V. Hoyer,* Wiederverehelichung 620 (reserving the possibility of such a distinction); FRANCE: *Audinet* 182; ITALY: *Vitta* II 188 n. 51; SWITZERLAND: *von Overbeck,* Remariage 51-52 (cf. the ENGLISH case cited *supra* n. 746, where the other intending spouse was of Spanish nationality and domiciled in Switzerland but where no attention was given to SPANISH law or to the question of its relevance under SWISS conflict of laws). See also for WEST GERMAN law *Dieckmann,* Eheschliessung 106.

754. Cour Bruxelles 14 Dec. 1955, Rev. crit. d.i.p. 1957, 68 with a critical note by Rigaux; also criticised by *van Hecke and Rigaux* (1953 à 1960) 369-370. For a similar FRENCH case see Trib. Montpellier 18 March 1920, Rev. crit. d.i.p. 1921, 79. This decision has been the subject of much adverse comment; see the references *infra* n. 794. But see for approval (in the result) *Champcommunal,* Un conflit de lois nouveau. L'exclusion du divorce entraîne-t-elle l'interdiction d'épouser des étrangers divorcés?: Rev. crit. d.i.p. 1921, 41-57; cf. *Bischoff* no. 33-39; *Niboyet* V 317-319. And see for a MOROCCAN decision holding the same way, Cour Rabat 14 March 1958, Clunet 1961, 510 with an approving note by Decroux.

755. Under art. 3 par. 1 of the convention the only case in which the celebration of a marriage may be permitted contrary to the applicable *lex patriae* is where the prohibition of that law is "exclusively founded on reasons of a religious character". This provision, as generally understood, does not cover the impediment resulting from a prior marriage which is still subsisting in the eyes of the *lex patriae.* Support for this interpretation is derived, *inter alia,* from a juxtaposition of art. 3 and art. 2 par. 3 of the convention. The latter provision, which deals with the converse question of interference of local public policy to forbid a marriage permitted by the relevant foreign law, specifies that resort to such public policy may be had if the proposed union is prohibited by the local law either "by reason of a prior marriage" or because of "an obstacle of a religious character"; cf. *supra* n. 634, 639 and 674.

756. See, e.g., *Beck,* ESchlKonv. art. 1 no. 12, art. 3 no. 8; *Böhmer* 90-91; *De Winter,* Nationality or Domicile? – The Present State of Affairs: Rec. des Cours 128 (1969-III) 347, 457; *Gamillscheg,* Kommentar, art. 13 no. 300-301, 312, 958; *Jayme,* Der Entwurf einer Novelle zum EGBGB und

accepted by courts in several countries when deciding cases within the scope of the convention.[757] The position adopted by the prevailing opinion is not self-evident, however, nor has it remained uncontradicted or been consistently followed in practice.[758]

87. *Rationale.* The arguments invoked by the proponents of the wide reference approach run along two main lines, one predominantly dogmatic and the other more policy-oriented.[759]

On the first score, the *lex causae* is held to prevail simply because this is regarded as a necessary consequence of the fact that capacity to marry is made subject to an independent conflicts regime and to its own proper law, differing from that applicable to divorce. It is common ground that it falls within the scope of the law governing capacity to decide in the abstract whether an existing marriage constitutes a bar to a second union. If a divorce has been granted in respect of the prior marriage, therefore, its validity only becomes relevant because it is made so by the applicable foreign law, which (it is assumed) insists on monogamy.[760] The question

---

das Haager Eheschliessungsabkommen: StAZ 1965, 145-148; *idem*, Nochmals – Eheschliessung geschiedener Italiener in Deutschland und Haager Eheschliessungsabkommen: FamRZ 1967, 197-198; *F. Kahn* 114; *Lewald* 118-119; *Makarov*, Remariage 654; *van Sasse van Ysselt* 193.

757. E.g., WEST GERMANY: OLG Karlsruhe 3 Sept. 1962, IPRspr. 1962/63 no. 70; KG 9 Dec. 1968, IPRspr. 1968/69 no. 70; and cases cited *infra* n. 789; NETHERLANDS: Hoge Raad 26 Sept. 1918 (Heeremans v. Grob), *Kosters and Bellemans* 154; Rb. Rotterdam 8 April 1968, N.J. 1969 no. 164, N.T.I.R. 18 (1971) 88; Rb. Arnhem 10 Jan. 1974, N.J. 1974 no. 122; SWITZERLAND: BG 11 Nov. 1954, BGE 80 I 427, 435-436; Regierungsrat Kanton St. Gallen 4 Feb. 1964, SJZ 64 (1968) 292; BG 3 June 1971, BGE 97 I 389, 411-412.

758. For DUTCH decisions permitting an Italian national to remarry on the authority of a DUTCH divorce decree, contrary to ITALIAN law which applied under the convention, see Rb. Amsterdam 30 May 1961, Clunet 1969, 955, note Kollewijn; Rb. Alkmaar 1 Feb. 1968, N.T.I.R. 18 (1971) 87; Rb. Dordrecht 2 Feb. 1972, N.T.I.R. 21 (1974) 84, note Verheul. And see among writers: *Dieckmann*, Eheschliessung 105-106; *R. Lüderitz*, Stellungnahme (reply to *Jayme*, Nochmals, *supra* n. 756): FamRZ 1967, 198-199; *Nussbaum* 163 n. 2; *von Overbeck*, Remariage 61-63; *Picone* 70 n. 70; *Undén*, Studier 31-32, 35, 63.

759. Only a summary of these arguments will be given here. See more fully: *Gamillscheg*, Kommentar, art. 13 no. 298-315; *Makarov*, Remariage 661-664; *Pålsson*, Haltande äktenskap 430-434, 499-503 (with a critical examination); *Wengler*, Vorfrage 191-213 (with regard to the incidental question generally).

760. The position would be different if the foreign law permitted polygamy and the application of that law was excluded by virtue of the public policy of the *lex fori* (cf. *supra* s. 78).

being raised by that law, it is inferred that the answer must be supplied by the same law, *i.e.* by applying its conflicts rules; for if the forum were to reserve this issue for independent determination by its own law, it would (in the situations interesting us here) come to affirm a person's capacity to marry in the teeth of the *lex causae* of that matter, thereby distorting the applicable law and violating its own conflicts rule. The problem is thus reduced to a question of the proper application of the *lex causae*.

The appropriate solution being prima facie established, courts and writers usually proceed to discuss whether this solution ought to be rejected in the end for reasons of public policy or otherwise. In particular, attention is drawn to the objection, advanced by opponents of the wide reference approach, that this approach compels courts and marriage authorities to ignore their own divorce decree (or a foreign decree recognised by the forum). As against this, it is pointed out that the denial, on the strength of the relevant foreign law, of a person's right to marry again does not amount to denying the validity of the divorce for other purposes.[761] Although a valid decree of divorce normally carries with it the right of remarriage, this effect is held to be separable from others and not to be necessarily inherent in the decree; it is only produced by virtue of and to the extent sanctioned by the applicable rules of substantive law, the reach of which in its turn depends on the rules of the conflict of laws. In so far as capacity to marry is referable to foreign law under those rules, the implication is that the forum has in advance accepted that the authority of its divorce decree may be limited in this respect by the law so designated.[762] Consequently, it is argued, it is no true inconsistency for the forum, on the one hand, to affirm the validity of the divorce and, on the other, to deny the right of remarriage of one or both of the ex-spouses. Nor is there, in the opinion of courts and writers reasoning on these lines, any other tenable ground for excluding the normally governing foreign law from application.

761. Though this distinction is apparently ignored by some courts and writers, chiefly in FRANCE, basing their opinion on *la théorie distributive* (*supra* n. 751).

762. Cf. *Wengler*, case note: JZ 1964, 621, 622, coining the term *kollisionsrechtliche Relativität der Rechtskraft* to denote the fact that the authority of a judgment may vary with the law applicable to its different effects under the rules of the conflict of laws. For a critical appraisal of this concept see particularly *von Overbeck*, Relativität.

These arguments, it is submitted, fail to carry conviction.[763] Admittedly, foreign law ought to be applied "properly" or "faithfully", but this is only to the point in so far as such law applies at all, *i.e.* within the scope of the reference effected by the forum's conflicts rule. The argument is irrelevant in the present context unless and until it has been established that the determination of the validity of a divorce of a prior union is included within the ambit of the *lex causae* of capacity to marry, which is precisely the problem to be solved. Similarly question-begging is the allegation that the reference to foreign law on capacity to marry implies that the forum is prepared to tolerate the corresponding limitation on the authority of its divorce decree, or that the forum by deciding otherwise would, in part, be depriving the foreign law of the scope already assigned to it; again, this can only be true if an initial choice in favour of the *lex causae* has been made, which is the point to be proved.

It may thus be seen that there is no "logical necessity" to give priority to the position of the *lex causae.* Nor do other dogmatic considerations (several of which have been left out here) seem to be of much assistance in choosing between this approach and that based on the *lex fori.* A meaningful discussion of this problem, it is believed, must rather centre on the merits and demerits of each solution, viewed in the light of relevant policies and desiderata, and end up in an evaluation based on such factors.

The main argument of this kind adduced in support of the wide reference approach is that it tends to prevent the creation of limping marriages and thereby to promote international uniformity of decision.[764] The purpose, or at least one of the chief purposes, of any conflicts rule referring capacity to marry to the personal law (whether determined by domicile or by nationality) is to ensure that the marriage will be recognised as valid universally, or in any event in the country whose law is designated as applicable. This purpose would obviously be frustrated if the forum were to permit the celebration of a second marriage on the authority of a locally valid divorce which is not recognised by the relevant foreign

763. See for criticism: *van Hoogstraten,* Le droit international privé néerlandais et la question préalable: De Conflictu Legum, Mélanges offerts à Kollewijn et Offerhaus (Leyden 1962) 209, 215-216; *Pålsson,* Haltande äktenskap 140-146.

764. See among decisions elaborating this argument, WEST GERMANY: BGH 12 Feb. 1964, BGHZ 41, 136, 139, 145-147; SWITZERLAND: BG 11 Nov. 1954, BGE 80 I 427, 437. For a critical discussion see *Dorenberg* 139-142.

law; for such a marriage would be invalid for bigamy in the country of that law, and possibly in third countries as well.

Strong language has often been used by courts and writers to warn against the creation of this type of limping marriages, which have been denounced as a "scandal"[765] and as "devoid of meaning".[766] It is true that such unions are a potential source of legal difficulties and uncertainty and that they may create hardship both on the spouses themselves (or on one of them) and on their children, because their status and the rights flowing from it are more precarious than otherwise. The human aspect of this is highlighted by cases in which a foreigner who had remarried in reliance on a locally valid divorce, on return or on a wedding-trip with his new bride to his home country, was prosecuted and sentenced to imprisonment there for bigamy.[767]

Fortunately, however, such cases seem to be rarer in actual life than in the teachings of jurists. On the whole, there has been a tendency to exaggerate the dangers attendant upon limping marriages.[768] In truth, the position varies greatly with the circumstances of each case, in particular with the degree of probability of the relationship being "confronted" with a legal system which does not recognise it as a valid marriage. Such a confrontation is chiefly to be feared if the parties make their home in, or if one or both of them at some later time move to, a country possessing such a system, though even in these cases the dangers incurred will to some degree depend on the severity of the sanctions envisaged by the law in question (whether it holds the union to be void or merely voidable, what significance it attaches to the good faith of the parties, whether it treats children of an invalid marriage as legitimate or as illegitimate, etc.).[769] On the other hand, as long as

765. See the ENGLISH case of R. v. Brentwood Marriage Registrar, [1968] 2 Q.B. 956, 971.

766. *Süss* 250.

767. A case full of drama is told by *Ferid*, book review: FamRZ 1961, 401.

768. Cf. *Arndt* 242-243; *G. Holleaux*, book review (*supra* n. 537) 637, assuring us that countless people are living quite cosily ("ganz gemütlich") in limping status relationships. See also *Heldrich*, Internationale Zuständigkeit und anwendbares Recht (Berlin & Tübingen 1969) 242-243.

769. It has often been assumed by courts and writers without proper inquiry that the children of a bigamous marriage would be illegitimate according to the foreign law concerned. This, however, is by no means always true. See, for instance, for a clearly erroneous assumption with regard to SWEDISH law, the WEST GERMAN case decided by the President of OLG Hamburg 27 Sept. 1963, IPRspr. 1962/63 no. 77.

the parties live in a country where they are regarded as lawfully married, the fact that they are not so regarded by one foreign law or another, with which they do not have any substantial contact, will typically only be of theoretical interest, inasmuch as their status will not, or will only in exceptional circumstances, come within the reach of such laws.[770]

These considerations certainly do not warrant the conclusion that the desire to achieve international uniformity of decision should lack relevance in the present context. Even if, at the time of celebration of the proposed marriage, the chances seem remote that the parties will ever get into contact with the foreign law which is opposed to their union, that risk cannot be completely excluded because events may later come to take a course which was not to be foreseen (for instance, if the party subject to the foreign law decides to return to his home country, perhaps after many years when the marriage has broken down). The only way in which this uncertainty can be avoided is if, following the wide reference approach, the marriage is not allowed to be celebrated.

It remains for consideration, however, whether this is a reasonable price to pay for the advantage of preventing limping marriages. The policy of promoting international uniformity of decision must therefore be weighed against policy factors pulling in the opposite direction. This question will be resumed later on (*infra* s. 90).

Furthermore, even assuming that uniformity of decision is held to carry such weight as to prevail over other desiderata, this policy can only be effectively pursued to the extent that it operates to preclude the solemnisation of a proposed marriage. If the union has already been celebrated, it is much more difficult to find a tenable policy justification for invalidating it afterwards by applying foreign law. The reason is in part that, whatever course is adopted by the forum, uniformity of decision often cannot be reached at this stage, in part (and more important, it is submitted) that the countervailing policy of validation comes into operation.[771] This shift of the balance between the relevant policies is clearly borne out by the West German practice previously referred to (*supra* s. 85).

770. This, it is true, depends to some extent on the attitude of the forum to the incidental question in other connections where the validity of the union may be relevant to the decision of a main issue (for instance, a claim to inheritance by the surviving spouse) governed by such a foreign law. In so far as the wide reference approach is adopted in these situations, the position of the foreign law will prevail.

771. Cf. *Gotlieb* 546; *Hartley*, Bigamy 690; and *supra* at n. 434.

abbb. Narrow Reference Approach

88. *Recent Developments in West German Law.* In opposition to the prevailing opinion in West Germany, it was being contended by a minority of writers, with the support of some judicial decisions, that a person validly divorced in West Germany (or by a foreign decree recognised in that country) could not be refused the right to marry again solely because the divorce was not recognised by the foreign law governing his or his intended partner's capacity to marry.[772] A provision to this effect figured among the proposals for reform of the conflicts law of marriage put forward by the German Council on Private International Law in its draft statute of 1962.[773] A bill proposing legislation on this particular point in accordance with the draft was also introduced in the Federal Parliament, but action on this initiative was deferred pending efforts to solve the problem by international conventions.[774]

Meanwhile, the need for reform voiced in various quarters was in part obviated by a decision of the Federal Constitutional Court rendered in 1971.[775] That case presented the typical "Spanish problem", namely, a proposed marriage between a Spaniard, who had not been married before, and a German woman divorced from her first husband (also of German nationality) in West Germany but regarded by Spanish law as still married to him. The trial court held the marriage to be barred in accordance with Spanish law, but this decision was quashed by the Federal Constitutional Court on the ground that it infringed the constitutional rights of the pro-

772. See, e.g., *Dorenberg* 138-155; *Ficker* 311-314; *Kegel,* Kommentar, art. 13 no. 18-25; *Kegel and A. Lüderitz; K. Müller,* Zum Begriff der "Anerkennung" von Urteilen in § 328 ZPO: ZZP 79 (1966) 199, 235-241; *Nussbaum* 134, 163; *Stöcker,* Religion 40-41 (with distinctions). For decisions see: LG Hannover 19 April 1961, IPRspr. 1960/61 no. 90; OLG Stuttgart 12 Nov. 1962, IPRspr. 1962/63 no. 71; OLG Braunschweig 10 Oct. 1963, IPRspr. 1962/63 no. 78; cf. OLG München 25 Feb. 1963, IPRspr. 1962/63 no. 192, and 2 April 1964, IPRspr. 1964/65 no. 264 (concerning the position after a foreign divorce recognised in West Germany). Further references are given by *Gamillscheg,* Kommentar, art. 13 no. 287-288.

773. *Vorschläge und Gutachten* 1 (text), 12-13 (comments), cf. 51-52, 71-72 (*H. Müller*). See *Kegel,* Reform 203-205; and for criticism *Gamillscheg,* Gleichberechtigung der Frau und Reform des internationalen Eherechts: RabelsZ 33 (1969) 654, 690-704.

774. See BVerfG 4 May 1971, BVerfGE 31, 58, 64; *Jayme,* Entwurf (*supra* n. 756); *idem,* Su un recente disegno di legge germanico in tema di matrimonio degli stranieri: Riv. dir. int. proc. 1965, 670-674. On the results of the work carried out at the international level see *infra* s. 89 at n. 804-806.

775. BVerfG 4 May 1971, BVerfGE 31, 58, IPRspr. 1971 no. 39, RabelsZ 36 (1972) 145, Rev. crit. d.i.p. 1974, 57.

spective spouses, specifically the freedom to marry protected, in regard to citizens and aliens alike, by the German Basic law.[776] The parties were therefore entitled to get married in West Germany.[777]

This decision set the matter at rest in cases of the type before the court. Its effect is to exclude the application of the foreign law governing the capacity of one of the intending spouses in so far as that law denies the validity of a divorce granted to the other party in a purely domestic case (from the German point of view, the divorce being pronounced by a German court in respect of a marriage between spouses of German nationality). To that extent the position of the foreign law is indeed distinctly exorbitant, inasmuch as it purports to interfere with a question which is wholly unrelated to it and which can properly be said to be "none of its business".[778]

It is far from clear, however, whether and to what extent the principle enunciated by the court applies to other situations involving the present problem. The decision seems rather to have been a source of confusion and to have given rise to a divergent

776. This right or freedom was interpreted into art. 6 par. 1 of the Basic Law, which is couched in vague and general language ("Marriage and family enjoy the special protection of the State"). Support for this interpretation was derived from art. 12 of the European Convention for the Protection of Human Rights and Fundamental Freedoms of 4 Nov. 1950, art. 16 par. 1 sent. 1 of the Universal Declaration of Human Rights of 10 Dec. 1948 and from the preamble of the UN Convention on Consent to Marriage, etc., of 10 Dec. 1962.

777. Among the numerous comments on this decision see those collected in RabelsZ 36 (1972) 2-140 (contributions by *Henrich, Jayme, Kegel, A. Lüderitz, Makarov, K. Müller, Neumayer, Siehr, Wengler* and *Neuhaus*) and, e.g., *Gamillscheg,* Kommentar, before art. 13 no. 63; *Müller-Freienfels* 84-98; *Stöcker,* Ordre public; *Sturm,* Durchbruch der Grundrechte in Fällen mit Auslandsberührung: FamRZ 1972, 16-22. The decision has also attracted much attention abroad. See: *Ballarino* 123-132; *Bucher* 178-187; *Juenger,* The German Constitutional Court and the Conflict of Laws: 20 Am. J. Comp. L. 290-298 (1972); *Kahn-Freund,* Problems 86-88; *Labrusse,* Droit constitutionnel et droit international privé en Allemagne fédérale: Rev. crit. d.i.p. 1974, 1-46; *Pi-Song Tsai* 272-285. Most commentators endorse the result of the decision in the particular case, though with many reservations as to the means used to achieve it. The main part of the discussion is devoted to the much larger problem of the implications of the decision with regard to constitutional review of GERMAN conflicts rules generally and of foreign laws applicable under those rules.

778. Cf. *Henrich,* Die Bedeutung der Grundrechte bei der Anwendung fremden Rechts: RabelsZ 36 (1972) 2, 7-9.

practice among the authorities administering this part of the law.[779]

It should first be noted that the decision left the choice of the appropriate means of achieving results compatible with the constitutional guarantee of freedom of marriage to the discretion of the competent courts. True, the Federal Constitutional Court suggested that any risk of violating the Basic Law could be avoided by treating the validity of the divorce as an independent question determinable by the *lex fori,* that is to say, by endorsing the narrow reference approach, but the court did not (and for that matter had no power to) enjoin other courts to adopt this particular course.[780] Nor have the courts faced with the problem in later cases been much disposed to follow this suggestion. On the contrary, they have generally remained committed to the principle that the validity of the divorce must be decided by the *lex causae* of capacity to marry (wide reference approach) and treated the interference of constitutional public policy merely as an exception to that principle, an exception which has predominantly been given a relatively limited scope.[781]

The first condition for the operation of this corrective is that the case presents a sufficiently strong connection with West Germany. The relevance of this factor may be illustrated by a case which came before an intermediate appellate court and which again raised the typical "Spanish problem", though in circumstances different from those of the case decided by the Federal Constitutional Court.[782] A Spaniard, who was single, sought to marry a Yugoslav woman divorced from her first husband, likewise of Yugoslav nationality, by a Yugoslav court, both parties to the projected union being residents of West Germany. The divorce was invalid by Spanish law but valid in West Germany since it emanated from a court of the country of the common nationality of the spouses. It might have been expected that the principle sanctioned by the Federal Constitutional Court would apply correspondingly to such a case, for the claim of Spanish law to prevent the marriage was equally excessive here.[783] This view was rejected by the

779. See *Otto,* Die Wiederverheiratung in Deutschland geschiedener Ausländer: StAZ 1972, 157-160.

780. BVerfGE 31, 58 at 86.

781. See the cases cited *infra* n. 782, 785, 789-791. Cf. also the decision of BGH 7 April 1976, IPRspr. 1976 no. 151.

782. OLG Hamm 8 Dec. 1975, IPRspr. 1975 no. 41.

783. Cf. the interpretation of the decision of the Federal Constitutional Court advanced by *Siehr,* Grundrecht der Eheschliessungsfreiheit und internationales Privatrecht: RabelsZ 36 (1972) 93, 112-115.

court, however, holding that the German Basic Law had no application to the instant case, inasmuch as the only contact with West Germany was that the intending spouses were resident there and, moreover, could be expected to return to one of their home countries at some future date. Effect was therefore given to the rule of Spanish law precluding the marriage.

Most other cases concern the remarriage of a foreigner who has himself been married before and whose West German divorce in respect of that union is not recognised by his national law. Since in these cases the divorce is not a purely local affair, it was contended by several writers that the decision of the Federal Constitutional Court had no application at all, with the result that the foreigner must be refused the right to marry again.[784]

Such a very narrow interpretation was rejected, however, by the Federal Supreme Court in a case involving a proposed marriage between a Spaniard, who was divorced from his first wife (of German nationality) by a West German court, and a German woman who was not previously married.[785] The Federal Supreme Court refused to draw any distinction between this case and that decided by the Federal Constitutional Court. Reversing its own earlier position on the subject, the court held that the Spanish rule denying effect to the divorce must be excluded from application and the marriage permitted, here too, by virtue of German constitutional public policy.[786] The local contacts were considered strong enough to justify such resort to the German Basic Law because, apart from the Spanish nationality of one of the intending spouses, all other connecting factors, including that party's habitual residence, pointed to West Germany.

On the other hand, the strength of the local connection is usually not regarded as the only relevant factor in deciding such

784. See *Dölle*, IPR 88; *Gamillscheg*, Kommentar, art. 13 no. 298; *Jayme*, Grundrecht der Eheschliessungsfreiheit und Wiederheirat geschiedener Ausländer: RabelsZ 36 (1972) 19, 22, 24, 26. Cf. *Siehr*, Grundrecht (*supra* n. 783) 96-97; *Wengler*, Die Bedeutung der verfassungsrechtlichen Bestimmungen über die Eheschliessungsfreiheit und den Schutz der Familie für das internationale Privatrecht: RabelsZ 36 (1972) 116, 122-124.

785. BGH 19 April 1972, IPRspr. 1972 no. 41, NJW 1972, 1619, note Otto, RabelsZ 37 (1973) 130. This decision has since been extended to a case where neither the first nor the intended second spouse of a divorced Spanish party was of German nationality but where both intending spouses were habitually resident in West Germany: BGH 23 Feb. 1977, IPRspr. 1977 no. 49.

786. For an approving comment, as regards the result of the decision, see *Sturm*. For critical views see *Jayme*, case note: StAZ 1972, 227; *Wuppermann* 107. See further *Pi-Song Tsai* 285-291.

issues. At least in the practice of lower courts available so far, the above decisions of the Federal Constitutional Court and of the Federal Supreme Court have been construed to be confined to cases where the foreigner's national law does not know the institution of divorce at all.[787] The position is held to be different where the foreign law admits divorce, though for some other reason it does not recognise the divorce granted by the German court or makes such recognition subject to some further condition, like the grant of an exequatur, still to be fulfilled. The ground of this distinction is that, here, it is in the power of the divorcee himself to remove the impediment existing under his national law and that it can be required that he should take appropriate action to do so before he is permitted to marry again.

This view has notably been adopted in several cases involving Italian law. In contrast with Spanish law, Italian law has since recently permitted divorce in certain cases (*inter alia,* where a spouse of foreign nationality has already obtained a divorce abroad from his Italian spouse) and is also prepared to recognise foreign divorces of Italian nationals on certain conditions, such recognition being accorded by a judgment of exequatur by an Italian court.[788] This being the position under Italian law, it has been held by West German courts that an Italian national divorced from his first spouse in West Germany is not entitled to remarry there unless and until he has procured either an exequatur of the German decree or a new divorce judgment in Italy in compliance with the requirements of Italian law.[789] In the opinion of the courts so holding, this restriction on the effect of the forum's divorce decree

787. See the cases cited *infra* n. 789 and 791.

788. See the ITALIAN Divorce Act of 1 Dec. 1970, particularly art. 3 no. 2 *lit.* e. On the requirement of an exequatur for the recognition of foreign judgments see *supra* s. 81-82.

789. OLG Hamm 13 Jan. 1972, IPRspr. 1972 no. 39; OLG Karlsruhe 21 Aug. 1972, IPRspr. 1972 no. 43; OLG Hamm 5 Oct. 1972, IPRspr. 1972 no. 44, FamRZ 1973, 143 with an approving note by Jayme; OLG Hamm 14 June 1974, IPRspr. 1974 no. 49. Contrast the DUTCH case of Rb. Arnhem 10 Jan. 1974, N.J. 1974 no. 122, where the remarriage was likewise held to turn on the recognition by ITALIAN law of a divorce granted by the forum but where the question was answered in the affirmative after the court had satisfied itself that the substantive conditions of such recognition were (probably) met, the court holding itself at liberty to anticipate the decision of the ITALIAN court in the light of the relevant provisions of ITALIAN law.

does not violate the constitutional provision on freedom of marriage.[790]

The same position has been taken even where the country of the divorcee's nationality, while admitting divorce in its domestic law, is opposed to any recognition of foreign divorces of its nationals because it claims exclusive jurisdiction for its own courts in such matters. An illustration is afforded by a case involving an Iraqi Moslem divorced from his German wife in West Germany.[791] This divorce being invalid under Iraqi law, by which exclusive jurisdiction was vested in religious tribunals, the man was held to be debarred from concluding another marriage with a German woman until he had secured a new divorce in accordance with Iraqi law. Here, too, the court was of the opinion that the party's freedom of marriage was not thereby restricted to such a degree as to come into conflict with the German Basic Law.

In conclusion, it appears that the intervention of the Federal Constitutional Court has scarcely had the success and the impact one might have expected. While this intervention was justified to correct a rather outrageous development in West German practice, it is difficult to avoid the impression that most courts and writers have so far been unwilling to pay it whole-hearted respect. The present state of the law, as represented by reported decisions, is hardly satisfactory. Apart from the complications attending it, the merits of the distinctions drawn by the courts are open to doubts. It is paradoxical, for instance, that a German divorce decree should be sufficient for remarriage in the case of a Spaniard, whose national law outright forbids divorce, but not in the case of an Italian, whose national law admits divorce.[792] It is easy to imagine that this distinction may come to involve the courts in difficulties in several situations and that it may necessitate further and more refined distinctions and complications. It remains to be seen whether such a system can be maintained in the long run. In any

790. A constitutional complaint filed against the decision of OLG Hamm 5 Oct. 1972, IPRspr. 1972 no. 44, was turned down by a decision of the competent committee of the Federal Constitutional Court of 23 Jan. 1973 on the ground that it did not have sufficient prospect of success; see *Jayme*, Zu Scheidung und Wiederheirat von Italienern: NJW 1973, 934-935; *Otto*, Die Wiederverheiratung bei "hinkender" Scheidung eines Ausländers: StAZ 1973, 78.

791. OLG Hamm 10 Aug. 1973, IPRspr. 1973 no. 36.

792. For criticism along these lines see *Sturm; Pi-Song Tsai* 291-294. See also *Raape und Sturm* 206-208, 291-293 and the writers cited *supra* n. 772 supporting the narrow reference approach.

event the German experience tends to show that an appropriate solution to the problem under examination should preferably be worked out by the "ordinary" means of the conflict of laws rather than by having recourse to the blunt instrument of constitutional law.

89. *Other Countries.* The position in other Continental European countries is much simpler. In so far as the problem has arisen for decision, the narrow reference approach seems everywhere to predominate.[793] This is clearly the case, for instance, in *France,*[794] *Belgium*[795] and *the Netherlands.*[796] In general, this solution has been arrived at along less arduous routes than those travelled by West German courts and writers. Whether the principle of public

793. References *infra* n. 794-796, 800, 802-803. See also for ITALY: *Sperduti,* Riflessi nell'ordinamento italiano di conflitti fra leggi e sentenze di più Stati in materia matrimoniale: Foro it. 1959 I 1364, 1365, 1369-1370; *Vitta* II 188-190; for TURKEY: Supreme Court 15 Jan. 1966, Clunet 1974, 178. For views to the contrary see *supra* s. 86.

794. For decisions upholding a marriage between a Spaniard and a divorced Frenchwoman see Trib. Seine 5 May 1919, Rev. crit. d.i.p. 1919, 543; Cour Aix 24 Jan. 1924, Clunet 1924, 670, Rev. crit. d.i.p. 1924, 99. For a decision upholding the second marriage of an Italian national divorced in France see Trib. Seine 17 March 1948, Rev. crit. d.i.p. 1948, 112 with an approving note by Niboyet; see also Trib. Belfort 19 March 1952, D. 1952.J.657 (*obiter dictum*) with a note by Loussouarn. And see among writers: *Batiffol and Lagarde* I 438, II 80-81; *Elgeddawy* 230-234; *Jean Foyer and Jacques Foyer,* Divorce et séparation de corps (Rép. dr. int. I) no. 172; *Francescakis,* La théorie du renvoi (Paris 1958) 215-218; *Francescakis and Gaudemet-Tallon,* Divorce: J. Cl. dr. int., Fasc. 547-B no. 96-98; *G. Holleaux* 154, 195, 199, 201, 228-229; *Lerebours-Pigeonnière and Loussouarn* 586-587; *Louis-Lucas,* Qualification et répartition: Rev. crit. d.i.p. 1957, 153, 170-173; *Mayer,* La distinction entre règles et décisions et le droit international privé (Paris 1973) 143-148; *Vincent and Ponsard* no. 110-113.

795. See for decisions upholding a marriage between a divorced woman of Belgian and a man of foreign nationality, notwithstanding that the man was by his personal law incapable of entering into the union: Civ. Bruxelles 17 July 1913, *Kosters and Bellemans* 121; Civ. Liège 5 Nov. 1958, Jur. Liège 1958/59, 171. And see for a decision permitting the remarriage of an Italian national divorced in Belgium contrary to his personal law, Civ. Bruxelles 9 April 1968, J.T. 1968, 566, Clunet 1971, 866. Among writers see: *Abrahams and Putters,* La loi belge du 27 juin 1960 sur l'admissibilité du divorce lorsqu'un conjoint au moins est étranger: Clunet 1966, 765, 777-779; *Rigaux,* DIP I 303-306; *idem,* Les tendances actuelles du droit international privé belge: R.B.D.I. 11 (1975) 1, 25-26.

796. For older cases see Rb. 's-Gravenhage 10 Dec. 1929, N.J. 1930, 237; Rb. Rotterdam 14 April 1930, N.J. 1930, 783. A summary of these two cases is given in RabelsZ 6 (1932) 849. For recent decisions see those cited *supra* n. 758. See further *Joppe* 5-6, 31.

policy or some other dogmatic justification has been invoked, the view that a divorce granted or recognised by the forum must be treated as valid, for the purpose of remarriage as in other contexts, whatever position is taken by one foreign law or another, is usually regarded as an elementary expression of the authority of the *lex fori,* dictated by common sense and not requiring to be buttressed by too laborious or sophisticated arguments.[797]

It is of particular interest to note that the narrow reference approach has in recent years also come to be accepted in *Austria* and *Switzerland,* where the opposite view formerly prevailed.[798] This development has been parallel both in time and in the result to that in West Germany, though it has gone further than there.

As regards Switzerland, the decision of the Federal Tribunal in the *Caliaro* case (*supra* at n. 741) provoked a strong negative reaction and became the target of severe and persistent criticism in almost all quarters.[799] This criticism bore fruit, for the next time the question came before the Federal Tribunal, in the *Dal Bosco* case decided in 1971, the court after setting itself to a thorough review of the criticisms levelled at *Caliaro* and of the merits and demerits of the different approaches reached the conclusion that that decision must be overruled.[800] Relying on the narrow reference approach, the court upheld a second marriage of an Italian national celebrated in Denmark (a Tondern marriage) after a divorce from

797. Though it has been suggested by some writers that a distinction should be drawn according to whether the divorce was granted by the forum or was granted by a foreign court and is recognised by the forum: *supra* n. 752.

798. See *infra* at n. 799-803, cf. *supra* at n. 740-745.

799. See, e.g., *P.M. Gutzwiller,* Grundsätzliche Überlegungen zur Wiederverheiratung des in der Schweiz geschiedenen Angehörigen eines Staates, der keine Ehescheidung kennt: ZZW 1969, 181-190; *Lachenal* 40-41; *von Overbeck,* Remariage 56-61; *idem,* Wiederverheiratung 350-356; *Stauffer,* Die Ehefähigkeit des geschiedenen Italieners in der Schweiz: SJZ 67 (1971) 117-121; *Pi-Song Tsai* 217-228; *Vischer,* "Mariage mixte" 414-416, 426; *idem,* Ordre public 328. Further references are given in the decision of BG 3 June 1971, BGE 97 I 389, 394-397.

800. BG 3 June 1971, BGE 97 I 389, Clunet 1976, 439, note Lalive, RabelsZ 36 (1972) 358, note Neuhaus, Schw. Jb. Int. R. 28 (1972) 357, note Lalive. See: *Bucher* 167-178; *Dutoit and Mercier,* La nouvelle jurisprudence du Tribunal fédéral suisse concernant le remariage de l'italien divorcé en Suisse: Riv. dir. int. proc. 1972, 5-21; *von Overbeck,* Relativität 283-284; *Pi-Song Tsai* 228-242. For an earlier decision which, although concerning a different issue, seems to foreshadow this turn of the tide, see BG 11 July 1968 (*Cardo*), BGE 94 II 65, Rev. crit. d.i.p. 1969, 303, note Knoepfler, Schw. Jb. Int. R. 26 (1969/70) 259, note Lalive.

his first wife in Switzerland, which had not been and which possibly would not be recognised in Italy. The Federal Tribunal, it is true, expressly refused to extend this solution to cases falling within the ambit of the Hague Convention on Marriage, which in the opinion of the court did not permit such disregard of the party's *lex patriae.*[801] As a consequence of this exception, divorced Italian nationals still could not remarry validly in Switzerland itself unless the divorce had been formally recognised in Italy by a judgment of exequatur, as required by Italian law, the convention being applicable in such cases.

A few years later, however, this last barrier, too, was removed by the denunciation of the Hague Convention (with effect from 1 June 1974) by Switzerland. In consistency with this development the Federal Tribunal, confirming and further clarifying its new position, has since held that an Italian woman divorced in Switzerland was entitled to conclude another marriage there without having to comply with the condition of Italian law as to the grant of an exequatur.[802] It was considered immaterial that strong connections existed with Italy, both the first and the second husband being, like the remarrying party herself, of Italian nationality.

In conclusion, it seems clear that the narrow reference approach now forms part of Swiss law and that it is not subject to any qualifications or distinctions of the kind adopted in West German practice. The same rule appears to be deducible from recent Austrian decisions on the matter.[803]

The tendency referred to here has also found expression in two recent international conventions governing, *inter alia,* the recognition of foreign divorces. The first of these is the C.I.E.C. Con-

801. BGE 97 I 389 at 411-412; cf. *supra* at n. 757. The convention is limited to marriages solemnised on the territory of the Contracting States (art. 8). Since Denmark is not, and has never been, a party to the convention, the *Dal Bosco* case was outside the scope of the convention.

802. BG 5 Feb. 1976 (*Paiano*), BGE 102 I b 1, Rev. crit. d.i.p. 1976, 519, note Knoepfler, Schw. Jb. Int. R. 33 (1977) 280, note Lalive. See *Dutoit and Mercier,* A propos d'un nouvel arrêt important du Tribunal fédéral suisse concernant le remariage de l'italien divorcé en Suisse: Riv. dir. int. proc. 1976, 515-517; *von Overbeck,* Relativität 285-290.

803. BMfJ 30 Aug. 1971, EFSlg 8 (1971) 211 no. 15,733; BMfJ 23 Dec. 1971, EFSlg 8 (1971) 213 no. 15,734; BMfJ 14 Feb. 1975, EFSlg 12 (1975) 247 no. 24,918; BMfJ 2 June 1976, EFSlg 13 (1976) 250 no. 27,296. See *Schwind,* IPR 143-144. In favour of the narrow reference approach see also *Matscher,* Zur Theorie der Anerkennung ausländischer Entscheidungen nach österreichischem Recht: Festschrift Schima 265, 284-285. For a proposal of a compromise solution see *V. Hoyer,* Scheidung.

vention of 1967 on the Recognition of Decisions Involving Marital Relations (not yet in force), which provides that when a decree of dissolution or annulment of marriage has been recognised in a Contracting State by virtue of the convention, the celebration of a new marriage cannot be refused in that State by reason only that the law of another State does not permit or does not recognise the dissolution or annulment in question.[804] The second provision forms part of the Hague Convention of 1970 on the Recognition of Divorces and Legal Separations, pursuant to which a State obliged to recognise a divorce under the convention may not preclude either spouse from remarrying on the ground that the law of another State does not recognise that divorce.[805] This latter convention came into force in 1975 and is so far binding on the following States: Czechoslovakia, Denmark, Finland, Norway, Sweden, Switzerland and the United Kingdom.[806]

Although these two provisions are limited to the problem of remarriage following the dissolution of a previous marriage by a foreign decree recognised by the forum, to the extent that they have come into force they will afford the strongest possible persuasive authority for the same solution in the more frequently occurring case of a divorce validly granted by the forum itself.[807] It is indeed difficult to imagine a distinction between the two cases to the effect that a domestic divorce decree would not be

804. Convention of 8 Sept. 1967, art. 9. See *von Overbeck*, Wiederverheiratung 357-358; *Schwind*, Das Übereinkommen der Internationalen Kommission für das Zivilstandswesen über die Anerkennung von Entscheidungen in Ehesachen: ZfRV 9 (1968) 161, 173-174 (critically); *Simitis*, Die internationale Kommission für Zivilstandswesen (C.I.E.C.): RabelsZ 33 (1969) 30, 57-58.

805. Convention of 1 June 1970, art. 11. For the *travaux préparatoires* bearing on this provision see Act. Doc. La Haye 11 (1968) II 23-24, 68-69, 152-154, 221 and *passim*. For further comments see: *Anton*, The Recognition of Divorces and Legal Separations: 18 I.C.L.Q. 620, 639-640 (1969); *Bellet and Goldman*, La Convention de La Haye sur la reconnaissance des divorces et des séparations de corps: Clunet 1969, 843, 850; *Dutoit and Mercier*, La onzième session de la Conférence de la Haye de droit international privé: N.T.I.R. 16 (1969) 125, 154-155; *von Overbeck*, Remariage 48-50; *Schwind*, Die Haager Konvention über die Anerkennung von Scheidungen dem Bande nach und von Tisch und Bett: Festschrift Schima 377, 386-387 (critically); *Pi-Song Tsai* 329-330, 332-333; *Vischer*, Abkommen über die Anerkennung von Scheidungen und Trennungen: Schw. Jb. Int. R. 25 (1968) 117, 126-127.

806. See Rev. crit. d.i.p. 1978, 212.

807. See, e.g., *Böhmer*, Die Übereinkommen der Commission Internationale de l'État Civil (CIEC): StAZ 1967, 313, 318; *von Overbeck*, Remariage 49-50; *Sturm* 69.

entitled to the same degree of authority as a foreign one for the purpose of remarriage.

The above-cited provision of the Hague Convention of 1970 has been followed in the *United Kingdom* by the Recognition of Divorces and Legal Separations Act 1971, which was adopted with a view to permitting acceptance of the convention by that country.[808] Where a foreign divorce is entitled to recognition under the 1971 Act, "neither spouse shall be precluded from marrying in the United Kingdom on the ground that the validity of the divorce would not be recognised in any other country."[809] This provision overrules previous English cases denying a party's capacity to remarry when the divorce was not recognised by the appropriate law for that issue.[810] It seems that the principle embodied in this provision applies *a fortiori* where the divorce has been granted by a court in the United Kingdom.[811]

In *Sweden,* too, a special statute has been enacted to implement the 1970 Hague Convention.[812] Here, however, it was not even considered necessary to reproduce the provision of the convention dealing with capacity for remarriage, which was held to follow as a matter of course from the obligation to recognise divorces obtained in accordance with the convention.[813] The position is the same where the divorce is entitled to recognition independently of the convention or where it has been pronounced by a Swedish court.[814]

By way of conclusion, there is no mistaking the general tendency in favour of the narrow reference approach in regard to the present problem. While attention has almost exclusively been directed

808. See *Karsten; North* 164-165.

809. Recognition of Divorces and Legal Separations Act 1971, s. 7, as amended by the Domicile and Matrimonial Proceedings Act 1973, s. 2 (3) and 15 (2). See *Cheshire and North* 350-351; *Dicey and Morris* 36, 274, 335, 337; *Graveson,* Conflict 300; *Lipstein* 105-106; *North* 191-193.

810. See *supra* at n. 746. But the new provision does not cover cases where the remarriage has taken place outside the United Kingdom. Here, it seems, no change has been made in the common law rule, by which the second marriage must be held invalid despite the validity of the divorce according to ENGLISH law. See *Karsten* 302; *North* 193-194.

811. See *Cheshire and North* 351; *Karsten* 302; *North* 195. Cf. *Hartley,* Bigamy 690-691; *Lipstein* 94-95; *Webb,* Thoughts 828.

812. Act of 14 Dec. 1973 on the Recognition of Certain Foreign Divorces and Legal Separations. For the legislative history see NJA 1973 II 612-622.

813. See NJA 1973 II 620.

814. See NJA 1973 II 580 and, with regard to the law prior to the amendments made in 1973, *Pålsson,* Haltande äktenskap 491-494.

to cases of a prior marriage dissolved by divorce, the principle probably applies to the same extent where that union is invalid in the eyes of the *lex fori,* whether because it is so *ipso jure* or because it has been properly annulled. Hence, even if the prior marriage is valid and, where a nullity decree has been granted, that decree is not recognised by the law governing the capacity of one or both of the parties to the fresh union, the latter will presumably not be barred on this ground.[815]

90. *Rationale.* The narrow reference approach has been defended on a variety of grounds, both dogmatic and policy-oriented.[816] Some arguments of the former type, such as the reasoning that the problem pertains to the domain of conflicts of jurisdiction rather than choice of law and that it must be resolved by applying the *lex fori* because of the "procedural nature" so attributed to it, seem too conceptualistic to be of much value and will not be dwelt upon here.[817] As pointed out earlier, it is more profitable, in any event for comparative purposes, to discuss the matter in terms of policies and desiderata, weighing the advantages and disadvantages of each solution against each other.

All arguments in favour of the narrow reference approach ultimately come down to the proposition that this approach alone guarantees internal consistency within the *lex fori.*[818] The simplest way of describing this advantage is by pointing to the "internal dissonances" produced by the opposite method of solution, *i.e.* the wide reference approach. The latter compels the forum to commit a sort of "legal hara-kiri",[819] inasmuch as it must treat a prior marriage as still in force despite a divorce pronounced or recognised by the forum and whose validity it is bound to affirm

815. For an express provision to this effect see art. 9 of the C.I.E.C. Convention of 1967 (*supra* at n. 804). For SWEDISH law see *Undén,* Studier 31-32, 35, 63. Cf. for WEST GERMAN law *supra* n. 733.

816. See, e.g., *Dorenberg* 142-150, 153-154; *Pålsson,* Haltande äktenskap 439-441, 503-507; *Pi-Song Tsai* 299-302.

817. Among writers relying on the allegedly procedural nature of the problem see: *Kegel,* Reform 203-204; *Kegel and A. Lüderitz; von Overbeck,* Remariage 58-59. For criticism see the SWISS decision of BG 3 June 1971, BGE 97 I 389, 403-404, and *Pi-Song Tsai* 224-225. Another distinction, equally scholastic and amorphous, which has chiefly been relied upon by GERMAN writers, is that between *Vorfrage* and *Teilfrage;* see the survey of opinions given by *Pi-Song Tsai* 258-259.

818. On the concept of internal consistency in the conflict of laws see, for example, *Neuhaus,* Grundbegriffe 164, 347-349; *Wengler,* Principles 398-416; *Wolff,* PIL 209-210.

819. *von Overbeck,* Remariage 59.

in other connections. By contrast, the narrow reference approach ensures a uniform evaluation of the divorcee's status for whatever purpose the question falls for consideration in the forum country.

A conspicuous and particularly objectionable aspect of the inconsistency resulting from the wide reference approach is the inequality it creates between the ex-spouses in all cases where the divorce is valid by the personal law of one of them only. Typically these cases involve divorces from marriages between a party subject to the *lex fori* as his personal law and a foreigner whose personal law declines to recognise the divorce. While the former party is free to marry again (so far as the prior union is concerned), the latter will find himself condemned to a "forced celibacy".[820] This situation resembles the bizarre phenomenon known as "semi-divorce", which affects one of the spouses only and leaves the other still married.[821] Such legal constructions fail to take account of marriage as an indivisible social fact which, from the point of view of each legal system, must reasonably either exist or not exist for both parties.[822]

This particular objection has no reference to cases in which both of the divorced spouses are regarded as still married by their personal law applicable to their capacity for remarriage.[823] Here too, however, the wide reference approach leads to "legal schizophrenia",[824] since the parties will be precluded from remarrying on the ground that their marriage still subsists, notwithstanding that they are validly divorced.

The inconsistency of this approach appears in a different shape in cases where the divorce is invalid, not by the personal law or laws of the ex-spouses themselves but by the law governing the capacity of the intended partner to a second marriage. Here neither of the divorced spouses is generally prohibited from remarrying but only restricted in their choice of a partner, seeing that the latter's personal law must be taken into consideration. Neverthe-

820. *Wolff,* IPR 212. Some writers speak of a "perpetual" celibacy; see *Hartley,* Bigamy 691. This is an exaggeration, however; for the impediment may be overcome in different ways (to be discussed below).

821. Such divorces are the result of the *théorie distributive* formerly cherished in FRENCH law (*supra* n. 751).

822. See, for instance, *Vischer,* "Mariage mixte" 415.

823. Such was the situation, for instance, in the SWISS case of *Paiano,* BG 5 Feb. 1976, BGE 102 I b 1, where both parties to the dissolved marriage were of Italian nationality and where the divorce had not been recognised in ITALY (*supra* at n. 802).

824. *W. Goldschmidt,* Sistema y filosofía del Derecho internacional privado I (ed. 2, Buenos Aires 1952) 291.

less, it seems even less justified to give effect to the foreign *lex causae* in this instance than in those previously mentioned, because to do so would amount to allowing that law to impose its value judgment upon a question with which it never had any contact.[825]

A common feature to all cases in which the wide reference approach is adopted, thereby preventing a remarriage by reason that a valid divorce of one of the parties is not "sufficiently valid" for this purpose, is that the decision is likely to appear legalistic and unintelligible to the parties as well as to the public in general.[826] Indeed, unless the parties happen to be lawyers specialised in the conflict of laws, they will reasonably expect that a divorce pronounced or recognised by the forum disposes once and for all of the question of the subsistence of the prior union so as automatically to carry with it the right to marry again, at least in the forum country. To defeat these expectations will tend to broaden the gap, which is already more than sufficiently wide, between the rules of the conflict of laws and the climate of public opinion and sense of justice.

It might be objected that "internal dissonances" of a similar kind are tolerated in certain other connections as a result of the application of various rules and mechanisms of the conflict of laws. One instance is the treatment of polygamous marriages, which are often recognised for some or for most, but not for all, purposes.[827] Nevertheless, if internal consistency is to be sacrificed, there must at least be some convincing reason before the forum should accept to do so. This reason, as we have seen, could only be the desire to avoid multiplying the cases of limping marriages (*supra* s. 87). But can this policy factor be given so much weight as to justify a course whereby the forum will thwart one of the main purposes of a divorce which it regards as valid? It is proposed to discuss this question by considering the choices left to the parties when faced with a decision that they may not wed:

(1) The parties may accept the decision and renounce their relationship. While this alternative avoids further legal problems, it is most unlikely to be realised. It is scarcely to be expected that the parties should recognise that prohibiting the projected union is to their best interest because they need protection against the dangers of a limping marriage. Much more probably they will

825. Cf. *supra* at n. 753 and 784.

826. Cf. the opinion expressed in the WEST GERMAN *Vorschläge und Gutachten* 12. Similarly *von Overbeck*, Relativität 292.

827. See *Pålsson*, Marriage, s. 256-263.

feel this course to be unbearably harsh and try to defy the decision in one way or another.

(2) They may evade the impediment by marrying in a suitable foreign country. This device has been resorted to in numerous cases, as exemplified by the stream of "nuptial refugees" from West Germany to Denmark.[828] At least in this example the evasion has almost invariably been successful in the sense that the foreign celebrated marriage was treated as valid afterwards in the country where the parties would have married in the normal course of things but where they were debarred from doing so. This fact tends to deprive the prohibition upheld in respect of local celebration of such rational meaning as it may otherwise have; for the result is that the rule can only be effectively enforced as to couples who lack the initiative or the financial resources to circumvent it.

(3) The divorced party may try to "regularise" the situation by seeking recognition of the divorce in the foreign country concerned. This possibility is only available in the rather special situation where the relevant foreign law is not opposed to recognising the divorce in question but where it insists on the necessity of an exequatur. In practice, this alternative chiefly comes into consideration for Italian nationals, whose divorces are now susceptible of recognition in Italy subject, *inter alia,* to the condition of the grant of an exequatur by an Italian court.[829]

Another way in which the situation may be "regularised" is by procuring a new divorce in the foreign country. This is only possible if the courts of that country are prepared to assume jurisdiction in the circumstances and if, in addition, the law applied by them admits divorce and holds a sufficient ground for a decree to exist in the particular case. In the case of Italy, this method is alternative to that of obtaining an exequatur.[830] It may, however, also be used in a number of other instances where the foreign law knows the institution of divorce but where it refuses to recognise the divorce granted by the forum for some other reason, as for example because it claims exclusive jurisdiction over its nationals in such matters.

In so far as these means are available, recourse to them will effectively obviate any danger that the new marriage will be denied recognition in the foreign country. It does not follow, however, that it should be appropriate for the forum to require an exequatur

828. Cf. *supra* s. 63 and 85.
829. See *supra* n. 687 and s. 82.
830. Cf. *supra* at n. 788.

or a new divorce to be procured in the foreign country as a condition to be met before the remarriage is allowed to take place. Such a position, as we have seen, receives support in West German practice in so far as the personal law of the remarrying party admits divorce at all (*supra* s. 88). This might be unobjectionable if, as a rule, the foreign judgment of exequatur or divorce could be obtained without any major difficulty in a swift and inexpensive procedure. In fact, however, experience tends to show that this is seldom so but that the foreign procedure, in so far as it leads to the goal at all, usually involves considerable inconvenience, costs and delays.[831] It seems excessively stringent to put such obstacles in the way of the remarriage of a person who is already validly divorced in the eyes of the *lex fori.* Nor does the West German solution become more palatable by the distinction it entails to the effect that a divorcee's right of remarriage will be so restricted when his personal law admits divorce, but not if that law is absolutely inimical to divorce, so that a Spanish national, for instance, will be treated much more liberally than an Italian.[832]

(4) The parties may postpone the celebration of the marriage until the foreigner whose personal law fails to recognise the divorce has acquired the nationality of the forum country (or become domiciled there, if this is the relevant test).[833] This piece of advice has now and then been given by West German courts to foreign divorcees who were denied the right to marry again because their divorce was invalid by their *lex patriae.*[834] The idea is that such a change of nationality operates to substitute henceforth the *lex fori* for the foreign law as the law to decide on the party's capacity to marry, thereby restoring full authority to the divorce decree pronounced or recognised by the forum.

While this course may be open to the parties in certain cases, there are strong objections to the view that a change of nationality

831. This experience, with regard to proceedings for divorce or to validate a foreign divorce in ITALY, was expressly relied upon by the AUSTRIAN Federal Ministry of Justice in a decision whereby a woman of Italian nationality was permitted to remarry on the authority of her AUSTRIAN divorce decree alone: BMfJ 23 Dec. 1971, EFSlg 8 (1971) 213 no. 15,734. Of the same opinion in respect of ITALIAN law see for SWITZERLAND *Knoepfler*, case note: Rev. crit. d.i.p. 1976, 525, 528.

832. Cf. *supra* at n. 792.

833. *Mutatis mutandis*, what is said below concerning a change of nationality also holds true in respect of a change of domicile, where capacity to marry is to be tested by the party's *lex domicilii.*

834. See, for example, the decision of the President of OLG Hamburg 5 Aug. 1955, IPRspr. 1954/55 no. 84.

should be made a condition for permitting the second marriage.[835] In the first place, such a condition is likely to create hardship in many cases, either because the interested party is not eligible for naturalisation and will only become so eligible, if at all, at some time in the possibly distant future (depending on circumstances which have little to do with the proposed marriage), or because he finds himself put to the election between the marriage and his present citizenship, which he may otherwise have neither reason nor desire to exchange for another. Secondly, to require such a change is not at all related to the proclaimed *ratio* of the forum's refusal to permit the marriage as long as the party retains his foreign nationality, namely, the desire to prevent limping marriages. Indeed, this danger survives the change of nationality, which only has the effect that the law of the party's former nationality needs no longer to be considered in determining his capacity to marry under the forum's system of the conflict of laws but which alters nothing in the fact that the divorce of the prior union is invalid by that law. One cannot help but feel that the true motive of the view criticised here lies, not so much in concern for the fate of the marriage as in veneration for an abstract principle of law (the principle of nationality).[836] Human and social interests are sacrificed to this principle, apparently without too many scruples and occasionally even with a touch of cynicism.[837]

(5) The last possibility, which is presumably the one most often resorted to, is that the parties take to living together in a concubinage, or a "paperless marriage". This alternative brings with it all the disadvantages of a limping marriage, though in every respect in a higher degree.[838] The parties will nowhere be treated as lawfully married. Even if they remain in one country during all their life, they will not even in that country have any mutual rights to support or to inheritance, etc., nor will any children born of the union have the status of legitimacy. By comparison, a limping marriage is certainly a minor evil. Typically such a union gives the parties and their children the full protection accorded to other lawful marriages in the country that permitted its celebration.[839]

835. This does not mean, however, that the degree of connection with the forum country should be completely disregarded; cf. *infra* at n. 842.

836. See *Dorenberg* 145, 149-150.

837. For a rather extreme example see the WEST GERMAN decision of OLG Hamm 14 June 1974, IPRspr. 1974 no. 49.

838. See, for instance, the opinion of the SWISS Federal Tribunal in the *Dal Bosco* case, BG 3 June 1971, BGE 97 I 389, 407-408.

839. Cf. *supra* n. 770.

In numerous instances the fact that the marriage limps is likely to remain a purely theoretical statement of what would be the legal position in a hypothetical case (namely, if the parties or one of them decided to settle in the foreign country prohibiting their union, or if the effects produced by the marriage in that country would otherwise be of interest to them). In the case of a "paperless marriage", on the other hand, the precarious situation of the parties is an inescapable reality wherever and whenever questions concerning their rights and position present themselves.

In conclusion, the arguments advanced in favour of permitting the remarriage greatly preponderate. Perhaps the opposite solution was more easily defensible in earlier days when the principle of the personal law had a stronger position than today and when, quantitatively, less harm could ensue from its application to the present matter because the number of mixed marriages and of limping divorces was relatively insignificant. With present-day population movements in Europe and the greatly increased number of mixed marriages, with the overall tendency to facilitate divorce and the parallel tendency in favour of applying the *lex fori* alone in proceedings for divorce involving mixed marriages (and often even as to marriages between two foreigners), the problem has acquired a new dimension so as now to stand out as one of the most important of all in the conflicts law of marriage.[840] Seeing that the principle of the personal law has lost much of the sway it used to hold (at least in the Continental countries of Europe) in matters of divorce, it seems necessary also to accept the consequence that a foreigner divorced contrary to his personal law must be entitled to remarry whatever that law may say. Tensions are likely to become unbearable in the long run if, on the one hand, the courts of a country are to disregard foreign law more or less systematically when divorcing foreigners but, on the other, to "resurrect" the personal law once the divorcee wants to marry again, refusing him the right to do so owing to the non-recognition of the divorce by that law.

It is certainly desirable, in these as in other cases of limping marriages, that the authorities of the country of celebration should

840. These changes in the factual and legal background of the problem, as well as a corresponding change in the climate of public opinion, were a moving factor behind the decision of the SWISS Federal Tribunal in the *Dal Bosco* case, whereby the wide reference approach adopted in its earlier decision in the *Caliaro* case was overthrown; see BG 3 June 1971, BGE 97 I 389, 408-410. See also *Knoepfler*, case note: Rev. crit. d.i.p. 1969, 312, 314-315; *Pi-Song Tsai* 228-230.

inform the parties of the danger that their union will not be recognised abroad and as to the possible consequences thereof.[841] If, however, the parties choose to accept these risks with open eyes, no further protection should be forced upon them.

While it is submitted that remarriage should be permitted as a rule, a different evaluation may be appropriate in some exceptional cases where the proposed union lacks any connection with the country of intended celebration.[842] Suppose, for instance, that the man is of Spanish and the wife of Swiss nationality. They make their matrimonial home in Spain, where they live together until the wife obtains a divorce in Switzerland. The man then wants to enter into a second marriage with a Spanish woman. Since he cannot do so in Spain where the divorce is not recognised, the parties decide to go to Switzerland on a short visit in order to get married there, intending to return to Spain and to live there afterwards. In such a case there appears to be scant justification for permitting the union to be solemnised, contrary to Spanish law, just because the divorce has been pronounced by a Swiss court. For while it is undesirable that the forum should assume the role of the guardian of the intending spouses by protecting them against their will from the dangers of a limping marriage, it does have a legitimate interest in protecting itself against the risk of becoming a "marriage haven" and in being able to ward off marriages which are clearly in evasion of the foreign law applicable under its conflicts rules.

If such an exception is admitted, its exact delimitation may give rise to some difficulties. This question will not be further pursued here, except to say that any departure from the rule should be narrowly confined. Obviously, for instance, the point of view advanced here cannot justify a refusal to permit the remarriage by reason only of the foreign nationality of the intending spouses.

In so far as it is accepted that a divorce valid in the eyes of the *lex fori* prevails, as a rule, over any foreign law at the stage of celebration of the second marriage, it goes without saying that the same must hold true if the validity of that union is later challenged in the same country. This is an argument *a fortiori* since, in addition

841. See, for example, *Ficker* 313; *Kegel and A. Lüderitz* 60. Cf. for similar requirements in other connections *supra* n. 273 (DANISH law) and the text after n. 536 (FRENCH law).

842. For writers supporting one distinction or the other based on the strength of the local contacts see, e.g., *Bucher* 177-178, 187-189; *Lalive*, case note: Schw. Jb. Int. R. 33 (1977) 284, 286; *Müller-Freienfels* 91-92, 97-98; *Pi-Song Tsai* 241-242, 294. Against any such distinction see, e.g., *von Overbeck*, Relativität 292.

to other considerations, the policy of validation comes into play once the marriage has been created. Even if, contrary to the position advocated here (or in accordance with the exception suggested above), the attitude of the foreign law should be held relevant so as to bar celebration of the second marriage, it is very difficult to imagine any case where it would seem appropriate to adopt this approach in order to defeat that union if already entered into in contravention of the foreign law.[843]

The preceding considerations and conclusions also apply, in the main, to the much rarer situation where the prior marriage has not been dissolved by divorce but where it suffers from an initial defect rendering it invalid according to the *lex fori,* though it is valid from the point of view of the *lex causae* of the capacity of /one of/ the parties to the second union.[844]

ac. *Effect on Second Marriage of Subsequent Dissolution of Prior Union*

91. The situation to be considered here is where a person has remarried while he was bound by a prior union, which was admittedly valid and subsisting under all relevant laws at the time of celebration but which has been terminated, whether by the death of the other spouse, by divorce or otherwise, at some later time, though before any proceedings to annul the second marriage or to declare it invalid for bigamy were instituted. Many legal systems, for example in the countries of Eastern Europe and Scandinavia, provide that such a subsequent dissolution of the first marriage operates, generally or in certain circumstances, to cure the defect initially vitiating the second, or to exclude or restrict the right to petition for a nullity decree.[845]

Such rules may give rise to conflict of laws problems chiefly when they form part of a foreign law invoked as applicable in defence to nullity proceedings in a country whose domestic law is unfamiliar with this kind of validation and where a bigamous marriage therefore remains void or liable to annulment, notwithstanding any subsequent dissolution of the prior union. This is the rule, for instance, in England and West Germany, respectively.[846]

843. Cf. for [WEST] GERMAN law *supra* at n. 512-514 and 735-739.
844. Cf. *supra* n. 733 and 815.
845. For a comparative survey see *Dölle,* Familienrecht 271-272.
846. ENGLAND: Matrimonial Causes Act 1973, s. 11 (*b*) (bigamous marriage void; cf. s. 13, enumerating the bars to the grant of a nullity decree,

continued on page 264

What is, or what should be, the approach in such countries to foreign rules of the present type?

This question should be regarded as a facet of the wider problem of the choice of law to determine the grounds on which an originally invalid marriage may become valid as a result of subsequent events.[847] Such validating force is attributed to a variety of facts – as, for instance, lapse of time, approbation by the parties (sometimes inferred from cohabitation with knowledge of the defect in question for a specified length of time), ratification by a third person whose consent was lacking, or the pregnancy of the wife – by different laws in different circumstances.[848]

On principle, there is little doubt as to the proper approach to conflicts of laws with regard to such questions. The connection between any particular cause of nullity and the grounds on which it will be "neutralised" is too tight to admit of any solution whereby the two matters would be assigned to different laws. Accordingly, the law by virtue of which the marriage is held to suffer from a defect rendering it invalid should also be entitled to decide what facts are sufficient to cure that defect. This is the generally prevailing view, at least in *Continental European* and *Scandinavian* countries.[849] It does not, and should not, make any difference whether the curative rule is phrased in substantive or – as often happens – in procedural language, providing for example that a petition "shall not be entertained" after the expiration of a certain period of time.

There is a paucity of cases and literature dealing with the problem specifically in relation to the issue considered here. On the other hand, there is no reason to believe that this issue would not be classified and treated along with other grounds of subsequent validation of a marriage. Since the defect of bigamy relates to capacity to marry, it may therefore be assumed that the healing

---

continued from page 263

all of which are limited to voidable marriages); WEST GERMANY: Marriage Act of 1946, § 20, 24; see *Hoffmann and Stephan* § 5 no. 15, § 20 no. 5. For further references see *Dölle*, Familienrecht 270-272.

847. These problems bear a certain resemblance to those, already covered, which result from a subsequent change of the relevant connecting factor or in the applicable rules of the *lex causae* (*supra* s. 53-57).

848. For a comparative survey see *Dölle*, Familienrecht 284-286, 341-346.

849. See generally *Rabel* 309-310, and for particular countries, e.g., FRANCE: *Bischoff* no. 163; *G. de La Pradelle* 183-188; WEST GERMANY: *Gamillscheg*, Kommentar, art. 13 no. 489-490, 868; ITALY: *M. Miele* 118-119; SWITZERLAND: *Beck*, art. 7 f no. 110, 138, 149.

effect of a subsequent dissolution of the prior marriage would be determined in accordance with the law governing the party's capacity.[850]

As regards *England* and other *common law countries,* however, it is very doubtful whether and to what extent this principle would be followed. These doubts are in part prompted by the tendency displayed in other connections to give a wide scope for the concept of procedural law referable to the *lex fori.*[851] There is *Scottish* authority for the view that foreign rules of the particular type under examination cannot be given effect by the forum, either because their application would violate public policy or because they are classifiable as procedural.[852]

> In that case H first married W(1) in Poland. This marriage still subsisted in 1940, when H went through a ceremony of marriage with W(2) in Scotland. W(1) then died in 1949. In 1953 W(2) brought an action for declarator of nullity of her marriage with H on the ground that it was void for bigamy. H claimed in defence that Polish law was applicable, because both he and W(2) had been domiciled in Poland at the time of their marriage in 1940, and that by Polish law the marriage could no longer be annulled after the death of W(1). On the assumption that Polish law was the proper law to apply, the court nevertheless rejected this defence on two alternative grounds:[853] If the effect of the Polish rule in question was to give retrospective validity to bigamous marriages upon the cessation of the prior marriage, then it was not a rule which the courts of Scotland would be under any duty to recognise, "for its substantial effect would be to make every bigamous or polygamous marriage potentially and conditionally valid." If, on the other hand, the rule only meant that in Poland an action to nullify a bigamous marriage must be brought during the subsistence of the prior marriage, that was "no more than a detail of the procedural requirements of the foreign *forum*", dealing with a matter "not of substance but of process, not of the right but of the remedy."

850. Expressly in favour of this view see for WEST GERMAN law *Gamillscheg*, Kommentar, art. 13 no. 491.

851. For some instances see *Pålsson*, Marriage, s. 236, 307 and 410 (at n. 557).

852. Prawdzic-Lazarska v. Prawdzic-Lazarski, 1954 S.C. 98.

853. 1954 S.C. 98 at 102.

Neither of these grounds, it is submitted, carries conviction. It is difficult to understand that foreign rules of the type before the court, even where unknown to the domestic system of the forum, should evoke a degree of odium sufficient to exclude them from application.[854] Admittedly, such rules can be analysed as implying recognition of a kind of "legal bigamy" in the past, inasmuch as both marriages must be regarded as having lawfully coexisted until the first was dissolved. While this concept may violate inherited dogmas of matrimonial law endorsed by the *lex fori*, it seems very questionable to infer that recognition must be denied to foreign rules based on a different policy. This policy is no other than that generally underlying the present-day tendency in many legal systems to restrict, or sometimes even to abolish completely, the notion of a retroactively invalid marriage, namely, that it is socially undesirable and out of touch with the realities of life that a union which has been celebrated in due form and which has been treated as valid by the parties themselves and by others for a longer or shorter period of time should afterwards be declared never to have existed at all.

Nor is it very appropriate to dispose of the problem by classifying rules of this type, even where they happen to be couched in terms of a restriction on the right to bring proceedings for nullity, as concerned "merely with procedure". This approach is too much *lex fori*-oriented and, while attaching weight to the often purely accidental wording of the foreign rule, fails to take account of the purpose of that rule and of the function it fulfills in its foreign setting.

ad. *Restrictions on Remarriage Applicable After Termination of Prior Union*

92. *Introductory.* Under the laws of many countries the right of ex-spouses to marry again is or may be limited in various ways, although their marriage has admittedly come to an end, at least for all other purposes. The conflict of laws problems involving such restrictions that have arisen in countries where capacity to marry is determinable by the personal law are in part similar to but in

854. But extrajudicial opinion in ENGLAND seems to lean in favour of the same view; see *Hartley*, Bigamy 681; *North* 122, 131. See, too, the AUSTRALIAN case of Stankus v. Stankus (1974), 9 S.A.S.R. 20 at 24-25 (S.C.) (*obiter*).

part different from those encountered in American law (as to which see *supra*, particularly s. 21 and 23).

In dealing with these questions it is necessary to distinguish between different types of restraint. As in American law (*supra* s. 23), one dividing line of primary importance is to be drawn according to whether the ban is imposed on both parties to the dissolved union (*ada*) or on one of them alone (*adb*).

In the nature of things, restrictions of the former kind only come into question where the prior union has been terminated by divorce or by annulment. Conflicts problems concerning such prohibitions, which are common in American practice, have relatively seldom fallen for consideration in the countries to be examined here (*infra* s. 93).

The usual type of restraint against remarriage occurring in the practice at least of Continental European countries is that bearing exclusively on one of the parties to the dissolved union. Several provisions within this category are more or less distinctly in the nature of a penalty, their typical purpose and effect being to prevent or postpone the remarriage of a party against whom a divorce was pronounced for matrimonial offences, usually adultery (*infra* s. 94). Other restrictions on remarriage, although directed against one of the ex-spouses only, have nothing to do with the notion of a penalty and are also applicable when the prior marriage was ended by the death of the other spouse. Chief among these restraints is the waiting period imposed by numerous legal systems on the remarriage of a widow or a divorced woman with the object of avoiding *turbatio sanguinis* (*infra* s. 95). In addition, there are a few "odd" types of prohibition against remarriage figuring in certain legal systems. They play a minimal part in the conflict of laws and will only be briefly adverted to here (*infra* s. 96).

ada. Restrictions Affecting Both Parties to Dissolved Marriage

93. Statutes prohibiting either party to a divorce from remarrying before a certain period has elapsed from the date of the decree are to be found in many common law countries.[855] The purpose of such a restraint is usually, and has been in all conflict of laws cases dealt with below, to prevent a premature remarriage in case

855. See the cases cited *infra* n. 857-863. For AMERICAN law see *supra* s. 23.

the decree is reversed on appeal.[856] The ban is accordingly framed so as to last during the time allowed for appealing or, if an appeal is brought within that time, until it has been dismissed.

The question of whether such limitations on the right of remarriage are entitled to extraterritorial effect has come before the courts in *England* and other *Commonwealth* countries on a number of occasions. In *Warter* v. *Warter,*[857] which is the leading English case on the matter, the parties to the first marriage were divorced in India. The relevant Indian statute, under which the proceedings were taken, provided that it should be lawful for either party to marry again when six months after the date of the decree absolute had expired and no appeal had been presented, but not sooner. The wife came to England and remarried there within the prohibited time. It was held that this marriage was invalid because it was so by the Indian *lex divortii.*[858]

This decision has been followed in *Australia* and *Canada.*[859] Like the English case, these cases involved a second marriage celebrated locally, or in a third country, which was held invalid because it violated a prohibition of remarriage within the time for appeal laid down by the law of the country where the decree of divorce had been pronounced.

Such questions may, of course, also arise for decision in the country itself whose law provides the restriction, that is to say, in

856. A different purpose is pursued by certain AMERICAN statutes which, in forbidding divorced persons to marry again within a specified time from the date of the decree, seek to discourage the use of divorce by thwarting any hope the parties may have for an immediate remarriage (*supra* s. 21, 23). Apparently, however, the treatment of such prohibitions has never come in issue in conflicts cases decided by courts in EUROPEAN countries.

857. (1890), 15 P.D. 152.

858. For later ENGLISH cases holding the same way see: Le Mesurier v. Le Mesurier (1930), 46 T.L.R. 203 (P.); Boettcher v. Boettcher, [1949] W.N. 83 (P.). A SCOTTISH decision to the same effect is Martin v. Buret, 1938 S.L.T. 479. And see among writers: *Cheshire and North* 352; *Dicey and Morris* 266-267, 334-335; *Graveson,* Conflict 261, 288; *Hartley,* Bigamy 694-698; *North* 191; *Wolff,* PIL 378-379.

859. AUSTRALIA: Miller v. Teale (1954), 92 C.L.R. 406 (H.C.A.), noted by *Webb*: 5 I.C.L.Q. 137 (1956); see *Nygh* 443; *Sykes,* Conflict 126; CANADA: In re Eaton, [1922] 1 W.W.R. 236 (B.C.S.C.); Turner v. Turner (1953), 9 W.W.R. 684 (Alta. Sup. Ct.); Bevand v. Bevand, [1955] 1 D.L.R. 854 (N.S. Div. Ct.); Sakellaropoulo v. Davis (1960), 24 D.L.R. (2d) 524 (Ont. H.C.); see also *Castel,* Conflict of Laws. Cases, Notes and Materials (ed. 3, Toronto 1974) 234, and *infra* n. 861. And see for NEW ZEALAND, *Webb and Davis* 294.

situations where the *lex divortii* coincides with the *lex fori*.[860] The attitude of the courts of that country is even a matter of primary importance; for the courts of other countries cannot be expected to recognise that the restraint has extraterritorial effect unless it is treated as having such effect in its country of origin.[861]

It seems clear that the domicile of the divorced party, or of any other party, at the time of the remarriage is immaterial for the present purpose.[862] This implies that the law governing capacity to marry has no say in the treatment of prohibitions of the kind under consideration.[863] In other words, these prohibitions constitute an independent category, which falls outside the usual "form and capacity" dichotomy in the conflicts law of marriage and for which the *lex divortii* is the appropriate law to apply.[864]

The basis and the scope of this rule, however, are not settled beyond doubt. Most of the relevant decisions seem to rely on a

860. For an early ENGLISH case see De Thoren v. Att.-Gen. (1876), 1 App. Cas. 686 (H.L.). In that case one of the parties to an English divorce remarried in Scotland before the time fixed for appeal against the decree had run out. Although this marriage was initially invalid by ENGLISH law (as it then stood), it was held to have become valid by a presumed exchange of new matrimonial consent in Scotland after the prescribed time had elapsed. This means of validation plays an important part in AMERICAN law (*supra* s. 25).

861. For CANADIAN cases decided in British Columbia and involving the interpretation and constitutional validity of the relevant statute of that province, see Gill v. Gill, [1947] 2 W.W.R. 761 (B.C.S.C.); Brown v. Brown (1956), 6 D.L.R. (2d) 693 (B.C.C.A.); Hellens v. Densmore (1957), 10 D.L.R. (2d) 561 (S.C.C.). For criticism on constitutional grounds see *Kennedy*, case note: 34 Can. Bar Rev. 825 (1956).

862. In the ENGLISH case of Warter v. Warter (1890), 15 P.D. 152, for instance, no finding was made as to the divorced wife's domicile (although it appears that she was domiciled in England, as was her second husband). And in the AUSTRALIAN case of Miller v. Teale (1954), 92 C.L.R. 406 (H.C.A.), where the divorce had been obtained in South Australia, effect was given to a restraint against remarriage imposed by the law of that state, notwithstanding that both parties to the new marriage were at the time of celebration domiciled in New South Wales, which was also the place of celebration and of the forum.

863. The question was approached as a matter of capacity referable to the *lex domicilii* in the AUSTRALIAN case of Pezet v. Pezet (1946), 47 S.R. (N.S.W.) 45 (F.C.), but this decision was overruled in Miller v. Teale (1954), 92 C.L.R. 406 (H.C.A.).

864. The *lex divortii* is taken to mean the law governing the procedure by which the divorce was obtained, *i.e.* the internal law of the country where the decree was pronounced, as distinct from the law applicable to the substantive aspects of divorce. Although this distinction is unknown in the COMMON LAW countries dealt with here, it is of importance from the point of view of many other countries where foreign law may have to be applied in matters of substance.

construction of the provision of the *lex divortii* that restrained the parties from remarrying, to the effect that the divorce was not yet final and conclusive or, while final and conclusive in other respects, that it was not so for the purpose of determining the validity of the new marriage. In *Warter* v. *Warter,* for instance, where the divorce had been pronounced by virtue of Indian law, that law was construed to imply that the tie of marriage was not completely dissolved until the time for appealing had passed and that the restriction on remarriage formed "an integral part of the proceedings by which alone both the parties can be released from their incapacity to contract a fresh marriage."[865] On this view it follows that a second marriage entered into while the prohibition runs is void for bigamy, regardless of the place of celebration or of the domicile of the parties.[866]

Whether the construction thus placed upon the provisions of the *lex divortii* is appropriate must be determined separately for each legal system containing a prohibition of the type examined here. In several instances opinions have been divided over this question.[867] In yet other and perhaps even in most cases, however, it is clear that the restriction on remarriage in no way affects the full operation of the divorce decree, which ends the marriage for all purposes from the moment it is made absolute.[868] In these cases the disability of the divorced parties to marry again until the lapse of the time limited for appealing from the decree springs, not

865. (1890), 15 P.D. 152 at 155.

866. Similarly for AMERICAN law see *supra* at n. 123-126.

867. See, for instance, the AUSTRALIAN cases of Pezet v. Pezet (1946), 47 S.R. (N.S.W.) 45 (F.C.), and Miller v. Teale (1954), 92 C.L.R. 406 (H.C.A.), where substantially similar statutes forming part of the *lex divortii* were construed differently. Moreover, the South Australian statute involved in the latter case was construed differently by the majority of four judges and by Kitto J. in a concurring opinion. A similar conflict of opinion, relating to the construction of the relevant statute in British Columbia, appears very clearly in the various judgments delivered in the CANADIAN case of Densmore v. Densmore (1956), 5 D.L.R. (2d) 203 (B.C.C.A.), reversed *sub nom.* Hellens v. Densmore (1957), 10 D.L.R. (2d) 561 (S.C.C.). And see for AMERICAN law *supra* at n. 118-121.

868. So held by the Privy Council, on an appeal from JAMAICA, in Marsh v. Marsh, [1945] A.C. 271; cf. *Hartley*, Bigamy 698. This is certainly the majority position in AMERICAN law (*supra* at n. 121). As regards ENGLISH law, there is not normally any right of appeal from a decree absolute of divorce; see Supreme Court of Judicature (Consolidation) Act 1925, s. 31 (1) (*e*). Even in those exceptional cases where such an appeal lies, however, this does not alter the fact that the marriage is at an end for all purposes: Dryden v. Dryden, [1973] Fam. 217, 239.

from the continued existence of the prior union, but from the prohibitory statute itself.

If this is the position under the *lex divortii,* it is much more doubtful whether the prohibition will receive extraterritorial effect so as to invalidate a marriage celebrated outside the enacting country. There are some indications that such a prohibition would be disregarded altogether or, possibly, that it would be treated as affecting capacity to marry, to be taken into account only where it is recognised by the relevant domiciliary law.[869] In any event the "bigamy theory" apparently embraced by the courts in most cases so far decided could not be invoked to support the extraterritorial application of a prohibition against remarriage which survives the complete dissolution of the prior union. On the other hand, there is some court language pointing to the conclusion that such a prohibition would be treated on a par with those construed to postpone the dissolution of the first union.[870]

This latter view, it is submitted, is greatly to be preferred. Whether a temporary ban on remarriage in order to allow for an appeal is "only" what it purports to be or whether it implies that the prior marriage "has not yet been dissolved in so far as the new marriage is concerned" is a tenuous distinction which can often be drawn at will. It is scarcely satisfactory that the determination of a serious question such as a divorced person's right to marry again should turn upon such exercises in mumbo-jumbo.

If this distinction is rejected, the only adequate solution is to govern all prohibitions of the kind under consideration by the *lex divortii.* Such prohibitions, regardless of whether they are construed to have any effect on the subsistence of the prior marriage, are too closely linked to the procedure for divorce to admit of any choice of law separate from that applicable to the latter. If the forum is prepared to recognise the jurisdiction of the foreign court to grant a divorce, then surely it must also recognise that the decree can be

869. In favour of such an approach see AUSTRALIA: Pezet v. Pezet (1946), 47 S.R. (N.S.W.) 45 (F.C.); CANADA: Densmore v. Densmore (1956), 5 D.L.R. (2d) 203 at 215-216 and 217-221 (B.C.C.A.).

870. See, e.g., AUSTRALIA: Miller v. Teale (1954), 92 C.L.R. 406 at 421 (H.C.A., concurring judgment of Kitto J.); CANADA: Bevand v. Bevand, [1955] 1 D.L.R. 854 (N.S. Div. Ct.); Hellens v. Densmore (1957), 10 D.L.R. (2d) 561 at 568-569 (S.C.C., *per* Rand J.). These opinions clearly endorse the view that the first marriage was completely ended with the divorce decree but that a second marriage within the time allowed for appeal against the decree was nevertheless invalid owing to a prohibition of remarriage during that time established by the *lex divortii.* See also *Hartley,* Bigamy 697-698; *M. Mann* 138-139. Cf. for AMERICAN decisions to the same effect *supra* n. 140, 142.

set aside on appeal if this is possible under the *lex divortii*. Since the restraint against remarriage is designed to prevent difficulties on this contingency, it is only reasonable for the forum to treat it as equally effective as other rules forming part of the foreign procedure.[871]

In no circumstances, it is submitted, is there any point in submitting this matter to the personal law decisive for the capacity of the parties to marry. Whatever regulation that law may contain concerning waiting periods for remarriage so as to safeguard the right to appeal from a decree of divorce is unlikely to have any reference whatsoever to decrees pronounced under another law.[872] If, for instance, a domiciled German national has obtained a divorce in England, his general capacity to marry again may well be subject to German law, but it seems preposterous to suggest that the scope of that law should extend to any question of whether he must await the expiry of a certain period during which an appeal may be taken from the divorce decree. This particular point can only be decided by reference to English law as the *lex divortii*.[873]

The problems under review have attracted scant attention outside the common law world, but they could well present themselves in other countries, too. Suppose, for instance, that a person seeks to marry again in a Continental European country shortly after a divorce from his first spouse in the United States and contrary to the terms of the divorce decree by which both divorced parties are subject to a temporary ban on remarriage. Assuming that the decree is final and that it is recognised by the forum, will effect also be given to this restraining provision in accordance with the *lex divortii*?

It is not possible to answer this question with any certainty. There are a few *West German* cases in which such issues were approached as affecting capacity to marry referable to the party's *lex patriae* (including its conflicts rules).[874] For the reasons set

871. See the opinion of Kitto, J., in the AUSTRALIAN case cited *supra* n. 870.

872. Cf. for AMERICAN law *supra* at n. 146-152.

873. By ENGLISH law a second marriage is now valid even if an appeal should be available from the decree absolute dissolving the first; see Dryden v. Dryden, [1973] Fam. 217, 237-239; cf. *supra* n. 868.

874. OLG Karlsruhe 3 Oct. 1968, IPRspr. 1968/69 no. 69 (ban on remarriage within twelve months of divorce in Texas, USA); AG Zweibrücken 14 May 1970, IPRspr. 1970 no. 46 (do. within 60 days of divorce in Kansas, USA). In both cases the prohibition existing under the *lex divortii* was dis-

out above, however, it is submitted that preference ought to be given to the *lex divortii* if the prohibition is of the kind designed to give time for appeal against the divorce decree.

No such problems seem capable of arising in the case of a divorce granted in a Continental European or Scandinavian country, for the laws of those countries do not contain any rules specifically dealing with remarriage within the time for appeal against a judgment of divorce. In general, the position is that a marriage is not regarded as dissolved for any purpose until the divorce has become final and conclusive, *i.e.* when the judgment is no longer open to ordinary means of attack.[875] The point of time at which this happens is, of course, a matter for the law of the country where the judgment was rendered.

adb. Restrictions Affecting Only One Party to Dissolved Marriage

94. *Restrictions Having Penal Connotation.* The restraints upon remarriage to be considered here are directed against one party only in divorce proceedings and imposed by reason of that party's marital misconduct. These restrictions are in the main of two kinds:

The first is that whereby a spouse against whom a divorce is pronounced for matrimonial offences is forbidden to remarry at all within a certain time of the decree.[876] Such a typically penal disability is prescribed by the laws of a few states in the United States.[877] In Europe, the best known example is provided by Swiss law, which requires the court granting a divorce to place on the guilty party a *Strafwartefrist* (penal waiting period) of a length ranging from one to two years, or in certain cases up to three years, during which that party is precluded from entering into another marriage.[878]

The second and more common type of restraining provision is

---

regarded because the proposed marriage would be recognised as valid by the relevant personal law if it complied with GERMAN law as the *lex loci celebrationis* (which was thus applied by way of *renvoi* from the *lex patriae*). The result would apparently have been the same under the *lex divortii*.

875. See, e.g., FRANCE: CC art. 260; WEST GERMANY: Marriage Act of 1946, § 41; ITALY: Act of 1 Dec. 1970, art. 10.

876. For comparative surveys see *Dölle*, Familienrecht 129, 136, 588-589; *Gamillscheg*, Kommentar, art. 13 no. 393-394.

877. See the references *supra* n. 132.

878. SWISS CC art. 150 and 104. Similar provisions are to be found in the TURKISH CC art. 142 and 96, respectively.

limited to the intermarriage of a person divorced for adultery and his accomplice, which is banned either for a specified term of years or indefinitely.[879] Until some time ago such prohibitions existed in different variants in several parts of the United States as well as in a large number of countries in Continental Europe, Latin America and elsewhere.[880] In recent decades, however, this kind of restraint has been on the decline; as regards Europe, it is only to be found today in a relatively small minority of countries.[881]

Although these restrictions affect capacity to marry, on the whole the notion of the personal law has been overshadowed by that of territoriality in determining their effect in the conflict of laws. This is borne out by the prevailing attitude both in situations (1) where the marriage takes place in a country whose law contains such a restriction and (2) where domiciliaries or nationals (as the case may be) of such a country marry in some other country.

(1) As regards the former situation, *Swiss* practice may be held out as affording a typical example. The provisions of Swiss law concerning a temporary ban on the remarriage of the guilty party to a divorce suit have been held to express a public policy compelling the courts to take them into account in all cases where the divorce and (the proposed) remarriage occur in Switzerland. The restraint is accordingly pronounced by the Swiss divorce court whenever so required by the terms of those provisions, and then operates to prevent the person subject to it from marrying again in Switzerland within the stated time.[882] The nationality of the parties to the divorce or to the new marriage is immaterial, and so is the law otherwise applicable in those matters.

Similarly, prohibitions against the intermarriage of a person

879. A variant of this impediment, known to the laws of certain Mediterranean and Latin American countries with a strong CANON LAW tradition, is that declared against the intermarriage of persons one of whom has been found guilty of an attempt against the life of the other's spouse with the intention to marry the survivor (*impedimentum criminis*). See *Dölle,* Familienrecht 128.

880. For comparative surveys see the references *supra* n. 132 (for AMERICAN law) and 383. See also *Fritzsche,* expert opinion reproduced in SJZ 48 (1952) 378.

881. The prohibition is unknown in the countries of EASTERN EUROPE and SCANDINAVIA, as well as in ENGLAND and other COMMONWEALTH countries. It was abolished long ago in FRANCE and more recently, for instance, in the BENELUX countries and WEST GERMANY, but still obtains, *inter alia,* in AUSTRIA (Marriage Act of 1938, § 9), GREECE (CC art. 1363) and a number of countries in LATIN AMERICA.

882. See: *Beck,* art. 7 c no. 54, art. 7 h no. 233; *Götz,* art. 104 no. 12, art. 107 no. 19; *Vaucher* 544.

divorced for adultery and his paramour have often been held to form part of the public policy of the enacting country so as to command application to all locally celebrated marriages, notwithstanding the absence of any such restriction in the personal law of the parties generally governing their capacity to marry.[883] In the past, this position was taken, for instance, by *Dutch* courts.[884]

In so far as statutes of this latter kind still remain in effect, however, the force of their policy seems less strong at the present day than it once was. Provision is usually made for the grant of dispensation from the prohibition in appropriate circumstances. This is an indication that the public policy of the enacting country might not be opposed to the application of foreign laws knowing of no such restriction at all.[885] In *West Germany,* for instance, where the restraining provision was recently abolished, that provision was not regarded as a bar to the celebration of a marriage permitted by the national laws of the parties.[886] On the other hand, even without resort to public policy such prohibitions are usually given a rather broad range as a result of their being treated as bilateral, *i.e.* applicable whenever enunciated by the personal law of either party to the proposed union.[887]

(2) Where the marriage takes place outside the country whose law contains the restraining provision and to which the divorced party belongs by domicile or nationality (whichever is relevant in identifying his personal law), the restraint will usually be treated as ineffective because of its penal character.[888] In *England,* for instance, it has been held that an incapacity to remarry imposed

883. The same holds true of the *impedimentum criminis* (*supra* n. 879). See, for instance, the HAGUE CONVENTION of 1902, art. 2 par. 1 no. 2 and 3; BUSTAMANTE CODE art. 38 (cf. art. 40, dealing with foreign celebrated marriages); BRAZIL: Act of 4 Sept. 1942, art. 7 par. 1 in conjunction with CC art. 183 (no. VII and VIII) and 207; ITALY: CC art. 116 par. 2 in conjunction with art. 88; VENEZUELA: CC art. 104 in conjunction with art. 55 and 107.

884. Hoge Raad 16 April 1908, W. no. 8718, Clunet 1912, 293; Hoge Raad 2 June 1936, N.J. 1936 no. 1013, Bull. I.I.I. 36 (1937) 511. See *Lemaire* 391; *van Sasse van Ysselt* 193. For a similar view in AUSTRIA see *Klang and Gschnitzer* 244, 490; but see now *Schwind,* IPR 145.

885. Cf. the HAGUE CONVENTION of 1902, art. 2 par. 1 no. 2, pursuant to which only an "absolute" prohibition based on adultery is sufficient to entitle the country of celebration to forbid a marriage which is permitted by the *lex patriae;* see *supra* at n. 634 and 639.

886. See *Gamillscheg,* Kommentar, art. 13 no. 377, 381; *Massfeller* 224; *Wolff,* IPR 191. Similarly for BELGIUM: *Graulich* 157 n. 11.

887. See *supra* at n. 384-386.

888. For the same tendency in AMERICAN law see *supra* at n. 137-138.

by foreign law "by way of punishment, discipline or example", and therefore only attached to the guilty party to the dissolved union, must be disregarded when the new marriage is celebrated in England.[889] This is also the position in other *Commonwealth* countries.[890] A similar view prevails in several *Continental European* and *Scandinavian* countries whose domestic laws do not recognise this kind of restriction.[891]

Nevertheless, opinions have been, and to some extent still are, divided in some Continental countries, particularly as concerns the treatment of penal waiting periods of the type figuring in Swiss law. In some older *French* and *German* cases, where a divorce was granted between spouses of Swiss nationality, the courts even went to the length of themselves pronouncing a *Strafwartefrist* against one of the parties in compliance with Swiss law, which was the law governing the divorce.[892] These decisions have not been followed in more recent cases, however, and in all probability no longer represent the law either in France or in West Germany.[893] It is somewhat more doubtful what attitude will be taken to such a penalty when it is imposed by the courts of the foreign country itself and forms part of a divorce decree otherwise recognised by the forum. Both in France and in West Germany some support exists for the view that effect must be given to the foreign restric-

889. Scott v. Att.-Gen. (1886), 11 P.D. 128, as explained in Warter v. Warter (1890), 15 P.D. 152 at 155. See *Cheshire and North* 352; *Dicey and Morris* 73, 231-233, 266-267, 274-275, 335; *Graveson,* Conflict 177-178, 262, 288; *Holder* 948; *North* 131, 191; *Wolff,* PIL 172, 339, 378. So also for SCOTLAND, *Anton* 283. For distinctions see *M. Mann* 140-146; cf. *Ryan* 991.

890. AUSTRALIA: Lundgren v. O'Brien (No. 2), [1921] V.L.R. 361 (F.C.) (where the principle was carried beyond the limits of penal prohibitions as that notion is normally understood, see *infra* at n. 921); Miller v. Teale (1954), 92 C.L.R. 406, 415 (H.C.A.) (*obiter*); see *Nygh* 275, 443; *Sykes,* Conflict 125-126; NEW ZEALAND: *Webb and Davis* 294, 513-514.

891. See the references *infra* n. 895-900. For the countries of EASTERN EUROPE see *Korkisch* 620 n. 69.

892. FRANCE: Cass. req. 27 Nov. 1934, D.P. 1935.1.89, critical note Carbonnier (a case decided under the particular conflicts rules for MOROCCO and probably not extensible to metropolitan FRANCE); cf. *Batiffol and Lagarde* II 81 n. 86; [WEST] GERMANY: OLG München 17 March 1921, OLGR 42, 16; KG 16 March 1931, IPRspr. 1931 no. 81; see *Nussbaum* 157-158, 390; *Raape,* IPR 308; further references are given by *Gamillscheg,* Kommentar, art. 17 no. 477.

893. For GERMAN decisions refusing to pronounce such an order see, e.g., KG 27 June 1932, IPRspr. 1932 no. 86; OLG Hamburg 22 March 1934, IPRspr. 1934 no. 56; KG 30 May 1938, JW 1938, 2750. See *Gamillscheg,* Kommentar, art. 17 no. 478 with further references.

tion in this situation, at least as a rule.[894] The prevailing trend of opinion, however, especially in modern literature on the conflict of laws, is in favour of rejecting any application of such penal restraints on remarriage.[895] In any event the penalty cannot be enforced against a person possessing the nationality of the forum country.[896]

There is also some split of opinion with regard to rules of foreign law forbidding the intermarriage of a person divorced for adultery and his accomplice. Modern *French* writers, for instance,

894. For FRANCE see the decision of Trib. Seine 17 Oct. 1961, Clunet 1962, 708 (prohibitions of AMERICAN law held not contrary to FRENCH public policy, but interpreted as not impairing the validity of a violating marriage celebrated in Lebanon) with an approving note by Ponsard (cf. for a BRAZILIAN decision likewise recognising an AMERICAN prohibition upon remarriage of the guilty party, *Garland* 28 (at n. 80), 97-98, 106). And see among writers: *G. Holleaux* 200; *Vincent and Ponsard* no. 114. These writers, emphasising the intimate tie between restraints on remarriage and divorce, lean in favour of dealing with the former by reference to the law governing the latter. [WEST] GERMAN writers, on the other hand, insist that the law for capacity to marry is the appropriate law to apply; see *Gamillscheg*, Kommentar, art. 13 no. 397, 399, 401-404; *Massfeller* 224-225; *Raape*, Kommentar 237, 425, 429.

895. In one FRENCH case where a restriction on remarriage contained in a foreign nullity decree was held to be incompatible with French public policy, the court went to the length of inferring that recognition must be refused to the decree as a whole; see Trib. Marseille 25 Nov. 1925, Clunet 1926, 388, Rev. crit. d.i.p. 1926, 537. A similar position was adopted in a GERMAN case, see LG Berlin 29 June 1937, StAZ 1937, 300. This is unnecessary, however; for the ancillary order as to remarriage can be separated from the main part of the decree dealing with the status of the parties (cf. art. 1 par. 2 of the Hague Convention on Divorce of 1970). See for WEST GERMAN writers of the opinion that the foreign decree should only be excluded from recognition in so far as it purports to forbid remarriage: *Dölle*, Familienrecht 136 n. 20; *Kegel*, Kommentar, art. 17 no. 102; *Lauterbach* 28; *Wolff*, IPR 69. For further references and criticism of this view see *Gamillscheg*, Kommentar, art. 13 no. 395-396. For an ITALIAN decision rejecting such a prohibition see Trib. Catania 5 Dec. 1908, Clunet 1910, 670.

896. For decisions to this effect see FRANCE: Trib. Versailles 26 Feb. 1947, Rev. crit. d.i.p. 1947, 457 with a critical note by Batiffol; Trib. Seine 14 May 1956, Clunet 1957, 146; GERMANY: AG Lörrach 10 Sept. 1907, BadRpr. 1908, 133; LG Berlin 14 Dec. 1923, JW 1924, 722; SWEDEN: HD 21 Feb. 1902, NJA 1902, 288 and 1903, 317, Clunet 1904, 457. The result in these cases is the same whether the matter is treated as referable to the law governing capacity to marry (see the GERMAN writers cited *supra* n. 894) or whether such restraints are considered wholly unrecognisable (*supra* n. 895). Even the proponents of the *lex divortii* (see the FRENCH writers cited *supra* n. 894) seem to concede that the rule must suffer an exception in the case of a national of the forum country.

lean towards the view that such prohibitions must be denied effect because they involve an intolerable violation of the principle of freedom of marriage.[897] In *Switzerland*, too, public policy has been called in aid to exclude the application of such foreign rules, though only where the restraint on remarriage was permanent and absolute (*i.e.*, not susceptible of dispensation) and the new marriage had a substantial connection with Switzerland.[898] In *(West) Germany*, on the other hand, restrictions of this kind established by the relevant foreign law on capacity to marry have been honoured even where they were considerably more far-reaching than the corresponding prohibition until recently sanctioned by West German law itself, in particular because they did not admit any possibility of dispensation.[899] This practice, however, seems no longer to be maintainable today. Very probably the application of foreign laws providing for a disability based on adultery must now be circumscribed along much the same lines as those just mentioned for Swiss law.[900]

The fact that restrictions on remarriage of the kind described here are usually denied extraterritorial operation makes it relatively easy for parties subject to such restrictions under their personal law to escape them by marrying in a suitable foreign country. In itself, this is a typical "false evasion", for when the parties return to their home country whose law they sought to foil that law resumes control (*supra* s. 63). Hence the marriage will be liable to annulment if that law so provides.[901] As a practical

897. See *Batiffol and Lagarde* II 41; *Bischoff* no. 68. But see for writers questioning this position: *G. Holleaux* 200; *Ponsard* 13.

898. Circular Letter of the Federal Department of Justice of 30 June 1928, SJZ 25 (1928/29) 183 no. 121; decision of Regierungsrat Kanton Zürich 16 Oct. 1952, SJZ 48 (1952) 376 (with an expert opinion by Fritzsche), RabelsZ 19 (1954) 659; *Beck*, art. 7 c no. 51, 54, 59; *Götz*, art. 104 no. 13, art. 107 no. 21 g; *Schnitzer* 343; *Vaucher* 544-545; *Vischer*, Ordre public 326-327.

899. LG Aachen 11 March 1931, IPRspr. 1932 no. 67; OLG Frankfurt 28 Feb. 1956, IPRspr. 1956/57 no. 5. See *Gamillscheg*, Kommentar, art. 13 no. 377, 380; *Neuhaus*, Grundrechte 611. For a critical appraisal see *Arndt* 251-252.

900. The question must be judged in the light of the decision of the Federal Constitutional Court of 4 May 1971, BVerfGE 31, 58 (*supra* at n. 775-777). See *Gamillscheg*, Kommentar, art. 13 no. 380, 402; *Stöcker*, Ordre public 106.

901. See, e.g., [WEST] GERMANY: RG 14 Jan. 1935, JW 1935, 1403; *Gamillscheg*, Kommentar, art. 13 no. 372; NETHERLANDS: Rb. Amsterdam 27 Feb. 1936, N.J. 1936 no. 1023, RabelsZ 11 (1937) 205. Both these cases involved a marriage celebrated in England contrary to a prohibition of the *lex patriae* based on adultery.

matter, however, these evasions have been successful in the vast majority of cases, because the prohibition in question was merely directory, so that a violative marriage was immune from attack. This is the case, for instance, with the penal waiting period prescribed by Swiss law, which has been successfully evaded on numerous occasions, often by the device of celebrating the forbidden marriage in England.[902]

95. *Waiting Periods for Remarriage of Wife.* By the laws of most Continental European and of several Latin American countries, a former wife is forbidden to marry again until a short time, usually ten months or 300 days, has elapsed from the date on which her previous marriage was ended.[903] Although imposed on one party only, this incapacity is independent of any notion of guilt, as may be seen from the fact that it attaches to widows and to divorced women alike. Its purpose is to resolve doubts and to minimise the risk of disputes as to the paternity of any child borne by the ex-wife within the time fixed for the delay. It is another matter that a ban on remarriage is scarcely an effective means of achieving this purpose.[904]

Generally speaking, these rules have now been losing ground for some time. They have recently been abolished in certain countries, including those of Eastern Europe and of Scandinavia.[905] In a number of other countries they have been modified by exceptions in cases where a pregnancy of the former marriage can be excluded or is unlikely. Especially where that marriage was dissolved by divorce, the waiting period is often computed from an earlier date, such as the day when the petition for divorce was presented, or when a legal separation was granted, or when the spouses ceased cohabiting, so that the prescribed period, or a part of it, may already have run out when the marriage comes to an end. Another means often used to soften this restriction is by providing for the

902. See *supra* at n. 584. For a BELGIAN case see Civ. Bruxelles 16 Dec. 1967, J.T. 1970, 68, upholding a marriage of Belgian nationals celebrated in San Marino before the expiration of the delay prescribed by BELGIAN law (as it then stood) for the intermarriage of an adulterer and his paramour.

903. For comparative surveys see *Dölle,* Familienrecht 135-136, 588; *Gamillscheg,* Kommentar, art. 13 no. 387; *Götz,* art. 103 no. 20.

904. The prohibition seems superfluous if the rules and presumptions concerning the paternity of children born within the critical time are framed in such a way as to take account of the great weight of probability in favour of the second husband's paternity. See, for example, for WEST GERMAN law, *Dölle,* Familienrecht 138-139; for SWEDISH law, NJA 1968 II 618-619.

905. ENGLISH law has never had such rules. The same is true of nearly all states of the USA. See the references *supra* n. 903.

possibility of dispensation, which may be granted more or less generously. On these and other points of detail there are many variations among the laws concerned. Conflicts problems therefore arise, not only as between laws which do and those which do not require a waiting period but also as between different laws within the former class.

It is generally agreed, in principle, that such questions fall to the personal law governing capacity to marry.[906] More particularly, the prevailing opinion is in favour of treating restrictions of the kind under consideration as unilateral, so that they only apply where imposed by the personal law of the wife herself whose capacity is in issue.[907] On this view, and seeing that a waiting period is prescribed, for example, by West German law but not by English law, this requirement must be complied with in the case of a marriage in West Germany between a divorced woman of German nationality and an Englishman but not in the case of a marriage between a divorced Englishwoman and a German man.[908]

On this point, however, there is a rival view propounded by *West German* writers, according to which waiting periods for the wife ought to be treated as bilateral, with the consequence that the requirement of West German law would also apply in the latter hypothesis.[909] The argument in favour of this solution is derived from the objective pursued by the restriction, which, as we have seen, is to avoid doubts as to the paternity of children born within the prohibited time. Such a restriction, it is convincingly reasoned,

906. The *lex divortii* does not afford a viable alternative here, inasmuch as the restriction in question, in contrast to those dealt with *supra* s. 93-94, is not limited to cases in which the previous marriage was ended by divorce. Cf. *Niboyet* V 447-448.

907. See *Rabel* 290-291; AUSTRIA: *Schwind,* Nachsichterteilung 39; BELGIUM: *Graulich* 108; [WEST] GERMANY: *Hoffmann and Stephan* no. 4 before § 1, no. 2 before § 4, § 8 no. 18; *F. Kahn* 63; *Lauterbach* 26; SWITZERLAND: *Beck,* art. 7 c no. 21; *Muret* 24-25.

908. For judicial decisions proceeding, as a matter of course, on the view that such requirements are to be treated as unilateral see ITALY: Trib. Alba 27 Feb. 1922, Giur. it. 1922 I 2, 155, Clunet 1922, 1045; NETHERLANDS: Rb. Rotterdam 9 Aug. 1933, W. no. 12, 685, RabelsZ 11 (1937) 205. Both of these cases were decided with reference to the HAGUE CONVENTION of 1902. In both, a woman of foreign nationality was permitted to marry a man of local nationality on the strength of a dispensation, granted by the appropriate authorities of her home country, from the waiting period prescribed by her *lex patriae.* The corresponding requirement of the man's personal law, coinciding with the *lex fori,* was held to have no application.

909. See *Frankenstein* 89; *Gamillscheg,* Kommentar, art. 13 no. 388; *Scholl* 169-174.

affects the interests of the future husband in an at least equally high degree as those of the wife.[910]

This particular problem is avoided in certain Continental European countries where the principle of public policy has played an overriding part, requiring the waiting period laid down by the *lex fori* to be observed, regardless of the nationality of the parties, in all cases where the marriage is celebrated locally. A statutory provision to this effect exists in *Italian* law.[911] The same solution is, or in any event was in the past, supported by the weight of judicial and extrajudicial opinion in *France, the Netherlands* and *Switzerland.*[912] Any foreign law is thus excluded from application if it is less stringent than the *lex fori,* whether because it does not provide for any waiting period at all, or because it admits an exception (by operation of law or by dispensation) in the particular case, or because the restriction imposed expires at an earlier date than that prescribed by the *lex fori.* On the other hand, if the *lex fori* is held to prevail for such reasons, the party concerned will also benefit from such rules concerning dispensation etc. as may be contained in that law.[913]

A mitigation of the demands of public policy was brought about by the Hague Convention on Marriage of 1902, which – as usually construed – does not allow the Contracting States to deviate from the rule of the *lex patriae* in order to enforce locally prescribed

910. One SWISS writer even goes to the length of suggesting that the man's personal law alone should be applied, to the exclusion of that of the woman, on the ground that the restriction is only superficially linked to her person and in reality concerns the future husband's legal position; see *Levis,* Die Wartefrist des Art. 103 ZGB. im internationalen Recht: SJZ 33 (1936/37) 29-30.

911. CC art. 116 par. 2 in conjunction with art. 89. See *A. Miele* 119.

912. FRANCE: Cour Paris 13 Feb. 1872, S. 1873.2.112, Clunet 1874, 31; *Batiffol and Lagarde* II 38; *Bischoff* no. 63; *Niboyet* V 344-345, 448; *Vincent and Ponsard* no. 114-115; NETHERLANDS: Rb. Amsterdam 19 Nov. 1925, N.J. 1926, 391 (but see for a case where the requirement of DUTCH law was "adapted" to the rules of the foreign law by virtue of which the wife's former marriage had been dissolved, Rb. Rotterdam 5 Feb. 1937, N.J. 1937 no. 482; NORWEGIAN divorce based on the ground of a decree of legal separation followed by one year's non-cohabitation, held to offer sufficient guarantee that the wife was not pregnant at the time of the divorce, so that a further waiting period was unnecessary); SWITZERLAND: ObG Zürich 7 July 1951, ZR 54 (1955) no. 167; *Beck,* art. 7 c no. 53-54; *Götz,* art. 103 no. 17-19; *Schnitzer* 343; *Stauffer,* art. 7 c no. 5; *Vaucher* 544.

913. See, for instance, the SWISS decision cited *supra* n. 912.

waiting periods.[914] In some countries whose courts otherwise insist on such recourse to public policy, this requirement has therefore been waived when the convention is applicable.[915]

Recent legislative action in many countries, as we have seen, evinces a tendency to soften the restriction under review, or to reduce its scope, if not to abolish it altogether. In such circumstances it seems incongruous, even more so than in the past, that this restriction should be elevated to the dignity of representing public policy so as to prevent the solemnisation of a marriage, permitted by the otherwise applicable law, in countries where it is still in force.[916] In so far as the forum holds capacity to marry to be a matter for the personal law, surely no exception ought to be admitted by reason only that that law is less stringent than the *lex fori et celebrationis* on the present point. This position is taken, for instance, in *West Germany* and seems to be gaining ground in modern law.[917]

As regards the converse situation, where the requirements of the relevant foreign law are stricter than those of the *lex fori*, it seems never to have been doubted in Continental European countries that effect must be given to the foreign rules.[918] *French* and *West German* courts, for instance, have refused to grant a dispensation to a divorced wife of foreign nationality whose *lex patriae*, in contrast to the *lex fori*, did not vest such power in them.[919]

914. Such requirements are probably not covered by the exception admitted in art. 2 par. 3 of the convention, which refers to cases where the proposed marriage would contravene the local law, *inter alia*, "by reason of a prior marriage". See, e.g., *Beck*, ESchlKonv. art. 2 no. 17; *Buzzati* 254; *Frankenstein* 112; *Gamillscheg*, Kommentar, art. 13 no. 953; *F. Kahn* 84; *Levis* (*supra* n. 910) 30; *A. Miele* 112-114; *Scholl* 172, 174. But see for the view that this exception includes waiting periods of the present type: *Götz*, art. 103 no. 17; *Travers* I 323-361.

915. See the DUTCH and ITALIAN decisions cited *supra* n. 908. But the balance of opinion in SWITZERLAND (which, like the NETHERLANDS, is no longer a party to the convention) was to the contrary; see the references *supra* n. 912, 914.

916. Cf. *Rabel* 300, who speaks of "exaggerated mandatory local requirements".

917. See for WEST GERMANY: *Gamillscheg*, Kommentar, art. 13 no. 389; *Lauterbach* 28; *Wolff*, IPR 191. Similarly for AUSTRIA: *Klang and Gschnitzer* 508-509; NETHERLANDS: *van Sasse van Ysselt* 193; SPAIN: *Aguilar Navarro* 300; *Miaja de la Muela* II 267. For a differentiated position see BELGIUM: *Graulich* 157.

918. This is affirmed by several writers cited *supra* n. 912 and 917.

919. FRANCE: Cour Paris 30 Nov. 1934, Clunet 1935, 927; WEST GERMANY: President of LG Regensburg 9 July 1949, IPRspr. 1945/49

It is somewhat uncertain, however, whether and to what extent provisions of the personal law embodying a waiting period would be enforced in countries to whose domestic law this kind of restraint on remarriage is wholly unknown, as for instance in *England* or in the *Scandinavian* countries.[920] The only case in point is one decided in *Australia,* where the court refused to give effect to such an incapacity imposed on a divorced woman by the law of Belgium, where the divorce had been granted and where she (possibly) was still domiciled.[921] Unfortunately, the reasons for this decision given by the court are highly unsatisfactory: the court was impressed by the fact that the disability in question attached to one of the divorced spouses only and inferred that it was within the same category as penal and discriminatory prohibitions against remarriage, which fall to be disregarded in English and Commonwealth courts (*supra* s. 94). This classification makes mockery of the foreign law concerned, by which the waiting period was only designed to prevent *turbatio sanguinis.*[922]

Despite the objections to which this decision gives rise, it may well be that it represents the law of England and of other Commonwealth countries. One pointer in this direction is that England seems often to have been chosen as the place of celebration of marriages in evasion of a waiting period prescribed for a former wife by the law of her domicile and nationality (the law of a Continental European country).[923] These evasions are regularly successful, because the validity of the marriage cannot be challenged afterwards even in the country whose law was violated, the requirement of a waiting period being merely directory.[924]

96. *Other Prohibitions.* Where a marriage is dissolved by the death of one of the spouses, the only restriction on the remarriage

---

no. 14; see *Gamillscheg,* Kommentar, art. 13 no. 392. Cf. the DUTCH decision of Rb. Rotterdam 30 Oct. 1972, *Joppe* 62 no. 30, where such a dispensation was granted on the strength of the relevant foreign law (at the time of this decision DUTCH law itself no longer required any waiting period at all in the case of the wife's prior marriage being ended by divorce).

920. No doubts exist as to the position in countries bound by the HAGUE CONVENTION of 1902. Art. 3 of that convention unequivocally excludes any interference of permissive public policy on the present ground.

921. Lundgren v. O'Brien (No. 2), [1921] V.L.R. 361 (F.C.).

922. See for criticism along these lines: *Hartley,* Bigamy 699; *Morris* 108; *Webb and Davis* 294 (n. 82), 513.

923. See, for instance, as regards evasion of the *Frauenwartefrist* prescribed by SWISS law, *Götz,* art. 103 no. 16, art. 130 no. 4.

924. See *Dölle,* Familienrecht 138, and for SWISS law, the references in the preceding note.

of the surviving party that is still relatively current is that of a waiting period for the wife (*supra* s. 95). In the past, it was not unusual for a temporary ban on remarriage to be placed on the surviving spouse, whether the husband or the wife. This prohibition (known as the *impedimentum luctus*) was dictated by reasons of decency, its purpose being to ensure that a period of mourning elapsed before the widow or widower married again.[925] This kind of prohibition is now practically extinct. It has never played any prominent part in the conflict of laws; but there is no doubt that, subject to the public policy of the forum, it fell to be governed by the surviving party's personal law determining his capacity to marry.[926]

Lastly, mention may be made of the impediment, deriving its origin from the dogmas of the Orthodox Church, whereby a person who has already been validly married three times cannot conclude a further marriage (*the prohibition against a fourth marriage*). This prohibition still forms part of *Greek* law.[927] According to Greek conflict of laws, it applies to prevent a fourth marriage by a party of Greek nationality, whatever the nationality of the intended partner (though, apparently, it does not interfere with the intermarriage of a foreigner, who has already been married three times but who is free to remarry under his national law, and a Greek national who has not himself been so married).[928] Whether this incapacity would be respected in other countries whose conflicts rules for capacity to marry refer to Greek law as the party's personal law, is a more doubtful question.[929] It is conceivable or even probable that it would be rejected in certain countries, either because any marriage impediment of a religious

925. See, e.g., *Klang and Gschnitzer* 498-500, 509; *Travers* I 328-330, 343.

926. See, for instance, as to the position under the HAGUE CONVENTION of 1902: *Frankenstein* 112; *Travers* I 349-361.

927. GREEK CC art. 1355. See *Stefanopulos,* Die Eheschliessung nach griechischem Recht: ÖJZ 1959, 451, 453-454.

928. In other words, the impediment is considered unilateral; see *Bendermacher-Geroussis* 3; *Maridakis* 216; cf. *F. Kahn* 63. But see in favour of the view that it is to be treated as bilateral (so as also to apply in the second situation), *Ehrenzweig, Fragistas and Yiannopoulos* 72.

929. The question has been considered by WEST GERMAN writers, who predominantly seem inclined to give an affirmative answer. See *Gamillscheg,* Kommentar, art. 13 no. 306, 449, 951; *Neuhaus,* Grundbegriffe 349-350; *idem,* Grundrechte 611; *Raape,* Das Verbot der vierten Ehe: StAZ 1959, 127; comment in StAZ 1969, 135, 136. But see *Frankenstein* 121 and, for SWISS law, *Stauffer,* art. 7 e no. 14 (to be disregarded as contrary to public policy).

character is held to be contrary to public policy or because it would be classified as penal and discriminatory.[930]

b. *Other Requirements or Impediments*

ba. *Consent of Parties*

97. *Law Generally Applicable.* In *Continental European* and *Scandinavian* countries, matters affecting the consent of the spouses, although not falling within the notion of capacity proper, are generally treated on the same lines as other questions pertaining to the substantive validity of a marriage, *i.e.* by reference to the personal law of the parties at the time of celebration.[931] More particularly, the bulk of judicial and extrajudicial opinion is in favour of applying the personal law of the party whose consent to marry is alleged to be defective, whether by reason of duress, fraud, mistake, unsoundness of mind or otherwise.[932]

930. Cf. *infra* s. 107-109. For ENGLAND and other countries following ENGLISH law see also *supra* at n. 889-890 and 920-922.

931. See the references *supra* n. 370-372, 522 and *infra* n. 932, 935. *Adde,* FRANCE: *Vincent and Ponsard* no. 54-58, 82; ITALY: Trib. Milano 11 June 1971, Riv. dir. int. proc. 1972, 533, 538; *Morelli* 105.

932. In other words, defects in the consent of the spouses are to be treated as unilateral; see *Rabel* 286-287 and the references *supra* n. 370-371. For a minority view claiming that such defects are bilateral so as to require a cumulative application of the two laws involved, see *supra* n. 372. A special aspect of this problem arose for decision in the BELGIAN case of Civ. Arlon 16 Jan. 1973, Rev. crit. d.i.p. 1973, 322, note Verwilghen. That case concerned the validity of a *posthumous* marriage celebrated in France, between a man of French and a woman of Belgian nationality, the man being deceased at the time of the ceremony. This type of marriage is countenanced, albeit only in exceptional circumstances, by certain legal systems, including FRENCH law (CC art. 171); see *Dölle,* Familienrecht 244-249; *Gamillscheg,* Kommentar, art. 13 no. 183-187. In the case at bar the marriage was good by FRENCH law, according to which there was in the circumstances a presumption in favour of a valid consent having been given by the deceased, but bad by BELGIAN (domestic) law, which did not know the institution of posthumous marriage. The court nevertheless upheld the union, adopting the "orthodox" principle that each party is only subject to the conditions of consent imposed by his own *lex patriae,* and not to those of the other party's law. The requirement of BELGIAN law that both parties to a marriage must be alive at the time of the ceremony was thus treated as unilateral, *i.e.* confined to the party of Belgian nationality. With regard to the corresponding requirement in WEST GERMAN law, the opposite position (bilateral) is advocated by *Gamillscheg, ibid.* no. 193. On this view it would not have been possible to recognise the marriage at issue in the BELGIAN case if the female party had been of German instead of Belgian nationality.

In practice, the issue which has occupied the courts most frequently is that of the effect of a mistaken belief by one of the parties as to the identity or the personal attributes of the other, or as to the nature or the legal effects of the ceremony undergone, on the validity of the marriage. These questions are approached in a variety of ways in the domestic laws of different countries.[933] It has been held on many occasions, particularly by *(West) German* courts, that the annulment of a marriage on the ground that a spouse's consent is vitiated by such a mistake depends exclusively on that party's *lex patriae.*[934] Hence, for instance, where that law, in contrast to the *lex fori,* did not recognise error as to the personal qualities of the other spouse as a ground for annulment, a decree was refused.[935]

In *England* and other countries following English law, the position is more open. Courts and writers have expressed their preference for a number of different solutions, but no firm stand has so far been taken on the point.[936] In addition, there are a number of cases involving lack of consent where foreign elements were present but where that complexion was completely ignored both by the parties and by the court, so that in effect the *lex fori* was applied.[937] These decisions, however, are not very conclusive, as the choice of law issue was not adverted to.

933. For comparative surveys see *Dölle*, Familienrecht 313-331; *Gamillscheg*, Kommentar, art. 13 no. 466-467; *Neuhaus*, Verhältnis 351-352.

934. See the decisions cited *supra* n. 371, nearly all of which deal with different kinds of mistake, sometimes claimed to be induced by fraud.

935. GERMAN cases so holding include: KG 14 June 1913, OLGR 27, 108; RG 6 Oct. 1927, IPRspr. 1926/27 no. 68; OLG Frankfurt a.M. 11 July 1929, IPRspr. 1929 no. 11; RG 23 June 1930, IPRspr. 1930 no. 65; OLG München 20 Nov. 1930, IPRspr. 1931 no. 60; BayObLG 13 May 1931, IPRspr. 1931 no. 61. See *Gamillscheg,* Grundrechte 341-342; *idem,* Kommentar, art. 13 no. 468.

936. Nearly all conceivable solutions have been canvassed in this context; see *infra* at n. 938-948 and 951.

937. ENGLAND: Cooper v. Crane, [1891] P. 369; Valier v. Valier (1925), 133 L.T. 830 (P.); Hussein v. Hussein, [1938] P. 159; SCOTLAND: Lendrum v. Chakravarti, 1929 S.L.T. 96; MacDougall v. Chitnavis, 1937 S.C. 390; Orlandi v. Castelli, 1961 S.C. 113; CANADA (common law provinces): Kokkalas (or Rokana) v. Kokkalas (1965), 50 D.L.R. (2d) 193 (Sask. Q.B.); Johnson v. Smith (1968), 70 D.L.R. (2d) 374 (Ont. H.C.); Iantsis v. Papatheodorou (1971), 15 D.L.R. (3d) 53 (Ont. C.A.); (Quebec) Ovadia v. Basette, [1954] C.S. 337. In all these cases the place of marriage was in the country of the respective forum. In most, though not in all, of them it is also clear or at least possible that the party whose consent was claimed to be nullified was domiciled in that country. However, neither of these factors was relied upon to justify the application of the *lex fori.* For cases involving a foreign celebrated marriage see *infra* n. 942 and 948.

At least as regards English law itself, the weight of such authority as there is supports the application of the law generally governing the essentials of marriage, *i.e.* the law of the antenuptial domicile of the spouses.[938] This is also the solution usually favoured by writers.[939] There is some conflict of opinion as to the exact meaning of this rule. Most writers take the same view as that prevalent in Continental and Scandinavian law, namely, that each party is only subject to the consent requirements of his own personal law, so that the wife's consent cannot be negatived by her husband's law, or *vice versa.*[940] While this clearly seems to be the better view, there is also some support for applying the two laws cumulatively, with the result that the marriage will be held invalid for want of consent if it is so by either party's law, regardless of whether the defect relates to that party himself or to the other.[941]

Although the rule of the *lex domicilii* is consistent with most of the relevant decisions, there are some English and Commonwealth cases where matters of consent were determined without any reference to foreign law, notwithstanding that at the time of the marriage the parties were (or at least the non-consenting party was) domiciled in a foreign country.[942] In an attempt to rationalise

938. Apt v. Apt, [1947] P. 127, 146-147, [1948] P. 83, 88 (C.A.) (*obiter*); Way v. Way, [1950] P. 71, 78-79, reversed on another ground but approved *obiter* on this point *sub nom.* Kenward v. Kenward, [1951] P. 124, 133 (C.A.); Szechter v. Szechter, [1971] P. 286, Clunet 1973, 417, note Lipstein; see also *P.B. Carter* (1970-1971) 406-408. The rival theory that the essentials of marriage are to be referred to the law of the intended matrimonial home (*supra* s. 54) can probably be excluded here; though see Kenward v. Kenward, [1951] P. 124, 143-146 (C.A.). Nor is there any support or justification for giving preference to the law of the husband's domicile (though this solution is advocated for SCOTTISH law by *Anton* 292-293, as regards defects rendering the marriage voidable, as distinct from void, according to the *lex causae*). See, for example, *Dicey and Morris* 277.

939. ENGLAND: *Cheshire and North* 400-403, 407; *Dicey and Morris* 275-279, 359-360; *Graveson,* Conflict 252-253, 271; *North* 124-125, 130; *Wolff,* PIL 327-328; *Woodhouse* 454-465; AUSTRALIA: *Nygh* 413-416; *Sykes,* Conflict 93-94; CANADA: *Falconbridge* (ed. 1) 626; NEW ZEALAND: *Webb and Davis* 246-247.

940. References *supra* n. 370.

941. References *supra* n. 372. A third solution has been proposed by *Hartley,* Policy Basis 580-581. This also involves a cumulative application of the two laws, but with opposite effect to that mentioned in the text: the marriage should be upheld unless there is no valid consent by the laws of both parties' domiciles. Such a rule, which is based on the policy of validation, has no support in the decided cases.

942. E.g., ENGLAND: Kassim v. Kassim, [1962] P. 224 (noted by *Turpin,* Marriage – Mistake as to Resulting Status – Mistaken Belief that

continued on page 288

the whole body of decisions it has been suggested that consent in marriage must be subdivided into at least two categories with a different choice of law.[943] On this view a distinction is to be drawn between the different grounds on which the reality of a party's consent to marry may be challenged; while for some of them, including mistake as to the attributes of the other spouse, the premarital domiciliary law of the interested party is appropriate, the *lex fori* alone is considered applicable to a number of other issues, such as those concerning duress, fear, fraud and mistake as to the legal nature of the ceremony performed, apparently because in these latter cases the element of fact-finding (which, as a matter of procedure, is referable to the *lex fori*) is predominating.[944]

Yet another proposal, which has been adopted in some English and Scottish cases, is that the consent of the parties is to be judged by the *lex loci celebrationis* (to the exclusion of their personal law or laws).[945] This choice of law is apparently based

---

continued from page 287

Marriage Polygamous: [1963] C.L.J. 48-50; *Webb*, Mistake as to the Nature of the Marriage Created by the Ceremony: 26 M.L.R. 85-87 (1963)); Buckland v. Buckland, [1968] P. 296; AUSTRALIA: Di Mento v. Visalli (1973), 1 A.L.R. 351 (N.S.W. Sup. Ct.). In these cases the marriage was also celebrated in the foreign country of the domicile of the parties, but the *lex fori* was applied nonetheless without consideration of the choice of law issue.

943. *Webb*, "Shot-Gun" Marriages 202-204.

944. This distinction seems capable of explaining all ENGLISH cases on the matter (though see Kassim v. Kassim, [1962] P. 224, where the *lex fori* was applied to determine the validity of a marriage claimed to be void by reason of the husband's mistaken belief, not as to the fact that the ceremony undergone was one of marriage but as to the monogamous or polygamous character of the union created by the ceremony; cf. *supra* n. 942). Nevertheless, such a distinction is open to criticism because, whatever the ground on which the reality of a spouse's consent is alleged to be destroyed, the court is never exclusively concerned with fact-finding; there are also the legal problems of whether the facts found amount to a defect in consent and of the effects of this on the validity of the marriage. Cf. *Cheshire and North* 401 and, for a similar observation with regard to AMERICAN cases, *supra* s. 28.

945. ENGLAND: Parojcic v. Parojcic, [1958] 1 W.L.R. 1280, 1283 (P.); see also H. v. H., [1954] P. 258 (which is the only one among these cases where the *lex loci celebrationis* was a foreign law, but where that law was also the *lex domicilii* of the wife petitioning for nullity and where no indication was given of in what capacity it was taken into account); SCOTLAND: Di Rollo v. Di Rollo, 1959 S.C. 75, 78 (criticised by *North* 265-266); *Anton* 292-293 (who, however, confines this solution to cases of a marriage which is void, rather than voidable, under the *lex loci celebrationis;* cf. *supra* n. 938). See also *F.G. Carter*, Proxy Marriages: 35 Can. Bar Rev. 1195, 1198 (1957); *Ryan* 992 (where the *lex loci celebrationis* coincides with the *lex domicilii* of one party).

on the concept of want of consent as a "contractual" rather than a "personal" defect.[946] At least in England, however, this solution is predominantly rejected; for while it is common ground that the method of giving consent is classifiable as a formality governed by the *lex loci celebrationis,* that law is usually considered inappropriate to determine the more fundamental questions of what is necessary to constitute a true consent and of the consequences flowing from the absence of these requirements.[947] Nor are the English and Scottish authorities relying on the *lex loci celebrationis* in such matters very convincing, for in all of them the decision would have been the same if the law of the antenuptial domicile of the parties had been applied. Furthermore, there are several cases in which the validity of a marriage attacked for lack of consent was decided without any reference to the foreign law of the place of celebration.[948]

Despite the dubious merits of the *lex loci celebrationis* for matters concerning the reality of matrimonial consent, this solution has also gained some adherence elsewhere, particularly in *Latin America.* An illustration is afforded by the *Bustamante Code* which, although referring capacity to marry to the personal law of the parties, provides that coercion, fear and abduction as causes of nullity of marriage are to be governed by the law of the place of celebration.[949]

98. *Influence of Lex Fori.* Whatever the basic choice of law rule for consent in marriage, the *lex fori* seems everywhere to exercise a strong power of attraction. In the first place, there are many instances of a "spontaneous" application of that law in cases where one would normally have expected foreign law to come into consideration but where the problem was passed over in silence. Occasional expressions of such a tendency are to be found

946. See *Cheshire,* PIL 320-322 (but this view has been abandoned by *Cheshire and North,* see *supra* n. 939).

947. See the references *supra* n. 938-939, particularly the *dictum* in Apt v. Apt, [1948] P. 83, 88 (C.A.), where the distinction between the method and the fact of consent is clearly made.

948. In addition to the cases cited *supra* n. 942 see: Mehta v. Mehta, [1945] 2 All E.R. 690 (P.); Way v. Way, [1950] P. 71; Silver v. Silver, [1955] 2 All E.R. 614 (P.). In *Way,* the application of ENGLISH law was based on the non-consenting party's domicile in England (*supra* n. 938). This factor could also explain the decision in *Mehta.*

949. Art. 48. Cf. the BRAZILIAN case cited by *Garland* 42 n. 144.

in the practice of *Continental European* countries.[950] Above all, however, this tendency is remarkable in the *English* and *Scottish* cases on the matter. Indeed, the application of the *lex fori* is the only solution which is consistent with the actual decisions in all those cases (though the reasoning of the courts in some cases contradicts such a rule).[951] It is no doubt true that the decisions applying the *lex fori* as a matter of course can be explained away on various grounds and that they are usually not regarded as representing the true state of the law. Nevertheless, the case law does leave a strong impression of a homeward trend.

Secondly, even where the applicability of some foreign law, selected by the aid of a "neutral" connecting factor such as domicile or nationality, is recognised in principle, the scope given for that law is often narrowly circumscribed when it differs from the *lex fori.* The reason is that the public policy of the forum usually plays a prominent part in matters affecting consent to marry.

This is particularly true of cases where the marriage is celebrated locally. In such cases the forum is often likely to insist on compliance with its own standards of consent, so that foreign laws will in effect be excluded from application to the extent that they are less exacting (prohibitive public policy). In *France,* for instance, the consent requirements of French law are considered to represent a minimum level below which it is not possible to go when the marriage takes place in that country.[952] In several other countries it is provided by statute, or held by courts and writers, that at least certain domestic rules on consent, such as those concerning duress, insanity or mental infirmity as an impediment to marriage, must

950. For an example see the BELGIAN decision of Cour Bruxelles 28 May 1955, Rev. dr. fam. 1955, 61; criticised by *van Hecke and Rigaux* (1953 à 1960) 364-365. See also the FRENCH decision of Trib. Grenoble 7 May 1958, G.P. 1958.2.82, applying FRENCH law to determine the validity of a marriage attacked on grounds of want of consent, although both parties were of foreign nationality. This decision proceeds on a scarcely convincing analogy with divorce, for which the law of the common domicile of the spouses prevailed in cases of different nationality (*supra* at n. 340-341). For cases involving sham marriages see *infra* s. 99.

951. In two cases, it is true, foreign law was taken into consideration: H. v. H., [1954] P. 258, and Szechter v. Szechter, [1971] P. 286. In both of them, however, the foreign law was found or presumed – not too convincingly, cf. *Hartley*, Policy Basis 580 – to be the same as ENGLISH law, which in the end was the only law to which the court gave full attention.

952. *Batiffol and Lagarde* II 39-40; *Bischoff* no. 66; *Vincent and Ponsard* no. 82.

be complied with in all cases where the marriage is celebrated locally, regardless of the otherwise applicable law.[953] Presumably no country would be prepared to permit the celebration within its borders of a marriage, or to uphold it afterwards, if it would be invalid under its own law for violation of some fundamental requirement of consent, as for instance if one of the parties was manifestly insane or agreed to the marriage under duress or coercion, even should the relevant foreign law be more tolerant.[954]

The position is somewhat different in the case of a marriage, valid by the relevant foreign law or laws, that has already been celebrated abroad. Although decisions bearing on these questions are almost completely lacking, it seems reasonable to assume that public policy will not interfere to require the annulment of such a marriage, except perhaps in extreme cases, on the ground that it does not meet the standards of consent imposed by the *lex fori* in domestic cases.[955]

Cases are also conceivable where, conversely, the (validating) public policy of the forum would be opposed to the application of a foreign law which is more stringent than the *lex fori*, rendering a marriage liable to annulment by reason of a defect in consent unknown to the latter law. In several countries it is uncertain, for

953. E.g., BULGARIA: FC art. 91 par. 3 in conjunction with art. 9 *lit.* b); ENGLAND: *Dicey and Morris* 278; *Hartley*, Policy Basis 580; *Woodhouse* 456; WEST GERMANY: *Gamillscheg*, Kommentar, art. 13 no. 182, 213, 818; ITALY: CC art. 116 par. 2 in conjunction with art. 85; SWITZERLAND: AppG Baselstadt 8 Feb. 1935, SJZ 32 (1935/36) 9 (dealing with the requirement of *Urteilsfähigkeit* laid down by SWISS CC art. 97); *Beck*, art. 7 c no. 44-45, art. 7 f no. 60, 153; *Götz*, art. 97 no. 25, art. 107 no. 19; *Muret* 76-77; *Stauffer*, art. 7 c no. 5; *Vaucher* 542; YUGOSLAVIA: BMA art. 73 par. 2. Cf. for AMERICAN law *supra* s. 28. But there are a number of cases in which the appropriate foreign law was given effect although its grounds of annulment for want of consent were more restrictive than those of the *lex fori*. The chief instance is the GERMAN practice with reference to mistake as to attributes; see *supra* n. 935; *Gamillscheg, ibid.* no. 474; *Wolff*, IPR 191, 195 n. 1. For another example see the BELGIAN case cited *supra* n. 932.

954. Note in this context that the policy of freedom of consent to marriage has found expression in the New York Convention, of 10 Dec. 1962, on Consent to Marriage, etc. Pursuant to art. 1 par. 1 of this convention, "no marriage shall be legally entered into without the full and free consent of both parties".

955. The statutory rules cited *supra* n. 953, which provide for the application of the *lex fori* to certain aspects of consent to marriage, have no reference to this situation. See also for WEST GERMANY: *Gamillscheg*, Kommentar, art. 13 no. 818 (concerning the special case of a proxy marriage in which the proxy has a discretion in the choice of a partner, *Stellvertretung im Willen;* cf. *Pålsson*, Marriage, s. 319); for SWITZERLAND: *Beck*, art. 7 f no. 60, 153.

instance, whether effect will be given to provisions of a foreign law which, in contrast with the *lex fori,* entitles the petitioner to obtain a nullity decree on the ground that he entered into the marriage under a mistaken belief as to the respondent's virginity, moral qualities, health, financial standing or other conditions.[956] Generally speaking, however, the prevailing tendency is to draw narrower limits for the demands of public policy in these cases than in those previously considered, so that the application of foreign laws differing from the *lex fori* will more easily be tolerated here.[957]

99. *Specifically on Sham Marriages.* The problems of sham marriages, or marriages of convenience, are akin to those concerning consent to marriage, but they present some special features justifying separate consideration. A sham marriage is one where the parties have voluntarily and with open eyes gone through the proper procedure for creating a marriage but where one or (usually) both of them lacked any intention of founding a marital community of living or of assuming the normal obligations of marriage, their sole or primary object being to bring about some particular and secondary effect of marriage. Cases decided in different countries provide a rich variety of such extraneous motives in marrying, for example marriages celebrated solely in order to win a bet, to obtain an engagement open only to married persons, to avoid military call-up, to legitimate a child, to procure a name for the woman or to give her the man's nationality.[958]

Domestic laws are at considerable variance as to whether such

956. For the doubts existing on this point in ENGLISH law see *Dicey and Morris* 278, 279 (Illustration 9), 363-364; *Hartley,* Policy Basis 580.

957. For the view that public policy does not prevent the forum from giving effect to the appropriate foreign law where that law invalidates a marriage on grounds of defective consent exceeding those of the *lex fori,* see FRANCE: *Batiffol and Lagarde* II 40; *Bischoff* no. 67; WEST GERMANY: *Gamillscheg,* Kommentar, art. 13 no. 474. It is also noteworthy that *foreign* decrees annulling a marriage for want of consent have been recognised in several countries even where the decree was based on a ground which would (probably) not have been sufficient under the *lex fori.* See ENGLAND: Mitford v. Mitford, [1923] P. 130 (recognising a GERMAN nullity decree granted to the wife on the ground of her mistaken belief as to the husband's personal qualities, namely, his "masculine indolence and unbearable selfishness"); FRANCE: Trib. Seine 6 April 1951, Rev. crit. d.i.p. 1953, 586, note Batiffol (AMERICAN nullity decree based on grounds of fraud); ITALY: App. Bari 9 March 1949, Riv. dir. matr. 1950, 145; NETHERLANDS: Hof Amsterdam 6 March 1963, N.J. 1963 no. 199, Clunet 1969, 1017.

958. See, for instance, the survey given by *Jackson* 290-297.

unions are valid.[959] The most common position seems to be that motive in marrying is immaterial and that a marriage of the present kind is therefore fully valid even after its purpose has been achieved. This is, for instance, the rule in *English* law, subject to the qualification that a party's consent may be negatived if it was given in circumstances amounting to fear or duress, such as where a sham marriage was chosen as a means enabling a woman to acquire the man's foreign nationality and thereby to escape from her native country where her life or liberty was imperilled.[960] A partly different attitude is taken by the laws of some Continental European countries, including *French* and *Belgian* law, which to a varying extent acknowledge sham or simulation as an independent concept rendering a marriage invalid for want of true consent.[961] An intermediate position is taken by some other Continental systems which, although generally hostile to considering the motives that may have prompted the parties to enter into a marriage, seek to combat certain types of sham marriage, especially those where acquisition of the man's nationality by the wife was the real object in view (nationality marriages). According to *Swiss* law, for instance, this is the only case where a marriage is liable to annulment for sham.[962]

959. For comparative surveys see: *Dölle*, Familienrecht 143, 276-277; *Gamillscheg*, Kommentar, art. 13 no. 418, 420, 422-423.

960. See the cases cited *infra* n. 973 (but see for SCOTLAND: Orlandi v. Castelli, 1961 S.C. 113). So also in the common law provinces of CANADA: Kokkalas (or Rokana) v. Kokkalas (1965), 50 D.L.R. (2d) 193 (Sask. Q.B.); Iantsis v. Papatheodorou (1971), 15 D.L.R. (3d) 53 (Ont. C.A.) (overruling a decision to the contrary in Johnson v. Smith (1968), 70 D.L.R. (2d) 374 (Ont. H.C.), on which see a critical comment by *Bromley* in 15 McGill L.J. 319 (1969)); Feiner v. Demkowicz (1973), 42 D.L.R. (3d) 165, 171-173 (Ont. H.C.), critically noted by *Bates*: 53 Can. Bar Rev. 359 (1975) (but see for QUEBEC: Ovadia v. Basette, [1954] C.S. 337). SOUTH AFRICA: Martens v. Martens, 1952 (3) S.A. 771 (W.L.D.). For other countries see *infra* n. 978.

961. See the BELGIAN and FRENCH cases cited *infra* n. 975, 976, 982, 989 and 991. For a critical analysis of the position in FRENCH law see *Foulon-Piganol*, Le mariage "simulé": Rev. trim. dr. civ. 1960, 217-251. For YUGOSLAVIA see BMA art. 43 and *Blagojević* 98. Cf. for AMERICAN law, where the problem has chiefly been encountered in the context of evasion of immigration laws, *supra* s. 28.

962. SWISS CC art. 120 no. 4; see *Götz*, art. 107 no. 14, art. 120 no. 1, 18-26, art. 121 no. 6; *Knapp*, Cent ans 294-296. See also for AUSTRIA: Marriage Act of 1938, § 23 (covering marriages solely or predominantly designed to enable the wife to obtain the husband's name or nationality); *Klang and Gschnitzer* 582-585. Another instance was the WEST GERMAN Marriage Act of 1946, § 19 (repealed in 1976), which was limited to *Namensehen* (marriages to procure the wife the husband's name); see *Dölle*, Familienrecht 142-146, 276.

In the conflict of laws this latter type of sham marriage presents a particular interest because, by definition, it involves parties lacking a common nationality at the time of celebration, so that a question of choice of law automatically arises, at least from the point of view of countries using nationality as the relevant test to identify the personal law. While other kinds of sham marriages have occasionally raised such problems, they are by far outnumbered by those concerning a nationality marriage. The ulterior purpose pursued by the parties in such cases is usually to evade the immigration or emigration laws of a country, the change of nationality being intended to make it easier for the wife to secure admission into, to remain in or to leave a particular country, or to escape the effect of other "hostile" rules of public law directed against persons of a certain nationality (as, for example, rules providing for the internment of enemy aliens). Although a sham marriage has often been successfully used to such ends in the past, this device is likely to lose in importance with the tendency in present-day legislation to exclude any automatic effect of marriage on the wife's nationality.

In so far as conflicts problems with regard to sham marriages have been adverted to, the weight of opinion at least among writers favours much the same position as with consent to marriage generally, *i.e.* the application of the personal law of each party at the time of celebration.[963] Most (though not all) decisions of courts in Continental European countries are at least reconcilable with, and some of them seem clearly to support, this approach.[964]

Among the partisans of this view, there is some divergency of opinion as to whether the defect of sham should be treated as unilateral or as bilateral. In contrast to the usual attitude in other matters of consent to marriage (*supra* s. 97), the latter alternative is often supported by writers.[965] This amounts to saying that it

963. See *Rabel* 294-295 and, e.g., AUSTRIA: *Schwind,* IPR 145; BELGIUM: *Graulich,* Nullité du mariage conclu à des fins étrangères à cette institution: Rev. crit. belge 1957, 184, 188; WEST GERMANY: *Gamillscheg,* Kommentar, art. 13 no. 419; *Kegel,* Kommentar, art. 13 no. 27; *Schwimann,* Zur Behandlung der Staatsbürgerschaftsehe im internationalen Privatrecht: FamRZ 1958, 303, 305-307; *Wengler,* Gutachten no. 18 and 19; expert opinion in IPG 1967/68 no. 20 (Munich).

964. See the cases cited *infra* n. 966, 968, 975, 976, 979, 982, 988 and 991. But see for decisions inconsistent with this view, *infra* n. 978, 980 and 991 (decision of Civ. Bruxelles 30 March 1976).

965. Particularly so in WEST GERMANY; see *Gamillscheg,* Kommentar, art. 13 no. 419, 421, 424 with criticism of this view; *Steinle* 73-74; cf. *Wengler,* Gutachten no. 19. See also for AUSTRIA, *Klang and Gschnitzer* 585-586.

should be sufficient for the annulment of a marriage on grounds of sham if a rule to this effect exists in the personal law of one of the parties even though that party's own consent was genuine and that of the other party alone was fictitious.[966] In practice this question is unlikely to be of much significance because, as a matter of domestic law, sham will normally only be recognised as an independent ground of nullity, if at all, where both parties took part in it, so that otherwise the marriage cannot be impugned on this ground whatever the applicable law.[967] If, on the other hand, this latter condition is met, the marriage must clearly be held bad if it is so by either party's law, regardless of whether the defect in question is considered unilateral or bilateral, for in any event the consent of one of the parties will be vitiated under his own law, which is sufficient to exclude the creation of a valid marriage (cf. *supra* s. 48). Example:

> A woman of Belgian nationality came to England in 1954 and took to working as a prostitute in London. In the same year she went through a ceremony of marriage there with a domiciled Englishman. The parties did not know each other, and the sole purpose of the marriage was to enable the woman to obtain British nationality so that she could not be deported as an undesirable alien. Several years later she petitioned a Belgian court for a decree of annulment on the ground of simulation. Although the marriage was valid by English law, the court granted the decree sought on the strength of Belgian law, which was held to govern the reality of the wife's consent in accordance with the principle of determining such matters as to each of the parties by reference to the law of his nationality at the time of the marriage.[968]

966. This situation may be illustrated by two SWISS cases, in each of which a marriage between a man of Swiss and a woman of German nationality was annulled on the ground, supplied by SWISS law alone, that the woman had entered into it solely in order to obtain Swiss nationality, the man being unaware of the fact that she had not intended marital community: BG 18 Oct. 1940, BGE 66 II 225; BG 15 Dec. 1942, BGE 68 II 273.

967. See *Gamillscheg,* Kommentar, art. 13 no. 419. Where, as in the SWISS cases cited in the preceding note, one of the spouses was in good faith, the marriage may however be open to attack on other grounds, such as fraud or mistake. This is usually held to depend exclusively on the law of the party claiming to be the victim of fraud, etc.; see *supra* at n. 370-371, 932.

968. Cour Gand 26 April 1973, RW 1973/74, 1886; see *van Hecke and Rigaux* (1970 à 1975) 226-227, 236. Before bringing the proceedings in this case the wife had unsuccessfully sought to obtain a decree of nullity in

continued on page 296

In general, it is submitted, the view referred to here commands approval. The purpose of rules or principles of domestic law directed against sham marriages is usually to prevent abuse of the institution of marriage and to ensure that the parties consent to a "genuine" relationship. It is difficult to see any reason why such issues should not be dealt with by reference to the law or laws otherwise governing the substantive validity of a marriage.

A different approach seems to commend itself, however, in respect of provisions specifically directed against selected types of sham marriage only, in particular against nationality marriages. It has been suggested that the application of such rules should exclusively depend on the law of that party's (normally the man's) nationality which is intended to be acquired by the other (normally the woman) as a result of the marriage.[969] The reason is that statutes providing for the annulment of nationality marriages are designed, not primarily to ensure the true consent of the spouses or even to prevent abuse of the institution of marriage – as may be inferred from the fact that no attempt is made to interfere with the validity of other kinds of sham marriage – but rather to protect the enacting State itself. The chief motive for such legislation seems to be the desire to counter evasions of the immigration laws of that State, including its laws concerning expulsion of undesirable aliens.[970] If the purpose is to safeguard such public interests of the State whose nationality is "invaded", then surely the law of that State has the strongest claim to application.[971] It follows that the other law involved, normally that of the wife's premarital nationality which she wants to throw off by the marriage, can be left out of consideration.

This conclusion may even emerge without any need for resorting to rules of the conflict of laws at all. If the object pursued by a statute against nationality marriages is to protect certain public interests of the enacting State, it stands to reason that the provision

continued from page 295

ENGLAND, *inter alia* on various grounds of defective consent; see Messina v. Smith, [1971] 3 W.L.R. 118 (P.).

969. *Gamillscheg*, Kommentar, art. 13 no. 424 (see also, with regard to *Namensehen*, no. 421); *idem*, book review: RabelsZ 32 (1968) 548, 551 n. 7.

970. An alternative and, it is submitted, more adequate means of fighting such evasions is by refusing the particular incident sought to be enjoyed (the effect of marriage on nationality) while leaving the marriage intact in other respects. Cf. for AMERICAN law *supra* at n. 201-205.

971. At least where the question arises in that State itself. It is more doubtful whether laws pursuing such objectives are or should be entitled to application in other countries, see *infra* at n. 986.

should be confined, or interpreted as confined, to marriages performed in order to acquire the nationality of that State itself. Such a self-limitation must probably be read into, for example, the *Swiss* provision on the matter (*supra* at n. 962). While this provision is aimed at invalidating marriages between a woman of foreign and a man of Swiss nationality entered into for the sole purpose of giving her Swiss nationality, it does not, apparently, purport to interfere with a Swiss woman's marriage to a foreigner in order to obtain his nationality.[972] In so far as this is the appropriate construction to be placed on the relevant statute, there can obviously be no question of extending it beyond its own limits in any other country. To that extent the choice of law by the forum is really immaterial.

The decisions of courts in most cases involving the validity of a sham marriage support, or are at least not inconsistent with, the above submissions. As in other matters of consent to marriage, however, there is an overall tendency in favour of applying the *lex fori* which occasionally defies rationalisation, the more so as many cases have been decided without any consideration of choice of law problems.[973] This holds good both for countries which do and for those which do not recognise the concept of sham as affecting the validity of a marriage in their domestic law. In the further discussion of these problems, which will in the main be devoted to nationality marriages, it is proposed to distinguish

972. See *Knapp,* case note: Clunet 1951, 956, 960. The same interpretation was placed on the prohibition against nationality marriages contained in § 23 of the GERMAN Marriage Act of 1938 (repealed in 1946); see *Letzgus,* Die Eheschliessung im deutschen internationalen Privatrecht: AcP 145 (1939) 177, 188-189. This provision is still in force in AUSTRIA where, however, the contrary interpretation (as including marriages between a woman of Austrian and a man of foreign nationality) has been proposed; see *Klang and Gschnitzer* 585-586.

973. For ENGLISH law it suffices to refer to what has been said on this topic *supra* s. 97-98. Among the ENGLISH cases cited in that context – which, as will be recalled, were all decided by the *lex fori,* though two of them also placed some reliance on foreign law (*supra* n. 951) – the following deal with marriages which might elsewhere be held to come under the rubric of sham: H. v. H., [1954] P. 258; Silver v. Silver, [1955] 2 All E.R. 614 (P.); Buckland v. Buckland, [1968] P. 296; Szechter v. Szechter, [1971] P. 286; see also the case cited *supra* n. 968. Marriages alleged to be void by reason of sham were, too, involved in the SCOTTISH and CANADIAN cases cited *supra* n. 960, in all of which the *lex fori* was applied as a matter of course. In favour of this solution specifically for sham marriages see *Webb,* "Shot-Gun" Marriages 202.

three groups of cases according to the relationship between the country of the forum and the personal laws of the parties.[974]

(1) The first and largest category consists of cases decided by the courts of the country whose nationality the woman sought to acquire by marrying a man already possessed of it. In these cases the preponderance of the *lex fori* is almost total.

To begin with, this appears from decisions of, for instance, *Belgian, French* and *Swiss* courts pronouncing against the validity of a marriage entered into only with the object of giving the woman the man's nationality, *i.e.* that of the forum State.[975] In nearly all such cases the courts have relied on their own law alone, often even without any reference to the possibility of a conflict of laws.[976] Here, it is true, the solution left little or no room for doubt, for on almost any conceivable theory the appropriate law to apply was the *lex fori* coinciding with the personal law of the party whose nationality the other sought to obtain.[977] Although

974. This division is chiefly of interest in analysing the problem from the point of view of CONTINENTAL EUROPEAN and other countries where, as will be assumed in the text, the personal law is determined by the test of nationality.

975. BELGIUM: Civ. Bruxelles 18 June 1949, Pas. 1950.III.7; Cour Gand 25 Feb. 1956, Rev. crit. belge 1957, 179, note Graulich, Clunet 1958, 1152, see *van Hecke and Rigaux* (1953 à 1960) 365; FRANCE: Trib. Seine 7 Jan. 1948, J.C.P. 1948.II.4430, note Jean Mazeaud, see *G. Lagarde* in Rev. trim. dr. civ. 1948, 461; Cour Lyon 16 June 1952, G.P. 1953.1. Tables, Mariage no. 1; Trib. Melun 20 Jan. 1954, G.P. 1954.1.272; see *Audit* 260-261; *Foulon-Piganol* (*supra* n. 961) 219-220, 225-228; *Vincent and Ponsard* no. 55. SWITZERLAND: BG 9 Nov. 1939, BGE 65 II 133, Clunet 1951, 954, note Knapp; BG 10 July 1941, BGE 67 II 63; and cases cited *supra* n. 966 and *infra* n. 977. The same view prevailed in earlier ITALIAN cases, e.g. Trib. Milano 4 April 1957, Foro pad. 1957 I 610, 862; but later decisions have held that sham is no good ground for annulling a marriage in ITALIAN law, see *infra* n. 978, 981.

976. An exception is the BELGIAN decision of Civ. Bruxelles 7 April 1945, Pas. 1946.III.83, applying POLISH law (which did not differ from BELGIAN law), apparently *qua* the law of the wife petitioner's premarital nationality, to annul her marriage to a man probably of Belgian nationality. In another BELGIAN case in which consideration was given to the conflict of laws issue, Civ. Bruxelles 18 June 1949 (*supra* n. 975), BELGIAN law was applied, though not in its capacity as the personal law of either party but because it was the law of the country where the fictitious marital relationship was created and where it was designed to produce legal effects; cf. *Spanoghe* 60-61. See also the FRENCH decision of Trib. Melun 20 Jan. 1954 (*supra* n. 975) where the court subsidiarily relied on GERMAN law as the law of the common domicile of the parties (cf. *supra* at n. 340).

977. True, in most of the relevant cases the place of celebration of the marriage was in a foreign country. But the *lex loci celebrationis*, which

the wife's premarital *lex patriae* was not taken into consideration, on the facts the decisions can also be reconciled with the view that each party's personal law controls; for as the marriage was invalid by the law of one of the parties there was no need to go into the other.

Secondly, the *lex fori* has been applied to sustain a marriage attacked on the ground that it was only to confer the man's nationality on the wife. Courts in several countries, for example in *Italy* and the *Netherlands*, have so held on the strength of their own law (again coinciding with the man's *lex patriae*) which did not recognise this as a sufficient ground of nullity.[978] No attention was usually given to the other law involved, that of the woman's premarital nationality.[979] The same holds true of decisions from certain other countries refusing to grant a nullity decree, not because nationality marriages were generally regarded as valid but because some condition of annulment laid down by the *lex fori* was not met in the case at bar (for example, because only one of the spouses lacked the intention of founding a marital community or that acquisition of nationality was not the sole object they had in view).[980] Here, too, the question of the validity of the union according to the wife's premarital *lex patriae* was not even posed.

These decisions are more difficult to explain than those holding against the marriage. They are clearly inconsistent with the "orthodox" view that the validity of a marriage in respect of consent

---

receives some support in matters of consent in ENGLISH law *(supra* at n. 945), can usually be left out of account for CONTINENTAL EUROPEAN countries. Some doubts in this respect have been entertained in SWITZERLAND, because of the rule in NAG art. 7 f par. 1 (*supra* s. 69). See the decision of ObG Zürich 8 March 1939, ZR 40 (1941) 36, RabelsZ 16 (1950/51) 73, applying SWISS law in part because the *lex loci celebrationis* (which was ENGLISH law) was found to refer back to that law as the man's *lex domicilii*. But see BG 9 Nov. 1939, BGE 65 II 133, 140, holding the particular ground of nullity under consideration here to fall outside the scope of NAG art. 7 f.

978. ITALY: Trib. Firenze 10 March 1960, Giur. tosc. 1960, 616; cf. *infra* n. 981; NETHERLANDS: Hof 's-Gravenhage 29 Nov. 1934, N.J. 1935, 402. See also for NORWAY (where, however, the starting-point is different inasmuch as the substantive conditions of marriage are generally tested by the *lex domicilii* rather than by the *lex patriae*, see *supra* at n. 291): HD 8 June 1926, NRt 1926, 426; *Hambro* 324.

979. But see the GERMAN decision of KG 2 May 1932, IPRspr. 1932 no. 21, where reference was also made, albeit rather perfunctorily, to that other law (SOVIET RUSSIAN law).

980. E.g., AUSTRIA: OLG Wien 15 Jan. 1974, EFSlg 11 (1974) 251 no. 22,675; SWITZERLAND: BG 19 April 1951, BGE 77 II 1; ZivG Basel 13 June and 22 Oct. 1973, BJM 1973, 284.

depends on each party's personal law at the time of celebration; for if so it would have been necessary to ascertain that the marriage was good by the woman's law as well as by the man's. It is no doubt true that the decisions in question can be rationalised on the footing that the law of the country of the "invaded" nationality prevails. On the other hand, there is nothing in the reasoning of the courts indicating support for such a rule. However this may be, it is difficult to avoid the impression of a bias in favour of the *lex fori*. There are some indications that the public policy of countries whose domestic law does not know the concept of a marriage invalid for reasons of sham will readily be opposed to the application of foreign laws providing for annulment on such grounds.[981]

(2) Only on rare occasions have questions of the present type arisen for decision in the country of the wife's premarital nationality which she desired to change by her marriage to a foreigner. One *Belgian* and one *French* case may be cited, in each of which the wife successfully petitioned for a decree of annulment of her marriage to a foreigner on grounds that the sole object of the union was to give her foreign nationality and thereby to avoid, respectively, deportation from the foreign country concerned or internment as an enemy alien in a third country.[982] No other law than the *lex fori* was taken into account.

Although these decisions are in line with the homeward trend already referred to, the application of the *lex fori* was quite unobjectionable in the circumstances, seeing that that law was the woman's *lex patriae* at the time of the marriage. The decisions afford some support for the usual rule that a marriage is invalid if it is so by either party's personal law. On the other hand, they are clearly inconsistent with the opinion that preference should be given to the law of the party whose nationality was (sought to be) acquired. This solution would indeed have been inappropriate in the cases under review, for there was no good reason for excluding

981. This is particularly clear for ITALY, where the courts have even refused to recognise foreign nullity decrees based on such grounds because to do so would be contrary to public policy: Cass. 21 Jan. 1958, Foro it. 1958 I 723; App. Roma 8 March 1960, Temi rom. 1960, 249; App. Roma 5 April 1966, Temi rom. 1966, 255; see *Vitta* II 283.

982. BELGIUM: Cour Gand 26 April 1973, RW 1973/74, 1886, see *supra* at n. 968; FRANCE: Trib. Grenoble 11 July 1923, G.P., Tables Quinquennales 1925/30, Mariage no. 37 (marriage of a Frenchwoman and an American citizen in Turkey during the First World War, at a time when the United States was still a neutral country).

the woman's personal law which had a legitimate claim to control the genuineness of her consent. The position would have been different, of course, if the relevant provisions of that law had only been concerned with marriages contracted with a view to obtaining the nationality of the enacting State.[983]

There are apparently no decisions by courts in the country of the wife's premarital nationality dealing with cases where, conversely, a marriage is valid by her but invalid as a sham marriage by the man's personal law. On principle, the latter law must prevail in this situation, whether the effect of sham is held to depend on each party's personal law or on that of the party alone whose nationality is "invaded", with the result that the validity of the marriage must be denied.[984] At least in some countries, however, this result would probably be rejected as contrary to public policy.[985] Where the invalidating rule of the foreign law is of the type specifically directed against nationality marriages, an additional reason for refusing to give effect to it may be derived from the purpose of such rules. This, as has been seen, is primarily to protect certain public interests of the enacting State. It is at least possible that courts outside that State would say that it is no part of their function to further such interests and so decline to hold against a marriage coming within the foreign provision.[986] Such an attitude would be in keeping with the predominating tendency to ignore foreign law in this matter.[987]

(3) Finally, there is a small group of cases decided in a third country, the nationality of which was neither that to be thrown off nor that to be obtained through the marriage. Here the courts have been more willing to apply foreign law, as may be seen from *Belgian, West German* and *Swiss* decisions annulling a nationality

983. Presumably, for instance, the provision of SWISS law against nationality marriages would not be applied even by a SWISS court to defeat a marriage between a woman of Swiss and a man of German nationality contracted solely in order to procure her the latter nationality, the provision in question being directed against abusive acquisition of Swiss nationality only; see *supra* at n. 972.

984. The situation would be the same as in the cases cited *supra* n. 975, except that the question arose in a different forum.

985. Cf. *supra* at n. 978-981.

986. Cf. *supra* at n. 524 and *infra* at n. 1185-1187.

987. But see the FRENCH decision of Trib. Melun 20 Jan. 1954, G.P. 1954.1.272, where the court was prepared to give effect to a provision of foreign law specifically directed against nationality marriages (*supra* n. 976). This is also the prevailing opinion in WEST GERMANY, see the references *supra* n. 963.

marriage in reliance on the *lex patriae* of one or both of the parties at the time of celebration.[988] In the main these decisions seem to support the proposition that such a marriage is invalid if it is so by either party's personal law, but they can also be reconciled with the view that the only relevant law is that of the party whose nationality was acquired.

Nevertheless, even in this situation the *lex fori* has exerted a certain power of attraction for reasons of public policy or otherwise. In a *French* case, for instance, which involved a marriage in France between a woman of Polish and a man of Italian nationality, French law was applied without more to grant the husband a nullity decree for absence of consent, the only object of the union being to give the woman Italian nationality.[989] On the other hand, it is very doubtful whether and to what extent the courts of countries whose domestic law upholds such marriages would be prepared to give effect to rules of foreign law providing for their annulment.[990]

In conclusion, the *lex fori* has prevailed in the great majority of cases dealing with an alleged nationality marriage. The same tendency is to be observed in those relatively few cases in which a marriage has been claimed to be a nullity on other grounds of sham, as for example where (allegedly) its sole or predominant

988. BELGIUM: Civ. Bruxelles 30 Jan. 1970, J.T. 1970, 498, Clunet 1975, 344 (marriage in Bulgaria, between woman of Bulgarian and man of French nationality; FRENCH law applied); WEST GERMANY: LG München 10 Dec. 1957, IPRspr. 1956/57 no. 104 (marriage in Hungary, between woman of Hungarian and man of Italian nationality; ITALIAN law applied; note that ITALIAN law has since been interpreted to be opposed to the annulment of sham marriages, *supra* n. 978, 981); see also BGH 11 June 1958, BGHZ 27, 375, IPRspr. 1958/59 no. 5 (involving BELGIAN and ENGLISH law), and *Wengler,* Gutachten no. 19; SWITZERLAND: BezG Zürich 14 June 1956, SJZ 53 (1957) 25 (marriage in Germany, between woman of German and man of Italian nationality, held to be invalid both by GERMAN and by ITALIAN law; note that the position is different today under both of those laws, see *supra* n. 962, 972, 978, 981). Cf. the ENGLISH case of H. v. H., [1954] P. 258 (where, however, the ground of annulment was duress).

989. Cour Paris 16 Oct. 1958, J.C.P. 1958.II.10897, noted by *Desbois* in Rev. trim. dr. civ. 1959, 75. Although the court in that case did not give any reason for its application of FRENCH law, the decision could be explained on the footing that the woman was a political refugee apparently domiciled in France. Cf. for AUSTRIAN law *Klang and Gschnitzer* 586, claiming that the prohibition of that law against nationality marriages must apply, on grounds of public policy, to all marriages celebrated in Austria whatever the nationality of the parties.

990. Cf. *supra* at n. 981 and 985.

purpose was to give the woman the man's name.[991] On the facts, it is true, most of the relevant decisions can be brought within an "objective" choice of law rule referring to the personal law of each party, or of the husband alone (whose nationality or name was to be acquired by the wife). Nevertheless, the main impression is that of a strong homeward trend, which leaves little scope for the application of foreign laws, especially where such laws differ from the *lex fori.* Significantly, there appears to be no case in which a marriage was upheld by virtue of foreign law in circumstances where it would have been annulled as a sham marriage according to the *lex fori.* Nor, it seems, has foreign law ever been applied to grant a nullity decree for reasons of sham where such grounds of annulment were entirely unknown to the *lex fori.*[992]

bb. *Physical and Mental Capacity*

100. *Introductory.* Prohibitions against marriage on account of certain physical or mental deficiencies of either party are or have been known to the laws of numerous countries. Many restraints of this kind are based on grounds of eugenics. This is usually the *ratio* behind provisions directed against the marriage of persons suffering from insanity or other forms of mental incapacity, epilepsy, venereal disease or some other transmissible illness. Such impediments are or were until recently to be found in the laws of

991. See for WEST GERMAN cases dealing with marriages claimed to come within the category of *Namensehen*: LG Aachen 23 Oct. 1961, IPRspr. 1960/61 no. 88; OLG Saarbrücken 12 March 1970, IPRspr. 1970 no. 84; but see LG Frankfurt 9 May 1958, IPRspr. 1958/59 no. 116, applying FRENCH law, which was the husband's *lex patriae,* to reject his petition for annulment on this ground. For BELGIAN decisions relying on BELGIAN law alone to annul marriages on grounds of sham (other than nationality marriages) see: Cour Bruxelles 25 Nov. 1959, Rev. crit. d.i.p. 1962, 76, note Rigaux (marriage in France, between a man of Belgian and a woman of Spanish nationality, the only purpose of which was to legitimate a child); Civ. Bruxelles 30 March 1976, J.T. 1976, 427, Clunet 1979, 176 (marriage in Belgium, between parties both of Greek nationality, for the sole purpose of facilitating for the man to obtain a work permit enabling him to remain in Belgium). The last-cited BELGIAN case, in contrast with the others, is obviously inconsistent with any rule referring the validity of sham marriages to either party's personal law.

992. The closest to this seems to be that WEST GERMAN courts have been prepared to give effect to rules of foreign law requiring the annulment of nationality marriages, although the corresponding provision of the *lex fori* was limited to marriages of the kind known as *Namensehen;* see particularly the decision of LG München 10 Dec. 1957, IPRspr. 1956/57 no. 104.

several European (chiefly Scandinavian and East European) and Latin American countries, as well as in the statutes of many states in the United States.[993] Another type of physical incapacity is that of impotence which, as a heritage from the canon law, is recognised as a bar to marriage, for instance, in England, Italy, Spain and in several parts of the United States.[994] This incapacity is imposed in the interest of the parties themselves; unlike most impediments of a eugenic nature it usually does not prevent the celebration of a marriage but is only treated as a ground for annulling it afterwards at the instance of one of the parties.

There are, however, great variations as to the purpose and function as well as the wording and scope of the provisions referred to. In addition to, or occasionally in place of the objectives mentioned, several of those provisions pursue a purpose akin to that of rules going to the matter of consent to marriage. This is perhaps most conspicuous in the case of restrictions on marriage imposed by reason of mental incompetency (insanity, feeble-mindedness, imbecility, unsoundness of mind, etc.), which are often primarily, and sometimes even exclusively, designed to ensure the voluntary character of marriage, preventing the afflicted party from marrying because he is deemed incapable of giving true consent.[995]

In a number of other cases the purpose is rather to protect the other spouse who does not himself suffer from any disability of the kind under consideration. Obvious examples are afforded by provisions to the effect that proceedings for nullity on the ground in question may only be brought by that spouse and only where he or she had entered into the marriage unaware of the respondent's affliction. Provisions of this type are not uncommon in respect of impotence as a ground for annulment. By Italian law, for instance, impotency to procreate (*impotentia generandi*) is in certain circumstances regarded as a cause for nullity, but it can only be pleaded by the other spouse and only where that spouse had no

993. For comparative surveys see *Dölle*, Familienrecht 94-98, 170; *Gamillscheg*, Kommentar, art. 13 no. 427-428. For AMERICAN law see *Clark* 38, 86-87; *Vernier* I 172, 188-191, 199-203.

994. ENGLAND: Matrimonial Causes Act 1973, s. 12 (*a*); for other parts of the BRITISH ISLES and the Republic of IRELAND see *North* 125, 335, 361. ITALY: CC art. 123; SPAIN: CC art. 83 no. 3; USA: *Clark* 87-91; *Vernier* I 196-198.

995. See *Dölle*, Familienrecht 169-170, 265-270, and for AMERICAN law: *Clark* 95-99; *Vernier* I 171, 188-191.

knowledge of the defect before the marriage.[996] Another illustration may be taken from English law where a marriage is voidable, *inter alia,* on the grounds that at the time of the marriage the respondent was suffering from venereal disease in a communicable form or was pregnant by some person other than the petitioner, provided in either case that the latter was at that time ignorant of the facts alleged.[997] Such provisions are analogous to those, already considered under the heading of consent to marriage, whereby a spouse may obtain a decree of nullity on grounds of fraud or error as to the personal attributes of the respondent. This resemblance must be borne in mind when discussing the treatment of such rules in the conflict of laws (*infra* s. 101-102).

All bars to the constitution of a valid marriage so far mentioned relate to the physical or mental state or condition of the parties at the time of the marriage (although the defect may not have been discovered until later). Deviating from this usual pattern, English law (followed by some related systems of law) recognises the postnuptial fact of wilful refusal to consummate the marriage on the part of one of the spouses as entitling the other to a decree of nullity (rather than divorce).[998] Conversely, antenuptial matters which would normally render the marriage invalid are sometimes treated as grounds for divorce, in the alternative to or even to the exclusion of nullity.[999] Many such anomalies are to be found in American law, *inter alia* as concerns mental incompetence, venereal diseases and impotence, which often qualify as grounds for divorce even where they have existed from the inception of the marriage.[1000] Both types of departure from the ordinary pattern of delimitation between annulment and divorce give rise to special problems in the conflict of laws (*infra* s. 103).

101. *Choice of Law: Eugenic Marriage Impediments.* It is common ground in *Continental European* and *Scandinavian* countries that eugenic marriage impediments fall within the general notion of capacity to marry determinable by the personal law of

996. CC art. 123 par. 2; see *Haller,* Nichtigerklärung einer Ehe nach Art. 123 Abs. 2 CCit. (impotenza di generare): SJZ 61 (1965) 351-354; *Jayme* 43. Contrast the rules cited *infra* n. 1037-1038.

997. Matrimonial Causes Act 1973, s. 12 (*e*) and (*f*), in conjunction with s. 13 (3). See *North* 125-126, 335.

998. Matrimonial Causes Act 1973, s. 12 (*b*). See *North* 125, 335, and for a critical discussion, *Cretney,* Principles of Family Law (London 1974) 71-75.

999. See generally *Gamillscheg,* Kommentar, art. 13 no. 514, art. 17 no. 458; *Neuhaus,* Verhältnis 357-358, 361.

1000. See *Clark* 88, 95, 356-358.

the parties at the time of the marriage.[1001] Having regard to the purpose of such impediments, it is usually agreed, further, that they must be treated as bilateral so as to require application whenever existing in the law of one of the parties irrespective of which of them is affected by the illness in question.[1002] Hence, even if the afflicted party's own law does not provide for any incapacity of this kind, the marriage is precluded if the healthy party's law does.

As in any other matter, the public policy of the forum may interfere as a corrective in particular instances. Of this little or nothing can be said with certainty. There are some indications, however, that in countries insisting on eugenic marriage impediments in their domestic law those impediments, or some of them, may be held to extend to all locally celebrated marriages regardless of the personal law of the parties.[1003]

In *England,* as well as in other countries following English law, these questions have been very little adverted to, presumably because eugenic marriage impediments are unknown to the domestic laws of those countries. As concerns mental incompetency, it has been suggested that since English domestic law regards this as a matter of consent to marriage it should also be so treated in the conflict of laws.[1004] On this view, the proper law is that applicable to the consent of the party labouring under the alleged infirmity, which apparently means the law of the domicile of that party alone (to the exclusion of the domiciliary law of the healthy spouse).[1005] This solution is unobjectionable in so far as it relates to rules which, in dealing with the effect of mental incompetency and similar questions, are solely concerned with ensuring the true consent of the afflicted party. While this seems to be the case with, among others, the relevant provision of English domestic law, other rules on the matter are clearly also based on considerations of eugenics. It is submitted that in these latter cases the bilateral approach involving a cumulative application

1001. See *Gamillscheg,* Kommentar, art. 13 no. 429, 432, and the references *supra* n. 378.

1002. *Supra* at n. 378.

1003. See, e.g., BULGARIA: FC art. 91 par. 3 in conjunction with art. 9 *lit.* b) and c); *Jessel* 153-154; NORWAY: *Gaarder* 133.

1004. *North* 125. See also *Falconbridge* 700-701; *Sykes,* Conflict 138.

1005. See the ENGLISH writers cited *supra* n. 370.

of the personal law of each party is to be preferred. This distinction is usually drawn by Continental writers on the subject.[1006]

The position is similar with regard to cases where the annullment of a marriage is sought on the ground that, at the time of celebration, the respondent was suffering from venereal disease in a communicable form. By English domestic law this ground is only available if the petitioner was at that time ignorant of the fact (*supra* at n. 997). It has been argued that this provision is in effect a statutory exception to the common law rule that mistake as to the attributes of the other spouse does not affect the validity of a marriage and that the matter should therefore be classified as relating to consent to marriage cognisable by the law governing such questions.[1007] This seems to mean the *lex domicilii* of the healthy party (the petitioner) alone.

Once more, this reasoning is convincing in so far as it concerns provisions of the type figuring in English domestic law. The borderline between such rules and those authorising annulment by reason of fraud or mistake as to personal attributes is too floating and tenuous to admit of any distinction between them in the conflict of laws.[1008] If, for instance, a domiciled Englishwoman has married a domiciled German national who unknown to her suffered from venereal disease, she is and certainly should be able to rely on the English provision in order to seek a nullity decree on this ground, just as the man would be entitled to invoke the rule of German law concerning error as to personal attributes in proceedings for nullity brought by him.[1009] The law of the party in whose person the defect is alleged to exist (the respondent) should be left out of consideration in both situations. These solutions, it is submitted, are appropriate whether the issue comes before an English or a German court or arises in any other country recognising the principle of the personal law in the matters under discussion.

It does not follow, however, that the same solution should be accepted for provisions treating venereal or other diseases as an "objective" impediment to marriage based on eugenic reasons, especially where it is imposed independently of any question of the healthy party's knowledge of the fact. Here again the bilateral

1006. See, e.g., *Beck*, art. 7 c no. 21, 23; *Gamillscheg*, Kommentar, art. 13 no. 210, 431; *Kegel*, IPR 346; *Knapp*, Essai 211; *Muret* 25-26; *Rabel* 292; *Steinle* 68-69.

1007. *Dicey and Morris* 360; *North* 126.

1008. Cf. *Gamillscheg*, Kommentar, art. 13 no. 430; *Wolff*, PIL 327.

1009. See *supra* at n. 370-371, 932, 934-935.

approach is more in keeping with the purpose and spirit of the domestic rules involved. Such rules ought therefore to be taken into account whenever they form part of either party's personal law.

102. *Choice of Law: Impotence and Related Matters.* The prevailing view in *Continental European* countries is that impotence as a bar to marriage is to be classified as a matter affecting capacity to marry referable to the personal law of each party at the time of celebration.[1010] In practice, questions of this kind seem chiefly to have been encountered in respect of marriages between parties of Italian nationality sought to be set aside by reason of the impotence of one of them. *Dutch, French* and *Swiss* courts have granted nullity decrees in such cases relying on Italian law, notwithstanding that impotence was not regarded as a ground for annulment by the *lex fori.*[1011] These decisions expressly or implicitly recognise that to do so is not incompatible with the public policy of the forum.[1012] Occasionally, however, it has been held or suggested to the contrary that no effect can be given to foreign laws providing, in contrast with the *lex fori,* for annulment on this ground.[1013]

In *England* and other countries following English law the position is rather different. Questions of the nullity of a marriage

1010. References *infra* n. 1011, 1012, 1034-1036, 1042. *Adde*, WEST GERMANY: *Gamillscheg,* Kommentar, art. 13 no. 429; ITALY: *Morelli* 105. The same classification prevails, in principle, for the requirement that the spouses are respectively male and female. On this point, however, foreign laws differing from the *lex fori* seem likely to be regarded as offensive to the forum's notion of public policy. See the WEST GERMAN decision of President of OLG Hamm 3 Dec. 1973, IPRspr. 1973 no. 39 (refusing to apply a foreign law recognising the transformation of the sex of one of the intending spouses). Similarly for FRENCH law, *Batiffol and Lagarde* II 38.

1011. FRANCE: Trib. Tunis 27 Nov. 1907, Clunet 1908, 811; Cour Grenoble 19 June 1963, Clunet 1964, 586, note Sialelli, Rev. crit. d.i.p. 1964, 520, note Déprez; NETHERLANDS: Rb. Rotterdam 12 Sept. 1966, N.J. 1967 no. 387; SWITZERLAND: BG 2 Dec. 1943, BGE 69 II 342, Clunet 1952, 618, note Knapp (this decision also held that the petition was not barred by the fact that it was presented after the expiration of the time limit prescribed for nullity proceedings by the *lex fori,* no such time limit being known to the applicable ITALIAN law). Cf. for ITALIAN practice concerning the recognition of foreign nullity decrees in such cases, *Vitta* II 282, 284.

1012. Among writers sharing this view see for WEST GERMANY: *Gamillscheg*, Kommentar, art. 13 no. 432; SWITZERLAND: *Schnitzer* 342. And see for the position under the HAGUE CONVENTION of 1902, *Travers* I 174-175.

1013. See for FRANCE: Cour Tunis 17 Oct. 1955, Rev. tunis. dr. 1956, 133, note Tallon; *Vincent and Ponsard* no. 97.

on grounds of impotence, or of the respondent's wilful refusal to consummate it (which, as has been seen, is a cause for nullity in English domestic law) are usually dealt with as a separate category, sometimes referred to as "essential validity other than capacity".[1014] There is a substantial number of cases involving foreign elements in which English courts have heard petitions for nullity based on one or both of those grounds. In most of them, however, jurisdiction was the main concern of the courts, and the issue of choice of law was not given adequate consideration. As a result, the law is in a state of confusion, and the authorities afford some support for a variety of conclusions.[1015]

As in the consent cases dealt with previously (*supra* s. 97-98), there is in the English cases of impotence and wilful refusal an obvious tendency to favour the application of the *lex fori* by some means or other. Until a relatively recent date (1947) questions of choice of law in these matters seem to have escaped notice completely, the *lex fori* being relied on as a matter of course once the court was satisfied that it had jurisdiction.[1016] Several later decisions, too, have assumed that this is the proper law to apply, or are at least consistent with such a rule.[1017] Some of the relevant decisions, it is true, can be explained on the footing that foreign law was not pleaded or proved.[1018] Significantly, however, even in those cases where the courts adverted to the problem of choice of law, and whatever rule they purported to lay down in this respect, they have almost invariably ended by applying the *lex fori*.[1019]

1014. *Dicey and Morris* 354, 355. Cf. *supra* s. 64.

1015. See *Cheshire and North* 403-406; *Dicey and Morris* 359-363; *North* 126-129; *Nygh* 416-419.

1016. Easterbrook v. Easterbrook, [1944] P. 10, noted in 60 L.Q.R. 115 (1944); Hutter v. Hutter, [1944] P. 95. In each of these cases the husband, of foreign domicile, was granted a nullity decree on the ground of non-consummation owing to wilful refusal on the part of the wife (who was domiciled in England at the time of the marriage), jurisdiction being assumed on the basis that the parties were resident in England. For criticism see, e.g., *Cheshire and North* 398-399; *Falconbridge* 696-697. But see for a defence of the decisions on the ground that the marriages in question had been celebrated in England, *Hamilton,* case note: 26 Can. Bar Rev. 875, 879 (1948).

1017. E.g., Ponticelli v. Ponticelli, [1958] P. 204 at 215-216 (where it was found unnecessary to come to a final conclusion as between the husband's *lex domicilii* and the *lex fori*); Ross Smith v. Ross Smith, [1963] A.C. 280, 306, 313, 322 (H.L.) (by implication).

1018. In addition to the cases cited *supra* n. 1016 see ENGLAND: Magnier v. Magnier (1968), 112 S.J. 233 (P.), Clunet 1973, 415, note Lipstein; CANADA: D. v. D. (1973), 36 D.L.R. (3d) 17 (Ont. H.C.).

1019. See the cases cited *infra* n. 1022 and 1027.

Although this tendency has been much criticised, some writers seek to justify a general application of the *lex fori.*[1020] The main argument advanced in support of such a rule is that suits for nullity on the grounds of impotence and wilful refusal are akin to those for divorce, which is admittedly governed by the *lex fori* in English conflict of laws. Such an analogy suggests itself for reasons derived from English domestic law, in part because these deficiencies render a marriage voidable only, which means that it is regarded as valid and subsisting until a decree of nullity is pronounced, in part because the effects of such a decree in respect of a voidable marriage are assimilated to those of a decree of divorce.[1021] No doubt this analogy carries particular force where, in addition, the annulment is based on an essentially postnuptial event, as in the case of wilful refusal to consummate the marriage.

Whatever merit this argument may have, the application of the *lex fori* as a general rule is clearly inconsistent with the reasoning of the courts in some of the cases on the matter. In two such cases, one English and one Northern Irish, the courts expressed their preference for the *lex loci celebrationis.*[1022] This solution is based on the view that physical incapacity is classifiable as a contractual defect, distinct from capacity to marry referable to the *lex domicilii*. In the English case the court gave as reason for

1020. ENGLAND: *Dicey and Morris* 359-363 (in the alternative to the husband's *lex domicilii* at the date of the marriage); *Garner*, Jurisdiction and the Choice of Law in Nullity Suits: 63 L.Q.R. 486, 489-490 (1947); *O.M. Stone*, Jurisdiction to Annul a Voidable Marriage: 18 M.L.R. 604, 606-607 (1955); *Webb*, Nullity Jurisdiction: 10 I.C.L.Q. 358, 365 (1961); *idem*, Thoughts 831; SCOTLAND: *Anton* 292, 294-295, 300 (who seems, however, to opt in favour of the husband's *lex domicilii* at the time of the proceedings rather than the *lex fori*); AUSTRALIA: *Sykes*, Conflict 136-138; cf. *Nygh* 417. As regards wilful refusal see also *infra* n. 1050.

1021. Matrimonial Causes Act 1973, s. 16. The same tendency prevails in other systems based on ENGLISH law; see, e.g., the AUSTRALIAN Matrimonial Causes Act 1959, s. 51.

1022. ENGLAND: Robert v. Robert, [1947] P. 164 (applying the law of GUERNSEY, which was also the country where both parties were at all times domiciled). For an approving comment see *Kennedy*, case note: 25 Can. Bar Rev. 1012 (1947); for criticism, *Garner* (*supra* n. 1020) and case note in 1 I.L.Q. 350, 352 (1947). NORTHERN IRELAND: Addison v. Addison, [1955] N.I. 1, 30 (Q.B.) (marriage in Northern Ireland, between a woman then domiciled there and a man at all times domiciled in England, annulled on the ground of the latter's impotence; NORTHERN IRISH law preferred to ENGLISH law, though the question was not pursued to the length of a decision as the two laws did not differ in substance), noted by *Webb*, The Twilight of the Doctrine of *Inverclyde* v. *Inverclyde*: 4 I.C.L.Q. 557-563 (1955).

applying the *lex loci celebrationis* that wilful refusal, which was the ground for annulment alleged in that case, must be considered "an error in the quality of the respondent".[1023] In other words, this defect was regarded as something akin to mistake as to personal attributes for which the proper law is that governing consent to marriage.

This reasoning has come in for criticism on various grounds.[1024] Although (contrary to these critics) there seems to be merit in the analogy drawn with consent to marriage, the conclusion reached by the courts in the two cases referred to here is open to the objection that such consent is probably a matter for the *lex domicilii* rather than for the *lex loci celebrationis.*[1025] However this may be, the decisions are of limited importance; for in one case the *lex loci celebrationis* coincided with the *lex fori,* and in the other the substance of the two laws was the same. Moreover, there are other English cases dealing with impotence and wilful refusal where the *lex loci celebrationis* was ignored or where reference to that law was expressly rejected.[1026]

In one of the last-mentioned cases, where the issue of choice of law was entertained at some length, the court leaned in favour of applying the law of the husband's domicile, either at the date of the marriage or at that of the commencement of the proceedings.[1027] While this decision stands out as the principal English authority on the matter, the merit of the solution adopted by it seems questionable, especially now that English law has abandoned the principle that the husband's domicile is automatically shared by the wife.[1028] Another English case suggests that the appropriate law to apply is

1023. Robert v. Robert, *ibid.* at 167-168.

1024. See, e.g., *Dicey and Morris* 361; *North* 126; *Sykes,* Conflict 137. But see in support of the *lex loci celebrationis, Hamilton* (*supra* n. 1016).

1025. See *supra* s. 97.

1026. Way v. Way, [1950] P. 71; Ponticelli v. Ponticelli, [1958] P. 204, 214-215.

1027. Ponticelli v. Ponticelli, *ibid.* at 214-216 (applying ENGLISH law, which was also the law of the intended matrimonial home, to annul a marriage of an English domiciled man to a woman domiciled in Italy on the ground of the wife's wilful refusal to consummate it), noted by *Webb,* Light At Last on De Reneville v. De Reneville?: 21 M.L.R. 416-419 (1958). See also Way v. Way, *ibid.* at 80, and the writers cited *supra* n. 1020. For other decisions affording some support for the *lex domicilii,* though without specifying either which party's domicile is relevant or as at what time the connecting factor is to be ascertained, see Robert v. Robert, [1947] P. 164, 168 (subsidiarily, if the *lex loci celebrationis* was to be considered wrong, cf. *supra* n. 1022); Ramsay-Fairfax v. Ramsay-Fairfax, [1956] P. 115, 125.

1028. See the criticism advanced by *North* 128.

"the law of the matrimonial domicile in reference to which the parties may have been supposed to enter into the bonds of marriage."[1029] That decision, however, is now generally explained on the basis that it was only concerned with a question of jurisdiction and that it has nothing to do with choice of law.[1030] The two solutions mentioned here may be seen in the light of the doctrine that capacity to marry as a whole should depend upon the law of the intended matrimonial home or, *in dubio*, upon the law of the husband's domicile (*supra* s. 54-55).

Yet another proposal, which is supported by the weight of extrajudicial opinion, is that impotence (though possibly not wilful refusal), along with other antenuptial defects, should be treated as affecting capacity to marry, *i.e.* by reference to the domiciliary law of each of the parties at the time of the marriage.[1031] Such a rule, which (apart from the question of domicile *v.* nationality) accords with the prevailing view in Continental countries, has never been directly endorsed by English courts. It seems, however, to be compatible with the actual decisions, if not with the reasoning, in all or nearly all English cases bearing on choice of law in this matter.[1032]

It is submitted that the best arguments militate in favour of this last solution. No satisfactory justification has ever been offered of why physical capacity should be taken out of the notion of capacity to marry and assigned to independent conflicts rules. While the analogy with divorce may be persuasive for the peculiar English rule of nullity on the ground of wilful refusal (see *infra* s. 103), sound principle demands that the relevant law to determine the effect of physical incapacity existing at the date of the marriage should be selected by criteria relating to that time. Moreover, as intimated in some English cases, there is the

1029. De Reneville v. De Reneville, [1948] P. 100, 114, 121-122 (C.A.). Followed in Casey v. Casey, [1949] P. 420, 429-430 (C.A.). See also the cases cited *supra* n. 1027 and *Ryan* 992 (for wilful refusal).

1030. See particularly *Morris*, De Reneville Revisited: 19 I.C.L.Q. 424-429 (1970); also, e.g., *Cheshire and North* 395-396; *Graveson*, Conflict 254, 266-267, 341-344; *Woodhouse* 460, 462-463.

1031. See: *Castel*, case note: 42 Can. Bar Rev. 474, 486, 488 (1964); *Cheshire and North* 403-406; *Falconbridge* 700-701; *Fleming*, Choice of Law in Nullity Proceedings: 11 M.L.R. 98-102 (1948); *North* 126-129; *Nygh* 419; *Wolff*, PIL 327-328, 337-338.

1032. In all cases where a decree of nullity was granted – except, possibly, in Magnier v. Magnier (*supra* n. 1018) – the law applied was that of a country in which at least one of the spouses was domiciled at the time of the marriage.

analogy with consent to marriage, in particular mistake as to personal attributes. In so far as such questions are held to fall to the law governing capacity to marry, some thorny problems of delimitation will be avoided if the same choice of law is adopted for impotence as a ground of nullity.

Not all problems are solved, however, by accepting the principle that each party's personal law at the time of the marriage applies. If the parties were then subject to different personal laws (whether determined by domicile or by nationality) and if impotence is a ground for annulment by one of the two laws involved, there is the further question of the requisite relationship between that law and the party alleged to suffer from the disability. This is a point on which a striking division of opinion exists but which has seldom been fully discussed in the light of comparative law.

According to one view, which is apparently espoused by the few English writers who have considered this question, impotence as a ground for annulment is to be tested by the personal law of the afflicted party himself.[1033] In other words, impotence is only relevant where it affects the party whose law regards it as constituting an incapacity. This is the same approach as that generally employed for impediments treated as unilateral, such as lack of age (*supra* s. 50). Most Continental writers, on the other hand, seem to be of opinion that the question depends exclusively on the personal law of the other spouse (the non-afflicted party, who is normally the petitioner).[1034] This view accords with the prevailing approach in respect of mistake as to personal attributes and similar defects in consent (*supra* s. 97). According to a third school of thought, impotence should be treated as a bilateral impediment operating to invalidate a marriage irrespective of whether the defect is that of the party whose personal law contains the invalidating rule or that of the other spouse.[1035]

It is submitted that none of these general formulas are acceptable in all cases. The problem should rather be solved in the light

1033. See *Cheshire and North* 396, 405; *North* 127, 128; *Ryan* 987, 992-993 (a similar opinion has been voiced in GERMANY by *Steinle* 69-70). But this is inconsistent with the actual decision in Ponticelli v. Ponticelli, [1958] P. 204, and with the view expressed by the court in Addison v. Addison, [1955] N.I. 1. In both these cases the law applied was in effect the personal law of the other spouse who petitioned for annulment, see *supra* n. 1022, 1027.

1034. See, e.g., *Albisetti* 49; *Frankenstein* 200; *Gamillscheg*, Kommentar, art. 13 no. 430; *Jayme* 43; *F. Kahn* 63; *Muret* 26; *Spivak* 43-44. Cf. *Rabel* 291.

1035. See *Betti* 413-414; *Wolff*, IPR 189; *idem*, PIL 336-337.

of the purpose and policy of the rule of domestic law involved in each case.[1036] Two main types of provision dealing with impotence should be distinguished:

(1) One class of provisions purport to say that impotence represents an incapacity in the party afflicted with it. A marriage of such a person may be annulled, at least as a rule, at the instance of either spouse. This is the position, for instance, in English law.[1037] Of a similar spirit is the rule of Italian law concerning *impotentia coeundi,* which (in contrast with *impotentia generandi*) is a ground for annulment available to each of the spouses.[1038]

It seems plain at the outset that provisions of this type, like other rules laying down an incapacity for marriage, must be taken into account whenever the disabled party is himself subject to the incapacitating law. Suppose, for example, that the man is of Italian and the woman (at the time of the marriage) of Swiss nationality. The husband is affected by *impotentia coeundi.* Clearly he should be able to rely on this ground in order to obtain a nullity decree in a Swiss court, as permitted by the relevant provision of Italian law governing his capacity to marry. Nor, it is submitted, is there any tenable reason why the wife should be precluded from setting up this ground for annulment, which by Italian law can be pleaded by either spouse.

This latter point has been contested by several Continental writers arguing that each of the spouses should only be allowed to petition for nullity on such grounds as exist under his own law but not on those existing under the law of the other spouse.[1039] The wife in our example could therefore only avail herself of the grounds supplied by Swiss law which does not include impotence.[1040] Such a restrictive attitude, however, seems neither warranted on principle, nor to be in accord with the decisions of courts in other matters of capacity to marry raising the same

1036. For distinctions largely similar to those proposed here see: *Beck,* art. 7 c no. 23; *Buzzati* 107-109; *Secrétan* 46. Cf. *supra* s. 51.

1037. By ENGLISH law a spouse is allowed to plead his own impotence in support of a petition for nullity, unless he is debarred from doing so under s. 13 (1) of the Matrimonial Causes Act 1973. For an earlier leading case on this question see Harthan v. Harthan, [1949] P. 115 (C.A.); followed in CANADA, see D. v. D. (1973), 36 D.L.R. (3d) 17 at 28-35 (Ont. H.C.) (*obiter*) with references. And see for AMERICAN law *Clark* 90.

1038. CC art. 123 par. 1. See also for SPAIN: CC art. 83 no. 3 in conjunction with art. 101 and 102 par. 2; *Weyers* (*supra* n. 513) 30-31.

1039. See *Frankenstein* 200; *Jayme* 43; *Secrétan* 62-63.

1040. Though she could invoke error as to personal attributes, which is recognised as a ground for annulment under SWISS CC art. 124.

issue.[1041] The better view is that the *lex causae* of capacity to marry (Italian law in our example) is the proper law to decide both whether there is a sufficient ground for annulment and, if so, who is entitled to bring suit on that ground.

What is the position in our example if the wife instead of the husband is the party suffering from *impotentia coeundi*? Can this ground be invoked, here too, to annul the marriage in reliance on Italian law, notwithstanding that it does not so qualify by Swiss law which is the law governing the wife's capacity? It is submitted that this question must be answered in the affirmative if the petition for nullity is brought by the husband.[1042] The reason is that the relevant provision of Italian law is not only concerned with the impotent party's capacity but also serves the purpose of protecting the other spouse by enabling that spouse to escape from a bond with a person so afflicted. A significant pointer in this direction is the fact that the right to plead this cause for nullity is vested in both spouses separately. Provisions so framed should reasonably be applied, not only where existing in the afflicted party's law, but also where they form part of the law of the other spouse impeaching the marriage on the ground of the respondent's impotence. To that extent a bilateral approach is appropriate.[1043] The situation considered here presents a strong analogy to cases where the petitioner alleges lack of true consent due to mistake as to the respondent's personal attributes; for if absurd distinctions are to be avoided the same law must decide whether the respondent's physical incapacity alone is a sufficient ground for annulment or whether it is only relevant where the petitioner entered into the marriage under a mistaken belief in this respect.

(2) The purpose and spirit of certain other provisions on the

1041. See generally: *Dölle*, Zur Behandlung der bigamischen Ehe im internationalen Privatrecht: Festschrift für Gustav Boehmer (Bonn 1954) 134, 136, 142 n. 23; *Gamillscheg*, Kommentar, art. 13 no. 494; *Kegel*, Kommentar, art. 13 no. 90; *Niboyet* V 325; *Pålsson*, Marriage (Encyclopedia) 169-170. Specifically in relation to impotence see *Travers* I 60-61.

1042. For a SWISS decision squarely in point see ObG Zürich 10 Sept. 1964, ZR 65 (1966) no. 94.

1043. See the writers cited *supra* n. 1035. Cf. the CHILEAN case mentioned *supra* at n. 255 where this approach was carried even further, the wife petitioner of German nationality being allowed to invoke CHILEAN law, which was the law of her husband's nationality, in order to obtain a nullity decree based on *her own* impotence. It would seem difficult, however, to justify such a position (unless it was prompted by the public policy of the forum).

matter are not to incapacitate the impotent party from marrying but solely to afford protection to the other spouse. Here too, as already noted, Italian law provides an illustration in so far as that law permits annulment of a marriage, at the instance of one of the spouses, on the ground of the other's *impotentia generandi.*[1044]

Since provisions of this type have in view the interest of the petitioning spouse alone, the proper approach is to treat them as unilateral, applicable when and only when they form part of the petitioner's personal law. This harmonises with the prevailing choice of law for cases of annulment based on fraud or error as to the respondent's personal attributes, to which once more there is a close analogy postulating such an identity of approach.

Applying this principle to our above example concerning a Swiss-Italian marriage, it is clear that the husband can rely on the relevant provision of Italian law if he seeks a nullity decree in a Swiss court on account of the wife's *impotentia generandi.*[1045] It is immaterial that this ground for annulment is unknown to the wife's own law. On the other hand, the wife could probably not invoke the Italian provision in order to obtain a nullity decree by reason of the same defect in the husband's person; for (in contrast with the rule concerning *impotentia coeundi*) that provision does not affect the capacity of the husband, to whom alone Italian law applies. Nor could the husband himself bring suit pleading his own impotency to procreate, because by Italian law the right to assert this ground for annulment is limited to the other spouse.

103. *Relation to Divorce.* While the proper law to apply in suits for annulment based on grounds of physical incapacity, as in other cases involving the substantive validity of a marriage, is that of the antenuptial domicile or nationality (as the case may be) of the spouses, other principles prevail for the choice of law in divorce. Broadly speaking, the latter is usually governed either by the *lex fori* alone or by that law in cumulation with the personal law of one or both of the spouses at the time of the proceedings.[1046]

1044. *Supra* at n. 996. There seems to be a good case for including the ENGLISH ground of wilful refusal to consummate the marriage within the same category (unless that ground is to be assigned to the law governing divorce, *infra* s. 103). ENGLISH writers, it is true, are opposed to classifying wilful refusal along with lack of consent for the reason that it does not depend on the petitioner's knowledge at the time of the marriage (*supra* n. 1024); but this does not alter the fact that the relevant ENGLISH provision is intended for the protection of that spouse alone.

1045. See the writers cited *supra* n. 1034-1036.

1046. See *Gamillscheg*, Kommentar, art. 17 no. 58-95; *Pålsson*, Marriage (Encyclopedia) 126-151; *Rabel* 419-422, 453-479.

This difference reflects the distinction typically drawn in domestic laws between annulment, which is granted for defects existing at the time of the marriage, and divorce (or legal separation, where that is the remedy provided for) which is based on postnuptial causes. As has been seen, however, there are many deviations from this pattern, mostly to the effect that certain antenuptial matters such as physical defects are to be treated as grounds for divorce rather than nullity (*supra* s. 100). The existence of such rules of domestic law is bound to produce problems touching the conflict of laws in certain situations, notably where the law applicable to the question of annulment provides for divorce as the proper remedy and *vice versa*. Example:

The wife was before her marriage domiciled in and possessed the nationality of country *X*, but she has now (by operation of law or otherwise) acquired her husband's domicile and nationality, that of country *Y*. She wants to get rid of the marriage because the husband is (and was at the date of the marriage) impotent. By the law of *X* this gives her a right to divorce, but by the law of *Y* it is a ground for annulment. A form of relief is thus available under either law. Nevertheless, the wife may be unable to obtain either type of relief if the normal principles of choice of law are applied strictly.[1047] The reason is that the law of *X* governing nullity does not annul the marriage in the circumstances and that the law of *Y* governing divorce does not treat the problem as one leading to a divorce.

Such a result is manifestly unsatisfactory. As a way out of the dilemma, it has been proposed that the conflicts rules of the forum should be suitably adapted. A persuasive solution, which has been advocated by *West German* writers in particular, would be to widen the scope of the law applicable to the nullity of marriage so as to embrace all antenuptial defects regardless of whether according to that law such defects constitute a ground for divorce or for annulment.[1048] If this solution is adopted the wife in our example would be able to obtain a divorce by virtue of the law of country *X*, notwithstanding that the ground invoked is not

1047. See *Raape*, Kommentar 390; *Rabel* 471-472.

1048. See *Gamillscheg*, Kommentar, art. 13 no. 515-516; *Kegel*, IPR 351-352, 378; *idem*, Kommentar, art. 13 no. 5-6, art. 17 no. 11. For slightly different views see *Jayme*, case note: RabelsZ 32 (1968) 323, 333-334; *Raape*, IPR 285-286; *Schröder*, Die Anpassung von Kollisions- und Sachnormen (Berlin 1961) 87-88, 113-116. Cf. *Rabel* 576-578.

recognised as a cause for divorce by the law normally controlling this matter.[1049]

Similarly, it would seem appropriate to refer all postnuptial grounds of matrimonial relief to the law governing divorce (or legal separation, as the case may be) even though by that law the only remedy available in the circumstances is a decree of annulment of the marriage. A solution along these lines has often been proposed in respect of the provision of *English* law concerning wilful refusal to consummate the marriage as a ground for annulment.[1050] On this view, for instance, an English court ought always to apply its own law when hearing petitions for nullity based on the respondent's wilful refusal, notwithstanding that at the time of the marriage the parties were, or one of them was, domiciled in a foreign country by the law of which this is only regarded as entitling the petitioner to a divorce or is not regarded as affording a cause for granting any form of matrimonial relief.[1051]

bc. *Age Requirements*

104. *Minimum Age for Marriage.* Rules as to the age of marriage are primarily intended to protect the parties by ensuring that they are physically and mentally mature for marriage and capable of giving true consent. In addition, broader considerations of morality and social expediency usually play a part in the framing of such requirements. There are wide variations in the age standards adopted in different countries.[1052] In part these variations can be

1049. An alternative means of overcoming the difficulty would be by admitting that a decree of nullity can be granted on the strength of the law of country *Y*, although the marriage is valid by the law of country *X* normally decisive for this question. In favour of such a solution for AUSTRALIAN law see *Nygh* 453; but see *Sykes*, Conflict 128.

1050. For writers dealing both with impotence and with wilful refusal see the references *supra* n. 1020. Other writers, while defending the application of the premarital *lex domicilii* as regards impotence, suggest that wilful refusal might properly be governed by the law of the postnuptial domicile (the relevant date being either that of the proceedings or that of the refusal) or by the *lex fori.* See *Cheshire and North* 405-406; *Falconbridge* 701; *North* 127-129; *Nygh* 419; *Woodhouse* 456.

1051. On the other hand, some arguments can be advanced for referring wilful refusal to the same law as applies to impotence. For support of this position see, e.g., Ponticelli v. Ponticelli, [1958] P. 204, 215; *Wolff,* PIL 337-338.

1052. For comparative surveys see: *Dölle*, Familienrecht 154-168; *Gamillscheg*, Kommentar, art. 13 no. 194; *Götz*, art. 96 no. 21. See also StAZ 1965, 26-27, and for AMERICAN law the references *supra* n. 207.

said to reflect differences in the natural conditions affecting the age at which physical and mental maturity is reached, but in part they are only explicable against the background of historical tradition, in particular a strong influence of religious law and concepts.

It is common ground that age qualifications form part of the subject-matter of capacity to marry referable to the personal law of the parties. As regards *Continental European* and *Scandinavian* countries, it is also generally agreed that these requirements are to be treated as unilateral, so that each party will only be subject to the age limit imposed by his own law.[1053] As noted earlier, a different position has been taken in *England,* where it has been held that a person of English domicile lacks capacity to marry a person who, though capable of marriage by the law of his own domicile, is under age according to English law.[1054] It is to be hoped that this double-barrelled approach, which seems to have little if any merit, will not be extended to cases where English domestic law is not involved.[1055]

As usual, the rule of the personal law is subject to such exceptions as may be compelled by considerations of public policy. This is of little significance in cases where the relevant foreign law is more stringent than the *lex fori,* whether because it requires a higher age for marriage or because, in contrast to the latter law, it does not admit the possibility of dispensation below that age. It is generally thought that the application of such rules is of no concern to the forum's public policy.[1056]

Where, on the other hand, the relevant foreign law is more liberal (permitting marriage at a lower age) than the *lex fori,* public policy is more likely to interfere, especially if the marriage is celebrated locally. In certain countries, including *England* and *France,* it has even been suggested that such a marriage can never be sanctioned by a registrar, or upheld by the courts, if either party is under the age required by the *lex fori,* whatever the per-

1053. References *supra* n. 361-363.

1054. Pugh v. Pugh, [1951] P. 482. See *supra* at n. 364-369.

1055. See *North* 120; but cf. *Dicey and Morris* 265.

1056. See, e.g., FRANCE: *Bischoff* no. 67, and the writers cited *infra* n. 1057; WEST GERMANY: *Gamillscheg,* Kommentar, art. 13 no. 199, 207; HUNGARY: *Réczei* 356; SWITZERLAND: *Beck,* art. 7 c no. 7, 9; *Knapp,* case note: Schw. Jb. Int. R. 7 (1950) 223, 224.

sonal law of the parties.[1057] In *Australia* this solution is embodied in statutory law.[1058]

In most countries, however, a somewhat more tolerant attitude is adopted.[1059] On the one side, it is agreed that foreign laws cannot be invoked to give sanction to child marriages prohibited by the local law.[1060] On the other, some scope is conceded for the application of foreign laws permitting marriage below the age prescribed in purely domestic cases. According to one view, which enjoys some support in *Continental* countries, the borderline for such tolerance ought to be drawn at the age under which the *lex fori* does not even provide for the possibility of granting dispensation.[1061] Another type of rule exists in *Swedish* law: while by Swedish domestic law the minimum age for marriage both for men and for women is eighteen years (subject to dispensation without any absolute lower limit), the threshold below which more permissive foreign laws will be refused effect is fixed at fifteen years (though even this limit is subject to dispensation).[1062] A very liberal position is taken by the *Hague Convention* of 1902, which does not in any case authorise the Contracting States to deviate from the rule of the *lex patriae* in matters of age of marriage.[1063] In a *Swiss* decision based on this convention it was held that an Italian girl aged fifteen could marry in Switzerland because by the applicable Italian law (as it then stood) she attained capacity for marriage at fourteen, notwithstanding that Swiss domestic law required an age of eighteen or, with dispensation, seventeen.[1064]

1057. See for ENGLAND the references *supra* n. 561; for FRANCE: *Batiffol and Lagarde* II 39; *Bischoff* no. 64; *Vincent and Ponsard* no. 80; but see for deviating views *Audinet* 186; *Audit* 299-300.

1058. References *supra* n. 636.

1059. See the references *infra* n. 1061-1064 and, e.g., BELGIUM: *Graulich* 157; WEST GERMANY: *Gamillscheg*, Kommentar, art. 13 no. 199; ITALY: *A. Miele* 117-118; *Morelli* 101-102; *Vitta* II 194; SWITZERLAND: *Muret* 75-76; *Schnitzer* 339; *Stauffer*, art. 7 c no. 2 and 5; *Vaucher* 542; YUGOSLAVIA: *Tchirkovitch* 223-224.

1060. Note the UN Convention on Consent to Marriage, etc., of 10 Dec. 1962, one of the aims of which is to eliminate child marriages.

1061. See e.g., CZECHOSLOVAKIA: *Bystrický*, À propos des problèmes fondamentaux du droit international privé de famille en Tchécoslovaquie: Bull. dr. tchécosl. 1958, 180, 181; SWITZERLAND: *Beck*, art. 7 c no. 40-43.

1062. Act of 8 July 1904 (as amended) ch. 1 § 3 no. 1.

1063. See art. 2 of the convention and the comments cited *supra* n. 634.

1064. BG 27 Jan. 1949, BGE 75 I 82, Clunet 1952, 670 with an approving note by Knapp, Schw. Jb. Int. R. 7 (1950) 222, note Knapp. For a critical comment see *Götz*, art. 96 no. 24, art. 107 no. 19.

Public policy will rarely prevent the recognition of a marriage entered into abroad in compliance with the relevant foreign law even if the parties are, or one of them is, well below the age of consent by the standards of the *lex fori.* An *English* decision furnishes a good illustration.[1065] That case involved a marriage celebrated in Nigeria, between parties domiciled there, the girl being only thirteen years and the man twice her age. Shortly after the marriage the parties came to live in England. Although manifestly this marriage could not have been solemnised in England, it was upheld by the court because it was valid by the applicable Nigerian law.[1066] Probably this must be regarded as a borderline case; for even as to foreign celebrated marriages it seems unlikely that the courts of countries rejecting child marriages could go much further in extending recognition.[1067]

105. *Parental Consents and Related Matters.* There is a sharp division of opinion as to the proper approach to questions of conflict of laws involving the consent of parents, guardians or other third persons to the marriage of persons below a certain age.[1068] While in *England* and other parts of the *British Commonwealth* such matters are predominantly classified as formalities referable to the *lex loci celebrationis,* in *Continental European* and *Scandinavian* countries they are almost invariably held to affect capacity to marry cognisable by the respective personal laws of the parties.[1069]

1065. Mohamed v. Knott, [1969] 1 Q.B. 1. For comments see *Karsten,* Child Marriages: 32 M.L.R. 212-217 (1969); *Schmitthoff* 89-90.

1066. The court further found that the girl was not "exposed to moral danger" within s. 2 of the Children and Young Persons Act, 1963, merely because she carried out her wifely duties, and proceeded to revoke an order committing her to a local authority on the ground that she was in need of care, protection or control within the meaning of the same provision. See Mohamed v. Knott, *ibid.* at 14-17.

1067. Cf. for ENGLAND: *Dicey and Morris* 73; *North* 131; FRANCE: *Bischoff* no. 72; WEST GERMANY: *Gamillscheg,* Kommentar, art. 13 no. 201; SCOTLAND: *Anton* 279; SWITZERLAND: *Beck,* art. 7 f no. 62.

1068. For comparative surveys of such requirements see *supra* n. 373.

1069. See *Pålsson,* Marriage, s. 409. For the Continental view, see the references *supra* n. 374-375, 507, 509, 511. Some dissent exists in Continental countries as to the proper classification of provisions which merely purport to postpone the ceremony, for instance by requiring the parties to demand the advice of their parents "by a respectful and formal act" (see *Pålsson,* Marriage, s. 409 at n. 550). Usually rules of this kind, too, are held to concern capacity to marry. See for decisions based on this view, e.g., BELGIUM: Civ. Bruxelles 3 Jan. 1913, Clunet 1914, 633; Civ. Bruxelles 7 July 1956, Clunet 1958,

continued on page 322

In so far as this latter position is taken, it means that questions of parental consent etc. will be treated on substantially the same lines as those concerning the age at which a person can marry at all.[1070] Typically, however, the policy embodied in provisions making the consent of parents, or of other third persons, a condition of marriage, or requiring the parties to notify and to seek the advice of such persons, is not nearly as strong as that applicable to the matter of minimum age for marriage. One aspect of this is that public policy has a minimal (if any) part to play as a factor disturbing the normal operation of the choice of law rule for the questions under consideration.[1071] In general, effect will be given to the appropriate foreign law not only where it is more stringent than the *lex fori*[1072] but also where it is more liberal, permitting the celebration of a marriage without parental consents etc. in

---

continued from page 321

1152; Civ. Liège 3 May 1967, Pas. 1967.III.99; FRANCE: Trib. Seine 21 Dec. 1885, Clunet 1886, 448; Trib. Seine 10 Jan. 1917, Clunet 1918, 1192; WEST GERMANY: OLG Frankfurt 31 Oct. 1950, IPRspr. 1950/51 no. 126; AG Hochheim 3 Jan. 1966, IPRspr. 1966/67 no. 57. But there are some suggestions that such rules, in contrast with those by which failure to obtain parental consent constitutes a bar to the proposed marriage, should be held to go to the form of marriage falling to the *lex loci celebrationis.* See for SWITZERLAND: *Beck,* art. 7 c no. 10; *Vischer,* IPR 590. This distinction apparently underlies the provisions on the matter in the VENEZUELAN CC art. 106; see *Lombard* 41 n. 132.

1070. Each of the parties is only subject to the requirements imposed by his own law (unilateral approach): *supra* at n. 374-375. It is also clear that the relevant law is that of the intending spouse himself and not that of the person whose consent is required. For a different view with regard to rules requiring parental advice rather than consent see *Marín López* 39. For a unique BELGIAN decision applying, in the absence of a common nationality of the intending spouse and her mother who opposed the marriage, the law of their common domicile coinciding with the *lex fori,* see Civ. Liège 21 Dec. 1973, Jur. Liège 1973/74, 228. This decision is criticised by *van Hecke and Rigaux* (1970 à 1975) 225-226.

1071. See, e.g., FRANCE: *Audinet* 183, 185-186; *Batiffol and Lagarde* II 40; *Vincent and Ponsard* no. 83 (with some reservations); WEST GERMANY: *Gamillscheg,* Kommentar, art. 13 no. 221; SWITZERLAND: *Beck,* art. 7 c no. 46; *Götz,* art. 98 no. 16, 18; *Knapp,* case note: Schw. Jb. Int. R. 7 (1950) 223, 226-227; *Muret* 77.

1072. See, e.g., AUSTRIA: OLG Wien 3 Oct. 1973, EFSlg 10 (1973) 240 no. 20,306; FRANCE: Trib. Seine 8 March 1920, Clunet 1920, 206; WEST GERMANY: LG Berlin 10 March 1947, IPRspr. 1960/61 no. 89; LG Nürnberg-Fürth 28 Feb. 1951, IPRspr. 1950/51 no. 65; KG 22 April 1968, FamRZ 1968, 466. See also the SCANDINAVIAN Convention of 1931 (as amended) art. 1 par. 2 (*supra* at n. 265).

circumstances where this would have been necessary according to the *lex fori* or providing for exemption from such requirements on easier terms.[1073]

Issues of parental consent have presented themselves with particular frequency in the context of evasion. Almost invariably these cases involved false evasions (*supra* s. 63), the parties having left their home country only temporarily in order to get married in a country, such as Scotland, whose domestic law did not insist on parental consent and where rules of foreign law containing such requirements were ignored. In some cases of this type the parties failed to achieve their purpose, inasmuch as their marriage was annulled by the courts of their home country once they were back in that country.[1074] Mostly, however, these evasions have been successful, either because the circumvented provision of the relevant personal law was only directory or because no proceedings to set the marriage aside were taken.[1075]

bd. *Consanguinity and Affinity*

106. Prohibitions against marriage between certain categories of relatives seem to be of universal existence, but there is a wide range of variations as to the kinds (by blood, by marriage or by adoption) and the degrees of relationship covered by such prohibitions, as well as on a number of other particulars, such as the possibility of dispensation and the sanctions imposed for violation.[1076] Generally speaking, there has for a long time been a tendency to narrow the limits of this kind of disqualification, which were once very broadly drawn, as exemplified above all by the classic canon law. A rather extreme instance of the modern tendency is afforded by Swedish law, where the list of absolute prohibitions has been reduced so as to include only persons related by blood in the direct line of ascent and descent or as full brother and sister, the intermarriage of half-brother and half-sister being permitted if

1073. See, e.g., BELGIUM: Civ. Bruxelles 3 Jan. 1913, Clunet 1914, 633; Civ. Liège 3 May 1967, Pas. 1967.III.99; FRANCE: Trib. Seine 30 Jan. 1923, Rev. crit. d.i.p. 1922/23, 494; Trib. Paris 15 March 1972, Rev. crit. d.i.p. 1973, 509, note D. Alexandre; GERMANY: KG 22 March 1906, KGJ 32 (1906) A 28, 33-34.

1074. *Supra* at n. 507, 516-517.

1075. *Supra* at n. 509, 511, 519-520.

1076. For comparative surveys see *Dölle*, Familienrecht 101-113, 272-273; *Gamillscheg*, Kommentar, art. 13 no. 231-234, 383. For AMERICAN law see the references *supra* n. 229.

special leave is obtained.[1077] As in Swedish law, so in several other systems, all impediments to marriage based on connection by affinity have recently been abolished.

It is common ground that these rules fall within the category of capacity to marry referable to the personal law of the parties, *i.e.* the law of their domicile or nationality (as the case may be) at the time of the marriage. It follows that the parties are debarred from marrying each other if they are within the prohibited degrees of relationship set out by their personal law or laws.[1078] It is well settled that this holds equally true for cases where the law of one of them alone regards their relationship as constituting an impediment to marriage even if this impediment is unknown to the other party's law or has been removed by dispensation according to that law.[1079] In both situations it is immaterial that the marriage may be permitted by some other law such as the *lex loci celebrationis.*[1080] A marriage will therefore only be lawful, so far as matters of consanguinity and affinity are concerned, if the parties are outside the prohibited degrees of their common personal law or, where they are subject to different laws, of both those laws.[1081] On the other hand, where this condition is met it is immaterial, at least as a rule, that an impediment of this kind may exist according to some other law such as the *lex loci celebrationis*.

These principles, however, are rather heavily qualified by exceptions, usually in favour of the *lex fori.*[1082] The reason is that

1077. Marriage Code of 1920, as amended, ch. 2 § 3.

1078. For examples of cases where both parties were subject to a law invalidating their marriage on such grounds see ENGLAND: Brook v. Brook (1861), 9 H.L.C. 193, [1861-73] All E.R. Rep. 493; Sottomayor v. De Barros (No. 1) (1877), 3 P.D. 1 (C.A.); In re De Wilton, [1900] 2 Ch. 481; SCOTLAND: Robertson v. Channing, 1928 S.L.T. 376; CANADA: Dejardin v. Dejardin, [1932] 2 W.W.R. 237 (Man. K.B.); Feiner v. Demkowicz (1973), 42 D.L.R. (3d) 165 (Ont. H.C.).

1079. See the decisions and writers cited *supra* n. 379-381.

1080. For an exception in ENGLISH law see *supra* s. 70, cf. *infra* at n. 1100-1101.

1081. For examples of such cases see ENGLAND: decisions cited *infra* n. 1094; AUSTRALIA: In the Will of Swan (1871), 2 V.R. (I.E. & M.) 47; CANADA: Crickmay v. Crickmay (1966), 60 D.L.R. (2d) 734 (B.C.C.A.); Reed (*alias* Frew) v. Reed (1969), 6 D.L.R. (3d) 617 (B.C.S.C.).

1082. In addition to the issues considered below, the problem of the incidental question may present itself in certain circumstances, namely, if the *lex fori* and the *lex causae* disagree as to the validity or the continued existence of a marriage or of an adoption alleged to create a forbidden relationship between the parties. In this respect, too, the *lex fori* is likely to prevail, at least in many situations. See *Dorenberg* 170; *A. Miele* 120-123;

the considerations of religion, morality and social policy underlying the rules as to prohibited relationships are often held to carry such force as to demand the application of those rules in respect of all marriages celebrated within the enacting country and to exclude the enforcement of foreign laws based on different policies.

This tendency is chiefly noticeable in cases where the relevant foreign law is more liberal than the *lex fori,* authorising the intermarriage of parties who are within the prohibited degrees as defined by the latter law. In some countries, for instance in *England* and *Australia,* the position seems to be that all incapacities on account of consanguinity and affinity laid down by the *lex fori* must be taken into account when the marriage is celebrated locally.[1083] To that extent public policy does not leave any scope at all for the application of more permissive foreign laws. Although, for example, West German law allows marriages between uncle and niece, parties so related probably cannot marry each other in England even if they are both domiciled in West Germany whose law would therefore normally decide their capacity to marry by English standards of the conflict of laws, such a marriage being proscribed by English domestic law.[1084]

Usually, however, a somewhat less rigorous approach is adopted, especially in countries whose domestic law permits the grant of dispensation from prohibitions affecting certain kinds or degrees of relationship. In general, such prohibitions are not considered to evince a policy strong enough to override the normal principles of choice of law and will not be invoked to prevent the application of more liberal foreign laws permitting the marriage without dispensation. This concept underlies the Hague Convention of 1902, which draws a distinction between local prohibitions, imposed by reason of consanguinity or affinity, of an absolute nature and

---

in part otherwise *Gamillscheg,* Kommentar, art. 13 no. 385. No decisions in point are known.

1083. See for ENGLISH law *supra* at n. 561, for AUSTRALIAN law the statutory provisions cited *supra* n. 636. For rules to the same effect on the present issue in FINNISH, HUNGARIAN and YUGOSLAV law, as well as in certain bilateral treaties concluded by YUGOSLAVIA, see the references *supra* n. 635. A similar view has been voiced in FRANCE: *Audinet* 187-188, and in SWITZERLAND: *Götz,* art. 100 no. 14, art. 107 no. 19; but see for the prevailing opinion in these countries *infra* at n. 1086 and 1090-1091, respectively.

1084. For the ENGLISH prohibition see the Marriage Act 1949, s. 1 (1) and Sched. 1, Part I, as amended.

those capable of dispensation; the former alone can justify a refusal on the part of the local authorities of the Contracting States to celebrate a marriage between foreigners which would be allowed by their *lex patriae.*[1085] A delimitation of the range of prohibitive public policy along substantially similar lines has been endorsed by statutes, or received the support of courts and writers, in a considerable number of countries, including *Belgium, France, West Germany, Italy, Norway* and *Sweden.*[1086] Probably, for instance, German nationals related as uncle and niece can get married in France, as permitted by their *lex patriae,* notwithstanding that they are within the prohibited degrees of French law; for by French law (in contrast to English law in the earlier example) this impediment is dispensable.[1087] By and large, the use of this criterion tends to restrict the scope of prohibitive public policy to cases involving an attempted marriage between members of the nuclear family, which hardly ever occur in the practice of conflict of laws.

Essentially similar results are sometimes achieved even in countries where, as a matter of domestic law, all marriage impediments based on consanguinity and affinity are treated as absolute. In *Bulgaria,* for instance, it is provided by statute that parties of foreign nationality desiring to marry in that country are subject to the conditions of their respective *leges patriae* and, in addition, to the local prohibitions of marriage between ascendants and descendants in the direct line of consanguinity and between brother and sister; but such parties are exempt from the more far-reaching impediments of this kind laid down, without any possibility of dispensation, by Bulgarian domestic law.[1088] The same position seems to prevail in *Greece.*[1089] In *Switzerland,* too, such a restrictive view of the demands of public policy has been advocated by several writers.[1090] Other Swiss writers, however, claim a

1085. Art. 2 par. 1 no. 1. See the comments cited *supra* n. 634.

1086. BELGIUM: *Graulich* 157; FRANCE: *Batiffol and Lagarde* II 38-39; *Bischoff* no. 65; *Vincent and Ponsard* no. 89-91; WEST GERMANY: *Dölle,* IPR 108; *Gamillscheg,* Kommentar, art. 13 no. 236, 238, 384; *Henrich* 303, 304; *Stöcker,* Ordre public 105-106 (but see for stricter views, *Raape,* Kommentar 808; *Wolff,* IPR 191); ITALY: CC art. 116 par. 2 in conjunction with art. 87; NORWAY: *Gaarder* 133-134; SWEDEN: Act of 8 July 1904, as amended, ch. 1 § 3 no. 2. For certain LATIN AMERICAN countries see *supra* n. 630-632.

1087. FRENCH CC art. 163, 164 no. 3.

1088. FC art. 91 par. 3 in conjunction with art. 10.

1089. See *Bendermacher-Geroussis* 6-7.

1090. See *Muret* 78-79; *Schnitzer* 340-341; *Spivak* 57-58; *Vaucher* 540.

broader scope for this notion, urging that no effect can be given to foreign laws which would permit the celebration in Switzerland of a marriage of uncle and niece or aunt and nephew, or between persons allied in the direct line of affinity, such relations being absolutely disqualified for marriage by Swiss law.[1091]

Another mitigation of the demands of public policy was introduced by the Hague Convention of 1902: even if a country is opposed, on grounds of public policy, to the celebration of a marriage within the absolutely prohibited degrees of relationship as specified by its own law, it cannot refuse to recognise the validity of such a marriage if it has been solemnised nevertheless in accordance with the *lex patriae*.[1092] On this point, too, the example of the convention has been of some importance as a source of inspiration for similar solutions in certain Continental and Scandinavian countries.[1093]

The interest of protecting existing marriages which is expressed in these rules is of greater significance in cases where the marriage has been entered into in a foreign country in compliance with the appropriate foreign law. Such a marriage will almost invariably be upheld even if the parties are within the absolutely prohibited degrees of relationship of the *lex fori* and its celebration in the country of the forum would have been refused for reasons of public policy. In an *English* case, for instance, where a marriage celebrated in Egypt, between a Jewish uncle and niece domiciled there, was recognised because it was valid by the relevant Egyptian law, the court expressly declined to accede to the view that such a marriage, although absolutely forbidden by English domestic law, must be rejected as contrary to English public policy.[1094] The

1091. SWISS CC art. 100 no. 1 and 2. See *Beck*, before art. 59 no. 80, art. 7 c no. 47-49; *Götz*, art. 100 no. 14, art. 107 no. 19. Of the same opinion for cases of consanguinity (CC art. 100 no. 1), but not for those of affinity (CC art. 100 no. 2), see *Stauffer*, art. 7 c no. 5. It appears to be common ground that the demands of public policy do not extend to such relationships created by adoption as constitute an absolute impediment to marriage by SWISS law (CC art. 100 no. 3).

1092. Art. 2 par. 2. See the comments cited *supra* n. 634 and the text pertaining to n. 638-639.

1093. See the FINNISH and SWEDISH provisions cited *supra* n. 635, cf. n. 638. And see for SWISS law: *Beck*, art. 7 f no. 153; *Spivak* 58.

1094. Cheni v. Cheni, [1965] P. 85, 92-100. See also In re Bozzelli's Settlement, [1902] 1 Ch. 751 (marriage in Italy between a woman and her deceased husband's brother recognised because it was valid by ITALIAN law, the law of the common domicile of the spouses, although it was invalid by

continued on page 328

same position would doubtless be taken in those Continental countries whose domestic law is opposed to marriages between uncle and niece (aunt and nephew), or between persons even more distantly related.[1095]

A different course seems only conceivable in extreme circumstances. A possible example occurs in the case of a marriage between a half-brother and half-sister. Assuming that parties so related, both Swedish nationals domiciled in Sweden, have married in that country on the strength of a dispensation obtained in conformity with Swedish law (*supra* at n. 1077), their union will be valid in Sweden the law of which governs their capacity to marry by any test that may be employed. Nevertheless, such a marriage would possibly be refused recognition for most purposes in countries whose domestic law regards it as incestuous, at all events if the parties came to live in such a country.[1096]

Interventions of public policy are rare in the converse type of situation where the parties are within the prohibited degrees of the applicable foreign law, although they would be free to marry by the standards of the local law. It is usually thought that effect must be given to rules of foreign law importing a more stringent regulation of this matter than the *lex fori,* as may be the case either because those rules establish wider degrees or other kinds of prohibited relationship or because, in contrast to the latter law, they do not contemplate the possibility of a dispensation.[1097]

---

continued from page 327

ENGLISH domestic law as it then stood). For comments on these cases see: *P.B. Carter* (1962-1963) 474-475; *Cheshire,* Husband and Wife 143; *Cheshire and North* 349; *Kahn-Freund,* Reflections 41-42; *Latey* 848-849; *Morris* 113; *Swan* 35-37; *Sykes,* Conflict 76-77; *Webb,* Potentially Polygamous Marriages and Capacity to Marry: 12 I.C.L.Q. 672, 677-679 (1963).

1095. See, e.g., FRANCE: *Bischoff* no. 72; WEST GERMANY: *Gamillscheg,* Kommentar, art. 13 no. 238; *Raape and Sturm* 216; SWITZERLAND: *Beck,* before art. 59 no. 80, art. 7 c no. 47, art. 7 f no. 61, 153; *Vaucher* 553-554. But see for a considerably stricter rule art. 40 of the BUSTAMANTE CODE, cf. *supra* at n. 640.

1096. See, e.g., ENGLAND and SCOTLAND: *Anton* 279; *Dicey and Morris* 73, 261-262; *North* 131; FRANCE: *Batiffol and Lagarde* II 39; *Bischoff* no. 72; SWITZERLAND: *Beck,* art. 7 f no. 61. But see for NORWAY, *Gaarder* 133-134.

1097. See, e.g., BELGIUM: *Graulich* 157 n. 7; ENGLAND: Sottomayor v. De Barros (No. 1) (1877), 3 P.D. 1 (C.A.); FRANCE: *Bischoff* no. 68; *Vincent and Ponsard* no. 89; cf. the decision of Cour Chambéry 7 Feb. 1885, Clunet 1888, 796; WEST GERMANY: OLG Düsseldorf 8 April 1969, IPRspr. 1968/69 no. 72; *Gamillscheg,* Kommentar, art. 13 no. 235, 384; *Raape,* IPR 256-257; *Wuppermann* 86-87; SWITZERLAND: *Götz,* art. 100 no. 14; *Vaucher* 540.

Although, for instance, marriages between uncle and niece are lawful in West Germany, persons so connected will be precluded from marrying there if they are, or if one of them is, of Greek nationality, for the application of the prohibitory rule of Greek law does not offend against the German notion of public policy.[1098]

Nevertheless, it may be doubted whether this traditional attitude will prevail in all cases. It can scarcely be excluded that the overall tendency in modern law to cut down the list of prohibitions because of consanguinity and affinity will have repercussions in the conflict of laws, contributing to the build-up of a more vigorous policy against foreign laws extending those prohibitions far beyond the limits prescribed by the *lex fori* and possibly conceived as out of keeping with current notions of the matter. Although such a policy could not justify a course whereby the relevant foreign law was set aside in cases lacking a substantial connection to the forum country, the position might be different if, for instance, one of the parties was a domiciled national of that country and the parties intended to make their home there.[1099] At least if a marriage has already been celebrated in such circumstances, there would seem to be a good case for refusing to give effect to the foreign law requiring its invalidation.

The only decision bearing exactly on this point is that, already considered in another context, of the *English* court in the second *Sottomayor* case.[1100] That case, it will be recalled, was concerned with choice of law in relation to consanguinity, the spouses being first cousins incapable of intermarriage according to the law of Portugal where one of them was domiciled at the time of the marriage. The court, ignoring the foreign incapacity, upheld the marriage in reliance on English law which was the *lex loci celebrationis* and the *lex domicilii* of the other spouse.[1101] Despite all criticisms that have been levelled at this decision, it is not difficult to feel sympathy for the result reached by the court, and the time may indeed be ripe for a revaluation of the decision in the light of modern ideas of consanguinity and affinity as impediments to marriage.

1098. For the GREEK prohibition, which extends to collaterals of the fourth degree, see CC art. 1356.

1099. See for NORWEGIAN law *Gaarder* 134. Cf. for SWISS law *Vaucher* 540.

1100. Sottomayor v. De Barros (No. 2) (1879), 5 P.D. 94. See *supra* s. 70.

1101. Note, however, that the scope of the rule established by this decision seems to be narrowed by s. 1 (3) of the Marriage (Enabling) Act 1960; cf. *supra* at n. 418 and 602.

be. *Religious Marriage Impediments*

107. *Introductory.* Numerous marriage impediments forming part of the secular law of various countries derive their origin from, or have been profoundly influenced by, religious laws. Here it is only proposed to deal with a "residue" of such impediments, not treated elsewhere, which involve a limitation of the right to marry on account of religious affiliation.

The most important of these limitations is that based on difference of religion (*impedimentum disparitatis cultus*), which seems to figure in every developed system of religious law.[1102] The laws of the Roman Catholic and of the Orthodox Churches, for instance, forbid marriages between a Christian and a non-Christian.[1103] In the past, up to the years around the Second World War, this prohibition was recognised as part of the secular law of several Continental European countries, such as Austria, Bulgaria, Poland and Yugoslavia, and also played a rather prominent role in the conflict of laws.[1104] With the secularisation of the matrimonial law of these countries, however, the impediment of difference of religion disappeared from their laws. Today it only remains in force in a few Mediterranean countries, including Greece and (as part of the canon law applicable to Catholic marriages) Spain.[1105]

Other examples of this impediment are afforded by Jewish and Islamic law.[1106] Jewish law prohibits, and treats as null and void, marriages between Jews and non-Jews. Islamic law distinguishes between men and women: while a Moslem woman lacks the

1102. See *Scheftelowitz* 91-94, 105-106. For other comparative surveys see *Gamillscheg*, Kommentar, art. 13 no. 436-437; *Mergenthaler* 135.

1103. For the law of the Roman Catholic Church see CIC canon 1070; cf. canon 1060, which contains a prohibitive (dispensable) impediment to the intermarriage of two Christians one of whom belongs to the Catholic Church and the other to an heretical or schismatic sect (*impedimentum mixtae religionis*). See *Dieckmann*, Eheschliessung 108; *Scheftelowitz* 45-46, 93-94. For the Orthodox Church see *Bergmann(-Ferid)*, Die religiösen Eherechte – Das Eherecht der orthodoxen Kirchen, *sub* 3 b) hh).

1104. See for AUSTRIAN law (ABGB § 64) as it stood until 1938, *G. Walker* 599-602.

1105. GREECE: CC art. 1353; SPAIN: CC art. 42 and 75 (referring to the canon law). The same rule prevails in ITALY in so far as concordat marriages are concerned, those marriages being governed by the canon law (*supra* n. 548), but with the essential difference that the parties can always escape the impediment by choosing the civil form of ceremony alternatively available under the law of that country.

1106. See *Scheftelowitz* 38, 52-53, 91-92. For HINDU law see *idem* 56, 58.

capacity to marry any other than a Moslem partner, a Moslem man is allowed to marry, in addition to his co-religionists, women belonging to "the people of the book", *i.e.* those professing the Christian or the Jewish religion, but not otherwise. These restrictions still retain their vigour and are accepted (sometimes in a slightly modified form) as part of the law of the land in Israel, Egypt, Iraq, Morocco, Pakistan and elsewhere in the Islamic world.[1107]

Problems of the conflict of laws in regard to marriage impediments based on difference of religion have presented themselves with some frequency and are still a matter of practical interest, largely owing to the increased present-day contacts and population movements between certain Mediterranean and Arab countries, on the one side, and European countries where such impediments are unknown, on the other. These questions will be examined in what follows (*infra* s. 108).

There are many other typically religious prohibitions or restrictions on marriage, some of which played a considerable part in the past.[1108] Few if any of them, however, are of much significance today, at any rate in the context of conflict of laws. The problems relating to these matters will only be briefly adverted to here (*infra* s. 109).

Before turning to the issues of conflict of laws, however, it should be recalled that efforts have been made at the international level with a view to securing recognition of the right to marry as a human right to be enjoyed without distinction on grounds such as religion. This work has resulted in several conventions and other international instruments which are likely to have repercussions both in domestic law and in the conflict of laws concerning disabilities to marry of the kind under consideration.

The starting-point of this development is the Universal Declaration of Human Rights adopted in 1948, which proclaims that "men and women of full age, without any limitation due to race, nationality or religion, have the right to marry and to found a family" and that "everyone is entitled to all the rights and freedoms set forth in this Declaration, without distinction of any

1107. For ISRAEL see *Scheftelowitz* 178. For various ISLAMIC countries see the surveys cited *supra* n. 1102 and *Bergmann(-Ferid),* Die religiösen Eherechte – Das islamische Eherecht, *sub* 3 b) dd).

1108. For comparative surveys see *Dölle,* Familienrecht 93; *Gamillscheg,* Kommentar, art. 13 no. 446-451.

kind," *inter alia* on grounds of religion.[1109] While this declaration did not create immediately binding law, the principles embodied in it have been endorsed by later conventions concluded both within and outside the framework of the United Nations and accepted by a considerable number of States.

The first instance of such transformation into binding rules of law is the European Convention for the Protection of Human Rights and Fundamental Freedoms of 1950. In dealing with the right to marry this convention, it is true, refers to "the national laws governing the exercise of this right" (art. 12), thereby apparently depriving the right to be protected of any independent element. This provision, however, must be read in conjunction with the non-discrimination clause contained in the convention (art. 14), which forbids discrimination on any ground, including religion, with regard to the enjoyment of the rights secured by the convention. Read together, these provisions seem to create an obligation on the part of the Contracting States to eliminate religious obstacles to marriage from their domestic laws.[1110]

Another instrument of some interest is the UN Convention on Consent to Marriage, etc., concluded in New York in 1962. In the preamble to this convention the Contracting States "recall" the principle of the right to marry stated in the Universal Declaration and "reaffirm" their commitment to a policy of ensuring complete freedom in the choice of a spouse.[1111] Clearer language is used in the International Covenant on Civil and Political Rights of 1966, which has now come into force and which has so far been accepted by some 50 States.[1112] In substance, this Covenant reproduces both the provision on the right to marry and the prohibition of

1109. Art. 16 (1) and art. 2 par. 1, respectively. For comments see *Goldman* 451, 459; *Neuhaus*, Europäisches Familienrecht 421-422 (proposing a restrictive interpretation); *Scheftelowitz* 112-114 (do.); *Serick* 402-403, 404.

1110. See, e.g., *Dieckmann*, Eheschliessung 108; *Fawcett*, The Application of the European Convention on Human Rights (Oxford 1969) 225; *Gamillscheg*, Kommentar, before art. 13 no. 66; *Guradze* 192-193, cf. 181; *A. Miele* 152-153, 160-161; *Moser* 159; *Opsahl* 190-191; *Partsch*, Die Rechte und Freiheiten der europäischen Menschenrechtskonvention (Berlin 1966) 213-217; *Schwelb* 119. But see for a restrictive interpretation, excluding the impediment of *disparitas cultus* from the scope of prohibited discrimination: *Neuhaus*, Europäisches Familienrecht 421-422; *Scheftelowitz* 114-116.

1111. Par. 2 and 4 of the preamble. On the interpretation and legal significance of these parts of the preamble see *Schwelb*, Marriage and Human Rights: 12 Am. J. Comp. L. 337, 371-376 (1963). In accord, *Guradze* 192.

1112. For a list of ratifications etc. see the annual publication of *Multilateral Treaties in respect of which The Secretary-General Performs Depositary Functions* (UN Doc. ST/LEG/SER. D).

discrimination set out in the Universal Declaration.[1113] As in the case of the European Convention of 1950, it seems to follow that marriage impediments based, *inter alia,* on grounds of religion are incompatible with the Covenant.[1114]

Admittedly, the interpretation of the above-cited human rights provisions leaves room for doubt, not least as to their impact on issues of conflict of laws. Nevertheless, there is no mistaking their general policy, which is clearly adverse to any discrimination in respect of the right to marry, religious affiliation being regarded as one among other invidious grounds of distinction. The provisions in question thus reflect and themselves tend to reinforce a policy which has now for a rather long time prevailed in large parts of the world, including nearly all European countries. In this way, if not more directly, they are likely to affect the attitude towards foreign laws, referred to by the conflicts rules of the forum, which sanction distinctions on grounds such as religion.

108. *Difference of Religion.* In the normal course of things, prohibitions against the intermarriage of persons of different religion would be applicable when, and only when, provided by the personal law of either spouse at the time of the marriage. In fact, this is the minimum scope claimed for such incapacitating rules in countries where they form part of the *lex fori.*[1115] Clearly, for instance, a marriage between a Christian and a non-Christian cannot take place in Greece if either party is of Greek nationality, since such a marriage is forbidden by Greek law which applies as the personal law of that party.[1116] Similarly, a Moslem woman of

1113. Art. 23 (2) and 2 (1), respectively.

1114. See *Schwelb* 118-119. Cf. *Tornaritis,* The Right to Marry and Found a Family Especially under the Law of Cyprus: Mélanges offerts à Polys Modinos (Paris 1968) 320, 329-330.

1115. Some doubts existed as to the interpretation of the earlier rule of AUSTRIAN law in ABGB § 64 (*supra* n. 1104). In the opinion of some writers, the spirit of this provision was to prevent a Christian from marrying a non-Christian (rather than conversely), with the consequence that the prohibition was limited to cases where the former party's capacity was governed by AUSTRIAN law; see *F. Kahn* 64; *Muret* 26-27; *Spivak* 44, 45 n. 13. By the weight of opinion, however, the provision was to be construed as bilateral, applicable whenever either the Christian or the other party was subject to AUSTRIAN law as his personal law; see *Gamillscheg,* Kommentar, art. 13 no. 438 with references, and the decisions of the POLISH Supreme Court (applying the prohibition as part of the then POLISH law) 22 July 1924, Rev. crit. d.i.p. 1925, 440, and 28 Nov. 1933, Z. osteur. R. 1934/35, 444.

1116. For the view that the prohibition in GREEK CC art. 1353 is to be treated as bilateral see: *Bendermacher-Geroussis* 3; *Ehrenzweig, Fragistas and Yiannopoulos* 72-73; *Maridakis* 216.

Egyptian nationality cannot marry a non-Moslem foreigner in Egypt, nor will such a marriage, if entered into abroad, be recognised as valid in Egypt, where the rule of Egyptian law (adopted from Islamic law) proscribing and invalidating disparate unions of this kind will prevail.[1117]

Usually, however, impediments founded on difference of religion are carried beyond the limits of the personal law and often enforced in respect of all locally solemnised marriages, regardless of the domicile or nationality of the parties.[1118] In an *Egyptian* case, for instance, the court annulled a marriage, celebrated at the British consulate in Cairo, between a Christian British subject and a Moslem woman of Turkish nationality, notwithstanding that the union was valid by the personal laws of both parties.[1119] To sanction such an interreligious marriage was held to be repugnant to the Egyptian notion of public policy, which was identified with that of Islamic law. Similarly in *Israel* the prohibition of marriage between a Jew and a non-Jew applies to all parties marrying within the country, whatever their domicile or nationality.[1120] To that extent the principle of territoriality prevails. A more liberal position has, however, been adopted in a *Greek* case, where the court upheld a marriage, celebrated in accordance with Turkish law before a Turkish consul in Greece, between two Turkish nationals one of whom was a member of the Orthodox Church and the other of the Jewish religion, although the union would have been invalid by Greek domestic law.[1121]

The attitude to *foreign* laws containing rules of this kind varies

1117. Mixed Court of Appeal 11 June 1913, *Elgeddawy* 154-155. Today the same result would be reached by applying the conflicts provision of the EGYPTIAN CC art. 14, see *supra* at n. 336. And see to the same effect for MOROCCO: *Bourely*, Le droit international privé du Maroc indépendant (suite et fin): Rev. crit. d.i.p. 1962, 445, 468-469; *Decroux*, case note: Clunet 1961, 518.

1118. Under art. 2 par. 3 of the HAGUE CONVENTION of 1902 the State of celebration is entitled to prohibit a marriage which would contravene its laws "by reason of an obstacle of a religious character", and to invalidate such a marriage if already celebrated within its territory (though this is subject to the proviso in art. 6 par. 1 sent. 2, according to which the State in question cannot object to the solemnisation of such a marriage in diplomatic or consular form within its territory). See *supra* at n. 634 and 639.

1119. Court of Cairo 6 Oct. 1953, Rev. Egypt. 10 (1954) 147. See *Benattar* 58-59; *Elgeddawy* 154-156; *Linant de Bellefonds* 830, 840.

1120. *Scheftelowitz* 162, 178.

1121. Court of Appeals of Athens 1937 no. 2462, Clunet 1938, 904, note Tenekidès; see, approvingly, *Maridakis* 171-172.

with the forum's own policy in the matter. Where a corresponding disability is known to the *lex fori*, there would seem to be no difficulty in giving effect to the foreign rule referred to by the conflicts system of the forum. In *Egypt*, for example, a marriage performed at the French consulate in Cairo, between a Jewish man of Tunisian and a Christian woman of French nationality, was held invalid because it was so by Jewish law, which applied in the particular case as part of the law of Tunisia governing the man's capacity to marry.[1122] A different position has been taken where the prohibition of the relevant foreign law, in contrast to Islamic law, extended to the intermarriage of a Moslem man and a Christian or Jewish woman. Thus in another Egyptian case involving a marriage between an Englishman of the Moslem faith and a Christian woman of Greek nationality, the court refused to grant a decree of nullity for *disparitas cultus* as required by the normally applicable Greek law, because to do so would have violated what was regarded as a fundamental principle of Islamic law recognised as an integral part of the *lex fori.*[1123] This view would probably be endorsed in Arab countries generally.[1124]

In countries where impediments owing to difference of religion are wholly unknown as a matter of domestic law, such impediments provided by foreign laws are usually denied any recognition. Various reasons have been advanced in order to justify the exclusion on this point of the law otherwise appropriate for capacity to marry.

One line of argument is to be found in some *English* and *Scottish* decisions. It is, in substance, that difference of religion does not represent a general disability to marry and therefore is not in the same class as impediments such as consanguinity or affinity which create a true incapacity to marry and which, as part of the law of the domicile, British courts are bound to recognise.[1125] Similarly the *Italian* Court of Cassation in one case took the view that a provision forbidding interreligious marriages falls outside the

1122. Court of Cairo 30 Dec. 1952, *Elgeddawy* 151-152. For another similar decision see *idem* 108.

1123. Court of Cairo 5 Jan. 1954, *Elgeddawy* 153-154.

1124. See *Benattar* 58.

1125. ENGLAND: Chetti v. Chetti, [1909] P. 67, 78; SCOTLAND: Lendrum v. Chakravarti, 1929 S.L.T. 96, 103; MacDougall v. Chitnavis, 1937 S.C. 390, 402-404, 407. Cf. *supra* s. 64, especially at n. 532. And see among writers, who usually rely on public policy to reach the same result: *Anton* 283; *Dicey and Morris* 231-233, 274-275; *Falconbridge* 709; *Holder* 948; *North* 131; *Nygh* 410; *Pearl* 132-133; *Wolff*, PIL 338.

notion of capacity to marry and therefore does not have any claim to consideration even though it forms part of the personal law (the *lex patriae*) governing that matter.[1126]

This reasoning fails to carry conviction. It is true, of course, that impediments due to difference of religion do not purport to affect a person's general capacity to marry but only his right "to make selected marriages".[1127] This, however, is no more than a way of saying that such impediments are relative rather than absolute, and does not afford any tenable ground for excluding them from the notion of capacity to marry. It would surely be preposterous to suggest that all relative impediments (including consanguinity and affinity which, just as difference of religion, only restrain a person from entering into "selected marriages") should be denied extraterritorial effect on the allegation that they do not concern capacity to marry.

More appropriately, the principle of public policy has been invoked to reject foreign incapacities imposed by reference to religion. At least in Continental Europe this is the usual line of defence against foreign laws prohibiting a marriage because of difference of religion.[1128]

The view that impediments of this kind must be repudiated as contrary to public policy has prevailed for a long time in countries such as *Belgium, France, Italy* and *Switzerland.*[1129] The attitude of those countries is reflected in the Hague Convention of 1902, which – as the only "permissive" exception from the rule of the

1126. Cass. 1 Aug. 1946, Giur. Compl. Cass. Civ. 21 (1946) I 440, note Messina. Cf. the ITALIAN cases cited *infra* n. 1129.

1127. MacDougall v. Chitnavis, 1937 S.C. 390 at 407.

1128. See *Gamillscheg,* Kommentar, art. 13 no. 440-441.

1129. See among relevant decisions and opinions, many of which have reference to religious marriage impediments generally: BELGIUM: Civ. Liège 5 Nov. 1958, Jur. Liège 1958/59, 171; *Graulich* 156; FRANCE: Cour Paris 17 Nov. 1922, Clunet 1923, 85, Rev. crit. d.i.p. 1922/23, 437 (*contra:* Trib. Seine 15 July 1920, Rev. crit. d.i.p. 1922/23, 778); *Batiffol and Lagarde* II 40-41; *Bischoff* no. 68; *Elgeddawy* 131, 234-235; *Maury* 149-151; *Niboyet* V 343, 349; *Vincent and Ponsard* no. 93-94; ITALY (as regards marriages in civil form): Trib. Livorno 5 May 1894, Clunet 1898, 415; App. Venezia 7 Dec. 1910, Clunet 1911, 1326; App. Trieste 17 Feb. 1942, Foro it. 1943 I 290, aff'd Cass. 19 May 1943, Foro it. 1943 I 930 (see also the cases cited *supra* n. 1126 and *infra* n. 1144); *Giardina* 28-29; *A. Miele* 39, 91-92, 149-159; *Monaco* 162; *Vitta* II 195-196 (*contra: Morelli* 102); SWITZERLAND: Regierungsrat Kanton Zürich 11 Nov. 1943, cited by BG 26 May 1950, BGE 76 I 172, 173; BG 29 March 1950, BGE 76 IV 109, 116-117 (*obiter*); *Beck,* art. 7 c no. 26, 56-57; *Muret* 82-84; *Schnitzer* 341, 350; *Stauffer,* art. 7 c no. 5 (Nachtrag), art. 7 e no. 14; *Vaucher* 541; see also *supra* n. 744.

lex patriae – admits that a marriage between foreigners may be celebrated on the strength of the local law of a Contracting State if the prohibition of the *lex patriae* is based exclusively on grounds of a religious nature.[1130]

In some other countries, particularly in *(West) Germany,* opinions have been much divided on this issue.[1131] Until a rather recent date the weight of (West) German opinion was in favour of respecting foreign incapacities by reason of difference of religion, especially where the effect was to preclude the celebration of a proposed marriage.[1132] Even where the question arose after the marriage had come into existence, (West) German courts were usually prepared to annul it on the strength of the *lex patriae.*[1133] The allegation that to do so violated the public policy of the forum was rejected, *inter alia* on the ground that the impediment under review does not involve any discrimination against either party on account of his religion because (in contrast with distinctions based on race or colour) it does not express any idea of the superiority of one or the inferiority of another religion but is only intended for the spiritual welfare of the members of the religious community concerned.

In recent years, however, there has been a clear shift of the balance of opinion in West Germany. In a leading case, decided by the Federal Supreme Court, it was held that the impediment of difference of religion imposed by the *lex patriae* of one of the parties to a proposed marriage in West Germany must be disregarded as contrary to public policy where, as in that case, the other intending spouse is a German national.[1134] In the opinion

1130. Art. 3. For comments on this provision see: *Beck,* ESchlKonv. art. 3 no. 1-18; *Buzzati* 226-253; *Gamillscheg,* Kommentar, art. 13 no. 956-959; *F. Kahn* 114-122; *A. Miele* 142-143; *Rabel* 301-303; *Travers* I 361-380.

1131. See *Gamillscheg,* Kommentar, art. 13 no. 439, 442-444; *Wuppermann* 79-84.

1132. For older practice see the communication reproduced in RabelsZ 4 (1930) 390, 398-399. More recent decisions holding the same way include: OLG Oldenburg 11 April 1967, IPRspr. 1966/67 no. 68; OLG Hamm 17 Nov. 1970, IPRspr. 1970 no. 48 (reversed by the decision cited *infra* n. 1134). And see among writers: *Gamillscheg,* Grundrechte 335-336; *Henrich* 301-302; *Neuhaus,* Religionsverschiedenheit; *idem,* Grundbegriffe 373-374; *Serick* 403-404.

1133. OLG Karlsruhe 28 March 1917, LZ 1917, 1012; RG 16 May 1931, RGZ 132, 416, 418, IPRspr. 1931 no. 59; RG 10 Oct. 1935, RGZ 148, 383; LG Bremen 12 July 1966, IPRspr. 1966/67 no. 60. But see for an early decision to the contrary, OLG Hamburg 6 Oct. 1908, NiemeyersZ 18 (1908) 541, Clunet 1909, 785.

1134. BGH 12 May 1971, BGHZ 56, 180, IPRspr. 1971 no. 40.

of the court, such impediments cannot be viewed as solely concerned with the spiritual welfare of the adherents of the particular religion; they also serve as an instrument of protection of the religious community itself by keeping its members separate from non-believers and thus do indeed have a discriminatory effect. The view that public policy bars the enforcement of prohibitions of this kind, at least where the case presents a strong connection with West Germany, has been adopted by several other decisions[1135] and is now also shared by most writers.[1136] This development has been inspired by both by constitutional provisions for the protection of basic rights and freedoms and by the bans on religious discrimination laid down by various international conventions on human rights.[1137] Still, however, it is somewhat doubtful how far the new practice will be carried, in particular in cases where both parties are foreign nationals.

In other countries, too, possessing a secularised system of substantive matrimonial law, the prevailing tendency is today to set up public policy as a bar to the application of rules of foreign law sanctioning religious impediments to marriage such as *disparitas cultus*. This is so almost everywhere in Western Europe and

1135. For cases involving a proposed marriage in West Germany see: OLG Karlsruhe 6 May 1965, IPRspr. 1970 no. 44 (where, however, the decision was rested on the ground that the marriage would be recognised as valid in the foreign country concerned despite the violation of its prohibition, cf. *infra* n. 1142); OLG München 1 June 1970, IPRspr. 1970 no. 47 (relying on public policy); OLG Hamm 3 Sept. 1976, IPRspr. 1976 no. 33 (do. in a case where both intending spouses were of foreign nationality but habitually resident in West Germany, one of them having very strong connections with that country). And see for a decision refusing to annul a marriage already celebrated in a foreign (third) country, OLG München 25 Feb. 1969, IPRspr. 1968/69 no. 71, cf. the expert opinion in IPG 1967/68 no. 19 (Hamburg).

1136. See, e.g., *Böhmer*, Die Traubereitschaftserklärung, Ein Beitrag zur DA 1968: StAZ 1968, 178, 179, 181; *Dieckmann*, Eheschliessung 108; *Kegel*, Kommentar, art. 13 no. 111; *Mergenthaler* 134-137; *Raape and Sturm* 205-206, 220; *Stöcker*, Ordre public 106; *idem*, Religion 39-40; *Wengler*, case note: JZ 1964, 621, 623; *Wolff*, IPR 64, 190; *Wuppermann* 84.

1137. In the latter respect see particularly the decisions of OLG München 1 June 1970, IPRspr. 1970 no. 47, and of BGH 12 May 1971, BGHZ 56, 180 at 190, both invoking the preamble to the UN Convention on Consent to Marriage, etc., of 1962 (*supra* at n. 1111). There is a divergency of opinion as to the relevance of the European Human Rights Convention of 1950 to this issue: do the provisions of this convention dealing with the right to marry extend to cases governed by the law of a foreign country which is not a party to the convention? For some different answers see the writers cited *supra* n. 1110.

Scandinavia,[1138] in the socialist countries of Eastern Europe,[1139] as well as in various parts of Latin America.[1140]

A marriage created by virtue of the public policy of the country of celebration, in defiance of a prohibition for difference of religion laid down by the personal law, will normally not be recognised as valid in the foreign country whose law was ignored.[1141] An exception occurs in *Israel* where such a marriage will be upheld by the temporal courts in reliance on the *lex loci celebrationis* even if the spouses are, or one of them is, of Israeli domicile or nationality.[1142]

If a nullity decree has been granted to the spouses in their home country because of difference of religion, the further question may be presented as to whether such a decree will be recognised in a country whose public policy would have been opposed to the grant of the decree and which, possibly, was invoked to permit the celebration of the marriage. In most countries the answer to this question is uncertain in the absence of authority. For *English* law, however, it is well settled that the recognition of the decree will not be affected by the grounds on which it is based.[1143] The contrary has been held by an *Italian* decision extending the principle of public policy so as to preclude recogni-

1138. Among countries not mentioned already see AUSTRIA: *Schwind*, Ehen von Griechen 176; *idem*, IPR 141, 147; NETHERLANDS: Rb. Rotterdam 13 Nov. 1967, N.J. 1969 no. 46, *Joppe* 50 no. 12; SWEDEN: *Eek* 242.

1139. See generally *Szászy* 345; and for CZECHOSLOVAKIA: *Knapp and Eliáš* 162; EAST GERMANY: *FGB-Kommentar* 447; HUNGARY: *Réczei* 357; YUGOSLAVIA: *Tchirkovitch* 224, 237.

1140. E.g., VENEZUELA: CC art. 105.

1141. Cf. *supra* at n. 1117.

1142. See: *Arndt* 250-251; *Bergmann(-Ferid)*, Die religiösen Eherechte — Das jüdische Eherecht, *sub* 1; *Scheftelowitz* 179. This "self-limitation" on the part of ISRAELI law, in its turn, has been invoked by some WEST GERMAN courts as a ground (additional to that of public policy) justifying their refusal to take the prohibition of that law into account when deciding on the permissibility or on the validity of a marriage involving an Israeli national. See OLG Karlsruhe 6 May 1965, IPRspr. 1970 no. 44; OLG München 25 Feb. 1969, IPRspr. 1968/69 no. 71; cf. BGH 12 May 1971, BGHZ 56, 180 at 186 (left open). This question bears a certain resemblance to that formerly raised by the provision of the AUSTRIAN ABGB § 4, the effect of which used to be discussed in terms of a problem of *renvoi;* see *Gamillscheg*, Kommentar, art. 13 no. 56-59.

1143. See generally *Pålsson*, Marriage, s. 285. An ISRAELI decree granted for difference of religion was recognised in Corbett v. Corbett, [1957] 1 All E.R. 621 (P.). In favour of the same solution for WEST GERMAN law see *Gamillscheg*, Kommentar, art. 13 no. 445.

tion of a foreign decree obtained on the ground of *disparitas cultus.*[1144]

109. *Other Impediments.* By the laws of the Roman Catholic and of the Orthodox Churches priests, monks and certain other persons who have taken a vow of chastity are forbidden to marry at all (*impedimenta ordinis* and *voti*).[1145] Those prohibitions are still recognised as part of the law of the land in a few European countries, including Greece and Spain.[1146]

Where such an impediment is prescribed by the *lex fori* it will clearly apply whenever the party labouring under the disability is himself subject to that law (by reason of his nationality), whether the marriage is celebrated locally or abroad. In *Spain,* for instance, a marriage of a Spanish priest, entered into in a foreign country in defiance of the prohibition of Spanish law, has been refused recognition.[1147]

A somewhat more doubtful point is whether these incapacitating rules are to be treated as bilateral, *i.e.* whether they can also prevent a national of the enacting country from marrying a priest etc. who, by his own personal law, is free to marry. The prevailing view is in favour of extending the disability to such cases.[1148] At least as regards *Spain,* however, the practical significance of this question is probably limited to marriages entered into outside the country; for as concerns marriages solemnised in Spain there is scarcely any doubt that the prohibitions of Spanish law demand

1144. App. Firenze 17 April 1953, Foro pad. 1954 I 69, note Biscottini; see *supra* n. 627.

1145. For the law of the Roman Catholic Church see CIC canons 1072-1073; *Scheftelowitz* 45, 90. For the Orthodox Church see *Bergmann(-Ferid),* Die religiösen Eherechte – Das Eherecht der orthodoxen Kirchen, *sub* 3 b) mm).

1146. GREECE: CC art. 1364. In SPAIN this impediment applies not only to Catholic marriages, which are entirely governed by the canon law (CC art. 75 in conjunction with art. 42), but also to marriages in civil form, CC art. 83 no. 4. For earlier AUSTRIAN law (ABGB § 63) see *G. Walker* 607-608.

1147. D.G.R.N. 4 June 1962, Rev. Esp. Der. Int. 17 (1964) 428, note Pecourt García, and earlier decisions cited in that note.

1148. GREECE: *Ehrenzweig, Fragistas and Yiannopoulos* 72-73; SPAIN: *Aguilar Benítez de Lugo* 243-245; *von Hoffmann and Ortiz-Arce* 664. A different view was often maintained in relation to the former rule of AUSTRIAN law; see Act. La Haye III (1900) 169; *Beck,* art. 7 c no. 22-23; *Buzzati* 104, 109-110; *F. Kahn* 64-65; *Spiwak* 44. Here too, however, the bilateral approach was endorsed by the weight of opinion, see *G. Walker* 609-610. See also *Gamillscheg,* Kommentar, art. 13 no. 446.

general application, whatever the domicile or the nationality of the intending spouses.[1149]

As with *disparitas cultus,* impediments of this kind will generally be ignored for reasons of public policy in countries to whose domestic law they are alien.[1150] The objections generally raised against rules of foreign law sanctioning a limitation of the right to marry due to religion seem to apply with added force here, since the effect of the *impedimentum ordinis* (or *voti*) is not only to bar a marriage across religious borders but to prevent a person from marrying at all.[1151]

In the past, numerous problems of the conflict of laws were caused by the impediment known as *impedimentum catholicismi,* which formed part of Austrian law until 1938 and which remained in force in Liechtenstein until 1974.[1152] The provisions concerning this impediment were to the effect (1) that a person belonging to the Roman Catholic Church, although he could in certain circumstances be validly divorced, could not marry again during the lifetime of the other spouse and (2) that such a person could not marry a partner divorced from a former spouse as long as the latter was alive. The difficulties created by those rules were in part similar to, but in part different from, those still occasioned by the laws of some Catholic countries, chiefly Spain, which do not recognise foreign divorces and which regard an existing marriage

1149. See *Aguilar Benítez de Lugo* 243-245; *Aguilar Navarro* 298-300.

1150. See the references *supra* n. 1125, 1129, 1130, 1136 and 1138-1140, most of which are also relevant to the *impedimenta ordinis* and *voti*. Specifically for those impediments see further ENGLAND: Sottomayor v. De Barros (No. 2) (1879), 5 P.D. 94, 104 (*obiter*); *M. Mann* 142-146 (with distinctions); FRANCE: *Bischoff* no. 32; *Elgeddawy* 132; *Vincent and Ponsard* no. 96 (*contra: Audinet* 184); ITALY: *A. Miele* 159-161; *M. Miele* 106-107; SWITZERLAND: *Beck,* art. 7 c no. 22, 56, 58. Only in WEST GERMANY, it seems, has this view met with major opposition in recent decades; see *Gamillscheg,* Kommentar, art. 13 no. 447 with references. There is little doubt, however, that the prevailing opinion is represented by a decision of OLG Hamm 26 Nov. 1973, IPRspr. 1973 no. 38, rejecting the *impedimentum ordinis* in the case of a proposed marriage between a Spanish priest and a German woman. For comments on this decision see *Brodach and Jayme,* case note: FamRZ 1974, 600 (critically); *Wuppermann* 85.

1151. Cf. *Neuhaus,* Grundbegriffe 373-374 who, while rejecting any general principle to the effect that religious impediments must be excluded from application, subscribes to the prevailing view in this particular case.

1152. See *Gamillscheg,* Kommentar, art. 13 no. 322; *Schwind,* Das "Ehehindernis des Katholizismus" in der Entwicklung des österreichischen Rechts: FamRZ 1966, 3-9; *G. Walker* 603. In LIECHTENSTEIN the impediment was abolished by the Marriage Act of 1973, which came into force on 1 June 1974.

as a bilateral impediment to a further marriage (*supra* s. 49-52, 84-90). The proper approach in this matter was much disputed, both in Austria itself and in certain other Continental countries, particularly in Germany, whose courts had frequent occasion to come into contact with the Austrian rules.[1153] In the course of time there grew up a marked tendency to restrict the scope of application, originally very wide, of the impediment in question.[1154] However, since all this now belongs to history, it is not proposed to go into the details of the development.

bf. *Impediments Based on Race*

110. Impediments against marriage due to race or colour have played a significant role, chiefly in the past, in various parts of the world.[1155] A well-known instance is the United States, where "anti-miscegenation" statutes were in force until a relatively recent date in a substantial number of states (*supra* s. 32). In Europe the most obvious example is afforded by one of the disreputable Nuremberg Laws in Nazi Germany, the Act of 15 September 1935 "for the Protection of German Blood and Honour", whereby an impediment was set up against marriages between Jews and "subjects of German or kindred blood" ("Aryans").[1156] This statute came to serve as a model for similar legislation in some other Continental countries then under dominant German influence.[1157] While these enactments were abolished towards or shortly after the end of the Second World War, legislation against interracial marriages obtaining even at the present day was introduced, as a link in the policy of *apartheid*, in South Africa in

1153. See for AUSTRIA: *G. Walker* 604-607; GERMANY: *Gamillscheg*, Kommentar, art. 13 no. 57-59, 323-326; *Raape*, Kommentar 243-245; SWITZERLAND: *Beck*, art. 7 c no. 24, 57.

1154. See particularly *Schwind*, Ehehindernis (*supra* n. 1152) 8-9. For LIECHTENSTEIN see the decision of the Supreme Court of 21 March 1964, FamRZ 1966, 33, note Beitzke.

1155. See *Habermalz* 9-41.

1156. Act of 15 Sept. 1935, § 1, and implementing orders made under the Act. Together with other enactments, the Nuremberg Laws imposed heavy restrictions on the personal and political rights of the "non-Aryan" population. See *Rowson*, Some Private International Law Problems Arising out of European Racial Legislation, 1933-1945: 10 M.L.R. 345, 345-346 (1947).

1157. In Fascist ITALY, for instance, an impediment of the same type was established by art. 1 of the Decree-Law of 17 Nov. 1938, no. 1728; see RabelsZ 12 (1938/39) 900. For a survey of this legislation see *Habermalz* 16-18.

1949. This was done with the passing of the Prohibition of Mixed Marriages Act, which forbids and declares invalid marriages between "Europeans" and "non-Europeans".[1158] In contrast with the general conflicts rule for marriage in South African law, as has been seen (*supra* s. 37), that statute claims to have extraterritorial operation inasmuch as it applies wherever the marriage is celebrated, if the male party is a citizen of or domiciled in South Africa.

In general, prohibitions of this kind have been regarded as odious and been refused application outside their country of origin, although the law of that country was the law normally governing the parties' capacity to marry according to the conflicts rules of the forum.[1159] In *England* and other countries following English law, foreign disabilities caused by race are held to be of no effect, either because they are classified as penal and discriminatory or because recognising and enforcing them would be contrary to public policy.[1160] The same attitude, based on considerations of public policy often bolstered by principles of constitutional law, has for long prevailed in a number of Continental European countries, such as *Belgium, France, Italy* (apart from the interlude of Fascist racial legislation in that country) and *Switzerland.*[1161] French and Italian courts have been confronted with American "anti-miscegenation" statutes on a few occasions where a marriage between a local and an American national was sought to be annulled by virtue of such a statute forming part of the latter spouse's personal law. In rejecting these petitions the courts held that the American statutes invoked must be disregarded for various reasons, chiefly because their application would amount to a violation of the forum's notion of public policy.[1162]

During the Nazi era in Germany, nevertheless, the position of

1158. Prohibition of Mixed Marriages Act 1949, s. 1 (1). See *supra* n. 281.

1159. For a comparative survey see *Habermalz* 54-63.

1160. Sottomayor v. De Barros (No. 2) (1879), 5 P.D. 94, 104 (*obiter*); *Rowson* (*supra* n. 1156) 347, 355-359, 361-362; *Ryan* 991; *Wolff,* PIL 339; and other writers cited *supra* n. 1125.

1161. BELGIUM: *Rigaux,* DIP I 359; cf. *infra* n. 1166; FRANCE: *Batiffol and Lagarde* II 40-41; *Bischoff* no. 68; *Delaume* 84; *Vincent and Ponsard* no. 93-94; ITALY: Cass. 19 May 1943, Foro it. 1943 I 930 (relating to the time before the Decree-Law of 17 Nov. 1938, *supra* n. 1157); *Giardina* 28-29; *A. Miele* 42-44, 161; *Monaco* 161-162; *Vitta* II 194-195; SWITZERLAND: BG 29 March 1950, BGE 76 IV 109, 116-117 (*obiter*); *Schnitzer* 341; *Vischer,* IPR 586; cf. *infra* n. 1164-1166, 1171.

1162. FRANCE: Trib. Pontoise 6 Aug. 1884, Clunet 1885, 296; see *Audit* 304-305. ITALY: Trib. Torino 22 April 1959, Riv. dir. matr. 1959, 736, note Cortese.

courts and other authorities in neighbouring countries with regard to the Nuremberg prohibition of marriages between Jews and "Aryans" was somewhat more hesitant and vacillating. In part this may have been due to political factors, but there were also legal difficulties for countries such as *the Netherlands* and *Switzerland* which, like Germany itself, were bound by the Hague Convention of 1902, which does not include impediments imposed by reference to race among those warranting an exception to the rule of the *lex patriae* for capacity to marry.[1163] These difficulties were in particular experienced by *Dutch* registrars of marriages and courts, which were rather frequently faced with problems involving the German prohibition.[1164] Although obviously reluctant to enforce that prohibition, in some cases they felt compelled to do so, refusing to permit the celebration of a marriage contravening the relevant German statute where the parties were, or the non-Jewish party was, of German nationality.[1165] Nevertheless, in what appears to be the majority of cases some means or other was found enabling the courts to ignore the prohibition.[1166] The techniques used to this end are open to objections from a strictly legal point of view, and the fact that recourse was had to them seems only explicable by the desire of the courts to avoid applying an odious

1163. The only case where a prohibition of the *lex patriae* may be disregarded is where it is based exclusively on grounds of a religious nature; see art. 3 of the convention and *supra* at n. 1130. Cf. *Maury* 100-102.

1164. For surveys of decisions see *Meyer-Collings,* Die niederländische Rechtsprechung auf dem Gebiete des internationalen Privatrechts in den Jahren 1933-1936: RabelsZ 11 (1937) 194, 206-207; Note, 8 I.L.R. 201 (1935/37). For SWITZERLAND see *L'application en Suisse de la loi allemande sur les mariages entre Juifs et Aryens*: Bull. I.I.I. 35 (1936) 284-287.

1165. Rb. Dordrecht 20 May 1936, N.J. 1936 no. 456, Bull. I.I.I. 35 (1936) 84; Rb. Arnhem 10 May 1938, Bull. I.I.I. 40 (1939) 92, 11 I.L.R. 23 (1919/42, Suppl. Vol.), and two other decisions briefly reported *ibid.* This was the prevailing solution in HUNGARY, see Bull. I.I.I. 34 (1936) 221, and partly in SWITZERLAND, see *supra* n. 1164.

1166. Rb. Rotterdam 29 May 1936, Rev. crit. d.i.p. 1936, 703, note Rehbock; Rb. 's-Hertogenbosch 16 June 1936, N.J. 1936 no. 479, Bull. I.I.I. 35 (1936) 281; Rb. 's-Hertogenbosch 31 July 1936, N.J. 1936 no. 860, Bull. I.I.I. 36 (1937) 41; Rb. Amsterdam 6 Jan. 1937, Bull. I.I.I. 38 (1938) 33. In BELGIUM, which was not a party to the Hague Convention, no doubts seem to have been entertained about the appropriateness of this solution; see statement by the Minister of Justice reproduced in Bull. I.I.I. 34 (1936) 220. For SWITZERLAND cf. the post-war decision of BG 14 June 1946, BGE 72 I 407, 413, repudiating another piece of the Nuremberg legislation whereby Jews residing abroad were deprived of their German citizenship.

foreign rule without openly violating the obligations incumbent on the Netherlands as a party to the Hague Convention.[1167]

Since the end of the Nazi regime, the climate of opinion in *West Germany* has undergone a radical change. It is now generally agreed that impediments to marriage based on race are incompatible with constitutionally protected basic rights and that foreign laws sanctioning such impediments cannot be enforced, at all events if the parties have, or one of them has, a substantial connection with West Germany.[1168] The question became of practical importance with the stationing of United States troops in West Germany after the Second World War, which led to the conclusion of many marriages between German women and coloured American soldiers. Although in several instances these marriages appear to have been forbidden by "anti-miscegenation" statutes then still in force in the American party's home state, this obstacle was disregarded and the marriages allowed in West German practice.[1169]

Today this view seems to be well established everywhere, and it is scarcely possible to find any country where a ban on interracial marriages, such as that contained in South African law, would be recognised so as to prevent or invalidate such a marriage.[1170] Indeed,

1167. One line of reasoning was that the relevant GERMAN statute must be construed as applicable only where the Jewish party was of German nationality and that it therefore had no reference to a marriage between a German "Aryan" and a foreign Jew – a self-limitation clearly absent both from the letter and from the spirit of the statute. Another equally untenable argument was that, while the GERMAN prohibition might be applicable in principle, it did not fall to GERMAN law to decide whether the intended non-German partner was a Jew, this being a matter for that party's own personal law. See for critical reviews of these and other reasons invoked by the DUTCH courts, *Habermalz* 59-60; *Steinle* 59-62. In other countries, too, courts unwilling to give effect to statutes of the present type have been known to use dubious legal means to achieve their end. As regards ITALY, this seems to have been the case even with the statute enacted in that country itself; see for an account of decisions under art. 1 of the Decree-Law of 17 Nov. 1938, *Cortese, supra* n. 1162.

1168. See, e.g., *Gamillscheg,* Kommentar, art. 13 no. 453; *Habermalz* 64-92; *Henrich* 302; *Stöcker,* Ordre public 106.

1169. See *Mergenthaler* 136; *Neuhaus,* Religionsverschiedenheit 280; It is not known, however, whether or to what extent the result was reached by relying on the principle of *renvoi;* cf. *Habermalz* 48-49.

1170. In addition to the countries mentioned already see, e.g., AUSTRIA: *Schwind,* IPR 141, 147; JAPAN: *Sato* 322; NORWAY: *Gaarder* 134, 136; SPAIN: *Miaja de la Muela* II 268; *Portero Sánchez* 515-516; VENEZUELA: CC art. 105. For the countries of EASTERN EUROPE see the references *supra* n. 1139; for POLAND see also the decision of the District Court of Krakow 21 Dec. 1970, Clunet 1974, 359, note Jodlowski.

this is one of the very few aspects of capacity to marry where one may with some confidence speak of the development of a truly international public policy, which is usually considered to be of such vigour as to override normal conflict of laws principles even in the absence of any substantial connection with the forum country.[1171]

The build-up of such a policy has been furthered by the work of the United Nations and other international organisations in the field of human rights. Distinctions on account of race or colour, *inter alia* in respect of the right to marry, figure among those combated and forbidden by all the international conventions etc. on this subject referred to in an earlier context.[1172] In addition, racial discrimination is specifically contemplated and condemned by the International Convention on the Elimination of All Forms of Racial Discrimination of 7 March 1966. By the terms of that convention the Contracting States undertake to prohibit and to eliminate such discrimination in all its forms and to guarantee the right of everyone, without distinction as to race, colour, or national or ethnic origin, to equality before the law, "notably in the enjoyment of . . . the right to marriage and choice of spouse."[1173] It is thus made very clear that impediments against mixed marriages between persons of different races are incompatible with the convention.

bg. *Impediments of a Political or Administrative Nature*

111. It is proposed to deal under this rubric with certain prohibitions or restrictions on marriage closely allied to the political or administrative interests of the enacting State. Of course, this is not a hard-and-fast criterion permitting any category of impediments against marriage to be absolutely distinguished from others, if only for the reason that the desire to protect public interests in

1171. Though some writers insist on the necessity of a durable connection if a marriage is to be celebrated in defiance of a prohibition of the appropriate foreign law. See for WEST GERMANY: *Habermalz* 91; SWITZERLAND: *Beck*, art. 7 c no. 59; *Vaucher* 543.

1172. *Supra* s. 107 at n. 1109-1114. Specifically as to the incompatibility of racial impediments to marriage with the European Human Rights Convention of 1950 see also *Castberg*, The European Convention on Human Rights (Leyden & Dobbs Ferry, N.Y. 1974) 140; *Guradze* 191-192.

1173. Art. 5 (d) (iv). For comments see *Lerner*, The U.N. Convention on the Elimination of All Forms of Racial Discrimination (Leyden 1970) 66, 69; *Schwelb*, The International Convention on the Elimination of All Forms of Racial Discrimination: 15 I.C.L.Q. 996, 1007, 1026 (1966).

a broad sense is an aspect of all rules limiting the right to marry in one way or another. Nevertheless, this feature is more dominant in the provisions to be considered here than in others.

One distinct type of such rules embodies a *general restraint on marriages between nationals of the enacting State and aliens.*[1174] Provisions making mixed marriages of this kind dependent on official authorisation or even forbidding them completely were a characteristic of the post-war laws of nearly all socialist countries in Eastern Europe.[1175] Requirements of official approval for marriages with a foreigner are still in force in some of those countries (Albania, East Germany, Rumania) and also figure in the laws of various Islamic countries (for example, Iran and Saudi Arabia).[1176]

Other restrictions are directed against marriages of *selected classes of persons in a special relationship to the enacting State.* This category includes provisions, which were quite common in the past and of which instances are still to be found in many countries, requiring the consent of the Sovereign, the Government or some other authority to marriages of members of the royal family, foreign service officials, members of the armed forces, or other groups of citizens who, because of their personal position or the nature of their functions, owe special loyalty to the State and whose marriages are deemed to be of particular importance to it.[1177] A similar restriction is sometimes imposed on persons who have not yet performed their military service.[1178] Most of these provisions are framed so as to apply equally to any marriage of

1174. For a comparative survey see *Gamillscheg,* Kommentar, art. 13 no. 455-456, 917.

1175. See *Korkisch* 620-622. For the development of SOVIET RUSSIAN law see the WEST GERMAN decision of LG Stuttgart 5 Aug. 1964, IPRspr. 1964/65 no. 80.

1176. ALBANIA: Decree of 5 Dec. 1966, noted in RabelsZ 31 (1967) 716; EAST GERMANY: RAG § 18 par. 1 sent. 2; *FGB-Kommentar* 170, 448; IRAN: CC art. 1060 (for marriages between women of Iranian and men of foreign nationality), see StAZ 1966, 72, 73; RUMANIA: CC art. 134 (as amended in 1950); Supreme Court 30 Aug. 1969, Clunet 1971, 620, note Nestor and Capatina; *Capatina,* Les règles matérielles dans les conflits des lois: R.R.S.J. 18 (1974) 87, 88-89; SAUDI ARABIA: Decree of 15 July 1973, see StAZ 1974, 276.

1177. For a comparative survey see *Dölle,* Familienrecht 98-100. For older provisions see *Travers* I 135-140.

1178. Such restrictions were at issue in some of the decisions cited *infra* n. 1185, 1190, 1196-1198. For older laws see *Buzzati* 84-85; *Travers* I 140-141.

their addressees, regardless of the nationality of the intended partner. In some cases, however, they are limited to marriages with foreigners or involve more severe restrictions against such unions, occasionally even to the extent of absolutely forbidding them for the "special subjects" concerned.[1179]

Another class of persons in a special position often entailing a disability for marriage is those lawfully deprived of their liberty, such as prisoners and convicts, or subject to other coercive rules or measures falling within criminal or administrative law.[1180] The reason for restrictions being placed on the right of such persons to marry, or on the exercise of that right, is normally that this is considered necessary in order to achieve the purpose or to secure the effective enforcement of the punishment or other measure involved.

While most provisions of this latter kind will apply to local and to foreign nationals alike, some of them are necessarily limited to marriages of or with persons of foreign nationality because the penal or administrative coercion justifying the restriction on marriage can only be directed against such persons. A decision of the Swiss Federal Tribunal from the time of the Second World War provides an example: an officer of the Polish armed forces, who was lawfully interned in Switzerland in accordance with the rules of the law of nations concerning the rights and obligations of neutral States in times of war, was held to be debarred from marrying while so interned, except with the consent of the Swiss authority in charge of the internment camp, on the grounds that marital life would be incompatible with the restraints on his liberty flowing from the state of internment and with the order and discipline to be enforced in the camp.[1181] In another decision the same court held that a Swiss man was precluded from marrying

1179. See, e.g., IRAN: CC art. 1061 and implementing provisions (official authorisation required for marriages of Iranian foreign service officials, army officers, etc., with women of foreign nationality); SAUDI ARABIA: Decree of 15 July 1973 (absolute prohibition against certain classes of Saudi nationals marrying an alien).

1180. See, for instance, for SWISS law: BG 2 March 1942, BGE 68 I 73, 81-82 with references; *Götz*, Vorbemerkungen zum Zweiten Abschnitt no. 6-7 (p. 47), art. 105 no. 27; *Knapp*, Cent ans 302-303; *Vaucher* 545-546. On the compatibility of such restrictions of the right to marry with the European Convention on Human Rights see the decision of the European Commission on Human Rights of 13 April 1961, 4 YB Human Rights 240, 254-256 (1961).

1181. BG 2 March 1942, BGE 68 I 73, Clunet 1951, 970, note Knapp. See *Götz*, Vorbemerkungen zum Zweiten Abschnitt no. 8 (p. 48), art. 105 no. 26; *Vaucher* 546; *Vischer*, IPR 588.

a German woman because she had been deported from Switzerland for an indefinite time (for reasons of national security) and because the projected marriage would have the effect of automatically giving her Swiss nationality so as to entitle her to return to and to live in Switzerland, thereby flouting the deportation order.[1182] The impediment established by this decision is akin to that against sham marriages, existing in Switzerland and certain other countries which thereby seek to protect themselves against abusive acquisition of their nationality (*supra* s. 99).

Conflicts problems in regard to the disabilities treated here are scarcely conceivable in the country itself whose law contains such a disability. Most of the prohibitions or restrictions in question are primarily directed to that country's own nationals, or to particular classes of such nationals, whether or not marriages with foreigners are specifically envisaged. In those relatively few cases where the exercise of a foreigner's right to marry is directly affected, the impediment set up seems invariably to be well beyond the bounds of the notion of capacity to marry possibly governed by foreign law.[1183] There is little or no doubt that all restraining rules considered here are of "immediate" application, to be enforced by courts and other authorities in the enacting State whenever so required by their own terms and without any reference to the conflict of laws.

1182. BG 3 Feb. 1949, BGE 75 II 1, Schw. Jb. Int. R. 7 (1950) 227, note Knapp, Clunet 1952, 674, note *idem.* Cf. BG 5 Dec. 1946, BGE 72 I 354. In this case the man was refused a certificate of capacity to marry to be used in West Germany where the ceremony was intended to take place. For cases in which a deported foreigner was held to be prevented from marrying in Switzerland (regardless of his actual presence in that country in contravention of the deportation order) see: BG 23 Oct. 1947, BGE 73 I 330, Clunet 1952, 660, note Knapp; BG 18 Nov. 1948, BGE 74 I 420, Clunet 1952, 668, note *idem.* And see *Götz,* Vorbemerkungen zum Zweiten Abschnitt no. 9-10 (p. 48), art. 105 no. 28, art. 107 no. 15, art. 113 no. 23, art. 114 no. 11; *Knapp,* Cent ans 296-302; *Vaucher* 546-547; *Vischer,* IPR 588. Similarly for AUSTRIA: KrG Steyr, ÖStA 16 (1962) 90; OGH 19 March 1963, ÖStA 17 (1963) 51; *Hintermüller,* Landesverweisung und Aufenthaltsverbot als Ehehindernis: ÖStA 16 (1962) 89.

1183. This holds good for rules restraining the exercise of the right to marry of foreigners lawfully detained in or deported from the country of intended celebration (*supra* at n. 1180-1182). The question was considered in the SWISS decision of BG 2 March 1942, BGE 68 I 73 at 83 (*supra* at n. 1181), where – rightly, it is submitted – the refusal to permit an interned alien to marry was held not to be in violation of the HAGUE CONVENTION on Marriage, although by art. 1 of that convention the party's right to marry was a matter for his national law.

The next question is what effect, if any, is to be given to such rules in other countries.[1184] This touches upon an old controversy opposing two schools of thought committed to the principle of territoriality and to that of extraterritoriality, respectively.

The "territorialist" approach has its stronghold in *France*, where the prevailing view has traditionally been that the reference to the personal law for capacity to marry is limited to questions within the domain of private law.[1185] Although a person's right to marry may be affected by rules pertaining to public or to criminal law, such rules are not included within the scope of the personal law but must be treated as confined to the territory of the enacting State. It follows that disabilities produced by foreign rules of this kind will be ignored, at all events if the marriage takes place outside the country of their origin. Since this result is reached without any need for relying on the doctrine of *ordre public*, it is immaterial that similar provisions may exist in the forum's own legal system. Besides France, this view receives a varying amount of support in several other Continental countries.[1186] In all probability *English* law (and other legal systems based on it) is the same in substance, although slightly different language might be used to express the position; disabilities of the kind will most likely be classified as penal, *i.e.* discriminatory, so as to be excluded from recognition or enforcement by English courts.[1187]

The rival view, which has in particular been propounded in *(West) Germany*, is that the personal law controls all questions affecting the right to marry, independently of whether the rules involved are classifiable as private or as public law (subject only to such exceptions as may be necessary for reasons of public

1184. Though for some of the rules under review, especially those limiting the right to marry of prisoners or internees (*supra* at n. 1180-1181), this question can hardly arise because of the fact situation presupposed.

1185. The problem has chiefly been canvassed in relation to provisions interposing checks on marriages of certain categories of civil servants, deserters from military service, etc., without official approval. For an early FRENCH decision refusing to give effect to such a provision of the *lex patriae* (GERMAN law) on the ground that it did not affect capacity to marry, see Trib. Malmédy 1 Dec. 1896, Clunet 1897, 348. And see among writers: *Batiffol and Lagarde* II 41 n. 9; *Bischoff* no. 41-43; *Niboyet* V 338-340; *Vincent and Ponsard* no. 84-86. See further *infra* n. 1191, cf. *supra* at n. 524.

1186. E.g., ITALY: *Morelli* 102-103; NETHERLANDS: *van Sasse van Ysselt* 193; SWITZERLAND: *Vischer*, IPR 588. See further *infra* n. 1193, 1198.

1187. See *Baty* 449 n. 14; *Dicey and Morris* 269-270, 275; *Wolff*, PIL 329-330, 339.

policy).[1188] This position appears to be endorsed by the Hague Convention on Marriage of 1902, which simply provides that a person's "right to marry" is governed by his national law without any distinction as to rules of private or of public law.[1189] Already at an early stage of the life of the convention, however, its interpretation in this respect became a bone of contention among the States parties to it, primarily between France and Germany. The origin of the dispute was that deserters from the German army (especially from Alsace-Lorraine, which then was a part of the German *Reich*) sought to marry in neighbouring countries, to which they had escaped, without the consent of the appropriate military authority prescribed by German law; while Germany insisted that this requirement, as part of the *lex patriae* governing the right to marry under the convention, must be observed in other Contracting States, this concept was unacceptable to France and Belgium.[1190] The controversy ended in France and Belgium withdrawing from the convention.[1191]

Today this problem has lost much of its edge. Although dogmatic differences still subsist, opinions on practical issues for a large part tend to converge in Western countries. In so far as the rule of the personal law is taken as the proper point of departure in dealing with impediments of the kind considered here, foreign

1188. For the prevailing [WEST] GERMAN view, which used to be shared in SWITZERLAND, see the references *infra* n. 1189, 1191, 1193-1194, 1196; cf. *supra* at n. 525.

1189. Art. 1. See: *Buzzati* 238; *Gamillscheg*, Kommentar, art. 13 no. 462, 957; *F. Kahn* 115-116; *Rabel* 303; *Travers* I 135-142; *G. Walker* 592-597. And see the decisions cited *infra* n. 1190.

1190. Though the appropriateness of the GERMAN interpretation was recognised in BELGIUM while that country was still a party to the convention; see the decision of Cass. 11 June 1914, *Kosters and Bellemans* 126, giving effect to the GERMAN requirement of military consent. So also in the NETHERLANDS: Hoge Raad 26 Sept. 1918 (Reiners v. Albert), *ibid.* 153 (but the majority of DUTCH decisions have held otherwise, see *infra* n. 1198).

1191. With effect from 1 June 1914 and 1919, respectively; see Rev. crit. d.i.p. 1913, 926, and 1919, 340. The official documents relating to the BELGIAN and FRENCH denunciation of the convention and to the controversy with GERMANY preceding it are reproduced by *Kosters and Bellemans* 22-41. See further: *Beer*, Die französische Kündigung der Haager Familienrechtskonvention und ihre Begründung: NiemeyersZ 25 (1915) 305-320; *La dénonciation des Conventions de la Haye du 12 juin 1902*: Rev. crit. d.i.p. 1914, 364-395; *Le mariage des déserteurs en Belgique et la dénonciation par la France des Conventions de la Haye:* Rev. crit. d.i.p. 1914, 5-23; *Niboyet* III 376; *Visscher*, La dénonciation par la Belgique des Conventions de la Haye relatives au mariage, au divorce et à la séparation de corps: Rev. crit. d.i.p. 1919, 624-630.

rules embodying such impediments are often rejected in the end because their application would violate the forum's public policy, or on some other ground, thereby producing results similar to those reached under the concept that foreign public law is not to be taken into account at all. Once again, this is largely due to the progress of the idea of marriage as a human right protected by international conventions as well as by national constitutional law, a notion with which at least some of the impediments in question are difficult to reconcile.

This is particularly true of rules involving a general prohibition or requirement of official authorisation of marriages across national borders.[1192] It is usually agreed today in West European countries that no effect can be given to such provisions, whether their public law nature or the public policy of the forum is invoked to support this conclusion.[1193] Scattered decisions to the contrary must now very probably be regarded as no longer representing the law.[1194] The position appears to be different, however, in the mutual relations between countries in Eastern Europe governed by bilateral treaties of legal assistance; for those treaties generally provide for the application of the *lex patriae* of each of the intending spouses in regard to all substantive conditions of marriage without any exception for impediments of the present type.[1195]

1192. For writers of opinion that such restrictions are outlawed by art. 12 and 14 of the European Convention on Human Rights see: *Goldman* 451; *A. Miele* 152-153, 160-161; *Moser* 159; *Opsahl* 190-191; *Schwind,* IPR 141; *Wähler,* case note: Clunet 1963, 1110-1113; *Wengler,* case note: NJW 1962, 347, 348.

1193. AUSTRIA: *Schwind,* IPR 141, 147; WEST GERMANY: decision of President of KG, cited in KG 22 April 1968, FamRZ 1968, 466; cf. LG Augsburg 10 Oct. 1952, IPRspr. 1952/53 no. 151 (by implication), and KG 14 Sept. 1961, IPRspr. 1960/61 no. 91 (left open); see *Beyer* 35; *Ferid,* Sind ausländische Verbote der Eheschliessung mit Nichtstaatsangehörigen zu beachten?: StAZ 1954, 19-20; *Gamillscheg,* Kommentar, art. 13 no. 457, 917; *Mampel,* Das Rechtsanwendungsgesetz der DDR: NJW 1976, 1521, 1525; *Mergenthaler* 134-136. ITALY: *A. Miele* 39-41, 161; NETHERLANDS: Rb. Almelo 18 June 1955, N.J. 1955 no. 774, Clunet 1959, 474, note Kollewijn, cf. *Gamillscheg,* Kommentar, before art. 13 no. 19, art. 13 no. 458. SWITZERLAND: *Vaucher* 543-544 (with distinctions).

1194. For such decisions see FRANCE: Trib. Bordeaux 18 Jan. 1882, Clunet 1882, 539; WEST GERMANY: OLG Oldenburg 11 April 1967, IPRspr. 1966/67 no. 68 (applying IRANIAN CC art. 1060, see *supra* at n. 1176).

1195. See the provisions cited *supra* n. 288. A few of those provisions expressly stipulate that the requirements so governed shall be deemed to include such authorisation by the competent authorities as may be prescribed

The dogmatic conflict may retain some practical significance for the treatment of rules requiring official approval for marriages of particular classes of public officials, persons in military service or who have not yet performed it, etc. At least in *West Germany* the weight of opinion seems still to be in favour of respecting such requirements (whether applicable to any marriage or only where the other party is an alien) of the relevant foreign law.[1196] Apparently, however, there is growing support for the view that such rules should be disregarded as obnoxious to public policy or because of their character of administrative law.[1197] This position prevails in most other European countries.[1198] Even where (as in West Germany) doubts may exist as to requirements of official permission, it is very unlikely that effect would be given to foreign provisions absolutely prohibiting certain subjects of the enacting State from marrying an alien.[1199]

---

by the law of the Contracting State of which the party is a national; see the treaties concluded by ALBANIA with HUNGARY on 12 Jan. 1960, art. 26 par. 2, and with RUMANIA on 12 Sept. 1960, art. 22 par. 2; cf. *Léh,* Le Droit international privé hongrois à la lumière des conventions bilatérales d'entraide judiciaire: Clunet 1964, 523, 534. The result seems to be the same, however, even without such mention; see *Lübchen* 84-85.

1196. KG 14 Sept. 1961, IPRspr. 1960/61 no. 91 (criticised by *Wähler* and by *Wengler,* case notes cited *supra* n. 1192); OLG Hamburg 29 Jan. 1962, IPRspr. 1962/63 no. 67. And see among writers: *Dölle,* Familienrecht 100 n. 92; *Frankenstein* 79-82; *Gamillscheg,* Kommentar, art. 13 no. 461 (but cf. *ibid.* no. 141, 459, 460); *Neuhaus,* Grundrechte 611. Similarly for SWITZERLAND: *Beck,* art. 7 c no. 14, 21 (but see *idem,* art. 7 c no. 60); *Vaucher* 541. For opinions to the contrary see *infra* n. 1197-1198.

1197. See the WEST GERMAN decision of OLG Köln 17 Jan. 1968, IPRspr. 1968/69 no. 62 (allowing a Portuguese national to marry although his national authorities would not issue a certificate of capacity to marry because he had not performed his military service; in the opinion of the court this was merely a matter of administrative law to be ignored in WEST GERMANY). And see *Kegel,* Kommentar, art. 13 no. 29, 111; *Wolff,* IPR 190; *Wuppermann* 87-91.

1198. See the references *supra* n. 1185-1187, 1191 and, e.g., BELGIUM: *Graulich* 156; ITALY: *A. Miele* 161-165; *Monaco* 161; NETHERLANDS: (cases involving foreign requirements of military or similar consent) Rb. 's-Hertogenbosch 4 Jan. 1917, *Kosters and Bellemans* 141; Rb. Dordrecht 4 Oct. 1917, *ibid.* 145; Rb. Haarlem 1 Sept. 1918, *ibid.* 151; Rb. 's-Gravenhage 4 April 1930, N.J. 1930, 1138; Rb. Arnhem 26 Jan. 1970, N.J. 1970 no. 423, N.T.I.R. 21 (1974) 84; SWITZERLAND: *Götz,* art. 105 no. 29 (but cf. *idem,* art. 107 no. 21 f); *Knapp,* case note: Clunet 1952, 678, 680; YUGOSLAVIA: *Tchirkovitch* 224.

1199. For an example of such a provision in SAUDI ARABIAN law see *supra* n. 1179.

E. Certain Problems Relating to the Administration of Foreign Law

a. *Dispensation from Marriage Impediments*

112. *Introductory.* Most legal systems permit a dispensation from certain requirements for or impediments to marriage to be given in appropriate cases. This is very usual in the case of rules fixing the minimum age for marriage or laying down a waiting period for remarriage (which may be cancelled entirely or curtailed) or creating an incapacity by reason of consanguinity, affinity or adultery.[1200] The power to grant dispensations from such or other rules is vested in the Head of State, the Government, some administrative agency, a judicial body or sometimes a religious authority.

There are some related kinds of provision which, although perhaps not properly classifiable as dealing with dispensation, present analogous problems in the conflict of laws and which may therefore conveniently be included under this heading. The chief example is provisions empowering a court or other authority to overrule a refusal by parents or guardians to give their consent for the marriage of a minor requiring such consent.[1201] A certain analogy with dispensation is also to be noted in the case of requirements of official approval for marriages with aliens or of selected classes of civil servants, etc. (*supra* s. 111); but these questions have already been sufficiently covered and will not be further dwelt on here.

The grant of dispensations, or of analogous official permissions, can give rise both to problems of jurisdiction and to substantive issues depending on the applicable law. For once it will be appropriate to start with the latter aspect.

113. *Substantive Matters.* It is generally agreed that the question of whether dispensation can be granted from any individual impediment to marriage and, if so, in what cases and on what grounds, must be decided by reference to the law establishing the impedi-

1200. See the comparative surveys cited *supra* n. 383, 876 and 903 (prohibitions or waiting periods based on prior marriage), 1052 (age requirements) and 1076 (consanguinity and affinity).

1201. See the comparative surveys cited *supra* n. 373. Another closely related question is that concerning the emancipation, or declaration of majority (*Volljährigkeitserklärung*) of a minor, which is or used to be a condition for dispensations of the requisite age for marriage in WEST GERMAN and kindred systems of law. See *Dölle*, Familienrecht 160-167; *Rabel* 187-188.

ment (the *lex causae*).[1202] Although the soundness of this principle is beyond doubt, some qualifications and distinctions may be called for.

The simplest situation is where the *lex causae* excludes any possibility of dispensation. This may be so either because that law regards the particular disability as absolute (*i.e.*, not susceptible of exemption in any circumstances) or because, while authorising the grant of dispensation in appropriate cases, it contains some absolute limit or condition for this (for example, by providing that the minimum age for marriage, fixed at eighteen years, may be dispensed with for grave reasons, but only if the applicant has attained the age of fifteen) which is not met in the instant case. In these cases it is too clear for argument that no dispensation will be available, wherever the question is raised and by whatever authority it falls to be decided.[1203]

This leaves cases in which the *lex causae* affirms the possibility of dispensation, provided that the competent authority is satisfied that there is a sufficient ground for permitting the marriage (as, for instance, if the applicant in the above case has completed his fifteenth year, so that the existence of "grave reasons" is the sole remaining issue). This latter question does not present any particular problem as long as the decision rests with the authorities of the country of the *lex causae* itself. The position is likely to be different, however, if the dispensation is sought in some other country, such as the intended *forum celebrationis*, whose authorities are prepared to assume jurisdiction.[1204] In this situation, too, to be sure, sound principle demands that the *lex causae* should be treated as authoritative for all substantive questions, so that an order should only be made if a sufficient ground exists under that law; for any other solution would amount to an encroachment upon the law once selected by the forum as applicable to the matter of marriage impediments. In practice, nevertheless, it is probably inevitable that the exercise of jurisdiction by a forum

1202. See, e.g., AUSTRIA: *Schwind*, IPR 142, 145; WEST GERMANY: *Gamillscheg*, Kommentar, art. 13 no. 158, 164, 204, 225, 380, 392; SWITZERLAND: *Beck*, art. 7 d no. 6. Further references are given *infra* n. 1212-1214. This view is generally shared by courts and writers permitting jurisdiction in such matters to be exercised by some country other than that of the *lex causae;* see *infra* at n. 1221, 1225, 1228, 1230.

1203. Subject, of course, to the overriding effect of the permissive public policy of the forum, where the impediment is imposed by foreign law.

1204. On the jurisdiction of the *forum celebrationis* see *infra* s. 114, particularly at n. 1221, 1223, 1225, 1228.

other than that of the *lex causae* will to some extent affect the determination of substantive issues as well, if only because of the formidable difficulties in applying the foreign law properly which may be encountered by such a forum. This point will be further illuminated when dealing with the problem of jurisdiction (*infra* s. 114).

Another point calling for some comment arises where the parties to the proposed marriage are subject to different personal laws. The grant of dispensation in such cases does not pose any particular problem if the incapacity sought to be lifted originates in one of the two laws alone. Assuming, for instance, that uncle-niece marriages are allowed by the uncle's but forbidden by the niece's personal law, then plainly it is for the latter law alone to decide whether the bar can be removed by dispensation.[1205]

The question is somewhat more difficult where the marriage is prohibited by each of the two laws involved. Cases presenting this complexion usually involve a single impediment figuring in both laws and held to "relate to" both parties (relative and other bilateral impediments, *supra* s. 49-52). Such a case occurs in the above example if uncle-niece marriages are forbidden by either party's law.

In this situation both laws must be taken into account in determining whether the impediment can be overcome by dispensation. More particularly, the marriage will only be allowed to be celebrated if such an order is possible and has in fact been obtained in relation to each of the laws setting up the bar.[1206] Hence if *H*'s law regards the incapacity as absolute, it will be of no avail that a dispensation can be or has been given under *W*'s law.[1207] Such an order will not affect the incapacity existing under *H*'s law, which is sufficient to prevent the marriage. Nor will it make any difference if *H*'s law, too, permits a dispensation as long as none has been issued in relation to that law.[1208] As a consequence of the

1205. See, e.g., AUSTRIA: *Hainzl* 19-20; *Schwind,* Nachsichterteilung 39; WEST GERMANY: *Gamillscheg,* Kommentar, art. 13 no. 159; *Hoffmann and Stephan* § 6 no. 44.

1206. See, e.g., *Gamillscheg,* Kommentar, art. 13 no. 158; *Lauterbach* 28.

1207. For illustrative cases see [WEST] GERMANY: LG Aachen 11 March 1931, IPRspr. 1932 no. 67; OLG Düsseldorf 8 April 1969, IPRspr. 1968/69 no. 72; NETHERLANDS: Hof 's-Hertogenbosch 21 Dec. 1937, N.J. 1938 no. 341.

1208. For cases apparently involving such a situation see, e.g., AUSTRIA: OGH 16 Dec. 1925, SZ 7 no. 398; POLAND: Supreme Court 28 Nov. 1933, Z. osteur. R. 1934/35, 444.

relevance of both laws in this respect, it may also become necessary to approach the authorities of both countries concerned. This depends on the rules of jurisdiction to which we shall now turn.

114. *Jurisdiction.* It is common ground that the dispensing power, if any, vests in the competent authorities of the country furnishing the applicable law (the *forum legis causae*).[1209] If, for example, a party's capacity to marry depends on his *lex patriae,* which provides that an obstacle to the proposed union existing under that law can be dispensed with, the right to do so belongs to the authorities designated by the same law. A dispensation given by those authorities will presumably be recognised as effective in any other country where the marriage is to take place, in so far as the *lex patriae* is held to be the controlling law for capacity to marry.[1210] This is almost self-evident since such an order is tantamount to saying that the applicable law has waived its objection to the marriage.

The question remains as to whether this jurisdiction is exclusive or whether jurisdiction may also be exercised by the authorities of some other country. This problem occurs where a foreigner approaches the local authorities of the country where he intends to marry, seeking exemption from some incapacitating rule of his personal law (usually his *lex patriae*). Will such a request be considered by the *forum celebrationis*?

> Example: A divorced woman of French nationality resident in West Germany wants to remarry there. By the relevant French law she is prohibited from marrying again until a waiting period has elapsed, but this bar can be removed by order of a judge if certain conditions are fulfilled.[1211] Assuming that no such order has been obtained from a French court, can the West German authorities exercise a "vicarious" jurisdiction to make the order?

By the weight of opinion in *West Germany* this question must be answered in the negative, it being considered that there must be concurrence (*Gleichlauf*) between jurisdiction and applicable law

1209. Whether or not that jurisdiction is regarded as exclusive; see the references *infra* n. 1210, 1212-1214, 1225, 1229.

1210. See, for example, *Gamillscheg,* Kommentar, art. 13 no. 164, 176. To the contrary for FRENCH law see *Ponsard* 11; but this view seems neither tenable nor representative of FRENCH law, cf. *infra* n. 1225.

1211. FRENCH CC art. 228, 261.

in this field.[1212] This amounts to saying that the jurisdiction of the *forum legis causae* is exclusive. The same view prevails in *Austria* and *Switzerland,*[1213] and probably in most other countries adhering to the principle of the personal law in substantive matters.[1214] While the authorities of these countries will exercise such powers to dispense with marriage impediments as exist under their own law wherever the marriage is to be celebrated, as a rule at least they will decline to do so in respect of foreign laws even if the marriage is to be celebrated in their own country. Nor will they be prepared to recognise foreign dispensations relating to impediments laid down by their own law (or by the law of a third country.

The reason for taking this position is primarily that the substantive and the procedural aspects of dispensation are so tightly interwoven as to be regarded as inseparable.[1215] The right to give exemption from requirements imposed by law is historically an attribute of the Sovereign in the exercise of his power over his own subjects. Although the right to sanction a marriage by dispensation now usually lies in the hands of administrative or

1212. See: President of LG Regensburg 9 July 1949, IPRspr. 1945/49 no. 14; KG 14 Sept. 1961, IPRspr. 1960/61 no. 91; OLG Karlsruhe 3 Sept. 1962, IPRspr. 1962/63 no. 70; OLG Bremen 16 May 1963, IPRspr. 1962/63 no. 74; OLG Hamm 10 Sept. 1963, IPRspr. 1962/63 no. 76; Service Instruction of 1968, § 156 (4), 157 (2), 161 (4), 163 (5); *Gamillscheg,* Kommentar, art. 13 no. 160-161, 435; *Hoffmann and Stephan,* before § 4 no. 9, § 6 no. 43, § 10 no. 25; *Keidel and Winkler,* Freiwillige Gerichtsbarkeit (ed. 10, Munich 1972) § 44 a no. 8, § 44 b no. 11-12, § 56 no. 3, 13 a; *Kropholler,* Das Haager Abkommen über den Schutz Minderjähriger (Bielefeld 1966) 73-74; *Lauterbach* 28; *Raape,* IPR 259 n. 38.

1213. AUSTRIA: OGH 16 Dec. 1925, SZ 7 no. 398; *Köhler* 42-46 (dealing with declarations of majority); *Schwind,* Nachsichterteilung. SWITZERLAND: BG 23 May 1912, BGE 38 II 1, Clunet 1913, 257 (declaration of majority); *Beck,* art. 7 c no. 9, 43, art. 7 d no. 13-15, art. 7 f no. 52; *Götz,* art. 96 no. 22, art. 98 no. 16, art. 100 no. 14, art. 103 no. 18; *Knapp,* case note: Schw. Jb. Int. R. 7 (1950) 223, 224-225; *Stauffer,* art. 7 no. 3, art. 7 c no. 3, art. 7 d no. 6 (for declarations of majority).

1214. See *Rabel* 308 and, e.g., HUNGARY: *Réczei* 357; POLAND: Supreme Court 28 Nov. 1933, Z. osteur. R. 1934/35, 444; *Jodlowski and Ponsard* 585 n. 147; HAGUE CONVENTION of 1902: *Travers* I 87-89, 305-307; SCANDINAVIAN Convention of 1931: NJA 1969 II 565.

1215. Similar problems are presented with regard to many other topics of the conflict of laws, particularly in the field of "non-contentious jurisdiction" (*jurisdictio voluntaria*). Among recent contributions supporting a modified principle of concurrence of jurisdiction and applicable law in such matters see: *Dölle,* Über einige Kernprobleme des internationalen Rechts der freiwilligen Gerichtsbarkeit: RabelsZ 27 (1962/63) 201-244; *Neuhaus,* Grundbegriffe 424-432.

judicial authorities, it still has largely the character of a prerogative power permitting a broad exercise of discretion. The authorising provisions usually afford little or no guidance as to their application in individual cases, the grounds for dispensation being left unspecified or indicated in vague and general language reading, for instance, that leave to marry may be granted "for grave causes", or "in extraordinary cases where justified by weighty reasons", or if the court is satisfied that "the circumstances of the case are so exceptional and unusual as to justify the making of the order", or unless there are "strong reasons against permitting the marriage."[1216] Although more fixed criteria for the exercise of the discretion so conferred may have crystallised through the development of practice, this will not much facilitate the task of authorities outside the enacting State, should they decide to assume a "vicarious" jurisdiction to apply such provisions. The difficulties are perhaps even more manifest in the case of provisions directing the competent authority to consider not only the likelihood of the parties making a successful marriage but also whether the intended union will be conducive to the public interest (a notion which must be taken to refer to the interest of the community or of the State of the *lex causae*).[1217]

Secondly, even the most "faithful" application of the *lex causae* will not afford any guarantee that a dispensation given by the *forum celebrationis* will be recognised in the foreign country concerned. As has been seen, most countries claim exclusive jurisdiction to make such orders in respect of impediments of their own law, with the consequence that a foreign order purporting to dispense with one of those impediments will be regarded as ineffective. It follows that a marriage celebrated on the strength of a locally granted permission runs the risk of being refused recognition, or of being annulled, in the country of the *lex causae* (and possibly in third countries as well). The exercise of jurisdiction

1216. See, respectively, FRENCH CC art. 145 (also art. 164 and 362), SWISS CC art. 96 par. 2, AUSTRALIAN Marriage Act 1961, s. 12 (2), and WEST GERMAN Marriage Act of 1946, § 6 (now repealed). For other examples see *Dieckmann*, Zuständigkeit 10 n. 13.

1217. See, e.g., the POLISH Family and Guardianship Code of 25 Feb. 1964, art. 10 § 1: permission to marry may, for grave reasons, be granted to a person below the prescribed marriageable age, "if, in all the circumstances, this is warranted by the proposed union being for the benefit of the family they will found, *and in the social interest*" (emphasis supplied). For the view that the social or political interest of the foreign country concerned cannot be considered or evaluated by the forum faced with provisions of this kind in the *lex causae*, see *Gamillscheg*, Kommentar, art. 13 no. 171-172.

by the *forum celebrationis* may thus contribute to increasing the number of limping marriages.

This risk, however, should not be overrated. It only exists in the case of rules to which the relevant foreign law attaches such weight as to sanction infringements in the manner mentioned. This seems unlikely to be so in most cases involving an impediment that admits of dispensation.

Furthermore, the argument based on the risk of creating limping marriages is wholly invalidated in those cases where the *lex causae* is prepared to recognise a dispensation obtained from the local authorities. In so far as such recognition can be predicted, it is indeed usually admitted, by way of exception to the basic rule, that a "vicarious" jurisdiction may be exercised by those authorities.[1218] Presumably, however, this is a rare situation; no reported case has been found where jurisdiction was assumed on this ground.

A related, but different, case occurring more frequently is that where the conflicts rules of the appropriate foreign law refer back to (or "are prepared to tolerate" the application of) the *substantive* rules of the local law, whether *qua* the law of the place of celebration or *qua* the party's domiciliary law (*renvoi: supra* s. 58-59). In so far as such a *renvoi* is accepted by the forum, it means that the local law will be substituted for the foreign law as the *lex causae* of substantive matters. Once this has been done it goes without saying that the forum will have jurisdiction to grant dispensations, since any such question will relate to prohibitions of its own law.[1219] Far from constituting any exception to the principle of the exclusive jurisdiction of the *forum legis causae*, the jurisdiction so exercised is entirely consonant with that principle.

The same holds good for other cases where, despite the presence of foreign elements, the *lex fori* is the proper law to apply to the substantive conditions of marriage, or to some of those conditions. One such case occurs where the foreign law referred to in the first instance is excluded, and replaced by the *lex fori*, for reasons of

1218. Expressly in favour of this view see AUSTRIA: *Schwind*, Nachsichterteilung 38, 39; WEST GERMANY: *Beitzke*, Ehevoraussetzungen 287-288, 289-290; *Gamillscheg*, Kommentar, art. 13 no. 165-166; SWITZERLAND: *Beck*, art. 7 c no. 9, art. 7 d no. 13; *Götz*, art. 103 no. 18; *Knapp*, case note (*supra* n. 1213) 225.

1219. See, e.g., AUSTRIA: *Schwind*, Nachsichterteilung 39; [WEST] GERMANY: KG 22 March 1906, KGJ 32 (1906) A 28, 33; AG Hamburg 22 Dec. 1966, IPRspr. 1966/67 no. 66; *Beitzke*, Ehevoraussetzungen 288-289; *Drobnig*, PIL 84, 143; *Gamillscheg*, Kommentar, art. 13 no. 165, 230; SWITZERLAND: *Beck*, art. 7 c no. 35, 43, art. 7 e no. 38, 48; *Götz*, art. 96 no. 22; *Knapp*, case note (*supra* n. 1213) 225.

public policy.[1220] Another example is the application of the *lex fori* (without any reference to foreign law) to determine the capacity to marry of stateless persons and political refugees domiciled or habitually resident in the forum country (*supra* s. 41). Since in all these cases the *lex causae* coincides with the *lex fori,* the jurisdiction of the forum to grant dispensations does not raise any problem.

While there are respectable reasons for limiting the jurisdiction of the forum to cases involving its own law, on the other hand a refusal to take jurisdiction in all cases where the applicant is subject to foreign law (except where that law is prepared to recognise an order made by the forum) inevitably brings with it some unsatisfactory practical consequences. This is particularly so if the party is habitually resident in the country of intended celebration and if he no longer entertains any connections with his home country providing the *lex causae.* An application to the authorities of that country may entail great inconvenience and long delays. In certain cases the party, even if he is not a political refugee in the legal sense, will in fact be prevented from approaching those authorities, so that a refusal on the part of the local authorities to consider a request for dispensation may amount to a denial of justice. These arguments militate in favour of the exercise of jurisdiction, at least to some extent, by the *forum celebrationis.*

The need for some mitigation of the basic rule has been recognised by *West German* courts and writers. It has been held that West German authorities may exempt a foreigner from marriage impediments imposed by his national law, provided that dispensation can be granted according to that law, where such exemption is warranted by reason of a pressing need for relief (*unaufschiebbares Fürsorgebedürfnis*).[1221] This is an ill-defined concept requiring the court to

1220. See, e.g., BELGIUM: Civ. Bruxelles 9 April 1968, J.T. 1968, 566, cf. *van Hecke and Rigaux* (1965 à 1969) 282; FRANCE: *Niboyet* V 341-342; SWITZERLAND: ObG Zürich 7 July 1951, ZR 54 (1955) no. 167; *Beck,* art. 7 e no. 39; *Götz,* art. 103 no. 19, art. 107 no. 19.

1221. OLG Hamm 19 Dec. 1968, IPRspr. 1968/69 no. 271. Among writers supporting the exercise of such a "vicarious" jurisdiction, though partly differing as to the criteria for this exception to the rule, see: *Beitzke,* Ehevoraussetzungen 288-290; *idem,* Zuständigkeit 596; *Dieckmann,* Zuständigkeit 10-11; *Gamillscheg,* Kommentar, art. 13 no. 167-173, 205, 225-226. See also, with regard to the analogous question of the jurisdiction of WEST GERMAN courts to emancipate minor aliens, *Beitzke,* Kommentar, art. 7 no. 77-92, and for decisions affirming this question: AG Saarbrücken 16 July 1947, IPRspr. 1945/49 no. 77; AG Hochheim 3 Jan. 1966, IPRspr. 1966/67 no. 57; AG Hamburg 19 Sept. 1966, IPRspr. 1966/67 no. 6.

examine and to weigh a variety of circumstances in each case.[1222] While it is clearly only intended to be used in exceptional cases, it is not possible to spell out any definite criteria for its application or to gauge the extent of the inroad made on the basic rule.

Among writers in West Germany there is now some support for a more radical solution requiring the traditional rule to be overthrown and favouring the acceptance of jurisdiction to grant dispensation by West German courts, independently of its recognition by the *lex causae*, whenever the applicant intending to marry in West Germany is habitually resident, or even resident *simpliciter*, in that country.[1223] This proposal is in line with a modern tendency to liberate jurisdiction in "non-contentious proceedings" (*freiwillige Gerichtsbarkeit, jurisdictio voluntaria*) generally from its dependency on the applicable law – a principle formerly espoused with few qualifications in (West) Germany.[1224]

This solution is indistinguishable from the view prevailing for a longer time in a few Continental countries, particularly in *France* and *Belgium*. The usual attitude in those countries is that the local authorities may give dispensation from foreign impediments whenever the marriage is to be celebrated before them, provided that the relevant foreign law so permits but without regard to whether an order made by the forum will be recognised in the foreign country.[1225] Dogmatically this position is defended by reference to the usual distinction in the conflict of laws between substance governed by the *lex causae* and procedure governed by the *lex fori*. The dominant practical concern is for the convenience

1222. For criticism of this concept see particularly *Dieckmann*, Zuständigkeit.

1223. See *Kegel*, Kommentar, art. 13 no. 100, 128, cf. *ibid.* art. 7 no. 23-25 (concerning declarations of majority).

1224. For recent contributions representing this tendency (as opposed to that mentioned *supra* n. 1215) see, e.g., *Heldrich*, Die Frage der internationalen Zuständigkeit im Bereich der freiwilligen Gerichtsbarkeit: BerGesVR 10 (1969) 97-132; *idem*, Zuständigkeit (*supra* n. 768) 165-274; *Schwimann*, Internationale Zuständigkeit in Abhängigkeit von der Lex Causae?: RabelsZ 34 (1970) 201-222. In a similar vein for ITALIAN law see *Tosato*, La giurisdizione italiana nel processo volontario (Milan 1971).

1225. BELGIUM: Civ. Tournai 10 Oct. 1962, J.T. 1962, 716, cf. *van Hecke and Rigaux* (1961 à 1964) 343; *Graulich* 108 n. 1; *Rigaux*, DIP 55-56; FRANCE: *Batiffol and Lagarde* II 42-43; *Bischoff* no. 73-76; *Bottini* 9; *Ponsard* 10-11, 38; *Vincent and Ponsard* no. 53, 64, 81, 92, 116-119 (*contra: Niboyet* V 341-342). See also for the NETHERLANDS: Rb. Rotterdam 30 Oct. 1972, *Joppe* 62 no. 30 (applying BELGIAN law to curtail a waiting period, imposed by that law, for the remarriage of a divorced wife of Belgian nationality).

of the parties, which demands that it should be possible to approach the local authorities with a request of this kind.

This view seems to be gaining ground in modern law. The recent development in West German law, just referred to, affords one indication. Another is to be found in an international agreement concluded under the auspices of the International Commission on Civil Status, the Paris Convention of 10 September 1964 to Facilitate the Celebration of Marriages Abroad.[1226] That convention deals, *inter alia,* with the topic of dispensations.[1227] It provides that the competent authorities of the country of celebration may, in the cases and subject to the conditions laid down by the personal law of the future spouse, grant him dispensation from impediments of marriage based on that law.[1228] The power thus conceded to the local authorities is limited to cases in which the applicant is a national of a Contracting State marrying in another such State where he is habitually resident. It is expressly provided that this power is without prejudice to the right of the State of the party's nationality to grant dispensations.[1229]

In conclusion, the present-day tendency is towards restricting, if not in favour of abandoning altogether, the principle of the exclusive jurisdiction of the *forum legis causae.* This leaves several problems as to which opinion remains divided:

In the first place, it is largely unsettled what positive criteria must be satisfied for the jurisdiction of the *forum celebrationis* to be affirmed. At one end of the scale, this jurisdiction is conceived as subordinate to that of the *forum legis causae,* to be exercised only in exceptional cases, as illustrated by the West German view confining it to cases which involve a "pressing need for relief" (whatever that may mean). At the other extreme is the position, apparently represented by French law, that this head of jurisdiction

1226. *Pålsson,* Marriage, s. 70. As mentioned there, the convention has been ratified by WEST GERMANY, the NETHERLANDS and TURKEY. In addition, it has since been acceded to by SPAIN, see StAZ 1977, 118. For comments on the convention see: *Gamillscheg,* Kommentar, art. 13 no. 975; *Massfeller,* Die Übereinkommen der Commision Internationale de l'État Civil (CIEC): StAZ 1965, 229, 230-231; *Simitis,* Die internationale Kommission für Zivilstandswesen (C.I.E.C.): RabelsZ 33 (1969) 30, 43-44.

1227. Art. 1-3. Two of the States parties to the convention (WEST GERMANY and the NETHERLANDS) have, however, availed themselves of a clause (art. 9) permitting them to exclude this part of the convention. See *Gamillscheg,* Kommentar, art. 13 no. 179.

1228. Art. 1. See also art. 2, which deals with the question of the proper authority to perform this task within the country of celebration.

1229. Art. 3.

is a fully equivalent alternative to that based on the *lex causae,* and not subject to any particular restrictions or conditions (additional to that of the marriage being intended to take place within the country). An intermediate solution providing a reasonable compromise is that of the Paris Convention of 1964, where the test of the applicant's habitual residence draws the line of permissible exercise of local jurisdiction to grant dispensations with reference to foreign laws.

Secondly, in so far as such jurisdiction is accepted by the *forum celebrationis,* there may be a problem as to the grounds on which a request for dispensation should be granted. The orthodox view is that these questions remain determinable by the *lex causae.*[1230] While sound principle requires that any decision on the merits should conform to that law, it has been submitted (*supra* s. 113) that this ideal is probably often beyond reach because the proper application of foreign provisions leaving the wide scope for discretion usually given by rules for dispensation may present insurmountable practical difficulties. At least in certain cases the reference made to the *lex causae* is likely to be little more than lip-service. Even apart from the technical difficulties canvassed already, there may be cases where it would scarcely be reasonable for the forum, once it has decided to take jurisdiction, to refuse a dispensation in reliance on the foreign law concerned. Supposing, for example, that the forum affirms its jurisdiction after satisfying itself that there is a "pressing need for relief" in the case at bar, it is virtually impossible to imagine the court proceeding the next moment to say that the request must be rejected because by the relevant foreign law there is not a sufficient ground for granting it.[1231] Here, indeed, the determination of the substantive issue is prejudged by the decision to accept jurisdiction. It may thus be concluded that the exercise of jurisdiction by any country other than that of the *lex causae* will inevitably have the effect of depriving that law of some of its exclusive authority in matters of substance.

A last and very doubtful issue is that of the recognition of foreign dispensations in respect of marriage impediments prescribed

1230. For support of this view in BELGIAN, DUTCH and FRENCH law see the references *supra* n. 1225, for FRENCH law also the decision of Cour Paris 30 Nov. 1934, Clunet 1935, 927, where the court relied on the relevant foreign law to refuse a request for curtailment of a waiting period for remarriage. For WEST GERMANY see: *Beitzke,* Ehevoraussetzungen 290; *idem,* Zuständigkeit 596; *Gamillscheg,* Kommentar, art. 13 no. 172.

1231. See *Dieckmann,* Zuständigkeit 9-10.

by the law of the country asked to recognise the order (or by the law of a third country). On principle it may be argued that the rules for recognising such orders should be symmetric with the rules for determining the forum's own right to give dispensations with respect to foreign laws. If and in so far as the forum claims such a right for itself, it should reasonably be prepared to recognise foreign orders made in parallel circumstances. It remains to be seen, however, whether and to what extent such a principle of reciprocal recognition will be accepted as good law.[1232]

b. *Proof of Foreign Law*

115. *General.* The system whereby capacity to marry is tested by the personal law, especially where that law is determined by nationality, leads to a relatively frequent application of foreign law. The problems connected therewith are general in character and will only be examined here in so far as they present special aspects. Such is the case when foreign law is to be applied by celebrants of marriages or other officials participating in the preliminaries to the act of celebration (as opposed to the judicial authorities passing on the validity of a marriage *ex post*). Those officials are generally ill-equipped to carry out investigations of their own into foreign law. Special devices have therefore been invented in order to facilitate this work and to ensure the correct application of the relevant foreign law.

The most important of these devices is the *certificate of capacity to marry* or *certificate of no impediment* (*certificat de capacité matrimoniale; Ehefähigkeitszeugnis*). This is, in essence, a document issued by the competent authorities of a party's home country (usually that of his nationality), intended for use in another country where the party desires to marry, and attesting that, under the law of the former country, no legal impediment stands in the way of the proposed union.[1233] The system of such certificates operates largely to transfer the burden of inquiring into the existence of marriage impediments under the appropriate foreign law from the authorities of the country of celebration to those of the foreign country itself.

1232. For writers expressly supporting recognition in certain circumstances see FRANCE: *Batiffol and Lagarde* II 42-43; WEST GERMANY: *Beitzke*, Ehevoraussetzungen 286-287; *Gamillscheg*, Kommentar, art. 13 no. 177-178, 224.

1233. See *Götz*, art. 105 no. 22; *Marquardt* 15-20.

This type of certificate, the use of which may be traced back to the first decades of the nineteenth century, plays a significant part in present-day practice, particularly in countries following the rule of the *lex patriae* in matters of capacity to marry.[1234] Provisions regulating various aspects of these certificates are to be found in the statutory law of numerous countries and also in several international treaties and conventions.[1235] This system will be somewhat more closely examined in what follows (*infra* s. 116).

There are various other kinds of document, with or without a denomination of their own, which are more or less commonly used to the same end and which are not always clearly distinguishable from certificates of capacity to marry proper.[1236] The most current type is that known as a "certificate of custom" (*certificat de coutume*), which is the usual means of proving foreign law particularly in *France.*[1237] Such a document differs in two respects from a certificate of capacity to marry. In the first place, it does not always emanate from an official authority of the foreign country concerned but may alternatively be issued by a lawyer of that country, or even by a lawyer of the country of celebration, or by an authority of that country, such as the Ministry of Justice or the Ministry of Foreign Affairs, depending on the local law, which itself decides, or leaves it to the local authorities to judge, who is qualified to deliver this form of certificate. Secondly, such a certificate is limited to reproducing the appropriate provisions of the foreign law, thus leaving the ascertainment of the facts as well as the interpretation and application of the provisions in question to the local authorities. Generally speaking at least, certificates of this kind are less satisfactory than certificates of capacity to marry, because they are often incomplete or inaccurate and involve

1234. For comparative surveys see *Marquardt* 51-67; *Rabel* 307-308.

1235. For statutory provisions see the references *infra* n. 1239, 1240, 1243 and 1244. See also the HAGUE CONVENTION on Marriage of 1902, art. 4; BUSTAMANTE CODE art. 37; and the SCANDINAVIAN Convention of 1931, as amended, art. 1 par. 1 sent. 3 (*supra* n. 263). For comments on the relevant provision of the HAGUE CONVENTION see: *Beck,* ESchlKonv. art. 4 no. 1-14; *Buzzati* 264-302; *Gamillscheg,* Kommentar, art. 13 no. 960; *F. Kahn* 122-124; *A. Miele* 45-59; *Travers* II 193-255. For certain bilateral treaties concluded by Continental European countries see *Dietz* § 10 no. 119-123; *Marquardt* 8, 54, 57, 78-79, 102; *A. Miele* 33-37, 48-49; *Vitta* II 191 n. 59.

1236. See *Marquardt* 21-27.

1237. For FRENCH law see: General Instruction of 21 Sept. 1955, no. 474; *Anton and Francescakis* 279-280; *Batiffol and Lagarde* II 36; *Bischoff* no. 82-84; cf. *supra* at n. 535-541. For other countries see *infra* n. 1243.

greater risks that the foreign law will be misinterpreted or misapplied.[1238]

116. *Especially on Certificates of Capacity to Marry.* Provision for the *delivery* of this form of certificate to nationals intending to marry abroad is made in most countries which themselves insist on compliance with the *lex patriae* for capacity to marry.[1239] The same is true of some countries, including *Denmark, Norway* and the *United Kingdom,* where the factor of nationality is immaterial in determining capacity to marry.[1240] In a number of other countries, however, for example the *United States,* most *Latin American* countries, the *Soviet Union, Greece* and *Spain,* no machinery exists for the issue of documents qualifying as certificates of capacity to marry.[1241]

Among the laws authorising the grant of certificates of this kind, there are considerable differences on a number of points.[1242] In many instances the certificate is given by the Ministry of Justice, a marriage registrar or some other domestic authority. In other countries this task is performed, at least in certain cases, by diplomatic or consular officers serving in the country where the marriage is to take place. The authorities designated as competent for the present purpose may be in a more or less favourable position to discharge the task assigned to them, and the inquiries actually undertaken by them may be more or less thorough. In some countries the certificate can only be obtained after a procedure as exacting as in the case of a marriage to be celebrated by or before the authorities of the issuing country itself. On the other hand, there are countries whose authorities are far more complaisant to the wishes of the parties, being prepared to deliver the certificate without any serious investigation. Significant differences exist as to the range of questions covered by the certificate. Sometimes it relates only to the applicant's general capacity to marry. In other cases it also takes account of possible incapacities for reasons inherent in the person of the intended partner, *i.e.* of

1238. Cf. *Anton and Francescakis* 284; *Marquardt* 23-24.

1239. For lists of countries and of authorities charged with this task see *Dietz* § 10 no. 47-117; *Gamillscheg,* Kommentar, art. 13 no. 714; *Marquardt* 151-155.

1240. DENMARK: Marriage Order of 18 Dec. 1969, § 25-27; NORWAY: *Lövold* 268 n. 8; *Marquardt* 63, 234; UNITED KINGDOM: *Anton* 285-286; 8 B.D.I.L. 593-603.

1241. See *Dietz, supra* n. 1239; *Gamillscheg,* Kommentar, art. 13 no. 715.

1242. See, besides the references *supra* n. 1239, *Götz,* art. 105 no. 22; *Marquardt* 71-87.

relative and other bilateral marriage impediments. It follows that the quality and reliability of certificates emanating from different countries vary greatly.

Where a certificate of no impediment is produced, it will generally be *accepted* as proof of the facts attested in the country of celebration. Mostly this means of proof is only optional in the sense that it does not exclude the use of other methods to establish the absence of any impediment to the projected marriage, in particular by the aid of "certificates of custom". This position is generally taken, for instance, in *England, France,* the *Benelux* countries and *Scandinavia.*[1243] A stricter rule obtains, however, in several Continental European countries, including *Austria, West Germany, Italy, Portugal* and some countries in *Eastern Europe.*[1244] In those countries the production of a certificate of no impediment, emanating from the country of the party's nationality, is a prerequisite to the marriage of foreigners in local form and, in principle, cannot be replaced by any other form of evidence. The position in *Switzerland* is essentially similar, such a certificate being normally required for the grant of a *Trauungsbewilligung* (marriage permit) by the respective cantonal authorities, which in its turn is compulsory for parties of foreign nationality, or of whom at least the male party is a foreigner, desiring to marry in local form.[1245]

In countries insisting on the submission of a certificate of no impediment some further problems are bound to arise. One group of questions concern the personal scope of this requirement. Is,

1243. For FRANCE see *supra* n. 1237; for ENGLAND and SCOTLAND: *Anton* 279; *Jackson* 245-246; 8 B.D.I.L. 593, 603-608; cf. *Anton and Francescakis* 281-285 (reform proposal for SCOTTISH law). And see for BELGIUM and NETHERLANDS: *Marquardt* 61; FINLAND: Implementing Order of 28 Dec. 1929; *Hakulinen* 364; NORWAY: *Gaarder* 133; *Holmøy* 16; cf. Regulations of 14 Sept. 1956, § 5, and Regulations of 1 July 1969, § 16 no. 6; SWEDEN: Ordinance of 14 Dec. 1973, no. 950.

1244. AUSTRIA: Marriage Act of 1938, § 14; *Klang and Gschnitzer* 514-523; *Köhler* 55-56; *Schwind,* IPR 146-147; BULGARIA: FC art. 92; *Jessel* 153-154; *Koschucharoff* 497; WEST GERMANY: Marriage Act of 1946, § 10; Service Instruction of 1968, § 166-169 a; *Dietz* § 10 no. 1-132; *Gamillscheg,* Kommentar, art. 13 no. 692-693, 697-722; *Hoffmann and Stephan* § 10 no. 2-14; HUNGARY: Act no. IV/1952 as amended by Act no. 1/1974, § 6; *Réczei* 356; ITALY: CC art. 116 par. 1; *A. Miele* 19-22; *Vitta* II 191-194; POLAND: Decree of 8 June 1955, art. 46; PORTUGAL: Decree-Law of 5 May 1967, art. 205; *Marquardt* 63-64.

1245. See NAG art. 7 e and Civil Status Order of 1 June 1953, art. 168, 170; *Beck,* art. 7 e no. 1-56; *Götz,* art. 105 no. 20-23; *von Overbeck,* Wiederverheiratung 347.

for instance, such a document necessary not only for parties of foreign nationality but also – and, if so, in what circumstances – in respect of stateless persons and political refugees?[1246] How are the provisions under consideration to be handled in cases where the interested party possesses more than one nationality?[1247] What is the position in cases involving a *renvoi* by the relevant foreign law, whether in the form of a reference back to the *lex fori* or on to the law of a third country?[1248] Without going into the details of these questions, it is submitted that they must be answered in the light of the purpose and function of the certificate, which is to facilitate the application of the appropriate foreign law. Rules requiring the production of a certificate are ancillary to conflicts rules prescribing the application of foreign law and should never be framed or applied in such a way as to become independent of their purpose. Obviously, for example, there is no point in demanding a certificate in the case of a stateless person whose capacity to marry is determinable by the *lex fori* by reason of his habitual residence in the country where he intends to marry.[1249]

Other questions concern the requirements to be met in order for the document produced to qualify as a valid certificate of capacity to marry. This includes matters such as the competence of the issuing authority, the requisite content of the document (what facts must be certified), formal requirements of legalisation and time limitations for the recognition of the certificate. Elaborate rules for these questions have been developed particularly in *West Germany.*[1250] Only one point will be mentioned here, namely, the competence of the issuing authority. While this question is usually held to fall exclusively to the foreign law involved, a more restrictive position is taken by *West German* and

1246. See, e.g., AUSTRIA: VwGH 24 Oct. 1946, JBl 1946, 509; *Schwind*, IPR 146; BULGARIA: *Jessel* 154-155; WEST GERMANY: *Gamillscheg*, Kommentar, art. 13 no. 704-709; *Marquardt* 98-99, 118-120; ITALY: *A. Miele* 31-32, 95. Cf. *supra* s. 41.

1247. See, e.g., *Marquardt* 91-93; AUSTRIA: *Klang and Gschnitzer* 527-528; WEST GERMANY: *Dietz* § 10 no. 19, 23; *Gamillscheg*, Kommentar, art. 13 no. 710. Cf. *supra* s. 40.

1248. See, e.g., *Marquardt* 93-97; AUSTRIA: *Schwind*, IPR 146-147; WEST GERMANY: *Gamillscheg*, Kommentar, art. 13 no. 701-703; ITALY: *A. Miele* 26-31, 57-59, 98-100. Cf. *supra* s. 58-59.

1249. See *Gamillscheg*, Kommentar, art. 13 no. 706 with pertinent criticism of the WEST GERMAN rule on this point.

1250. See *Dietz* § 10 no. 44-46, 118-131; *Gamillscheg*, Kommentar, art. 13 no. 711-713, 716-718.

Austrian law, which provide that only documents emanating from the domestic authorities of the country of issue can be treated as certificates of capacity to marry.[1251] Certificates delivered by officers of the diplomatic or consular service are thus excluded, apparently because they are not considered to offer sufficient guarantees of a serious examination of the pertinent questions.[1252]

Finally, it is usually envisaged that leave to dispense with the requirement of a certificate of no impediment may be granted in certain cases.[1253] Although the scope of these exceptions to the rule is not very well defined, it is easy to perceive their purpose and justification. It would indeed be impracticable and unreasonable to insist on the necessity of the certificate in question in all cases because, if so, a foreigner would often be precluded from marrying although he did not suffer from any incapacity to do so.[1254] In many cases the reason why a foreigner cannot produce a certificate of no impediment is simply that the authorities of his home country lack any power to issue such a document (*supra* at n. 1241) or that the certificates given by them do not meet the special conditions as to form required for their acceptance by the *lex fori*, for example where that law does not recognise consular certificates (*supra* at n. 1251). In other instances the certificate may not be obtainable without great difficulties or delays. In yet other cases the foreign authorities may refuse to grant the certificate for political or other reasons which have nothing to do with the party's capacity to marry as conceived by the *lex fori*, or on grounds of an incapacity, for instance due to religious affiliation, which is regarded as incompatible with the forum's public policy.

The power to dispense with the requirement of a certificate of

1251. See the references *supra* n. 1244 and 1250.

1252. See *Albers* 146. But such a generalisation certainly goes too far; cf., critically, *Marquardt* 18-20.

1253. See *Marquardt* 115-131 and the statutory provisions cited *supra* n. 1244. For further details see AUSTRIA: *Klang and Gschnitzer* 523-527; WEST GERMANY: Service Instruction of 1968, § 170-171; *Arndt; Beyer; Dietz* § 10 no. 133-175; *Gamillscheg*, Kommentar, art. 13 no. 723-744; *Hoffmann and Stephan* § 10 no. 23-43.

1254. In contrast to other systems, ITALIAN law does not envisage any possibility of exempting a foreigner from the submission of the certificate; see the references *supra* n. 1244 and the decision of Trib. Benevento 20 March 1953, Foro it. 1954 I 1292, 1296. In practice, however, this rigid system has given rise to such difficulties as to compel the courts to depart from it in certain instances. See Trib. Milano 11 Oct. 1947, Giur. It. D.I.P. (1942/66) 532, and among critical voices in literature: *Marquardt* 131-133; *A. Miele* 22-44, 82-101, 144-148; *Vitta* II 193-194.

no impediment necessarily leaves some room for the exercise of discretion by the local authorities, for example in judging whether the difficulties in procuring the certificate are sufficiently grave to justify a waiver of the requirement. Until recently it was often thought that the scope for this discretion extended to the substantive aspects of the matter, so that a waiver could be granted and the marriage permitted notwithstanding the existence of some impediment according to the relevant foreign law.[1255] Conversely, it has happened that a waiver was refused, and the marriage thereby in effect prevented, regardless of the party's capacity to marry under the foreign law, on the ground that the union was considered undesirable from the point of view of the public interest or that it was judged to stand small chances of success.[1256] Similarly, the local authorities held themselves at liberty to impose conditions for the grant of a waiver additional to those otherwise required to be satisfied by foreign parties and not relating to the party's capacity to marry.[1257] In part at least, the grant of exemptions was coloured by the notion that it involved the exercise of a prerogative (*Gnadenakt*).

This concept, however, is usually rejected today, in particular because the discretion it involves is difficult to reconcile with current ideas of the right to marry as a legally protected human right. On the one hand, it is now generally recognised that a waiver of the certificate of no impediment is quite distinct from a decision to dispense with impediments imposed by the applicable foreign law and that it implies only that the party's capacity to marry has to be examined by the local authorities without the help of such a certificate. A waiver will therefore only be granted if it is shown by other means that the requirements of the foreign law have been complied with, or that the only incapacity existing by that law is one which falls to be disregarded by the forum for

1255. For a representative of this view in WEST GERMAN law see *Guggumos*, Die Befreiung von der Beibringung des ausländischen Ehefähigkeitszeugnisses: StAZ 1954, 2-5; *idem*, Zum Problem der Befreiung von der Beibringung des Ehefähigkeitszeugnisses: StAZ 1964, 54-55. For SWITZERLAND, where opinion seems still to be divided on this issue, see the references *supra* n. 1245.

1256. AUSTRIA: VwGH 24 Oct. 1946, JBl 1946, 509, ÖJZ 1946, 489; [WEST] GERMANY: older practice cited by *Gamillscheg*, Kommentar, art. 13 no. 732.

1257. An important example is the AUSTRIAN, WEST GERMAN and SWISS practice requiring the production of a *Traubereitschaftserklärung* in the case of foreigners whose national law insists on religious solemnisation. See *Pålsson*, Marriage, s. 277 and *Gamillscheg*, Kommentar, art. 13 no. 737.

reasons of public policy.[1258] On the other hand, where this condition is fulfilled, it has been held at least in *West Germany* that the requesting party is entitled, as of right, to obtain a waiver, thus excluding any scope for a discretion to withhold the order.[1259]

It remains to consider the *probative force* of a certificate of capacity to marry, where produced. According to one view, which receives support particularly in *Italian* law, such a document must be treated as conclusive evidence of the facts attested, with the result that the local marriage authorities lack any right to conduct further inquiries into the foreign law.[1260] Usually, however, the certificate is only regarded as a rebuttable means of proof, which does not preclude an independent examination on the part of the local authorities.[1261] This, it is submitted, is the more appropriate position, not least in view of the uneven quality of the certificates invoked in different cases. For practical purposes, it is true, this difference will scarcely be of major importance. In the great majority of cases the accuracy of the certificate is unlikely to be questioned, if only for the reason that the local authorities rarely dispose of resources enabling them to undertake a critical review of the content of the document. Nor is it desirable, if the certificate is to fulfill its function smoothly, that additional investigations should be conducted unless there is some special reason to do so.

1258. See *Marquardt* 121 and for AUSTRIA: BMfJ 23 Dec. 1971, EFSlg 8 (1971) 213 no. 15,734; OLG Wien 3 Oct. 1973, EFSlg 10 (1973) 240 no. 20,306; *V. Hoyer,* Wiederverehelichung 618; *Schwind,* IPR 147; WEST GERMANY: BGH 12 Feb. 1964, BGHZ 41, 136, 140, IPRspr. 1964/65 no. 74, and cases cited *infra* n. 1259; *Gamillscheg,* Kommentar, art. 13 no. 725, 728-730 with references; POLAND: Supreme Court 16 Nov. 1971 and 22 June 1972, Clunet 1977, 136, note Jodlowski; SWITZERLAND: *Beck,* art. 7 e no. 40-44 (but opinion in SWISS law is divided, see *supra* n. 1245).

1259. KG 14 Sept. 1961, IPRspr. 1960/61 no. 91; BGH 12 May 1971, BGHZ 56, 180, 184, IPRspr. 1971 no. 40; *Dietz* § 10 no. 160-161; *Gamillscheg,* Kommentar, art. 13 no. 699, 732-733, 737 with references. Similarly for AUSTRIA: *V. Hoyer,* Scheidung 20; *Schwind,* IPR 147-148; SWITZERLAND: *Vischer,* IPR 590-591.

1260. App. Milano 1 Feb. 1949, Giur. It. D.I.P. (1942/66) 532; see also App. Milano 28 Dec. 1971, Riv. dir. int. proc. 1972, 311; *Monaco* 159. For criticism see *Balladore Pallieri* 167-168; *Marquardt* 28, 106.

1261. See *Marquardt* 105-108 and, e.g., AUSTRIA: *Klang and Gschnitzer* 515, 527; *Schwind,* IPR 146; WEST GERMANY: Service Instruction of 1968, § 172 (1); LG Hannover 19 April 1961, IPRspr. 1960/61 no. 90; BGH 14 July 1966, BGHZ 46, 87, 92-93, IPRspr. 1966/67 no. 59 b; *Gamillscheg,* Kommentar, art. 13 no. 698, 719-721 with references; SWITZERLAND: BG 2 March 1942, BGE 68 I 73, 80-81; *Götz,* art. 105 no. 22. See also the provisions of the HAGUE CONVENTION and of the BUSTAMANTE CODE cited *supra* n. 1235.

In those exceptional cases, however, where the local authorities know of an impediment, it would be very unsatisfactory if they were bound to allow the marriage to proceed nevertheless, solely because the existence of the impediment is not revealed by the certificate. Nor should an independent examination be barred if there is some reason to doubt the accuracy of the certificate. Obviously such an examination is necessary in respect of matters which are not covered by the certificate, particularly as concerns requirements or impediments imposed, in addition to those of the foreign law, by virtue of the forum's own public policy.[1262]

1262. See, e.g., *Marquardt* 111-114, and for ITALIAN law *Vitta* II 192-193.

INDEX

Note. References are to section numbers, not to pages. Where the subject-matter is treated in a footnote, or in the text in direct connection with a footnote, the number of that footnote is given within parentheses. A footnote number followed by an asterisk (*) indicates the nearest footnote preceding the passage in the text where the question is considered.

Examples: 74 (639) means that the question is treated in s. 74, either in footnote 639 or in the text pertaining to that footnote. 113 (1202*) refers to the part of the text of s. 113 following footnote 1202.

Italics are used to indicate a passage where a question is given principal consideration.

ABOUT THE AUTHOR

Lennart Pålsson is professor of international law at the Institute of International Law, University of Lund, Sweden. He has published extensively in Swedish and previously published with S & N, *Marriage and Divorce in Comparative Conflict of Laws*, 1974. In addition, he is a contributor to the *International Encyclopedia of Comparative Law*, where he wrote the chapter on "Marriage and Divorce" in the volume dealing with private international law.

COLOPHON

letter: baskerville 10/12 and 8/10
setter: H. Charlesworth
printer: Samson Sijthoff Grafische Bedrijven
binder: Callenbach
cover-design: Bram de Blécourt